KU-163-946

LIVERPOOL POLYTECHNIC
TRUEMAN STREET BUILDING
THE LIBRARY
15-21 WEBSTER STREET
LIVERPOOL L3 2ET
TEL. 051 207 3581 ext. 4022/4023

Mentally Abnormal Offenders

Mentally Abnormal Offenders

EDITED BY

MICHAEL CRAFT
MD, FRCP, FRCPsych, MRANZCP, DPM
Consultant Psychiatrist, Bryn-y-Neuadd Hospital
Llanfairfechan, Gwynedd, Wales

AND

ANN CRAFT
BSc(Econ), CQSW
Evaluation Research Officer, School of Education
University of Bath, England

FOREWORDS BY

ROBYN DAVID
QC, DL
Circuit Judge, Cheshire and North Wales

AND

KENNETH RAWNSLEY
CBE, FRCPsych, FRCP, DPM
Professor of Psychological Medicine
Welsh National School of Medicine, Cardiff

Baillière Tindall
LONDON PHILADELPHIA TORONTO MEXICO CITY
RIO DE JANEIRO SYDNEY TOKYO HONG KONG

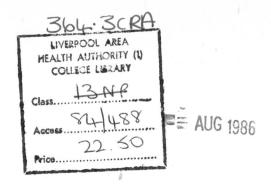

364.3CRA

LIVERPOOL AREA
HEALTH AUTHORITY (1)
COLLEGE LIBRARY

Class.........13NP........
Access......84/488......
22.50
Price........................

AUG 1986

Baillière Tindall   1 St Anne's Road
Eastbourne, East Sussex BN21 3UN, England

West Washington Square
Philadelphia, PA 19105, USA

1 Goldthorne Avenue
Toronto, Ontario M8Z 5T9, Canada

Apartado 26370—Cedro 512
Mexico 4, DF, Mexico

Rua Evaristo da Veiga, 55-20° andar
Rio de Janeiro—RJ, Brazil

ABP Australia Ltd, 44 Waterloo Road
North Ryde, NSW 2064, Australia

Ichibancho Central Building, 22-1 Ichibancho
Chiyoda-ku, Tokyo 102, Japan

10/FL, Inter-Continental Plaza, 94 Granville Road
Tsim Sha Tsui East, Kowloon, Hong Kong

© 1984 Baillière Tindall
Chapter 4 (Mr G. R. Walmsley) © 1984 Crown Copyright reserved

All rights reserved. No part of this publication may be reproduced, stored in a retrieval system or
transmitted, in any form or by any means, electronic, mechanical, photocopying or otherwise,
without the prior permission of Baillière Tindall, 1 St Anne's Road, Eastbourne, East Sussex
BN21 3UN, England

First published 1984

Typeset and printed in Great Britain by
Butler & Tanner Ltd, Frome and London

British Library Cataloguing in Publication Data

Mentally abnormal offenders.
  1. Insane, Criminal and dangerous
  I. Craft, Michael   II. Craft, Ann
  364.3′8   HV6133
  ISBN 0-7020-1003-0

Contents

Contributors

D.A. Black MMA(Cantab)
Consultant Clinical Psychologist and Head of Department of Psychology,
Broadmoor Hospital, Crowthorne, Berkshire RH11 7EG.

A.D. Brooks AB, JD(Yale)
Distinguished Professor of Law, Rutgers University Law School, 15 Washington Street,
Newark, New Jersey 07102, USA.

A. Craft BSc(Econ), CQSW
Evaluation Research Officer, School of Education, University of Bath,
Claverton Down, Bath BA2 7AY.

M. Craft MD, FRCP, FRCPsych, MRANZCP, DPM
Consultant Psychiatrist, Bryn-y-Neuadd Hospital, Llanfairfechan,
Gwynedd LL33 0HH.

D.A. Crawford BSc, MSc(Clin Psych), PhD ABPsS
District Clinical Psychologist, Whitecroft Hospital, Sandy Lane,
Newport, Isle of Wight, PO30 3EB.

G.W. Fenton MB BCh, FRCP(Ed), FRCPsych, DPM
Professor of Psychiatry, Ninewells Hospital, Dundee DD1 9SY.

P. Gerber LLB, DJur
Member, Taxation Board of Review; Honorary Lecturer in Medical Jurisprudence and
Ethics, Medical School,
University of Queensland, St Lucia, Queensland 4067, Australia.

L. Gostin BA, JD
General Secretary, National Council for Civil Liberties, 21 Tabard Street, London
SE1 4LA; *Formerly* Legal Director of MIND (National Association for Mental Health).

J. Higgins MB ChB, MRCPsych, DPM
Consultant in Forensic Psychiatry to the Mersey Regional Health Authority, 36 Rodney
Street, Liverpool L1 9AA, and to the Home Office; Honorary Clinical Lecturer in
Forensic Psychiatry, University of Liverpool.

W.K. Lawson MB ChB(Glas), MRCPsych
Senior Medical Officer, HM Remand Centre, Risley, Warrington, Cheshire
WA3 6BP; Visiting Psychiatrist, Red Bank School, Newton le Willows,
Merseyside.

M.B. Spencer BCL, MA(Oxon)
Barrister of the Inner Temple, 4 Paper Buildings, Temple, London EC47 7EX.

S. Spencer DM, FRCPsych, DPM
Locum Consultant Psychiatrist, Oxfordshire Health Authority;
Clinical Lecturer in Psychiatry, University of Oxford; Visiting
Psychotherapist, HM Prison Grendon; *Formerly* Consultant Psychiatrist,
Oxfordshire Health Authority.

W.B. Spry MB ChB, DPM, DMJ, ABPsS, AFOM, FBIM
Consultant Psychiatrist, Bryn-y-Neuadd Hospital, Llanfairfechan, Gwynedd LL33 0HH;
Honorary Consultant, West Glamorgan Health Authority.

G.R. Walmsley MA(Oxon), MPhil
Principal Research Officer, Home Office Research and Planning Unit,
Queen Anne's Gate, London SW1H 9AT.

Foreword

Judges have long recognised that those appearing before the Criminal Courts include both the bad and the mad. Some are just bad, some just mad, but many are partly bad and partly mad. The perennial questions are how to distinguish between the bad and the mad and, given that distinction, how to sentence appropriately.

Psychiatry now plays an essential part in the judicial process. In homicide cases, the question will often be whether the defendant was fully responsible for his actions. However, the defendant's state of mind is frequently under consideration in different contexts and in a whole range of other less serious cases. In the area of sentencing, one of the most important objectives is to ensure, so far as may be possible, that the offender does not re-offend. If a medical disposal is under consideration, the Court will need to know what can and should be done and what is likely to be achieved.

In the past, Judges have been hampered by an inadequate understanding of mental disorder in its various forms. They have found psychiatrists remarkably coy when asked about the specific nature of a 'treatment' proposed, and positively evasive when asked to give some assistance on what that treatment may be expected to achieve. Lack of knowledge, both general and specific, leads to lack of confidence and that, in turn, militates against constructive and enlightened sentencing.

The Crafts and their colleagues have opened the door to understanding. Here, in eminently readable form, are to be found the answers to all the questions that have worried Judges in the past. The chapters on psychopaths and sex offenders are particularly illuminating and interesting. The reader will be fascinated with the chapter on genetic endowment and the XYY syndrome. There is a typically forthright review of the mentally abnormal offender in prison by Dr Lawson.

This book will herald a new and much more constructive approach to sentencing. A change long overdue.

Robyn David QC, DL

Foreword

The world looks very different when seen through the professional eye of the lawyer, as against that of the psychiatrist. Legal philosophy prefers a black or white answer in matters of human conduct; the psychiatrist deals in shades of grey. Not surprisingly, therefore, lawyers and psychiatrists may jar on each other when considering issues such as seriously diminished responsibility for a crime.

In the land of Erewhon people were punished for their illnesses and treated for their crimes. The value systems operating in most contemporary societies broadly speaking adopt a contrary viewpoint, but then what are we to do when a crime is committed by a mentally ill person?

Michael and Ann Craft have endeavoured to lead us through this jungle by the skilful deployment of chapters written by experts, themselves included. These are arranged under broad headings to consider firstly the Offence both from the epidemiological and the clinical standpoint; the Offender from the genetic angle, and from the association with specific psychiatric syndromes; the Law with emphasis upon recent legislative policy in the U.K. and in the U.S.A. concerning mentally abnormal offenders; the Court and its relationship to the mentally ill; and, finally, issues of Treatment.

Michael Craft has written a neat appendix on the Professional Criminal and Paul Gerber an epilogue on Psychiatry in the Dock (which made me apoplectic).

I believe that this book will appeal not only to the professionals of all disciplines whose task is to deal in one way or another with the mentally disordered offender, but also to the thoughtful citizen who must have been concerned and puzzled by the many such cases which hit the headlines with monotonous regularity.

Kenneth Rawnsley
CBE, FRCPsych, FRCP, DPM

Preface

The need for this book became apparent from our work and research in that particular area of practice which is shared by psychiatry and the law. Although the disposal of mentally abnormal offenders involves practitioners from both professions, they are not always clear about what each can contribute towards an outcome which best satisfies the criteria of community protection and humane treatment of the offender.

The contributors to this book write with experience acquired from a variety of disciplines – jurisprudence, forensic psychiatry, prison medical service, clinical psychology, and research. The aim is thus to offer cross-professional insights to those who try to pick their way through this complex field.

The first part of the book reviews the statistics of mental disorder and criminal offence and finds that the incidence of both is high, and is becoming higher. Thus for many reasons, including chance, they will frequently coincide in the same person. Crimes such as sexual offences, murder, and shop-lifting, which are most commonly associated with mental abnormality, are surveyed.

The section on offenders analyses current knowledge of the various factors known to play a part in the mental abnormality evidenced by some offenders. From this comes a discussion of that most pertinent of issues – the prediction of dangerousness, with its implication for offenders, courts, care and treatment agencies, and the community at large.

The ethical, practical and social principles of law in this field are reviewed in the U.K. and the U.S.A. It is still early days for Britain's new Mental Health Act and the changes it has introduced to the management of mentally abnormal offenders, but probable consequences are discussed.

A major part of the book considers aspects of treatment. One might be forgiven for thinking that there are almost as many 'treatment' regimes as people available to treat, but these chapters introduce interested professionals to what might be on offer to their clients. In the last resort, however, the issue is one of what resources are available, who is prepared to treat, and what treatment venues the court will accept. A review of long-term follow-ups of treated mentally abnormal offenders shows that the picture may not be as black as is sometimes painted. People can and do improve. However, it would seem that variables such as quality of aftercare can play as significant a part in a mentally abnormal offender's 'success' or 'failure' as the treatment itself.

Durkheim's sociological insights told us that crime in society is a normal occurrence. The Appendix on the professional criminal is included for the sake of balance, reminding the reader that criminals are not mentally abnormal _per se_; indeed many possess an abundance of judgement and forethought, in marked contrast to the subjects described in this book. The Epilogue gives warning to the unwary professional – very little in life is clear-cut, less still where psychiatry and the law encounter each other in court!

It is our hope that this volume will be of constructive use to those professionals brought into contact with offenders whose disposal needs to take into account their personality disorder or mental state.

December 1983   _Michael Craft_
                                                                                     Ann Craft

Acknowledgements

We would like to thank Dr William B. Spry and Mr Martin Spencer, both for their contributions and also for reading the manuscript and giving much valuable advice. To our secretaries, Mrs Margaret Miller, Mrs Anne Williams and Mrs June Cooper, we have nothing but praise for their unstinted work and numerous typescripts.

This book is the property of
LIVERPOOL AREA HEALTH AUTHORITY (T)

1

The Mentally Abnormal Offender and His Society

James Higgins

Forensic psychiatry embraces the assessment and treatment of mentally abnormal offenders. Who should be considered a mentally abnormal offender is, however, much more difficult to determine. Various types of behaviour and disability lead to inclusion in this category: the florid psychotic who in a deluded state has committed an antisocial act; the chronic psychotic whose social competence has deteriorated to such a low level that his ill-judged attempts at survival lead him to be charged; those of low intelligence who know no better or whose judgment is poor; the non-mentally ill of dull or normal intelligence who offend because of neurotic conflicts or because of abnormalities of personality structure. These groups have little in common. Some of them can co-exist and one may be replaced later by another. Perhaps the only things in common are that many such individuals present at courts and do not seem to be normal criminals. Courts then seek medical advice to try and understand them and to advise on how to dispose of them. Appropriate facilities have then to be provided somewhere to cater for them.

All countries have developed legal, medical and penal systems to deal with such offenders. These systems are quite different, reflecting different traditions, social climates and mores. They have all changed with time. Change, however, rarely follows research, improvements in therapy or proven success of a particular measure. It more often follows sea-changes of public and political opinion and subsequent committees of enquiry, but the efforts of individuals can be decisive, whether they be notorious offenders, charismatic therapists or enthusiastic reformers.

Mentally ill and severely intellectually handicapped patients who do not offend are invariably seen as the province of a health service, wilful predatory criminals the province of a penal service. The place of the mentally abnormal offender has, however, always been much less clear, particularly when the sole or principal psychological abnormality is a neurosis or a personality deviation. In some countries the offending neurotic or psychopath is treated in the penal system as an ordinary prisoner or in some specialised penal treatment facility; in other countries a place in a hospital, either ordinary or specialised, is chosen; in some, a disposal to either a hospital or a prison is possible. Recent concern about the treatability of psychopathy and its status as a psychiatric entity, and concern about indeterminate detention for treatment on the ground of dangerousness, particularly when the predictability of future dangerousness is low,

1

have caused considerable shifts in policy and practice. A brief review of the development of the law relating to mentally abnormal offenders and the penal, hospital and community facilities for their management in various societies can introduce the problems facing forensic psychiatry.

ENGLAND AND WALES

The first statutory provision for recognising complete exemption from criminal responsibility in Britain was the Criminal Lunatics Act, 1800. This was superseded by the judgment of the House of Lords in McNaughton's case in 1843. Absolute non-responsibility was the only psychiatric defence available to a criminal charge and it resulted in indeterminate detention in a psychiatric hospital. County asylums had been introduced in 1808 to cater in part for such offenders and for those mentally ill already detained in prison whose sad plight had been described by John Howard thirty years earlier (Howard, 1777). The county asylums, however, soon refused to take some patients on the grounds of inadequate security; they accumulated in the prisons, and as a result Broadmoor was opened in 1863 as a criminal lunatic asylum. Contemporary definitions of psychiatric illness in the statutes were vague and only the severest forms came within the McNaughton Rules or warranted transfer to a psychiatric hospital. The mentally handicapped were excluded, but the Mental Deficiency Act of 1913 rectified this omission and large numbers were subsequently transferred from prison to hospitals.

Despite early difficulties in the placement of some mentally abnormal offenders, by the early twentieth century the system of county asylum, criminal lunatic asylum and prison was working reasonably well; the only group not being adequately catered for were the psychopathic or neurotic offenders. There was considerable debate about where the suggested treatment for this group should take place, for, despite reservations expressed by some, there was considerable confidence that psychotherapeutic intervention would be beneficial. Various bodies recommended that prisoners should be screened to see if treatment rather than punishment would be of value, and a number of experimental regimes were tried. In 1939 the report of the East–Hubert Committee, formed to investigate this area, recommended the setting up of a specialised treatment unit for abnormal and unusual types of criminal and it firmly expressed the view that this unit should be within the penal, and not the hospital, system (East and Hubert, 1939). The East–Hubert report was not implemented until 1962 with the opening of Grendon Prison, which has a therapeutic community orientation albeit in a secure prison setting, and a Medical Superintendent as Governor (Gunn et al, 1978).

In 1957 the defence of 'diminished responsibility' was introduced into English Law, though it is limited to cases of murder. Its introduction extricated courts both from the restrictions of the outmoded concepts of the McNaughton Rules and the fixed penalty for murder, thus enabling a conviction for manslaughter with subsequent flexibility in sentencing, including the option of any form of psychiatric treatment. However, the Mental Health Act of 1959 had a far greater bearing on the management of mentally abnormal offenders. This Act was a complex piece of legislation, outstanding for its time, and despite recent amendments is a piece of enlightened legislation unmatched elsewhere, copied or adapted in many English speaking countries.

Unfortunately the expectation that the Mental Health Act, 1959 would result in the removal of large numbers of mentally abnormal offenders from prison and ease disposal difficulties at court was ill-founded. Marked changes of psychiatric philosophy and practice were occurring at the same time and these changes gathered momentum over the next fifteen years. New psychotropic drugs were controlling the more bizarre behaviour of psychotic patients and it came to be realised that some of the unwanted behaviour of the patients in hospital was as much due to the restricted and impoverished regime under which they were being treated as to their illnesses themselves. Effective drug treatments and an awareness of the effects of institutionalisation brought great optimism and therapeutic endeavour in the climate of increasing liberalism of the 1950s and 1960s. Mental hospitals, as the county asylums became known, had been holding gradually increasing numbers of patients since their opening, but in 1955 numbers started to decline. The spirit of the Mental Health Act, 1959, that psychiatric patients should as far as possible be treated no differently from physically ill patients, spawned informal admissions, out-patients departments, day hospitals and psychiatric units in large district general hospitals. As a result, new groups of patients presented themselves for psychiatric treatment, particularly those with neurotic and personality difficulties, and they were vigorously assailed with psychotherapy, minor tranquillisers and anti-depressants. Mental hospitals became almost entirely open door institutions despite early warnings about the hazards of such a development in 1961 (Ministry of Health, 1961). The 'open door policy' became the vogue and some even suggested that within a couple of decades mental hospitals might no longer be needed. These changes proved markedly beneficial to the image of psychiatry and to the vast majority of patients. Large numbers of chronic patients were transferred to the community but for many the expected provision of hostels never materialised. Admissions became briefer and more numerous and the 'revolving-door policy' quickly evolved. Those who required long-term asylum were often seen as therapeutic failures who blocked beds.

Uncooperative, difficult or violent patients fitted uneasily into the new philosophies of treatment and their removal or exclusion was sought. Two broad groupings of patients emerged, the 'nice' and the 'not nice'. The 'nice', no matter how minimal their disability, cooperated in treatment, behaved in a socially acceptable way, had somewhere to live in the community, and frequently got better or stopped pestering the doctor. Psychiatrists and psychiatric nurses liked them. The 'not nice' patients were more time-consuming, were mostly friendless and had nowhere to go, were demanding and disruptive and rarely responded well to the new treatment regimes. Psychiatrists and psychiatric nurses did not like them. Further, if there was no evidence of frank mental illness or severe intellectual deficit, the 'not nice' could be described as psychopathic and consequently not in need of further psychiatric attention; confidence that psychopathy could be treated within the new regime having quickly faded, and the less the patient responded, obviously the greater the degree of his psychopathy. Unfortunately, this reasoning spilled over on to the management of some chronic psychotics with the result that comments like 'he has never really been schizophrenic, his schizophrenia has burned out and it is his personality disorder that is causing the problems, in any event he is not suitable for treatment in our hospital' were not infrequently made in reports to court.

The Mental Health Act, 1959 also transferred the management of the criminal lunatic asylums from the Home Office to the Health Service and these hospitals were renamed special hospitals, because they offered a special level of security for those of a dangerous, violent or criminal propensity. There were, by this time, three special hospitals with approximately 2000 beds in total. Also, patients no longer needed to commit an offence to be admitted to a special hospital. They could be transferred from a mental hospital because their behaviour was intolerable and a considerable number of such patients were transferred. The facilities in mental hospitals that previously contained them were dismantled and skills in the management of difficult patients were lost. Their subsequent return was resisted. Courts also began to experience increasing difficulties in finding a bed for clearly mentally disordered defendants. Mental hospitals refused to have them on the grounds that they were too difficult or were untreatable or that they were both. The increasingly overcrowded special hospitals belatedly raised their criteria for admission and refused to take them on the grounds that they were not difficult or dangerous enough to warrant their special high security, especially as they were just the patients whom mental hospitals had taken years before without remark. Many psychotic petty offenders then received short penal sentences and came to be a well recognised group in local prisons. The fewer more serious psychotic offenders became the subject of unseemly wrangles at court and were usually eventually given a bed in a special hospital though some were sentenced to long periods of imprisonment in the hope that they would subsequently be transferred to a hospital.

As has already been mentioned, confidence in the treatment of psychopaths in ordinary psychiatric hospitals had quickly waned except in a few centres like the Henderson Hospital (Whiteley, 1975), Balderton Hospital or Garth Angharad (Craft, 1966). Special hospitals also still retained some confidence in the efficacy of medical treatment. The general view was that psychopathy was not a true psychiatric illness and could only be treated on a voluntary out-patient basis but even such recommendations for offenders were made with declining frequency. A diagnosis of psychopathy in an offender usually resulted in a disposal at court little different from that a non-psychopathic offender would receive. It was even suggested by some that imprisonment could be beneficial: in prison time would pass and would allow possible maturation, individual psychotherapy could be given in prison; or the prisoner could even be transferred to Grendon Prison where he could receive treatment unobtainable within a psychiatric hospital. Subnormal offenders, or rather those of limited intellectual ability who in earlier paternalistic days would have been given asylum for their own, if not society's good, became more difficult to place. They fitted ill with the hopes that subnormality hospitals would be things of the past, those few patients requiring residential care being looked after in small units within their local community. Again, many such defendants were sentenced to imprisonment or unjustifiably admitted to special hospitals for want of any appropriate place in ordinary subnormality hospitals.

By the early 1970s the problems had become acute and in 1972 a Committee on Mentally Abnormal Offenders under the chairmanship of Lord Butler, commonly known as the Butler Committee, was set up to inquire into all aspects of the law relating to mentally abnormal offenders and into the provisions necessary for their treatment (Home Office and DHSS, 1975). The Committee took the unusual step of issuing an interim report in 1974 describing in strong terms the plight of patients and of courts, the overcrowding in special hospitals, the number of mentally disordered offenders in prison and the lack of a coherent policy to rectify these deficiencies. It recommended that regional secure units be set up with a degree of security intermediate between psychiatric hospitals and special hospitals and pressed that the facilities for the mentally abnormal offender at all stages in his criminal or psychiatric career should be co-ordinated. It suggested that special monies should be provided to help overcome some of the expected resistance to the concept of such units. Among very many other issues, most comprehensively dealt with, the Butler Committee discussed the treatability of psychopathy and the prediction of future dangerousness. After a detailed historical overview it concluded quite firmly that there was little evidence to suggest that psychopathy was treatable by medical means or in a medical setting, and it was rather more confident than most criminologists and forensic psychiatrists of the value and accuracy of the prediction of dangerousness. To cater for psychopaths who had committed serious offences and who were expected to repeat them it suggested a new disposal of an indefinite but reviewable sentence and special psychopathic treatment units within the prison system to be run on social and psychological lines. This last suggestion, unlike that for regional secure units, has not met with much favour and is unlikely to do so in the future.

The Mental Health Act, 1959 has recently been amended and a consolidated Mental Health Act 1983 recently introduced. It still recognises four forms of mental disorder: mental illness, mental impairment, severe mental impairment and psychopathic disorder, though the definitions of the last three have been changed. Included in many other changes there are a number of alterations in the sections dealing with mentally abnormal offenders and some entirely new provisions, originating from the Butler Committee, have been introduced. The principal sections which now deal with offenders are: S35, a remand to hospital for psychiatric report; S36, a remand to hospital for treatment; S37, a hospital order, committing an offender to hospital for potentially indefinite compulsory treatment; S38, an interim hospital order; S41, an order restricting the discharge of a dangerous offender; S47, allowing the transfer to hospital of a mentally disordered prisoner; S48, allowing the transfer to hospital of a mentally ill or severely mentally impaired remanded prisoner; S49, an order restricting the discharge of S47 and S48 patients.

A hypothetical but unlikely sequence of events could be that a defendant at a lower court could be admitted to a psychiatric hospital for a report; if a ready disposal to a hospital was not indicated he could be remanded for treatment during the wait for his appearance at a higher court. Following his conviction, if there was still uncertainty about the wisdom of making an hospital order, he could again be detained in hospital for a trial of treatment before final decision for or against a medical disposal had to be made. How these new and elaborate provisions will work is uncertain but it seems likely that most minor psychotic offenders will be dealt with speedily at a lower court after the first report, most psychotic serious offenders at the time of their conviction at a higher court, with interim hospital orders only being used in cases of severe diagnostic uncertainty and in cases where psychopathy is felt to be worthy of a trial of treatment. Seriously mentally impaired defendants will probably be dealt with like psychotics, those only mildly intellectually impaired more like those suffering from psychopathic disorder.

Although it is intended that most minor offenders will be assessed and subsequently treated in non-secure psychiatric facilities, those who are currently refused bail and are assessed in prison are only committed into custody because of characteristics which do not endear them to open psychiatric units. It is probable, therefore, that these new provisions can only be implemented where specialist forensic psychiatry facilities exist, such as interim and regional secure units.

The frequency of mental health review tribunals has been virtually doubled by the new Act. This will considerably increase the work-load of secure units, particularly as legal aid is to be available to any detained patient to permit him to employ a lawyer. Tribunals are likely to become much more adversarial. Further, those patients who are thought dangerous and who are detained under Section 41, will now have access to a special mental health review tribunal with powers of discharge, chaired by a judge. This is in response to a judgment of the European Court of Human Rights, which concluded that there should be a judicial review of detention rather than the bureaucratic review under the previous procedures.

Forensic psychiatry in England is thus in a state of flux at present and more recent developments, particularly with regard to regional secure units and regional forensic psychiatry services, will be discussed later.

SCOTLAND

Though part of the British Isles, Scotland has a legal tradition quite different from that of England and Wales. The clinical practice of forensic psychiatry, the facilities for treatment, and the legal concepts have progressed along similar lines to England but there are considerable variations.

The concept of diminished responsibility in Britain originated from the practice of Scottish judges of the nineteenth century who introduced it to deal with the clearly mentally abnormal offender who did not fit the very narrow

McNaughton Test. The judges were prepared to substitute a verdict of culpable homicide for those defendants whose abnormality amounted almost to insanity, with resultant flexibility in sentencing options, including a committal to hospital. The Scottish Mental Health Act, 1960 does not have the four sub-categories of mental disorder of the English Act. There are only two, mental illness and mental deficiency. The omission of psychopathic disorder is interesting especially as a number of eminent Scots, D.K. Henderson in particular, were very much in the forefront of the development of the concept of psychopathy. Nevertheless, despite this omission, Scottish courts have allowed mental illness to embrace highly dangerous and extremely psychopathic offenders who would be dealt with within psychopathic disorder in England though this trend is on the wane following homicidal assaults on staff and patients in an escape bid by psychopathic patients from the state hospital, Carstairs, in 1978.

Scottish psychiatric practice has in general developed somewhat differently from that in England, though the differences have perhaps been more marked in the past. Scotland was in the forefront of the provision of mental hospitals and a surprising number of well endowed hospitals with a Royal Charter were built to serve quite small populations. Scotland still has more beds and more psychiatrists per head of the population than England and Wales. The same applies to the state hospital at Carstairs, the Scottish special hospital. The Scottish legal system has an element of the continental inquisitorial system, a public prosecutor, the Procurator-fiscal. In his inquiries into a case he can call for psychiatric investigation from any psychiatrist of his choosing, usually a local general psychiatrist of standing. Because of this policy and the much smaller size of the Scottish prison system, a Scottish prison medical service has not developed to provide psychiatric reports on remanded prisoners, although there is a small number of prison medical officers working in Barlinnie Prison, Glasgow, dealing mostly with the physical welfare of the inmates. This lack of a prison medical service has had a number of results. General psychiatrists, regularly reporting on mentally abnormal offenders, have not so readily rejected them and espoused the entirely open door policy of the hospitals in England. Secure facilities have always been a feature of Scottish mental hospitals and they have not been seen as facilities of low prestige, probably because of the status of the senior staff using them. As a consequence the need for the new secure facilities as described in the Butler Report have in general been felt to be unnecessary. General psychiatrists and forensic psychiatrists regularly visit and work in prisons and have perhaps been more able to influence the workings of the Scottish penal service, within the smaller and much more integrated administrative system of the health and penal services, and to encourage a radical innovation like the Special Unit at Barlinnie Prison (Boyle, 1977). This unit was opened to help reduce the serious level of endemic violence in the Scottish prisons on the premise that, if the most seriously disturbed and violent prisoners were treated in a more sensitive and psychotherapeutically orientated regime with adequate numbers of specially selected and trained prison officers, they would become less violent and the violence in the prisons as a whole would drop. This unit has attracted a great deal of publicity and has been reasonably successful in achieving its aims.

The unit is almost invariably peaceful and some very disturbed and very violent individuals have been successfully rehabilitated. Its regime, however, has been criticised and its existence repeatedly threatened by those who see its success as having been bought at too high a price of élitism and pandering to the inmate.

In general, therefore, Scottish forensic psychiatry has remained part of mainstream psychiatry to an extent much greater than in England. Scottish forensic psychiatrists spend a larger proportion of their time looking after convicted prisoners, supplying support and guidance to penal establishments. Forensic psychiatry has not spawned regional forensic psychiatry centres with specialised hospital units, secure or non-secure, nor the extensive out-patient departments that have been evolving in England over the last fifteen years.

DENMARK

Because of the inquisitorial system of justice in Denmark, differences of psychiatric opinion, diagnosis and disposal in cases of mental abnormality are not aired at court. Psychiatric reports are prepared for the court solely by recognised expert psychiatrists. Cases of difficulty or of particular seriousness can, however, be further referred to a state board of forensic psychiatrists. Most of the Danish penal code dates from 1866. The current legislation came into force in 1933 but has been amended subsequently, most recently in 1974. There is in Denmark the customary clear distinction between a psychiatric hospital system and a public prosecution, police, prison and probation system run by the Ministry of Justice. Within the hospital system a special hospital has not developed, though in 1918 a special security facility was set aside for the dangerous psychiatrically ill. However, with the advent of effective drug treatments and the disposal of psychopaths and borderline or intermittently psychotic patients to Herstedvester, the special detention centre in the penal system, the numbers declined so spectacularly that no special secure hospital facility was found to be necessary.

In dealing with the mentally abnormal offender two concepts underpin the Danish system; eligibility for punishment, and susceptibility to punishment. Under Section 16 of the Danish Criminal Code persons who are completely non-responsible by reason of insanity or because of pronounced mental deficiency are not eligible for punishment. Under Section 17, 'if at the time of committing the punishable act, the more permanent condition of the perpetrator involved defective development or impairment or disturbance of his mental faculties, including sexual abnormality . . . a court shall decide, on the basis of a medical report and the other available evidence, whether he may be considered for punishment.' Under Section 70 of the same code, the court may decide, having regard to public safety, what measures will be applied to those coming within Sections 16 and 17 to prevent further offending; the aim is to adopt the minimum number of custodial disposals for treatment, such as to hospital or special detention, probation and outpatient treatment being preferred, particularly as custodial treatment measures are of an indeterminate nature. The future handling of Section 16 and 17 cases, such as discharge from an institution or removal of restrictions in the community, are determined by a further referral to the original court.

Under the Danish system seriously mentally ill and severely mentally handicapped offenders coming within Section 16 are, in practice, handled little differently from those in Britain, being sent to hospital for treatment. However, for many years, psychopaths, though psychopathy is not mentioned in Section 17, were given an indefinite sentence for treatment in a 'special detention centre', Herstedvester, which was opened for this purpose in 1936. Its long-time director, Stürup, has described at length the selection procedures, the inmate population, and the type of treatment offered at Herstedvester (Stürup, 1968). It was run as a therapeutic community offering 'individualised, integrating growth therapy', by means of individual or group psychotherapy and somatic therapies such as hormone therapy and even castration for certain sexual offenders. Under the direction of Stürup, Herstedvester achieved a world-wide reputation. However, in the late 1960s confidence in the success of treatment of psychopaths under indeterminate detention started to become outweighed by scepticism about the results of treatment, concerns about the prediction of further offending and concerns about indeterminate sentencing as a principle, particularly as Stürup, even in 1965, was stating, 'I would like to present a clear description, complete with statistical figures, of the final outcome of our work at Herstedvester but I cannot do so'. Statistics, however, did show that only 40 per cent of inmates had committed violent or sexual offences, the majority being recidivist property offenders, and that the success of treatment for violent, sexual or property offenders was little different from ordinary imprisonment. As a result fewer and fewer were made the subject of special detention and it was finally abolished in 1974 and replaced by ordinary determinate imprisonment. Indeterminate sentences were retained for only a small number of the most serious offences. Herstedvester now operates within the prison rules as a prison, but is still run on hospital lines. It takes selected psychologically disturbed prisoners from the other regional prisons as well as acting as a remand centre. While there are two forensic assessment units within the hospital system in Denmark, for disturbed psychotics, the number of places is small and there is a long waiting list. The numbers of psychotic patients in Herstedvester are therefore increasing, particularly as psychiatric hospitals have become more and more reluctant to admit them and are even taking such patients who commit antisocial acts to court to have them removed from the hospital system.

Since the change in the law in 1974 removing special detention, the number of psychiatric assessments for court has dropped dramatically. Psychopaths now go to prison and are treated in the usual way unless they are subsequently transferred to Herstedvester. Many more mentally ill offenders are admitted to prison, ending up in Herstedvester. The similarities to England are obvious.

HOLLAND

The Dutch hospital and penal system and the law dealing with mentally abnormal offenders is difficult to describe simply, especially as there are so many differences from elsewhere. Health care in Holland is principally private with state care only for those not covered by insurance or for those who require long-term and consequently expensive treatment.

The private system is organised by religious denominations, though narrow sectarian demarcation is on the wane. Denominational psychiatric hospitals have no obligation to admit any patient, even from their immediate catchment area, and state provision for unwanted patients is patchy and in general inadequate. A full range of psychiatric facilities is provided by denominational hospitals and admissions can be voluntary or compulsory via a civil court. The proportion of detained patients is small and these patients tend to be found more in older mental hospitals than in urban general hospitals or university units.

The Dutch attitude to ordinary offenders is remarkable, first because of the reluctance to adopt any punitive measures at all, especially in first and petty offenders, and second because of the brevity of sentences imposed even on repeated offenders and very serious offenders. The prison population is therefore quite low. Many mentally abnormal offenders do not reach a criminal court. The public prosecutor may abandon prosecution, the case being dismissed and the patient admitted to a hospital on a voluntary basis or via a civil court. Serious cases, however, are almost invariably brought to a criminal court.

The principal issue in a Dutch court is the degree to which the defendant can be reproached for his offence. Dutch law recognises two main disposals of court, a punishment and a 'measure'. A 'measure' is a disposal for treatment in order to prevent a recurrence. Under the Penal Code of 1886 the measure imposed for a defendant who is wholly not responsible for his act is compulsory detention in a psychiatric hospital for a period of one year. During this year the patient may be discharged by the responsible medical officer if he has improved, but if necessary he may be detained further under civil procedures. In cases where criminal responsibility is diminished but not absent, the proportion to which the defendant can be reproached must be determined and the punishment appropriately reduced. However, in the case of seriously abnormal offenders, particularly psychopaths, such a reduction might increase the risk to the general public. To cater for this circumstance a second 'measure' was introduced in the Psychopaths Act, 1928. This is detention at the government's pleasure, 'terbeschikkingstelling van de regering', commonly known as TBR (Detention at the Government's Pleasure, 1977).

TBR allows indefinite detention for treatment, the detention being reviewed every one or two years by the criminal court imposing it. It can be applied to a non-responsible offender whose case has been discharged or who has been committed to a mental hospital. However, the majority are applied to those who are found to be of diminished responsibility and psychopathic rather than psychotic. As the degree of reproach is crucial, the defendant of diminished responsibility must be sentenced to an appropriate punishment; the TBR is imposed in addition. A conditional discharge may even be given, enabling the TBR procedure to start forthwith, but in general, as the punishment is reduced by diminished responsibility, the prison sentence is short, even by Dutch standards, and the TBR measure implemented shortly. In recent years, however, very long sentences have been imposed, with the TBR only coming into force at the date of release. The reasons for this development will be discussed later.

To provide facilities for the treatment of TBR patients, specific institutions have been set up under the general direction of the Minister of Justice: five private institutions, the two best known being the Dr Henri Van der Hoeven Clinic in Utrecht, and the Prof. Mr W.P.J. Pompe Clinic in Nijmegen; two state institutions, the most well known and the most secure of all the units being the Dr S. Van Mesdag Clinic in Gronigen. These TBR establishments range in size from 35 to 85 patients and the total number of places is approximately 260. The placement of each TBR patient is usually determined by the Selection Institute in Utrecht after a 4–6 week period of observation. The general philosophy of care in all the establishments is social and personal retraining by means of individual and group psychotherapy provided by psychiatrically, socially or psychologically trained therapists. The duration of stay is expected to be relatively short. Discharge usually follows increasing amounts of parole and leave and it has been unusual for a patient to obtain a second extension of his TBR. The TBR continues after discharge but invariably the staff of TBR units pass the management of the patient over to the probation service in his home locality and lose contact with him. The regime in each unit is quite different as each unit is free to indulge its preference: the Van Mesdag Clinic has a psychoanalytical approach under medical direction; the Van der Hoeven Clinic individual treatment programmes by social therapists; the Pompe Clinic, initially at least, a very permissive therapeutic community.

Each clinic was built at considerable cost. The cost per patient is extremely high because of very high staffing levels. They were built mainly in the 1960s, when it was confidently expected that such institutions and regimes would have a markedly beneficial effect on both recidivist property offenders with personality abnormalities and markedly psychologically disturbed sexual and violent offenders. Many more TBRs were imposed then than more recently. Between 1965 and 1976 they declined from 183 to 104 and they have declined further since. In addition, the percentage of older property offenders has diminished and those now made the subject of a TBR are usually young sexual or violent offenders. Public interest in discharged patients and their success or failure is therefore much greater.

Throughout the 1970s a number of attempts have been made to pass amending legislation on mental health in the Dutch parliament. None has been successful, though yet another bill is currently under consideration. The problems which demand changes are already familiar. Private psychiatric establishments which can refuse are reluctant to admit offender patients. The state mental hospital which was then obliged to take them narrowed its catchment area to its more immediate area and many parts of the country as a result now lack secure psychiatric provisions. The type of facilities and the quality of treatment in state psychiatric hospitals have been much criticised, especially when they are compared with the TBR units. A report published in 1980 has suggested the need for regional secure units similar to those proposed for England. Confidence has waned in the theoretical basis of the TBR and the results of its application in practice. The much larger proportion of younger more disturbed individuals has caused difficulties in the units. There have been some marked difficulties, to the extent that the most liberal unit, the Pompe Clinic, was occupied for a while more by discharged patients intent on a haven from which they could pillage the neighbourhood than by official patients. It was severely damaged and was eventually closed in 1976. It was reopened later with a considerably changed regime after a large number of the original staff had departed.

The TBR, interpreted by the units as a treatment rather than a detention measure, has been losing the confidence of the courts particularly when, as part of a gradual rehabilitation scheme, many patients are reintroduced to the community at an early stage and then reoffend. To prevent early release a short or conditional sentence with a TBR is being replaced either by a long prison sentence with a TBR and the recommendation of an immediate transfer from prison to a TBR unit, or even by a prison sentence alone, during which the prisoner may be transferred to a TBR unit via the Prison Rules. These long-term prisoners fit ill with the others in the TBR unit and have a deleterious effect on their regimes. It is generally accepted now that a TBR is not indicated for property offenders, even quite psychiatrically disturbed recidivists, and there has been much discussion about the indeterminacy of a TBR, contrasting it with the results of finite sentences, particularly in the case of dangerous psychopathic offenders. Opposing views are held on whether the TBR is indefinite detention for treatment or indefinite detention for dangerousness, psychiatrists more espousing the former, jurists and courts the latter. Finally despite long experience, many patients, elaborate structural and staffing provisions and diversity of regimes, there has been surprisingly little hard statistical information about the effectiveness of the units.

SUMMING UP

Reviewing the provisions available for the management of mentally abnormal offenders in Britain, Denmark and Holland and the subsequent changes over time, several common themes become apparent.

1   The increasing liberalisation of mental health legislation;
2   the continuing decline of mental hospitals in both numbers and security and the subsequent rejection of disturbed and difficult patients;
3   the shift of mentally abnormal offenders, psychotic and intellectually handicapped, away from prisons to hospitals, which has now to some extent been reversed;
4   the dilemma of the psychopath, his degree of responsibility, his need for

treatment and his response to it, has not been resolved, no matter whether he has been placed in an ordinary prison, in a specialised unit inside the penal system, in a hospital, or even in an entirely separate system;

5 the disturbance of the settled, cosy and pragmatic relationship between psychiatrists, courts and the bureaucracy by the appearance of civil liberties lawyers and criminologists raising issues such as: the right to be punished; the right not to be punished; the right to be treated; the right not to be treated; the justice of indeterminate sentences especially when associated with treatments of debatable efficacy; and the poor predictability of dangerousness.

Developments in the USA from where many of these last issues have originated and where the effects of them are most marked, are particularly influential and are discussed later in this book.

Is it really a paradox that during a period of rapid advance in the understanding and treatment of psychiatric illness, the shift of practice from the large, custodial and paternalistic mental hospital to the much more permissive and medically orientated practice in general hospital clinics should result in increasing intolerance of a few difficult patients and in increasing numbers of mentally ill on the street and in the prisons? Perhaps, for the benefit of many, a few should be neglected or rejected: but this is easier if they can be seen as a discrete category of offender-patients. Perhaps it is the price of progress but care must also be taken to ensure that the 'not nice' patients in the interests of their civil liberties should not become equally deprived and be compelled to 'rot with their rights on'. The civil liberties approach has quite correctly drawn more attention to the rights of patients but if carried too far can lead to a preoccupation with legalism with resulting interference or delay in treatment or in precipitate discharge. Acutely disturbed and resistant patients will be transferred by cautious staff even more readily to the 'not nice' group and so swell the numbers of mentally abnormal offenders. There will be an increasing reluctance to use restraint of either a physical or chemical variety and psychiatric hospitals offering security and long-term care will be under even more fire than they have been of late. Proposals for much more frequent reviews of detention orders and mandatory second opinions for many forms of compulsory treatment, which are incorporated in the new English Mental Health Act, will further threaten secure hospitals, will certainly lead to the adoption by the hospitals of a much narrower remit and the disposal of even more borderline cases to the penal system.

Success of treatment measures for psychopathic offenders has not been clearly demonstrated. The swing away from a treatment approach has been most marked in Denmark but even in Holland, where the most elaborate provisions have been made, enthusiasm is waning. Treatability has become intertwined with prediction of dangerousness and indeterminacy of detention. Two polar views have emerged: a clinical one that, even as an act of faith or of compassion, the treatment of psychopathy must be undertaken and such treatment must logically be indeterminate; an academic, criminological and legalistic one that, as there is little proof of the benefit of treatment and, as dangerousness is not predictable, society in practice and in theory is better protected by determinate sentences whose length reflects the extent of the breach of the social contract by the offender. There has been a definite shift towards the latter view throughout the 1970s. This change has produced considerable uncertainty among clinicians and courts, the unhappy grasping of the nettle that, in the absence of effective treatments, those of diminished responsibility as a result of personality abnormality require longer sentences. To salve consciences, treatment is often mentioned, but only to take place during or even at the end of a very long prison sentence. In Denmark no treatment orders for psychopathy are now made, in Holland long prison sentences with treatment orders provide for flexibility but those psychopaths detained solely within a hospital setting, such as the British special hospital, now present considerable difficulties. The revised legislation will provide a means by which their continuing detention can be more effectively questioned and their discharge more vociferously demanded. Whether, as a result, enforced experiments on the prediction of dangerousness will be undertaken, as in the Baxstrom experiment in the United States (Steadman and Cocozza, 1974), or whether the new Act will still allow the continued detention of dangerous but untreatable patients, remains to be seen.

Without doubt the role of the psychiatric expert will continue to be questioned within the next few years, probably increasingly so. Pressures to examine the bases for recommendations and to erode clinical freedom and clinical responsibility are now considerable. Increasing involvement of laymen in the monitoring of a patient's treatment and his need for continuing detention, such as is proposed by the Mental Health Act Commission and the increased frequency of mental health review tribunals, will increase these. Unfortunately laymen have little experience or training and require guidance. Complex legal issues are involved and laymen are allegedly notoriously susceptible to the blandishments of doctors. A lawyer is thus considered by many to be essential. However, his different frames of reference can give rise to difficulty in reconciling the needs of patients with the concepts of personal freedom and individual responsibility. As such concepts come to carry increasing weight there will be even fewer detained patients in psychiatric hospitals. It seems likely that increasing numbers of mentally abnormal individuals will accumulate in the community, will offend, and the result will be even more mentally abnormal individuals in the penal setting.

One can predict that a reaction to this will come. For psychotic offenders perhaps the reaction is already being seen with the advent of regional secure units in England and Wales and the suggestion of similar units in Holland, but unless some new treatments appear for psychopaths and the intellectually limited, effective care or help for them seems a long way off.

REFERENCES

Boyle, J. (1977) *A Sense of Freedom*. Glasgow: MacLehose.
Craft, M. (1966) *Psychopathic Disorders and Their Assessment*. Oxford: Pergamon.
Detention at the Government's Pleasure, Treatment of Criminal Psychopaths in the Netherlands (1970) The Central Recruitment and Training Institute of the Prison Service and the Care Criminal Psychopaths Service.

East, W.N. & Hubert, W.H. de B. (1939) *The Psychological Treatment of Crime*. London: HMSO.

Gunn, J., Robertson, G., Dell, S. & Way, C. (1978) *Psychiatric Aspects of Imprisonment*. London: Academic Press.

Home Office and DHSS (1975) *Report of the Committee on Mentally Abnormal Offenders* (Butler Report). *Cmnd. 6244*. London: HMSO.

Howard, J. (1777) *The State of the Prisons in England and Wales*. Warrington.

Ministry of Health (1961) *Report of the Working Party on Special Hospitals*. London: HMSO.

Steadman, H.J. & Cocozza, J.J. (1974) *Careers of the Criminally Insane: Excessive Social Control of Deviance*. Lexington: D.C. Heath.

Stürup, G.K. (1968) *Treating the Untreatable: Chronic Criminals at Herstedvester*. 2C68-12901. Baltimore: Johns Hopkins.

Whiteley, J.S. (1975) The psychopath and his treatment. *Brit. J. Psychiat.*, **121,** 159-169.

2

Who Are
Mentally Abnormal Offenders?

Michael Craft

Crime is common and so is mental abnormality. Two such common things would be expected to occur together in some individuals, and this is the case. There may be circumstantial evidence of the mental abnormality existing before a crime, sometimes immediately antecedent to it; or evidence of mental disorder present after the crime, possibly the result of the arrest, or the crime itself. In addition, mentally ill people commonly behave in a way which is unlawful. Florid mental illness or psychosis with resultant criminal behaviour are relatively easy for both lawyer and psychiatrist to disentangle, and were it not for the life-long personality disordered or psychopathic, the relationship between the two professions would be more straightforward than it is.

THE JUDGE'S VIEWPOINT

Lord Justice Ormrod, himself a doctor, reminds us that although justice has always been engaged in dealing with the results of a wrong act, the advance of civilisation in the country can be reflected in the interest it takes in the mental state or intent behind the act, and the sophistication and resources it will devote to the care of the perpetrator, as well as the victim (Ormrod, 1975). Criminal offences, like 'other legal concepts, such as domicile, desertion and the interpretation of contracts came to depend as much or more on the state of mind as on the acts in question.' However, the forensic difficulties of defining states of mind are formidable, so that, 'Today there is a discernible tendency to avoid defining legal obligations too precisely in terms of states of mind, and to leave the judges more discretion to "take into account all the circumstances of the case".' In effect, this leaves the professional advising on the mentally abnormal offender with a series of options, more options being open to the defence than the prosecution in England and Wales. Defending lawyers and professional witnesses may decide on one of the rebuttals of 'intent' or 'guilt', declaring either that the client was 'unfit to plead', or 'without the intent to commit the crime'. They may advance the plea of 'diminished responsibility', or seek to show that the client committed the crime under extreme circumstances, or that resulting illness is so temporary or so treatable as to proceed to a sentence following conviction which ensures best care for the client. Providing dangerousness to the public is not overriding the defence may obtain a favourable hearing. The rest of this book is concerned with the infilling of factual knowledge for professionals, so that each knows better what the other may be talking about, and the ends to be achieved.

MENTAL ABNORMALITY AND OFFENCE

Both mental disorder and crime are common. To examine their interrelation we need to examine the incidence of each in society and the problems of definition. There are three areas in which we can examine such definitions and incidence.

1 The frequency of mental abnormality in the general population. This is the subject of the first part of this chapter.

2 The frequency of crime in the general population. This is the subject of the next two chapters.

3 The frequency of mental abnormality and crime in institutionalised populations such as (a) residents of ordinary psychiatric hospitals, (b) prisoners, (c) maximum security psychiatric hospitals, those like Broadmoor, Rampton, Moss Side, etc., caring for mentally abnormal offenders who are dangerous.

Mental Abnormality in the General Population

Estimations of the extent of mental abnormality or illness in a general population are as difficult to make as estimations of criminality, discussed in the next chapter. There are many parallels. Serious crime is filtered out from less serious crime by passage along the court system, in the same way as mental illness is filtered by the levels of psychiatric care. Depending on severity, there will be different figures for mental illness or abnormality at each level of complaint. I am indebted to Goldberg and Huxley (1980) for the data appearing in *Mental Illness in the Community* now to be drawn upon.

Figure 2.1 represents the filters screening out mental illness in a family doctor's practice. The square represents the entire population on his list. Circle A represents the two-thirds of his practice who will consult him sometime during a year, and circle B those who themselves feel mentally unwell. Not all of these will complain of *mental* ill health, so circle C represents those identified by their family doctor as psychiatrically ill. Table 2.1 gives the numbers at issue, the final filter, or level of severity, here representing those requiring hospital admission. A similar filter system could be drawn up for physical illness, for a legal practice in civil or criminal law, indeed for any professional practice.

It is perhaps a surprising finding that as many as two-thirds of the general population consult their doctor each year, and a sizeable minority do so with mental illness. Women are over-represented in circle B. More than half of them will not tell their doctor the extent of their sorrows, he will not ask them and the speedy prescription shows that the mental illness component is unrecognised and untreated. Of course, as with many physical illnesses, these mental illnesses will mainly be of short-term duration, most recovering with or without medical treatment. The more prolonged or more serious are likely to pass through the

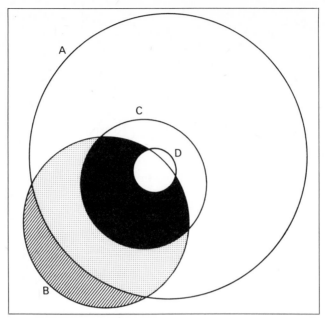

Figure 2.1 Venn diagram showing mental illness in an urban UK community. (From Goldberg and Huxley, 1980, with kind permission.)

A = *Consult their doctor during year*
B = *Psychiatrically ill during year (level 1)*
C = *Identified by their doctor as psychiatrically ill (level 2)*
D = *Referred to a psychiatrist (level 3)*
  Do not pass 1st filter (ill, but do not consult)
  Do not pass 2nd filter (illness unrecognised by doctor)
  Do not pass 3rd filter (not referred to a psychiatrist)

filters of recognition and referral on to psychiatric outpatients clinics. At each of these levels some clients will by-pass the filter, for instance some patients are referred to a psychiatrist by a solicitor, or may even be admitted to hospital as emergencies (not shown in Figure 2.1).

Table 2.1 provides the figures and explanations behind the Venn diagram. The annual incidence of 250 and 230 per thousand population at the first two levels may seem high, but include all episodes of mental ill health in a population having available a free National Health Service, and the figures are well authenticated by repeated surveys. For more detail readers should consult the original book (Goldberg and Huxley, 1980), itself a small and readable summary of the numerous world-wide investigations among different populations. The figures and flow diagram show averages for typical British middle-class general practices, and would be different for black-dominated suburbs of Birmingham where unemployment and poverty increase stress to depressed housewives, or Carshalton Beeches, where alcoholism is a major problem among stockbrokers. It is of interest that at similar levels of affluence, the total figures are found to be similar among suburbs in Beverly Hills or suburban Canberra, but the flow would be different. Both the latter places have higher proportions of self-referrals

Table 2.1 The filter system at work in psychiatry.

	The community	Primary medical care		Specialist psychiatric services	
	Level 1	Level 2	Level 3	Level 4	Level 5
One-year period prevalence, median estimates	Morbidity in random community samples	Total psychiatric morbidity, primary care	Conspicuous psychiatric morbidity	Total psychiatric patients	Psychiatric inpatients only
	250 per 1000	→ 230 per 1000	→ 140 per 1000	→ 17 per 1000	→ 6 per 1000
Characteristics of the four filters		*First filter* Illness behaviour	*Second filter* Detection of disorder	*Third filter* Referral to psychiatrists	*Fourth filter* Admission to psychiatric beds
Key individual		The patient	Primary care physician	Primary care physician	Psychiatrist
Factors operating on key individual		Severity and type of symptoms	Interview techniques	Confidence in own ability to manage	Availability of beds
		Psycho-social stress	Personality factors	Availability and quality of psychiatric services	Availability of adequate community psychiatric services
		Learned patterns of illness behaviour	Training and attitudes	Attitudes towards psychiatrists	
Other factors		Attitudes of relatives	Presenting symptom pattern	Symptom pattern of patient	Symptom pattern of patient, risk to self or others
		Availability of medical services	Socio-demographic characteristics of patient	Attitudes of patient and family	Attitudes of patient and family
		Ability to pay for treatment			Delay in social worker arriving

From Goldberg and Huxley, 1980.

direct to private psychiatrists – also higher proportions of self-medication by alcohol. Alternatively, places as far apart as Uganda and Johannesburg can have high incidences of mentally (and physically) unwell black Africans, their sorrows compounded by poverty, unemployment and autocracy, but alleviated by native practitioners, 'primary care government staff', or even witch doctors.

It is a consolation that surveys show that mental health statistics get better with the improvement of each of the environmental variables, such as housing, employment, etc., so that in the affluent Western societies a high level of mental and physical health can be reached, beyond which minor variables of genetic endowment, ageing, spouse, seem to play a major part. Thus, best placed females in Australian and other surveys had an incidence of 11 per cent of mental ill health in the year surveyed, compared with 67 per cent in the environmentally worst placed – quite a difference! Interesting political questions emerge. What is the most cost-effective way of alleviating human ills: housing or health practitioner, sex education, mental health teaching at school? and so on. Developed societies can afford to compromise, with most western societies outside Russia having rising life expectancies – and rising suicide rates. Russia has a falling life expectancy – and rising alcohol rate – so in 1972 stopped issuing figures of life expectancy (discussed Ryan, 1982).

It is important to note the effect of the filter system on the distribution of the mentally ill. As might be expected, the common mild illnesses are treated successfully in the community, the more severe and persistent are forwarded to psychiatric outpatients clinics and to hospital. Thus, the family doctor treats minor depressive illnesses, anxiety neuroses, and counsels the oddities of the personality disordered and the mentally handicapped. A psychiatric inpatient ward is likely to have a greater proportion of personality disordered, especially if the consultant is interested in court work. There will also be a higher proportion of severe depressive and schizophrenic disorders in the inpatient ward than the general practitioner's office. Some of the severe personality disorders, the repeatedly offending psychopaths and sociopaths may be found in an ordinary psychiatric hospital if the consultant wants to treat them and the nursing staff are willing. Many more will accumulate in maximum security hospitals like Broadmoor and Rampton which exist for their treatment, and in long-term prisons.

The Frequency of Crime in the Ordinary Psychiatric Hospital Population

Unfortunately, any investigation of the proportion of psychiatric hospital populations sent there after conviction runs into three serious pitfalls. In the first place, in most developed countries police avoid prosecuting people, especially for minor and moderate crimes, if they are assured that the person concerned is entering a psychiatric unit. This is not only because of sympathy for the patient, or respect for his medical supervisors, it is also the thankful avoidance of the degree of paperwork involved and the knowledge that, even if this paperwork is completed, many courts will pay little regard to it if they can accept with relief an institutionalisation which most know to be almost as all-caring as penal care.

In the second place, once more for 'mild' or 'moderate' offences, the injured party will often not press charges if the offender enters hospital. Again, this is not only out of sympathy for the offender; most aggrieved persons have a disinclination to go through the paperwork and court procedure themselves. Thirdly, there has been a strong tendency over recent years for hospitals to avoid taking patients direct from the courts. This is not only because the open door policy of most modern hospitals means lack of security, but the increasingly bad press and publicity given to hospitals who do treat convicted patients ranks high in the scale of things psychiatrists wish to avoid. For instance, although indict-able offences rose from 536 653 in 1962–4 to 907 267 in 1972–74, an increase of 69 per cent, admissions to psychiatric hospitals under Part V (hospital court orders) of the 1959 Mental Health Act fell 12.5 per cent for females (from 415 to 363 cases) and rose by only 4.2 per cent for males (2270 to 2365) (Parker and Tennent, 1979). Put another way, per 10 000 offenders, disposals under Part V dropped 40 per cent over this period of time. In 1974 mental handicap hospitals took three times as many Part V admissions as did mental illness hospitals (1.7 per cent of total admissions as opposed to 0.5 per cent). Clearly the mental handicap hospitals play an important part in court disposals. Special hospitals (Broadmoor, etc.) had 76.5 per cent of all 1974 admissions under Part V.

It is probable that the number of patients on probation in psychiatric hos-pitals has risen 1961–77, but there are no available figures from the Home Office on this point.

Mental Abnormality among Prisoners

For a proportion of inmates in developed countries it has long been known that chance plays a part as to which of the two total institutions, prison or mental hospital, cares for them. In Britain Penrose's Law is commonly adduced as showing the inverse relationship between mental hospital and prison population numbers. Penrose's pre-Second World War research demonstrated that de-veloped countries with large penal populations had small psychiatric hospital populations, and vice versa; additionally, the number of prisoners, the murder rate, the suicide rate and the country's mortality rate had an inverse relationship with the rate of psychiatric hospital admission. The force of his arguments has become very clear in England and California in recent times when the number of psychiatric hospital places has been sharply reduced, and the number of prison places has had to be increased. Conversely, in more traditional areas such as Scotland and Queensland, where large mental hospitals have kept beds open, the rise in prison populations has not been so great.

There have been a number of studies into the degree of mental abnormality shown by resident penal populations both in Britain and in America. There are causal factors here, for instance, a long prison sentence can produce a degree of personality damage. One of the first surveys was that of Gibbens (1963), who found that 27 per cent of his sample of English Borstal boys needed psychiatric treatment, despite the fact that, following medical examination on intake, frank psychiatric illness had been screened out. West (1963), looking at 100 recidivists (preventive detainees) who were then in prison for at least seven years following repeated offences, found that ten were psychotic, two epileptic, nine had had previous mental hospital treatment and a majority of the remainder had inadequate, unstable or aggressive personalities. Later, Bluglass (1966) examined a quarter of the admissions of convicts to Perth prison over eleven months. Out of 300 sampled, he called 2 per cent psychotic, 2 per cent neurotic, 11 per cent alcoholic (one drug addict), 14 per cent 'subnormal' or 'borderline subnormal', 1 per cent epileptic, 2 per cent organic states, and 13 per cent 'psychopathic'. In all, 46 per cent needed psychiatric treatment in his opinion. Gunn (1974) confirmed this in a one-in-ten sample of convicts in south eastern England. Of 629 questionnaire replies from 811 men in all, he and his interviewing team of trainee psychiatrists found 31 per cent needing psychiatric treatment, including such severe cases as: two psychoses, nine neuroses, three sex deviations, 13 alcoholic and 22 personality disorders. He comments that the 31 per cent should be set against the 14 per cent of the general population consulting their doctors for psychiatric reasons at any one time, although, of course, an additional proportion have psychiatric and physical complaints.

Of the American studies into the incidence of mental abnormality among prison populations, most have found even higher frequencies than in Britain. One of these series was described by Guze (1976), who arranged for a team of psychiatrists using standardised psychiatric questionnaires to survey 223 consecutive discharges from prison. He found 90 per cent of the men had a psychiatric diagnosis, 78 per cent having a sociopathic personality disorder. However, only 32 per cent of this prison population were thought amenable to treatment, among these being the one per cent schizophrenic, one per cent epileptic and the alcoholic. In passing, it is worth while noting that one per cent is the incidence of schizophrenia in the general population too. This incidence of mental handicap (under IQ 70) in the general population is three per cent, but Guze did not find any of these in the male prison population surveyed. Among the female prisoners he and his team found that all deserved a psychiatric diagnosis, some earning more than one; 65 per cent had sociopathic personalities, 31 per cent hysteria, and many were at the time secondarily depressed.

One can conclude this survey of mental abnormality found among penal populations by noting that most surveys find a substantial proportion with degrees of mental abnormality. Syndromes of chronic brain damage with or without alcoholism, and degrees of personality disorder make up the major contribution. Depressive episodes are common, usually secondary to the underlying personality disturbance.

The Frequency of Mental Abnormality and Crime in Maximum Security Psychiatric Hospitals

The survey of 1974 referred to above showed 76.5 per cent of all English special hospital admissions to be direct from the courts, most of them following conviction for serious crime. This high proportion of conviction among patients has not changed subsequently. The remaining 23.5 per cent were transfers under compulsory order from ordinary psychiatric hospitals, some of whom would also have been convicted earlier. The Department of Health must be satisfied that all admissions present outstanding danger or violence. The proportion of personality disorders is also high among this population, as Table 2.2 shows.

Table 2.2 Mental Health Act classification of special hospital admissions.

	1962–64		1972–74	
Males	n	%	n	%
Mentally ill	238	38.7	311	43.3
Psychopathically disordered	156	25.4	247	34.5
Subnormal	120	19.5	95	13.3
Severely subnormal	47	7.6	37	5.2
Multiple classification	54	8.8	24	3.4
Not known	0	—	2	0.3
TOTAL	615	100.0	716	100.0
	1962–64		1972–74	
Females	n	%	n	%
Mentally ill	41	25.0	70	32.9
Psychopathically disordered	29	17.7	56	26.3
Subnormal	27	16.5	18	8.5
Severely subnormal	48	29.2	38	17.8
Multiple classification	17	10.4	28	13.1
Not known	2	1.2	3	1.4
TOTAL	164	100.0	213	100.0

From Parker and Tennent, 1979.

Of special hospital admissions 43 per cent of males and 33 per cent of females are mentally ill, predominantly schizophrenic and depressed persons who commit serious crime during the course of, or as a result of, oncoming illness. A further 3.4 per cent of males and 13 per cent of females have multiple diagnoses, more common in females than males, as Guze (1976) noted above for prisoners.

A considerable proportion of special hospital patients have psychopathy (35 per cent male, 26 per cent female) or subnormality (13 per cent male, 9 per cent female). In a survey of the use of the term 'subnormal' to be described in detail in Chapter 12, 'subnormality' was said to be an interchangeable diagnosis with 'psychopathy' among special hospital patients who had personality disorder and were below average (IQ 100) intelligence. If one adds these diagnostic groups together 48 per cent of males and 35 per cent of females in special hospitals have extreme personality disorder.

PERSONALITY DISORDER, PSYCHOPATHY, SOCIOPATHY

In case the reader is bemused by a surfeit of labels for the personality disturbed, a short discussion on this subject may be welcomed. People with personality disorders of varying severity appear before courts more commonly than do the mentally disordered with other diagnoses.

The more severe forms of personality disorder combined with anti-social behaviour are commonly labelled *psychopathy* in the UK and *sociopathy* in the USA. Indeed, the more severe the personality disorder and the greater the number of convictions, the greater the proportion of psychiatrists likely to label the individual as a psychopath. All the above entities are discussed at length in the chapters that follow, but because there has been much confusion over the meaning of the term 'psychopath'[1] a simple model of frequency is advanced here to place it in the range of behaviour disorders (see Figure 2.2). Just as severe mental illness affects only a small proportion of the mentally ill population, or very serious offences have been committed by only a small minority of those in prison at any one time, so the 'true' or 'essential' psychopath is in the minority

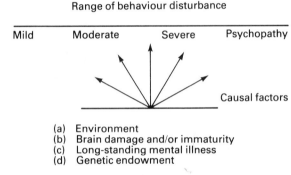

Range of behaviour disturbance

Mild   Moderate   Severe   Psychopathy

Causal factors

(a) Environment
(b) Brain damage and/or immaturity
(c) Long-standing mental illness
(d) Genetic endowment

Figure 2.2   Causal factors in behaviour disturbance.

(a) *Environment;* i.e. highly disturbed or missing family life, absence of adequate controlling or socialising factors. There may be a close interaction with (b) and (d) below when a minimally brain damaged or chromosomally abnormal baby is continually fretful and rejects comfort, thereby calling forth an antagonistic rearing pattern.

(b) *Brain damage;* partial or complete destruction of the frontal lobes by accident, surgery, tumour or infection. Among other abilities, these areas of the brain are responsible for careful judgement, forethought, feeling for others and steady application to tasks.

Brain immaturity; EEG studies have shown that slow wave activity in the cortex is present in 15 per cent of normal men, but three times more common in psychopaths (MacKeith, 1975).

(c) *Long-standing mental illness;* e.g. diminution of mental ability due to schizophrenia. Although most schizophrenia sufferers recover with modern treatment, a few are left with affective coldness, impulsivity, low tolerance threshold or paranoia.

(d) *Genetic endowment;* chromosomal abnormalities such as XYY can have an association with personality disorder, linked with cortical immaturity.

---

[1] 'Deeply ingrained maladaptive patterns of behaviour generally recognizable by the time of adolescence or earlier and continuing throughout most of adult life, although often becoming less obvious in middle or old age. The personality is abnormal either in the balance of its components, their quality and expression or in its total aspect. Because of this deviation or psychopathy, the patient suffers, or others have to suffer, and there is an adverse effect upon the individual or on society.' (World Health Organisation, 1978.)

In the English and Welsh 1983 Mental Health Act: ' "Psychopathic disorder" means a persistent disorder or disability of mind (whether or not including significant impairment of intelligence) which results in abnormally aggressive or seriously irresponsible conduct on the part of the person concerned'.

of those with personality disturbance and disorder. There would undoubtedly be disagreement as to where along the population continuum the curve should begin, and where on the severity scale *mild* becomes *moderate* and *moderate* shades into *severe*. It is even more complex when we remember that severity of behaviour is unlikely to be constant over time in any one individual. However, at any survey point in time, the population will contain a small group of those for whom the label 'psychopath' is appropriate, distinguished from others on the personality disorder scale by the extremity of their behaviour and the frequency of offence (not necessarily of conviction). The International Classification of Diseases (World Health Organisation, 1978) describes their disorder as being characterised by:

disregard for social obligations, lack of feeling for others, and impetuous violence or callous unconcern. There is a gross disparity between behaviour and the prevailing social norms. Behaviour is not readily modified by experience, including punishment. People with this personality are often affectively cold and may be abnormally aggressive or irresponsible. Their tolerance to frustration is low; they blame others or offer plausible rationalization for the behaviour which brings them into conflict with society.

A clinical model of psychopathy will be subject to disagreement concerning the importance of the various traits that lead psychiatrists to such a diagnosis. Indeed, some would not wish to make such a diagnosis at all, while others are perhaps over-inclusive. This was strongly brought home to me very early on when I did an analysis of the diagnostic practice of consultants at the Maudsley Teaching Hospital. I found that one psychiatrist (an ex-Guards Colonel with firm eugenic views concerning the unfit in society) characterised over a third of all his outpatients as psychopaths. Another, much more sympathetic and with left wing views, used the label not at all, feeling that society had been unfair to most of his patients! Being conscious of the need for testimonials from both, the analysis was left unpublished.

A recent survey of British psychiatrists on this subject was carried out by Davies and Feldman in 1981. They wrote to 35 forensic experts asking them to rate 22 traits for their importance in coming to a diagnosis of psychopathy. Table 2.3 shows the level of agreement between the 31 willing to rate. Interestingly, the first three signs on the Davies and Feldman list also scored highly on the earlier postal survey of Canadian psychiatrists, Gray and Hutchison (1964), who mailed their questionnaire to all 1366 English- and French-speaking doctors classified as psychiatrists with the Federal Department of National Health and Welfare. Detailed replies were available from 677, with results very similar to those of Davies and Feldman among British forensic psychiatrists. The first ten traits of the former are very much a rearrangement of those of the latter. Davies and Feldman go on to say that signs 16–22 on their list were considered by many respondees to be irrelevant to psychopathy. While psychiatrists may disagree about the relative importance of various traits, most would rate as significant:

1   Anti-social behaviour from childhood onwards and manifest over long periods of time;
2   An inability to adapt behaviour in the light of past experiences;
3   A quality of lovelessness, and an inability to have feelings for other humans,

Table 2.3   The importance of 22 signs of psychopathy as rated by a mixed sample of 31 forensic specialists.

	Sign	Mean	SD
1	Not profiting from experience	8.25	1.46
2	Lacking control over impulses	8.22	1.41
3	Chronically or recurrently antisocial	8.16	1.80
4	Lacking a sense of responsibility	7.53	2.09
5	Behaviour unaffected by punishment	7.50	2.02
6	Inability to form meaningful relationships	7.28	2.59
7	Emotional immaturity	7.28	2.33
8	Inability to experience guilt	7.25	1.81
9	Lack of moral sense	6.75	2.71
10	Deficiency in goal-directed behaviour	6.31	2.38
11	Self-centred	6.25	2.77
12	Frequent law-breaking	5.81	2.58
13	Frequent lying	5.75	2.51
14	Is aggressive	5.63	2.71
15	Occupationally unstable	5.45	2.57
16	Irresponsible sexual behaviour	4.03	2.51
17	Excessive alcohol consumption	3.84	2.30
18	Shows pronounced swings in mood	3.13	2.55
19	Abnormal EEG	3.00	2.90
20	Hyperactivity	1.25	1.67
21	More intelligent than average	1.19	2.13
22	Homosexuality	1.13	1.58

Rating: 10 = very important; 0 = not at all important.
From Davies and Feldman, 1981.

or sometimes themselves. Parallel to this is an inability to appreciate others' feelings. Cleckley (1976) has a graphic analogy: A man who has never understood visual experience would lack appreciation of what is sustained when the ordinary person loses his eye;

4 A high impulsivity or liability to over-react to provocation or stimulus;

5 Sometimes a degree of viciousness or wish to hurt others.

Such characteristics, present to a greater or lesser extent, make the psychopath an unattractive, usually unwanted patient.

Psychopathy, like schizophrenia, depression, diabetes or a fractured femur, results from a number of causes. It can be more or less severe, it may be affected by complications, in short, like any other medical/social entity affecting humans, it leads to a patient with an individual set of problems (see Figure 2.2). Many varying weights can be given to the causal factors. For each individual there will be a unique interplay of personality and life events. However, weighing causes is an academic exercise when one is faced with an individual who has offended and who is highly likely to present difficulties and to offend again. 'What to do now' is more pertinent than 'Why' at our present level of knowledge. As John Gunn, currently Maudsley Professor of Forensic Psychiatry, reminds us, the diagnosis of 'psychopath' tells one nothing specific about a particular patient (except perhaps that he is not liked). An amplified picture is needed of a man's problems, their seriousness and their time-span, together with an assessment of his strengths. Only then can a treatment pattern be considered (Gunn, 1974).

A second, vital consideration, is a psychiatric assessment of current or potential dangerousness – itself fraught with difficulties (see Chapters 15 and 20) and compounded by the present availability of custodial, treatment, or supervisory facilities. However, not all psychopaths are dangerous all the time or to everybody. Age, circumstances known to provoke aggressive response, abuse of disinhibiting drugs or alcohol, recent behaviour patterns, are all factors to be considered.

CONCLUSION

Mental illness and mental abnormality are very common in the community. Minor mental illnesses and upsets bring a significant proportion to a general practitioner's surgery, but during the filtering process from family doctor or court to differing levels of psychiatric care, the end points of special hospital and prison will accumulate the most severe mental and personality disturbances. Nearly half of the males in maximum security hospitals for mentally abnormal offenders suffer from psychopathic disorder or its variant 'subnormality'.

RERERENCES

Bluglass, R.S. (1966) *A Psychiatric Study of Scottish Prisoners*. MD Thesis.
Cleckley, H. (1976) *The Mask of Sanity* (5th edition). St Louis: C.V. Mosby.
Davies, W. & Feldman, P. (1981) The diagnosis of psychopathy by forensic specialists. *Brit. J. Psychiat.*, **138**, 329–31.
Gibbens, T.C.N. (1963) *Psychiatric Studies of Borstal Lads*. London: Oxford University Press.
Goldberg, D. & Huxley, P. (1980) *Mental Illness in the Community*. London: Tavistock.
Gray, K.C. & Hutchison, H.C. (1964) The psychopathic personality: a survey of Canadian psychiatrists' opinions. *Can. Psychiat. Ass. J.* **9**, 452–61.
Gunn, J. (1974) Management of patients who have committed offences. *Medicine*, **30**, 1783–5.
Guze, S.B. (1976) *Criminality and Psychiatric Disorders*. New York: Oxford University Press.
MacKeith, J. (1975) Sociopathic personality disorders. *Medicine*, **11**, 497–502.
Ormrod, R. (1975) The debate between psychiatry and the law. *Brit. J. Psychiat.*, **127**, 193–203.
Parker, E. & Tennent, G. (1979) The 1959 Mental Health Act and mentally abnormal offenders: a comparative study. *Med. Sci. L.*, **19**, 29–38.
Ryan, M. (1982) Aspects of male mortality, *Brit. Med. J.*, **284**, 181–182.
West, D.J. (1963) *Habitual Offenders*. London: Macmillan.
World Health Organisation (1978) *Mental Disorders; Glossary and Guide to their Classification in Accordance with the Ninth Revision of the International Classification of Diseases*. Geneva: WHO.

3

The Criminal Statistics of England and Wales 1980 and Sentencing Policy

Michael Craft

To counter-balance the previous chapter, which was concerned with mental abnormality in the parent population, the incidence of criminality is now discussed. Figures are taken from the Criminal Statistics, England and Wales, 1980 (Home Office, 1981). Trends are followed, and particular emphasis is laid on the high incidence of crime amongst juveniles. Sexual offenders, among which the highest proportion of psychiatric court reports are requested, are analysed in more detail in the next chapter.

Among the parent population of 50 million in England and Wales, there were in 1980 2.5 million serious offences recorded by the police, close to the previous peak recorded in 1977 (1981 saw a 10 per cent increase). Because several offences may be the work of one person, the number of offenders is always substantially less than offences recorded, and a yet smaller number of offenders are actually 'dealt with', for some at least will be under ten years old, the age of criminal responsibility. Still smaller numbers, 556 000 in 1980, are actually found guilty or cautioned for indictable offences. Although the population is not increasing to the same extent, the average annual increase in offenders dealt with for indictable offences is 3 to 4 per cent per year, approximately half of all offenders being juveniles. To cope with this increasing workload of some 4 per cent a year, a growing proportion of juveniles are cautioned and not taken to court, this amounting to 20 per cent in 1980. Together the total number of offenders found guilty or cautioned amounted in 1970 to almost 1.8 million and nearly 2.4 million in 1980. Set against a population rising slower than offences, this translates into 4 offenders per 100 of population in 1970 and 5.5 in 1980, excluding those below the age of ten. McClintock and Avison (1968) estimated that one in six males and one in ten females in the United Kingdom would at some point in their lives be sentenced to a term of imprisonment. This proportion is likely to have increased to date.

The number of offenders being convicted may have increased, and this may be due to increased reporting of crime. Research surveying 'victims' has recently been reported by Sparks et al (1977), and has been amplified by the Government Housing Surveys of 1972, 1973, 1979 and 1980. These surveyed 10 000 households in England and Wales, with some 3 per cent recording offences of burglary and household theft in each particular year. Although this amounts to half a million burglaries throughout the country, the proportion of burglaries notified to police were 239 000 in 1972 rising to 307 000 by 1980. The number of burglaries reported for each of the years of the General Household Survey was about 3 per cent, but there was an increased frequency of offences recorded by the police, rising to 4 per cent in 1980. Part of the reason for the discrepancy is that victim surveys are notoriously subjective, but also because, in one quarter of the household enterings, nothing was stolen and victims did not bother to report such crimes. This seems to show that in England burglary is not on the increase, although its reporting to the police is. Burglary is only one contributor to the steady and persistent increase in serious offences recorded by the police per 100 000 population from 1950 to 1980. These amounted in the 1950s to just on 1000 and in 1980 to some 5000 indictable offences per 100 000 population per year.

As might be expected, crime differs considerably between geographical areas. Urban areas such as London, Manchester and Merseyside each recorded over 7000 and most rural areas recorded under 4000 serious offences per 100 000 population in 1980. There were also considerable differences between police forces for individual offence groups, so that in London there were over 100 recorded offences of robbery per 100 000 in 1980, whereas in mid-Wales only 2 per 100 000 were recorded.

Considerable variation also occurs with offences such as violence against a person. There was a 10 per cent increase in recorded offences of violence against a person during the decade 1970-9, which was over and above the annual rate of increase for crime in general at 4 per cent per year. There were 620 homicides in 1980, but this number varies considerably from year to year, due to chance factors. In 1980 these included a large number associated with deliberate arson and each incident involved several persons. A change in the law may also affect figures, so that after September 1977 when a verbal threat to kill became an offence under the Criminal Law Act of 1977, the numbers of offences of threat or conspiracy to murder went up to 530 by 1980 compared with a mere 250 in 1978. During 1979-80 about 15 per cent of recorded homicides or threats involved violence between spouses, while in the same years 6 per cent of wounding and assault was between married partners. Theft and the handling of stolen goods was by far the largest group of indictable (now called serious) offences, recorded at 1.46 million in 1980. Some 22 per cent of these were for theft of motor vehicles, a further 20 per cent thefts from vehicles and 14 per cent shoplifting. These particular offences appear to be increasing at the rate of about 5 per cent a year and in the vast majority (85 per cent) the amount was less than £100. Sexual offences amounted to some 21 000 serious offences in 1980, of which 11 500 were indecent assaults on females. The total of sexual offences was the lowest recorded figure during the last decade, and there has not been an increase in this type of crime comparable with that in other categories (the figure was lower still in 1981). Approximately one-fifth of sexual offences concern homosexuality. At 1230 the number of recorded offences of rape has increased over recent years, but this is thought to be due to the growing willingness of victims to report such offences, following the anonymity of victims allowed under the Sexual Offences Amendment Act 1976. Rape is analysed in more detail later in this book to illustrate the differing viewpoints of perpetrator, victim and community. Sexual offenders form one of the largest groups of clients referred for psychiatric reports. Although amounting to about 1 per cent of total indictable offences for 1980, they comprise some 20 per cent of reports requested for offenders (Gibbens et al, 1977).

Firearms are seldom used in the UK, in contrast to the US. During 1970–80 incidents involving firearms have never represented more than 10 per cent of offences recorded. In 1980 there were 6500 serious offences recorded by police in which such a weapon was used as a blunt instrument or threat, or actually fired. Two-fifths of these offences involved violence to people, two-fifths criminal damage, and one-fifth robbery. The increase per year has been approximately 19 per cent annually up to 1979. Within individual categories of crime, there are considerable variations over the years, for instance in 1980 there were less than 70 burglaries involving firearms, as opposed to between 80 and 100 in 1977–9, and the number of homicides, 24 in 1980, was also lower than in any of the ten previous years. Attempted murder, at 250, was lower than the peak of 300 recorded in 1975, and there were similar variations in other categories.

Recorded homicide (the term covers the offences of murder, manslaughter and infanticide) amounted to 621 in 1980 (557 in 1981). Although the number varies from year to year, the average was 55 per cent higher during the 1970s than in the 1960s. This compares with the increase of 170 per cent in the averages between the same decades for recorded offences of violence against a person. As with other offences, some of the initial number recorded by the police as homicide are later reduced by police or court to a lesser offence, and a further 10 per cent are decided by the court to be no offence at all. Of the 564 homicides remaining 28 per cent involved a sharp instrument, 16 per cent strangulation and a small percentage (3.4 per cent in 1980) firearms. Many of the remainder were by arson. In about 70 per cent of all homicide offences, the victim was a member of the suspect's family (this includes cohabitants and lovers). About half the offences recorded were committed during quarrels or temper outbursts. Some 50 were caused during robbery or housebreaking, this number remaining much the same throughout the decade. One police officer was killed on duty in England and Wales in 1980. Children under one year are the age group at greatest risk at 50 non-accidental deaths per million population in 1980. The age group least at risk was that between 5 and 16 years of age, at 3 per million of the population per annum. Homicide rates have varied only slightly over the decade.

By age boys under 17 provided a third of the total found guilty of, or cautioned for, indictable offences in 1980. The proportion was highest for offences of burglary, where it was just under half, and for theft and handling of stolen goods, or criminal damage, each being just under two-fifths. Young people aged 17 and under 21 provided a fifth of all those found guilty of or cautioned for indictable offences in 1980. They provided one-third of those involved with robbery. The highest rate of offenders is in males aged 14 and under 17, at 7.5 per 100 population in 1980. For males aged 17 and under 21 the rate is nearly 7 per 100 population per year. The average rate of increase in the rate of male offenders was about 2.5 per cent for these two age groups.

Females provide 17 per cent of the total number of people found guilty of or cautioned for indictable offences in 1980. Their peak age for offence is 14, although for males it is 15. This peak rose at the time when the compulsory school leaving age was raised to 16 in 1972. The approximate proportion of females aged 10 to under 14 cautioned for indictable offences rose from 40 per cent in 1960 to 85 per cent by 1980; for males of the same age it rose from 28 per cent to 65 per cent during the same time. These are the highest proportions of offenders to be cautioned, and compare with a 30 per cent caution rate for females of all ages, and a 17 per cent caution rate for all males.

COURT DISPOSAL

During 1980 some 2.4 million defendants were arraigned in some 650 Petty Sessional Divisional Courts in England and Wales. This was an increase of 16 per cent over each of the three previous years. Over a longer period of time this represents an average increase of some 4 per cent per year, and a doubling in the total number of defendants since 1952. Of the increase of 1.5 million defendants between 1952 and 1980, one million was accounted for by the increased number of motoring offences. During this period of time indictable offences also increased, being in 1980 half a million for the first time.

Magistrates' courts deal with the vast majority of offenders. They deal with offenders on petty (summary) offences, where trial must be at the magistrates' court, and also sit as examining justices to determine if there is sufficient evidence to justify a committal to the Crown Court. Offenders may be arraigned either on indictment or summarily; offenders arraigned for summary offences can also be tried at the magistrates' court. The numbers involved in summary procedures increased between 1952 and 1980, either doubling or more than doubling.

Crown Court work increased at much the same rate as magistrates' courts. Some 74 000 defendants of all ages were tried at Crown Courts in 1980, this number being considerably less than those disposed of at magistrates' courts (2.4 million) but still a record. The increase was spread throughout the categories of offences, except that of violence where numbers fell by 800 between 1979 and 1980.

The increase in criminal work handled by the courts has been paralleled by the increase in work done by other community agencies in the disposal or prevention of crime. Sentencing to imprisonment and otherwise is discussed later in this chapter, but is usually regarded by courts as only the final outcome of a number of community solutions to a particular offence, taking into account the often differing needs of community, perpetrator and victim. In developed societies where crime increases apace and resources more slowly, courts more and more turn to the intent behind the crime, and constructive methods of handling law breakers. Table 3.1 shows some of the viewpoints on criminal behaviour, and some of the community solutions for it. For a large area a civil code disposal is possible before punishment becomes necessary. Social services are increasingly called in to resolve disputes or deal with unlawful behaviour,

Table 3.1　Community solutions to criminal behaviour.

	Agency system				
Agency viewpoint	*Penal*	*Psychiatric*	*Probation*	*Compensation*	*Social services*
The ideal	Remorse and penance	Mental well-being	Non-reconviction	Just evaluation	Peace between parties
Direction of intervention	Community protection and retribution	Treatment for mental ill health	Counselling and supervision	Compensation for damage	Conflict area
Agent activation	Police	Psychiatrist and nurse	Probation Officer	Lawyer and client	Social worker
Subject	Accused	Patient	Probationer	Perpetrator	Disputant
Overall target	Punishment community protection	Restoration of mental well-being	Useful citizenship	Restitution in work, repair or money	Resolution of dispute

particularly of young or disordered people, before the matter requires court punishment. Where there is no question of mental disorder, compensation or probation disposals may satisfy both parties. A psychiatric disposal is being increasingly sought where the intentions of the perpetrator are disordered or unclear, or where this seems the most constructive way to prevent the perpetrator committing further misdeeds. Above all the table shows the differing motives of agency principals, and the potential areas of conflict between them, if mutual endpoints are not harmonised. It is inevitable that the targets of the various agencies are different and sometimes in conflict. More commonly, the differing agencies do not explain to each other either what they intend or how they hope to go about it, so that confusion is worse confounded. In addition, the multiplication of agencies and professional disciplines able to offer help to the court, and the degree to which they are prepared or not prepared to accept responsibility may be confusing. Many of these methods of disposal are discussed later in this book, but before psychiatric and other agencies are reviewed, a survey of court sentencing policy may set the court room background.

SENTENCING

All court adjudicators, whether they be religious in Iran, military in Africa or judges and magistrates nearer home, have a tariff of sentence for disposal of the convicted. Indeed, it was to bring more extreme sentences into line with the average that the Court of Criminal Appeal was set up. The first publicised comprehensive analysis of sentences given for all types of offences in England and Wales appeared in *Principles of Sentencing* (Thomas, 1979).

　　Basing his information on millions of court verdicts, Thomas describes the general tariff of penal sentences for 'ordinary' criminal acts. He also shows that mentally abnormal offenders receive individual consideration for appropriate sentencing. What this is will depend not only on how responsibility for the crime is undoubtedly diminished by mental disorder, but on the gravity of the actual crime, what treatment is available, or is likely to prevent repetition; in short, the dangerousness of the individual himself. If the judge (or the Court of Criminal Appeal behind him) can be persuaded that the mentally abnormal offender is very ill, can be treated, and there is somebody prepared to take responsibility for his care so that no further danger to the public is threatened, then some kind of order for treatment not only should ensue, but on appeal would be made to ensue. Alternatively, if imprisonment is merited, if treatment is unavailable and danger to the public is likely, the judge will be entitled to pass a penal sentence even of life imprisonment, and be fortified in doing so by the Court of Appeal (*R. v. Pecker* [1970]).

Probation with a Condition of Treatment

This is the widest ranging measure allowing treatment for a mentally abnormal offender. Based on a number of Acts culminating in the Powers of the Criminal Courts Act 1973, Section 3, a court making a probation order can include a requirement ... 'that the offender, during part or all of the period on probation up to three years, undergoes treatment by, or under the direction of a duly qualified medical practitioner, with a view to achieving an improvement in his mental condition.' Only one approved medical practitioner (not necessarily a psychiatrist) is required, and it is noteworthy that the doctor does not have to give the treatment himself or even see the patient, so long as it is under his direction. The nature of the treatment does not have to be specified, it does not have to be in a hospital, and the responsibilities of compulsory treatment under Section 60 hospital orders (as recently extended) do not have to be satisfied. What is called a 'psychiatric probation order' is slightly more specific in that it requires both that psychiatric treatment is available and that the client is pre-pared to accede to it, but this neither requires the psychiatrist nor the hospital to have custody of the patient, nor does it require the probationer to accede to treatment such as electro-convulsive therapy, if that 'would not be reasonable' for an ordinary man to agree to. The Criminal Courts Act, 1923, Section 6 (7) allows such refusal if this 'was reasonable having regard to all the circumstances'.

So far as the court is concerned, some advantages of a psychiatric probation order are that it can be used with offenders such as alcoholics or addicts who are not otherwise eligible for hospital orders; it allows the decision on treatment to be passed to the proper hands, that is the doctor concerned; it allows an after-care system to be built in, and the court, through the probation officer, to be kept informed. Disadvantages of both orders are that they can only last for up to three years, and they cannot protect the community if the mentally abnormal offender presents a serious risk (for instance by arson, or because of recurrent depression) or ensure custody, until an actual event occurs that allows breach of probation to be proved.

Psychiatric probation orders, as Thomas's (1979) analysis makes clear, have been made for murder, manslaughter, blackmail, arson, and numerous other less serious offences. An analysis of psychiatric probation orders has recently been made by the Cambridge Institute of Criminology (Lewis, 1980). Lewis sampled 120 such orders made in Nottingham, finding that for many of these much-convicted mentally disordered offenders they were indeed a viable alternative to jail. Their success depended on the high expectations and hard work of the probation officers and psychiatrists concerned, with adequate backing by prompt court action when necessary. Not all three elements were always available or in harmony.

Hospital Orders

A decreasing number of hospital orders have been issued by English courts in recent years. This is in part due to the decrease in locked wards in ordinary psychiatric hospitals, the decrease of beds in special hospitals and disagreements between doctors as to treatability. It has been relatively common in recent years for diagnoses to be proffered and treatment not be available. For instance, in *R*. v. *Thornton* an appeal against a sentence for arson was refused. Although the subject was agreed to be a psychopathic personality, he was not thought to be treatable (see also *R*. v. *Bland*). In *R*. v. *Bringins* the accused was agreed to be mentally subnormal, but a life sentence was upheld on the grounds that treatment was unlikely to prevent him re-committing buggery on small boys. In *R*. v. *Ashdown*[1] robbery of £2 from a passerby on a road after threats with an air pistol was felt to merit life imprisonment, upheld on appeal because of the appellant's impulsivity. The accused was agreed to be psychopathic, agreed to have 'abnormally high sexual drive ... pursues a deviant course', but no treatment offered 'permanent and guaranteed improvement'. Alternatively, in *R*. v. *Smith* a life-long inmate of mental handicap hospitals had been imprisoned for minor theft and on appeal a hospital order was substituted when a local psychiatrist offered admission.

Life Imprisonment

As Thomas (1979) says, this 'was not created legislatively as a special measure for dangerous offenders. It emerged as the maximum sentence for a considerable number of offences as the result of amendments, consolidations and partial codifications of the criminal law at various times.' It has recently emerged as an indefinite preventative sentence 'as a result of judicial initiative after the enactment of provisions enabling a person subject to a sentence of life imprisonment to be released by the Home Secretary subject to conditions and recall at any time.' Thus it can be used for relatively trivial offences meriting imprisonment (subject to certain safeguards) to protect the public against an emotionally unstable offender or an inadequate offender who repeatedly offends sexually

---

[1] Robbery is defined in section 8 subsection 1 of the Theft Act 1968 as theft using force or fear of force.

against children; to enable the Parole Board to ensure that conditions after release are adequate to safeguard the public; or to ensure by means of discharge on licence that supervision is maintained. This licence may be revoked by the Crown Court on re-offence, by the Parole Board, or indeed by the Home Secretary without any recommendation if considered expedient.

The result is that such a life sentence is very similar to a restriction order. Both are usually used for those who commit offences of substantial gravity, who suffer from continuous disorder of personality or instability of character, and who need continuous supervision. Both may use the probation service for aftercare, although mental health restriction orders can also use local authority social workers or psychiatric nurses in the community.

THE INDIVIDUALITY OF CIRCUMSTANCES

The professional advising the court following the finding of 'guilty' and before the passing of sentence may also need to bear in mind the individuality of circumstances which guide judges in considering treatment or care orders as opposed to the tariff for 'normal' offenders. Thomas (1979) describes four of the individualisation principles which guide the sentencers in determining the care for special groups of offender, to which might be added a fifth resulting from the increasing numbers of aged in the community.

The young offender is entitled to the mitigation of age, because the effects of maturity, marriage and responsibility are least likely to have been operative. Probation is a common tariff measure, especially for first offences, and is often used for serious offences.

The term 'intermediate recidivist' is used by Thomas to describe 'an offender in his twenties or early thirties who has acquired a substantial history of convictions and findings of guilt as a juvenile, who has undergone various individualised measures, such as probation and borstal training, and is now steadily adding terms of imprisonment to his record.' If psychiatric evidence shows personality inadequacy, immaturity or minor instability and the chance that extra care, treatment or supervision will break the sequence of ineffective imprisonments, courts will often take community methods of care and treatment, if given a chance. Thomas also describes the *inadequate recidivist*, similar in definition but more pronounced in personality failing as opposed to social failing, with numerous legal examples which may be useful for professionals to cite (see particularly pages 20–3).

Clear need of psychiatric treatment and availability of such treatment stand out in Thomas's analysis as impelling judges to forgo the tariff system. Obviously this needs evidence all 'to go one way', and disagreement between medical witnesses in the witness box or documents submitted rarely fails to fill the judge with concern.

The writer would add *the aged* as a relatively new category to warrant classification as mentally abnormal offenders needing psychiatric care or treatment. Some causes of dementia are treatable, such as that due to alcohol, tobacco, diabetes or hypertension, and documentary evidence of investigations into brain function by the CAT scanner, the electroencephalograph and air studies mean that professional witnesses are in a far better position to show corroborative evidence supporting mental abnormality in its relation to crime. Extra services help the court to avoid penal measures, for instance in shoplifting where day care, supervision by relatives, or even mental improvement following medication, decrease likelihood of opportunity for further offence. A decrease in anoxia by reducing tobacco consumption or alcohol intake may assist.

More might be written about the important variable of 'dangerousness of the offender' except that many of the topics discussed in this chapter, including dangerousness, receive more detailed treatment later. The same applies to that most treatable of syndromes of mental abnormality, depression. The reader is reminded that more than one professional viewpoint can be requested. This subject is treated at different points in the book, so the reader is advised to check the index.

CONCLUSION

Chapter 2 showed mental abnormality to be more common among females, Chapter 3, crime more common among males. Yet both variables are common in the general population. McClintock and Avison (1968) estimated that one in six males and one in ten females were likely to be convicted for an indictable offence at some time in their lives. This proportion is certainly greater now. One in six women and one in nine men in the current estimation are likely to have psychiatric inpatient treatment in their lifetime. Yet among some individuals the likelihood of both events occurring is known to be much higher. The next chapters attempt to tease out some of the variables involved.

CASE

R. *v.* Pecker [1970] 54 Cr. App. R 330.

APPEALS

Ashdown 01.11.73 3001/C/72 1974 Crim. L.R. 130.
Bland 21.09.71 1018/C/71.
Bringins 05.05.75 421/C/75.
Smith 13.01.76 5919/B/75.
Thornton 11.10.74 2404/C/74 (1975) Crim. L.R. 51.

REFERENCES

Gibbens, T.C.N., Soothill, K.L. & Pope, P.J. (1977) *Medical Remands in the Criminal Courts.* Maudsley Monographs No. 25. London: Oxford University Press.
Home Office (1981) *Criminal Statistics, England and Wales, 1980*, Cmnd 8376. London: HMSO.

Lewis, P. (1980) *Psychiatric Probation Orders*. Cambridge: Institute of Criminology.
McClintock, F.M. & Avison, N.H. (1968) *Crime in England and Wales*. London: Heinemann.
Sparks, R.F., Genn, H.G. & Dadd, D.J. (1977) *Surveying Victims*. Chichester: John Wiley.
Thomas, D.A. (1979) *Principles of Sentencing*. London: Heinemann.

4

Recorded Incidence and Sentencing Practice for Sexual Offences

Roy Walmsley

The first half of this chapter describes the recorded incidence of sexual offences in the thirty-five years since the end of the war. Any account of the recorded incidence of offences must commence with a reminder that there may – and in most cases there will – be a considerable difference between the *recorded* incidence of offences and their *actual* incidence. Only a proportion of all offences committed come to the notice of the police, and changes in the recorded incidence may reflect a variety of factors totally unconnected with the actual incidence. There may, for example, be changes in public practice in reporting an offence, or in police practice in investigating it, or in the ways in which particular forms of behaviour and particular acts of lawbreaking are classified. For this reason the following description of the recorded incidence of sexual offences contains very little comment on the causes or the significance of the trends noted. For the most part the information is merely presented; the reader may decide for himself its interpretation.

The second half of the chapter indicates the patterns of sentencing for sexual offences and in particular draws attention to the varying levels of seriousness which are attached by the courts to different types of sexual offence. Again, the material is predominantly descriptive; explanations for the patterns of sentencing noted would have been highly subjective, and indeed speculative, without extensive careful investigations.

RECORDED INCIDENCE OF SEXUAL OFFENCES

Sexual Offences and Other Offences

In 1946 less than half a million indictable (now known as 'serious') offences of all kinds were recorded as known to the police; in 1980 the figure exceeded 2.5 million, a five-fold increase.

Most serious crime can be subsumed under two headings: 'offences against the person' and 'offences involving property'. Offences against the person are customarily divided into offences of violence against the person and sexual offences. The recorded incidence of the former has increased dramatically since the war but the number of sexual offences recorded has risen much more slowly. In 1946 less than 10 000 sexual offences were recorded as known to the police; by 1959 over 20 000 were recorded, but after a peak of over 25 000 in 1973 the average over the last five years has been under 22 000 and the 1980 total was 21 107 – just two and a quarter times that of 1946. This compares with a current figure of offences of violence against the person which is almost 24 times that of 1946 and a figure for all indictable (serious) offences of more than five times that of 1946. Table 4.1 helps to illustrate the point.

Table 4.1   Indictable offences.

	Sexual offences (1946 total = 100)	Offences of violence against the person (1946 total = 100)	All indictable (serious) offences (1946 total = 100)
1946	9 329 (100)	4 062 (100)	472 489 (100)
1951	14 633 (157)	6 516 (160)	524 506 (111)
1956	17 103 (183)	9 307 (229)	479 710 (102)
1961	20 404 (219)	17 601 (433)	806 900 (171)
1966	23 308 (228)	26 716 (658)	1 199 859 (254)
1971	23 621 (253)	47 036 (1158)	1 646 081 (353)
1976	22 203 (238)	77 748 (1914)	2 135 713 (452)
1980	21 107 (226)	97 246 (2394)	2 520 628 (533)

The trend in the number of persons found guilty is similar. The number found guilty of sexual offences has doubled since 1946,[1] the number found guilty of offences of violence against the person is 24 times the 1946 figure and the number found guilty of all indictable (serious) offences is more than four times what it was in 1946.

Sexual offences recorded as known to the police rose from being two per cent of all recorded offences in 1946 to almost four per cent in 1955; since then they have been falling as a percentage of all recorded offences and in 1980 constituted less than one per cent.

The number of persons found guilty of sexual offences rose from being about three per cent of all persons found guilty of indictable offences in 1946 to five per cent in 1955; since then they have been falling as a percentage of all persons found guilty and in 1980 (after adjusting for the already mentioned change in the presentation of the Criminal Statistics) the comparable figure was below 1.5 per cent.

Different Types of Sexual Offence

Consistently about half the sexual offences recorded are indecent assaults on females. Since 1960 another 15–20 per cent have consistently been offences of unlawful sexual intercourse with girls of 13 but under 16 and another 10 per cent have been indecent assaults on males. These three offences, which with certain exceptions are not regarded by the courts as the most serious sexual offences,

---

[1] If one excludes summary convictions for solicitation by a male and gross indecency with a child, which were included for the first time in 1979 in statistics of persons found guilty of sexual offences.

thus comprise at least 80 per cent of all sexual offences recorded. By contrast, the offences which the courts tend to regard seriously – rape, incest, buggery, and unlawful intercourse with a girl under 13 – rarely comprise more than about 10 per cent of recorded sexual offences. Figure 4.1 indicates the distribution of recorded sexual offences in 1980.

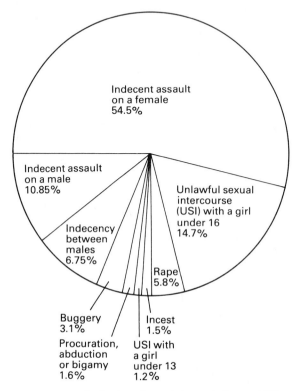

Figure 4.1   Distribution of recorded sexual offences, 1980.

Let us now consider the main homosexual offences (buggery, indecent assault on a male, indecency between males) and the main heterosexual offences (rape, indecent assault on a female, unlawful sexual intercourse and incest). Recorded homosexual offences trebled between 1946 and 1955 but have now fallen back and stood in 1980 at just under twice the 1946 figure. Recorded heterosexual offences reached a peak in 1973 (at nearly three and a half times the 1946 figure) but now stand at less than three times the 1946 figure.

The figures for the three homosexual offences have not changed uniformly. The *buggery* total quadrupled between 1946 and 1954, but then fell, so that by 1972 it was only twice the 1946 figure; in the last three years (1978–80), in which offences of attempted buggery have also been included, it seems to have stabilised at around two and three-quarter times the 1946 figure. The Sexual Offences Act 1967, which amended the law so that homosexual acts are no longer illegal if they take place between consenting adults in private, seems to have made no difference to the number of offences recorded. The number of recorded offences of *indecent assault on a male* (until 1978 cases of attempted buggery were also included in this classification) more than doubled between 1946 and 1951; it then remained fairly stable until 1974, since when it has fallen steadily so that in 1980 it stood at one and a half times the 1946 figure. Here too there is no indication that the 1967 Act had any effect on the figures. The figures for the offence of *indecency between males*, however, have fluctuated considerably and do seem to have been affected by the 1967 Act. The number of such recorded offences quadrupled between 1946 and 1955, then fell to only one and a half times the 1946 figure in the late sixties, but had doubled again by 1974. The figures for 1979 and 1980 have been slightly lower, the latter being just over two and a half times the total in 1946. The fall in figures between 1955 and the late sixties may well be attributable to the Wolfenden enquiry, set up in 1954, which resulted in the law prohibiting all homosexual acts between males being called into question. The 1967 Act reaffirmed the unlawfulness of homosexual acts in public and thus provided the police with a basis on which action could more confidently be taken against those involved in such behaviour; this particular offence is almost always recorded only as a result of police activity. The same Act introduced summary trial for indecency between males, thus making it easier to bring prosecutions. It seems likely that the substantial rise in the figures for the offence can for these reasons be attributed to the Sexual Offences Act 1967 (see Walmsley, 1978).

By contrast, the figures for most of the heterosexual offences rose fairly steadily between 1946 and 1973, since when they have fallen. There is no obvious reason for the increase. In the 35 years since 1946 about two-thirds of the heterosexual offences recorded have been offences of *indecent assault on a female*. The 1973 figure for this offence was nearly three times that of 1946 but the 1980 figure was less than two and a half times the total in 1946. Likewise the 1973 figure for *unlawful sexual intercourse with a girl under 13* was three times the 1946 figure; the 1980 figure was just under two and a half times that total. By 1973 the number of recorded offences of *unlawful sexual intercourse with a girl under 16* had risen to seven and a half times that in 1946; since 1973, however, the figures have fallen sharply and in 1980 the number recorded was only four and a half times the 1946 figure.

Unlike indecent assault and the unlawful intercourse offences, the figures for *rape* have not fallen since 1973. In 1973 the recorded incidence of rape was four times that in 1946 and in the years 1978–80 it has not been far short of five times the 1946 level. However, in order that this increase be kept in perspective two facts particularly should be noted. First, rape differs from other sexual offences in that violence is often an important component part of the act. The figures for offences of violence not only continue to increase but are increasing at a rate far greater than that for rape. Second, the Sexual Offences (Amendment) Act 1976 enabled rape victims to remain anonymous in court and limited the right to cross-examine as to past sexual experience. These may have led to a greater willingness of victims to report offences of rape. (However, publicity for the part which the victim has to play in the criminal justice process may have dissuaded others who might otherwise have reported the offence from doing so (Walmsley, 1980).)

The figures for *incest* do not follow the pattern of the other heterosexual offences. They had more than doubled by 1953 since when they have fluctuated between two and three times the 1946 figure. In 1980 the number of incest offences recorded was two and a half times that figure.

Table 4.2, in which the 1946 figure is taken as 100, summarises the changes in recorded incidence within the 35-year period for each of the main sexual offences.

Table 4.2 Recorded incidence of sexual offences.

	1946	1951*	1956*	1961*	1966*	1971*	1976*	1980*
Buggery	100	183	367	295	233	240	268	265
Indecent assault on a male	100	215	220	212	206	190	177	150
Indecency between males	100	205	345	295	169	183	280	253
Rape	100	133	131	200	257	312	436	488
Indecent assault on a female	100	156	175	201	235	266	234	247
Unlawful intercourse with a girl under 13	100	177	158	210	276	204	271	233
Unlawful intercourse with a girl under 16	100	175	231	574	608	740	631	455
Incest	100	165	224	264	187	242	266	246
The eight main sexual offences	100	173	205	245	257	285	268	254
All sexual offences	100	157	183	219	228	253	238	226

* Percentages of 1946 figures.

SENTENCES IMPOSED ON SEXUAL OFFENDERS

Different Degrees of Seriousness

The seriousness with which the different sexual offences are regarded by the courts may be measured by considering the proportion of custodial sentences passed on adults. Sentences imposed on juveniles cannot be used so readily as an indication of the seriousness of the offence because of the more limited availability of custodial sentences for juveniles and the principle that the courts in sentencing juveniles must have regard to the welfare of the offender. It is, of course, true that a serious offence may on occasion be dealt with by means of a non-custodial penalty because of special circumstances associated with the offender; but this does not negate the general validity of the method.

Examination of the Criminal Statistics (Home Office, annually) reveals that of the eight main indictable sexual offences four are regarded as much more serious than the rest. There is a clear distinction between those four (rape, incest, buggery and unlawful sexual intercourse with a girl under 13), for which at least half the adults convicted receive a custodial sentence, and the four less serious offences (unlawful intercourse with a girl under 16, indecent assault on male or female, and indecency between males), for which less than a quarter of adults convicted receive a custodial sentence.

Of the four more serious sexual offences it is quite clear that *rape* is regarded as the most serious. Over the five years 1976–80, 93 per cent of adults convicted of that offence received a custodial sentence. Over the same period custodial sentences were passed on 72 per cent of adults convicted of *incest*, 60 per cent of adults convicted of *buggery* and 59 per cent of adults convicted of *unlawful intercourse with a girl under 13*. The custodial rates for the less serious offences were 23 per cent for *unlawful intercourse with a girl under 16*, 20 per cent for *indecent assault on a male*, 16 per cent for *indecent assault on a female* and 1 per cent for *indecency between males*.

The figures given relate to the offence classifications used in the Criminal Statistics but each classification embraces a variety of different types of offence, each with a different sentencing pattern. A research project carried out by the Home Office Research Unit has enabled light to be thrown on some of these differences.[1]

Rape

As stated, the custodial rate for adults convicted of rape is currently (1976–80) 93 per cent. It seems to be equally likely that a custodial sentence will be imposed whether the act of rape is completed or only attempted. In the year studied (1973) 92 per cent of adults convicted of full rape received custodial sentence as against 90 per cent of adults convicted of attempted rape. However, prison sentences for the full offence tended to be about two years longer than for the attempt. The nature of the pre-existing relationship between the offender and the victim appeared not to affect the custodial rate, but offenders who were complete strangers to their victims were more likely to receive sentences in excess of four years' imprisonment.

Of adults sent to prison for rape (including all offences whether completed or attempted) over the period 1976–80, sentences of two years or less tended to be imposed on about 15 per cent, sentences of three years but no more than four on about another 20 per cent and sentences of five years or more on the remaining 30–35 per cent. Sentences of life imprisonment were imposed on an average of six offenders per year.

Incest

The custodial rate for adults convicted of incest over the period 1976–80 has already been quoted as 72 per cent. But this figure masks the great difference

---

[1] The research, which was undertaken partly in order to provide information for the Criminal Law Revision Committee and the Policy Advisory Committee on Sexual Offences in their current review of sexual offences, is written up more fully in Walmsley and White (1979, 1980).

between sentencing practice for paternal incest (incest by a father with his daughter) and that for sibling incest (by brother with his sister). In the year studied 74 per cent of fathers received a custodial sentence as compared with only 21 per cent of adult (over 17) brothers. Sibling incest, it seems, is regarded as on a par with the less serious offences such as indecent assault and unlawful intercourse with a girl under 16. And when convictions for paternal incest were examined in relation to the age of the daughter concerned it became clear that the paternal incest figure of 74 per cent itself masked considerable differences. Incest with a daughter aged 16 or over had a custodial rate of 56 per cent, and incest with a daughter aged 13–15 a rate of 74 per cent. But incest with a daughter aged under 13 was regarded as seriously as an offence of rape; 88 per cent of fathers so convicted received a custodial sentence. It is noteworthy that, although incest is an offence whether it takes place consensually or not, consensual incest tended to be dealt with by means of less severe penalties than the non-consensual offence, both in respect of paternal and sibling incest.

Buggery

As with incest, so buggery – despite its overall custodial rate in 1976–80 of 60 per cent – comprises several varieties in terms of sentencing practice. Buggery (by a man of 21 or over) with a boy under 14 seems to be treated as akin to rape or incest with a daughter under 13. Of those convicted of such an offence of buggery in the study-year, 86 per cent received a custodial sentence. But buggery (by a man of 21 or over) with a male aged 14–20 only had a custodial rate of 56 per cent, and buggery with a male of 21 or over (only an offence if non-consensual or not committed in private) did not lead to a single custodial sentence in the year studied. In general, as one might expect, consensual buggery seemed to be regarded less seriously than non-consensual, offences with men less seriously than offences with boys and offences of attempted buggery less seriously than offences of completed buggery.

Unlawful sexual intercourse

The custodial rate (over the period 1976–80) for unlawful sexual intercourse with a girl under 13 was 59 per cent but with this offence also there were wide variations. Only 36 per cent of offenders aged under 25 received custodial sentences as against 69 per cent of offenders aged 25 or over. And offenders aged 25 or over whose offence was committed with a girl under 12 had a custodial rate of 89 per cent, again similar to the rate of rape, for incest with a daughter under 13 and for buggery with a boy under 14.

The custodial rate between 1976 and 1980 for unlawful intercourse with a girl under 16 (in practice almost all such offences are with girls aged 13–15) was 23 per cent. The variations here too are dependent on the age of the offender and the victim. In the study year (1973) when the comparable overall figure was 21 per cent, the custodial rate for offenders under 30 convicted of the offence with a girl of 15 was only 10 per cent; by contrast the rate for offenders aged 30 or over with a girl of 13 or 14 was 44 per cent.

Indecent assault

The custodial rate for indecent assault on a male over the period 1976–80 was 20 per cent. In the study-year the main variation was between offences committed by men aged 30–49 with boys under 14 (custodial rate 30 per cent) and offences committed by men aged 50 or over with boys of 14 or over (custodial rate 5 per cent).

The same pattern is evident in the penalties imposed for indecent assault on a female, for which the custodial rate over the period 1976–80 was 16 per cent. Offences committed in the study-year by men aged 30–49 with girls under 13 led to a custodial rate of 24 per cent whereas offences committed by men aged 50 or over with girls of 13 or over had a custodial rate of only 3 per cent.

Indecency between males

The offence of indecency between males is mainly committed in public conveniences or in open spaces. It is clearly regarded by the courts as comparatively trivial and is invariably dealt with summarily by means of a small fine. In the period 1976–80 it had a custodial rate of 1 per cent. In the year specially studied in which the overall custodial rate was also 1 per cent it was noticeable that the courts distinguished between offences between two men of 21 or over and offences where a man of 21 or over was involved with a young man under the age of 21. The custodial rate for the former was below 1 per cent whereas for the latter it was 4 per cent.

Trends in Sentencing

Table 4.3 sets out the custodial rates for the main sexual offences over five-year periods since 1946. It is immediately obvious that in respect of the less serious offences the trend is sharply away from custodial sentences. The custodial rates

Table 4.3 Custodial rates for sexual offences.

Offence	1946–50	1951–55	1956–60	1961–65	1966–70	1971–75	1976–80
Buggery	71	64	53	50	61	59	60
Indecent assault on a male	46	38	31	24	18	17	20
Indecency between males	37	25	16	9	4	1	1
Rape	90	86	87	85	89	89	93
Indecent assault on a female	42	35	27	21	15	13	16
USI with a girl under 13	90	77	73	65	57	53	59
USI with a girl under 16	50	42	30	24	23	20	23
Incest	75	73	73	70	74	64	72

for the indecent assault offences and for unlawful intercourse with a girl under 16 have more than halved between the late forties and the late seventies. And the rate for indecency between males has dropped almost to nothing. By contrast the custodial rates for the three most serious offences, rape, incest and buggery, have changed very little over the same period. The only offence not so far mentioned, unlawful sexual intercourse with a girl under 13, shows a steady decrease in its custodial rate but not of the proportions of the less serious offences.

One feature of Table 4.3 which is particularly worthy of note is the sudden increase in the use of custodial sentences for sexual offences in the last five years. Every offence except indecency between males showed a higher custodial rate in 1976–80 than in 1971–5. In the case of buggery the increase (1 per cent) was insignificant but the increases in the other six offences cannot be so easily dismissed. The increases in the custodial rates for the less serious offences are perhaps especially remarkable. In contrast to the trend towards less and less use of custodial sentences for these offences, a trend which is quite clear-cut over a period of thirty years, the custodial rates for the two indecent assault offences and for unlawful sexual intercourse with a girl under 16 suddenly jumped, in each case by 3 per cent. The reason for this change is not clear, but an examination of the year-by-year figures for these offences in 1976–80 shows that the increased custodial sentencing for USI 16 occurred only in 1977 and 1978, years in which a very marked increase was recorded. Since 1978 the figures have again fallen back. The indecent assault offences reveal a different pattern, both of them showing a consistently higher level of custodial sentencing over the five-year period (compared with 1971–5), although the rate for indecent assault on a male (like that for USI 16) was especially high in 1977 and 1978. (The rate for indecent assault on a female was exceptionally *low* in 1978.)

There were similar increases in the rates of custodial sentencing for the more serious offences. The rate for unlawful sexual intercourse with a girl under 13, which had been falling steadily, leapt by 6 per cent. The rate for rape, consistently between 85 and 89 per cent since 1950, rose to 93 per cent and the rate for incest, which had been consistently between 70 and 75 per cent until a sharp fall in 1971–5, rose 8 per cent to return to its regular path. Again there is no obvious explanation for this increased use of custodial sentencing. The year-by-year figures show that for USI 13 – as was found with its less serious counterpart USI 16 – the increased use of custody occurred only in 1977 and 1978, in which years it was very marked. The higher incest figure for 1976–80 does not appear to require special explanation. Figures for the offence regularly fluctuate considerably from year to year (e.g. 82 per cent in 1978, 61 per cent in 1979) and the 1971–5 figure was unusually low. The custodial rate for rape, however, like those for the indecent assault offences, does show a consistently higher level of sentencing over the five-year period 1976–80. Successive years showing custodial rates for rape of over 90 per cent had occurred in 1947–8 and 1951–2 but not since then. In all five years 1976–80 the rate exceeded 90 per cent. It was 93 per cent in 1976, 94 per cent in 1977, 95 per cent in 1978, 93 per cent in 1979 and 92 per cent in 1980. One may speculate that public concern about the offence in the mid 1970s contributed to the courts taking a tougher line. Reflections of this public concern were the Home Secretary's decision to set up an Advisory Group on the Law of Rape[1] and the subsequent passing of the Sexual Offences (Amendment) Act 1976.

Hospital Orders and Restriction Orders

The use of hospital orders and restriction orders under Sections 60 and 65 of the Mental Health Act, 1959 as a means of dealing with persons convicted of sexual offences has declined considerably in the last ten years. In the period 1964–70 (full figures for the earlier years are not available) an average of 117 sexual offenders per year were dealt with in this way, 90 being made subject to Section 60 (hospital) orders and 27 to Section 60/65 (restriction) orders. The pattern was fairly stable from year to year with the maximum being 128 (in 1964) and the minimum 107 (in 1965). Two per cent of persons convicted of sexual offences were dealt with by means of such orders. In the following five years, 1971–5, the average number of sexual offenders made subject to hospital orders and restriction orders was 73, 48 to Section 60 orders and 25 to Section 60/65 orders. Thus

Table 4.4   Hospital orders for sexual offences.

Offence		1964–70 Average per year	1971–75 Average per year	1976–80 Average per year
Buggery	S60 S60/65	2 9 } 11	1 4 } 5	2 1 } 3
Indecent assault on a male	S60 S60/65	28 3 } 31	12 6 } 18	5 1 } 6
Indecency between males	S60	2	1	0
Rape	S60 S60/65	3 6 } 9	1 6 } 7	1 4 } 5
Indecent assault on a female	S60 S60/65	53 4 } 57	29 6 } 35	15 4 } 19
Incest	S60 S60/65	1 3 } 4	1 0 } 1	0 0 } 0
Other	S60 S60/65	1 2 } 3	3 3 } 6	3 1 } 4
TOTAL	S60 S60/65	90 27 } 117	48 25 } 73	26 11 } 37

[1] Under the chairmanship of the Hon. Mrs Justice Heilbron DBE (in July 1975; the group reported in November 1975).

the number of persons made subject to hospital orders without restrictions regarding release had fallen by almost 50 per cent while the number made subject to 60/65 orders had remained constant. One per cent of persons convicted of sexual offences were dealt with by means of such orders. In the last five years, 1976–80, there has been a further 50 per cent fall in the use of such orders for sexual offenders. This level of decrease applies equally to Section 60 and to Section 60/65 orders; only an average of 37 persons per year were so dealt with, 26 receiving Section 60 orders and 11 Section 60/65 orders. Only one half of one per cent of persons convicted of sexual offences were made the subject of such orders.

An examination of the use of hospital orders and restriction orders offence by offence shows that the reduction in the use of Section 60 orders over the period 1964–80 was due to a reduction in the use of such orders for offenders convicted of indecent assaults. But since 80–90 per cent of such orders are imposed on persons convicted of indecent assaults, this is not an important finding. The fall in the last five years in the use of restriction orders is particularly marked in respect of persons convicted of homosexual offences but the numbers are too small to rule out the possibility that the changes noted are merely the result of chance.

Table 4.4 summarises the details on which the above discussion is based. It is not surprising that the more serious offences, especially rape, are more often dealt with by means of the Section 60/65 order, which places restrictions on the offender's release.

CONCLUDING SUMMARY

Recorded Incidence of Sexual Offences

The number of sexual offences recorded as known to the police in 1980 was two and a quarter times the 1946 figure. This compares with a 1980 figure for offences of violence against the person which was 24 times that of 1946 and a 1980 figure for all indictable offences which was 5 times the 1946 figure. In 1980 sexual offences constituted less than 1 per cent of all offences recorded.

Recorded homosexual offences trebled between 1946 and 1955 but in 1980 were less than twice the 1946 figure; recorded heterosexual offences reached a peak in 1973 (at nearly three and a half times the 1946 figure) but in 1980 were less than three times the 1946 figure. The recorded incidence of rape, however, has continued to increase since 1973 and in the years 1978–80 has been approaching five times the 1946 figure.

In respect of the eight main homosexual and heterosexual offences the recorded incidence in 1980 is two and a half times that of 1946. Only three of the eight offences show increases which differ significantly from this overall picture. Offences of indecent assault on a male are recorded at only one and a half times the 1946 figure and falling; offences of unlawful intercourse with a girl under 16 are four and a half times the 1946 figure but falling rapidly; offences of rape, as already mentioned, are now recorded at nearly five times the 1946 figure.

Sentences Imposed on Sexual Offenders

Rape is undoubtedly regarded by the courts as the most serious of the sexual offences. Over the last five years (1976–80) 93 per cent of adults convicted of the offence have received a custodial sentence. At the other end of the scale only 1 per cent of adults convicted of indecency between males receive custodial sentences.

Each offence classification embraces a variety of different types of offence which are regarded by the courts with differing degrees of seriousness. For example paternal incest is regarded very much more seriously than sibling incest and unlawful sexual intercourse by a man of over 30 with a girl of 13 or 14 much more seriously than the same offence by a man under 30 with a girl of 15.

The proportion of persons found guilty who receive a custodial sentence has remained fairly stable since 1946 in respect of the most serious sexual offences (rape, incest, buggery) but in respect of the other offences the custodial rate has dropped sharply. Despite this there has been a sudden increase in the use of custodial sentences for sexual offences in the last five years.

The use of hospital orders and restriction orders as a means of dealing with persons convicted of sexual offences has dropped by more than two-thirds in the last ten years.

© 1984. Crown copyright reserved.

REFERENCES

Advisory Group on the Law of Rape (1975) *Report* (Chairman the Hon. Mrs Justice Heilbron, DBE) Cmnd. 6352. London: HMSO.

Home Office (annually) *Criminal Statistics, England and Wales*. London: HMSO.

Walmsley, R. (1978) Indecency between males and the Sexual Offences Act 1967. *Criminal Law Review*, July, 400–407.

Walmsley, R. (1980) Rape: Rates, Trends and Sentencing Practice, *Research Bulletin* 10, Home Office Research Unit.

Walmsley, R. & White, K. (1979) Sexual Offences, Consent and Sentencing. *Home Office Research Study* No. 54. London: HMSO.

Walmsley, R. & White, K. (1980) Supplementary Information on Sexual Offences and Sentencing. *Research Unit Paper* 2, Home Office.

Wolfenden (1957) Report of the Committee on Homosexual Offences and Prostitution (Chairman Sir John Wolfenden, CBE) Cmnd. 247. London: HMSO.

5

Shoplifting

Michael Craft & Martin Spencer

Shoplifting is big business (*Daily Telegraph*, 23 March 1982). F.W. Woolworth and Company stated in their Annual Report that it can account for up to 10 per cent of takings. Segal (1977) quotes an estimate that this amounts to an increase of 2 per cent in the price of all goods sold in the shops, whilst Gibbens (1981) points out that shoplifting is only one part of the wastage (goods not accounted for by sales) occurring in shops. A recent estimate (Wescott 1971) gave wastage as short delivery (35 per cent), shop soiling of goods (15 per cent), shop assistant loss at point of sale (25 per cent), and shoplifting (25 per cent). The error at point of sale includes marking up and marking down; marking down occurs when the shop assistant passes out goods not charged; marking up occurs when the purchaser is charged more than the price of goods bought. This latter can occur when shoplifting has become excessive and the manager wishes to compensate himself. Within firms shoplifting can become endemic. During a recent dockers' strike in Britain resulting from the introduction of container stores, London dockers asked for an extra 10 per cent on wages to allow for food items they had previously obtained from ships being discharged, no longer possible as a result of the introduction of containerisation. Some stores have tried to eliminate this kind of illegal 'perk' by giving a substantial mark-down to their shop assistants for purchasing their own store goods.

High street shoplifting varies substantially with time, place and clientele. The sweet shop outside the comprehensive school soon learns to protect its goods; since adolescents from 10 to 21 comprise 'far in excess' of expected numbers convicted (McClintock and Avison, 1968, p. 276) they are very high on the incidence of shoplifting. Woolworth Stores countered the substantial rise in shoplifting in the 1940s by glassing-in counters; the newer Superstore is more vulnerable to shoplifting, because of open shelves and fewer staff. Although this led to a substantial rise in the number of housewives shoplifting, with recent unemployment the male contribution has risen substantially. From London, Gibbens (1981) reports, 'When every fifth woman entering a department store and a supermarket was followed a few years ago, 1 in 84 was seen to steal; made up of 1 in 131 in department stores, and 1 in 49 in supermarkets, from a total of 1000 cases. Using their sixth sense detectives do rather better, arresting 1 in 34 in department stores and 1 in 10 in supermarkets. In the USA 1 in 15 randomly followed stole.'

THE LEGAL POSITION

So much for statistics. In Britain there are a number of Acts under which theft is chargeable. Shoplifting itself is thought petty, but when charged under Section 1 of the Theft Act 1968, 'A person is guilty of theft if he dishonestly appropriates property belonging to another with the intention of permanently depriving the other of it.' Accordingly, it becomes clear that the intention to steal (*mens rea*) is in practice more important than the act (*actus rea*) which might consist of walking out of a shop with unpaid goods. Thus, obtaining a confession at an early stage is an essential part of a shop detective's work. Such employees are not prepared to risk their jobs or mental peace by proceeding with a case in which the intent is not admitted, and the reasoning forever remains locked in the accused's mind. In practice, most people caught in the street outside the shop with unpaid goods in hand or coat pocket confess very rapidly, the punishment is usually a small fine, and they are not prepared for the shame and upset of a long trial.

How the word 'dishonestly', used in Section 1, is to be construed was considered by the Court of Appeal in the case of *R. v. Feely* (1973). It was decided that the word 'dishonestly', being a word in common use, is not for judicial definition, but whether the defendant acted dishonestly is a question for the jury, applying the current standards of ordinary, decent people. Lord Justice Lawton said in the course of his judgment:

In Section 1(i) of the Act of 1968, the word 'dishonestly' can only relate to the state of mind of the person who does the act which amounts to appropriation. Whether an accused person has a particular state of mind is a question of fact which has to be decided by the jury when there is a trial on indictment, and by the magistrates when there are summary proceedings . . . Jurors, when deciding whether an appropriation was dishonest can be reasonably expected to, and should, apply the current standards of ordinary decent people. In their own lives they have to decide what is and what is not dishonest. We can see no reason why, when in a jury box, they should require the help of a judge to tell them what amounts to dishonesty.

This appears to us to have a profound bearing on the legal effect of psychiatric illnesses/disorders with respect to shoplifters. If the evidence is that the defendant was suffering from a severe depressive illness, that his or her act in taking goods from a shop without paying for them was a 'cry for help', an attention-seeking act where the purpose and hope was to be caught, it would be perfectly open for a jury to find the essential element of dishonesty was lacking and the defendant was therefore not guilty of theft. The example can be widened and elaborated considerably; the point is that, given medical evidence of this kind, it is not open to the judge to direct the jury that the defendant had the necessary *mens rea*; in all cases, whether the defendant was dishonest is a matter for the jury (or for the magistrates in summary trial). It can be seen, therefore, that medical evidence can have a considerable effect, not just at the sentencing stage but at the earlier stage of determining liability. It can constitute a defence. Nor does this defence amount to a defence of insanity under the McNaughton rules; this was the misapprehension of the Assistant Recorder in the case of *R. v. Clarke* (1972) and the Court of Appeal soon put him right. The judgment of Lord Justice Ackner is particularly informative; he outlined the nature of the defence:

The appellant's defence was that she had no intention of stealing these goods. She had not been feeling well on the morning in question nor for quite some time. She suffers from sugar diabetes. In the previous year she had gone down with 'flu and on the Friday previous to that occurrence her husband had broken his collarbone. He had to look after her and was in fact, because of his own condition, off work for several months. What with one thing and another, she had become very depressed. On a number of occasions she had been very forgetful; for example, she had put sugar in the refrigerator instead of in the cupboard and the sweeping brush in the dustbin and then put the dirt where the brush should have been put. In her own words 'everything seemed to get on top of me'.

On the morning in question she woke up with a very bad headache which persisted despite her taking her pills. Her husband rang up at about 11 00 am to say that he would be home for lunch late. She put their meal in the oven on a low flame and went out to fetch the groceries. She had no recollection of putting these three items into her shopping-bag and as for the jar of mincemeat neither she nor her husband ever ate this. In short, her defence was that she had not intended to steal these articles but in a moment of absent-mindedness had put them in her own shopping-bag.

... to support the validity of her explanation medical evidence was called. These witnesses were her GP and a consultant psychiatrist. These two gentlemen spoke to the fact that she was suffering from depression, which one of them accepted to be a minor mental illness. The GP described the symptoms. The patient feels a lack of energy – he finds it difficult to concentrate – he may be short-tempered or absent-minded. The psychiatrist stated that the condition can produce states of absent-mindedness in which the patient would do things he would not normally do, in periods of 'confusion and memory lapses'. All this evidence was entirely consistent with the appellant's story. ...

The effect of this evidence on the assistant recorder was to convince him that the defence was in truth a defence of 'not guilty by reason of insanity' under the McNaughton Rules ... The McNaughton Rules relate to accused persons who by reason of a disease of the mind are deprived of the power of reasoning.

They do not apply and never have applied to those who retain the power of reasoning, but who in moments of confusion or absent-mindedness fail to use their powers to the full. The picture painted by the evidence was wholly consistent with this being a woman who retained her ordinary powers of reason but who was momentarily absent-minded or confused and acted as she did by failing to concentrate adequately to use her mental powers.

The case thus illustrates how medical evidence can be used to support a *defence* to a charge of shoplifting without necessarily getting into the realms of McNaughton insanity, with all its drastic effects. A further illustration of where medical evidence might support a defence to a charge is given by Cox (1968):

It can be clearly seen that the defence of absent-mindedness does not hold water if the method of taking (e.g. the surreptitious concealment of the article) negates absence of intent ...

The position is however frequently complicated by the fact that at the time of the taking the defendant is under some unusual stress. A lady of 51 years of age, suffering from severe menopausal symptoms, on the anniversary of the death of her son goes into a store, picks up something that her son might have found useful, of trivial value, walks to another counter, pays for a second article and leaves the store without having paid for the first. When interviewed and asked whether she intended to steal the first article she says 'she doesn't know but she doesn't think she wanted to steal it'. Asked if she remembers picking it up she says 'Yes'; asked why she picked it up she says, 'I don't know, it's of no use to me or anyone else I know'. It is possible that the lady's actions might have resulted in the store losing a small article if she had not been stopped, but whether such a person is guilty of theft is extremely difficult to decide.

The point is that for a person to be guilty of theft, he or she must have the requisite intent or *mens rea*; whether one focuses on the 'dishonesty' aspect of the *mens rea*, or simply on whether the defendant had the necessary intent in more general terms, does not matter, although it helps that dishonesty in particular is the exclusive province of the jury. What matters is that a person's state of mind, as evidenced by medical evidence called on his or her behalf at trial, may mean that he or she lacks *mens rea* and is hence not guilty of the offence.

In the opinion of one of us (M.S.), the medical evidence as a defence in shoplifting cases is not used enough, even though there is clear authority that it can constitute a defence. More usual is the use of medical evidence as a mitigating circumstance, very often when the defendant has pleaded guilty to the substantive charges. Here, there is clear authority that medical evidence can play a major role in reducing the sentence imposed, and will often have the effect of preventing the implementation of an immediate custodial sentence. One such example is the case of:

R. v. *Walker* (1974). A female aged 32, Walker pleaded guilty to two charges of theft and asked for 22 other offences to be taken into consideration. Over a period of six weeks she and another woman carried out a series of planned shoplifting expeditions, using a car. The value of the property, all recovered, was over £2000. At the time she was on probation for shoplifting, with a condition of outpatient treatment at a hospital. She had five previous convictions for shoplifting. The Court of Appeal paid attention to the following considerations: She was married with two children and had started shoplifting in 1966 after the death of her step-father. She had a compulsion to steal attractive objects, which she stored in her house, and derived sexual satisfaction thereby. She had responded to treatment but started shoplifting again when the doctor who was treating her, and with whom she had become closely identified, left the district. Psychiatrists were of the view that if she served her prison term she would return to compulsive shoplifting but there was a chance of improvement if she received treatment. The Court of Appeal said that, but for the medical position, the sentence would have been a proper one having regard to the gravity of the offences and her record for shoplifting. As it was, the public interest and that of Walker coincided. The result was a three years' probation order with a condition of inpatient treatment at hospital.

An older example of an immediate prison sentence being reduced so that the defendant could be released immediately, on account of the circumstances of mental strain on the defendant, is *R. v. Dobson Shade* (1961). The court took account of the fact that the defendant Dobson had an invalid husband and six children, and as a result of these difficulties had undergone a period of mental strain.

We would conclude that medical matters can now directly impinge upon the offence of shoplifting, both as a significant mitigating circumstance and also, in particularly strong cases, as a defence.

FREQUENCY OF MENTAL ILLNESS AMONG SHOPLIFTERS

To help in the preparation of this chapter, we researched Western literature over the last twenty years. Articles in the early 1960s dealt predominantly with individual cases of medical interest, such as a man of 25 with cerebral tumour. Research reports in the early 1970s comment on the lack of large-scale analysis of series of shoplifters. The most recent reports give both analyses of groups and a follow-up to see whether treatment has been effective with such groups. Thus, much more information is available now than was the case five years ago. Most recent research reports comment that the main motivation for shoplifting is greed, particularly among adolescents. Desperate need, as reflected by single mothers stealing for their infants, does occur, but is rare in Britain. Oscar Wilde once said that the simplest way of dealing with temptation is to yield to it, and many adolescents would be in agreement with him, in one way, if not in another! For those who shoplift, there is an explanation if not a psychological interpretation for almost everybody. In this vein is a psychoanalytic paper by

Castelnuovo-Tedesco (1974), who psychoanalysed three cases and found that the motivation of each was due to earlier maternal deprivation of love or goods at some point in the past. Others, notably Davis (1979), can find evidence of depression or mental ill-health among almost all of 17 patients referred, although he does not make it clear whether the anxiety and depression occurred after arrest or before. Yet others comment on the number of elderly people on drugs which can lead to confusion (Todd, 1976). It is a feature of middle-aged and older people that a substantial number may be on drugs and confused as to timing and dosage of medication. In an age incidence analysis of shoplifters, there is a notable bulge in numbers of middle-aged housewives, who steal mainly from food shops, and older men, who steal from bookshops. Multiple drug-taking and lapses of concentration in these age groups are both common in the general population.

The most useful recent research concerns the analysis of large numbers of shoplifters. One of the earliest large-scale series was that carried out by Gibbens and Prince concerning 500 London shoplifters in 1959 (see Gibbens et al, 1971). Of the 500 seen, 20 per cent had significant ill-health or psychosomatic illness, 8 per cent had a significant physical illness, mainly gynaecological. London hospital admissions were researched by way of follow-up (Gibbens et al, 1971) and by 1981 Gibbens was able to report:

The situation seems to have altered quantitatively rather than qualitatively ... [over the years]. The presence of depression in such cases seemed to be confirmed when we studied their subsequent convictions for any offence in the next ten years, and also admissions to mental hospitals, although this was only possible in the second quinquennium ... At least 5.8 per cent of those (the great majority) with only the one offence in 1959 had since been admitted, 12.2 per cent with a subsequent offence, 12 per cent of those with a previous offence, and 19.6 of those with both previous and subsequent offences (which often included other types of offence) – an overall 8.4 per cent. The age specific rate of admission in those years was 2.5 per cent, so it assumed that ex-shoplifters had two or three times the expected rate. Most of the admissions had been for depression or attempted suicide. It suggested that shoplifting in these women was the earlier symptom in a gathering depression; but there are certainly some who are pushed further into depression by the shame of arrest.

As with minor sex offences in men, which they resemble in many respects, it is sometimes a response to serious mental illness in someone else. All depressed patients, however, are aggressive, either to themselves or others, and the element of well concealed resentment and spite is detectable. In 1959 we thought that 10 to 15 per cent of cases fell into the disordered group, but I understand that a modern fully clinical study of a large group suggests 5 per cent. One can understand that shopkeepers weary of the popular assumption that all shoplifters are of this type.

The results of other series seem to vary with the orientation of the writer and the circumstances of referral. For instance, Neustatter writing in 1953 says that of 338 shoplifters referred to the Chicago Psychiatric Institute, 77 per cent showed definite depressive symptoms. Of the 338, 313 were women. From Germany Englert (1972) reports that among 50 shoplifters referred, 18 had a degree of mental ill-health, with 5 depressive, many with cerebral degeneration or atrophy. He says the majority were women with an average age of 43.8. From New York City where the rate of drug addiction is high, James et al (1979) report an analysis of 268 females imprisoned for theft; most shoplifted to obtain money for drugs. These authors thought most addicts had abnormal personalities in a larger series of 457 women released consecutively from New York penal units.

They found that 75 per cent were narcotic addicts; some shoplifted, others gained the money for drugs by prostitution.

Some writers are not convinced that shoplifters need psychiatric referral. Bockner (1976) points out that in thirty years of London psychiatric practice he had come across only one compulsive stealer. For many years a steady stream of shoplifters had been referred to him for psychiatric opinion by courts. He writes, 'Very rarely indeed have I found any psychiatric disorder in these cases . . . True, there is the occasional case of menopausal depression . . .' He complains bitterly about Segal's (1976) listing medical causes of confusion as possible defences to shoplifting, which he thinks is psychiatric presumption. On the other hand, because of Bockner's known views on shoplifting no one refers such cases to this Harley Street psychiatrist.

Medical and Psychiatric Causes of Shoplifting

Most writers agree that the conviction rate for shoplifting closely follows in its age incidence that of convictions in general, but that there is an important bulge in the later groups concerning middle-aged housewives, many of whom are suffering from depression, and older men, some of whom are senile, forgetful and lacking in concentration. In fact, shoplifting can be found as an incidental feature of mental handicap or mental illness at any age. Together with person-ality disorders, drug abuse and confusional states, it can occur in the whole range of illnesses found in the psychiatric textbook. Such individual cases form the basis for most of the fifty or so articles on shoplifting in the western literature over the last ten years, usually concerned with fascinating individual cases such as stealing for sex (Revitch, 1978); the XYY syndrome (Wiedeking et al, 1979); narcolepsy (Zorick et al, 1979); or cerebral atrophy in a 25-year-old (Khan and Martin, 1977).

Who to Refer for a Medical Report?

A psychiatric referral by a solicitor or medical referral to the family doctor is warranted on certain particular indications. Clear illness or obvious confusion represent two of these, together with the first offence for no very obvious reason, in a person of otherwise impeccable habits. In Britain only 10 per cent of all first offenders are ever re-convicted, and, as Gibbens (1971) has shown, it is among those who are re-convicted that the need for hospital admission for a depressive illness becomes most likely. Further indications for medical or psychiatric refer-ral concern the motiveless nature of theft, apparently compulsive repetition (the old kleptomania), the apparent need for drugs, or bizarre sexual motivation, such as bras, panties or swimming costumes.

Clinical Groups Needing Help

In practice, as Segal (1977) noted, almost any condition causing severe mental confusion can coincide with shoplifting. Episodes of confusion are common in the elderly and, since most elderly women are in fact living alone, daily shopping is essential whether they are confused or not. In addition, many are poverty-stricken, and confusion may sap the moral balance.

General medical conditions which are common, which cause confusion and which have convinced lawgivers to accept medical evidence include diabetes, post-influenzal states, multiple drug taking, post-alcoholic hangovers and diar-rhoea, leading to gross loss of water and hypoglycaemia from lack of food. Rare causes have included post-comatose confusion, post-epileptic confusion and myxoedema, either natural or drug (lithium) induced. Obviously in all cases medical evidence should prove cause and effect; one per cent respectively of the general population are epileptic and diabetic, and some of these people will maliciously steal.

Psychiatric causes can start with mental handicap. Many of these people and young children may lack adequate parental training against theft; some of each continue a degree of personality impulsivity into adulthood for various reasons. Immature juveniles commonly shoplift and there may be good reason for referral to a child guidance clinic if there are other indications such as depression, hallucination, or bizarre sexual interest. Having said this, a number of juveniles shoplift at some time, either as part of the general pattern of delinquency, or by way of a 'dare', or to satisfy greed or need such as smoking. Some develop expensive habits such as gambling or drug taking.

The psychotic shoplifter is easily recognised. The schizophrenic, who believes that the store belongs to him, or the hypomanic rushing in and out of stores cramming his pockets full of goodies, may be diagnosable by the neighbourhood policeman (if he can catch up with the hypomanic!).

Depression, particularly in the middle-aged housewife, may not be so readily recognisable. The vague and ineffectual woman stopped on the street outside the store, who breaks down weeping and dejected, may present a very similar picture to the 'normal' reaction pattern of somebody caught thieving for greed. All second convictions for shoplifting among middle-aged housewives should be carefully assessed, and the enquiring solicitor, or for that matter doctor, should check for depression of vital functions: sleeplessness, lack of appetite, loss of weight, early morning waking, apathy, thoughts of suicide. These all need direct, but tactful, questioning to be brought out. It must not be forgotten that some depressed patients are vague and ineffectual; some may be agitated, tense and excited, others noisy and blustering. These are the face-to-face manifestations of particular types of character; it is the depression of vital functions common to all characters which is indicative of the depressive illness.

Confusional states are common in the elderly, and often associated with the taking of drugs, either self-administered or from doctors. The lapse of concen-tration in the elderly bibliophile, the wandering of a housewife after a sleepless night, even the minor confusion of the middle-aged man whose blood alcohol level remains above the legal driving limit although 12 hours have elapsed since his last drinking bout – all these may have valid medical reason, if not for acquittal, for consideration by the court. Nor must other illnesses be forgotten. An episode of bronchitis in the heavy smoker with resultant de-oxygenation of the brain, the sudden spasm of diarrhoea, the urinary problems prostatic-enlarg-ened, all have been brought to the attention of courts as the reason for leaving a shop in haste. One in four adult women are said to be on tranquillisers which, like alcohol, 'can similarly impair the social judgment of persons under stress' (Oswald, 1982).

Senile dementia, according to the latest research, might be expected to occur in one in six of the population over the age of 60. Some, such as the man of 25 quoted above, can be demonstrated by air encephalograms (X-rays of air intro-duced in their skulls) to have a substantial loss of brain mass. Once syphilis was the most common cause of brain wastage, now it is alcohol. One in ten of all heavy drinkers will have demonstrable loss of brain mass by the age of 55. Some dementia is reversible, such as that due to grossly deficient diet, high blood pressure, excess smoking, excess alcohol or lack of thyroid. All need investigation so that treatment may be started and the court may have a full picture of the current position.

A psychiatric probation order can be a constructive court disposal to ensure psychotherapy and drugs. Courts are very mindful of suicide following depres-sion in shoplifting, and are also well aware that they may not have been supplied with all the background relevant to the case. A probation officer is a court official who can continue counselling, aid a housewife with her marital difficulties and perhaps also ensure the uncovering of any concealed depressive illnesses. A psychiatric report may be used to ensure that the probationer can be returned for treatment to the psychiatrist should this be necessary; most psychiatrists who are in local practice will be prepared to have cases re-referred to them by the probation officer if an undiagnosed depressive illness later becomes manifest.

A grudge, or an obsession, is usually found to be responsible for the more spectacular examples of accumulation of unused goods from shoplifting. In a recent personally known example in Wales, a lifetime's results filled a household, and later the police station; the shoplifter had had a long-standing concealed grudge against his merchant employers. The justices were content to see pictures of the vast collection, and placed him on a psychiatric probation order. In another case, a professor of archaeology was diagnosed as 'obsessional' and given a similar probation order, for travelling the museums of Europe as a distinguished researcher to find articles to fill the gaps in his own collection which he had willed to his old university. His 'shoplifting' was discovered only by chance, as few checked the State collections he rifled.

Paranoid jealousy of a rival store has been known to motivate other shop-keepers to shoplift. Alternatively, a Woolworth shareholder in the practice of one of us thought his dividends were insufficient. Lodged in a mental hospital on a compulsory court order in an earlier era, for years he was allowed out on parole only on Sundays. It took two decades of this before senile dementia resulted in his being uninterested even in shoplifting.

TREATMENT

Most psychiatric illnesses now respond to treatment by drugs, by psychotherapy, or by other means. Most depressive illnesses can be treated at family doctor or outpatient level without hospital admission. For many of the others, and even for those caught in a 'situational maladjustment', to use a social work cliché, aid by National Health or social services department means is possible. Psychology departments may offer behaviour therapy (see Chapter 27 and Keutzer, 1972).

Relief by reassurance and the comfort of somebody being interested in their problems often helps overwrought housewives in a difficult marital situation. The diagnosis of a treatable condition, which can be alleviated by drugs at outpatient or family doctor level, is enough to start others on the road to recovery. General counselling, as any solicitor knows, plays a substantial part in the resolution of environmental difficulties. Sometimes the rearrangement of the day's work, the coaxing of a spouse to play more part in a difficult marriage, the engagement of the attention of grown-up children or relatives may all help to brighten the family outlook.

For the lonely, the elderly or the senile, the reorganisation of eating, living or day occupation pattern may be necessary. Here the social services or meals on wheels service may help. For the confused, the senile and the demented, it may be necessary for their shopping to be done by others, or for them to go with a partner on shopping expeditions. This does not have to be done in an autocratic way; by the time people reach the stage of assisted shopping, their general frailties are all too recognisable.

As Lord Justice Ormrod (1975) said, 'Courts have always to deal with individuals, and their need – sometimes it is almost a desperate need – is for information, knowledge and advice on an individual basis.' It may be that some psychiatrists are more helpful to solicitors than others, whilst a few may be frankly antagonistic, but the courts do not always have to take the advice of the first one sought. The practising solicitor soon comes to know the psychiatrists in his neighbourhood, and can suit the opinions available to his needs or those of his client.

CASES

R. *v*. Clarke (1972) 1 All England Report p. 219.
R. *v*. Dobson Shade (1961) Criminal Law Review, 724.
R. *v*. Feely (1973) IQB 532.
R. *v*. Walker (1974) Criminal Law Review, 323.

REFERENCES

Bockner, S. (1976) Psychiatric aspects of shoplifting. *Brit. Med. J.*, **i**, 710.
Castelnuovo-Tedesco, P. (1974) Stealing, revenge and the Monte Cristo complex. *Int. J. Psychoanal.*, **55**, 2, 169–81.
Cox, A. E. (1968) Shoplifting. *Crim. Law Rev.*, **425,** 429.
Davis, H. (1979) Psychiatric aspects of shoplifting. *S. Afr. Med. J.*, **55,** 22, 885–7.

Englert, H. (1972) The psychopathology and criminal psychology of shoplifting: Report on 50 expert opinions. *Oeff. Gesundheitswes*, **34**, 8, 466–73.

Gibbens, T.C.N. (1981) Shoplifting. *Brit. J. Psychiat.*, **138**, 346–7.

Gibbens, T.C.N., Palmer, C. & Prince, J. (1971) Mental health aspects of shoplifting. *Brit. Med. J.*, **3**, 612–15.

James, J., Gosho, C. & Wohl, R.W. (1979) The relationship between female criminality and drug use. *Int. J. Addict.*, **14**, 2, 215–29.

Keutzer, C.S. (1972) Kleptomania: a direct approach to treatment. *Brit. J. Med. Psychol.*, **45**, 159–63.

Khan, K. & Martin, I.C. (1977) Kleptomania as a presenting feature of cortical atrophy. *Acta Psychiat. Scand.*, **56**, 3, 168–72.

McClintock, F.H. & Avison, N.H. (1968) *Crime in England and Wales*. London: Heinemann.

Neustatter, L. (1953) Psychiatry and Crime. *Practitioner*, 170, 391–9.

Ormrod, R.G.F. (1975) The debate between psychiatry and the law. *Brit. J. Psychiat.*, **127**, 193–203.

Oswald, I. (1982) The poor sleeper. *Psychiatry in Practice*, **1**, 8–13.

Revitch, E. (1978) Sexually motivated burglaries. *Bull. Am. Acad. Psychiat. Law*, **6**, 277–83.

Segal, M. (1976) Psychiatric aspects of shoplifting. *Brit. Med. J.*, **i**, 523–4.

Segal, M. (1977) Psychiatry and the shoplifter. *Practitioner*, **218**, 823–7.

Todd, J. (1976) Pharmacogenic shoplifting? *Brit. Med. J.*, **i**, 150.

Wescott, R. (1971) In: Gibbens, T.C.N. (1981) *Brit. J. Psychiat.*, **138**, 346–7.

Wiedeking, C., Money, J. & Walker, P. (1979) Follow-up of 11 XYY males with impulsive and/or sex offending behaviour. *Psychol. Med.*, **9**, 2, 287–92.

Zorick, F.J., Salis, P.J., Roth, T. & Kramer, M. (1979) Narcolepsy and automatic behaviour: a case report. *J. Clin. Psychiat.*, **40**, 4, 194–7.

6

Sexual Offences: Intent and Characteristics

Ann Craft, Michael Craft & Martin Spencer

In 1980 sexual offences represented only one per cent of all offences recorded by the police, but as Bluglass (1982) comments, 'Sex offenders are among the smallest group of offenders, but in many ways they arouse the most concern, anxiety and alarm among those who have to manage or sentence them. As a result of this, perhaps a relatively high proportion are remanded for psychiatric assessment and many accept psychiatric treatment or an attempt at treatment.'

The label 'sexual offender' is a very broad one and can place together the most violent and sadistic of rapists with the most inoffensive of exhibitionists. Rape, attempted rape, indecent assault, child molestation, homosexual activity with males under 21, buggery, bestiality, procuration and indecent exposure are all sexual offences (although the latter is no longer indictable). The variety in such a list should remind us that circumstances, offenders and victims are going to be very different.

The vast majority of sexual offences are committed by males and the bulk of this chapter is therefore devoted to an examination of the male offender.

INTENT: PSYCHIATRY AND THE LAW

There are over thirty separate indictable sexual offences, most of which are contained in the Sexual Offences Act, 1956, and numerous summary sexual offences such as exhibitionism, which may involve the psychiatrist. Each offence is separately defined, and therefore the criteria for guilt in respect of the necessary *mens rea* differ between them, and there is no such thing as a general criterion of *mens rea* in sexual offenders.

Psychiatric evidence can only come in at the stage of determination of the accused's guilt where there is some mental criterion which could be affected by mental abnormality. This could be a lack of knowledge, or an appreciation or belief on the part of the accused stemming from his mental condition and rendering him unable to appreciate facts or circumstances which would have been obvious to a perfectly normal person. Under these circumstances, the scope for psychiatric evidence being used to exonerate the accused at the stage of trial is limited in most sexual offences. Most of these do not require any particular *mens rea* on the part of the accused – in fact, many are of 'strict liability'. For example, by Section 12 of the Sexual Offences Act, 1956, the offence of buggery is stated as follows.

It is an offence for a person to commit buggery with another person or with an animal.

From this, it appears that there is no scope for psychiatric evidence to come in at the stage of ascertaining the accused's guilt – the simple question is whether the accused did the act of buggery. Many other sexual offences are of a similar nature: the offence is complete by the mere doing of the act prohibited. The fact that the accused is suffering from a mental illness is no defence, only mitigation.

Even in respect of those offences where there is some special mental element required in the definition of the offence, it is difficult to see how mental abnormality could be a defence. Thus, the offence of incest is defined in Section 10 of the Sexual Offences Act, 1956 as follows:

It is an offence for a man to have sexual intercourse with a woman whom he knows to be his grand-daughter, daughter, sister or mother.

The mental abnormality would have to be exceptional to deprive the accused of the knowledge necessary in this offence. The same goes for the offence of trading in prostitution, defined in Section 30 as follows.

It is an offence for a man knowingly to live wholly, or in part, on the earnings of prostitution.

There is, however, one major exception to this general truth that mental abnormality can be no defence to most sexual offences, and that concerns the offence of rape. The *mens rea* in rape was considered by the House of Lords in the case of *DPP* v. *Morgan* [1975] 61 Cr App R 136. In this case, the judge had directed the jury that on a charge of rape, a defendant was not entitled to be acquitted on the grounds that he may have believed the woman was consenting, unless the belief would also have been reasonable. By a majority, the House of Lords held that this direction was wrong. The result is that if a man, on whatever unreasonable grounds, believes the woman to be consenting, he cannot be guilty of rape. This decision was subsequently enshrined in the Sexual Offences Act 1976 which provides by Section 1(2):

It is hereby declared that if at a trial for a rape offence the jury has to consider whether a man believed that a woman was consenting to sexual intercourse, the presence or absence of reasonable grounds for such a belief is a matter to which the jury is to have regard, in conjunction with any other relevant matters, in considering whether he is so believed.

Thus, if a defendant states in evidence that he believed the victim was consenting, the question for the jury to decide is whether that statement is true or not. In deciding that question, the presence or absence of reasonable grounds for such belief is one factor for the jury to take into account; but the absence of reasonable grounds is not conclusive, as would have been the case if the judge's direction in *Morgan* had been the law. Reasonable grounds here mean all relevant surrounding circumstances, such as whether the victim resisted, what, if anything, she had done to encourage the defendant, etc.

It seems to us that the words 'in conjunction with any other relevant matters' are significant. For example, if a psychiatrist were, in a rape trial, to give evidence that the accused's state of mind is such that he may not have appreciated the woman was not consenting, even though such belief would not have been objectively reasonable, then this would surely be another 'relevant matter' for them to consider in determining whether the accused did in fact believe that the woman was consenting; if they find that he did, then he is, of course, entitled to be acquitted.

However, it should be remembered that a medical witness cannot be called to give his opinion as to the state of the accused's mind at the time of the commission of the alleged offence: it is always for the jury to decide whether, in fact, the accused appreciated that the victim was not consenting, on the basis of the evidence they have heard. This is a distinction which has become blurred in murder trials. Since *Byrne* (see p. 96–7), an expert witness may say that, in his opinion, the accused was suffering from diminished responsibility, a matter which is strictly for the jury to decide. However, in sexual offences, a medical witness can simply give his opinion as to what (if any) mental illness the accused is suffering from, and how that might affect his knowledge, or appreciation, or belief in a general sense.

It can be seen that the extent to which medical evidence as to the accused's state of mind can help towards his acquittal depends on the extent to which the test of liability is subjective or objective. In so far as the House of Lords in *Morgan* opted for a subjective test, so that the question now is what the accused acutally believed as opposed to what a reasonable person would have believed, they have, in our opinion, opened up the possibility of medical evidence being relevant to the issue of the accused's guilt in the case of rape.

Women

Very few sexual offences are committed by women; indeed, many cannot be. See, for example, Section 1 of the Sexual Offences Act 1956: 'It is an offence for a *man* to rape a woman.' Sometimes this is illogical: for example, there is no reason why the offence of procuring others to commit homosexual acts should be limited to men, but it is – see Section 4 of the Sexual Offences Act, 1956. Those offences which may be committed by women are, particularly, incest under Section 11 of the Sexual Offences Act, 1956 and indecent assault on a man, under Section 15; for example, a woman commits an offence if she indecently assaults a man, and if he is a boy aged 15 or less, his consent thereto is irrelevant. Depending on the circumstances, this could mean that an act of sexual intercourse between a woman and a boy aged 15 or less was an offence on the part of the woman, if her actions could also be said to amount to an indecent assault.

OFFENDER CHARACTERISTICS

Stereotypes of 'typical' sex offenders abound, ranging from the dirty old man in his shabby raincoat who haunts public parks, to the social isolate who sits in his lonely room, fuelling his hatred with hard porn. In all stereotypes there is a kernel of truth, for while we seldom come face to face with such characters, it is, as Crawford (1979) points out, '... equally unusual to find a well-adjusted family man, happily married with a satisfactory sex life, who has a responsible and enjoyable job, leads an active social life and rapes women.'

Studies indicate that sex offenders show signs of a wide variety of problems in their lives, particularly in the social and sexual areas. Many sexual offenders have also been in trouble for other crimes. Fowles (1977) found in a 1971–4 survey of Rampton Special Hospital patients that, of 73 men admitted for a sexual offence, only 10 per cent had previous convictions for sexual crimes alone; 77 per cent had previously been convicted of a variety of other crimes (43 per cent for non-sexual offences only). These percentages were more or less matched in a comparison with other patients already resident at the time of survey, also admitted as a direct result of a sexual offence.

Perhaps not surprisingly, difficulties in establishing the relationship that normally precedes a sexual interaction and general immaturity are reported features in studies of sexual offenders. In a survey of 500 non-aggressive such offenders, Pacht and Cowden (1974) concluded that they were 'less capable of establishing satisfactory relationships leading to socially approved sexual behavior with mature persons of the opposite sex'. Goldstein and Kant (1973), in a study undertaken for the United States Commission on Pornography and Obscenity, concluded that:

Sex offenders are more like teenagers in their sexual orientations, still highly stimulated by fantasy objects and fixated upon masturbation as a sexual outlet. This appears to be but one aspect of a generally lower level of social competence and adequacy when contrasted with the controls.

Howells and Wright (1978), using personality tests to compare a group of aggressive sexual offenders in Broadmoor Special Hospital with a sample of patients admitted for non-sexual crimes, found that the sex offenders group had poor impulse control in the sexual area and showed tendencies to act out dangerously. They were less satisfied with their sexual contacts, were more worried about sex and reported more sexual difficulties than the non-sex offenders. For both groups sexual problems were associated with shyness, social avoidance and social anxiety. Taylor (1972) reported that deficient social skills was the second most frequent reason given by sexual offenders to explain their behaviour. All of the above have implications when treatment programmes are considered.

It may be a truism to say that sexual offences occur as interactions between two or more people (voyeurism and bestiality are the exceptions); it should alert us to what has until recently been a neglected area, the role of the victim. We shall consider this in relation to the various offences.

Homosexuality

While homosexuality itself is not illegal, certain homosexual *acts* in England and Wales do contravene the law (in Scotland and many of the States in America *all* homosexual acts are illegal). It is therefore relevant to look briefly at homosexuality and the areas in which the male[1] is liable to come up against the law.

Although there had been surveys of homosexuality before the Kinsey study it was this report that revealed how relatively common such sexual behaviour is. The findings may not be representative of America as a whole, nor are they current, but they remain the most extensive data available.

Kinsey and his colleagues (1948) found that approximately 4 per cent of the surveyed adult males were exclusively homosexual in both physical contact and erotic interests. About 60 per cent of prepubertal boys had had homosexual experience and, between the age of puberty and 45, about 37 per cent of males had had at least one homosexual encounter leading to orgasm (this figure was 50 per cent for single men). The data was conceptualised on a heterosexual–homosexual behaviour rating scale which is better thought of as a continuum (see Table 6.1).

Table 6.1 Heterosexual – homosexual behaviour scale.

Category	Definition
0	Entirely heterosexual experience
1	Mainly heterosexual, but at least some homosexual experience
2	Mainly heterosexual, more than incidental homosexual experience
3	Equal heterosexual and homosexual experience
4	Mainly homosexual, more than incidental heterosexual experience
5	Almost exclusively homosexual but some heterosexual experience
6	Exclusively homosexual experience

Compiled from data in Kinsey et al, 1948.

As Katchadourian and Lunde (1972) comment, the Kinsey researchers were quite aware of the implications of placing people on a continuum and thus 'contaminating' large segments of the population who would like to think of themselves as exclusively heterosexual, but they were unrepentant, stating clearly:

Males do not represent two discrete populations, heterosexual and homosexual ... It is a fundamental taxonomy that nature rarely deals with discrete categories. Only the human mind invents categories and tries to force facts into separate pigeon-holes. The living world is a continuum in each and every one of its aspects. The sooner we learn this concerning human sexual behavior the sooner we shall reach a sound understanding of the realities of sex. (Kinsey et al, 1948)

The first obvious point, then, is the sheer numbers of males engaging incidentally or preferentially in homosexual acts which may or may not come to the attention of the police.

The second point is the way in which homosexuality is regarded in society. For centuries in Western culture homosexual behaviour, whether thought of as

---

[1] Female homosexuality between adults is not legally proscribed in Britain and although many American statutes do not distinguish between male and female homosexuals, lesbians seem to be rarely prosecuted. The Kinsey researchers (1953), reviewing arrests in New York over a ten-year period, found 'tens of thousands' of arrests and convictions for male homosexuals but only three for female homosexual offences and all three cases had been dismissed.

a life style, an illness, or an offence, was generally seen as a threat to norms and morality. It was deemed 'unnatural' because it contravened the Judaeo-Christian position which holds that sexual activity is only legitimate within marriage for the purpose of reproduction. Many people still hold this view, and to a great extent it is enshrined in the legal code. Although the Wolfenden Report (1957) had far-reaching consequences in establishing an adult individual's right to engage privately in consensual homosexual acts which were formerly illegal, it was still felt necessary for the law to protect young men until they reached the age of 21.[1] They were considered not to be mature at the same age as young women, who can give valid consent at 16. Homosexual males are thought to be a bad influence on young males at a time when they are not mature enough to have a fixed sexual orientation. Lesbians are not seen as a threat to young women because such relationships tend to arise later in life.

In practice in England and Wales custodial sentences are very rare for consensual buggery and indecency between males where both are 18 or over. In 1962 the American Law Institute drew up and approved a Model Penal Code which did not contain any prohibitions against any kind of sexual behaviour among consenting adults in private. However, most states have not altered their statutes relating to consensual sexual behaviour (Myren, 1975). There has been much discussion that the application of such laws may be unconstitutional, particularly in regard to homosexuals (Barnett, 1973). The grounds for challenge are threefold: the independent rights doctrine, which holds that the constitution imposes certain restrictions on state laws that might interfere with personal liberty; the right to privacy doctrine, which has been used to uphold the concept that what people do in private should not be the concern of prohibitive laws unless someone is being harmed; and the equal protection doctrine, which requires states to apply laws equally to all citizens (sodomy laws are often *not* applied equally, but used particularly to proceed against homosexuals).

Finally, the lifestyle of males with homosexual preferences may inevitably put them at risk of contravening the law. 'Homosexual relationships tend to be impermanent and may be transient and promiscuous' (Bebbington, 1979). The latest Kinsey survey of the year 1970 (published 1978) indicated that two-thirds of the male homosexual subjects had developed venereal disease and two-fifths had each had more than five hundred sexual partners. If relationships are short, a man may be driven at frequent intervals to find new partners, which can be a hazardous business, although the following Californian experience may be atypical.

One survey of the Los Angeles area indicated that 90–95 per cent of all homosexual arrests were violations under Section 647 (a) of the Californian Penal Code which makes a person guilty of the misdemeanour of disorderly conduct 'who solicits anyone to engage in or who engages in lewd or dissolute conduct in any public place or in any place open to the public or exposed to public view.' What makes the Californian arrests different is that the majority had involved the use of attractive young policemen as decoys to entice homo-

---

[1] The Criminal Law Revision Committee (1980) favoured reducing the age of consent to 18 years.

sexuals into the 'lewd' behaviour proscribed by the statute. There was some outcry that this strategy was itself an outrage to public decency! (Hoffman, 1968). It should, however, be noted that in Britain it is not necessary for a member of the public to take offence at a homosexual act, say in a toilet, for the police to proceed. Indeed, the 1967 Sexual Offences Act reaffirmed the illegality of public homosexual acts, and introduced summary trial, thus giving the police confidence to act and making prosecution easier. The recorded incidence has more than doubled since 1967, the number of persons prosecuted has trebled, and the number convicted has quadrupled in the UK. Having a homosexual orientation is not illegal, but the actions manifesting those preferences are implicitly risky, either *per se* as in Scotland, or where the venue is public and/or the partner is unable to give valid consent.

Sexual Offences and Mental Handicap

The early view was unequivocal:

... there is no investigator who denies the fearful role played by mental deficiency in the production of vice, crime and delinquency ... Not all criminals are feeble-minded, but all feeble-minded are at least potential criminals. That every feeble-minded woman is a potential prostitute would hardly be disputed by anyone (Terman 1916).

When Alfred Binet first developed his original IQ test it was to distinguish between illiterate criminals labelled mentally defective – many for sexual crimes – and others. Even now, depending on the social and IQ variables used, the proportion of convicted offenders found to be defective can range from 2.6 to 39.6 per cent from one American state to another (MacEachron, 1979). This researcher found that when IQ testing of all convicts was done the prevalence rate of mentally retarded adult male offenders under IQ 70 is only slightly higher than the prevalence rate of retarded male adults in the general population. She concludes, 'Social and legal variables are more germane to the problem of being an offender than is intelligence.'

No study to date has satisfactorily explored the subject of sexual offences committed by mentally handicapped persons. Brown and Courtless (1968) looking at jailed offenders under IQ 55 did not separate out sexual offences from other crimes against the person, such as homicide and assault. They make the general observation that offences of a sexual nature were the least frequently committed crime by incarcerated offenders under IQ 70.

Walker and McCabe (1973) using Mental Health Act, 1959 classifications found that males labelled as subnormal (SN) and severely subnormal (SSN) made up one-third of their sample of offenders, but accounted for 50 per cent of sexual offences. This may seem a clear enough indication, but Parker (1974), in her survey of special hospital patients, found 69 per cent of those with a Mental Health Act classification of SSN had IQs above 50, which is the normally accepted cut-off IQ point. Of this 69 per cent, 3 per cent had IQs above 80. Of those patients with a Mental Health Act classification of SN, 51 per cent had scores above the normally accepted cut-off point of IQ 70. As Fowles (1977) points out, the classification 'subnormal' is commonly interchangeable with 'psychopath' in court practice and bears little relation to intellectual retardation, so all British analyses of offences committed by subnormals should be regarded with suspicion in the absence of an IQ rating which would confirm mental handicap.

Two other germane points concern police action. First, it is often easy to persuade the handicapped to a confession of doubtful veracity. Only recently have confessions by a mildly mentally handicapped person without a guardian or professional present been questioned by British courts. Secondly, motivation: when is an offence a perversion or done with malicious intent, and when is it a result of ignorance and lack of training? Often, many 'crimes' look much worse on paper than they are in fact. For example, a charge of indecent exposure may result from a retarded man not knowing how to locate a toilet when he is out and urinating in the street. It is impossible to tease out from criminal statistics those 'indecent exposures' from men who deliberately expose themselves for the thrill they get from the reaction of others, or from a retarded adolescent who used an antisocial behaviour which happened to be sexual to get his neighbourhood to notice him. All give cause for concern, but require a different response from parents and professionals (Craft and Craft, 1979).

THE OFFENCE

Bluglass (1982) makes the important point that some offences are basically sexual, while others are basically violent acts. Indecent exposure, voyeurism and most instances of child molesting are predominantly sexual crimes; but rape, serious sexual assault, many cases of unlawful intercourse under 13, sometimes buggery, and a minority of assaults on children have an inherent element of violence. Incest may fall into either category, or somewhere between the two. The presence or absence of violence is a factor in both prognosis and treatment.

While the likelihood of a repetition of the offence is small, a series of reconvictions makes a further one much more likely (although not nearly so likely as for traffic offences or dishonesty). However, Gibbens (1981) describes a disturbing difference between sexual and other offences. If a property offender is not reconvicted within five years he probably never will be again, but sex offenders, although not very often reconvicted for several years, seem to have a low but persistent tendency to be reconvicted even after many years. One explanation might be that, 'Sexual maladjustment is probably an "Achilles heel", which determines how an offender breaks down under the variable stresses of life' (Gibbens et al, 1980).

Even though deviant sexual behaviour brings a man into conflict with the law, at times the personal rewards of tension release, control over others, or orgasmic achieval are overwhelmingly urgent, and probably come to be sexually arousing in their own right.

Rape

In Britain rape is defined as sexual intercourse with a woman who, at the time, does not consent to it, and who, to the defendant's knowledge, does not consent or is reckless as to whether she consents. In some American states the term 'statutory rape' applies to sexual intercourse where one participant was not able to give a legally valid consent due, for example, to mental incompetency or being a minor (these constitute a large proportion of rape cases). In Britain and America a man still cannot be charged with the rape of his wife unless there are special circumstances, such as the existence of a court separation order.

The legal definition makes it clear that rape does not always require force; the use of drugs, alcohol, the impersonation of a husband, or sliding into the bed of a married woman while she is asleep have all been the subject of rape convictions.[1] However, some degree of force is usual. In Wright's (1980) East Anglian study, physical violence had been used on about 80 per cent of the victims. This was commonly rough handling such as pushing or slapping but 13 per cent were severely beaten and 6 per cent severely injured. The age (and thus size) and reaction of the victim are relevant to the degree of violence used. In Wright's (1980) study, two-thirds of the victims were under 20, 30 per cent being under 16 years old. Intimidation alone is far more likely to be used in such cases. Where the victims were aged less than 13, 65 per cent of the rapes had been effected by threat alone as opposed to only 8 per cent of those involving females over 13. The female victim faces a paradox: although she is more likely to avoid rape if she fights as hard as she can, she stands in greater danger of being rendered unconscious or worse in the struggle. The paradox does not end there, for although the police may advise women not to resist to the extent of endangering their lives, some proof of violence and resistance to it are often important factors in the decision to prosecute. Rape counselling centres have sprung up, partly in response to this paradox.

Rape is regarded as the most serious of sexual crimes, with 93 per cent of convicted adults in Britain receiving a custodial sentence (maximum life imprisonment). But in America it is stated that something like 80 per cent of accused rapists walk free from the courts as in a defence dominated system the jury is more easily persuaded not to convict when long penal sentences would destroy family men with good local reputations (Evans, 1982). It is generally accepted that many rapes go unreported anyway; a reliable estimate for the USA suggests that less than 30 per cent of those committed are the subject of complaints to the police. In Britain the Sexual Offences (Amendment) Act 1976 enabled rape victims to remain anonymous in court, but the number of reportings has not increased significantly.

Bluglass (1982) states that rape is generally agreed to be a crime of healthy, sexually unsatisfied and inexperienced young men. In Wright's (1980) study just

---

[1] The Criminal Law Revision Committee (1980) has provisionally concluded that sexual intercourse induced by threats (other than of force) or other intimidation or by fraud should not be considered rape. Also that the offence of rape should be extended to include the instance of a man having sexual intercourse with his wife without her consent, whether they are cohabiting or not.

over half the suspected rapists were under 25 years old, and three-quarters were in unskilled occupations.

In most surveys there are a proportion of rapists who do not have previous criminal records. Of those who do, the majority have committed offences other than rape, such as theft or burglary or, occasionally, indecent exposure. The incidence of reconviction is low. Soothill et al (1976) found that of 86 convicted rapists only 2 had previous rape convictions, and over a follow-up period of 22 years, only 5 had subsequent rape convictions. But against this should be set the fact that many rapes go unreported, and that there is also a low rate of prosecution and of conviction (Evans, 1982). Of course, the more serious the sexual crime, the more depends on the predictability of future dangerousness. In North America Abel and his colleagues (1978, 1979) devised a method of monitoring penile response to assess dangerousness in rapists. While their Rape Index retrospectively identified those who had committed the most rapes and had been the most aggressive, only long-term follow-up (as yet unavailable) will show whether a decrease on the index from 'dangerous' to 'safe' levels is matched by a reduction in likelihood of offending.

Crawford (1980) directs attention to an essential element in any consideration of rape – the motivation. There is well documented evidence to suggest that in many instances rape is primarily an aggressive, not a sexual act (Howells, 1980). Here the man is motivated by a basically anti-female feeling manifesting itself in a desire to terrify, cause pain, or humiliate the victim. Other rapes are primarily sexually motivated; here the offender is attracted to women but was willing to use force to effect intercourse. It must then be asked, was the force *instrumental* in achieving the sexual satisfaction or, more dangerously, was the use of force *itself* sexually arousing? Gebhard et al (1965) found that 30 per cent of rapists in his study needed sex *and* violence in order for it to be maximally gratifying. If violence is necessary for sexual stimulation there is far more danger to the victim for it will be used even if she is compliant through fear. If force was used only as a means to the end, Crawford (1980) then asks why the rapist could or did not obtain a willing partner through socially acceptable channels. Part of the answer may relate to his anxiety, abuse of alcohol or social and sexual competence generally; but another part of the answer is that he may have thought he *did* have a willing partner. Frequently victims and offenders are known to each other before the offence occurs, and it is within this group that tragic misunderstandings or morning-after changes of attitude happen. Amir's (1971) study showed that over one-third of rapes took place between acquaintances, and many were located in one of the participants' homes. Wright (1980) found that about 40 per cent of victims and assailants were quite well known to each other; a further 20 per cent knew each other slightly. Alcohol consumption by the rapist immediately prior to the assault has been reported in between 30 and 50 per cent of cases (Evans, 1982).

As a postscript to a discussion of rape Kanin and Parcell (1977) found that sexual aggression was a common experience for American college females. Approximately 50 per cent reported being offended by the degree of aggression used by their male dating partner, and about 32 per cent of the intercourse aggressions were reported to be successful. The researchers went on to look at the characteristics of offended females. 'She was asking for it' is the archetype from which stems a myriad of verbalisations that not only explain but also serve to mitigate the male's role in his enthusiastic pursuit of sexual activity. They found that the offended female demonstrated an overall history of being sexually victimised more frequently than her peers both in her high school and college years, but in this study could find no significant evidence to associate with any social and personal characteristics.

Child Molestation

Overt sexual behaviour with children is illegal. Those under the age of 16 are not legally capable of giving consent to sexual activity. In Britain a young man must attain the age of 21 before he can validly consent to private homosexual behaviour. It would seem, however, that adult-child sexual interaction is a relatively common event. Tsai and Wagner (1978) say that a conservative estimate places the annual occurrence of reported child sexual abuse in the USA at 100 000 cases. As these predominantly occur within affinity systems (involving relatives, close friends and neighbours) the phenomenon may be largely unreported and have a hidden incidence of anywhere between five to ten greater than comes to light. Kinsey et al (1953) reported that 9.2 per cent of their female sample had been physically molested prior to puberty by a post-adolescent male at least five years older. For female children in the lower socio-economic bracket this figure was 40 per cent. Fritz et al (1981) found a molester rate of 7.7 per cent for female children and 4.8 per cent for male children among college students surveyed.

Bluglass (1982) says there is a basic division between homosexual and heterosexual paedophiles (very few choose boys *and* girls), with a distinct sub-group of violent individuals. Crawford (1980) suggests that offenders against boys are more likely to have been frequently involved with children, to have a sexual preference for children and show deviant sexual arousal patterns. Offenders against girls are more likely to be situationally motivated, that is they prefer adult women, but under environmental stress or pressure such as marital difficulties, sexual problems, social rejection, or alcohol abuse, turn to a child. In Massachusetts Groth and Birnbaum (1978) surveyed 175 males convicted of sexual assaults on children and found two distinct 'types'. The *fixated* subjects (83) were characterised by a temporary or permanent arrestment of psychological maturation. From adolescence the offender had been sexually attracted primarily or exclusively to significantly younger persons. The average age was late 20s and 88 per cent had never married. The *regressed* subjects (92) were temporarily or permanently manifesting 'primitive behaviour' after more mature forms of expression had been attained. Socio-sexual interests had focused on peer-age or adult persons primarily or exclusively. The average age was the middle 30s, and 75 per cent were or had been married. The *fixated* offenders' victims were 42 per cent exclusively male, 34 per cent female; the victims of the *regressed* offenders were 71 per cent exclusively female, 16 per cent male.

Girls are more likely than boys to be victims of sexual abuse. DeJong et al (1982) found that, of 416 alleged assaults of children under 16, 82.7 per cent were girls, 17.3 per cent were boys. Rinsza and Niggeman (1982) similarly found that 86 per cent of their 311 victims were female, 14 per cent male. These figures reflect assaults which are reported or come to light, and it must be borne in mind that boys are not so likely as girls to talk about the molestation with family members (Fritz et al, 1981).

Use of violence

Because of the media coverage which inevitably attends sadistic or murderous attacks the public probably over-estimates the degree of violence typically involved. The *British Medical Journal* (1966) estimated an incidence of about four sexual murders of children per year in a population of 50 million. Studies suggest that about half the offenders use a degree of force, but Finkelhor (1979) suggests that affection is the more common motivating factor. Gebhard et al (1965) found that physical damage to the child had occurred in only 2 per cent of instances, though threat of force or some degree of physical restraint was present in about one-third of cases where arrest and conviction followed. Groth and Birnbaum (1978) report that 30 per cent of surveyed offenders enticed by bribe, trick or use of adult authority; 49 per cent intimidated or threatened the victim; 20 per cent of the incidents involved brutal and violent attack with the specific aim of hurting the child. DeJong et al (1982) found that violence was more likely to be used against boys (in 55.6 per cent of incidents) than girls (31.7 per cent). Fritz et al (1981) report that in cases where coercion was a factor, boys were much more likely to have experienced positive coercion (i.e. rewards) than females. This may be explained by the fact that molesters of the girls tended to be relatives with substantial interpersonal power in a position to use status and authority to demand compliance, while molesters of the boys tended to be non-familial individuals, needing to use more subtle, positive inducements.

Where violence is used, Crawford (1980) says that, as with rapists, the distinction needs to be made between those who use force as a means of obtaining compliance; and those for whom the sadistic infliction of pain and terror is its own reward. It is vital in any consideration to make this distinction between aggressive and non-aggressive paedophiles because

... at one extreme one is dealing with someone whose problem is an overpowering love of children and at the other extreme someone who has an overpowering hate of children. Clearly there will need to be differences in the assessment and treatment of such cases (Crawford, 1980).

Motivation

Why, either for preference or under situational pressure, does an adult turn to children for sexual gratification? Howells (1977) suggests that it is not simply a question of the paedophile being sexually excited by the physical stimulus of a 'young' bodybuild, or the absence of adult characteristics such as pubic hair or developed breasts. Several sociological studies have indicated the importance of the social interaction between the paedophile and the child. In their study Gibbens and Prince (1963) report that only one third of assaults on children were by complete strangers; friends and relations were the usual offenders. Virkunnen (1975) reviewed the evidence and found that a majority of victims and offenders were known to each other. He concluded:

Aggressive behaviour was not as a rule characteristic of these offenders ... they seemed to be in a pronounced manner gentle, fond of children and benevolent. Obviously these characteristics contributed to the parents generally consenting to the children's visits to persons of this kind.

Gebhard et al (1965) also found that in about 85 per cent of such incidents the paedophile was either a relative or otherwise known to the child; 79 per cent of contacts occurred in homes, 13 per cent in public places, 8 per cent in cars. Rinsza and Niggeman (1982) reported that, of 311 sexually abused children aged 2 months to 17 years old, 18 per cent had been assaulted by strangers (mostly teenage victims); 42 per cent of the assailants were relatives (usually fathers). Thirty per cent of the victims reported multiple assaults over a time period of one week to nine years. Among a self-selected group of women needing therapy because of childhood molestation, Tsai and Wagner (1978) found that 97 per cent had had a prior relationship with the perpetrator (nearly half were fathers or stepfathers). The findings of DeJong et al (1982) were slightly different. Of 416 alleged sexual assaults 53.9 per cent were by strangers, 22.8 per cent by acquaintances and 23.3 per cent by relatives (just over half of those were parents, stepparents or siblings). Younger children were particularly likely to be molested in their own home by relatives or family friends. Most forensic psychiatrists will also be familiar with the offender who has been regarded as a fond and generous 'uncle' until by chance, an offence comes to light.

The question then becomes, why do these adults appear to interact with children rather better than with other adults? In a study of 10 American molesters of girl children Howells (1977) looked at the way such offenders perceived other adults. He found that the paedophiles were more likely than the controls to view both men and women in terms of dominance and submission, and went on to ask what kinds of social difficulty might predispose the paedophile to find others domineering and overbearing. If, for example, he lacks the strength of personality and the social skills to stand up for himself and to initiate or control social interaction he might well '... find the company of children rewarding in that it might provide him with a situation in which he is relatively dominant, an initiator rather than a follower.' Howells goes on, 'The current results do suggest that paedophiles see their victims as more passive and less dominant than other people on the grid.'

Crawford (1977) makes the point that the social skills necessary to relate to children are easier than those needed to sustain an adult relationship. Also children are not usually in a position to compare sexual performance and make far less threatening sexual partners. Pacht and Cowden (1974), in their survey of 500 sex offenders, suggest that non-aggressive offenders were

... less capable of establishing satisfactory relationships leading to socially approved sexual behavior with mature persons of the opposite sex. Perhaps because of their failures and frustrations in this area, they appeared to be striving to establish some type of relationship with socially inappropriate

– i.e. immature or same sex victims. At the very least they seemed interested in evoking a positive response from their victim, rather than simply using them as vehicles for immediate sexual gratification or as objects for aggressive impulses.

Children are usually considered to be the most innocent of sexual victims, yet in their review of the literature Gibbens and Prince (1963) estimated that two-thirds of child victims participate in sexual offences in that they co-operate in one or more assaults. Virkunnen (1975), too, found that many victims actively precipitated the offence.

Background

Ingram (1979) studied 74 children, aged 6–14, who mostly came from families with multiple problems and were at Catholic summer schools. They had had a total of 83 sexual contacts, the vast majority with professional workers, family friends or relatives. Two contacts were with strangers, another four were by promiscuous children who picked up strangers for reward and/or pleasure. Eleven of the adult men involved were counselled and showed a striking similarity of family background to that of the children although from a high socio-economic class. They all viewed their own sexual development with disgust and thought childhood was a sort of perfection. They were impotent with men and women alike. Most were doing valuable work in the community and suffered much anxiety about their indiscretions 'but complained that the children were so provocative or seductive, and they had found abstinence impossible'.

Mohr et al (1964) found that the age of heterosexual paedophilia victims was usually 6–11 years, whereas homosexual victims were more often aged 12–15 years. They link this to Kinsey's findings that childhood sex play increases in boys up to the age of 12, but is predominant in girls between 5–9 years. Other studies confirm that girl victims are frequently aged about 5–7 (Tsai and Wagner, 1978) but DeJong et al (1982) report a second peak at the age of 14–15. Both DeJong et al and Rinsza and Niggeman (1982) report younger male victims than Mohr et al (averaging 6–7 years old and 7–8 years old respectively), but this may be a function of the clinical settings of the studies, with parents or welfare workers more concerned with younger children.

Effects of abuse

The effects of childhood sexual abuse are not very well documented. Tsai and Wagner (1978) report on therapy groups for 50 self-selected women who were sexually molested as children. The mean age at first sexual contact was 6.5 years, and the duration of the abuse ranged from one incident to 12 years of continual occurrences. For all of them the childhood event(s) had had long-term effects on the quality of personal adjustments and interpersonal relationships. Several key issues were raised repeatedly in the group discussions. Firstly, the guilt experienced at being pressured to keep the abuse a secret; and/or at the pleasurable physical feelings sometimes occurring which were at odds with intellectual repugnance; and/or the feeling that they must have been responsible in some way if the contacts continued over time. Secondly, feelings of negative self-image and depression, linked to the guilt and 'constantly carrying something with you that can't be talked about'. The women also had problems in interpersonal relationships taking the form of mistrust of all males; and/or inadequate social skills and a feeling of isolation; and/or repetitive compulsion for relationships with unworthy men; and/or sexual dysfunction, either being non-responsive sometimes to the point of sexual abhorrence, not enjoying orgasm because of the unpleasant memories associated with arousal, which inhibit a pleasurable response, or experiencing arousal only if they were in control of the act. In addition, many experienced 'flashbacks' to their molestation during sex play and intercourse which detracted from or prevented sexual pleasure. Lastly, for the 31 women who had been molested by father or stepfather, resentment and bitterness towards the molester were matched or superseded by the intensity of similar emotions towards their mother for consciously or inadvertently perpetuating the pathological sexual relationships.

Fritz et al (1981) in a survey of 952 college students found that of 42 females who had been molested as children 10 (23 per cent or 1.8 per cent of the total female sample) were experiencing problems in adult sexual adjustment. Of the 20 molested males 2 (10 per cent or 0.5 per cent of the total male sample) were experiencing problems. Interestingly, 60 per cent of the cases of male molestation were heterosexual in nature. The authors suggest that the profound differences in the sexual socialisation process mean that 'males are likely to view pre-pubescent contacts as sexual *initiation* while females view such encounters as sexual *violation*'.

On a final note, while the popular assumption is that homosexual males represent an ever-present threat to young boys, the studies indicate that adult homosexuality and homosexual paedophilia are not synonymous; indeed they may be mutually exclusive (Groth and Birnbaum, 1978). Underage children are at far greater risk from heterosexual males, and girls are at more risk than boys. Fritz et al (1981) found a hetero-homosexual molestation rate of 9:1 among their college population, but it should be noted that within this ratio is an unusually (among the literature) high proportion of adult female molestation of pre-pubescent boys (60 per cent of the incidents). Estimates of the girl:boy ratio range from 10–12:1 (De Francis, 1969) to 2:1 (Fritz et al, 1981).

Unlawful Sexual Intercourse with Young Girls

Unlawful sexual intercourse (USI) with a girl under the age of 16 is far more common than USI with a girl under the age of 13 (3109 offences recorded by the police in England and Wales in 1980 as opposed to 254). In the nature of things most cases are undetected and therefore never reach the court. In 1977, for example, more than 5000 pregnancies were recorded in Britain among girls below 16, but the number of offences coming to the notice of the police was well under 4000 (Working Party on the Age of Consent, 1979). Where there is little age difference between the parties in unlawful sexual intercourse under 16, the question of mental abnormality seldom arises.

The two separate offences have very different maximum penalties in English law – two years' imprisonment for USI with a girl under 16, and life imprisonment for USI with a girl under 13. While in law no consent given by a girl under 16 is valid, the courts implicitly recognise that the albeit under-age consent of girls aged 13, 14 and 15 may be a mitigating circumstance. Offences with girls under 12 are regarded particularly seriously. There is an unusually high degree of discretion in the decision to prosecute. Broadly, for every adult prosecuted in the years 1967–77, two were cautioned; the ratio for juveniles was 1:10 (Criminal Law Revision Committee, 1980). The Home Office Research Unit found that the younger the girl and the older the offender, the more likely it was that a custodial penalty would be imposed (Walmsley and White, 1979). Where the offender is under 21 and the offence was committed with a girl of 15, the court very rarely awards sentences of over six months (Walmsley, 1980).

Gibbens et al (1980) surveyed the careers of 121 men convicted in 1951 and 1961 of USI under 13, and were able to follow up 48 men for 22 years and 62 men for 16 years. None of the offenders was related to the children (although some may have been stepfathers, common-law husbands and lodgers) and the extreme youth of some of the girls was a surprising finding (10 being six years old or under). Of the 1951 cohort, 4 per cent had previous convictions for sexual offences compared with 16 per cent of the 1961 cohort. Subsequently 29 per cent of those convicted in 1951, and 10 per cent of those convicted in 1961, were charged with other sexual crimes. These included attempted rape, incest, USI under 13, USI under 16 and indecent assault. Again, the existence of previous convictions was a good indicator for subsequent offence. Those with no previous convictions were rarely reconvicted.

Incest

'Incest is one of the oldest crimes, and numerous references to it in mythology and literature emphasise the cultural and legal prohibitions against incestuous behaviour that have existed in most countries for a very considerable period of time' (Bluglass, 1979). There is, however, wide variation in different states in the degrees of relationship that are forbidden, Ford and Beach (1951) finding that 72 per cent of societies surveyed had more extensive incest prohibitions than is common in the West. Manchester (1978) states that there are three elements common to the offence in all jurisdictions.

a the individuals concerned must be within a specified degree of relationship;
b at least one of them must have been aware of that relationship;
c sexual intercourse must have taken place between them.

In earlier times in England and Wales incest was thought to be an offence against God (like adultery, witchcraft and bestiality) and was dealt with by ecclesiastical courts. It became a criminal offence with the passage of the Punishment of Incest Act, 1908, the substance of which was incorporated into the Sexual Offences Act, 1956. The law in Scotland is based on Leviticus, Chapter 18, although modification in its application is slowly taking place (Noble and Mason, 1978).

It is generally agreed that incest is a far more common occurrence than would appear from the number of cases brought to the attention of the police (about 300 annually) or the numbers of offenders found guilty or cautioned by the police (171 in 1980 in England and Wales). Gebhard et al (1965) estimated that 3.9 per cent of the average population of the USA had experienced incest. Such behaviour may only be known to doctors, priests or social agencies.

Father–daughter incest is the most commonly reported type, but it is probable that sibling incest is the most frequent (Weiner, 1964). Other possible associations involving mother–son, grandfather–granddaughter, uncle–niece, aunt–nephew are much less frequently reported in the literature. The courts of England and Wales appear to take a more serious view of father–daughter incest that of sibling relationships. Walmsley (see p. 44) found that 74 per cent of fathers received custodial sentences (88 per cent where a daughter under 13 was involved), as against only 21 per cent of adult (over 17) brothers. Where fathers receive custodial sentences, the tariff usually lies in the 3–5 year bracket.

Bluglass (1979) lists 7 predisposing psychological and sociological factors.
1 A man returning home after a long absence now finds an ageing wife and a young daughter who seems almost like a stranger and also a temptation.
2 The loss of a wife leaves a bereaved father alone with an adolescent daughter who becomes a substitute wife, providing love, solace and sexual comfort.
3 Gross overcrowding, physical proximity, and alcoholism leading to sexual intimacy.
4 A lack of social contact outside the family, perhaps as a result of poverty or geographical remoteness.
5 Anxiety associated with a lack of sexual potency.
6 Marital disharmony and rejection or a decrease in marital sexual activity.
7 Psychopathic characteristics of poor impulse control, aggressiveness, and lack of guilt feelings, with or without any of the above.

Most would agree that father–daughter incest indicates a complex and distorted intrafamilial pattern and that the offender should not be seen in isolation from the family unit. In the 'endogamous' family everything is outwardly normal, with the incest serving to maintain the tenuous structure and reduce family tension by satisfying sexual need. In some instances the father may rationalise that adultery is more abhorrent than incest. He may be tacitly encouraged by his wife who by various means 'offers' her daughter as a sexual substitute, while denying that anything out of the ordinary is occurring. Meisleman (1978) reports that 75 per cent of mothers failed to act effectively to terminate the incest.

The child may well feel ambivalent about the sexual attention, experiencing it as one pleasurable aspect of a valued relationship, but also anxiety-provoking because it is furtive and 'peculiar' (Rosenfeld, 1981). In some instances the father is the more supportive and nurturing of the parents, which has important implications if he is subsequently sent to prison. Guilt and long-standing tension may take their toll. Lukianowicz (1972) reported that of his 26 victim patients, four showed some frank psychiatric symptoms (one acute anxiety neurosis, three depression with repeated suicidal attempts), eleven developed character disorders (promiscuous, anti-social activity, alcohol and drug abuse, thieving), and five frigidity or aversion to sexual relations with their husbands. Only six daughters showed no apparent ill effects.

Brother–sister relationships are less commonly reported and, as we have seen, less severely dealt with by the courts. As a background note, sexual play between siblings is not uncommon. In a survey of 796 undergraduates at six New England colleges, 15 per cent of females and 10 per cent of males reported some kind of sexual experience involving a sibling. Fondling and genital touching were the most common activities; one-third happened only on one occasion, but 27 per cent continued with varying frequency for over a year. A quarter could be described as exploitive as force was used, or there was a large age discrepancy between partners. Few participants ever told anyone (Finkelhor, 1980).

Of the studies of sibling incest, the most consistent finding is that the children have lacked adult supervision, particularly of their sex-play activities (Meisleman, 1978). Weinberg (1955) stressed that the father's absence from the family is often a key factor. Lukianowicz (1972) found in his County Antrim study that the brothers' ages ranged from 12 to 19 (mean 15.5); the sisters' ages ranged from 8 to 18 (mean 13). The duration of the relationship was from 2 to 14 years (average about 4 years); it ended when each participant found a sexual partner outside the family circle. Only one of the sisters developed any psychiatric symptoms, and her reactive depression was not a result of the incest itself but due to her brother's later rough treatment of her, and to her anger, frustration and humiliation when he began bringing other women to their home and having intercourse with them under her very eyes.

Incest, because it is primarily a family problem, is usually considered to be of a different order of sexual offence. However, Abel et al (1979) suggest that some incest cases may be more similar to paedophiles than had previously been thought, choosing their own children because of easy access, but having sexual arousal in respect to all children. There are many conflicting views on the subject, some of which were reflected in the Criminal Law Revision Committee's Working Paper on Sexual Offences (1980): 'We are at present divided on the question whether incest should continue to be a criminal offence at all ages or whether it should constitute an offence only where one (or each) of the parties is below a specified age.' Some of the committee members favoured 18 as the specified age for father–daughter incest, others 21. There was a similar division of opinion concerning brother–sister relationships.

Buggery

Until 1967 in England and Wales anal intercourse, whether between males or with a female, and whether consensual or not, constituted the crime of buggery, punishable with a maximum penalty of life imprisonment. The Sexual Offences Act 1967 altered the law, so that anal intercourse between consenting males over 21 in private was no longer an offence (save in certain special circumstances); non-consensual buggery on a male of 16 or over became punishable with a maximum of 10 years in prison. Non-consensual buggery where the victim is a female or a boy under 16 remains a very serious offence, akin to rape. Walmsley (see Chapter 4) found that 86 per cent of offenders received custodial sentences when the boy was aged under 14.

Heterosexual buggery seems to fall into three main types: offences with young girls (aged 10 or under) by close relatives who usually receive long prison sentences; offences with young women aged 16–25 in circumstances akin to rape, which are similarly penalised; and offences with wives or cohabitees (usually reported by the women after a row or separation) and not followed by custodial sentences (Walmsley, 1977). Cases of non-consensual, assaultive buggery between males seems to be rare – there were only three convictions in 1973, each resulting in a three-year prison sentence.

In the USA anal intercourse is termed sodomy, and is defined as criminal in virtually every state of the union. No distinction is made between hetero- or homosexual acts, nor is consent relevant. In 1965 a woman in Indiana quarrelled bitterly with her husband and in the heat of her anger filed a complaint of sodomy against him. She did not accuse him of using force, and before it came to trial she changed her mind and tried to get the case withdrawn. She was not allowed to do so because sodomy is an offence against the state, and the state proceeded to prosecute. The husband was convicted and sentenced to a term of from two to 14 years in the state prison. After serving three years he was released when the US Seventh Circuit Court of Appeals overturned the conviction on a technicality in the proceedings. The law itself was not challenged (Katchadourian and Lunde, 1972). What became of the marriage is not related!

Bestiality

At present under the Sexual Offences Act, 1956, it is an offence for a man or a woman to have intercourse with an animal. The maximum penalty is life imprisonment. The offence is usually called bestiality to distinguish it from other forms of buggery. It is an offence which rarely comes before the courts. In 1973 there were five convictions, all of men whose ages ranged from 17 to 60. Only one man received a custodial sentence (two years). The Criminal Law Revision Committee (1980) were of the opinion that if bestiality was retained as an offence, the maximum penalty should be greatly reduced (to six months). It was felt by the Policy Advisory Committee that total abolition would be unacceptable to the public, and interestingly, '. . . to retain bestiality as an offence punishable with imprisonment would ensure that those who needed treatment for engaging in sexual conduct with animals would be able to receive it under a hospital order'. Some members, however, considered that the need for treatment was an insufficient reason for retaining the offence. The matter is still under discussion.

Kinsey et al (1948) found that eight per cent of adult males and three per cent of females reported sexual contact with animals, but that it was more common among some groups than others. Among boys raised on farms as many as 17 per cent had had at least one orgasm through animal contact after puberty.

Indecent Assault on a Female

Under the Sexual Offences Act, 1956 it is an offence for a person (male or female) to make an indecent assault upon a female. The maximum penalty is two years' imprisonment where the victim is aged 13 or over, five years when the girl is under 13. It includes homosexual (lesbian) acts where the female is under 16. In 1980 almost one-half of the sexual offences recorded were indecent assaults on females and about one-third of all known sexual offenders that year were cautioned or found guilty of this offence.

Walmsley (1980) found that where the female victim was 13 or over, the custodial rate was 10 per cent, where she was under 13, the rate was 15 per cent. An average of 10 hospital orders a year were made for this offence in the period 1976–80.

The term 'indecent assault' covers a very wide range of behaviour, from the relatively minor act of touching a woman's breasts without her consent, to forcible fellatio or vaginal or anal penetration with a bottle or other object.

Indecent Assault on a Male

The Sexual Offences Act, 1956 makes it an offence, punishable with 10 years' imprisonment, for a person (male or female) to make an indecent assault upon a male. The Criminal Law Revision Committee (1980) proposed a change in that any form of non-consensual indecent assault should have a maximum penalty of five years' imprisonment.

Consent is no defence to a charge of indecent assault on a person under the age of 16, but Walmsley and White (1979) found that in 1973 the custodial rate was 13 per cent if the male victim was over 14 years old, 25 per cent if he was under 14.

An average of six hospital orders a year were made in respect of this offence for the years 1976–80, a drop of two-thirds from the previous five-year period (see Walmsley, Chapter 4).

Most professionals whose work brings them into contact with men charged with sexual offences involving young boys will be familiar with the youngster from a deprived background who offers sexual favours as a means of obtaining money or other reward. There have been very few studies of male prostitution, but Allen (1980) gives an interesting review of recent work. What is very relevant to our discussion is that the majority of these male prostitutes are under 21 and thus under the legal age of consent of males to homosexual acts.

Several precipitating factors are mentioned: broken homes, indifferent or hostile parents, poor vocational skills and the chance of easy money have all been cited. Craft (1966) found a number of sons of prostitute mothers in his series and felt that parental attitudes and behaviour were of prime importance in preparing a child for misconduct and motivating him to seek affection and reward through prostitution. Allen (1980) found much variation among his 98 subjects' family background, educational attainment, criminal career and social status. Russell (1971) suggested that the psychopathology of young male prostitutes involved a combination of factors including normal adolescent sex drive, a need for identification with older men and a withdrawal from family ties. Allen's own study (1980) found that between the ages of 14 and 19 was the most active period, which is coincidental with the years of the most intense sexual arousal.

Allen's three-year study identified four main groups of young men: full-time street and bar hustlers; full-time call boys or kept boys; part-time hustlers, usually students or unemployed; peer delinquents who use prostitution and homosexuality as an extension of other delinquent acts such as assault and robbery. As might be expected, there were many differences between the groups. For example, the mean age at entering prostitution was 14 years overall, but the kept/call boys had started younger at 12.6 years. They were mainly runaways and had been picked up and cared for by an older male. Often these relationships were described as warm, affectionate, needed and desirable, sometimes even as life-saving. By contrast the members of the peer-delinquent subculture were mostly aged between 14 and 17 and their activity was directed towards the exploitation of adult homosexuals by threat, assault or blackmail.

Allen also looked at the age at which his subjects had had their first sexual experience, and at the gender of the partner. The age range was 5 to 16 years with an average of 12.9 if the partner was male, and 12.2 if the partner was female. In fact one-third of the subjects had their first sexual experience with females, 66 per cent of these being seduced by an older woman. Two-thirds had their first sexual experience with males, 56 per cent being seduced (usually receiving money or favours); 44 per cent either initiated the sexual act or entered into it by mutual agreement.

A heterosexual adult male may buy sexual favours from females of 16 or over with impunity (the prostitute being the 'guilty' party), but his homosexual counterpart cannot do the same without risk to himself, for in practice, although both break the law, if the young prostitute is under the age of consent, it is the adult who is the more 'guilty' party.

Indecency Between Males

In 1980 in England and Wales about one-sixth of all known sexual offenders were cautioned or found guilty of committing indecency with other males. The Sexual Offences Act 1967 retained as an offence homosexual acts in public, 'public' meaning where more than two people take part or are present, or places to which the public has access (including lavatories). The maximum penalty where the parties are consenting adults is two years' imprisonment. It seems a reflection of society's ambivalence towards homosexuality that most of the persons convicted are aged 18 or over, committing the offence with other males over the age of 18 (legally adult in all other respects).

Police activity plays a significant part in the reporting of the offence. In one police area, following the formation of a new vice squad, prosecutions rose from about 40 to about 200 in the year. In general, however, it is regarded as a trivial offence, with a custodial rate dropping to below one per cent and no hospital orders being made for the period 1976–80.

Indecent Exposure

The Vagrancy Act of 1824 asserts that 'every person who wilfully, openly, lewdly and obscenely exposes his person with intent to insult any female is a rogue and a vagabond'. The offence is limited to males, and the second 'person' here means 'genital organ'. Prosecution is also possible under Section 25 of the Town Police Clauses Act, 1847, where 'insult to a female' is not an essential element. Indecent exposure can also be an offence under the Indecency with Children Act, 1960, and under various local Acts and by-laws. It is also an offence at common law. It is one of the commonest of sexual offences, with approximately 3000 court cases a year in England and Wales. There is some indication that, while it is a common behaviour, the number of prosecutions is decreasing, which suggests a greater tolerance on the part of the public and a reduction in the reporting of cases (Gittleson et al, 1978). It is usually regarded as a nuisance, not a danger, with a fine being the usual penalty for first offenders. Most (70–80 per cent) do not offend again (Rooth, 1971; Bluglass, 1982), but as with other offenders the chances of further reconviction greatly increase with a second offence. It is at this stage that psychiatric and social assessments are usually requested.

Bluglass (1982) says that indecent exposure is fundamentally an offence of sexual immaturity and inadequacy, occurring mainly in the 25–35 age group. There have been few studies on the family background of exhibitionists, but Gebhard et al (1965) report that their subjects showed a clear preference for their mothers, and that it is unusual to meet an exhibitionist who speaks well of his father. They also found the exposers as a group tended to have less petting experience at any age, to be less successful in obtaining intercourse with girl friends, to make greater use of prostitutes and to rely more on masturbation. Married exposers masturbated more than any other form of sexual outlet, increasing this behaviour from the late teens to early thirties, in direct contrast to the usual trend noted for the controls. Premature ejaculation and impotence are common problems for exposers who do have regular heterosexual relationships. The sexual act fails to satisfy them or their wives. Sexual inadequacy is almost always the rule in men with long histories of exposing (Rooth, 1971). Bluglass (1980) in his series of 100 exposers reports that just over half reported difficulties in forming relationships with women and had rarely or never had a girl friend. Many had never experienced heterosexual intercourse and none for at least a year prior to referral (according to their own account).

Rooth (1973) looked in detail at the sexual behaviour of 30 persistent exposers, only 4 of whom did not display deviant sexual interests other than exposure (see Table 6.2). Rooth points out that this behaviour is dominated by the immature goals of genital display, inspection and manipulation. Adolescent peer-group homosexuality was rare, the subjects' adolescent homosexual activity had mainly occurred with older men. Their adult homosexual behaviour seemed to be mainly exhibitionist in nature – they enjoyed displaying their genitals and having them handled, less frequently participating in mutual masturbation or fellatio. Genital exploration and display is a characteristic feature of normal

Table 6.2　The distribution of abnormal sexual behaviour in 30 persistent exhibitionists.

Category	No. of subjects	Total involved in each category
Sexual violence or assault		
Rape or near rape	1†	
Sexual assault with some use of force	1	
Indecent assault conviction	4	
'Touching'	5	7
Frottage		
Occasional	4	
Repeated	8	12
*Paedophilia**		
Adult (incestuous)	2	
Adolescent	4	5
*Hebephilia**		
Adult	3	
Adult (incestuous)	1	3
Peeping		
Occasional	1	
Repeated	5	6
Cross-dressing		
Occasional	6	
Repeated	2	8
Homosexual		
Adult	8**	
Adolescent	9	
Adolescent with adults	5	
Exhibitionistic	5	12
No. of subjects not in any of above categories		4

* Only subjects who had engaged in physical contact are recorded.
† Long Y chromosome.
** Includes one case of homosexual hebephilia.

From Rooth, 1973.

childhood, with Kinsey et al (1948) finding that genital exhibitionism is the commonest homosexual or heterosexual activity among American adolescents, with genital manipulation the next commonest activity.

Bluglass (1980) found no psychiatric diagnosis to be applicable in 26 of his 100 referrals, but 59 were considered to exhibit personality disorders of varying severity. Six patients were considered to suffer primarily from sexual deviance, two were schizophrenic, one subnormal and one was given the primary diagnosis of situational crisis. Seven were alcoholics and seven more had a past history of alcoholic dependency.

Sexual aggression appears to be rare, in keeping with the timidity and unassertiveness often commented upon in the literature. This passivity may be linked to difficulties in expressing aggression constructively. Rooth (1971, 1973) comments upon the frequent discrepancy between the demure and submissive exterior life the exposer presents to the outside world, and the bullying, petulance, moods and tantrums displayed at home. This difficulty in expressing aggression may explain why their angry feelings commonly lead to self-destructive behaviour which often amounts to a need to be arrested (Gunn, 1976, suggests that perhaps this is exposure in another sense). Exposers may hang around after the offence, display from their own homes and gardens, or use their own cars with easily traceable registration plates. Exposers often report activity and recklessness increasing in proportion to mounting tension and distress in their life situation: '. . . it seems that capture means more than punishment for themselves or someone else: it also means escape from an increasingly intolerable life situation' (Rooth, 1971).

From his examination of the literature Rooth (1971) describes two main groups of offender. Type I is an inhibited young man of relatively normal personality, who struggles against an irresistible impulse to expose. He feels anxious, guilty and humiliated because of his behaviour. He exposes with flaccid penis, does not masturbate, and derives little if any pleasure from the act. In contrast, Type II exhibitionists are less inhibited and more sociopathic. They generally expose in a state of great excitement, with an erect penis and often masturbating at the time of exposure. They get great pleasure from the act and show little shame or guilt. A sadistic element is not uncommon and their personalities show signs of disturbance in other areas. Rooth says that clinically these classifications are not always helpful because a majority of exposers have features of both types. However, Bluglass (1980) was able so to divide his 100 exhibitionists, finding 44 Type I men and 56 Type II men.

Bluglass classified his series of 100 indecent exposers referred to the out-patient clinic of the Midland Centre for Forensic Psychiatry according to the age group of the victims. There was quite a settled pattern; 28 have exposed to children only, 25 to adolescent girls only, and 33 to women only; 4 men had exposed to a mixed age group (age of victim not known in 10 cases). The men who exposed only to children tended to be older, of higher socio-economic status, more intelligent and had a more stable work record than others in the sample. They were also the most co-operative in treatment and at follow-up had the lowest reconviction rate (21.4 per cent). By contrast Mohr and Turner in their 1960 study found that a preference for exposing to children was associated with a worse prognosis. The men who exposed to adolescents included a majority of the married individuals and were younger than the other groups. They had a worse record of previous convictions and 60 per cent reported a poor sexual adjustment. A majority (68 per cent) were exposers of the more aggressive kind (Rooth Type II). The men who exposed to adult women were mainly single young men with a marked history of disturbed and unhappy early lives. They were the least co-operative in treatment, and were the most likely to re-offend (45.4 per cent).

The classification of offenders according to type and victim preference may well be important as Bluglass (1980, 1982) found at 5-year follow-up that 6 of the 7 who had 'progressed' to more serious sexual offences (rape, child molesting, buggery) were aggressive exposers; 6 had a preference for women victims (one for a boy). All 7 had been diagnosed as having a personality disorder. The escalating exhibitionist is untypical, but possibly may be distinguished by the aggressive display and assaultative fantasies marking his exposure.

The reaction of the witness to the exposed penis is an essential factor. If the desired response is not elicited, the exposer will continue until it is. (Understandably, indifference is the most disliked reaction.) Rooth (1971) gives us an insight into the complex meanings which make the act so significant to the individual: '... the exhibitionist, usually timid and unassertive with women, suddenly challenges one with his penis, briefly occupies her full attention and conjures up in her some powerful emotion, such as fear and disgust, or sexual curiosity and arousal. For a fleeting instant he experiences a moment of intense involvement in a situation where he is in control.' He therefore gets '... powerful reassurance as to his worth and importance, (which) must stand out vividly in a life where feelings of inferiority and inadequacy are the norm' (Rooth, 1971).

Voyeurism

Voyeurism is essentially a passive act, involving no physical involvement with or molesting of the victim(s). Sexual relief, usually by masturbation, is obtained from the solitary observation of others undressing or being sexually active. Such 'Peeping Toms' are usually regarded as nuisances; the offence is not considered serious in itself. It may, however, be a symptom of other personality or sexual disturbance. Rooth (1973) found it was linked with indecent exposure in a few of his sample. Bluglass (1982) reports the case of a voyeur who eventually acted out his violent and bizarre sexual fantasies by murdering and mutilating a female student.

The typical voyeur is not interested in ogling his own girl friend or wife; Gebhard et al (1965) found in 95 per cent of incidences that it was strangers who were observed. In this study the voyeurs tended to be young men (average age 23 at first conviction), unmarried (25 per cent married, 9 per cent divorced, separated, widowed), with little evidence of serious mental disorder, drug or alcohol abuse (16 per cent were drunk at the time of the offence, none under the influence of drugs). The single most common characteristic of this group of sex offenders was a history of grossly deficient heterosexual relationships (both in quantity and quality). Many had histories of minor misdemeanours, but few had committed serious crimes.

CONCLUSION

As Kinsey and his colleagues have reminded us, human sexual behaviour is best seen as a continuum, or in fact a whole range of continuums. Upon these, social and legal systems superimpose arbitrary dividing lines which label certain behaviour as immoral and/or illegal. The points where the dividing lines rest on the continuum are not constant over time and are, of course, subject to review and debate within societies. In practice too, sentencing policies may have the effect of blurring the boundaries. The Kinsey survey (1948) revealed that the number of sex offenders among the American male population exceeded 95 per cent of all males. The researchers were highlighting the fact that many long-standing American statutes seek to regulate private sexual behaviour between consenting adults, prohibiting, for example, premarital sexual intercourse, oral-genital contact and extramarital affairs.

Any discussion of sexual offences and mental abnormality should be set in context. One per cent of offences recorded by the police in England and Wales in 1980 were sexual in nature, annually about two per cent of imprisonment sentences are for sex crimes and at any one time sex offenders make up about five per cent of the prison population. But by no means all of the offenders could or should be labelled mentally abnormal. What proportion might appropriately be so labelled would be open to debate, but for our purposes is beside the point. Sexual crimes, particularly repeated ones, often *are* associated with personality disorders of differing severity and these are the offenders who are quite rightly referred for psychiatric and psychological assessments and treatment. Treatment options are discussed in Chapter 28.

REFERENCES

Abel, G.G., Becker, J.V., Blanchard, E.B. & Djenderedjian, A. (1978) Differentiating sexual aggressiveness with penile measures. *Crim Justice Behav.*, **5**, 315–32.

Abel, G.G., Becker, J.V., Murphy, W. D. & Flanagan, B. (1979) *Identifying dangerous child molesters*. Paper presented at the 11th International Conference on Behavior Modification, Banff.

Allen, D.M. (1980) Young male prostitutes: a psychosocial study. *Arch. Sex. Behav.*, **9**, 5, 399–426.

Amir, M. (1971) *Patterns of Forcible Rape*. Chicago: University Press.

Barnett, W.E. (1973) *Sexual Freedom and the Constitution*. Albuquerque: University of New Mexico Press.

Bebbington, P. (1979) Sexual disorders. In *Essentials of Postgraduate Psychiatry*. Hill, P., Murray, R. & Thorley, A. (eds). London: Academic Press.

Bluglass, R. (1979) Incest. *Brit. J. Hosp. Med.*, **22**, 2, 152–57.

Bluglass, R. (1980) Indecent exposure in the West Midlands. In *Sex Offenders in the Criminal Justice System*. West, D.J. (ed.). Papers presented to the 12th Cropwood Round-Table Conference, Dec. 1979. Cropwood Conference Series No. 12. Cambridge.

Bluglass, R. (1982) Assessing dangerousness in sex offenders. In *Dangerousness: Psychiatric Assessment and Management*. Hamilton, J.R. and Freeman, H. The Royal College of Psychiatrists Special Publication 2. Gaskell.

British Medical Journal Leader (1966). **i**, 626.

Brown, B.S. & Courtless, T.F. (1968) The Mentally Retarded Offender. In *Readings in Law and Psychiatry*. Allen, R.C., Ferster, E.Z. & Rubin, J.G. (eds.). Baltimore: Johns Hopkins University Press.

Craft, M. (1966) Boy prostitutes and their fate. *Brit. J. Psychiat.*, **112**, 111–15.

Craft, A. & Craft, M. (1979) Personal relationships and partnerships for the mentally handicapped. In *Tredgold's Mental Retardation*. (*12th edition*). Craft, M. (ed.). London: Baillière Tindall.

Crawford, D.A. (1977) A social skills training programme. In *Sex Offenders – A Symposium*. Gunn, J. (ed.). Special Hospitals Research Report No. 14.

Crawford, D.A. (1979) Modification of deviant sexual behaviour: the need for a comprehensive approach. *Brit. J. Med. Psychol.*, **52**, 151–56.

Crawford, D.A. (1980) *Problems for the Assessment and Treatment of Sexual Offenders in Closed Institutions: and Some Solutions*. Paper presented at the British Psychological Society Conference, London, Dec. 1980.

Criminal Law Revision Committee (1980) *Working Paper on Sexual Offences*. London: HMSO.

De Francis, V. (1969) *Protecting the Child Victim of Sex Crimes Committed by Adults*. Denver: The American Humane Association.

DeJong, A.R., Emmett, G.A. & Hervada, A.R. (1982) Sexual abuse of children: sex, race and age dependent variations. *Am. J. Dis. Child.*, **136**, 2, 129–34.

Evans, C.M. (1982) Alcohol and sexual assault. *Brit. J. Sexual Medicine*, **9**, 89, 40–2.

Finkelhor, D. (1979) *Sexually Victimised Children*. New York: The Free Press.

Finkelhor, D. (1980) Sex among siblings: a survey on prevalence, variety and effects. *Arch. Sex. Behav.*, **9**, 3, 171–94.

Ford, C.S. & Beach, F.A. (1951) *Patterns of Sexual Behavior*. New York: Harper and Row.

Fowles, M.W. (1977) Sexual offenders in Rampton. In *Sex Offenders - A Symposium*. Gunn, J. (ed.). Special Hospitals Research Report No. 14.

Fritz, G.S., Stoll, K. & Wagner, N.N. (1981) A comparison of males and females who were sexually molested as children. *J. Sex. & Marital Therapy*, **7**, 1, 54–59.

Gebhard, P.H., Gagnon, J.H., Pomeroy, W.B. & Christenson, C.V. (1965) *Sex Offenders*. New York: Harper and Row.

Gibbens, T.C.N. (1981) Incest and sexual abuse of children. *Brit. J. Sexual Medicine*, **8**, 81, 23–6.

Gibbens, T.C.N. & Prince, J. (1963) *Child Victims of Sex Offences*. London: Institute for the Study and Treatment of Delinquency.

Gibbens, T.C.N., Soothill, K.L. & Way, C. (1980) Child molestation. In *Sex Offenders in the Criminal Justice System*. West, D.J. (ed.). Papers presented to the 12th Cropwood Round-Table Conference, Dec. 1979. Cropwood Conference Series No. 12. Cambridge.

Gittleson, N.R., Eacott, S.E. & Mehta, B.M. (1978) Victims of indecent exposure. *Brit. J. Psychiat.*, **132**, 61–66.

Goldstein, M.J. & Kant, H.S. (1973) *Pornography and Sexual Deviants*. Berkeley: University of California Press.

Groth, A.N. & Birnbaum, H.J. (1978) Adult sexual orientation and attraction to underage persons. *Arch. Sex. Behav.*, **7**, 3, 175–81.

Gunn, J. (1976) Sexual offenders. *Brit. J. Hosp. Med.*, **15**, 1, 57–65.

Hoffman, M. (1968) *The Gay World: Male Homosexuality and the Social Creation of Evil*. New York: Basic Books.

Howells, K. (1977) Construct types in paedophiles and non-sexual offenders. In *Sex Offenders - A Symposium*. Gunn, J. (ed.). Special Hospitals Research Report No. 14.

Howells, K. (1980) Social reactions to sexual deviants. In *Sex Offenders in the Criminal Justice System*. West, D.J. (ed.). Papers presented to the 12th Cropwood Round-Table Conference, Dec. 1979. Cropwood Conference Series No. 12. Cambridge.

Howells, K. & Wright, E. (1978) The sexual attitudes of aggressive sexual offenders. *Brit. J. Criminol.*, **18**, 179–84.

Ingram, M. (1979) Sociological aspects: the participating victim: Part I. *Brit. J. Sexual Medicine*, **6**, 44, 22–26.

Kanin, E.J. & Parcell, S.R. (1977) Sexual aggression: a second look at the offended female. *Arch. Sex. Behav.*, **6**, 1, 67–76.

Katchadourian, H.A. & Lunde, D.T. (1972) *Fundamentals of Human Sexuality*. New York: Holt, Rinehart and Winston.

Kinsey, A.C. (1978) *The Modernization of Sex*. New York: Harper and Row.

Kinsey, A.C., Pomeroy, W.B. & Martin, C.E. (1948) *Sexual Behavior in the Human Male*. Philadelphia: W.B. Saunders.

Kinsey, A.C., Pomeroy, W.B., Martin, C.E. & Gebhard, C.H. (1953) *Sexual Behavior in the Human Female*. Philadelphia: W.B. Saunders.

Lukianowicz, N. (1972) Incest. Part I: paternal incest. Part II: other types of incest. *Brit. J. Psychiat.*, **120**, 301–13.

MacEachron, A.E. (1979) Mentally retarded offenders: prevalence and characteristics. *Am. J. Ment. Defic.*, **84**, 2, 165–76.

Manchester, A.H. (1978) Incest and the law. In *Family Violence*. Eekelaar, J.M. & Katz, S.D. (eds.). Toronto: Butterworths.

Meisleman, K.C. (1978) *Incest*. San Francisco: Jossey-Bass.

Mohr, J.W. & Turner, R.E. (1960) *Exhibitionism and Pedophilia*. Toronto: University of Toronto Press.

Mohr, J.W., Turner, M.B. & Gerry, M.B. (1964) *Pedophilia and Exhibitionism*. Toronto: University of Toronto Press.

Myren, R.A. (1975) Sex: the law and the citizen. *SIECUS Report*, **3**, 43–5.

Noble, M. & Mason, J.K. (1978) Incest. *J. Medical Ethics*, **4**, 2, 64–8.

Pacht, A.R. & Cowden, J.E. (1974) An exploratory study of 500 sex offenders. *Criminal Justice Behav.*, **1**, 13–20.

Parker, E. (1974) *Survey on Incapacity Associated with Mental Handicap at Rampton and Moss Side Special Hospitals.* Special Hospitals Research Report No. 11. Special Hospitals Research Unit.

Rinsza, N.E. & Niggeman, E.H. (1982) Medical evaluation of sexually abused children: a review of 311 cases. *Pediatrics*, **69**, 1, 8–14.

Rooth, F.G. (1971) Indecent exposure and exhibitionism. *Brit. J. Hosp. Med.*, **5**, 4, 521–533.

Rooth, F.G. (1973) Exhibitionism, sexual violence and paedophilia. *Brit. J. Psychiat.*, **122**, 705–10.

Rosenfeld, A.A. (1981) Treating victims of incest. *Brit. J. Sexual Medicine*, **8**, 70, 5–10.

Russell, D.H. (1971) On the psychopathology of boy prostitutes. *Int. J. Offender Ther.*, **15**, 49.

Soothill, K.L., Jack, A. & Gibbens, T.C.N. (1976) Rape: 22 year cohort study. *Medicine, Science and the Law*, **16**, 26–39.

Taylor, L. (1972) The significance and interpretation of replies to motivational questions: the case of sex offenders. *Sociology*, **6**, 23–39.

Terman, L. (1916) *The Measurement of Intelligence.* Boston: Houghton Mifflin.

Tsai, M. & Wagner, N.N. (1978) Therapy groups of women sexually molested as children. *Arch. Sex. Behav.*, **7**, 5, 417–27.

Virkunnen, M. (1975) Victim-precipitated paedophilia offences. *Brit. J. Criminol.* **15**, 175–80.

Walker, N. & McCabe, S. (1973) *Crime and Insanity in England.* Vol. 2. Edinburgh: University Press.

Walmsley, R. (1977) Sentences imposed on sexual offenders. In *Sex Offenders – A Symposium.* Gunn, J. (ed.). Special Hospitals Research Report No. 14.

Walmsley, R. (1980) Prosecution rates, sentencing practice and maximum penalties for sexual offences. In *Sex Offenders in the Criminal Justice System.* West, D.J. (ed.). Papers presented to the 12th Cropwood Round-Table Conference, Dec. 1979. Cropwood Conference Series No. 12. Cambridge.

Walmsley, R. & White, K. (1979) *Sexual Offences, Consent and Sentencing.* Home Office Research Study No. 5. London: HMSO.

Weinberg, S.K. (1955) *Incest Behavior.* New York: Citadel.

Weiner, I.B. (1964) On incest: a survey. *Excerpta Criminalogica*, **4**, 2, 137–55.

Wolfenden Report (1957) *Report of the Committee on Homosexual Offences and Prostitution.* Cmnd. 247. London: HMSO.

Working Party on the Age of Consent in Relation to Sexual Offences (1979) *Report.* London: HMSO.

Wright, R. (1980) Rape and physical violence. In *Sex Offenders in the Criminal Justice System.* West, D.J. (ed.). Papers presented to the 12th Cropwood Round-Table Conference, Dec. 1979. Cropwood Conference Series No. 12, Cambridge.

7

Homicide, Mental Abnormality and Offence

Seymour Spencer

The main impact of psychiatrists on homicide has, as will be shown, shifted since the Homicide Act, 1957 from the Special Verdict of McNaughton Insanity, to Diminished Responsibility, a subject intricate, complex, fascinating and controversial. It will therefore be the main concern of this chapter, after cursory glances at the issues of confidentiality, unfitness to plead or disability, infanticide, mercy killing, provocation and the special verdict.

It is hoped that not only will this chapter help psychiatrists to sift the issues that are liable to be debated in court in this area, particularly that of diminished responsibility; but that lawyers may also find it of use towards deciding whether or not to set up a psychiatric defence and, if so, the form the defence should take and the best medical ingredients of it. Can the defendant, for instance, be called psychopathic in law, and if so, in clinical practice also? Where might such special factors as premenstrual syndrome and hypoglycaemia come in? What is the contribution of explosive rage and behind it chronic 'sozzling'? By chronic sozzling is meant that state of subclinical alcoholism resulting from drinking regularly to pathological degree without evidencing obvious drunkenness. For instance, 80 mg per 100 ml of blood was the level for conviction on a charge of drunken driving, but the Royal College of Psychiatrists (1979) has noted that a steady *daily* consumption of more than 70 ml alcohol is likely to cause brain damage and bodily dysfunction.[1] This is the level meant by 'chronic sozzling'.

The author has included cases from his own experience as well as from the literature. This experience resides especially in the realm of explosive rage upon a background of longstanding 'subclinical' alcoholism. He has also discussed personally the issues behind the premenstrual tension syndrome with Dr Katharina Dalton.

HOMICIDE AND PSYCHIATRY

As Trick and Tennent (1981, pp. 35-6) point out, a proportion of killing (and indeed of saving from death) arises from chance acts designed for gain but needing violence for achievement, although violent burglars who kill cannot be

---

[1]There is recent evidence from Taylor (1981, p. 27) that brain damage is even more prevalent than liver damage in alcoholics. N.B. In Britain the measure is now 40 μg per 100 ml breath.

called 'abnormal' unless all criminals, or at least all violent criminals, are considered psychopathological.[1] Even limiting discussion to those that commonsense would regard as psychiatric cases, it will be noticeable from their table 1 that 44 per cent of homicide convictions in 1979 were of manslaughter on grounds of diminished responsibility, with all its psychiatric implications. Trick and Tennent's (1981) survey states that one-third of those committing homicide also commit suicide before arrest. The majority of these are domestic killers, mainly of spouse or child; most of the women victims, outnumbering men victims by about 3 to 2, are killed by husband, relatives or 'close associates'; and 75 per cent of child victims are killed by a parent or 'other relative'.

Reinforcing this view, Dell and Smith (1983) examined a representative sample of all male cases convicted of manslaughter on the ground of diminished responsibility between 1966 and 1977. They found that over the period the victim was previously known to his or her assailant in 87 per cent of all cases and cohabiting in 53 per cent, 38 per cent being wives or mistresses: a high proportion of homicide being the result, therefore, of intimate interpersonal altercation.

Forty per cent of their cases had a previous history of psychiatric intervention, 33 per cent (of all cases) as inpatients; 30 per cent (again of all cases) were under current general practitioner or specialist treatment for psychiatric conditions, 5 per cent as inpatients. It can be assumed that these figures are much higher than for homicides in general. Even so, they add up to an important contribution to homicide of abnormality in either the person or his relationship with others, or both.

HOMICIDE AND CONFIDENTIALITY

There is a story of a Catholic priest who, on hearing a patient confess to him that he had committed murder, replied, 'How many times, my son?' He knew the seal of confession protected the confidentiality of the situation. Contrary to widespread belief, though the psychiatrist might consider he had overriding duties as a citizen, he is not *legally* bound under the Criminal Law Act 1967 (part 1, 4 (1)), any more than is the priest, to inform the police on a patient disclosing homicide in confidence: he could not be thought to be assisting an offender, whatever the view taken by the police. It would be enough for him to advise the patient to see his solicitor in regard to disclosure and to annotate the fact of the advice; no more self-protection would be required. However, in court under subpoena, personal evidence must be given and full disclosure made of such documents as case notes.

---

[1]The author had heard Lady Wootton in a lecture assert that, if psychiatrists regarded all crime as 'psychiatric', they should make proper institutional provision for their incurables.

UNFITNESS TO PLEAD

The consideration[1] is not confined to homicide. It arose in the case of a demented patient who came under care after allegedly killing his wife (author's case 17, Table 7.1, legal case (LC) 31[2]). As episodic confusion and a possible hysterical overlay made variable his accessibility to reason, he was mercifully found in court rational enough to plead 'not guilty': a plea accepted after medical evidence had afforded assurance that he could be placed in long-term care under Part IV of the Mental Health Act, 1959 (to be called hereafter MHA, 1959).

At present the issue has to be tried by a jury at Crown Court. The Butler Committee's (1975, paras. 10.19–10.32) recommendations for rationalisations and simplifications of the procedure are sensible but still to be enacted. The criteria are described in Chapter 18.

R. v. *Podola* (LC21, described in Smith and Hogan, 1975) demonstrated in 1959 the difficulty that can arise in court over fitness to plead on ground of allegedly total amnesia leading to an insanity issue and inability to understand the nature of the trial proceedings well enough to make a proper defence. It can lead to a trial before the trial of whether this amnesia is organic, hysterical or malingered (and therefore not 'real'); and, in the process, put the psychiatrist on the spot, since exact appreciation is impossible. As the Butler Committee points out (paras. 10.4–10.11) amnesia, without other contiguous mental disturbance, should not be allowed to interfere with the course of justice. It must also be pointed out that if a defendant is found to be under such disability, the court *shall*, under the Criminal Procedure (Insanity) Act 1964, 5.5 (1), order his admission to 'such hospital as may be specified by the Secretary of State', who can *order* even an unwilling hospital to find a bed in which to receive and detain the patient under the equivalent of Section 60/65 (without limit of time).[3] Worse still, there is no compulsion on the Home Secretary to remit him for trial, even if his RMO[4] certifies him as fit to plead and the patient requests to be tried – and even though he has never been tried, much less convicted.[5] It is surprising that MIND has not inveighed harder against this unjust abrogation, on quasi-medical and humanitarian grounds, of habeas corpus.

---

[1] As the Committee on Mentally Abnormal Offenders (The Butler Committee, 1975, para. 10.2) points out, the term 'unfitness to plead' occurs only in the marginal note to paragraph 4 of the Criminal Procedure (Insanity) Act 1964, the preferred 'under disability' being used in the main section.

[2] Details of these legal cases appear at the end of the chapter (p. 113).

[3] The Warneford Hospital, Oxford was recently ordered by the Home Secretary to take such a patient within 24 hours from Winchester Prison (LC19).

[4] Responsible Medical Officer as defined in the Mental Health Act 1983 (hereafter called MHA 1983) 5.34 (1).

[5] See Gostin (1977, pp. 22 and 27).

Table 7.1 The author's homicide cases.

Case	Legal case (LC)	Sex	Special factors	Age group	Individual history	Amnesia (total or partial)	No psychiatric defence	Verdict	Disposal
1	9	M	Subnormal	22–35	CR, PB			Guilty, S2 manslaughter	Life imprisonment
2	4	M		22–35	CR, CS, ER, PB	/		Guilty, S2 manslaughter	Life imprisonment
3	29	M		22–35	CR, CS, ER, HI, PB	/		Guilty, S2 manslaughter	Life imprisonment
4	5	M	Killed deformed child	36–55	CR, PB			Guilty, S2 manslaughter	Probation
5	14	F	Subnormal	36–55	CR, PB			Guilty, S2 manslaughter	Imprisonment less than 10 yrs
6	24	M		36–55		/		Guilty, other manslaughter	Probation
7	17	M	Chronic schizophrenic	36–55	ER			Guilty, S2 manslaughter	MHA, 1959, S60/65
8	20	F	Killed baby	22–35	PB			Guilty, other manslaughter	Imprisonment less than 10 yrs
9	8	M	Sex killing	22–35	CR, ER, PB	/	/	Guilty of murder	Life imprisonment
10	7	M		22–35	CR, CS, ER, HI, PB	/		Guilty, S2 manslaughter	Life imprisonment
11	22	M		22–35	CR, CS, ER, HI	/		Guilty, S2 manslaughter	Imprisonment less than 10 yrs
12	12	M	Early cerebral arteriosclerosis	56+	CR, CS, ER, HI	/		Guilty, S2 manslaughter	Imprisonment less than 10 yrs
13	11	M		22–35	CR, CS, ER, HI, PB	/		Guilty, S2 manslaughter	Life imprisonment
14	1	M	Defence of provocation	36–55	CR, CS, ER, PB	/	/	Guilty of murder	Life imprisonment
15	15	M		22–35	CR, CS, ER, HI, PB	/		Guilty of murder	Life imprisonment
16	30	M		56+	CR, CS, ER, HI, PB	/		Guilty of murder	Life imprisonment
17	31	M	Gross dementia	56+	CR	/		Not guilty of murder	MHA S26 1959
Totals	M = 15 F = 2								

22–35 = 9   Criminal record (CR) = 13   Head injury (HI) = 7
36–55 = 5   Chronic sozzling (CS) = 9   Psychopathic background (PB) = 11
56+ = 3   Explosive rage (ER) = 11

INFANTICIDE

Infanticide, under the eponymous Act of 1938, Section 1 (1) and (2), relies on medical evidence to reduce the finding from murder to this verdict on ground of disturbance of the balance of the mother's mind resulting from the actual childbirth within the last 12 months or from continued lactation. While the Criminal Law Revision Committee Report (1980, paras. 100–104, 114.1) favours its retention, the Butler Report (1975, para. 19.26) would prefer its subsumption into diminished responsibility, in whatever form retained.

MERCY KILLING

In a valuable, brief review of forensic psychiatry, Bluglass (1980) has pointed out that cases of mercy killing always involve psychiatrists, and that the proposal of a special category of offence with limited sentence has been rejected by the Criminal Law Revision Committee (1980, para. 115).

PROVOCATION

Section 3 of the Homicide Act, 1957 states: 'Where on a charge of murder there is evidence on which the jury can find that the person charged was provoked (whether by things done or by things said or by both together) to lose his self-control, the question whether the provocation was enough to make a reasonable man do as he did shall be left to be determined by the jury; and in determining that question the jury shall take into account everything both done and said according to the effect which, in their opinion, it would have on a reasonable man.' Its success in defence will reduce murder to manslaughter. The burden of proof rests on the prosecution to negative this defence beyond reasonable doubt (see Williams, 1978, ch. 22, p. 477). The provocation, which can be verbal, need not necessarily emanate from the victim. The homicide has to be impulsive. It may be temerarious to adduce psychiatric evidence upon the defendant's capacity on psychiatric grounds to exercise self-control equal to that of reasonable man, since this could be thought for the jury to decide, without expert evidence, judging from *R.* v. *Terence Turner* (LC26). On the other hand it has been ruled by the Court of Appeal in *R.* v. *Newall* (LC18) that only persistent if not permanent characteristics could count to distinguish the provoked man from the normal or reasonable one. Thus, in relation to alcohol, temporary intoxication would not count, whereas chronic alcoholism would. The decision upon what constituted such a persistent state of alcoholism rather than transient intoxication with alcohol could well entail the invocation of psychiatric opinions on both sides: which could easily be contradictory.

THE SPECIAL VERDICT AND DIMINISHED RESPONSIBILITY

These are to be considered together for several reasons.
1 The special verdict ('not guilty by reason of insanity' – Criminal Procedure (Insanity) Act 1964, 5 (1)) was brought in in only two cases who were older than 21 years of age, one of each sex, in 1980 (Criminal Statistics, 1980[1]). It has been virtually taken over, therefore, by diminished responsibility.
2 Professor Nigel Walker, a member of the Committee which produced the Butler Report (1975) has since stated (Walker, 1982) that, if his suggestion from continental practice (Walker, 1981, p. 597) that 'extension of the defence by diminished responsibility to offences other than murder' were implemented in order not to lessen the offence (which would be illogical) but to mitigate the sentence, then the special verdict could disappear altogether.
3 The subsumption of all psychiatric defences (including 'insane automatism' – see Butler Report, 1975, para. 18.22) into the single one of diminished or absent responsibility on evidence of mental disorder would become still easier if implementation were made of the Butler Report's proposal that the mandatory life sentence for murder be abolished (1975, paras. 19.8–19.15).

The diminished responsibility defence to a murder charge was imported from Scotland in 1957 after it had filtered into Scottish common law through the 'bluidy' Mackenzie of Scotland (1636–91) diverging from Hale of England (d. 1676), then through Lord Deas in *R. v. Dingwall* (1867). Nothing came of the valiant attempt of Fitzjames Stephen to introduce in 1883 a similar defence into this country with his suggestion of the alternative verdicts of 'guilty; guilty but his power of self-control was diminished by insanity; not guilty on the grounds of insanity' (Walker, 1968, chs. 8 and 9). It took an independent legal committee (the Heald Committee) and further parliamentary debates to offset government shilly-shallying over the Gower Report's recommendations[2] and enact the Homicide Bill in 1957 (Walker, 1968, pp. 149–50). As Hamilton (1981) has pointed out, the term 'diminished responsibility' does not appear in the working of any legislation but as a marginal note to Section 2 of the Homicide Act, 1957, the relevant subsection (1) of which runs:

Where a person kills or is a party to the killing of another, he shall not be convicted of murder if he was suffering from such abnormality of mind (whether arising from a condition of arrested or retarded development of mind or any inherent causes or induced by disease or injury) as substantially impaired his mental responsibility for his acts and omissions in doing or being a party to the killing.

Despite its intrinsic snags, it has been widely and increasingly used, though with a tendency to 'plateau-off' in recent years. This rise has accompanied a rise in murder convictions (see Table 7.2). Criticism on semantic and moral–philosophical grounds and problems of practical and clinical interpretation have abounded.

---

[1] Supplementary tables, vol. 2, Tables 2.1 (E), p. 100.
[2] Royal Commission on Capital Punishment, 1949–53, Cmnd. 8932. London, HMSO.

Table 7.2   Convictions for manslaughter and murder.

Convictions	1964	1974	1979
Section 2 manslaughter	58	96 (year of big increase)	96
Mandatory life for murder	78	136	124

From Criminal Statistics, 1979 (Table 10.11)

The onus of proof

The onus of proof is on the defence and on a balance of probability as against under provocation (see p. 92) where the onus is on the prosecution and 'beyond reasonable doubt' (Williams, 1978, pp. 107, 623). This distinction in two similar areas of reduction from murder to manslaughter has been rejected by the Criminal Law Revision Committee Report (1980, para. 94) which agrees with the Butler Report (1975, para. 19.18) that the burden of proof in respect of both these matters should rest on the prosecution.

Rebuttal is rare

Walker (1968, ch. 9, p. 161) found that, as long ago as 1964, there was no prosecution rebuttal of the psychiatric evidence for defence in three out of four Section 2 manslaughter[1] cases.

Dell's (1982) researches have shown that in 1976–7 the plea, not guilty of murder but guilty to Section 2 manslaughter, was accepted in 80 per cent of such cases; in only 13 per cent of cases was the defence psychiatrist's evidence rebutted by the prosecution; presumably in the further 7 per cent there was non-acceptance of the plea but no rebuttal of the psychiatric evidence for the defence.

Dell and Smith (1983) have shown that when two psychiatric reports were presented, as became increasingly common in the latter years of their survey of changing sentences after Section 2 manslaughter convictions, the reports disagreed in only 10 per cent of all cases. The author has been involved in a number of these instances of disagreement.

Disregarding concurring medical evidence

As the Sutcliffe case has shown (see Appendix to this chapter),[2] there is no compulsion on the judge to concur with the acceptance by the Crown of a plea of not guilty to murder but guilty to Section 2 manslaughter, even when medical evidence of sufficient abnormality of mind is unopposed or agreed on both sides: he may insist on a trial of the facts.

---

[1] This term is used and will be so used in this chapter to denote manslaughter on ground of diminished responsibility as defined in Section 2 of the Homicide Act, 1957.
[2] Blom-Cooper (1982) has criticised the attorney-general in this case for over-meek acceptance of the judge's ruling when medical opinion was so unanimous.

The position of psychiatric evidence

(*i*) If, at a Section 2 manslaughter trial, there is unanimous psychiatric evidence from both sides, prosecution and defence, or uncontradicted medical testimony (likely to come from the defence only) that the defendant was of diminished responsibility, either the case must not go to the jury or the trial judge must rule the jury to find a Section 2 manslaughter verdict unless there 'be *some evidence* arising from other testimony or the circumstances of the case upon which "the jury" "can properly act" – to convict of murder' (*R. v. Vernage*, 1982 at 599, LC27). Diane J. Birch, from whose commentary the above quotation comes, added that under such circumstances of undisputed medical testimony and lack of outside contrary evidence, 'there does not seem to be a great deal of merit in the rule that the issue must go to the jury, even if it is conceded that that body must be free, if it wishes, to be perverse in favour of the *defence*' (ibid., italics the commentator's in both passages).

In the case in question (*R. v. Vernage*, 1982), the trial judge had permitted a murder verdict despite the prison medical officer reporting for the prosecution that he could not dispute the defence report in favour of diminished responsibility submitted by a consultant psychiatrist who ratified it in evidence. The Court of Appeal replaced the verdict with one of Section 2 manslaughter.

It is clear that, in the Sutcliffe case, Boreham J. held that the jury had such relevant outside evidence to consider as the possibility that Sutcliffe was bluffing all the doctors who examined him (see p. 109).

(*ii*) Nigel Hamilton, QC tried unsuccessfully to turn this ruling (or the rulings in parallel cases) the other way up. He argued that by the same token upon which a jury could overturn medical evidence if there was sufficient non-medical evidence to convict of murder, a jury could be asked to convict of Section 2 manslaughter without medical evidence submitted if there were sufficient outside evidence of substantial mental abnormality (*R. v. Dix*, 1982 at 311, LC6).

The circumstances were, as presumed by the legal commentator above, that, despite the highly bizarre circumstances surrounding the killing of the lady in question as admitted in statements by the defendant, the trial defence counsel (not Mr Hamilton) had not succeeded in obtaining a psychiatric report in favour of Section 2 manslaughter (*R. v. Dix*, 1982 at 310, LC6). He had therefore asked the judge to rule, in the absence of the jury, that, on the circumstantial evidence, the jury could reach a conclusion of diminished responsibility 'without the assistance or guidance of medical evidence as to the nature or source of the abnormality of mind from which the accused was suffering' (ibid.). Upon the judge ruling against this submission, the defendant changed his plea of not guilty of murder to guilty; but an appeal was lodged on the ground of judge's 'erroneous view of the law' (*R. v. Dix*, 1982 at 311, LC6).

At appeal Shaw L.J., while finding Mr Hamilton's argument attractive and that Section 2(1) of the Homicide Act, 1957 does not require *in terms* [author's italics] that medical evidence be adduced in support of a defence of diminished responsibility, nevertheless upheld the trial judge's ruling on the ground that this subsection makes it a practical necessity. Mr Hamilton's argument, it was ruled, would hold up only if the parenthesis in the subsection '(whether rising from a condition of arrested or retarded development of mind or any inherent causes or induced by injury or disease)' was descriptive of all forms of abnormality of the mind so that psychiatric evidence as to *what* sort was unnecessary. The appeal judge was of the opinion that Lord Parker, then L.J., in *R. v. Byrne* (1960 at 252, LC2) made it clear that the defence must show not only the existence of abnormality of mind but also that it does come into the realm of the above parenthesis and is substantial. What emerges from Lord Parker's statement is that scientific evidence of a medical kind 'is *essential* [author's italics] to establish what is referred to in the above parenthesis and under the term substantially impaired his mental responsibility . . .' (*R. v. Dix* 1982, at 311). A Section 2 manslaughter defence, therefore, without psychiatric evidence, seems impossible.

The psychiatrist in court

It is the author's experience that the full facts in an opposed Section 2 manslaughter case do not emerge until witnesses are examined and cross-examined, including the defendant when defence counsel has the courage (or temerity?) to call him. Depositions, proofs, social enquiry reports and examination of the defendant take the psychiatrist only so far along the road to understanding. Presence in court throughout the trial may add to it enormously, and also reduces the possibility of a strict judge ruling out elements of medical evidence as 'hearsay'. But, then, the psychiatrist must be in a position to attest to the evidence he has heard. To do so it is best for him to take down in writing, as it is produced, the evidence he hears, as does junior counsel. In this way, he can quote accurately what he has heard, give chapter and verse when required, and keep abreast of the full flavour of the emerging case.

Jury responsibility

There is also no compulsion on the jury, despite similar medical concurrence, to find that responsibility is diminished (see Appendix, pp. 106, 108), since the jury has to reach the verdict on all the facts and circumstances of the case, not just medical evidence, which the jury is, anyway, entitled to reject on its intrinsic merit, as the Privy Council decided in *Walton v. The Queen* (LC28).[2]

Abnormality of mind at issue

Contrary to future possibilities (see p. 106) and possible interpretation of *R. v. Sutcliffe* (see p. 108), the issue is of abnormality of mind, not insanity nor the MHA's (1983, Section 1) term, mental disorder. The accepted definition is that by Lord Parker, then L.J., in *R. v. Byrne*[1] as

. . . a state of mind so different from that of ordinary human beings that the reasonable man [earlier defined as 'a man with a normal mind'] would term it abnormal. It appears to us to be wide enough

---

[1] LC2, quoted by the Butler Committee (1975, para. 19.4).
[2] This case was originally *R. v. Walton* and is so listed.

to cover the mind's activities in all its aspects, not only the perception of physical acts and matters, and the ability to form a rational judgement as to whether the act was right or wrong, but also the ability to exercise will-power to control physical acts in accordance with that rational judgement.

It compels the psychiatrist to discuss in evidence the unwonted and 'unmedical' consideration of his patient's ability to (a) perceive physical acts and matters: this seems to amount to appreciation *mentally* of what he is doing and experiencing physically; (b) make rational moral judgements; (c) use will-power to control his actions on the basis of such judgements. Presumably, (b) cannot take place unless (a) is given, nor (c) unless (b) is.

The psychiatrist's report

It does not follow that the psychiatrist, in evidence, is exonerated from examination on the form of MHA-defined mental disorder that he has diagnosed. Indeed, it may be wise, if possible, to formulate both the Parker abnormality of mind and the MHA diagnosis in the original report. It is, perhaps, an additional argument for the change of MHA 1983, S. 1 (2) category from 'psychopathic disorder' to 'personality disorder' as propounded by the Butler Report (1975, paras. 5.24–6) that, again as implied by the Butler Report (para. 5.20), the orthodox clinical description of psychopathy is far more limited and extreme than the MHA's 'persistent disorder ... of mind ... which results in abnormally aggressive or seriously irresponsible conduct ...' It may be necessary to explain, therefore, in court that, while the defendant has to be classified, in MHA terms, as psychopathic under S. 1 (2), he would not, in extra-forensic clinical practice, be diagnosed a psychopath.

Alleged tautologies

Wootton (1981, pp. 90 and 87 respectively) criticises the semantics of both the MHA, 1959, S. 4 (4) and the Homicide Act S. 2 (1) definitions. Following Sir Aubrey Lewis, she writes '... the psychopath's mental disorder is inferred from his antisocial behaviour while the antisocial behaviour is explained by mental disorder ... the Homicide Act's definition of diminished responsibility is virtually tautological ... the offender suffers from diminished responsibility if anything has impaired his responsibility.' It may be on account of this second definition that cross-examining barristers criticise the psychiatrist who infers abnormality of mind from the bizarreness of the killing itself, making out that only evidence of such abnormality outside the area of the crime itself is admissible. This argument might have validity if *no* medical evidence of abnormality of mind were adduced other than from the crime itself. The diagnosis must result from the defendant's whole life history and his explanation, upon interview, of the crime and its circumstances, even amnesia counting significantly, especially when associated with alcohol. Moreover, the Homicide Act Section 2(1) definition (see p. 93) strongly implies that the evidence of the psychiatrist, who was highly unlikely to have known the defendant then and almost certainly could not have witnessed his act, must be directed to his mental state at the moment of commission of the crime. If, then, there is hard evidence, as there clearly was in Sutcliffe's case (see Appendix, pp. 108–9) that the killings bore the mark of an abnormal mind, surely it is legitimate evidence, perhaps the most legitimate and persuasive?[1] The curiously ritual way in case 13 (LC11) of the author's series (Table 7.1, p. 91) in which the accused stabbed without motive his sleeping girlfriend in three discrete places, then covered up her body with night-dress and bedclothes, was an important factor in determining his abnormality of mind.

Psychopathy and wickedness

Wootton (1960) also criticises the application of diminished responsibility to psychopathy on the lack of 'convincing demonstration that an intelligible distinction between psychopathy and wickedness can be drawn in terms of any *meaningful concept* of moral or criminal responsibility': a viewpoint in its turn criticised as exaggerated by Walker and McCabe (1973, pp. 226–8) as the result of their analysis of the diagnostic procedures of their Oxford Survey. Anyway, can 'wickedness', surely a value-judgement, be 'diagnosed'? Wootton (1959, p. 250) is right, even in non-judgemental terms, when she asserts elsewhere: 'Paradoxically ... if you are consistently ... wicked enough, you may hope to be excused from responsibility for your misdeeds; but if your wickedness is only moderate ... you must expect to take the blame ...' Certainly, as in the author's case 10 (LC7) (Table 7.1, p. 91), a classical 'psychopathic' history of child guidance, approved school, detention centre, borstal and prison, combined with sexual promiscuity, occupational instability, offences, amongst others, of arson and lack of restraint over drink and drugs, abutting in violently aggressive episodes, will be likely to lead to the verdict of Section 2 manslaughter, while her 'other-side-of-the-coin' argument (Wootton, 1960, p. 224) that the out-of-character homicidal deserves mercy at the jury's hands equal to that for the in-character psychopath may well prove true, albeit rare in practice. The 'diminished' plea succeeds better at each end of the spectrum of instability of personality than in the centre: logically so, in the opinion of Walker and McCabe (1973, p. 225).

Jurors' difficulty

The author's experience has left him with the impression that the technical medical issues, tossed between defence- and rebuttal-psychiatrists, worked over in opposing counsels' speeches and in the summing up, can be so overwhelming to the twelve reasonable men and women that they may well conclude on grounds more emotive and capricious than judicial. Hamilton (1981) suggests chance will decide as between success and failure of the plea when the psychiatrists disagree: undisputed psychosis may fail to reduce the verdict where psychopathy will succeed: a possibility strongly criticised by Bowden (1983).

---

[1] Yet it appears to have been inadequately stressed by his defence.

Issues of responsibility

Responsibility in psychiatry. This term is used in two other psychiatric settings and with two other nuances, as has been discussed elsewhere (Spencer, 1977). (i) Responsible Medical Officer[1] – meaning 'taking the buck'. (ii) Seriously irresponsible: part of the definition of psychopathic disorder (MHA 1983, 5.1 (2)) – lacking foresight, judgement and concern for others. (iii) There seems good agreement among the lawyers that in the Homicide Act S. 2 (1) context it means 'accountable in law'. Walker (1968, p. 152) after outlining the history of the term, construes it as 'impairment of some *mental* faculty which is called "responsibility" '; but it is unclear to which of the three senses defined above he is allocating 'responsibility'.

Impaired mental responsibility. But why 'mental' rather than 'legal' when the sense is clear in the Act that abnormality of mind can reduce the homicide's accountability before the law in the sense of his culpability upon verdict for sentence? Sparks (1964) suggests the drafter was alluding to that 'mental capacity which is morally a necessary condition of legal responsibility'. Williams (1978, p. 624) regarding the expression ill-chosen as 'a legal and ethical notion, not in itself a clinical fact ...', explained that the draftsman rejected the words 'moral responsibility' to avoid introducing moral questions into criminal law, while 'legal responsibility', in the sense of liability to conviction, either did or did not exist and could not therefore be 'impaired'. This argument can, however, be assailed if it is understood that the 'liability to conviction' means 'conviction for murder rather than manslaughter'; and it is liability in this linked sense that is impaired. Certainly it is easiest for the psychiatrist in practice to interpret 'mental responsibility' as meaning no more than 'liability to be convicted of murder rather than manslaughter'.

Substantial impairment of mental responsibility. When the author first gave medical evidence in diminished responsibility cases, he was advised by counsel not to offer an opinion on the substantiality of this impairment but to insist that it was – as ultimately indeed it is – for the jury to decide. However, there has been a shift, possibly since the Byrne case (LC3), of emphasis that has led to the psychiatrist being invited – perhaps even required – to offer his opinion on whether he found an abnormality of mind that *substantially* impaired responsibility. It is wise to incorporate this opinion in the medical report. The interpretation of 'substantially', which counsel prefer, derives from the words of Ashworth, J. in *R. v. D.W. Lloyd* (LC13) endorsed by Edmund Davies, J. (now Lord Edmund Davies) on appeal. Enjoining upon the jury that they were the judges of what 'substantially' means, the judge continued: 'This far I will go. Substantial does not mean total, that is to say, the mental responsibility need not be totally impaired, destroyed altogether. At the other end of the scale substantial does not mean *trivial or minimal*' (author's italics).

---

[1] As defined in Mental Health Act 1983, Section 34 (1).

Mental responsibility and abnormality of mind. The Criminal Law Revision Committee (1980, para. 91), commenting on the criticisms in the Butler Report (1975, para. 19.5), points out that while 'mental responsibility' is essentially a *legal* concept, psychiatric evidence on it is sought; while the issue of 'abnormality of mind', essentially a *medical* concept, is put to the jury, so paradoxical has become the practical work-out of this Act. 'It seems odd' says the Butler Report itself, 'that psychiatrists should be asked and agree to testify as to legal and moral responsibility' (1975, para. 19.5).

Philosophical objection. Wootton (1981, p. 90) argues, 'At a fundamental level, acceptance of mental disorder as diminishing or eliminating criminal responsibility demands an ability to get inside someone else's mind so completely as to be certain whether he acted willingly or knowingly, and also to experience the strength of temptation to which he was exposed.' But, albeit to less extent, could not much the same be said of McNaughton insanity and indeed of all psychiatric conditions requiring detention under the provisions of Part III of the MHA 1983? Wootton is epitomising the essential problem of psychiatric diagnosis.

Disposal

Wootton (1981, p. 66) perspicaciously following Sir Aubrey Lewis's concept of 'partial insanity' based on Hale, asserts that reduced culpability points not to the need for medical treatment as such, but to a less stringent custodial sentence: '... less than half the cases in which the defence succeeded' were detained under Section 60 of the MHA, 1959; the 'great majority' got imprisonment, as if some degree of criminal responsibility remained for punishment after extraction of the medical element. 'The idea that ability to conform to the law can be measured is particularly puzzling', says the Butler Report (1975, para. 19.5). In the author's first case (Table 7.1, p. 91, LC9) *R. v. Edgington*, the judge asked the author in evidence the degree in percentage of responsibility to be ascribed to the defendant.

Figures appear to bear out this concept of partial responsibility (see Table 7.3).

In a detailed research project covering the period 1966–77 Dell and Smith (1983) discovered that disposals progressively shifted from hospital orders to prison sentences. The main reasons discovered, after exhaustive analysis of factors, were:

1 Automatic availability upon request of special hospital places ceased and selection for these places became increasingly stringent; fewer 'psychopathic' cases were thought to be treatable.

2 Fewer psychiatrists were therefore prepared to recommend placement of such cases in regional NHS psychiatric hospitals. As a result, psychiatric reports progressively less frequently recommended any form of hospital order in Section 2 manslaughter cases, whether to special or regional hospital;

3 Therefore judges, bent on finding some sort of custodial institution for psychopathic cases, had no option but to impose prison sentences with increasing

Table 7.3   Disposal of Section 2 manslaughter cases.

Disposal	1969	1979
Imprisonment	16	52
Life	10	25
10 years + +	0[a]	0[a]
5–10 years	5	12
4 years or less	1	15
Other sentence	2	1
Suspended sentence	1	0
Hospital order	34	28
60/65	27	22
60 only	7	6
Probation/supervision	5	15
TOTAL	58	96[b]

[a] Unreported but 1 each in 1977 and 1978.
[b] Unfortunately the figure is given as 92 in tables 5(a), p. 346 and 10(a) p. 440.
From Criminal Statistics, England and Wales, 1979. Table 10–11, p. 199: no equivalent in 1980 when the total number of Section 2 convicted was 78 (Table S2–1(a), p. 6 of Supplement, vol. 2).

frequency. In other such cases, for example severe depression causing homicide followed by unsuccessful suicide attempt followed by recovery, the ground for the increase in custodial sentence appeared to be merely retributive.

The Sutcliffe case

This is discussed in detail in the Appendix to this chapter (pp. 106–13).

Premenstrual syndrome

At the other extreme, two recent women killers reported in *The Times* have been convicted of Section 2 manslaughter on the medical evidence of Dr Katharina Dalton. The first, reported in *The Times*,[1] was not of homicide but of carrying a knife and threatening to kill a police sergeant. However, Sandie Smith (formerly Craddock), who was placed on probation after evidence was adduced that it was misfortune which caused her to miss three successive days of her progesterone injections, had previously been put on probation in May 1980 for Section 2 manslaughter in a case of fatal stabbing in 1979 of a fellow-barmaid. By strange coincidence – and these are the only two cases involving homicide in which Dr Dalton has taken part (Dalton, 1982a) – on the following day *The Times* (11 November 1981, p. 6) reported the case of Christine English who was conditionally discharged for a year after her plea had been accepted of guilty to the Section 2 manslaughter of a man at whom she fatally drove her car. The argument propounded in both cases by Dr K. Dalton (1982a) is that the true

---

[1] *The Times*, 10 November 1981, p. 3 and Dalton (1982a).

premenstrual syndrome (PMS) (also called premenstrual tension, or the premenstrual tension syndrome in diametrical distinction from the oestrogen-
deficient menstrual distress leading to post-menstrual osteomalacia and arteriosclerosis) is a condition of progesterone deficiency, starting from ovulation and
reaching its peak seven days before menstruation as shown by the reliable
measurement of sex hormone-binding globulin (Dalton, M.E., 1981). This condition causes or is associated with:

1   A variety of physical symptoms in many bodily systems, including food- and
alcohol-craving, migraine or other headache, epilepsy, vertigo, fainting;
2   Such psychological symptoms as tension, depression, instability, lethargy;
3   Secondary hypoglycaemia countered by adrenaline upsurge and leading at
times to:
4   Such behaviour disturbance as suicidal attempt, assault, child abuse and
bouts of alcoholic intoxication, to which PMS sufferers are sensitive (Dalton,
1982b), the last enhancing the behavioural disturbance.

Dalton claims that crime associated with PMS tends to be unpremeditated,
motiveless, with tracks uncovered, often a *cri de coeur* and arising out of 'a
sudden and momentary surge of uncontrollable emotions resulting in violence
...' amongst other effects (Dalton, 1982b).

The condition responds adversely to oral progestogen but favourably to
progesterone administered intramuscularly, anally or vaginally (Dalton, 1981).
It is relevant that, on the day of the homicide, neither defendant had eaten
properly (Sandie Smith now keeps a daily food chart). Two psychiatrists agreed
with Dalton's diagnosis in the English case.

'Should PMT be a woman's all-purpose excuse?' asked *The Times*' legal and
medical correspondents after the Smith and English cases (12 November 1981,
p. 12), continuing, 'The medical evidence would have to be convincing that the
condition was strong enough to have resulted in reducing her responsibility for
her actions', particularly if it is considered more of a 'trigger' than a cause
(d'Orbain, 1983).

Dalton (1981) found that 49 per cent of 156 newly committed London
prisoners had committed their crime in the paramenstruum (i.e. four days before
and the first four days of menstruation), while, of 134 attenders at a special
London clinic for PMS, 34 per cent had attempted suicide or homicide (Dalton
1982c). The PMS clinic at University College Hospital, London, confirmed this
diagnosis 'in only half of the women claiming to have PMS' (Dalton, 1982b).
Dalton is confident that the accurate correlation of crime with symptoms associated with the paramenstruum, the careful annotation of both symptoms and
food intake, and the use of biochemical aids to diagnosis, will effectively differentiate the true sufferer from the 'false pleader' (Dalton, 1982b, c). There are
political overtones, already voiced, to any suggestion of psychological vulnerability among women to behavioural disturbance.

Explosive rage: a grey area

This condition, in America, is currently called the episodic dyscontrol syndrome
(Ratner and Shapiro, 1979). When – as invariably and in a particular way in the

author's series – it is associated with alcoholic abuse, it is called pathological intoxication or *mania à potu*. Explosive rage, in relation to head injury, was the term used by Hooper and his colleagues (1945) following Kaplan's (1899) phrase 'explosive distress', to describe violent episodes after head injury in cases, some predisposed to ill-temper, some not. Though in none of their eleven cases did homicide occur, two attempted stranglings might have succeeded but for outside intervention. The first description of the full condition seems to occur in the chapter 'The Dyscontrol Syndrome' in *Violence and the Brain* (Mark and Ervin, 1970) with later contributions by Bach-y-Rita et al (1971) and, particularly, by Maletzky (1973), and an earlier pointer to it by May and Ebaugh (1953).

As well as to head injury (and mania and depression), Hooper et al (1945) relate the condition to epilepsy, aggressive psychopathy and Kaplan's (1899) 'alcoholic degeneration'. Although loss of temper without alcoholic abuse must be presumed to result in occasional homicide, in most of the author's cases there has been a background of the form of drinking best called 'chronic sozzling': weeks, usually months or longer, of regular alcohol consumption, frequently night after night to well beyond the level of 40 µg per 100 ml of breath which is the driver's boundary for legal drinking. Can this condition constitute a defence?

The relation of *this* form of drinking to intent has never, it appears, received judicial comment. Murder is among the crimes of specific intent, as opposed to those of basic (or general) intent (Williams, 1978, p. 728). Therefore, as Williams tells us, '. . . the intent can be negatived by evidence of intoxication' to the extent that '. . . the jury are allowed to take intoxication into account'. The issue of the intention of an attacker under drugs was canvassed to the House of Lords in *R. v. Majewski* (Williams, 1978, pp. 423–5, LC16). In *R. v. Sheehan* (LC23) it was ruled that '. . . the mere fact that the defendant's mind was affected by drink so that he acted in a way in which he would not have done had he been sober does not assist him at all provided the necessary intention was there'. A drunken intent is nevertheless an intent: this seems to be Bluglass's (1979) argument when he alleges that alcohol and drugs would not normally affect the intent unless the defendant were unaware that he was consuming them. Hall Williams (1980) argues similarly.

It can be argued that all homicide, except in post-epileptic automatism, is organised enough to require some intention; but can chronic sozzling, often embarked on for neurotic reasons as in the author's case 11 (Table 7.1, p. 91, LC22), and often leading to low-grade brain intoxication unrecognised by the defendant, abut in such unpremeditated, explosive and homicidal rage as to diminish that intention? The failure to recognise the existence of 'chronic sozzling' may well be a major element in the unpredictability of verdict in the few cases in the literature. Such may have been the case of Walker's (1968, p. 180) unidentified man, who, after the death of his parents, went into mental decline which could well have been contributed to by chronic sozzling, killed two women while in some sort of drunken state and was convicted each time of manslaughter, with one year's imprisonment the first time but life the second. On the other hand, in *R. v. Fenton* (LC10) the Lord Chief Justice ruled that, even when there is a craving, self-induced drink or drug intoxication cannot of itself produce an abnormality of mind due to inherent causes – but the issue of chronic sozzling did not arise.

The amount of alcohol that actually precipitates the homicide is also uncertain and variable. Lishman (1978, p. 700) says that the release of '... irrational, combative behaviour ... can allegedly follow the ingestion of relatively small amounts in some individuals.' Mayer-Gross et al (1960)[1] also talk of 'a relatively small amount of alcohol' leading to 'a tendency to extreme violence'. Number 291.4 in the 9th revision of *The International Classification of Diseases* runs, 'Acute psychotic episodes induced by relatively small amounts of alcohol. These are regarded as individual idiosyncratic reactions to alcohol, not due to excessive consumption and without conspicuous neurological signs of intoxication.' The lack of conspicuous neurological signs concords with the concept of chronic sozzling. Coid (1980), however, in his PhD thesis, criticises this concept in that, from the literature, he found no consistency in the precipitating imbibement. If the concept of chronic sozzling is accepted, then the extent of the immediately precipitating drinking can, understandably, be a little, a lot or even none at all.

Some authorities insist on amnesia as a factor (e.g., May and Ebaugh, 1953, p. 200); others cite it as a variable factor (e.g., Maletzky, 1973). Coid (1980) found again no consistency. In the author's series, it was absolute in four cases (11, 12, 13 and 16, Table 7.1, p. 91, respectively LC22, 12, 11 and 30), with memory grossly and unchangeably distorted in one other (15, Table 7.1, LC15). In this case, the defendant claimed to remember but his story was radically inconsistent with the facts. This, again, would be consistent with the low-grade intoxication of the brain in chronic sozzling: analogous with the hazy and variable recollections of dream-states.

And where does head injury come in? It is accepted neuro-psychiatric belief that closed head injury 'sensitises' to alcohol, causing intoxication after less consumption than before; but to what degree of head injury does this apply? Must there be one with a clear-cut retrograde and post-traumatic amnesia? And what if the evidence for such head injury is of long ago and/or inconclusive? Furthermore, as in the author's cases 11 and 15 (Table 7.1, p. 91, LC22 and 15), Hovey and Rickler (1980) point out that the life-style of violence-prone individuals (chronic sozzlers would be special cases-in-point) leads to a high prevalence of head injury, resulting in a 'hen-and-egg' uncertainty as to causation between head injury and violence.

Then what of the contribution of hypoglycaemia? Reference has already been made above to the enhancement of PMS behavioural disturbance by food-lack, causing hypoglycaemia, causing compensatory adrenalin upsurge. Alcohol, especially in a sweetened drink like gin and tonic, acts like a carbohydrate in increasing the blood sugar, which may then fall rapidly ('bounce down') as insulin is produced and the alcohol metabolised. Marks and Clifford Rose (1980, p. 393) claim that 'alcohol, in addition to the other mechanisms by

---

[1] P. 350. The section, 'Pathological Drunkenness', in which it occurs is not replicated in the 3rd edition (Slater and Roth, 1969).

which it produces hypoglycaemia, has the capacity to increase insulin secretion in response to an oral glucose load, and so enhances the natural tendency to develop reactive (rebound) hypoglycaemia.' Coid (1980) found only two references to hypoglycaemia as a factor in homicide.

Lishman describes 'episodic dyscontrol' and 'reduced control of aggression' several times in his textbook *Organic Psychiatry* (1978, pp. 104–5, 200, 229, 334, 373–4, 700). Reduced control of aggression can occur in head injuries, epilepsy and as pathological intoxication. Sometimes it can be almost equated to temporal lobe epilepsy, and 'liability to attacks was usually worsened by alcohol'. He discussed Maletzky's (1973) 22 such patients all of whom 'had a history of increasing frequency and severity of attacks while drinking alcohol'.

It is likely that improved computerised tomography (CT) scan diagnosis will demonstrate changes in chronic alcoholics, including, perhaps, chronic sozzling. Although there is a long-standing equation by Hill and Watterson (1942) of aggressive psychopathy with electroencephalographic (EEG) 'immaturity', in the author's experience the EEG has proved too vague a diagnostic tool to be helpful in evidence.

The author's series (Table 7.1, p. 91) Of the eight pre-Sutcliffe male cases in which the author has submitted psychiatric evidence, seven were found guilty, after a murder trial, of Section 2 manslaughter. The two cases 15 and 16 (LC15 and 30) coming quickly after Sutcliffe, and leading to verdicts of murder, also involved special factors including transparent untruthfulness, which did not help their cases. In six of the 'diminished' cases and the final two found guilty of murder, chronic sozzling made an outstanding contribution both to the background of the offence and to the strangeness of the actual homicide. Case 14 (LC1) also showed chronic sozzling and seemed to the author to be defensible for Section 2 manslaughter. Counsel preferred to defend on ground of provocation alone; the defendant was convicted of murder. If it can be established as producing genuine abnormality of mind particularly, as in the author's case 10 (LC7), where there was gross poverty of judgement about the need to cut down consumption after earlier offences,[1] or, as in the author's case 11 (LC22), when the drinking was for neurotic purposes to assuage misery and escape from problems, chronic sozzling may feature increasingly as a homicide defence against conviction for murder.

Explosive rage remains a grey area associated with psychopathy, head injury, hypoglycaemia, brain disturbance (possibly temporal lobe epilepsy) and, above all, chronic alcoholic sozzling. If the sozzling, itself pointing to lack of judgement, can become as one factor amongst others, of background or circumstantial nature, which diminish responsibility, the condition may blossom increasingly as a psychiatric defence.

---

[1] Albeit no craving as alleged in *R. v. Fenton* (LC10).

The future

Unless the Butler Report recommendation (1975, para. 19.14) for the abolition of the mandatory death sentence – against the balance of judgement of the Criminal Law Revision Committee (1980, para. 76) – comes to enactment, diminished responsibility is likely to stay with us indefinitely, with all its blemishes or, perchance, with some removed – or even enhanced. When you try to improve on an Act, the worsening of the last state is always a danger.

The main alternative proposals are those of Walker, already discussed.

1 To subsume into it the special verdict which can then disappear; that at least has the merit of final burial of the moribund McNaughton dog (Walker, 1982);

2 To widen the plea of diminished responsibility beyond homicide, in order statutorily to reduce sentence, limiting its 'choice and severity'. Walker (1981) suggests the possibility, if the plea of diminished responsibility is accepted, of changing a conviction of simply 'guilty' to one of 'guilty but with diminished responsibility'.

This statutory limitation of sentence could, Walker (1982) explains, serve better psychiatrically than the current production of a psychiatric report and/or psychiatric evidence in mitigation, since mitigation leaves the decision regarding length of sentence entirely open to the judge, whereas the finding by the jury of the verdict of 'guilty with diminished responsibility' would limit the range of sentence open to the judge.

Finally, we return to the semantics. No one likes '. . . substantially impaired his mental responsibility'. The Butler Report prefers 'Where a person kills . . . he shall not be convicted of murder if there is medical or other evidence that he was suffering from a form of mental disorder as defined in Section 4 of the MHA, 1959 and if, in the opinion of the jury, the mental disorder was such as to be an extenuating circumstance which ought to reduce the offence to manslaughter' (1975, para. 19.17).

The Criminal Law Revision Committee (1980, para. 93) prefers, after several tries-out, '. . . the mental disorder was of such a degree as to be a substantial reason to reduce murder to manslaughter'. The two forms of words are not dissimilar; the Criminal Law Revision Committee one is a little simpler, the Butler one gets round the vexed 'substantial'. It is only if one or other change is enacted and tried out that we psychiatrists will discover whether it has made more or less comfortable our passages through the witness-box.

APPENDIX: FAILURE OF 'DIMINISHED RESPONSIBILITY' IN THE SUTCLIFFE CASE (LC25)

The conviction for murder of 13 women, and attempted murder of seven others aged 16–47 (summarised in Table 7.4), of Sutcliffe, the 'Yorkshire Ripper' (LC25), at Central Criminal Court on 22 May 1981 before Boreham, J., makes legal history

Table 7.4 The 20 women (aged 16–47) attacked by Sutcliffe.

Date	Name	Murder	Attempted murder	Stab or laceration	Head injury H = hammer S = stone in sock	Strangulation	Prostitute	Possible prostitute	Not prostitute	Sex component or other curiosity
1 July 1975	Anna Rogulskyj		✓		H			✓		
2 Aug 1975	Olive Smelt		✓		S			✓		
3 Oct. 1975	Wilma McCann	✓		✓			✓			
4 Jan 1976	Emily Jackson	✓		✓	Mode not ascertained		✓			
5 May 1976	Marcella Claxton (ESN girl)		✓	✓	?H			✓		
6 Feb. 1977	Irene Richardson	✓		✓	H		✓			
7 Mar. 1977	Patricia Atkinson	✓			H (claw-type)		✓			
8 June 1977	Jayne MacDonald	✓		✓ + rib fractures	H				✓	
9 Jul. 1977	Maureen Long		✓		H				✓	
10 Sept/Oct. 1977	Jean Jordan	✓			Mode not ascertained		✓			Re-attacked body at scene 9 days later
11 Dec. 1977	Marilyn Moore		✓	✓	H		✓			
12 Jan. 1978	Helen Rytka	✓			Body crushed – mode unclear		✓			Had intercourse with her before killing
13 Mar. 1978	Yvonne Pearson	✓		✓	H					
14 May 1978	Vera Millward	✓		✓	H					
15 April 1979	Josephine Whittaker	✓		✓				✓		Screwdriver used including vaginally
16 Sept. 1979	Barbara Jane Leach	✓		✓	H				✓	Bruises and abrasions
17 Aug. 1980	Marguerite (Margo) Walls	✓				✓			✓	Said intent was to kill
18 Sept. 1980	Upidha Bandara		✓			✓			✓	
19 Nov. 1980	Theresa Sykes		✓		H (metal)				✓	Breast attack
20 Nov. 1980	Jacqueline Hill	✓		✓	H				✓	Eye attack
	TOTALS	13	7	7			7	4	9	

in that the medical opinions of four psychiatrists[1] had agreed that he was of diminished responsibility, and the prosecution (but not the judge who set up a full trial of the issues) was prepared, therefore, to accept the Section 2 manslaughter plea. This conviction is likely, in the author's opinion, to make juries more wary in contested cases of finding 'diminished' except in extreme examples of near McNaughton insanity: the jury found rapidly against 'diminished' in both subsequent homicide cases (15 and 16, Table 7.1, p. 91, LC15 and 30) in which the author gave evidence in favour, though in both cases the defendants' ostensible lying made more difficult the psychiatric part of this defence.

The author had available the fifteen *Times* reports of the cases (*The Times* newspaper, 1981, usually on front page with more subsequent detail on a later page) and the help of a taping by a colleague of parts of the Old Bailey shorthand writers' transcript.[2] Close perusal confirmed the initial impression that what went wrong was that a 'diminished' defence was so allowed to become a McNaughton one that symptoms consistent in themselves towards abnormality of mind were made to appear discrepant.

There seem to be two main explanations:

1 Because, presumably, of the 'circular argument' proposition (see under 'Alleged tautologies', p. 97), the defence failed to introduce, as evidence of abnormality of mind, the bizarre evidence in the killings themselves; curiously it was the prosecution that stressed them against the schizophrenic possibility: at times along moralistic lines designed to suggest to the jury that, if Sutcliffe were not ostensibly schizophrenic, he must be not a severely disordered sadistic psychopath but a 'cruel, calculated and controlled killer because it afforded him a cruel satisfaction'[3] – and, therefore, of undiminished responsibility. *The Times* (23 May 1981, p. 13)[4] leading article made the point, 'It is ... an abuse of language to apply the term "normal" to a person who commits violent murders for years on end for no tangible gain. ...' But 'no tangible gain' is but the first intrinsic pointer of his crimes to abnormality. Others are:

(a) The fact that he could have had nothing *personal* against any of his victims since he knew none of them.

(b) The need to explain the high proportion of prostitutes (seven seem certain, three probable) and the fact that the last six were not.

(c) More specific factors:

i. The curious (and in the reports) unexplained bruises and grazes to the lower abdomen of Patricia Atkinson (6 May 1981, p. 4);

ii. the return after eight days to re-attack the body of Jean Jordan at the scene of the crime (6 May 1981, p. 4);

iii. the introduction of an 'evil' screwdriver into the vaginal area of Josephine Whitaker (all brought out in cross-examination of Dr Milne, 15 May 1981, p. 6);

---

[1] Three were called. The fourth opinion was that of Dr P.G. McGrath, now retired from the Physician Superintendency of Broadmoor Hospital.
[2] To be called T hereafter. As it is private, it is not among the references.
[3] Cross-examination of Milne by Ognell QC. (T).
[4] Dates and page numbers in subsequent references in parentheses will also refer to *The Times* newspaper (1981).

iv. the penetrating stab wound to the right eye of Jacqueline Hill, provoked, it was supposed, by her 'accusing stare' (15 May 1981, p. 6);

v. other sexual possibilities including mutilation of five victims and alteration of clothing in 'sex revenge' (15 May 1981, p. 6).

2   The virtual swing of line by the defence from 'diminished' to McNaughton insanity in that, presumably on ill-advised medical instruction, the defence became one of 'schizophrenia or nothing'.

The first clue as to why comes from the sequence of the first-day events. The judge expressed immediate anxiety, before even the Attorney-General opened to present the facts, as to whether the plea 'Section 2 manslaughter' should be accepted (T). The Attorney then explained why all four psychiatrists were agreed and, as the judge demurred, explained that after a private trial, before the trial, of all four doctors, he was satisfied that the diagnosis was of schizophrenia (T): he did not, however, persist against the judge's view (T) (see footnote 2, p. 94).

The judge's reservation was on the ground that the medical opinions, while expert in themselves, 'seemed to him to be based simply on what the defendant has told the doctors and nothing more', in contrast to reports in newspapers that he told the police that he held women in universal, homicidal hatred (T) – as if this, as the judge saw it, nullified both schizophrenia and 'diminished'. The factual basis, insisted the judge, of the medical unanimity of conclusion was what Sutcliffe told them (T) (this is in fact not true: his behaviour and demeanour at interview were also influential). '... If it were shown that the factual basis were wrong then the medical evidence would go.' (T).

Once the judge ruled that there must be a full trial, the collusion between the prosecution and defence which had permitted the 'pre-trial' by the prosecution of the psychiatrists, retailed by the Attorney-General, collapsed and the psychiatric issue had to be raised by the defence and assailed by the prosecution. At this point the psychiatric issue should have ceased to be one of 'schizophrenia or nothing' and become one of 'abnormality of mind', according to the Parker doctrine, allowing a completely new look at what constituted Sutcliffe's 'abnormality of mind'. But this did not seem to happen: the defence appears meekly to have taken over the collusion of 'schizophrenia or nothing', which in practice proved assailable on the very ground of poverty of factual basis that the judge impugned. Why was not psychopathy adduced as alternative?

The clue to the omission of the alternative may lie in the evidence-in-chief of Dr McCulloch, who expected to discover 'abnormality of personality including sexual deviation of some sort' (16 May 1981, p. 4), yet not amounting to substantial diminution of responsibility (T), but in fact, within the first half-hour of his interview with Sutcliffe, diagnosed schizophrenia on the basis of 8 'first rank signs' (only 6 of which were reported) (16 May 1981, p. 4).

The Times' (23 May 1981, p. 5) 'Comment', after the verdict, reports the Attorney-General, in his first day submission, as asserting that the 'experts were not deceived by Sutcliffe. They had expected to find a sadistic killer with a personality disorder', but had not unearthed the typically violent and delinquent psychopathic history outlined in 'Psychopathy and wickedness' (p. 98 above).

In fact, Sutcliffe's post-verdict biography did include two previous convictions,[1] eleven different jobs and, to say the least, sexual and marital instability; a man inscrutable, a 'cold smiler', said his friends. Perhaps not enough, but straws in the wind . . .

Nevertheless, Drs Milne, McCulloch and Kay (perhaps McGrath too) took their stand on schizophrenia, and Dr Milne added the curious 'Catch 22' (15 May 1981, p. 6) volte-face of Sutcliffe if he *had* been earlier feigning abnormality, in that, in evidence, he resolutely asserted his normality while insisting on his God-given mission to exterminate 'the scum of the earth . . . responsible for all these problems of his: the prostitutes' (12 May 1981, p. 4 and 21 May 1981, p. 5).

Dr Milne went so far as to produce 19 diagnostic features of Sutcliffe's paranoid schizophrenia (Table 7.5 (T)).

Of these, it might be considered that A, C, D, H and S point to paranoid thinking which might not be of schizophrenic origin; B, I, J, and K do not necessarily relate to schizophrenia, although, as Milne explained it, K referred to Sutcliffe interviewed, describing himself as if he were describing another

Table 7.5   Milne's 19 features of Sutcliffe's paranoid schizophrenia

A	Suspicion
B	Uncontrolled impulse
C	Paranoid ideas about prostitutes
D	Preoccupation with prostitutes to extent of delusion
	('Scum of earth', etc. Linked with 'C'.)
E	Ideas of grandeur (e.g. direct communication with God)
F	Hallucinosis (e.g. hearing God's voice)
G	Feelings of depression including suicide
H	Ideas of reference
I	Misidentification (e.g. of which women were prostitutes)
J	Over-controlled behaviour
K	Psychotic detachment (linked with 'J')
L	Lack of insight
M	Thought argument
N	Schizophrenic thinking (illogical thinking, deductions and conclusions; extensions of 'M'; ?distinct from 'thought disorder')
O	Devoid of insight (extension of 'L')
P	Primary schizophrenic experience
Q	Ideas of passivity and control
R	Mind control (inserted or broadcast)
S	Religious delusions (probably incorporated in 'E')

From taped transcript.

---

[1] The first, in 1969, 'fined £25 for visiting a brothel area equipped with a hammer' – for, Sutcliffe later admitted, homicidal purposes, on that occasion frustrated.

person(T); G only relates to that form of schizophrenia with accompanying affective features that is termed 'schizo-affective psychosis'; L, and its extension in time and/or degree, O, are derivative: the illness has to be present before insight into it can be lacked; on the factual basis for P, the cemetery incident, the issue of the whole hearing could be said to hinge; F, M, N, Q and R provided, if substantiated, pointers to front-rank symptoms of schizophrenia; but was Sutcliffe's masquerading some or all of them?

Furthermore, as to N, did Sutcliffe, in the opinions of the four psychiatrists, show clear-cut formal thought disorder? Dr Milne appeared to deny it (T); under cross-examination, Dr Milne replied, says the tape, 'He does not have that which is the very obvious thought disorder that many schizophrenics demonstrate' (T). Dr Milne, while, like his colleagues, taking his stand on schizophrenia rather than 'abnormality of mind', does not seem to have substantiated it in evidence. Repeatedly indeed, Dr Milne (and, it appears, Dr McCulloch) admitted that the diagnosis failed, he was duped, and Sutcliffe was a murderer (T) if:

(a) Sutcliffe's claim for his divine and hallucinatorily based 'mission' was an invention;

(b) Then his 'primary delusion' or 'primary experience' as Dr Milne called it (insisting that it was crucial to his diagnosis) (21 May 1981, p. 5), his experience of the voice of God and the special writing on the grave in Bingley cemetery in 1965 must also be an invention;

(c) He killed his non-prostitute victims knowing they were not prostitutes;

(d) Sutcliffe was masquerading schizophrenia since these ideas first came out as late as two months after his arrest and on Dr Milne's seventh interview with him.

Sutcliffe himself agreed he had lied protectively (13 May 1981, p. 6). Play was then made by the prosecution of his speaking to Prison Officer Fitzgerald of how he duped doctors, in the belief that he would serve only ten years in a loony bin (13 May 1981, p. 6): of his aping his wife Sonia's known schizophrenia (19 May 1981, p. 4) (but if it was schizophrenia it led to rapid remission and resumption of teacher-training); of an American experiment, showing how easily psychiatrists could be misled by masqueraders of schizophrenia (19 May 1981, p. 4).

Rather naive cold water, as it seems, was thrown by both prosecuting counsel and the judge on whether Sutcliffe displayed schizophrenic thought disorder (22 May 1981, p. 4) (one reported remark of Sutcliffe's in evidence pointed strongly to a knight's move in thinking) and whether he had too much drive for hebephrenia (15 May 1981, p. 6) (typical hebephrenia was never, it appears, alleged by the defence).

Then a wedge was successfully driven between categories to make them falsely appear mutually incompatible:

(a) Mental illness and mental disorder (even defence counsel talked of his having a 'diseased mind') (20 May 1981, p. 4);

(b) Schizophrenia and sexual psychopathy, allowing the Attorney-General not just to concede but assert the killings were 'sadistic' (6 May 1981, p. 1), 'horrible and sadistic beyond our ordinary comprehension' (20 May 1981, p. 4) yet insisting the issue was between Sutcliffe being 'mad or just plain evil' (7 May 1981, p. 6 – Milne's report cited by prosecution in opening speech).

The defence had to ignore the grotesquely paranoid development of Sutcliffe's homicidal vendetta against prostitutes. In 1974, estranged from Sonia, who was being unfaithful and possibly thought a prostitute, he went himself to a prostitute who showed up his impotence, diddled him out of £10 change from £20 and then humiliated him before her friends in a pub when he tried to reclaim it (11 May 1981, p. 4 – defendant's evidence-in-chief). Although, from this incident, unpleasant but trivial, came the apparent extension of his hatred for women which led to his killing or maiming twenty of them, it could not have been the origin of this hatred in view of the report of his unsuccessful attempt to kill a prostitute in 1969 by quite literally socking her: it appears that she decided against bringing a charge against him but the police had a note of the incident.

The later, avowedly compulsive, element, reported more in the summing up than in the account of Sutcliffe's evidence, making Sutcliffe increasingly 'random and indiscriminate' in his choice of victim, had also to be ignored by the defence as pointing away from schizophrenia. Did Sutcliffe *have* to believe all his victims were prostitutes, even the final six, to be of diminished responsibility? He reportedly said in relation to various victims, 'My desire to kill prostitutes was getting stronger than ever and it took me over completely . . . there was an urge inside me to kill girls . . . now practically uncontrollable . . . I had the urge to kill any woman. No woman was safe when I was in this state of mind . . . I realise she (? Yvonne Pearson) was not a prostitute but at the time I was not bothered and I just wanted to kill a woman . . . My urge to kill was totally out of my control . . . I was . . . in a world of my own, out of touch with reality.'

How came the defence to be so constituted that the judge could, summing-up, say '. . . the defence and medical experts are agreed that not too much notice should be taken of such comments because Sutcliffe was wanting to hide his divine mission'? (22 May 1981, p. 4).

The Times leading article (23 May 1981, p. 13) talks of 'the poor showing of the psychiatrists in the witness box'. No psychiatrist who has come under heavy cross-examination could cast the first stone or lack sympathy; but the psychiatrists failed to make it clear that there is a well-known form of schizophrenia that does little other than slowly change the developing adolescent into a strange and twisted being, sometimes with grotesque sexual disturbance. The writers of the best known English textbook of psychiatry (Slater and Roth, 1969, p. 157), discussing emotionally inadequate interpersonal reactions, coldness, insensitivity and social maladjustment, claim that, 'A more important cause is schizophrenia. In some cases the schizophrenic process may cause a destruction of some affective qualities of the personality, while leaving others almost unimpaired; and among emotionally callous psychopaths there are a small number who appear, after careful enquiry, to have had in earlier life a mild and usually clinically unclear mental illness, from which the unfavourable turn in character development can be traced.' In his apparent simulation of insanity, his alleged and God-inspired delusions and the sadistic undertones of his killings, Sutcliffe falls exactly half-way between the murderers John George Haigh and Neville Heath (Neustatter, 1957, pp. 124–51 and 111–23).

The defence might have fared better by positing that Sutcliffe suffered from clear-cut abnormality of mind of a strangely paranoid type. Starting in 1969 with an unexplained attack on a prostitute and enhanced in 1974 by trivial humiliation, it developed into a bizarre, homicidal hatred of women, particularly prostitutes or alleged prostitutes. It continued with a strongly sadistic overtone and possibly – perhaps probably – as the result of a low-grade schizophrenic process. Whether or not the basis was schizophrenic, there was surely substantially more than minimal or trivial (see p. 99) diminishment of responsibility?

ACKNOWLEDGEMENTS

The author's gratitude is extended to the editors, Professor Nigel Walker, Mrs Susanne Dell and Dr Nigel Eastman for criticism of the first draft of this chapter; to his son, Martin Spencer, Barrister-at-law, for help over recent case-law on provocation; and to Dr Andrew Ashworth, law tutor, Worcester College, Oxford, for help over recent case-law on medical evidence.

CASES

1   R. *v*. Barrett (1981) unreported.
2   R. *v*. Byrne (1960) 44 Cr. App. 246–55 at 252.
3   R. *v*. Byrne (1960) 2 QB 396–455 at 403.
4   R. *v*. Cox (1970) unreported.
5   R. *v*. Crofts (1972) unreported.
6   R. *v*. Dix (1982) 74 Cr. App. R. 306–11.
7   R. *v*. Dolan (1979) unreported.
8   R. *v*. East (1980) unreported.
9   R. *v*. Edgington (1962) unreported.
10 R. *v*. Fenton (1975) 61 Cr. App. R. 261.
11 R. *v*. Hussey (1980) unreported.
12 R. *v*. Jackson (1980) unreported.
13 R. *v*. Lloyd, D. W. (1967) 1 QB 175–81 at 175 and 178–9.
14 R. *v*. Loat (1973) unreported.
15 R. *v*. Macanaspie (1981) unreported.
16 R. *v*. Majewski (1977) AC 443.
17 R. *v*. Meaden (1971) unreported.
18 R. *v*. Newall (1980) 71 Cr. App. R. 331.
19 R. *v*. Nicholl (1980) unreported.
20 R. *v*. Oxley (1980) unreported.
21 R. *v*. Podola (1959) 3 All E. R. 418 described in Smith and Hogan (1975, pp. 157–60).
22 R. *v*. Reid (1979) unreported.
23 R. *v*. Sheehan (1975) 1 WLR 739–744 at 740.
24 R. *v*. Standen (1971) unreported.
25 R. *v*. Sutcliffe (1981) *The Times* newspaper, April–May, see reference.
26 R. *v*. Turner (1975) QB 834, see Williams (1978, p. 483, footnote 21).
27 R. *v*. Vernage (1982) Crim. L. R. 598–600.
28 R. *v*. Walton (1978) All E. R. 542.
29 R. *v*. Wilkins (1973) unreported.
30 R. *v*. Williams (1981) unreported.
31 R. *v*. Wines (1981) unreported.

REFERENCES

Bach-y-Rita, G. Lion, J. R., Climent, C.E. & Ervin, R.F. (1971) Episodic dyscontrol: a study of 130 violent patients. *Amer. J. Psychiat.*, **127**, 1473–8.

Blom-Cooper, L. (1982) Personal communication.

Bluglass, R.S. (1979) The psychiatric court report, *Med. Sci. Law*, **19**, 2, 121–9.

Bluglass, R.S. (1980) *New Issues in Forensic Psychiatry and the Law*. London: S.K. & F. Publications.

Bowden, P. (1983) Madness or badness? *Brit. J. Hosp. Med.*, **30**, 6, 388–94.

Butler Report (Committee on Mentally Abnormal Offenders) – see Home Office and DHSS (1975).

Coid, J. (1980) *Mania a Potu: a Critical Review of Pathological Intoxication*. PhD thesis, University of London. Privately circulated.

Criminal Law Revision Committee (1980) *14th Report: Offences against the Person*. Cmnd. 7844. London: HMSO.

Criminal Statistics, England and Wales (1979) Cmnd. 8098. London: HMSO.

Criminal Statistics, England and Wales (1980) Cmnd. 8376. London: HMSO.

Dalton, K. (1981) *A Guide to Premenstrual Syndrome and its Treatment* (privately published).

Dalton, K. (1982a) Personal communication.

Dalton, K. (1982b) Legal implications of PMS. *World Medicine*, **17**, 93–4, April 17.

Dalton, K. (1982c) Violence and the premenstrual syndrome. *Behaviour* (to be published).

Dalton, M.E. (1981) Sex hormone-binding globulin concentrations in women with severe premenstrual tension. *Postgrad. med. J.*, **57**, 560–1.

Dell, S. (1982) Personal communication.

Dell, S. and Smith, A. (1983) Changes in the sentencing of diminished responsibility homicides. *Brit. J. Psychiat.*, **142**, 20–35.

d'Orbán, P.T. (1983) Medicolegal aspects of the premenstrual syndrome. *Brit. J. Hosp. Med.*, **30**, 6, 404–9.

Gostin, L. (1977) *A Human Condition*, Vol. 2. London: MIND.

Hall Williams, J.E. (1980) Legal views of psychiatric evidence. *Med. Sci. Law*, **20**, 4, 276–82.

Hamilton, J. (1981) Diminished responsibility. *Brit. J. Psychiat.*, **138** 434–6.

Hill, D. & Watterson, D. (1942) Electroencephalographic studies of psychopathic personalities. *J. Neurol., Neurosurg., Psychiat.*, **5**, 47–65.

Home Office & DHSS (1975) *Report of the Committee on Mentally Abnormal Offenders*. (Butler Report.) Cmnd. 6244. London: HMSO.

Hooper, R.S., McGregor, J.M. & Nathan, P.W. (1945) Explosive rage following head injury. *J. Ment. Sci.*, **91**, 458–71.

Hovey, J.E. & Rickler, K.C. (1980) *Neurobehavioural characteristics of Patients with a History of Violent Behaviour*. Unpublished paper presented at the American Academy of Criminal Justice Society.

Lishman, A. (1978) *Organic Psychiatry*. London: Blackwell Scientific Publications.

Maletzky, B.M. (1973) The episodic dyscontrol syndrome. *Dis. Nerv. Syst.*, **34**, 178–185.

Mark, V.H. & Ervin, R.F. (1970) *Violence and the Brain*. New York: Harper and Row.

Marks, B. & Clifford Rose, F. (1980) *Hypoglycaemia*, 2nd edition. Oxford: Blackwell Scientific Publications.

May, P.R.A. & Ebaugh, F.G. (1953) Pathological intoxication, alcoholic hallucinosis and other reactions to alcohol: a clinical study. *Quart. J. Studies on Alcohol*, **14**, 200–27.

Mayer-Gross, W., Slater, E. & Roth, M. (1960) *Clinical Psychiatry*, 2nd edition. London: Baillière Tindall and Cassell.

Neustatter, W.L. (1957) *The Mind of the Murderer*. London: C. Johnson.

Ratner, R.A. & Shapiro, D. (1979) The episodic dyscontrol syndrome and criminal responsibility. *Bull. Amer. Acad. Psychiat.* **7**, 422–31.

Royal College of Psychiatrists (1979) *Report of a Special Committee on Alcohol and Alcoholism*. London: Tavistock.

Slater, E. & Roth, M. (1969) *Clinical Psychiatry*, 3rd edition. London: Baillière Tindall and Cassell.

Smith, J.C. & Hogan, B. (1975) *Criminal Law: Cases and Material*. London: Butterworths.

Sparks, R.F. (1964) 'Diminished responsibility' in theory and practice. *Modern Law Review*, **27**, 9–34.

Spencer, S.J.G. (1977) Psychological medicine, responsibility and crime. *The Month*, **9**, 301.

Taylor, D. (1981) *Alcohol*. London: OHE.

The Times Newspaper (1981) Daily reports on Sutcliffe Trial, 30 April and 6–23 May (Mondays excluded).

Trick, K. & Tennent, T.G. (1981) *Forensic Psychiatry: an Introductory Text*. London: Pitman.

Walker, N. (1968) *Crime and Insanity in England*, Vol. 1. Edinburgh: University Press.
Walker, N. (1981) Butler *v.* the CLRC and Others. *Crim. L.R.*, 596–601.
Walker, N. (1982) Personal communication.
Walker, N. & McCabe, S. (1973) *Crime and Insanity in England*, Vol. 2. Edinburgh: University Press.
Williams, G. (1978) *Textbook of Criminal Law*. London: Stevens and Sons.
Wootton, B. (1959) *Social Science and Social Pathology*. London: Allen and Unwin.
Wootton, B. (1960) Diminished responsibility: a layman's view. *Law Quarterly Review*, **76,** 224–39.
Wootton, B. (1981) *Crime and the Criminal Law*, 2nd edition. London: Stevens.

8

Genetic Endowment and the XYY Syndrome

Michael Craft

Nowhere in the field of medicine has advance been more rapid than in the understanding of genetics. The rules behind Mendelian inheritance were worked out in the late nineteenth century, and so generally accepted that during the twenties and thirties the transmission of traits by genetic inheritance was expected to lie behind many familial characteristics. It was in 1959 that technological improvements allowed Lejeune and his associates to map the 46 normal human chromosomes, and thus facilitate our understanding of the chromosomal misendowments which may affect individuals.

In the law court, arguments based on genetic misendowment have been unhappy battle grounds. The technical arguments are complex, the amount of research and available experts has been prodigious, and it has been repeatedly shown that an adequate environment is crucial for complete manifestation of a genetic endowment. For instance, if a child is not fed properly it will not grow, and cannot become as tall as its genes would endow it to be. In this chapter only a generalised and simplified account can be given of genetic predisposition, and rather than provide a survey of the literature, a few examples of interrelationships are described.

First, some background data for the non-medical reader. Every cell of the human body contains 46 chromosomes in 23 pairs in the nucleus. In preparing a 'map' or karyotype of the human nucleus, the chromosomes are teased out and arranged in order of size, the biggest pair called 'one' and the smallest 'twenty-two'. The twenty-third pair are the sex chromosomes, XX for the normal female, XY for the normal male. Each chromosome is a chain of deoxyribonucleic acid (DNA). Hereditary information is arranged on the DNA chain as a three base coding system. The protein molecules or nucleotides in the DNA chain are in sequences, which like a key, constitute the genes determining the characteristics of the individual. Biochemists are now half-way to synthesising genes by adding nucleotides together in the right sequence. A recent advance has been the discovery of special enzymes which cut up chromosomes by 'reading' nucleotide sequences, and allow the 'stitching' of genes together in new order. This is the basis for the new genetic factories recently financed by US and UK stock exchanges, with their mind-boggling possibilities (see Stoker, 1980 for details).

It is clear that molecular biology has recently advanced rapidly and precisely; unfortunately its application to the understanding of psychiatry is not so far advanced. Still, the reading of 'gene maps' has progressed and tells us about the location of gene pairs which determine predisposition to some abnormalities. So far these are for precise entities, such as disease sensitivity or errors of metabolism.

Because the chromosomes are arranged in pairs, genes also are in pairs which together act rather like reins upon a horse, equal pressure on either side guiding the animal straight forwards, but with imbalance of pressure an abnormal course is steered. Pairing constitutes some protection against abnormality. Not surprisingly for such a complex endowment, each human on average has one lethal, and three recessive genes, each of which if paired with another recessive gene, would be damaging for a child. The lethal gene may lead to a fetus dying in the uterus, whilst if the recessive gene is paired with a similar, it may cause serious childhood illness. The dominant lethal gene is sometimes responsible for the death of a developing fetus in the uterus and subsequent spontaneous miscarriage; the recessive genes for deaths in early childhood, such as the inherited phenylketonuria abnormality, where the infant is unable to detoxicate a normal protein constituent which accumulates to poison brain development. Huntington's chorea is an example of a dominant lethal gene, which because of increasing inability to process neurotransmitter substances, leads to death in early or middle age. Since this last example is the only clear-cut instance of dominant Mendelian inheritance, which leads to an increasingly aggressive and paranoid personality, it has some interest for the study of mentally abnormal offenders.

'BODY' CHROMOSOMAL ANOMALIES

Chromosomal abnormalities were discovered in some number after the technique for karyotyping was reported by Lejeune and his associates in 1959. The abnormalities reported to date, either too many (47, 48, 49 or even 50 chromosomes) or too few (45 chromosomes), are principally associated with intellectual retardation. This is not surprising in view of the complex nature of endowment. Detailed descriptions of the anomalies can be found in texts on mental handicap, such as *Tredgold's Mental Retardation* (Craft, 1979). In brief, absence of a 'body' chromosome (numbers one to twenty-two, which are concerned solely with physical and mental development) is incompatible with life. Such fetuses are aborted and constitute some of the sixteen per cent of ordinary pregnancies which are spontaneously miscarried. An *absence* of one of the two X chromosomes is compatible with life, as in the case of an individual with 44 body chromosomes and one X sex chromosome who is a normal-looking female, but lacking the ability to reproduce. Such a female is slightly retarded in mental and general bodily development. Absence of both X chromosomes is lethal, so a fetus with no X and one Y aborts, whilst with two Ys a tumour is formed and death of the fetus ensues. *Excess* chromosome anomalies are relatively common and viable.

Among newborn, one in two hundred are chromosomal abnormalities, half of these affecting body chromosomes, half affecting the sex chromosomes. Mongolism or Down's syndrome with its extra chromosome is the most common at one in seven hundred of ordinary births. This abnormality results in individuals who are retarded mentally and physically, but, thanks to modern antibiotics, now live almost as long as ordinary people. All 'true' Down's syndrome individuals are severely mentally handicapped, that is, with a mental age of less than seven, and thus, so far as the courts are concerned, although they can look after their needs and wants, they can be found 'unfit to plead' and could be protected under the 1957 Sexual Offences Act, which prohibits intercourse with the severely mentally handicapped. Other examples of excess body chromosomes are far less common and not usually associated with long life.

SEX CHROMOSOMAL ANOMALIES

In the past these have provided the courts with problems. The normal individual is XX female or XY male, the Y chromosome being dominant and determining male development for the purposes of this discussion. In all populations studied, approximately one in every four hundred live births have an extra sex chromosome, most being XYY, XXY, or XXX, each with a frequency of one to 1500 live births. The remainder, which are rare, have 48 or more chromosomes. The interest of the courts in these syndromes springs from the statistics for penal institutionalisation. Utilising recent research, we can calculate that in any one year, 86 normal men (XY) in every adult 100 000 are serving prison sentences, but some 150 out of every 100 000 XYY individuals are serving penal sentences. Obviously these figures can be argued both ways. Of the XYY individual, or the 'supermale' as some have dubbed him, it can indeed be proclaimed, as an advocate did to a murder court in Lyons, that 'every cell in his brain is abnormal' (he gained an acquittal verdict), but the later statistics showed that any tendency to abnormality required environmental factors before actual abnormal actions occurred. Since research in this area is of particular interest for a study of mentally abnormal offenders, and does affect a relatively high proportion of the population, the story is worthwhile giving in more detail.

XYY AND XXY MALES, XXX FEMALES

The early studies in the chromosomal abnormalities concentrated on institutionalised populations for ease of access by the investigators. In retrospect they can now be seen as a classic example of an argument being based on inadequate premises. The initial studies showed body chromosome abnormalities to be commonly found in mental handicap hospitals, whilst sex chromosome anomalies were common in penal units, including security hospitals. It was found that XYY men tended to be over 184 centimetres (6 feet) tall and inmates were more determined, aggressive and sexually active than peers. After ten years of research, in 1970, Kessler's authoritative review commented that XYY individuals seemed to constitute a unique group of uncontrollable psychopaths, going on, 'In some the evidence is impressive. In the relatively few years since the Jacobs' (1959)

Report, over one hundred XYY individuals have been detected, many of whom have been involved in criminal and other anti-social activities. Studies of certain institutionalised populations have obtained frequencies of XYY individuals ranging from one in 35 (Jacob) to one in 100 (Bartlett) representing a possible twenty-fold (Court Brown) or greater representation over the newborn incidence.'

Experts reviewing the literature gave a list of characteristics of personality which read rather like a roll call for signs of psychopathy, persuading many that here was a predominantly genetic causation for many psychopaths, and by implication there could be genetic reasons for others, if only time and resources were available to look. However, even at that time in the early 1970s, there were doubts. It was becoming increasingly clear that, apart from the many who were indeed convicted and in institutions, there were many others, apparently not offending and ordinary citizens in the community. Definitions of character traits have always been difficult to substantiate, and even a label like 'aggressive tendencies' is a vague criterion. Court Brown (1967) found that two XYY individuals judged to be aggressive had been convicted in one case for thieving a milk bottle and shirt, and in the other for committing a verbal 'breach of peace', both being a first conviction in retired men. In addition, there are important population group differences behind the incidence of chromosomal anomalies. For instance research shows that there is a statistical association between social class, violence and conviction. Other studies appeared to show that XXY males feminised because of the extra X chromosome were also more 'aggressive' (whatever this means) and likely to be hospitalised (Hunter, 1968a). In one study there were 19 individuals over 184 centimetres (six foot) tall in an English security hospital who were XYY, but three others were XXY. The researcher thought that because of feminisation they might have been provoked into reactive behaviour.

A similar argument was put forward to explain aggression in the XXX syndrome. The XXX syndrome was at one time wrongly called the 'superfemale'. In fact, subjects are usually under-developed, with menstrual disorder and delayed or absent breast and uterus development. Most clinical descriptions have been of institutionalised females, however, and although it is known that the greater the number of X chromosomes the greater the disorder of development, it is clear from the birth incidence of one in 1500 of live births that large numbers at least of the XXX syndrome must be walking about in the community and regarded as reasonably normal women. Yet, although the frequency of each of the common abnormalities, XXY, XYY and XXX is approximately one in 1500 live births, their frequency in state residential institutional surveys is much increased – six times greater than in the general population for XYY males, four times for XXY males and four times for XXX females. There are also substantially increased frequencies to be found in residential schools for the delinquent, maladjusted and retarded (Hunter, 1968b). However, against this it must be considered that among the 50 000 000 population of England and Wales there will be some 33 000 XYY and 33 000 XXY males and 33 000 XXX females, about 100 000 citizens in all.

One of the most sophisticated tools for the investigation of genetic endowment and crime comes from the use of twin studies. Monozygotic, or identical, twins originate from the fertilisation of one egg which splits to become two embryos, each with precisely the same genetic material. If in a series of monozygotic twins a particular characteristic demonstrated by one member of the twin pair is also developed by the other twin, then this constitutes the strongest possible argument for saying that this characteristic is genetically determined. The German criminologist, Lange, in his 1929 Leipzig study *Crime as Destiny* first investigated 13 identical twin pairs for crime. He found that of 13 twins, one member of whom was in prison, all but three of their twin partners had also been convicted. Among the three pairs with one unconvicted member, the partner had been convicted following brain damage. Other investigators followed Lange and reached much the same conclusion, but their studies would not be faulted because they were not in possession of the modern sophisticated blood sampling techniques to establish twin zygosity; some may have been binovular or fraternal twins. Early workers failed to take account of the fact that identical twins have a more similar upbringing than fraternal twins.

More recent studies have used the National Twin Registers of Denmark and Norway to pursue the investigation. In 1976 Dalgard and Kringlen were able to use nine blood indices to establish monozygosity. They searched the Norwegian Twin Register to find 6600 twins born 1900 to 1935, with 139 male twin pairs, one of whom was on the National Criminological Register. They also present the results of previous investigations of twin pairs and crime, in date order for monozygous twins. They show that the pre-war 100 per cent rate matching for identical twins has dropped to the most recent 33 per cent in a 1968 Danish study, and their own 23 per cent in Norway in 1976. Early studies for non-identical binovular twins had a concordance rate for crime which was nil, but the most recent Danish and Norwegian studies each show 18 per cent. Thus there is no statistical difference between the most recent concordance rate of 23 per cent for monozygous twin pairs and crime and the 18 per cent found for binovular twin pairs for crime. The result is that Dalgard and Kringlen concluded that genetic endowment is of little importance for criminal behaviour.

In studies of *sex* chromosome anomalies Witken et al (1976) used the Danish Twin Registry and the Copenhagen Birth Register for males born 1944 to 1947. Witken and his colleagues were able to study 4139 18-year-old Danish conscripts who were over 184 centimetres (6 feet) tall, among whom they expected to find most sex chromosome anomalies. They used blood samples and chromosomal maps from cell smears from the inside of the cheek to check their chromosomal state. Among them were 12 XYY and 16 XXY, a prevalence of three and four per thousand respectively for each tall 1000 conscripts. Using State Criminal Registers, they found that 9 per cent of the same-aged normal Danish males (XY), 42 per cent of their XYY group and 19 per cent of the XXY men had been convicted. This was statistically significant at a probability level greater than 0.01 for XYY, but not significant for the XXY group. Seventy-one of the XY (i.e. normal) male recruits, one of the XYY, and one of the XXY had convictions for violence, but the differences between these figures are not significant. Army tests of intelligence showed the 12 XYY and 16 XXY had scores significantly lower than the remaining XY subjects, and the scores of intelligence were themselves significantly related to conviction. These suggest a correlation of XYY and XXY with intellectual dullness, which itself correlates to conviction, rather than to any direct association between XYY, XXY and conviction. By way of corroboration they checked into past education records and found that a poor educational index (based on school grades reached) and a poor parental educational grade correlated with the conviction of their subjects at a highly significant level.

As a mathematical exercise, Witken and his colleagues produced a 180 cell contingency table of five categories for height, seven categories for intelligence, four for educational grade reached and seven for parental life achievement, in order to test each against probability of conviction. They found that the variables of tallness, intelligence, grade reached and parental achievement fitted an association of likely conviction better than the XYY and XXY syndromes themselves. In other words, any group of individuals with social and personal disadvantages would be likely to have such a conviction rate, whether they were XYY, XXY or not. A further analysis failed to support height as a relevant variable, as, with the tall normal conscripts (XY), height showed a small but statistically significant negative relation to reported crime. Intelligence showed the same. Witken et al also found that the electrical measurement of brain rhythm (EEG) of XYY subjects showed a greater number of immature rhythms than matched XY conscript controls. This suggests that the XYY syndrome might be associated with a delay in development. In conclusion they said, 'The elevated crime rate in the XYY sample reflects an elevated rate of property offences (which agrees with other studies, most of which have also shown that XYYs are not more likely to commit crimes against people than are XYs.' They go on to say, 'No evidence has been found that men with either of these sex chromosome complements are specially aggressive.' It seems, therefore, that as with other chromosomal anomalies such as Down's syndrome. which cause a delay in mental and physical development, there is a slight delay in development engendered by the sex chromosome anomalies. Indeed there is a significantly later puberty and completion of bone growth in normal boys compared with normal XX girls, suggesting that the Y chromosome itself causes delay in maturation; additional chromosomes, be they X or Y, cause further delay. It is known from other studies, as well as Witken's 180 Cell Contingency Table, that adverse environmental influences are associated with a tendency to conviction and most convictions are for property offences. There is no proven association with aggressive crime in Witken's study for the two sex anomalies. The writer concludes that here we have

1   A chromosomal anomaly causing delay in maturation;
2   Adverse environmental upbringing adding to delay in development;
3   Chance factors bringing about crime which are more likely to occur in association with adverse environmental circumstances and retardation.

Some of these subjects may need high security or institutionalisation, but in general most benefit from a place to mature and develop their abilities, so that on release they may make a constructive contribution to the community.

Similar arguments apply to so many of the rest of the population who get convicted that one therefore enters the interesting ethical argument as to whether one is justified in putting forward a chromosomal analysis of XYY, XXY or XXX syndrome, even if one's client does happen to be one of the 100 000 such people walking the streets in England and Wales. If one does put the argument forward, then the involved professional ought also to arrange counselling and genetic advice, so the client understands the odds of producing a child with similar endowment.

Acting on such arguments, three of the tallest, most determined, aggressive and successful among UK psychiatrists met for dinner. It transpired that two among the three had had their chromosomes checked, the third had refused. The two were 'normal'. It is of interest that two out of the three had made contributions to the literature concerning XYY. A special interest indeed!

THE INFLUENCE OF THE GENES

Research into the influence of genetic endowment on the development of mentally abnormal characteristics long antedates chromosomal analysis and the Mendelian hypothesis. Arguments on the relative importance of nature and nurture have also surrounded the issue of intelligence over the centuries. More sophisticated methods of measuring intelligence have developed over the last century than have been developed for the measurement of personality traits, so it is as well to take note of the current status of the arguments on inheritance of intelligence running parallel to inheritance of personality before discussion on the inheritance of mental traits underlying mental abnormality.

One of the best discussions on inheritance of intelligence is given in the book *Intelligence, the Battle of the Mind* by Professors Eysenck and Kamin (1979). Eysenck, who has written many books on the subject of the hereditability of intelligence, bases much of his argument on twin studies. In fact he and other writers find high correlation of intelligence between members of the family, and the closer the genetic constitution to the subject, the closer is the correlation of intelligence. This goes for the bright as well as the dull. Geneticists conclude that between 70 and 80 per cent of the variation in intelligence between people is inherited, and the reader is cautioned as to the closeness of the argument in this field when he is reminded that the above statement is different from saying that 70 to 80 per cent of intelligence itself is inherited.

Kamin is an environmentalist from New York who has written much on the demonstrated difference of intelligence among blacks and whites in the USA. He reminds his reader that many studies of twins are open to severe objections. There is difficulty in establishing concordance and further difficulties in the study of separated twins reared apart, who demonstrate some of the greatest differences in IQ but who in fact often have similar environments even if apart, because they are usually reared by different members of the same large family.

Kamin points out that even if intelligence is inherited, it can be changed by the environment in much the same way that weak eyesight can be inherited, but corrected by spectacles. He quotes studies showing that adopted children from different natural mothers, reared by the same foster mother, come to resemble her in IQ, whether or not they share her genetic endowment, and that black children from disadvantaged homes, if adopted when infants into advantaged white homes, have been shown to develop IQs nearer to their foster parents. Reviewing the same data on intelligence available to Eysenck, Kamin can come to the conclusion that differences are consistent with the influence of environment.

The two authors wrote alternate chapters in isolation for the first part of the book, then reviewed each other's chapters to demolish each other's arguments, and finally ended up demolishing some of the research articles alluded to. They had an enjoyable, if wordy, battle.

The assessment of intelligence by IQ tests has provided a sophisticated way to analyse over the years one particular human characteristic. If, even now, two reputable academics can review the literature and come to different conclusions, the professional reader could well decide that the issue is unresolved: it is likely that both genes and environmental influences have strong bearings on the development of intelligence, but that one cannot with present tools assess the true importance of each. Much the same can be said of personality characteristics and mental traits, for which measuring tools are far less sophisticated than IQ tests.

CONCLUSION

Any review of the genetic contribution to mental abnormality and to psychiatry itself has to conclude that advances in this field over the last few years are far less than in molecular biology with its decoding of gene locations for disease susceptibility and synthesis of genes for construction of human insulin. For schizophrenia, the extreme example of human mental abnormality, it seems certain that two, or probably more, genes determine susceptibility and, like other genetic predispositions, additional environmental variables are needed for disease manifestation. Thus, even the monozygotic twin partner of a fully fledged schizophrenic patient has only an 86 per cent likelihood of schizophrenia, despite identical genes. It must not be forgotten that with one environmental variable, modern drug treatment, most schizophrenics remain illness- (and conviction-) free most of their lives. Compare the possessor of a Y chromosome (e.g. an ordinary male) with his greater likelihood of penal incarceration than a normal XX female. In 1980 some 6500 males and 300 females were sentenced to immediate imprisonment by courts.

One can now answer the question, Will any fetus be born with a totally bad seed? The answer, in strictly accurate terms, is yes, in the sense that approximately one in six of fertilised eggs abort spontaneously and without manipulation of environmental variables (obstetric care); others cause some mothers to bleed to death. The same argument can be applied to certain stillbirths, remembering that one in two hundred conceptions are chromosomal anomalies, half of which do not survive birth. Of the half that do survive, most are not only 'abnormal' in personality development, but severely intellectually handicapped. Yet, once more, any genetic predisposition towards abnormality of behaviour is strongly influenced by environmental variables, such as a warped family upbringing. The same argument applies to a lesser extent to the inheritance of genes predisposing an individual to schizophrenia and to manic-depressive psychosis since, so far as is known, none of these genes causes death in the uterus or early life and, except rarely for Huntington's chorea and muscular dystrophy, do not cause severe personality abnormality with severe intellectual handicap in childhood. Thus, in the field we are discussing, one has to postulate a continuum of genetic predisposition for mentally abnormal offenders. These can be a chromosomal predisposition to immature development and aggressiveness, or a gene-influenced predisposition, such as Huntington's personality abnormality.

The conclusion which seems reasonable is that although totally 'bad' seeds are not likely to survive long after germination, the more hostile or unhelpful the world into which 'poor' human seeds are born, the less likely they are to flourish. Some that do will have a genetically endowed tendency to be warped, and others, originally of good stock, will be warped by unusually hostile environments. At a later date, it is often difficult to disentangle the effect of each, although the greater the knowledge of stock and environment, the clearer the contribution of variables will be. Yet, at the stage of needing assessment, say for a youth of 15 or 20, the availability of resources, such as retraining, the hazards of chance such as employment, can be at least as important, in future planning, as evaluation of the past. It is in the context of the chancy nature of the future that concepts like 'future aggressiveness' or 'liability to danger' must be judged.

REFERENCES

Court Brown, W.M. (1967) Genetics and Crime. *J. Roy. Coll. Phys.* **1**, 311–18.
Craft, M.J. (ed.) (1979) *Tredgold's Mental Retardation (12th edition)*, pp. 345–414. London: Baillière Tindall.
Dalgard, O.S. & Kringlen, E. (1976) A Norwegian twin study of criminality. *Brit. J. Criminol.* **16**, 213–232.
Eysenck, H. & Kamin, J. (1979) *Intelligence, the Battle of the Mind.* New York: John Wiley.
Hunter, H. (1968a) Klinefelter's syndrome and delinquency. *Brit. J. Criminol.*, **8**, 203–207.
Hunter, H. (1968b) Chromatin positive and XYY boys in approved schools. *Lancet*, **i**, 816.
Kessler, S. (1970) A review of chromosomal abnormalities. *J. Psychiat. Res.*, **7**, 153–170.
Lange, J. (1929) *Crime as Destiny.* Leipzig: Thieme.
Lejeune, J., Gauthier, M. & Turpin, R. (1959) Etudes de chromosomes somatiques de neuf enfants mongoliens. *C.R. Acad. Sci. (Paris)*, **248**, 1721–22.
Stoker, M. (1980) New medicine and new biology. *Brit. Med. J.*, **281**, 1678–1682.
Witken, H.A., Mednick, S.A., Schulsinger, F., Bakkestrøm, E., Christiansen, K.O., Goodenough, D.R., Hirschhorn, K., Lundsteen, C., Owen, D.R., Philip, J., Rubin, D.B. & Stocking, M. (1976) Criminality in XYY and XXY men. *Science*, **193**, 4253, 547–555.

9

Schizophrenia and Crime

William B. Spry

In any consideration of the possible causal relationship between schizophrenia and crime, it is first necessary to define as far as possible the terms being used before any conclusion can be reached.

DEFINITIONS

Crime

Crime may be simply defined as the breaking of the criminal law. This encompasses everything from most trivial motoring offences to murder. In fact, some 60 per cent of all crime is concerned with motoring. The changing views of society are reflected by Parliament, with legislative measures which may create new offences, modify others, or remove certain offences completely from the statute book. Examples of such changes include the law relating to attempted suicide, and that concerning homosexual behaviour which was at one time illegal under all circumstances.

Indictable (serious) offences have shown a steady increase in recent years (Criminal Statistics in England and Wales, 1978; Home Office, 1979). The total figure for indictable offences has steadily increased from 321 056 in 1969 to 435 550 in 1978. This represents an increase in indictable offences per 100 000 population for males from 1615 to 2125 in this period. Corresponding figures for females in 1969 were indictable offences 50 551, going up in 1978 to 95 354, and the rate per 100 000 population increased from 238 in 1969 to 434 in 1978.

The pattern of serious offences is similar in both men and women, and shows a steady increase from the age of 10 upwards, peaking between the ages of 14 and 17, slightly decreasing between the ages of 17 and 21, and then subsequently diminishing markedly. This is in itself of interest, as such a distribution pattern has little concordance with the distribution pattern of schizophrenic illness.

McClintock and Avison (1968), using standard list offences which include all indictable offences and those non-indictable ones regarded as of a similar nature to the indictable ones, estimated that approximately one in three of the male population and one in twelve of the female population would be convicted of such an offence during some time in their life.

Schizophrenia

The term schizophrenia covers a group of psychotic illnesses, not associated with any known form of brain damage, which characteristically show a marked tendency to produce disintegration of the personality. The first definition of this as a distinct syndrome, and its subsequent classification, was by Emil Kraepelin in 1896. It was, however, Eugene Bleuler who first introduced the term 'schizophrenia' in 1911. Bleuler stated: 'by the term dementia praecox or schizophrenia, we designate a group of psychoses whose course is at times chronic, at times marked by intermittent attacks, which stop or retrograde at any stage, but does not permit a full restituto ad integram. The disease is characterised by a specific type of thinking, feeling, and relation to the external world which appear nowhere else in this particular fashion.' The illness is thus typically episodic and in the acute phase showing marked disorder of thought, emotion, drive, and possibly movement. Between the episodes of acute disorder may be periods of comparative remission, but in the untreated case each recurrence increases the level of chronic disability until total social incapacity or chronic invalidism is reached.

During the acute stage, there is a change of personality with incoordination of thought, emotion and impulses, occurring in a setting of clear consciousness, memory and orientation. Normal association of ideas is often lost, and illogical or bizarre sequences frequently occur. Delusions or hallucinations are frequent symptoms, and the individual's behaviour may be a response to such phenomena. Emotional responses may often be incongruous and inappropriate. For instance, the individual may laugh or giggle in circumstances where grief would be more appropriate.

Schizophrenic illnesses affect both sexes equally. The commonest onset is in early adult life, although less frequently it may occur at adolescence or middle age. Schizophrenia is more commonly found associated with the lower social classes, but this is usually attributed to the tendency for the illness to cause a downward drift in both occupational and social levels.

The causes of schizophrenia are ill understood, but there is evidence (Shields and Slater, 1975) that certain hereditary factors are of importance, though their mode of inheritance remains unclear. Whilst, in addition, various biochemical and social factors would appear to play a role in both the precipitation and maintenance of the condition, it is apparent that the closer an individual is related to someone with schizophrenia, the higher the risk of developing the condition.

FREQUENCY OF SCHIZOPHRENIA

The prevalence of a disease is its frequency in the general population expressed as a rate. Point prevalence refers to data on a particular census day. Period prevalence refers to similar data over a given period. It is the latter that are generally used in studies of the prevalence of schizophrenia, and the usual period prevalence used is that of one year. A summary of the survey data on the prevalence of schizophrenia has been made by Cooper (1978). Most figures lie in the range of two to four per 1000 population. There would appear to be considerable consistency in the figures, which have been taken from all over the world. The pooled data give the mean prevalence of 3.3 per 1000. Two significant discrepancies may be noted, that of Böök (1953) who found a very high prevalence rate of 10.8 per 1000 in an isolated community in Northern Sweden, and Eaton and Weil (1955) who found a very low prevalence of only 1.1 per 1000 among Hutterite communities of North America.

In addition to the prevalence rate, the estimation of disease expectancy or morbid risk may be made. The usual method of collation is that of Weinberg (1927). This morbid risk means the likelihood that any individual who survives long enough to be exposed during the period of risk in life when the particular disease usually arises will develop the disease. The period of risk varies, and in schizophrenia is usually taken to be between the ages of 15 and 45. A number of investigations from all over the world have made estimates of this morbid risk, and pooled data from these surveys provides a mean rate for schizophrenia of 0.86 per cent (Shields and Slater, 1975). In the United States of America, however, where schizophrenia is diagnosed somewhat more readily than in Europe, the figure is between 1 and 2 per cent.

As with other psychiatric disorders, there have in the past been considerable differences between diagnoses from area to area, and from psychiatrist to psychiatrist. These differences have arisen partly from the varying conceptual philosophies of psychiatrists in different countries regarding the disease, and partly from difficulties inherent in assessing subjective symptomatology. The development of the Present State Examination (Wing et al, 1974) has rendered it possible for psychiatrists trained in the use of this technique to achieve very considerable degrees of agreement as to what symptoms are present, irrespective of culture or language. This technique has been used in international pilot studies on schizophrenia (WHO, 1973). For those readers who would like to read further on the subject of schizophrenia, the book *Schizophrenia* edited by J. K. Wing (1978) is recommended.

SCHIZOPHRENIA AND THE CRIMINAL POPULATION

As seen above, both crime and schizophrenia are quite common events, and thus it would be reasonable to anticipate, from chance alone, that a considerable number of people suffering from schizophrenia might also be criminal. Let us now look at the evidence as to whether there is any causal relationship.

Tennent (1975), in discussing aberrant or dangerous behaviour, outlined the three types of relationship that might exist. Firstly, the aberrant behaviour may occur as a result of mental illness. Secondly, patterns of aberrant behaviour may occur in those with mental illness but in whom successful treatment of the mental illness will have no effect on the pattern of behaviour, mental disorder being one of the many factors in their life pattern. Thirdly, aberrant behaviour may be present in individuals without any evidence of mental disorder.

Various attempts have been made to determine any possible relationships between schizophrenia and crime. Firstly, let us examine those studies of criminal populations that have been undertaken to determine the frequency of schizophrenia in criminals; this might point to some association.

One of the earliest of such studies was that of Glueck (1918) who examined 608 consecutive admissions to Sing Sing prison over a nine month period from August 1916. He gave a prevalence rate of 6 per cent for schizophrenia, but listed no diagnostic criteria. Bromberg and Thompson (1937) studied 9958 convicted prisoners in the psychiatric clinic to the Court of General Sessions in New York City. Ninety-six per cent of these prisoners were male, and the study lasted for four years between 1932 and 1935. Again, no diagnostic criteria are given, and schizophrenia is only included in the global term 'psychosis'. During the four years of the study, a total of 153 (1.5 per cent) were considered to be psychotic. Thompson (1937) made a study of all recidivists seen in a court of general session in 1935. Of 1380 in the group studied, 0.6 per cent were classified as psychotic. Diagnostic criteria were presented.

In a further American study, Guze et al (1962) examined 223 convicted male felons aged between 15 and 78 (average 23). Only two subjects (1 per cent) met the diagnostic criteria for schizophrenia. A British study of a highly selected population has been done by Gillies (1965) who examined 66 persons accused of a total of 70 murders in the Glasgow area. He found that 15 per cent of these were schizophrenic. In a further Scottish study, Bluglass (1966) took a sample of 25 per cent of the total admissions of convicted prisoners to Perth prison over an eleven-month period. Out of the 300, six (2 per cent) were regarded as psychotic. Woddis (1964) reports on 91 cases referred to courts as thought to be suffering from some mental abnormality. Nine of this selected group were diagnosed as suffering from schizophrenia. In another selected group, West (1965) reported on 78 murderers who subsequently committed suicide. Of these he found two males and two females whom he classified as schizophrenic, and two others who were labelled as morbidly jealous. Kloek (1969) reported a study of 500 cases in an observation clinic for non-sentenced criminals. In 30 of these, consideration was given to a diagnosis of schizophrenia but was regarded as doubtful. Only one case of the 500 met the fairly strict criteria laid down for schizophrenia. In another American study, Cloninger and Guze (1970) examined 66 female felons aged between 17 and 54 with a mean age of 27, and found only one case of schizophrenia in a person who was also mentally handicapped. Tupin et al (1973) report on 50 male murderers at a California medical facility which was the psychiatric institution of the California Department of Correction. Only 12 per cent of these highly selected individuals were considered to be psychotic.

In a more recent British study, Faulk (1976) studied 72 male consecutive discharges from Winchester prison. Of these, he found none with a principal diagnosis of schizophrenia, but two with this as a subsidiary diagnosis. The principal diagnosis was of personality disorder and alcoholism respectively.

Finally, Green (1981) reviews 58 admissions to Broadmoor for matricide by sons, finding 74 per cent schizophrenic, 16 per cent depressive and 10 per cent personality disordered. Chiswick (1981) comments on the selectivity of this sample, pointing out that thousands of schizophrenic sons live peacefully with their mothers! Other studies have looked at psychiatric populations to assess their degree of criminality. Guze et al (1974) studied 500 patients between July 1967 and October 1969. Twenty-two patients gave a history of felony conviction. This was 4 per cent of the entire sample (10 per cent of the men). Within this sample of 500, there were 200 patients with schizophrenia or primary affective disorder, and none of these reported a felony. From these figures one may deduce that the prevalence of schizophrenia in a criminal population is either at the same level as would be found in the general population, or only slightly raised.

Why is it, therefore, that schizophrenia is associated in many people's minds, particularly those of the lay public, with delinquency and even violent crime? To answer this, one may look at the types of criminal behaviour that may be found in schizophrenia. These have been outlined by Prins (1980). Firstly, schizophrenia may be associated with violent crime, and certainly such acts that may lead to considerable notoriety and publicity, especially if they involve a prominent person. Thus, whilst being rare, these individuals, who are usually deluded and paranoid, attract a great deal of attention. Well-known examples are those of McNaughton who in 1843 murdered Sir Robert Peel's secretary whom he had mistaken for the statesman. McNaughton had been, for some considerable while, suffering from a delusion that Sir Robert was persecuting him. More recently there has been the case of Ian Ball who, again acting on delusional thought processes, planned to kidnap Princess Anne. In both these incidents the crime was premeditated and well thought out. It is commonly thought that the behaviour of a schizophrenic must be impulsive, and that elaborate premeditation is indicative of sanity. This is not the case, and many schizophrenics with fixed delusional symptoms are capable of considerable premeditation. This is confirmed by the Royal Commission on Capital Punishment (1953) who expressed a similar opinion.

Secondly, schizophrenia may also be associated with bizarre crime, and in these instances the individual does not usually suffer from a fixed or consistent delusional system. Again, these incidents are rare and in these circumstances the individual may have a changing pattern of disturbance varying at frequent intervals. Behaviour in these circumstances may certainly be impulsive, and be incomprehensible to those investigating it. At times the amount of violence used may be quite appalling, and thus once more these crimes tend to receive considerable publicity, although their frequency is low.

Thirdly, schizophrenia may be associated with other offences because of a decline in social functioning competence. Here the individual succumbs to temptation which he would previously have resisted had he been in good mental health. These offences are seldom of an aggressive nature. In addition, schizophrenia leads to withdrawal of the individual from the community and may be associated with petty theft, begging, breaches of the peace and other similar delinquencies.

MOTIVATION IN SCHIZOPHRENIC CRIME

Serious crime may on occasion be the first or almost the first sign of schizophrenia. Gillies (1965), in commenting on the ten schizophrenics in his study of 66 murderers, highlights this point. He mentions a young schizophrenic who revealed the first signs of his illness when he killed a male neighbour over a disagreement in which he had no involvement. In two other cases, teenage schizophrenic boys showed the very first signs of their derangement by killing their mothers for no apparent reason. All four cases of matricide in this series were by schizophrenic males, and he regards matricide as being 'the schizophrenic crime'. The motives for such acts in the case of schizophrenic individuals are bizarre and typical of the disorder. They are distinct from so-called normal murders performed for sexual reasons, gain, or in fits of rage. They are also distinct from the disturbed motivation found in those with psychopathic personality disorder. Gillies lists the motives of the ten schizophrenic murderers in his series and these are sufficiently distinctive of the disorder to justify being repeated. The motives given by the ten schizophrenic murderers were as follows:

1 'To be manly.'
2 'I wanted to be a fourteen year old homosexual, but my wife laughed at the idea.'
3 'Because I was afraid I would be put in a mental hospital.'
4 'So I would be hanged and not have to go to a mental hospital.'
5 'I thought that after I'd killed my mother, there would be peace in the house.'
6 'The voice of the mother of God told me to kill my brother.'
7 'Because my wife was putting powder in my tea.'
8 'A mysterious power told me she was being unfaithful.'
9 'My mother taunted me and said I didn't even know if I was the father of my kids.'
10 'I just killed my mother, I don't know why.'

Matricide is a rare crime, but one which undoubtedly has a strong association with schizophrenic disorder (Green, 1981). To illustrate this point is the case of Edward Ball, quoted by Gaute and Odell (1979). Edward Ball was the 19-year-old son of a Dublin physician who was separated from his wife. Edward lived with his mother, and in February 1936 an empty bloodstained car was found that belonged to his mother. Searches in his home revealed considerable quantities of bloodstained clothing, and Edward gave a story to the police that his mother had committed suicide by cutting her throat and that he had subsequently disposed of her body by placing it in the sea. Her body was never found, but there was sufficient evidence to disprove his story of suicide and to point to murder. He was, however, found to be suffering from dementia praecox, or schizophrenia as it is now known, and a verdict of guilty but insane was brought in. No motivation for his behaviour was demonstrated.

There is thus a relationship between schizophrenia and various forms of criminal behaviour, albeit a slender one. However, many of us who deal with such offenders on a day-to-day basis in fact come across these people far more frequently that would be expected from the figures given above. This has been explained by Rollin (1969) who studied the population admitted in 1961–62 to Horton Hospital. He found that the typical mentally abnormal offender admitted was a man between 30 and 50, of no fixed abode, and very likely to be suffering from schizophrenia (83 per cent of his sample). These people constituted what Rollin has called a 'stage army' and thus tramp round and round between prisons, mental hospitals, and lodging houses making a much greater impression than their numbers warrant. He noted that usually they had committed only trivial offences, although serious crime was not unknown. Similar findings have been made by Tidmarsh and Wood (1972) who studied 8000 cases referred to a reception centre in London; 1200 of these were diagnosed as being mentally ill or mentally subnormal. It was found that most of those who had not been in prison had also not been in hospital, and likewise most of those who had not been in hospital had not been in prison either. However, those who had been in one or other type of institution had usually been in both. As long ago as 1939, Penrose demonstrated that countries with large prison populations tended to have small mental hospital populations and vice versa. He demonstrated the negative correlation between homicide rate, number of prisoners, birth rate, suicide rate and general death rate with the level of mental hospitalisation.

METHODS OF DEALING WITH SCHIZOPHRENIC OFFENDERS

What might happen to a schizophrenic who offends? Let us take the example of a person suffering from this condition who becomes disturbed, possibly due to a failure to take medication; consequently whilst living rough he steals some food and, when apprehended, engages in an argument with the police that leads to some physical violence.

He is taken into custody, but it may be apparent to the authorities that he is mentally disordered and as a result action may be taken under the Mental Health Act 1983 without recourse to prosecution. Whether this in fact occurs is largely a matter of local practice, and as such cases are not recorded in criminal statistics no figures can be given as to the frequency of disposal. It is likely, however, in areas where there is good liaison between the police, social services and the local psychiatric unit, that such practice may be frequent, and this has the advantage of offering the person concerned immediate and appropriate care and treatment.

Using the Mental Health Act 1983, the police may call upon a social worker, or the nearest relative if available, to make an application for urgent admission with a single medical recommendation. This recommendation may be by any doctor, though, if possible, the doctor should be one who has known the patient previously. The use of this procedure, under Section 4 of the Act, should be limited to emergency applications in cases of urgent necessity, where obtaining a second medical recommendation would give rise to undesirable delay. Such an application, when completed, may detain the individual in hospital for a period up to 72 hours, during which time a second medical recommendation may be sought, extending the period to 28 days from the time of admission.

Whenever possible a second medical recommendation should be obtained prior to admission. Such a second medical opinion must be by a doctor who is recognised under Section 12 by the Secretary of State as having specialist knowledge of mental disorder. The completed recommendations in this form are under Section 2 of the Mental Health Act, and constitute 'admission for assessment' for a period of up to 28 days. This type of admission is applicable to any form of mental disorder.

Occasionally Section 3 'admission for treatment' may be instigated in such circumstances. The procedure is similar to that required for Section 2, but with considerably fuller detail being necessary. This form of detention is for a maximum period of six months in the first instance. Because of its nature, Section 3 is usually only invoked after an initial period of assessment under Section 2.

A further method of dealing with the situation might be under Section 136 of the Mental Health Act. This Section refers to mentally disordered persons found in a public place and is comparatively little used. In many ways it is a most useful procedure, and the writer considers that it should be known more widely and used more frequently. The Section may be used by any constable who finds a person 'in a place to which the public have access' who appears to be mentally disordered and in immediate need of care or control. Under its provision, the person may be removed to a 'place of safety' where he may be detained for not more than 72 hours for the purpose of being examined by a medical practitioner and the making of any necessary arrangements for his treatment and care. Usually the 'place of safety' is a psychiatric hospital or unit, but there are a number of alternatives stipulated in the Act such as residential accommodation provided by the local authority, residential homes for the mentally disordered, or a police station.

Informal admission under the Mental Health Act may also be considered in suitable cases, provided the individual consents to admission. In a number of instances the criminal act may have been performed with a direct view to obtaining a return to hospital. There are many who find residence in a psychiatric unit, coupled as it is with adequate food, warmth and company, preferable to a grossly under-privileged life in the community. Reservations must, however, be expressed about this type of admission in the case of offenders, as they are free to leave hospital whenever they wish and, being by virtue of their illness unpredictable people, they may do so. In such circumstances repetition of criminal behaviour may occur and the social and other nuisance involved is such that informal care may not be appropriate.

Should it be considered that the offence should be dealt with in the normal judicial manner, the offender would be appropriately charged and the case would come to court. Occasionally there may be raised the question of the individual's competence as regards fitness to plead, the criteria for which are given in Chapter 16.

If a magistrates' court considers the person unfit, the case is referred to the Crown Court, where a jury after hearing evidence from two doctors makes the final decision. In such an event, the person is then detained 'pending Her Majesty's pleasure be known' in a place designated by the Home Secretary.

Usually a plea is taken from the accused person, and then the case is heard according to the nature of the plea. If the plea is one of guilty, or if, after hearing the evidence, a verdict of guilty is brought in, then there are a number of ways of dealing with the matter which the court may consider suitable, taking into account the schizophrenic illness of the accused. There are, of course, standard court procedures such as fines, conditional discharge, youth custody (previously borstal training), imprisonment, and deferred and suspended sentences. These are not of special reference to the schizophrenic offender and will not be discussed further, although in a number of cases it may be appropriate for one or other of these to be used. Examples of such use might occur if the schizophrenic illness were to be considered to be in remission and not in need of treatment or if, unfortunately, psychiatric facilities for undertaking care were not available. It has to be realised that the National Health Service has finite resources and that there must be instances when the services available are insufficient to meet the need.

When sentencing is undertaken, consideration should be given to the value of a probation order with psychiatric care as an inpatient or outpatient as a requirement of the order. Such an order may be made under Section 3, Powers of the Criminal Courts Act 1973 for a period of up to three years. It requires the consent of the accused and a medical recommendation from one doctor who must be approved under Section 12 of the Mental Health Act. A probation order cannot be made for a juvenile.

There are a number of advantages to the use of a psychiatric probation order, which is slowly increasing in popularity. At least one thousand orders are made annually for inpatient care, and about a further five hundred for outpatient care. Whilst in hospital the individual is an informal patient under the Mental Health Act. Such care offers the opportunity for close liaison between the Health Service staff in the psychiatric unit and the probation service, planning the objectives in the treatment and the management of after care. In many instances unemployment, with its economic and social consequences, may play an important part in the precipitation of relapse in schizophrenic illness, and may also be associated with further delinquency. It is, therefore, vitally important that planned after-care should exist which should aim at utilising the person's full potential, whether this be in open employment, sheltered workshops, or in simpler forms of occupational diversion according to need.

Should the individual fail to co-operate in the treatment programme being offered and leave the hospital without consent, he is then in breach of his probation order and would be returned to court for such breach when other alternatives could be considered.

The magistrates' court may make a Hospital Order under Section 37 of the Mental Health Act if they consider that this is the most suitable method of dealing with the case. To do this, they must have two medical recommendations (one from a doctor approved under Section 12 of the Mental Health Act) and be notified of the availability of a place for the person in a suitable hospital within

28 days of the order being made. Such an order under Section 37 has similar effect to an order under Section 3.

In certain circumstances the court may consider that some restriction is required upon the hospital order in order to protect the public where the disordered offender has been convicted of a serious offence, and it is thought likely that he might offend again once freed from detention. In such circumstances the magistrates' court refers the case to the Crown Court which also requires two medical recommendations, and one of these must give oral evidence to the court. In addition a place must also be available for the accused with 28 days at an appropriate hospital. In many instances where a restriction order is considered necessary, this may be in a special hospital, though a number of other units within the Health Service have limited facilities for accepting such persons. To obtain a vacancy in a special hospital, it is necessary to approach the appropriate branch of the Department of Health and Social Security with an application supported by medical reports which would indicate, after investigation, whether a vacancy can be found, and this information would be available to the court at the hearing. When a restricting order is made, then the power of discharge is lodged with the Home Secretary, or with a Mental Health Review Tribunal.

In rare circumstances a hospital order may be made when a person has not been convicted. In such circumstances the court must be satisfied that this is the most appropriate course of action and that no benefit would ensue from continuing the prosecution of the case to reach a guilty verdict.

The schizophrenic offender, if charged with murder, may well come within the definition in Section 2 of the 1957 Homicide Act as having an abnormality of mind induced by disease. The situation is in practice far from clear and uniform, and for a more detailed appraisal of the current situation the reader is referred to Hamilton's review of the subject (Hamilton, 1981). One such problem is that of the definition of 'substantial impairment'. Often the psychiatric evidence involves few or no contentious issues. However, where there is contention, or where for any reason the Crown does not accept the defence plea at the outset, then the evidence must be presented to a jury for their decision.

In the famous trial of the Yorkshire Ripper (*R.* v. *Sutcliffe*, May 1981) the psychiatric evidence of schizophrenia was not accepted by the jury, and this highlights the necessity for those psychiatrists appearing in court to give such evidence to have their case prepared in every detail and presented in a manner that is readily understood by a lay jury (see Chapter 7).

Bluglass (1981) refers to this difficult area in his letter 'Psychiatrists in the Witness Box' and further draws attention to the weaknesses of the Homicide Act, 1957 as regards the matter of diminished responsibility. It is mentioned that the Butler Committee on Mentally Abnormal Offenders made important recommendations to improve the law in this field that have not been implemented.

From this it can be seen that there are a number of ways of dealing with the schizophrenic offender, and that varying methods may be appropriate according to the particular circumstances. In all cases there should be a full evaluation of the circumstances available to the court in the form of a social enquiry report from the probation service, and medical reports. With the assistance of these, the court may then make the most appropriate decision. It is valuable to note, however, that with the development of better treatment methods and community services it is possible that in the future more such persons may be suitably contained in the community, possibly under a psychiatric outpatient probation order, than previously.

There is at present insufficient evidence to judge the long-term effectiveness of systems of inpatient and outpatient care of such offenders, and follow up and research will be needed. To those engaged in the work at first hand, the initial signs indicate that the methods applied are at least as effective as, and probably more so than, purely penal methods in terms of future delinquency and social competence.

DISCUSSION

The information that we have would show that overall criminal activity among schizophrenics is not materially different either quantitatively or qualitatively from that which would be found in the normal population. Silverman (1946) in a study of 500 psychotic criminals at the Springfield Medical Center compared his group with a similar number of non-psychotic criminals. He found no significant difference in family, personal or social background, or in the type of crime, between the two groups. Further evidence is given by Hafner and Boker (1973) who state that crimes of violence committed by the mentally ill (by which they mean schizophrenic and affective psychosis) are quantitatively proportional to the number of crimes of violence committed by the total population. There would appear to be general agreement that the frequency of criminal behaviour in the schizophrenic is very similar to that found in the normal population, or if raised is only by a very small amount. Wiersma (1966) who undertook a review of the German, Dutch and Scandinavian publications describing the psychiatric studies of criminals and crime in psychiatric patients, came to the conclusion that 'amongst schizophrenics, criminals are probably not more frequent than among so-called normal subjects'. Guze (1976), who has undertaken extensive study in this area, states – referring to schizophrenia – 'whilst no complete agreement, it is clear that it carried only a slightly increased risk of criminality, if at all'. Wyrsch (1955), in his German textbook of forensic psychiatry referring to schizophrenia, states 'even a very busy psychiatric expert may have to wait decades before he meets such a delinquent'. He goes on to state that 'on rare occasions, schizophrenics commit acts of violence which may then be serious, but as a rule their delinquency concerns petty acts, sometimes rather bizarre, and as a rule hardly worth the trouble of prosecution.'

The real problem concerning the schizophrenic and criminal behaviour lies in Rollin's 'stage army' referred to previously. These are the individuals who because of their illness have become socially incompetent and are sent from pillar to post, from prison to hospital to lodging house, with little effective activity being instituted towards any possible reform. Amongst these there are a number whose schizophrenic condition is such that they require 'asylum' in the true sense of the word. These people should be looked after by the Health Service in suitable accommodation. Others require and would benefit from active rehabilitation techniques. It is not appropriate that they should be accommodated within prisons. However, one must realise, as Gunn (1974) has stated, that prisons are part of the institutional network of most countries, and their populations contain a disproportionate number of people in need of chronic institutional care. The fact that this is so is really a reflection on the lack of available services outside prisons. There is undoubtedly a need within the mental health services to provide active rehabilitation for these individuals, with the aim of restoring social competence. It would appear that where this has been undertaken the results can be remarkably satisfactory. Brill and Malzberg (1949) in their study of former patients of New York State Mental Hospital found that their record of re-arrest in those who had previously committed offences compared favourably with figures available for persons in the general population who had an arrest record. Other studies, such as those of Cohen and Freeman (1945), Ashley (1922) and Pollack (1938) have all indicated that former psychiatric inpatients from hospitals catering for offenders have a lower arrest rate than for the general population. More recently Cook (1983) studied 78 young male psychiatric patients in the Bristol area (42 of them schizophrenics) and found the subsequent conviction rate to be comparable to that of men of the same age in the general population.

To conclude then, the relationship between schizophrenia and crime is only a tenuous one. A very few, but unfortunately notable and attracting attention, commit crimes of considerable violence which may be bizarre in nature and which may or may not be premeditated. Far more, however, infringe the criminal law by acts of petty delinquency related to their lack of social competence, and because of the repetitive nature of their problem they constitute a sizeable demand upon the services available. It is considered that the existing system of rotating between prison, hospital and lodging house is unsatisfactory. Thus, while the overall incidence of criminal behaviour associated with schizophrenia is very similar to that found in the general population, there is a considerable need to develop the health services available for the rehabilitation of this unfortunate group: from the evidence available such a project would be worthwhile.

REFERENCES

Ashley, C. (1922) Outcome of 1000 cases paroled from the Middletown State Homeopathic Hospital. *State Hosp. Quart.*, **8**, 64–70.
Bleuler, E. (1911) *Dementia Praecox, or the Group of Schizophrenics*, New York: Int. Univ. Press.
Bluglass, R.S. (1966) *A Psychiatric Study of Scottish Prisons*. MD thesis (unpublished).
Bluglass, R.S. (1981) 'Psychiatrists in the Witness Box', Letter to *The Times*, 28 May 1981.
Böök, J.A. (1953) Acta genet. *Statist. Med.* (Basel), **4**, 1.
Brill, H. & Malzberg, B. (1949) Statistical report based on the arrest record of 5354 male expatients released from the New York State Mental Hospital during the period 1946–48. Mimeographed manuscript.
Bromberg, W. & Thompson, C.B. (1937) The relation of psychosis, mental defect and personality types to crime. *J. Crim. Law and Criminol.*, **28**, 70–89.

Chiswick, D. (1981) Matricide. *Brit. Med. J.*, **283**, 1279–80.

Cloninger, C.R. & Guze, S.B. (1970) Psychiatric illness and female criminality: the role of sociopathy and hysteria in the antisocial woman. *Am. J. Psychiat.*, **127**, 303–11.

Cohen, L. H. & Freeman, H. (1945) How dangerous to the community are State Hospital patients? *Conn. State Med. J.*, **9**, 697–700.

Cook, D. A. G. (1983) A study of criminal behaviour in discharged male psychiatric patients. *Med. Sci. Law.*, **23**, 279–282.

Cooper, B. (1978) Epidemiology. In *Schizophrenia – Towards a New Synthesis*. Wing, J. K. (ed). pp. 31–51. London: Academic Press.

Eaton J. & Weil, R.J. (1955) *Culture and Mental Disorders*. Glencoe, Illinois: Free Press.

Faulk, M. (1976) A psychiatric study of men serving sentences in Winchester Prison. *Med. Sci. Law*, **16**, 244–51.

Gaute, J.H.H. & Odell, R. (1979) *The Murderers' Who's Who*, pp. 33–34. London: Harrap.

Gillies, H. (1965) Murder in the West of Scotland. *Brit. J. Psychiat.*, **111**, 1087–94.

Glueck, B. (1918) Study of 608 admissions to Sing Sing Prison, *Ment. Hyg.*, **2**, 85–151.

Green, C.M. (1981) Matricide by sons. *Med. Sci. Law*, **21**, 207–214.

Gunn, J. (1974) Prisons, shelters, and homeless men. *Psych. Quart.*, **48**, 505–512.

Guze, S.B. (1976) *Criminality and Psychiatric Disorders*. London: Oxford University Press.

Guze, S.B., Tuason, V. B., Gatfield, P. D., Stewart, M. A. & Picken, B. (1962) Psychiatric illness and crime with particular reference to alcoholism: a study of 223 criminals. *J. Nerv. Ment. Dis.*, **134**, 512–21.

Guze, S.B., Woodruff, R.A. & Clayton, P. S. (1974) Psychiatric disorders and criminality. *J.A.M.A.*, **227**, 641–2.

Hafner, H. & Boker, W. (1973) Mentally disordered violent offenders. *Soc. Psych.*, **8**, 220–9.

Hamilton, J.R. (1981) Diminished responsibility. *Brit. J. Psychiat.*, **138**, 434–6.

Home Office (1979) *Criminal Statistics in England and Wales, 1978*. Cmnd. 7670. London: HMSO.

Kloek, J. (1969) Schizophrenia and delinquency: the inadequacy of our conceptual framework. In *The Mentally Abnormal Offender*. De Rueck, A.V.S. & Porter, R. (eds.). London: Churchill.

Kraepelin, E. (1896) *Psychiatrie*. Leipzig: Thieme.

McClintock, F.H. & Avison, N.H. (1968) *Crime in England and Wales*. London: Heinemann.

Pollock, H.M. (1938) Is the paroled patient a menace to the community? *Psych. Quart.*, **12**, 236–44.

Prins, H. (1980) *Offenders, Deviants or Patients?*, pp. 65–7. London: Tavistock Publications.

Rollin, H.R. (1969) *The Mentally Abnormal Offender and the Law*. Oxford: Pergamon Press.

Royal Commission on Capital Punishment, 1949–53 (1953) Cmnd. 8932. London: HMSO.

Shields, J. & Slater, E. (1975) Genetic aspects of schizophrenia. In *Contemporary Psychiatry*, pp. 32–40. Silverstone, T. & Barraclough, B. (eds.). *Brit. J. Psychiat.*, *Spec. pub*. No. 9. Ashford, Kent: Headley Bros.

Silverman, D. (1946) Mentally disordered violent offenders. *Soc. Psych.*, **8**, 220–9.

Tennent, T.G. (1975) The dangerous offender. In *Contemporary Psychiatry*. pp. 308–15. Silverstone, T. & Barraclough, B. (eds.). *Brit. J. Psychiat. Spec. pub*. No. 9. Ashford, Kent: Headley Bros.

Thompson, C. B. (1937) A psychiatric study of recidivists. *Am. J. Psychiat.*, **94**, 591–604.

Tidmarsh, D. & Wood, S. (1972) Psychiatric aspects of destitution. In *Evaluating a Community Psychiatric Service*. Wing, J.K. & Hayley, A. (eds.). London: Oxford University Press.

Tupin, J.P, Mahar, D. & Smith, D. (1973) Two types of violent offenders with psychological descriptors. *Dis. Ner. Sys.*, **34**, 356–63.

Weinberg, W. (1927) Mathematisike grundlagen der probanden methode. *Ztschr. indukt. Abstamme V. Vereb.*, **48**, 179–228.

West, D.J. (1965) *Murder followed by suicide*. London: Heinemann.

Wiersma, D. (1966) Crime and schizophrenia. *Excerpta Criminalogica*, **6**, 168–81.

Wing, J.K. (ed.) (1978) *Schizophrenia – Towards a New Synthesis*. London: Academic Press.

Wing , J.K., Cooper, J. E. & Sartorius, N. (1974) *The Description and Classification of Psychiatric Symptoms: an instruction manual for the PSE and Catego System*. London: Cambridge University Press.

Woddis, G.M. (1964) Clinical psychiatry and crime. *Brit. J. Criminol*, **4**, 443–60.

World Health Organization (1973) *International Pilot Study of Schizophrenia*. Geneva: WHO.

Wyrsch, J. (1955) *Gerichtliche Psychiatrie.*, p. 194. Berne: Paul Haupt.

10

Depression and Crime: a Discursive Approach

William K. Lawson

DIAGNOSING DEPRESSION

Probably the most common illness with which the psychiatrist has to deal is depression. The term, to the lay mind, is often confused with unhappiness. Unhappiness is the lot of us all from time to time as the vicissitudes of life crowd in, and the problems of day-to-day living appear insurmountable. I am sure all the readers of this book have experienced such feelings and indeed at times may well have felt despair. However, it is only when these feelings of misery and gloom reach the stage whereby action on the part of the individual to deal with the problem becomes impossible, that the examining doctor can safely begin to feel his way towards the diagnosis of depression. The work of Sir Martin Roth, when he was Professor of Psychiatry at Newcastle upon Tyne, in differentiating that type of illness which arises from external stimuli from that type arising out of the blue is well known. Sir Martin and his colleagues, in carefully researched papers, support the differences in symptomatology between reactive and endogenous depression, which helps the psychiatrist treating a particular case to decide which drug to use, but tends to confuse the layman, be he either a judge, a magistrate, a barrister, a solicitor or a member of a social agency.

Generally speaking, the spectrum of symptoms of depresssion is wide, and the illness is usually clear cut. For example, the classic disturbance of sleep is a first rank symptom. A depressed individual has difficulty in sleeping and indeed may waken early in the morning only to find the problem which has caused his restless night is crowding in on him once again. This leads to a second symptom of the first rank numeration which is not often recognised as being of great importance. The symptom, of course, is rumination. If one thinks of a ruminant animal and the apparently interminable action of chewing the cud, one can clearly see how this phrase can be applied to the person with a troubled mind. Be it an unfaithful wife, an unfaithful husband, financial disaster, divorce proceedings, or even the behaviour of a wayward child, the problem becomes dominant in the thinking to the exclusion of all else. Quite naturally, sleeplessness and rumination lead on to a loss of appetite. I am quite sure that all readers of this book who have endured a sleepless night with some anxiety or other will accept at once that in the morning the last thing they wish to face is food. To the writer's mind the classical triad of sleeplessness, rumination and loss of appetite are paramount. The physiological changes brought about by sleeplessness and insufficient intake of food lead on to irritability. A depressed person may well be apathetic for long periods of time but attempts by well-meaning individuals who use the 'pull yourself together' approach are usually met with an irritable and apparently unreasonable response. One always takes note of the apparent apathy and listlessness of the depressed patient. This is described in psychiatric terms as retardation, and means the general slowing down of all the bodily processes, both physiological and psychological.

A patient presenting with these symptoms is undoubtedly depressed and one is concerned then to try and establish a cause. Usually the cause is obvious and easily identified. However, as was mentioned above, the question of endogenous and reactive depression occupies many brilliant psychiatric minds, and for the purposes of this book it is not appropriate to enter into the academic discussions which have taken place. Suffice it to note, there are patients who become acutely depressed, who have well-marked mood swings as the day goes on, and the illness arises from no apparent cause. Perhaps the best differentiation between reactive and endogenous depression is that in the individual who apparently has no reason to be depressed, the mood improves towards the end of the day; he tends to feel better towards the evening but regresses to an acutely depressed state by the following morning.

Like many medical terms 'depression' is misused, and care must be taken to establish a proper diagnosis. It cannot be over-emphasised that this is a time-consuming process and much depends, not only on the observations and statements of the patient, but on the objectivity of relatives and friends. A depressed patient may steel himself to face the day and act in a perfectly normal way. The patient may think that outwardly he or she appears perfectly normal but the observations of friends, relatives and colleagues, elicited by the psychiatrist, show that indeed all is not well. A general falling off of work standards, an apparent withdrawal from the communal life of the workplace by an individual who is usually very outward looking and cheerful at work, the prolonged silence of a spouse in the evening, when normally conversation does take place between husband and wife, the unhappiness and tetchiness of an adolescent approaching a public examination who suddenly becomes obsessed with failure and who cannot be comforted with regard to his or her ability and potential. Confirmation of the clinical impression by cross-checking with relatives and friends may be time consuming, but can also confirm the diagnosis.

The gravest sequel of depression, of course, is suicide. The legal phrase 'the balance of mind being disturbed', is extremely accurate. Despair, with an overwhelming sense of impending doom, can drive many a depressed patient into the ultimate step of taking his own life. Therefore, it can easily be seen that one is not dealing with unhappiness but rather with a condition which can have appalling consequences both for the patient and his or her immediate family. Nor must it be forgotten that a suicidally depressed patient could kill those nearest to him, prior to taking his own life.

DEPRESSION PRIOR TO OR AFTER CRIME

Very often in matters of serious crime in which a statutory defence can be advanced the expert witness, in describing a depressive illness to the court, will speak of the judgement of the accused being affected as a result of the illness. In other words, what he is saying is that an individual who, up to the commission of a serious crime, was regarded as a person whose actions in life were purposeful and logical, has, as a result of a depressive illness and possibly as a result of associated biochemical changes which are as yet not fully understood, reached a position where he can no longer properly judge either the reasons for his actions or the consequences of those actions. The effect of depression in matters which bring a patient before the courts is primarily lack of judgement.

The relation of depression to petty crime is very difficult to evaluate. One can only speculate as to the number of preoccupied and depressed people who unwittingly commit offences against the Road Traffic Act. Offences of speeding, driving without due care, failing to observe a traffic signal, failing to observe a road sign, even parking on double yellow lines, can all be carried out by an individual who is suffering from a depressive illness. It is not often advanced as a defence because the majority of offences against the Road Traffic Act are framed in such a way that such a defence would not be seriously considered by a responsible lawyer, even as a matter of mitigation. Most people charged with the minor offences which take place in their thousands upon our roads every day plead guilty and the penalty usually depends on the ability of the solicitor to present a credible and understandable plea in mitigation.

Depression in Shoplifting

The question of clinical depression at the time of the commission of a shoplifting offence is often raised. The famous play which was written some years ago about a black chiffon scarf brought this to public attention and, indeed, recently the untimely death of a well-known public figure prompted discussion at parliamentary level about the nature of the offence and what the attitudes of the court should be. The offence itself falls into several clear categories.

The first of these is the activity of the organised adult gang described in the Appendix (p. 454).

The second group is composed of bored teenagers who sweep through a store like Woolworths, where goods are openly displayed and where supervision at peak hours is extremely difficult. Again, this is organised theft and the answer does not lie within the province of the psychiatrist.

Finally, there are individuals who steal from shops and who are under stress of one kind or another. The author has had reason to examine approximately 50 cases over the past five years which have been referred to him by the magistrates of a large seaside resort.

In this group, females outnumber males accused of this offence by almost 10 to 1. The males, almost without exception, were charged with stealing alcohol of some kind or another. It was not difficult, from examination of the accused and perusal of their previous convictions, to establish that alcoholism was well established, and that because of social and economic pressures mounting on the individual he resorted, as part of his preoccupation with obtaining supplies, to theft from a supermarket. It was also sad to observe that the prognosis in these cases was poor, as the offender was usually beyond middle age and attempts made to treat him in the past both by inpatient admission to a suitable unit or contact with Alcoholics Anonymous had been unsuccessful. Inevitably these individuals go to prison for various terms, which is a sad reflection on society's inability as a whole to grapple successfully with the problem of alcoholism.

The female offenders fell into clearly defined groups. About half of them were habitual shoplifters. Previous convictions, in one case stretching over a period of 20 years, were on record. The goods stolen generally had some value to the individual, ranging from winter clothing at the upper end of the age range to cosmetics and costume jewellery at the lower end. The acts themselves were simple acts of dishonesty and none of these patients showed any clear-cut symptoms of depression, although many claimed they were depressed and indeed were receiving anti-depressants from their general practitioner. However, the author was never satisfied that a genuine depressive illness existed and was more inclined to the view that any depression was reactive to being arrested and charged, rather than an existing condition prior to the offence.

Another fairly large group were really tragic cases. These were single parents, usually with the responsibility for young children, whose efforts at raising children single-handed were totally inadequate. Even allowing for the fact that in most cases they were supported to a great extent by the social services, it was found on examination that their level of intelligence was below average and their ability to order their lives in a purposeful and reasonable way within the economic constraints imposed upon them was lacking. Nearly always they were in debt, either to the extent of serious rent arrears or gas and electricity bills outstanding to an amount whereby the respective boards were going to take action. Without exception the goods they stole were foodstuffs. Examination of the charge sheet showed that in many instances convenience foods and package foods, which are generally enjoyed by children, were the foods that were stolen. In other words, these somewhat inadequate mothers were making every attempt to protect their children and to ensure that they were well fed. The interviews were usually tearful and the individuals full of guilt and remorse. Arrogance was absent and resentment against the proprietors of the establishment concerned was lacking. Concern for their children was uppermost in their minds and as the majority were first offenders they viewed with considerable apprehension the judgement of the court. It was noted that attempts to reassure them along the lines that the magistrates had no intention of using their penal powers usually failed to achieve anything positive and, checking back with probation officers after the case, it was found that even after a kindly magistrate passed them over to the care of the probation officer they still could not believe their good fortune. While it is very early in terms of follow-up to decide whether or not these unfortunate ladies have made a satisfactory adjustment, at least the advice and guidance of a skilful probation officer has helped many of them to avoid further contact with the law. The majority of these patients had no conception of their legal rights under the Social Security Acts and in at least two cases, two years had elasped since their husbands had paid anything towards their maintenance in spite of court orders. It will be seen at once that the elimination of this offence, committed by this type of individual, is a matter for better education rather than psychiatric intervention.

Finally, there was the very small group, totalling approximately 10 per cent of the whole sample, in which one had to think very carefully about whether or not a genuine depressive illness was present at the time, and whether it would be appropriate for the court to deal with the matter as leniently as possible and refer the accused for psychiatric advice. The patients in this small group, without exception, were middle-aged. They indicated that menopausal symptoms were causing them great stress and this was substantiated by contact with each patient's general practitioner. What is particularly interesting is that one lady, who was under 40 and who had had irregular menses, flushes and marked irritability for at least two years, could not accept that she was menopausal because, as she put it, 'my periods are not yet finished'. The precise nature of hormonal imbalance at the menopause again is not a matter for this text but it is generally agreed after many years of debate, that the symptoms vary tremendously in intensity from a mild irritability and disturbance of equanimity, to florid symptoms of flooding, embarrassing flushing and mood swings of some intensity. In one case the patient had suffered from endogenous depression for many years. She described with great accuracy how periodically she developed sleeplessness, loss of appetite and irritability for no apparent cause, and that her symptoms subsided after a variable interval with no apparent intervention or action on her part. Another had been recently bereaved, and the loss of her husband had undoubtedly produced a reactive depression which she had felt to be a natural consequence of her loss.

A great deal of scorn has been heaped in the past on the picture of the middle-aged, menopausal woman who is charged with a single act of shoplifting and who is previously of impeccable character. The danger in cases of this kind is that the forensic psychiatrist, in whom familiarity can breed contempt, must be very careful not to overlook the possibility that the patient is depressed and that to establish this depression one must be patient, forbearing and tolerant. Most ladies of this type do not want any excuses offered as they are so anxious to avoid publicity. Without exception this group intended to plead guilty and were not at all keen about being legally represented. Consequently, care and patience are the virtues of the examining doctor in cases of this kind, but it must be said that a fatuous diagnosis of depression should never be advanced in cases where all the evidence shows the theft to be deliberate, in spite of the age and circumstances of the accused. A straightforward report to the court is much more effective in assisting the offender than an esoteric essay on psychopathology.

While the writer has experience of only one case, he has spoken to colleagues who have encountered the phenomenon, and the following is very rare indeed. There is a very small group of prosperous, middle-class and highly respected citizens who obtain some vicarious thrill from shoplifting. The case I was involved in concerned a professional person in a small village who was well known and respected throughout the whole community. The theft of half a pound of expensive cheese, a jar of rather exotic pickle and a packet of expensive biscuits was carried out more or less under the eye of the shop owner and it would seem to me that the thief was defying the shop owner to take action. Had this case come to court the offender would undoubtedly have been convicted and it would have attracted great publicity. The shop owner did not wish to prosecute and the thief agreed to take a psychological ticking off and was left in no doubt whatsoever as to what the result of any further dishonest act would be. Nothing similar has happened for four years. Why people court danger and professional ruin is not easily understood and one can only speculate, to quote an old saying, that the thrill is in the hunt, not the kill.

The views which have been expressed by well-known and sincere public figures, that a review of the law with regard to shoplifting should be undertaken and that in some way prosecution should be avoided, may perhaps be modified by a consideration of the matters that have been outlined above. Provided the accused person who is stealing either because of poverty or depressive illness is legally represented and that their legal adviser is aware of the fact that shoplifters fall into clearly recognised groups, then there is no reason to suspect that the decision of the magistrates will be unsympathetic. Their powers under Section 30 of the Magistrates' Courts Act, to remand individuals for psychiatric reports, are used very frequently in the catchment area of Risley Remand Centre and, provided a logical and trustworthy explanation can be offered to the Bench, the vast majority of these offenders are dealt with either by the making of a probation order or by a conditional discharge.

Depression in Homicide

Probably the most difficult cases with which the psychiatrist has to deal are cases of murder. By definition, murder is the unlawful killing of an individual with intent to cause him or her grievous bodily harm. This is an essential component of the charge and in order to prove it, a degree of intent, and ability to form an intent, must be shown by the prosecution. The crime itself is one at common law, although very frequently a warrant concerning an individual charge of murder is written as follows: 'That you, A.B., on such and such a day, did murder C.D., against the Peace of our Sovereign Lady the Queen, her Crown and Dignity.' From a legal point of view this is a very interesting indictment in that it illustrates that it is lawful to kill in wartime. In other words, when the Queen's peace is threatened or non-existent the defence of the realm is a lawful act.

The problem which the examining doctor has to face is usually one which involves the mental responsibility of the accused. Section 2 of the 1957 Homicide Act makes it clear that an individual who is mentally abnormal at the time of the offence to such a degree that his mental responsibility is substantially diminished, cannot be convicted of murder. However, if he indeed killed the victim, then he is guilty of manslaughter. This plea is often advanced by the defence and accepted by the Crown, and frequently it is advanced by the defence and contested by the Crown. The writer hopes here to offer some guidelines and to point out that the criteria for diminished responsibility in cases of depressive illness, must, by the very gravity of the offence, be set high, must be carefully considered and at no time should a trivial mental abnormality be advanced as an excuse. It is most important that all concerned with the examination of an individual charged with murder realise that there is a victim. A life has been taken and this must always be borne in mind. The rapport which develops between a doctor and his patient often puts the death of the victim out of perspective, and while one should never judge the act of an individual from a moral or personal point of view, it should always be remembered that a life has been lost as a direct result of a violent and unlawful act.

Murders, of course, vary tremendously in their types and nature. Murder comes about for many reasons. The most common type of murder is the domestic killing. This is the situation where a husband kills his wife or, conversely, a wife kills her husband. This section will be confined to domestic killing as in the experience of the writer it is this field which causes the most difficulty and gives rise to the most acute diagnostic problems. Frank psychotic illness, long established and well documented, presents little difficulty but psychoneurotic illness, inevitably of a depressive character, can be a different matter.

The background to domestic killing is depressingly similar in most instances. The common situations are that an unfaithful wife is killed by her husband's hand, or a drunken, brutal and sadistic husband meets his death at the hands of his wife. Usually, although not inevitably, the accused person is of previously good character and not known to the police. In cases of the wife being killed, as a general rule the home circumstances are good, the husband is a man of non-violent tendencies and the crime is unexpected. Very often in cases where the husband is killed the family are known to the social agencies, the husband very often has a criminal record, and social conditions are poor. The woman from social class I, II and III, who runs into violence in her marriage generally has sufficient wit and resource to consult a solicitor, or even the police. There is a tendency in social classes IV and V to mistrust the police, and to avoid seeking legal advice.

The police usually have no difficulty in completing their enquiries into domestic killings. Frequently the accused person telephones the police or surrenders to the police voluntarily. There is usually no question of denial. A voluntary statement is usually obtained without any difficulty whatsoever, and it is interesting to note that the vast majority of people accused of domestic murder speak highly of the police officers in charge of the case and of the kindness they receive at their hands.

The accused is usually remanded in custody and indeed it is misplaced kindness to remand anyone on a murder charge on bail. In all cases of murder there is a mandatory duty for psychiatric reports to be prepared for the Director of Public Prosecutions. The defence may also wish to take psychiatric advice. It is a feature of good psychiatric reporting that the report is based on a period of observation as well as examination. Doctors examining an accused person cannot forget their obligations and the need to test the statements of the patient – not to take the patient's account at face value. It is even more unwise in the case of the domestic killing. The suicide risk among people accused in this way is very high and they require to be observed very closely for some time after their arrest. Usually on reception into prison a patient, either male or female, speaks of being depressed. It is at this stage that the unwary can fall into the trap of assuming, without a detailed examination being carried out, that the depression existed prior to the offence. While this is often the case, it is not a matter which can ever be assumed.

An examination of a person accused of murder should be carried out as quickly as possible, preferably within hours of being received into custody. This allows an early assessment of the physical state of the accused. In the case of the battered wife who had turned on her husband it is essential that all bodily marks and injuries, if they exist, be clearly detailed and described. If at all possible they should be photographed. In the case of the male patient a similar exercise is often of value as many wives, particularly alcoholic ones, can be violent. In the best interests of the accused, their physical state and their general physical well being are sometimes of great importance in the diagnosis of depression.

From a personality point of view the husband who kills his wife falls into a fairly distinct pattern. One usually finds that he is a good provider; is a model father if there are children; that he has little, if any, experience of women outside the marriage; and there is strong evidence of sexual obsession with regard to his wife. Generally, the protests which he makes concerning the love he holds for his dead wife are indicative of very strong sexual feelings towards her which at times can verge on the morbid. Careful examination will usually disclose other obsessional features as well. Contact with his employer will show that he is punctilious in his attendance at work, a long-serving employee and that his work record over the years has been good. He is usually very neat in his appearance, tidy in his habits and meticulous with his personal hygiene. There is very seldom a history of excessive drinking or drug abuse. What is even more startling, in the case of the unfaithful wife, is his knowledge of his wife's behaviour going back over a considerable period in time. In a case I once dealt with, the husband had been aware of his wife's infidelity with at least four men and had forgiven her on three occasions.

Turning to the female accused of killing her husband, one finds a passive and generally inadequate type of personality. She is usually a woman from social classes IV and V who has married young and who was probably pregnant at the time of her marriage. She has several children and has gradually been over-whelmed by deteriorating social and economic circumstances within her home. A substantial history of the husband's violence towards her can be corroborated by members of her family, and even on occasion by members of the deceased's family. Clear evidence is usually forthcoming about the husband's drunkenness, violence and general sloth. Affection between the couple has been absent for some considerable time and the wife is deriving no pleasure or tenderness from sexual relations.

In both sexes there may also be at times a history of para-suicide. In my experience both male and female patients have taken an overdose or carried out some other act mainly to draw attention to the problem, rather than as a deliberate act of self-destruction. Occasionally one is informed of a domestic killing and learns that the accused is being treated in intensive care following an attempt on his or her own life, after the act of murder.

The word 'depression' is used so loosely in these days that it can be almost a term of abuse. However, as is well known, there is a definite spectrum or cluster of symptoms in this illness, and it is most important that these are clearly established beyond reasonable doubt. The neat classification of the type of depression – endogenous, reactive or whatever – is not so unimportant as to be completely overlooked, but it is more vital to the diagnosis of the case to establish that a depressive illness pre-dated the crime, without too much speculation as to the precise aetiology. In some cases clear evidence will be forthcoming that the accused has a cyclothymic type of personality with mood swings tending towards clinical depression for no apparent cause. On the other hand no such evidence may be forthcoming from any assessment of the pre-morbid personality. Consequently it is appropriate to remember that the pre-trial psychiatric examinations are a diagnostic exercise designed to establish a mental abnormality – namely depression – without esoteric speculations, which the trial judge may not understand, still less a lay jury. The doctor who is prepared to say that at the time of the killing the accused person was depressed, must understand that he may well be required to give that evidence on oath and while the taking of the oath is usually a matter of great significance to medical men, very few people really comprehend that the key phrase in the oath is the middle one. In other words, one must tell the whole truth, not only that part of the truth which may be of assistance to the patient.

The following examples illustrate, in a general way, the social circumstances and pathological features of the domestic killing in which depressive illness is present in the accused and there is an absence of planning, pre-meditation and even malice.

Case A

Male. Aged 35. Civil Servant. Married 11 years. Three children, ages 8, 6 and 4. Home owner. Proficient and well-liked employee having achieved two promotions during his career. Wife 3 years younger. Housewife, with no full-time occupation. Information from neighbours and friends gave no indication of serious tension within the marriage. Wife actively engaged with local drama group. Affair with member of the same group begun approximately six months before her death. Husband became suspicious when wife began to refuse intercourse which was something unusual. There was no reason to disbelieve the husband when he described his wife as highly sexed and while this could not be completely confirmed, it cannot be denied. Some three months before the wife's death, her husband was told by a friend that the affair was in progress. He did not tackle his wife at this stage, but went to see her lover, and in a very calm and reasonable way put his point of view. The lover then agreed to stop seeing the wife but was obviously either unwilling or unsuccessful in this venture because the relationship continued. One evening when the wife was ostensibly at a rehearsal the husband followed her, leaving the children in charge of his sister, in whom he had confided. He saw the wife enter her lover's car and returned home. He pretended to be asleep when his wife arrived home and did not discuss the matter with her until the following afternoon. At this stage the wife indicated that she wished to leave him, take the children with her and marry her lover. Her husband then consulted his general practitioner who offered him advice but wisely refrained from prescribing psychotropic drugs. However, the husband became preoccupied with his wife's conduct, becoming withdrawn and ruminative. He saw his brother and sister much more frequently than in the past. He would pour out his troubles to anyone who would listen and who he saw as someone who could help. However, he rejected any suggestion of legal advice because his lack of insight and judgement prevented him from analysing his situation in a logical way.

This situation persisted for some 4 to 6 weeks prior to his wife's death. The husband's obsessional nature was very apparent during this time and at every available opportunity he would challenge his wife about her intentions, although he made no threats, as far as we could ascertain. It was at this time that enquiries showed that his work was not up to standard, that he was becoming more irritable and his brother gave information to the effect that the husband came to him on several occasions and wept copiously as he discussed his affairs. Finally, after one altercation with his wife, he returned to the bedroom where he had been sleeping apart from his wife for some six weeks, took some Valium – about 20 mg – and went down to the kitchen. In the kitchen he selected a knife, went upstairs to his wife's bedroom and killed her with a single stab wound. He cleaned her body, changed her nightdress and had intercourse with her after death. He then returned to his bedroom, dressed himself, went downstairs and telephoned his brother, who came over to his house. The accused then dialled 999 and summoned the police and the ambulance. The investigating police officers reported him as tearful and ashamed but fully co-operative subsequent to his arrest. No ill effects were noted by the police surgeon as being due to Valium.

Case B

Female. Aged 36. A housewife, married for 18 years. Six children of the marriage ranging from 18 years to several months. Married when 4 months pregnant, living in appalling social conditions in a large conurbation and overwhelmed by financial problems, which had been present most of her married life. Husband known to be a violent man, a heavy drinker and with a criminal record, including prison sentences, for violence. The wife had suffered beatings at his hands for many years but had never taken an action except to complain to the district midwife following the birth of her youngest child. The district midwife informed the social services; a social worker was sent round, but achieved nothing at all. In fairness, the main reason for this was that the wife was literally terrified of her husband and anxious to avoid further trouble. As her husband's drunkenness increased with the passage of time, the wife's routine, particularly in the evenings towards closing time, became almost a ritual. She made every effort to get the younger children to bed and encouraged her 18-year-old son and 15-year-old daughter to either go to her mother's or her sister's on the nights she knew her husband would come home drunk. She was tense, frightened and totally unable to deal with these situations. She had been seeing her general practitioner for several years and was being prescribed tricyclic antidepressants, and sleeping pills. On the night her husband was killed she was feeling particularly low. He arrived home about midnight, began to verbally abuse her, accused her of being a near-prostitute (an interesting facet of alcoholic behaviour) and threatened to hurt her. He struck her several times with his fists, she retreated into the kitchen, selected a carving knife, re-entered the living room and stabbed him several times. At this stage she went across the road to a neighbour, who summoned the police. The husband was dead on arrival in hospital. The investigating police officers reported her as apathetic and hesitant, but fully co-operative.

Both patients were charged with murder and the police were correct at this stage to lay this particular charge. In the case of the husband, the mere fact of going downstairs and selecting a weapon – as was admitted by the accused in his voluntary statement – was sufficient for a senior detective to consider and establish intent. The same circumstances applied to the wife although a defence of provocation might well have succeeded at her trial. However, examination of both accused showed firm evidence of depression. In the male patient, agitation, preoccupation and despair seemed the predominant features, while in the other case, apathy, indifference and fear were predominant.

In each case it was agreed by both examining doctors, one of whom had been instructed by the defence, that on the balance of probabilities the responsibility of the accused was substantially diminished as a result of a depressive illness.

Histories of this nature can be obtained on many occasions, and a careful evaluation of the facts can lead the examining doctor to honourably report that at the time the mental responsibility of the accused was substantially diminished. However, it is important that the symptoms of depression in such cases are properly established and evaluated. The classic triad of disturbance of sleep, disturbance of appetite and restriction of thought content must be elicited carefully. Direct questioning in cases of this kind is not fair to either party as, no matter what compassion may be directed towards the accused the interests of justice demand that justice be done. In other words, if the examining doctor is not satisfied that a degree of depression sufficient substantially to diminish responsibility is present, then he must be prepared to say so. The most important word in Section 2 of the 1957 Homicide Act is the word 'substantially'. Substantially means less than complete, but on the other hand it means a lot more than a little. It is somewhere in between, and the definition of the word has proved very difficult in certain cases when the trial judge has summed up; indeed it has proved difficult even to the Lord Justices of Appeal. However, it must always be remembered that even although diminished responsibility is a matter to be raised by the defence, the burden of proof is less than is normally applied. The Crown must prove its case 'beyond reasonable doubt'. In diminished responsibility cases, the burden of proof is on the defence and only goes as far as 'on the balance of probabilities'. However, this should never be interpreted in a careless or reputation-seeking way.

In Case A His Lordship passed a sentence of two years' imprisonment. On passing sentence he observed that it was the least sentence he could pass viewing all the circumstances of the case, but he was satisfied that the accused's remorse for his action was genuine and that it would never have taken place had he been in a normal frame of mind.

In Case B His Lordship made a probation order for 3 years. He felt that the accused had suffered greatly over the years and he took this into account, but above all, he took into account the possibility that a fairly effective family unit might be destroyed forever were he to pass a sentence of imprisonment.

It should be observed that both cases were tried by different judges, both of whom have a reputation for severity where the case demands it, and in spite of all that is said to the contrary most High Court judges are considerate and courteous in their dealings with the mentally abnormal offender.

The two cases which have been outlined in some detail are typical of the many individuals charged with murder and who are found to be suffering from depression, and have passed through Risley Remand Centre in the last 15 years. Precise arithmetical details of what exactly happened to whom are not of great interest to the average reader and as statistics they are not particularly valuable because they are applied to one part of the country and not to the whole. However, no case has been the subject of a hospital order from Risley Remand Centre, where no evidence of a psychosis existed. Psychotic depression and the transfer of the accused person to a special hospital under Section 60/65 of the

Mental Health Act, 1959 has only taken place once in the last eight years, in the writer's recollection. The majority of depressed individuals recover rapidly without active intervention. In many cases the only medication which is prescribed is a sedative for the first night or two that they are in custody. The clamour for bail is often not in the best interests of the patient. No prison medical officer is going to oppose bail for the sake of mere opposition, as even one less inmate in his overcrowded establishment can be a relief, but the necessity for careful assessment and, above all, observation of the patient during a remand period cannot be overemphasised. Many solicitors feel they have a duty to apply for bail and indeed, in many cases it is granted. It is much more advisable to give the medical staff of a Remand Centre or Remand Prison time to properly assess a depressed patient than for that patient to be released on conditions of bail which contain no proviso for psychiatric care. Many individuals who feel strongly about bail being a right, and the writer includes himself in this group, are well advised to be cautious in the early stages and by consultation with the remand centre authorities a successful application can usually be made at the committal stage.

It should also not be forgotten that there are a few cases of depression where it is necessary to treat the individual intensively and from a policy point of view it is not a useful exercise to use electroconvulsive therapy (ECT) on any remand prisoner who is depressed. The ability to recall a sequence of events may make all the difference between a verdict of guilty to murder or guilty to manslaughter and the effect of ECT on memory is well known. Such cases, as in the writer's experience it has been necessary to treat, are approximately 10 to 20 per cent of all receptions and all of them, without exception, have responded to the use of antidepressant drugs in therapeutic doses. Each doctor, of course, has his favourite and the old axiom if you believe in a particular treatment it will have a beneficial effect on the patient is well illustrated. What is more interesting is that it is possible to withdraw drugs completely long before the individual goes to trial. Any doctor having charge of a patient who is to face a trial for murder and in whom the statutory defence of diminished responsibility can be properly advanced should make every effort to produce his patient in court in an alert, balanced and drug-free frame of mind. Depressive illness, no matter what its circumstances, is usually eminently treatable with patience, care, advice and support, and this should always be remembered by those who are involved in any way with an offender who is obviously ill.

In cases where there is overwhelming evidence of the accused suffering from a depressive illness and the medical evidence is not contested, then the proceedings should not take long. However, a situation can arise where a depression is advanced by the defence, and their medical experts are opposed by those instructed by the Crown. This can be a difficult situation but it is one which the examining doctor, from either side, may well have to face. The course of the trial then takes on a somewhat different aspect. Generally speaking, the defence does not contest the facts in that the accused did kill the victim and the situation revolves round the question whether or not the jury take the opinion of the defence or the opinion of the Crown. It is most important for medical witnesses in this situation to carefully consider all the aspects of the case. They must carefully differentiate between unhappiness, which is the lot of us all from time to time, and a genuine depressive illness. The establishment or otherwise of an illness in the accused can be firmly proved only by careful, detailed examination and corroboration of fact. This means a careful perusal of the witnesses' statements in the case, the necessity of speaking to relatives or friends and even, on occasion, travelling to the scene of the crime in order to get the feel of the household and some indication of the personality both of the deceased and the accused. All help will be offered to the doctor involved in such a case by the authorities, and one need not be afraid to carry out extensive enquiries. Indeed such enquiries can only assist the practitioner concerned to form a firm opinion.

One of the most important diagnostic procedures, however, is a period of observation by trained staff, preferably in a penal institution, who will report on a daily basis regarding the behaviour of the accused. It is very seldom that a patient charged with murder is psychotically depressed. As was indicated earlier, these cases usually present no difficulty and the value of observation is, strangely enough, in psychoneurotic depression, in recording the illness remitting spontaneously. Time and time again it is necessary to take full suicide precautions on the patient's initial reception into prison and it can be quite fascinating to see the improvement in the patient as the days go by. There are usually several reasons for this, not the least of which is the advice given by legal advisers. The patient's solicitor can often be a very great comfort to him, and in fairness to the legal profession the vast majority of solicitors attend to their duties punctiliously. The contact with other individuals who may be in the same position; the pouring out of their troubles to a sympathetic doctor; and the informal approach of prison hospital staffs all contribute to an increased sense of well-being in the accused. It is very seldom necessary to use antidepressant drugs or any other method of relieving the depression. It is also fair to say that the problem which has dominated the thinking of the accused for a considerable period of time, has been solved, albeit in a terrible way.

At the conclusion of any case where a defence of diminished responsibility on the grounds of a depressive illness, has succeeded, the trial judge has to pass sentence. In cases such as I have attempted to describe, the making of a hospital order is seldom, if ever, justified. By the time the case is over the patient is no longer depressed and there is really nothing in a psychopathological sense left to treat. Judges have a public duty to do, and very often a sentence of imprisonment is passed on a husband. This sentence varies but the tariff is usually between 18 months and three years depending on all the circumstances. In the case of wives, very often a custodial sentence is not imposed at all. In cases where there are children, and the trial judge is satisfied that the situation of the accused is unlikely to arise again, he very often makes a probation order in order that the family can be re-united. However, it is not for doctors to criticise sentencing policy. Nor is it for doctors to make impracticable recommendations to the court. So often a recommendation is made which is so fatuous when all the circumstances of the case are taken into account, that the individual may end up worse off than if the recommendation had not been made.

In cases of this kind the doctor's sole responsibility is one of diagnosis; the presentation of the case is a matter for learned counsel. The sentence of the court is a matter for His Lordship. Doctors who become experienced in this field of work, develop instincts which can often assist an accused person and provided the doctor maintains a reputation for honesty, he will be listened to with courtesy and appreciation. It is always useful for the forensic psychiatrist, or indeed the general psychiatrist involved in criminal matters, to remember that the only thing he has is his integrity, and once that is lost, so is his reputation.

EDITOR'S CONTRIBUTION

Manic Depressive Illness

The earlier parts of this chapter have been concerned principally with the form of depression usually called unipolar or reactive, that is resulting from situational crises. There are other people who have a constitutional predisposition to mood swings throughout their lives. Such cyclothymic personalities may have periods of mania, or the lesser version, hypomania, for a few months, then return to normal mood states even without treatment, often going on later the same year to a period of depression, the natural history of which is six to nine months, modifiable with treatment. These mood swings can occur without environmental provocation, and such unfortunate people may not know with what mood state they will wake up in the morning, thus making it very difficult to plan activities. Suicide is common. Treatment with lithium is particularly effective in this endowed personality type.

Mania and hypomania are mental abnormalities particularly likely to bring the patient into conflict with the law. Such people are madly merry, over-active by day and busy by night, with great numbers of new things urgently to do, usually involving them in clashes with relatives or next-door neighbours.

Case C

Fifty-year-old Mrs W. was forwarded to my clinic by the local police, having been arrested on the Australian Gold Coast beach for running naked along the water's edge, drying her night clothes in the air as she went. She had also made obscene remarks to young men as she passed them on their way to surf, suggesting that they were not up to the mark for failing to have intercourse with her at that beautiful time of the day. The police were prepared to drop charges if she took treatment. She had a long history of mood swings, and for one month past, as owner of a boarding house, had raised all her occupants at 4.00 am to go surfing with her. She had started to write three books, had broken certain windows in her house 'to let more air in', made long phone calls to relatives early in the morning, and brought traffic to a screeching halt because she was too busy to wait for traffic lights to change. She spent very freely and recklessly, dominated her friends and neighbours, and had crashed her car. At interview, she wept crocodile tears as she described her troubles, talked incessantly, twitched nervously. She had little complaint, but her daughter had obviously had enough. Replaced on lithium and treated with haloperidol she soon recovered, but two months later reappeared at the clinic in normal mood state, saying she had stopped her lithium because 'Doctor, you couldn't refuse me my "highs" now I'm good could you?'

Case D

Mrs W. rarely had severe depressive downswings, but Mr T. did. His was a severe agitated psychosis and, aged 60 in excellent physical health, he had a one-week history of sudden onset of agitation, weeping and depression and was severely suicidal. He was also the subject of police charges for dangerous driving, having agitatedly rushed out of his house after a row with his wife, collided with a car two blocks away and severely injured an old lady. He had recently retired to the Gold Coast from Brisbane where he had been a bank manager, but recurrent mood swings had led to an early retirement on medical grounds. On examination he was upset, severely depressed, hopeless as to the future, had lost weight, lost appetite and slept badly, waking early in the morning. He responded rapidly to tricyclic drugs and one month later was fit and well, although there were persistent financial problems dating well back into the past, and discussions were opened to make his wife administrator of the joint estate. A series of psychiatric court reports enabled him to avoid imprisonment.

Depressive illnesses can be arranged as a continuum, at one end of which are the reactive depressions which occur when a series of overwhelming catastrophes drive even strong men to drink and despair. At the other end of the continuum are those illnesses occurring 'out of the blue' without any apparent environmental provocation, in people with a strong constitutional tendency to recurrent depressive and possibly manic illnesses. The majority of illnesses are somewhere between these two poles. All are responsive to a greater or lesser extent to the new range of trycyclic, quadricyclic and monoamine oxidase drugs. The natural history of a depressive illness is some six to nine months, drugs being necessary to suppress, but not abolish the process. Obviously milder illnesses recover quicker, but for those with recurrent episodes lithium may be started, sometimes for life. Manic episodes are shorter in duration, drugs are needed to control the episodes for the four to eight weeks, and can be reduced thereafter as the natural history finishes.

Paranoia

Morbid suspicion is common in many mentally abnormal offenders. Not without reason they may feel that 'the police are always picking on them'. When such morbid suspicion dominates behaviour that subjects are not amenable to reason and fly in the face of reality then paranoia can be diagnosed. Morbid suspicion may occur in confused states such as delirium tremens, alcoholic psychosis, dementia in manic depressive illness (as described above) or in deaf old people. Deafness and blindness in old people with mental deterioration is particularly liable to lead to misinterpretation and minor crime, yet deafness, depression and paranoia are all eminently treatable. Paranoid personalities are also found among mentally abnormal offenders. After a lifetime of deprivation, poor treatment and lack of love, exacerbated by alcohol, their tendency to violence does not decrease with age as happens with most immature and unstable personalities, but becomes intensified by factors such as a degree of alcoholic dementia, hypoxia due to over-smoking, police harassment, and loss of friends and relatives to talk to and to reason with them. Living in a foreign environment can worsen the situation.

Case E

Mr Z. was a 72-year-old Yugoslav. One in six Australians are immigrants; in retirement areas such as the Gold Coast one in four come from other states. Mr Z. had been a political activist all his life, harried by police of all sorts of hues. When his immigrant daughter and her new husband offered him a Gold Coast home he was pleased to leave, and the Yugoslav authorities were surprisingly swift and helpful. The Gold Coast was not up to expectations. He still had trouble with the police who failed to understand his accent, the bank was unhelpful about his money, he was arrested, complained violently to fellow Aussies in a bar. When Mr Z. broke up his daughter's home after returning drunk, his Australian son-in-law had had enough. The local authority was keen to use the state mental hospital, but eventually a nursing home was found, his mental state improved on regular tranquillisers, injected monthly due to variable mood state. Not a happy end, but at least in Mr Z.'s case treatment of his alcoholism and his over-smoking was possible; and the imposition of a routine allowed resolution of the crisis and its aftermath.

Paraphrenia is a paranoiac state occurring particularly in older females, often living alone, perhaps partly deaf and with increasing eccentricities. The syndrome is known in literature as the old lady of impeccable past who keeps an immaculate house, but develops increasing suspicions of her neighbours, withdraws into her garden and looks under her bed for burglars.

Professor Martin Roth (1981) has made a special study of paranoid psychoses which he calls 'late paraphrenia'. He says the four main clues are:

1   The presence of well described paranoid delusions fortified by 'reasonable' observations;
2   It becomes obvious following an abrupt crisis;
3   The person's previous personality is often cold, suspicious, and lonely;
4   Deafness is common (40 per cent of all those over 60 are deaf to some degree), as is evidence of past strokes etc., which reduce mental ability.

Roth finds marked improvement on phenothiazines. The illness occurs in over 1 per cent of the general population over 65, and over 5 per cent of admissions to a psychiatric ward. Although police or solicitors may be called in as a result of an attack on neighbours, sexual accusation, boundary dispute or non-payment of debt, such people are rarely dangerous. They may be a long-term nuisance to courts and police alike, since insight deteriorates.

The views expressed by the author in this chapter are not necessarily those of the Home Office.

REFERENCE

Roth, M. (1981) Diagnosis of dementia in late and middle life. In *Epidemiology of Dementia.* Mortimer, J. A. & Schuman, L. M. (eds). London: Oxford University Press.

11

Mentally Abnormal Offenders in Prison

William K. Lawson

HYSTERICAL REACTIONS IN PRISON

Even to the most case-hardened criminal the passing of a prison sentence is a traumatic experience. Loss of liberty, a controlled and disciplined environment, and the regulation of his or her life to the degree necessary to maintain order, are factors which depress the prisoner; and while a vast number of sentenced individuals accept their punishment with philosophical resignation, there remains a small group who are completely unpredictable in their response to a judicial decision involving imprisonment.

Some of these individuals vent their immediate frustration once and for all by a tirade of abuse either directed at the trial judge or their unfortunate barrister. Some, in the interval between going from the court to the prison, will vent their abuse on the prison officer in charge of the escort or the police officers in charge of the case. By and large the matter ends there and it will probably come as a surprise to many readers to learn that the vast majority of individuals who are sentenced to imprisonment enter the institution in a perfectly rational way and settle down to what is essentially a very simple routine, with clear-cut ground rules and above all a regime, which by its very nature, makes little demands on the individual, provided he accepts the need to maintain standards.

The sentenced prisoner is usually easier to handle from the point of view of discipline and control than a remand prisoner. On the face of it this statement seems absurd, but nevertheless it is true. Any individual charged with an offence, who is remanded in custody to await trial, is under pressure which is mostly brought about by the uncertainty of his position. He may well intend to plead guilty, but what he does not know is what sentence he will receive. He may be firmly determined to plead not guilty in spite of incontrovertible evidence against him. A remand establishment can be a volatile place. The nature of the prison rules demands that certain individuals charged with particular offences shall come under psychiatric observation, and a great deal of difficulty is experienced by the medical staff in these cases. However, in addition, the unpredictability of certain individuals can bring about a series of reactions which are essentially hysterical in nature, and which cause great alarm to all concerned.

Hysteria, as such, is always difficult to define. Perhaps the best definition is to say that it is an overwhelming desire to escape from one's immediate environment. By accepting this premise one must automatically consider the alternative,

154

yet similar, type of behaviour. That is to say, in addition to a genuine hysterical reaction, the practitioner working in a penal institution must also be prepared to deal with malingering, and it is sometimes very difficult to separate the two. Colleagues who are called in to penal establishments, and whose main work is within the National Health Service framework, sometimes react a little angrily when an experienced prison medical officer firmly and without equivocation comes down on the side of malingering rather than hysteria. It must be remembered that as a general rule recidivists, that is, people who come into conflict with the law to a degree whereby they are imprisoned on more than one or two occasions, are basically unstable, feckless and idle. This must not be interpreted as a harsh or unjust judgement. It is an unfortunate fact of life. Such assistance and guidance as can be offered to people of this type must be given in a totally detached and objective way. It is very hard for an honest and well-motivated doctor to appreciate that there are times when his function must, to a greater or lesser degree, be a disciplinary one. He must preserve the life and well-being of his patient, yet at the same time he must not encourage him to continue behaving in a way that can lead to his own self-destruction.

The majority of hysterical acts carried out by prison inmates, either on remand or during sentence, are trivial. The reasons for the majority of these acts are usually perfectly clear. One of the main difficulties that the prison medical service face in their daily task is the need to remind themselves constantly that the men and women in their care are relatively isolated. Problems which, in the normal course of events, would present no difficulty in solving assume gigantic proportions to an unstable individual who cannot obtain an immediate answer. Much of the criticism directed against the penal system is ill-judged in the sense that the complainant has never worked in a penal establishment, and is unaware that, in order to maintain a reasonable and humane level of containment, the rules must be applied fairly across the board and with few exceptions. It must also never be forgotten that rejection by those nearest and dearest to the inmate can happen, and a letter from a wife indicating that she is instituting divorce proceedings, for example, can produce a state of affairs which is sudden, dramatic and could possibly have a fatal outcome. It would be perhaps appropriate at this stage to deal with attempted suicide in the penal setting, as probably this is the most common threat the practitioner has to face and one which, if it is successful, leads to adverse publicity and criticism, sometimes of a hostile nature.

Attempted Suicide

Threats of suicide are a fairly common occurrence, both in the remand and the custodial situation. The reasons for this are numerous. Rejection by a wife, threats by other inmates, loss of privileges because of some misdemeanour, a sudden realisation of the length of the sentence and, in a few cases, a genuine depressive illness can all lead to a suicidal impulse. However, it must be stressed that depression as a clinical entity is an infrequent finding in cases of this kind. Very often the injuries inflicted are trivial. For example, men must be allowed to shave. The control of razor blades in closed training or remand establishments is very strict indeed. However, no human system is perfect and very frequently a patient scratches his wrists with a razor blade. These injuries are usually trivial and very seldom require suturing. In fact, a useful diagnostic pointer as to whether or not the attempt is really genuine is simple inspection of the wound. Superficial scratches which require nothing more than a dry dressing are usually not indicative of a suicide attempt. On the other hand, a deep and penetrating wound which may have cut a blood vessel, and indeed may require transfer to the local general hospital for transfusion, should always be taken seriously and a full psychiatric assessment of this type of patient must be carried out as quickly as possible. Other methods include the preparation of a noose which is left in such a position that it will be easily found by staff before any act takes place. Threats in writing to relatives and friends are also fairly frequent, but the inmate knows perfectly well, if he is in a secure establishment, that the letter is going to be censored and the matter referred to the medical staff.

Examination of the patient with a trivial injury or one who has apparently taken steps to prepare a suicide attempt generally shows a tearful, unhappy and miserable man. It demands great patience at times to find out the precise reasons why he has behaved in this way. Very often there is no obvious psychiatric reason for this behaviour and the gesture is attention-seeking. This somewhat emotive phrase tends to be interpreted in a derogatory sense but frequently a perfectly genuine reason for the inmate's desire to see higher authority emerges. He may be under threat from his fellow inmates. He may be genuinely seeking a reconciliation with his spouse. He may be concerned at the fact that he has not heard from his family for some time. On the other hand he may wish a change of environment from the ordinary location to the hospital wing where life as a rule is easier, slower and more pleasant. All in all the feeble attempt at suicide, or the obviously contrived attempts, are fairly easy to deal with and experience shows that the individual who genuinely wishes to take his own life does so with dramatic suddenness and with no warning whatsoever.

Swallowing

This problem, while relatively uncommon, is one that can cause great concern. In all cases these individuals have marked hysterical features in their personality, and the articles they manage to swallow are amazing. Knives, forks, spoons, razor blades, lavatory chains, tooth brushes, pieces of plastic and almost any article that can get into the mouth can reach the alimentary tract. A vast number of them are known to the prison authorities as they are generally habitual offenders convicted of relatively minor offences, and swallowing is a habit they have been indulging in for many years. In many cases, they have carried out acts of this kind long before they came to prison, and careful research will probably show that this type of behaviour began at some time in their early adolescence. Their reasons are usually clear. They wish to leave the prison and are prepared to take considerable risks in order to achieve this. However, the management of these cases demands self-control on behalf of the doctor concerned and it is clear that his first step must be to establish the truth or otherwise of what the patient claims to have done. A straight X-ray of the abdomen establishes this fact beyond any doubt provided the object is radio-opaque. It is at this stage that the need for self-control and calmness on behalf of everyone concerned is vital. Expressions of alarm and fear on behalf of the medical staff will only exacerbate a situation which, in the vast majority of cases, nature will deal with in her own way. Razor blades have passed through the alimentary tract without any difficulty whatsoever and the normal action of the digestive juices will take the edge off most sharp implements. The danger, of course, is penetration of the gut and the difficulty in which this can place a surgical colleague. No surgeon likes operating in these conditions but, on the other hand, one must strike a balance between what is clinically necessary and what is clinically desirable. It is essential for the sake of the patient that he or she learns at once that the act of swallowing does not necessarily mean immediate surgery.

One is also faced with the problem of X-rays. The habit of daily X-rays in order to assess the progress of a foreign body through the alimentary tract is to be deplored and, particularly in the case of the female patients, should not be carried out. It is therefore obvious that careful examination of the abdomen at frequent intervals is required, together with the routine recording of temperature and pulse. From a dietary point of view the patient should be offered a bland diet, no quasi-disciplinary measures such as cotton wool sandwiches should be undertaken and provided all those concerned remain calm it is remarkable how often the situation can resolve itself within 48 to 96 hours. Of course, any evidence of peritoneal irritation should be a matter for a surgical opinion and this must never be delayed. However, it cannot be stressed too strongly that immediate surgery without any indication of peritonitis will almost inevitably lead to a repetition of the act. Successful treatment of the hysterical swallower depends on self-control on behalf of the medical adviser and a modicum of good fortune that the object will be passed naturally. This usually has the effect on the patient of persuading him or her that the action does not necessarily mean removal from the establishment. In the habitual swallower the dangers of excessive zeal with regard to surgical intervention are very real. Most experienced prison doctors have seen an abdomen with several surgical scars where exploratory operations have been carried out with a view to recovery of a foreign body. The dangers of adhesions, leading to complicated intestinal obstruction requiring urgent surgical intervention and with a grave risk to the life of the patient, cannot be overemphasised.

Self-mutilation

This is perhaps the most tragic and heart-rending act with which the practitioner can be faced. Generally speaking these patients are young, female and totally damaged in a psychological sense. Almost without exception their history reveals a rejected and unwanted child, who, during her formative years, has been shunted from pillar to post and whose life exhibits no continuity in care, teaching or affection. Of limited intelligence and ability, clear evidence is usually available from early adolescence on, that all the training in the world will never fit them to live an independent existence. Without exception they have spent periods either in a mental handicap or general psychiatric hospital. Their behaviour within these institutions is appalling, particularly with regard to aggressive outbursts against the staff, and their management without secure conditions is an impossible task. As young women they have never learned to make the best of their appearance and they are regarded with loathing by their fellow inmates. There is, of course, no justification for this attitude but nevertheless it exists and it cannot be eliminated. The staff of any penal institution can be tried to the limits of endurance by patients of this type and immediately they come into the clandestine possession of any sharp object they can inflict up to twenty severe lacerations on all parts of their body. The principal target, if the patient is right-handed, of course, is the left arm, but instances of mutilation of the breasts, the abdomen and the vulva have been noted. In other words, the patient is in such a hysterical state of mind that she is totally rejecting her own identity; and practitioners faced with a need to preserve life and the degree of control and supervision which must be exercised are compelled to impose a restriction of privileges, which cannot improve the situation. Promises of future good behaviour are absolutely worthless in cases of this kind and amazingly, in spite of repeated acts which to all intents and purposes are, in effect, immolation, death is relatively unknown. When the actual act is taking place it has to be conceded that the patient is in a highly abnormal frame of mind as he or she appears to be relatively insensitive to pain. A sharp knife accidentally cutting the finger of a normal person causes intense momentary pain, but patients of this type can inflict up to twenty wounds, each of which may require suturing, without any apparent distress. In the light of present psychiatric knowledge there is no specific treatment available, and to drug such patients into submission is neither ethically nor morally justified. This type of case is a living example of the limitations of our knowledge, and demonstrates the need for all who are concerned in their medical management to understand that there are certain patients who are beyond reach with regard to their behaviour, when they enter a hysterical phase.

Food Refusal

Food refusal, or hunger striking, as it is inaccurately described, can be a difficult problem. It is not proposed to discuss those whose refusal of food is politically motivated. Individuals of this kind are usually in full possession of their faculties and are so involved in the cause which they represent that their refusal of nourishment is clearly designed to obtain a specific end which is completely outside of the control of the prison staff. However, there are those who refuse food for personal reasons and reasons which need not become public knowledge. It must not be assumed that the refusal of food for a reason which on the face of it does not seem terribly important, is not a matter of concern. However, the cases of food refusal which the prison doctor has to deal with generally fall into two distinct groups. There are those who are attempting to manipulate the environment and whose rage at some decision which is not in their favour makes them refuse food. The individual who refuses his meals is noted from first refusal in that the regulations insist that a meal which is returned uneaten is properly recorded in the returned food book. The medical staff are usually alerted within 24 hours and it is at this stage that the assessment of the individual must take place. Generally speaking the reason is trivial in the extreme and can usually be resolved within a very short time by explanation. Hostility towards the inmate is a valueless exercise but at the same time an overly sympathetic approach is also unsuccessful. The inmate should be told that in the absence of mental illness, and since his judgement is unimpaired, the conscience of the doctor will not allow him to carry out the degrading task of feeding an individual by force until such time as he especially requests help. Artificial feeding is fraught with difficulties and in the past was a distasteful and humiliating experience, for all concerned. The management of a case of this kind turns once more on the question of self-control and determination on the part of the practitioner involved. If his conscience will not allow him to feed an individual artificially, then he must be prepared to put his point across to the patient consistently and without threat. The elimination of the cause of food refusal should be sought. This does not necessarily mean that the patient will be allowed his own way. What it does mean is that a clarification of the reasons for the original decision can be offered and the assistance of the staff should be sought. Very often careful enquiries will produce a member of the uniformed staff whom the patient trusts and whose assistance can very often end the demonstration. Those medical practitioners who may in the future work in prison, should always bear in mind that knowledge of the inmate and of his potential is at its most accurate amongst those officers who have day-to-day contact with him. It is also essential in the management of this type of case that the advice of a consultant psychiatrist and a consultant physician from the National Health Service should be sought at an early stage and their opinions and advice recorded.

The circumstances outlined above represent circumstances in which food may be refused by someone who is not mentally ill. Unfortunately prisons have to receive many individuals who are mentally disturbed. Paranoid schizophrenia may be a cause of law-breaking with subsequent admission to prison, at least in the early stages of the judicial process. Not infrequently the delusional system expresses itself in the belief that the patient's food is poisoned. One is faced, therefore, with a situation whereby the refusal to take nourishment is not designed to redress some real or imagined grievance but is a symptom of a serious mental illness, which, left untreated, will lead to the early death of the patient. All experienced practitioners who have worked in the penal setting will agree that the rapidity with which a mentally abnormal offender who is refusing food declines is very much more than the speed at which the mentally normal inmate declines. Within a very short time the practitioner can be faced with a totally dehydrated, deluded and hallucinated patient whose management, unless rigorously adhered to, can cause a tragedy. The immediate requirement in such a case must be an attempt to restore the mental equilibrium to such an extent that the patient will at least take fluid by mouth. The use of phenothiazines is sometimes very effective but more often than not the assistance of an NHS colleague is required. That there are difficult ethical questions in this situation goes without saying. The very vexed question of consent springs to mind and it must be remembered that no practitioner should embark on such measures without consulting a colleague of senior standing, or at least of equal standing. If the practitioners concerned are acting primarily to save life and neither the patient nor any relative who may be contacted is willing to give consent to treatment, then it is highly unlikely that either practitioner could be faulted. The most effective method of restoring a paranoid patient to a reasonable frame of mind, is, of course, by the use of ECT. This can either be carried out on an out-patient basis with the assistance of an NHS colleague, or by admission to an NHS psychiatric unit. However, it should always be remembered that the use of Sections 47 and 48 of the Mental Health Act 1983 can be cumbersome and there are powers in Section 22(b) of the Prison Act, 1952 whereby a prisoner can be transferred to National Health Service facilities which can be used in an emergency.

Hysterical Pseudo-Dementia

This can be another formidable problem facing the prison medical officer. Very often, and indeed most frequently, it occurs in prisoners on remand who are facing serious charges. Treatment of this condition (first described by Ganser (1898) is difficult. The description of 'the syndrome of approximate answers' given in textbooks is unknown to the writer. At no time have foolish and contrived answers to questions been noted. The impression created that the inmate who succumbs to this condition is a facile and indifferent individual is not correct. The change in behaviour is usually dramatic and alarming. Experience shows that some inmates received on a serious charge, usually involving serious violence, behave quite normally during the early stages of the remand period, but it must never be forgotten that the interval between arrest and trial can be considerable, extending possibly up to many months. It is, therefore, reasonable to assume that stress plays some part in the production of hysterical dementia, although why some individuals are so vulnerable as to be able to dissociate themselves completely from both their surroundings and their immediate predicament is difficult to evaluate.

While there may be a previous mental history in these individuals and indeed it is always wise to bear this in mind, there may be little else of significance in the mental history other than indications of vulnerability to pressure, lack of stability in their daily lives and a social history which illustrates an idle and feckless existence. Usually they are of below average intelligence, but on the other hand intelligence, or lack of it, does not appear to be of great importance.

The first indication is, of course, a change in behaviour. The patient may have been completely passive and obedient until the onset of the condition; he or she may have been overtly hostile to authority, or loquacious and garrulous or even have behaved in such a way as to draw no comment. The deterioration which one sees is, in the first instance, a deterioration of personal standards. In male patients the staff begin to experience difficulty in the normal routine of shaving and bathing. In the case of female patients, menstruation is ignored and the performance of natural functions where they stand or sit is common to both sexes. The smearing of excreta and a total rejection of advice and encouragement are notable aspects. Contact with the patient in any reasonable way is rapidly lost. The patient usually becomes totally mute, refuses to answer questions, refuses to give even personal details and withdraws into a huddled and miserable specimen of humanity, which can cause alarm among those responsible for providing care.

On the other hand, the patient may begin to talk utter nonsense. Foul language not directed against any individual in particular, but merely a monotonous series of repetitive obscenities can take place; the visit of their legal adviser or their priest results in a similar state of affairs and apparently it would seem that the patient is becoming hypomanic.

The active patient who is content to live in filthy conditions and to remain awake for some days at a time is not as difficult a problem as the patient who withdraws completely. The active patient continues to eat and drink, sometimes quite ravenously, and while such a state of affairs is not very pleasant, at least with careful supervision the risk of death is much less than when nourishment is refused.

Again, it is often said, how does one differentiate between schizophrenia, mania and hysterical pseudo-dementia? Unfortunately there is no easy answer to this and again it revolves round the diagnostic feelings which come only with experience. The treatment of the individual whose life is at risk by food refusal is to all intents and purposes identical with the individual who has a genuine paranoid illness. Electroconvulsive therapy is usually invaluable and the diagnostic criterion between a pseudo-dementia and a schizophrenic illness is the rapidity of recovery. Two, at the most three, applications of ECT usually restore the individual to the state of health which was present before the condition arose. Very often they will say they have no recollection of behaving in this way. To a certain extent this may be due to the effects of the ECT, but their total inability to recall, which must be accepted as genuine, suggests that they have regressed into a hysterical state rather than undergone an acute psychotic episode.

The hyperactive patient, of course, can be more difficult to manage. However, as long as the patient takes nourishment and a nursing staff attends to his daily needs, patience usually brings its own reward. The condition may persist up to, and during, the patient's trial.

There is, unfortunately, no easy way of differentiating between these conditions, and again it is a question of close observation and careful note taking. The hyperactive patient may respond in a perfectly normal way when offered a cigarette. When he or she thinks she is not being observed behaviour may be perfectly normal. In other words, it is very difficult to separate the hysterical from the contrived but behaviour disturbance which comes in the absence of any clearly defined psychiatric symptoms, is obviously calculated to gain some advantage, and must always be viewed with suspicion.

Mute of Malice

Very infrequently in the practice of forensic psychiatry one encounters the individual who, by feigning mental disorder, attempts to persuade the court that he or she is unfit to plead. The law clearly differentiates between those who are mute of malice and those who are mute by visitation of God, to use the legal phraseology.

Those who deliberately refuse to answer questions or to take any part in their defence from a malicious point of view present no difficulty to the experienced forensic psychiatrist. In fact, their behaviour can be dismissed in a very few words. Close observation of the patient will show an experienced doctor that there is nothing mentally wrong and that his behaviour is deliberate and designed to avoid his just deserts.

On the other hand, those who are mentally ill present different problems. The question as to whether or not an individual who is severely subnormal within the meaning of the Act, could follow the proceedings of the court, is debatable and each case must be judged on its merits. The schizophrenic patient, again, can present difficulties. However, no matter what mental condition is present and is agreed on by consultation with colleagues, every effort should be made for the doctors concerned to be able to say on oath that the prisoner is fit to plead. It must always be remembered that unfitness to plead does not mean the end of the matter. The Law Officers of the Crown can return a prisoner to trial when his mental health is restored, should they so wish. Certainly it is not a thing that is done very often, but nevertheless the powers exist and it is not necessarily in the patient's best interest for the psychiatrist to indicate that an individual is unfit to plead to an indictment.

A serious problem can arise in cases of hysterical pseudo-dementia and it is very often in these cases that differences of opinion between colleagues are aired in public. The merits of each particular doctor's opinion will have to be tested by a jury and this is the point which must always be borne in mind. It is no purpose of this book to instruct doctors as to how to behave in court but it is essential that a case for or against is meticulously prepared and, above all, translated into simple terms which are easily understood by lay persons. It is established in law that hysterical pseudo-dementia is no bar to trial. A case that springs to mind is *R. v. Garbutt* which was heard at Mold Crown Court in 1974. The accused was incoherent, unreachable, foul mouthed and continually interrupted the proceedings. Her learned counsel quite properly raised the issue of her fitness to plead, but it was held by a jury that because her mental state was essentially hysterical in type, this did not preclude the evidence against the accused eventually being heard. The condition was self-induced to a greater or lesser degree and there was a large component of malingering in her mental state. In other words, the argument put forward by those doctors who represented the Crown was that it is virtually impossible to separate hysteria from malingering, that in their opinion the patient could have communicated with them had she so wished, and that a prolonged period of observation had shown no evidence of any recognisable psychotic syndrome. It is interesting to note that, as soon as the jury announced their verdict that the accused was fit to plead, she pleaded guilty to the offence in a perfectly normal way, and has behaved normally since.

Perhaps under the heading of this chapter it is appropriate to add a few words about amnesia. Amnesia, as such, is no bar to trial. This was established twenty years ago in the case of *R.* v. *Podola* discussed by Gostin in Chapter 16. In Podola the accused shot a police sergeant dead and argued that, as he had no recollection whatsoever of carrying out the fatal act, he could not be held responsible. Many eminent medical men gave evidence for and against this hypothesis but eventually the court ruled that because an individual could not remember what he had done, it did not necessarily mean that he did not do it, or that he was not in full possession of his faculties at the material time. Very often an accused person claims total amnesia for an offence, particularly one which has serious consequences. Again, it is virtually impossible to establish whether or not the patient is being truthful. As is well known the mind can blot out an unpleasant experience very efficiently, especially if the act is contrary to the basic nature of the accused. Alcohol and drugs also produce retrograde amnesia and the argument that culpability is reduced in a person who has a retrograde amnesia because of alcohol or drug abuse does not really bear close examination. It is well known that an excess of alcohol consumption produces a period of unconsciousness rather than of natural sleep, and it stands to reason that amnesia to a greater or lesser degree must occur.

The whole question of hysteria in all its manifestations among people either awaiting trial or convicted of serious offences covers only few cases, which do not, as a rule, run to any consistent pattern. They represent, by and large, the personality of the accused coupled with the thinking of the individual in that he behaves as he thinks he should. The differentiation of these conditions from serious mental disorder is a task which calls for experience and expertise. Unfortunately, for all the millions of words that are written about prison, prisoners, penal policy, and penal reform, the only place where a doctor can really learn about crime, criminals and their behaviour is a penal institution.

PSYCHOPATHS IN PRISON

Of all the difficulties which face the forensic psychiatrist, the diagnosis and evaluation of this condition can be the most formidable. The behaviour of an individual whose personality development leads to his actions being regarded as abnormal can be capable of such wide interpretation as to make the diagnosis of 'personality disorder' meaningless. The term is not really scientific, not really psychiatrically accurate, and, without putting too fine a point on things, it can mean all things to all men. Human beings can be very cruel to one another and, indeed, the observation that the most predatory animal on the surface of the earth is man himself contains more than a grain of truth. One has only to look back in our recent history to the holocaust and the cruelty which was shown to the Jewish people during the last world war. I have often wondered whether or not the staff of an extermination camp like Belsen or Dachau were abnormal in the accepted sense of the word, or whether they were so blinded by their devotion to Nazism that they rationalised their behaviour in the name of duty. It is hard to believe that human beings could be so cruel, so ruthless and so cold-blooded. However, I think a broad view of that time in our history indicates that the conscience of many individuals can be suppressed by the application of a political ideal and the propaganda associated with that ideal. It is virtually impossible to look dispassionately at those times without a degree of moral judgement. By making that point it will be seen as a reinforcement of the necessity to any doctor who is faced with the problem of personality disorder to dissociate himself, or herself, from any moral judgement of the patient's behaviour.

There are certain matters which come to the attention of any forensic psychiatrist which are horrific in the extreme. To receive a set of papers, including photographs of a brutal crime, from the Director of Public Prosecutions, can be a traumatic experience even to the most case-hardened forensic psychiatrist. It becomes too easy to allow a moral judgement to make the diagnosis but no single act, however cruel or pointless, can ever support a diagnosis of personality disorder.

Recent diagnostic views indicate that the terms 'personality disorder', 'psychopathy' and 'psychopathic disorder' all tend to mean the same thing. In this chapter, the phrases will be used synonymously, in that no matter which diagnostic label is attached to a patient, in effect it means that the behaviour of the individual is the cause for concern, rather than a cluster or spectrum of symptoms. From a nosological point of view such a supposition may be incorrect, but so many complicating factors have come to surround the terms that it is better to use them in a simple and interchangeable way. While for the purpose of certification of course, 'psychopathic disorder' stands alone, the interchangeable use of terms is acceptable in any form of wide-ranging discussion.

Generally speaking, when psychiatrists are talking together and the phrase 'psychopath' is used, each knows instinctively what the other means. Basically this indicates that the patient is either 'impossible', or, in the phrase of the late Dr Peter Scott, 'unwanted'. In other words, the behaviour of these individuals is such that the normal compassionate and caring psychiatrist, while he instinctively feels that in some way his patients must be assisted to live a normal life, as yet has found no successful method of treatment, other than the passage of time.

One of the problems of the definition of psychopathic disorder, as stated in the English and Welsh Mental Health Act, is that it defines psychopathic disorder as a disease concept. As at present stated, it implies that the behaviour of the individual is without his or her control and that in some way these individuals are not fully responsible for what they do. To argue that the use of words such as 'persistent', 'disorder' or 'disability' mean something other than an illness is illogical. The other part of the definition, 'compulsory admission to hospital or guardianship', makes it abundantly clear that the 1983 Act makes psychopathic disorder an illness. Without putting too fine a point on things, such a concept is not acceptable to most psychiatrists who work in this field, and individuals who apparently fit into the category are described as untreatable. This would appear to be a useful point from which to start examining the whole question and trying to establish whether or not this is indeed the case, before passing on to any propositions as to how they should be dealt with and how they should be treated.

Many theories as to the causation of an abnormal personality, or indeed psychopathic disorder, have been advanced. Some years ago the phrase, 'failure of the learning process' was very much in vogue. To a great extent there is some meat on this suggestion. The behaviour of these individuals suggests without a doubt that they have failed to learn their responsibilities as citizens, failed to realise the responsibilities they have to the society in which they live, and failed to take advantage of the normal exposure to ethical matters which is given in the process of education. However, if we adhere strictly to the definition in the Mental Health Act, the inference must be that in some way an abnormal function of the brain is preventing these matters of ethics and conduct being properly assimilated and evaluated.

Experience, however, shows this not to be the case. Examination of notorious men and women shows that they fully understand the difference between right and wrong. It also shows that in the absence of mental illness they fully understand the nature and quality of their actions. Undoubtedly, in most legal cases where the question of personality disorder or psychopathic disorder is being considered, without exception these individuals understand that their behaviour is unlawful. Consequently, the idea that in some way they are mentally ill (if mental illness in any form is regarded as an illness which primarily affects judgement), no matter what the cause, should be disregarded and a more clear-cut definition requires to be applied.

I use the following diagnostic criteria for the psychopathic personality:
1   a poor development of conscience;
2   a lack of concern for the effect of their behaviour on others;
3   a failure to profit by experience;
4   the absence of any specific mental illness;
– all of which having been present for many years.

These concepts are clear, concise and to the point. They are written in simple language without any esoteric additions or leavening of unproven psychiatric theory. If each of the four criteria is examined on an individual basis and the diagnosis of the patient is based on them, the need to evaluate the single act which probably has brought the patient to the consultant becomes less important. The evidence will unfold with little difficulty, to reveal a degree of conduct which by normal standards is outside the scatter of acceptable behaviour.

The question of development of conscience is a matter for enquiry going back over the years. Usually with the assistance of the social agencies, or the psychiatric social worker, such information is readily obtainable. Conversations with the relatives and friends of the patient frequently reveal behaviour which is cold and callous. Such things may come to light as petty thieving from the home, lying to parents, difficulties at school, petty delinquency which may or may not have come to the notice of the police and a gradual intensification of the nature of the behaviour indicating that in effect, this individual does not care about anything at all, except the immediate gratification of his desires, and a surprisingly wilful ability to achieve them.

Lack of concern for others can again be shown as a trait which has existed over many years. Indifference to suffering, indifference to those nearest and dearest and a total inability to comprehend how easily people can be hurt, not only physically, but mentally as well, can be easily elicited. In criminal cases, perusal of their criminal record shows a total inability to profit by experience. Punishment appears to have no effect on them whatsoever; even in the armed forces, where punishment in a detention barracks can be extremely severe, this regime appears to have little effect, if any, on their behaviour. The absence of any other mental disorder, of course, is clearly illustrated in any examination and I do not think there is any need to elaborate on this particular aspect.

However, the term personality disorder as such cannot be applied only to criminals. A little thought will show that it applies to people in all walks of life and professions. There is little doubt that certain aggressive and successful entrepreneurs have an abnormal personality, mainly exhibited by a ruthless determination to achieve power at whatever cost and whatever hurt to those around them. Certain political leaders undoubtedly have highly abnormal personalities and in this field it is safe to say that intransigence and a lack of feeling for their people are particularly apparent. The behaviour of certain athletes and well-known public entertainers can also be classified as highly abnormal.

It would seem, therefore, that there is a group of individuals, not all of whom are necessarily criminal, to whom the personality features outlined above can be applied. History gives us the classic example of Adolf Hitler. Looking at the business world one or two examples spring readily to mind and the attitudes of many British manufacturers in the nineteenth century and several American manufacturers in the twentieth century, with regard to the evolution and formation of trade unions, undoubtedly show an unnatural degree of hostility or indifference to the needs of their labour forces, much beyond what one would expect as a normal reaction to change. The behaviour of certain well-known musicians is undoubtedly abnormal and the factor which appears to be missing from the violent and criminal psychopath when compared with more successful psychopaths is that of skill. The mere accident of birth can differentiate between an abnormal personality achieving great wealth and status or finishing his days in prison. It is often said that abnormal personalities lack judgement but this is very much open to question. If judgement is taken as the method whereby any situation is evaluated and consequently acted on, it cannot be said that because a criminal, with a highly abnormal personality, shoots a police officer in order to avoid arrest, he is incapable of judgement. His judgement of the situation is that the firing of a shot may well enable him to evade arrest. In a similar vein, the business man who commits fraudulent acts to manipulate the funds of his shareholders, thereby increasing the size of his empire, and enabling himself to return the money he has obtained by devious ways, has judged the risk to be worth it. It cannot, by any stretch of imagination, be said that individuals of this kind are incapable of judgement. What can be said is that their judgement, when viewed against the normal standards of the community to which they belong, is abnormal. It is interesting to note that in both types of case, when criminal proceedings are taken as a result of their judgement of the situation, one is faced with individuals who knew perfectly well what they were doing, knew perfectly well the risks that they were running, but yet considered the action they took to have merit in relation to the circumstances they were in at the time.

It is obvious that patients of this type are not influenced in any way by the checks and balances of society. While the Christian ethic of doing unto others as we would wish them to do unto us, is extremely difficult to live up to, it is nevertheless observed to a greater or lesser degree by the vast majority of the population. Spontaneous acts of kindness, spontaneous acts of generosity and an unwillingness to condemn are the more pleasant features of the British character and indeed tolerance is a trait which is admired. How one acquires tolerance is incapable of scientific explanation as it is an abstract virtue which probably comes about as a result of genetic factors and also the factors to which the developing child and adolescent are exposed. The influence on the growing child of parents, teachers, youth leaders, and what he sees going on around him, all play their part in producing a reasonably mature adult. The counter-attractions to these factors are, of course, the exploitation of young people by the purveyors of music, sex, cigarettes and alcohol, and adolescence is usually a painful experience for most young people. However, the vast majority come through adolescence without a great deal of difficulty and take their places in the world as well-behaved citizens. The majority of individuals acquire an ability to judge between good and evil, to put it in simple terms. The psychopathic individual has also the ability to judge between good and evil but of necessity seems to prefer evil. It is unfortunate in the modern practice of psychiatry that there is a tendency to disregard evilly disposed individuals as such and to offer explanations for their behaviour which really have no foundation in fact. It is easy to confuse cause and effect, and the argument that the deprived child becomes the depraved adult does not bear close examination. Criminal families are uncommon and best known in Italy and the United States, with the Mafia and Cosa Nostra syndicates.

THE RECIDIVIST IN PRISON

One of the more distressing features of penal administration is the behaviour of what is termed the 'recidivist'. I mean by this the habitual offender who indulges in pointless and useless acts, mainly of dishonesty, which over the years earn him longer and longer prison sentences. Perusal of the records of many of these men shows the distressing pattern of probation, detention centre, borstal training and finally, prison sentences of increasing severity. By no stretch of the imagination can these individuals be described as abnormal. Crime is a normal part of every society and if this were not the case, then surely it poses the question, 'Why have laws?' The recidivist appears to have fallen into a way of life which demands little effort on his part. He is generally inadequate. In other words, he is socially incompetent to a degree where the most satisfying feature of life, namely the holding of and enjoyment of a job, is quite beyond him. Perusal of his work record shows that he has rarely, if ever, been gainfully employed, and has represented a charge to the state for very many years. Eventually this behaviour stops, usually between 35 and 45 years of age. What happens to these individuals afterwards is relatively unknown. However, a large proportion of them form the derelict population of any large conurbation and usually vanish from human ken without anybody being concerned. Such marriages as they had have inevitably broken down, their children are unaware of their whereabouts and they present, in the latter days of their lives, as tragic individuals. Undoubtedly there is an element in this group who have simple schizophrenia. However, at this stage it is not appropriate to discuss this.

Another group of recidivists are undoubtedly the professional criminals. These are a fairly small group in terms of crimes committed, generally made up of perpetrators of the more successful robberies, the bulk of which take place in and around London. Among them are the hard men from the East End who are not averse to using violence on a security guard or bank clerk. They are usually highly articulate and have grown up in an area where crime is endemic. Their increasing strength and ability as they grow up has come to the notice of men who control and direct criminal operations. These individuals cannot be called psychopathic although their indifference to suffering and the callous way in which they attack their targets could be considered abnormal. However, they put an almost militaristic interpretation upon their actions and the thought processes which go into the planning and execution of a venture certainly indicate a degree of ruthlessness and determination which is not given to every individual, but nevertheless are purposeful and relevant. A definite objective is in mind and patience is a feature of all the individuals involved. It can take many weeks, or even months, to plan an operation to steal a factory payroll, for example. These men are, almost without exception, prepared to wait until all the details are in their possession. In other words, immediate gratification to the exclusion of all else is not a characteristic of offenders of this type.

That there are well-known exceptions to the general observations made above, goes without saying, but individuals which spring to mind in this context are the leaders and organisers, and in one or two cases abnormality of behaviour in relation to others can be deduced. The fear which this type of man can induce in his associates is remarkable. Their associates, in the confidential atmosphere of the consulting room, will describe these individuals as 'nutters', 'headbangers' or 'psychos'. In other words, it is apparent that, even to the average villain the dominance which these individuals can exert is so terrifying, and the consequences of betrayal or informing so definite, that they succumb to any pressure which is put on them and conform to a code of behaviour, which they may not particularly admire. The gang leader is usually a figure seeking respectability, who may well be on reasonable terms with well-known people but yet is vicious and wicked enough to callously disregard any normal feelings for others and ruthlessly exploit individuals for his own nefarious ends. Even the 'heavies' who work protection rackets in clubs and other public places are influenced by someone in the background who is able to dominate them.

The arrest of individuals such as I have described, of course, is always accompanied by a vast outgoing from the media and indeed, their behaviour and conduct while in prison is usually sought out by the press, and such notoriety makes the reason for the Home Office refusing to discuss individual cases abundantly clear. However, it cannot be said that these men are mad, so one must look at the possibility that they are bad. That is, have they learned over the years how to use threats, violence and a total disregard for anyone else in order to achieve the status they have among the criminal fraternity? I think the answer is 'yes' and that for too long we have disregarded the proposition that evil exists and perhaps have chosen to explain it away with some nebulous concept of a mental abnormality. If we turn from the leaders to the led, the 'heavy' is usually a member or an associate of any well-organised criminal gang. Perusal of his record inevitably shows a pretty appalling record of violence. The only difference between him and the leader is the quality of leadership. The 'heavy' does not usually possess the organising ability or the intelligence of his boss and is quite content, in a sycophantic way, to act as minder, or indeed, executioner as the occasion presents itself. Here again, is it wickedness or illness that psychiatrists are faced with? Rapport with people of this kind usually takes time, but once it is established it is perfectly clear that there is no evidence of mental illness in these individuals and they are doing what they do because they want to, in the full knowledge that what they are doing is wrong. One easily elicits characteristics like indifference, self-pity, self-righteousness and a total lack of remorse. Inevitably they accuse the police of beating them up, their lawyers of being crooked and the prison authorities of giving them a hard time. In many respects they are much of a muchness while in custody and it may be that several long sentences will have passed before they begin to mature.

In many ways prison doctors talking amongst themselves and using the term 'psychopathy' or 'personality disorder' will consider the degree of conformity which the person is showing towards the system as an indication of approaching maturity. It is often argued that the frequent breaking of the Prison Rules by these individuals in the early stage of the sentence is an attempt to establish themselves in the prison 'pecking order'. There may be a certain amount of truth in this, but on the other hand acts of violence against staff or fellow inmates, destruction of property and other offences suggest that this behaviour is irrational. Frequent discussions with the individual show that it is more an 'acting out', or a demonstration as to how he thinks he should behave, rather than a deep-seated desire to become the leader of the sub-culture within the prison.

Whatever the motivation for a refusal to conform to prison life, there is no doubt at all that in certain of these individuals mental abnormality can occur. The sophisticated offender, who is used to high living and who eventually receives a very long term of imprisonment, finds the prison regime extremely difficult to accept; the contrast between prison and his former life is dramatic. Women, gambling, drinking and, in short, a totally hedonistic way of life, may characterise the intervals between criminal operations. Many of them are, on the surface, respectable family men. The attitudes which they show to their children are genuine and in spite of the large-scale crime which they plan and execute, their greatest desire is for respectability and acceptance.

If we recognise that there is an unstable element in the make-up of these individuals, when they are taken from a criminal sub-culture where they are surrounded by obsequious sycophants, to a disciplined regime in which they are no different to any other inmate, it is obvious that breakdown of some kind can take place. The unwillingness of offenders of this type to serve their sentence, at least in the early stages, in a calm and rational way does lead to great difficulties in their management. While the doctors may be concerned to keep their behaviour under control by personal contact alone, the difficulties faced by the governor and his staff should never be disregarded. A great deal of criminal intelligence flows into the governor's department in any long-term prison and it is understandable if at times the information he has is not widely disseminated. Men of the calibre I have described are very escape prone and the escape of an offender of this type can cause great alarm to the public and also put them at risk. Consequently it may be necessary for the governor to apply the strictest measures which, if not accepted as part of the overall management of the individual, can cause affront to any psychiatrist concerned in the case. This is the dichotomy which exists on many occasions in prison and it is the duty of the doctor concerned to accept the governor's decision as he has ultimate responsibility for the man. However, a tactful approach will always ensure that at least the governor and his immediate staff are aware of any potential problem.

PARANOIA IN PRISON

As has already been indicated, self-righteousness is a marked feature of these individuals and very often this can develop into a paranoid type of illness. The inmate rapidly exhausts his avenues of appeal. The Appeal Court has usually ruled in favour of the trial judge with regard to sentence. Petitions to the Home Secretary are being rejected. Complaints to the Board of Visitors of the establishment have been investigated and rejected. The individual then comes to believe that he has been 'fitted up' for his crimes and conversations with this type of patient show undoubtedly that his attitude to the police officers investigating the case, his lawyers or even the trial judge are delusional in content and from an indifferent and hostile individual one begins to see a psychotic type of illness appearing. Or it may be that the mere duration of the sentence which is passed can cause mental breakdown. This may be characterised by irrational outbursts of violence against the staff, by determined suicide attempts or by a gradual withdrawal from the life of the establishment. Extraneous criteria differentiate between withdrawal, characterised by refusal of food, lack of personal hygiene and uncommunicative behaviour, which is due to mental disorder and that which is due to sheer bloody-mindedness. These extremes are easy to state but not so easy to diagnose and it cannot be overemphasised that experience is the great teacher in cases of this kind.

Quite naturally, any individual of this type who becomes mentally ill must be dealt with, if at all possible, by means of the Mental Health Act. Very often a transfer to a maximum security hospital for treatment is highly effective and the patient can then be returned to the prison to complete his sentence. On the other hand, it may well be that he remains in a maximum security hospital for the duration of his sentence. It is a question not so much of treatment as of management, and the judgement of the doctors concerned with regard to the best possible use of available resources.

DRUGS IN PRISON

It may be appropriate at this stage to make some comment regarding the accusations which are habitually made regarding the over-prescribing of psychotropic drugs, particularly in cases of this kind. The dilemma in which the prison medical officer finds himself is that on the one hand he has a difficult and disruptive individual to deal with and, on the other, he has the chemical resources to modify behaviour. Recent figures produced by the Home Office Prison Department indicate quite clearly that allegations of excessive prescribing of psychotropic drugs are quite unfounded when one accepts the number of individuals in prison. The doctor cannot withhold therapeutic relief. The main problem is that because of the use of phenothiazines in particular, the matter has been blown up out of all proportion. The use of powerful drugs to control behaviour as such is wrong and should not be countenanced.

THE SINGLE MINDED EXTREMIST

A small number of prisoners countable on the fingers of one hand, are those whose very notoriety marks them out from the moment of their arrest till the day they are eventually sentenced, as unusual and abnormal. These people generally work alone, and are convicted of crimes so bizarre and horrible as to cause revulsion to the population, including the criminal fraternity. Bizarre sexual acts, accompanied by murder or near-murder, occupy a vast amount of police time, attract the attention of the media in a most unhealthy way and present the prison authorities with a major problem. Again, the characteristics which one finds in the professional criminal are present in these individuals as well. They have little insight, show no remorse, are extremely cold-blooded and one gains the impression that they are going to take society on and are in full possession of their faculties. It is often said that many rapists cannot obtain sexual satisfaction unless force is used against a woman, and indeed sadistic trends are easily identified in these individuals. One needs only to read the witnesses' statements in the case, and the occasional confession made by the accused, for this point to be made perfectly clear. The treatment of these prisoners presents great difficulties; one of the more distressing features of penal life is the self-righteousness in the attitudes shown to either the sexual offender or the child molester, and they are undoubtedly targets for their fellow inmates. Consequently, from the point of view of maintaining discipline and good order, these individuals must be secluded, at least at the start of their sentence. While individuals of this type are few and far between, they can present a considerable challenge to psychiatrists involved. Rapport is usually extremely difficult, as even the most objective of psychiatrists will find difficulty in avoiding revulsion at their record. To maintain an air of detached objectivity when faced with such an individual is a task which calls for expertise and sagacity: these qualities are not acquired without a great deal of experience, not only of psychiatry but of life itself.

These offenders are often highly intelligent, and the planning and execution of their crimes is impeccable. Usually their arrest has come about either in the most fortuitous circumstances, or owing to the fact that someone close to them has decided that enough is enough and has quietly informed the police. Even the most experienced police officer will admit that the 'brilliant detective work', beloved by the popular press, cannot be applied in cases of this kind. Generally speaking, these individuals are not mentally ill but have highly abnormal personalities, particularly with regard to their sexual drive. The question of specific therapy designed to reduce sexual drive does not enter into cases of this kind as the sentence is of such duration that when it is finally decided to release the individual both their physical strength and their sexual drive will be diminished in the natural course of events.

Surprisingly, in time, they come to be accepted by their fellow inmates and while occasionally they may make the headlines as a result of somebody seeking to assist them, as an overall psychiatric problem no real difficulties ensue. They tend to be manipulative and indulge in various manoeuvres designed to keep them in the public eye, as it were, but overall their mental health remains good and they are a living illustration of the view that modification of psychopathic behaviour, if it does occur, only occurs with maturity.

The patients already described form but a tiny minority of those men and women who are actually serving prison sentences. Unless specific mental disorder appears they must remain the responsibility of the penal system. Not the least reason for this attitude is that, if at all possible, labelling them as mentally ill should be avoided. The tendency of any highly dangerous criminal serving a long sentence to seek any peg on which to hang his hat is all part of the game. It is folly to ignore the fact that while in prison many individuals persevere in a never-ending battle with authority. That their complaints, in many cases unjustifiable and ridiculous, are listened to goes without saying and because of a natural and understandable reluctance on the part of prison staff to discuss the behaviour of prisoners publicly, the bias of public opinion can turn in favour of the inmate.

THE INADEQUATE BORDERLINE OFFENDER

One must now turn to a larger group. While this group of individuals exhibit many, if not all, of the characteristics outlined above, they do not possess them to the degree of intensity which is shown by the notorious criminal. In other words, in the opinion of the writer, a borderline group exists who appear incapable of dealing with the vicissitudes of life in a reasonable and acceptable way. Offences are generally sexually related but of a trivial nature. Indecent assault of a timorous and fumbling nature, which is more exploratory than deviant is characteristic. Generally they are of limited intelligence, but not mentally impaired within the meaning of the Mental Health Act. Their offences can be described as trivial but none the less, are extremely distressing to the victim. In most cases an element of violence exists. This may take the form of very minor sexual assault against children, a tendency to annoy and distress older members of the female population without proceeding to sexual penetration, and a totally disorganised style of living which has brought them into contact with the social agencies for some years, before their eventual appearance before the court.

The psychiatric examination of these individuals shows clearly that basic intellectual defects have prevented progress at school, even in spite of special education. Perusal of the information available concerning them shows that they have failed to respond to those methods which are successful with the normally developing child. They may have a confused sense of what is right and what is wrong, and are consequently unable to judge a situation in which these principles are involved. Home backgrounds are very often not of the best and, indeed, the offender may well have been in care for some years, either in a children's home or with foster parents. Their first contact with the courts is usually in their late teens, although incidents of sexual misdemeanours may be recorded in the records of social services departments, whose officials have not reported the matter to the police. Some, labelled 'mentally handicapped', end up in hospitals.

In my view, as so often happens in the practice of psychological medicine, one cannot describe with any diagnostic accuracy precisely what constitutes this type of individual. One is back with the old gut feelings that in some way a particular patient may be salvaged. In other words, the doctor can discern a desire for change on the part of the patient even though, from a prognostic point of view, the experienced psychiatrist will be very cautious as to the successful outcome of any programme of rehabilitation which he may be willing to undertake.

Adolescence can be an extremely trying time for the most balanced teenager and very few parents can say that they were not presented with both emotional and educational difficulties experienced by their children during this difficult time. Teenage rebellion as such tends to be over-played but difficulties with sex, communication and parental relationships are so common as to be almost banal, and most honest adults when they look back over the years will accept that they underwent similar experiences themselves. Such an understanding of one's self is an essential part of the makeup of the psychiatrist who wishes to undertake the difficult, and at times the heart-rending task of guiding the teenager or young adult with abnormal personality features, which may be suitably modified under an appropriate regime.

As has been known since its inception, the National Health Service consumes a vast amount of the nation's wealth and in a perfect world its facilities would be instantly available on demand. Its financial resources are limited, however, and it follows that there must be a system of priorities; without putting too fine a point on things, the law-abiding citizen expects that his or her needs shall take priority over those of a group of individuals whose behaviour is reprehensible and who do not rate very highly in the public eye. This, of course, is human nature and it is unwise to ignore public feeling. However, certain small units do exist outside the confines of the large mental hospitals and these deserve to be encouraged and supported. The dichotomy which exists at the moment is that adolescent units exist, but principally they exist within large institutions, and it would be fair to say that the young patient can never really feel free of the stigma of mental illness. In many cases, on examining such patients after they have failed to progress in a National Health Service hospital and have come into the penal system, their recollection of the period spent in an adolescent unit is vague, hostile and rejecting. In other words, they feel they have made no progress at all. This is not a reflection on the staff, other than that they may have no clear concept of the object of the exercise and while they may be the most skilled psychiatric nurses, their limited experience of offenders makes it extremely difficult for them to understand the confusion that these young people feel. One of the more distressing features of the young patient who finds himself in conflict with the law over minor sexual offences is his low self-esteem. All these young-sters have a very low opinion of themselves, take their offences very much to heart and are the subject of ridicule and contempt from their peers. As is well known, most adolescents boast about their sexual adventures, whether or not they have taken place, but this group are, in many cases, genuinely ashamed of what they have done and at the same time their inarticulate and hesitant manner makes it virtually impossible for them to enter into a relationship with a young female which, although it may be fumbling and experimental, is at least one of mutual consent.

The provision of staff who are both mature and experienced enough to gain the confidence and trust of the patients, while at the same time ensuring that the security of the establishment is adequate, is of paramount importance. The unit does not necessarily need to be geared to analytical methods or even to in-depth counselling. It needs to be geared to normality. The first prerequisite of a normal life is, of course, the instillation of regular work habits which produce satisfac-tion and a sense of achievement. The patient's confidence in his ability to deal with difficulties which arise in his very restricted world is surely the primary therapeutic aim. The teaching of the habits of cleanliness and order which eventually will ingrain self-discipline and control goes without saying. The small communal institution, which above all is personalised, seems to hold out a much better chance of success than the large institution of the borstal type whose primary function is the rehabilitation of offenders through rewards and punish-ments. The punishment of the inadequate, mildly deviant offender should be clearly separated from that of the hard-core juvenile whose crimes are mostly directed against property and whose violence, if it exists, is directed mainly for personal gain rather than any frustrated sexual feeling. The young offender from a large conurbation who embarks on a series of burglaries or robberies must, with the best will in the world, be regarded as potentially a recidivist. From an early age he has got into the habit of acquiring other people's property and is not particular about how he achieves this. Certainly amongst this group are the leaders and the led, the bullies and the bullied, but the vast majority show a total disregard for authority of any kind and a wilful refusal to accept the rights of other citizens to retain their possessions. The offender with whom we are at present concerned is limited in ability, usually socially isolated, and it is because of his incompetence that he gets into trouble, rather than by any predetermined planning and execution of crimes. It is a fact that many members of the judiciary, including lay magistrates, show concern towards the young offender whose offences they regard as primarily due to personality defects rather than to determined criminal intent. Psychiatrists who are asked their advice on these patients must preserve a clear sense of objectivity and an ability to discern the hopeful therapeutic prospect from the offender with a determined and established criminal attitude.

The provision of small units which are neither hospitals nor penal institutions but yet are medically orientated, is worthy of further enquiry and experimentation. The most important consideration is the staffing of such establishments. The idealist, who can see no wrong in wayward adolescents, is valueless. The director of such an institution must be above all a pragmatist who by his personality can achieve success both with his patients and those who would criticise his task. Success is never welcomed by the media in any matter affecting criminal behaviour. Failure is much more newsworthy and has much more effect on public opinion. Consequently, from the medical director downwards, the staff must be carefully recruited and above all have the ability to live with failure. Success, with the subsequent boosting of the ego, is very pleasant. To have to account, perhaps in public, for a total failure is never a desirable or a happy situation. From the medical director to the domestics, the organisation must be welded into a formidable group of individuals whose approach to the patient is consistent, calm and rational. Above all, this approach must be understandable to the patient. As a rule, such establishments do not need to run on very high-powered lines and the staff must come to understand that even if they regard themselves as a team, there must be a captain. The word 'team' has become fashionable in therapeutic circles in recent years and one tends to forget its origin and its meaning, as far as the public is concerned. The word in the public mind is usually connected with sport in some form or another; in all team games there is a captain, and when he or she issues an instruction on the field, then that instruction is obeyed. In other words, the team treating the offender must be prepared to accept discipline themselves if they are going to have any hope at all of instilling self-discipline in their charges.

The provision of such facilities will, of course, be very expensive. The decision as to whether or not they will ever be established on a nationwide scale is a political one and must depend on the balance between the resources available to the community and the desire of the community as a whole to regard the type of patient who would benefit from such a regime as important. How important a single human being is has been a philosophical debating point for very many years. The Christian philosophy is that any human being is of value. Tending as we do to live in a more materialistic age, this concept is frequently ignored. However, in the last analysis it will depend on the nation itself and, above all, on the realisation that the incidence of crime reported to, and detected by, the police is but a reflection of the behaviour of society as a whole.

The views expressed by the author in this chapter are not necessarily those of the Home Office.

CASE

R. *v.* Podola (1960) L QB 325.

REFERENCE

Ganser, S.J.M. (1898) Mentioned in *Clinical Psychiatry*. 3rd edition. Slater, E. & Roth, M. (eds.). pp. 114–115. London: Baillière Tindall.

12

Low Intelligence, Mental Handicap and Criminality

Michael Craft

Estimations as to how many criminals are dull have always been bedevilled by problems of definition. Poor conditions of upbringing, school truancy and illiteracy were even more common among criminals at the beginning of this century than now; even today the proportion of convicts in British prisons who are illiterate is estimated at over twice the national average. When Alfred Binet started work on the first intelligence test, it was to estimate the proportion of criminals in Paris gaols who were of innately low intelligence as opposed to those who were poorly schooled. At this time, the term 'mental defective' and its French equivalent was usually defined with strong overtones of social deprivation, further compounding arguments which often became circular.

Even among experienced investigators, views such as the following were common. Terman, in his 1916 book on the measurement of intelligence, was widely read; '... there is no investigator who denies the fearful role played by mental deficiency in the production of vice, crime and delinquency ... not all criminals are feeble-minded, but all feeble-minded are at least potential criminals. That every feeble-minded woman is a potential prostitute would hardly be disputed by anybody.' Arguing from an imperfect understanding of genetics, some thought sterilisation of mental defectives was justified. In a judgment enacted in the USA Supreme Court, Justice Oliver Holmes: 'It is better for all the world if, instead of waiting to execute degenerate offspring for crimes, or to let them starve for their imbecility, society can prevent those who are manifestly unfit from continuing their kind. The principle that sustains compulsory vaccination is broad enough to cover cutting the fallopian tubes ... three generations of imbeciles are enough.' (*Buck* v. *Bell* 274 US 200 (1927)).

In England, following the passage of the 1913 Mental Deficiency Act, all counties were enjoined to build or use colonies for their mental defectives. These colonies were a more humane version of prisons, being unlocked, bisexual (but segregated), open air, with plenty of work and recreation. But, as certification of mental defectives following court conviction could be for a life-time on eugenic grounds, the proper definition of mental defectiveness was important, especially when in 1927 'moral defectiveness' was added to the other three English categories of defectiveness, namely 'feeble-mindedness', 'imbecility' and 'idiocy'. 'Moral defectiveness' was specifically enjoined by the Act to regulate those who were now called 'psychopathic'. Indeed, in the 1959 Mental Health Act in England, one definition for compulsory action was called 'psychopathic dis-

177

order', whether or not including subnormality of intelligence. Thus to the lay mind (and even many 1982 Crown Court Judges) confusion was worse confounded between low intelligence, mental handicap, subnormality and psychopathy. In 1983 in England and Wales 'mental impairment' will be the new term.[1]

It is said that in England, perhaps with a view to relieving prison overcrowding, it was the Home Office which insisted on a category such as 'mental impairment' with its lack of adequate definition of intellectual deficit, being included in the 1982 English Mental Health (Amendment) Act against heavy pressure from the DHSS and many community bodies. If so, these are shades of Alfred Binet indeed. For as long ago as 1954, Mary Woodward's survey of the role of low intelligence in delinquency greatly clarified the inter-relationship between low intelligence, poor environment and criminality. There have been advances since then. Woodward checked English-speaking research reports on the subject from 1900 to 1954, from the dawn of intelligence testing to the English Mental Health Act. Although not a legal definition at any time in that period, she defined 'feeble-minded' as under IQ 70, and, as Table 12.1 shows,

Table 12.1   Proportion of convicts found to be feeble-minded.

Years	No. of studies	% Feeble-minded in median survey	% Feeble-minded range
1910–14	50	51	4.96
1915–19	142	28	1.82
1920–24	104	21	1.69
1925–28	46	20	2.58

From Woodward, 1954.

the proportion of feeble-minded thus defined, of total criminals, gradually decreased in that period. She said, 'Over a period of 40 years, the extent to which test results underestimate the intelligence of delinquents in America has gradually diminished. Beginning in the defective range, the test results of delinquent groups have steadily approached the average, and this change is paralleled by improvements in tests and methods of sampling.'

Table 12.2 describes the number of people tested and further illustrates the decrease in proportion of those under IQ 70 found among criminal populations. It shows that in 1931 Snyder found that one-third of the convicted population scored below IQ 70 on the Stanford-Binet; their mean IQ was 71. Yet by 1950 the Gluecks in New York State, and Gittins in 1952 among 1000 schoolboys in the United Kingdom, noted that the mean IQ in both cases was 92 on the Wechsler, a much more sophisticated test. Again Woodward, 'All these lines of evidence therefore, indicate that the eight IQ points by which delinquents differ

---

[1] Defined in the 1983 Act as: 'A state of arrested or incomplete development of mind (not amounting to severe mental impairment) which includes a significant impairment of intelligence and social functioning and is associated with abnormally aggressive or seriously irresponsible conduct on the part of the person concerned.' 'Psychopathic disorder' is retained, but does not now need to be susceptible to medical treatment.

Table 12.2   Mean IQ of convicted prisoners.

Date	No.	Test used	Mean IQ	IQ <70	Source of sample	Investigation
1931	200	1916 Stanford-Binet	71.00	34.00	Institution	Snyder
1931	401	Not stated		5.9*	Institution	Frank
1931	300	1916 Stanford-Binet	82.00 (mdn)	18.65	Institution	Beane
1933	602	1916 Stanford-Binet	79.34		Court	McClure
1934	979	1916 Stanford-Binet		13.1	Court	Gluecks
1934	3584	1916 Stanford-Binet	82.2	13.9	Court	Rogers and Austin
1935	699	Otis Group Test	87.96	10.0	Institution	Lane and Witty
1937	152	Otis SA test 14 yr. norm.	75.5		Institution	Moore
1937	21 studies		82.4		Institution	Owen
1939	1731	Revised Stanford-Binet	84.45		Court	Mann and Mann
1945	463	Revised Stanford-Binet and Kulhmann-Anderson	86.74	10.4	Court and others	Kvaraccus
1947	300	1916 Stanford-Binet	86.7		Court	Merrill
1947	500	Revised Stanford-Binet	92.5	11.6	Court	Merrill
1950	500	Wechsler	92.28	4.2	Institution	Gluecks
1952	1000	Wechsler	92		Approved school	Gittens

* Per cent feeble-minded; not based on test only.
After Woodward, 1954.

from the general population norm are entirely attributable to the depressive effect on the test score constellation of factors which differentiate delinquents from the general population. In other words, there would be no difference in intelligence between delinquent and non-delinquent groups matched for all the cultural variables.' (p. 280).

The depressive environmental variables were analysed by Eleanor Glueck (1935) for her group of 1000 juvenile delinquents. As Table 12.3 shows, she divided them into two groups, with IQs above and below 80. Glueck found that those under IQ 80 had a greater number of adverse environmental factors than in the group over IQ 80, concluding that this followed 'from the mental deficiency of the delinquents themselves and from the sub-stream of delinquency in their families.' Today, one might argue the reverse in that there was a 'cause and effect', and given the concatenation of adverse factors, it was a surprise to have so few dull being convicted.

In Britain before the 1959 Mental Health Act there was no definition of 'mental defectiveness' in terms of an intelligence quotient. Indeed, in 1958 the writer, visiting Rampton Special Hospital, was introduced to a London University graduate schoolmaster, who had been convicted for repeated seduction of small boys, and was in care as 'morally defective' under the 1913 Mental Health Deficiency Act. 'Subnormality of intelligence' was not defined in terms of IQ in the 1959 Mental Health Act, nor is 'severe mental impairment' in the 1983 Act, so it is in this context one has to evaluate current usage of the term 'subnormal'

Table 12.3 Environmental factors associated with intellectual retardation.

		IQ 80 and under (%)	IQ 81 plus (%)
Factors occurring more frequently in low IQ group	Low intelligence in family	73.0	45.0
	Illiteracy in parents	40.7	23.9
	Parents without schooling	60.0	—
	Home overcrowded, dirty, shabby, etc.	78.0	55.4
	Near-poverty	84.6	72.9
	Parents unskilled workers	53.5	37.5
	Retardation (two years) at school	91.6	50.9
	Truancy or school misconduct	93.0	82.0
	Mother hostile or indifferent	22.2	16.5
	Father over-strict or no control	75.6	66.5
	Mother over-strict or no control	77.0	67.0
	Mother under 16 at marriage	7.2	2.3
	Poor health	51.2	40.1
	Over-suggestible or emotionally unstable	46.9	29.9
	Other members of family delinquent	92.0	86.0
	Continuance in delinquency after treatment	90.0	84.0
Factors occurring less frequently in low IQ group	Other mental abnormalities in family (not mental defect)	39.0	50.5
	Club membership	6.3	11.7
No difference between groups	Possibilities for culture conflict (native-born children of foreign-born parents)	70	70
	Father hostile or indifferent	33	33
	Psychosis, neurosis, epilepsy, etc.	—	—
	Mother working	40	40
	Parental incompatibility	37	37

From Glueck, 1935.

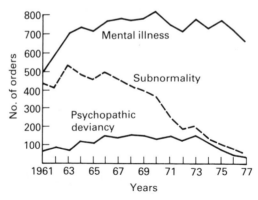

Figure 12.1 Section 60 disorders by diagnostic category. (From Robertson, 1981, with kind permission.)

in England today. In the flush of enthusiasm (see Figure 12.1) there were many such Section 60 mental health orders; nowadays most are made to the special hospitals of Rampton and Moss Side. Fowles (1977) carried out an analysis of admissions to Rampton. 'The bulk of the admissions (75.8 per cent) are classified as either subnormal or psychopathic disorder, and for Rampton patients, these two diagnostic categories are often interchangeable. Whether a patient is called psychopath or subnormal is often quite fortuitous. There was a small group of mental illness (15.1 per cent) ...'. Parker (1974) provided an analysis of intelligence quotients (mainly Wechsler) of all patients in the English special hospitals of Rampton, Broadmoor and Moss Side. 'IQs of 50 are usually considered to be Severely Subnormal, and those with quotients between 50 but under 70 are designated Subnormal ... only 31 per cent of the Severely Subnormal patients had intelligence quotients falling below 50 and 59 per cent of the group fell in the 50 but under 70 subnormal range. Three per cent had intelligence quotients of over 80. Nearly half, 46 per cent, of the Subnormal patients met the criterion of an intelligence quotient of at least 50 but under 70; 16 per cent had intelligence quotients of over 80.' Thus 69 per cent of the severely subnormal and 54 per cent of the subnormal had IQs well above the normally accepted levels, one subnormal patient scoring above 100. This last patient is likely to be among the group whose earlier intelligence assessments were depressed by lack of schooling, education or childhood deprivation. Craft (1958) describes a certified mental defective, who in the absence of psychiatric illness improved from IQ 35 to 85, given proper care.

Parker notes that less than half (43 per cent) of the special hospital patients had any IQ test at all, and the proportion is likely to be considerably less in provincial hospitals. Recent IQ estimates are rare in psychiatric court reports. As Fowles (1977) says of Rampton court reports, 'The surprising fact is that the majority of medical evidence is accepted without question, and indeed the courts do trust the experts. Their enthusiasm for psychiatry in a court of law can be quite startling at times.' However, trust of medical experts varies widely from state to state, as the Epilogue makes clear for Queensland. In their analysis of 1963 English court practice of hospital orders, Walker and McCabe (published 1973) were unable to use that part of their analysis dealing with intelligence quotients, due to the unreliability of tests and data given on their questionnaires. Between April 1963 and April 1964, they found English and Welsh courts had made 1332 hospital and guardianship orders under the new Mental Health Act, of which 330, or 26 per cent, were for subnormality. As might be expected, most patients were in their teens, and many were of near-normal intelligence; 93 had been to ordinary secondary modern schools, whilst one man and one woman were said to have attended technical colleges. They found that although those labelled subnormal did not often commit serious personal violence, they were responsible for more than their share of arson and sexual offences. It is not clear from their analysis whether some were labelled subnormal *because* psychiatric hospital treatment was thought a better disposal for those committing minor sexual offences, or whether those under IQ 70 are inherently more likely to commit such offences. They did carry out a follow-up two years after the initial order had been made, and found that 673 of the original inpatients had been discharged or absconded, and of these 23 had been re-convicted.

Of the total 350 'subnormals' on Order, five had been re-convicted for sexual offences, none serious. This proportion is the same as the group labelled schizophrenic. Walker and McCabe also did a breakdown of regional variation in usage of court hospital orders. Even between parts of London this varied between 1.94 per cent of all convictions in North East London to 11.87 per cent for South West London, whilst for 'subnormality' orders, the proportion of all hospital orders varied from 55 per cent in South West England to the Principality where at 9 per cent they said: 'Wales, nearly all of whose rates are low, has exceptionally small percentages for both schizophrenia and subnormality; the reason may be the over-representation of psychopaths, due to the attractions of Dr Craft's unit for them in North Wales' (p. 161). The impact of personality and specialised hospital unit on regional practice could hardly be better put!

This regional variation in Britain has been overtaken by a national decline in England and Wales in the use of hospital orders, shown in Figure 12.1. The decline in use of the compulsory court hospital order is, however, outweighed by an increase in psychiatric probation orders to hospitals over the same period of time, which more than makes up for the shortfall in compulsory orders and reflects the current community emphasis on treatment with consent, rather than treatment without consent.

Elsewhere in the English-speaking world, there have been three useful surveys on the subject in the United States. Tarjan and his colleagues in 1973 showed that the proportion of the United States general population scoring under IQ 70 varied from 0.2 to 2.4 per cent, depending on the type of test used. Among offender populations with high proportions of blacks, and of illiterates, proportions on the same tests scoring under IQ 70 varied from 2.6 in predominantly white states (Idaho, Montana and Nevada) to 24.3 per cent in Georgia in 1976. MacEachron (1979) described some of the other variables which lead to high rates of mentally handicapped under IQ 70 being found in different convicted populations in the United States. When offenders are tested immediately after conviction (and are presumably depressed) rates are consistently 4 to 7 percentage points lower than results based on total offender rates at a later date. Prevalence rates are also higher when all offenders take an intelligence test (this was 27 per cent in Atlanta for instance) compared with only a small proportion taking a test (it was 5.2 per cent in Kentucky and 7.9 per cent in South Carolina on this basis). The Georgia Department of Offender rehabilitation found that its prevalence rate varied by 8 per cent, merely by changing an intelligence test. Alternatively, in Texas the same criminal population given four different intelligence tests gave a prevalence ranging from 7 to 23.4 per cent who scored under IQ 70. Allowing for all these variables, MacEachron reached the conclusion that only a few states such as Maine which universally tested all offenders (rate 2.3 per cent) and Massachusetts (1.8 per cent) could be relied upon. Both these rates are very close to that found in the general population using the same tests, which in her analysis was close to 2.4 per cent. She concluded, as did Woodward earlier, that with increased control of variables, and using standardised tests,

'The prevalence rate of mentally retarded adult male offenders is only slightly higher than the prevalence rates of retarded male adults in the general population.' The results 'indicate that there is little empirical support for a conceptual linkage between retardation and criminality'.

A less detailed and therefore less reliable American analysis is provided by Brown and Courtless (1968) who carried out a postal questionnaire analysis of American penal units. Of the 90 477 replies they found 'a bewildering array of tests used by the institutions to measure intelligence' and a bewildering variety of people who administered them, including convicts! Of the returned questionnaires 1454 gave IQ scores below 55, which in Britain usually means that such a person is severely mentally handicapped, unable to read and write, often incontinent, and may not be able to dress properly. Yet in 99 per cent of these cases no question of competency to stand trial was raised, in 78 per cent no pre-trial psychological or psychiatric examination of the accused was made, in no case was an examination requested or ordered during the course of a trial, and any examination (usually by the probation department) was made in only 20 per cent of these cases. More tellingly, no appeal was made in 88 per cent of cases, and 84 per cent did not ask for 'post-conviction relief'. In 80 per cent the original charge for which the retardate was arrested was the same as that for which he was tried and convicted, in other words plea bargaining, which is common among those of average ability, was rare among the retarded.

The Brown and Courtless results may be unreliable in giving a picture of the prevalence of crime among the mentally handicapped, but they do give a damning indictment of the practicalities, as opposed to the theory, of law for the dull before many American courts of law.

In Britain a number of research reports over the years have suggested that the truly mentally impaired (under IQ 70) might be more likely to be 'shopped' by their brighter criminal colleagues, caught because they were not so adept at escape, confess whilst in police custody because they were suggestible, and convicted because they had less access to legal counsel than the financially more affluent. This last has been covered by recent extensions of legal aid in Britain which now (1982) is said to cover more than half of the population earning not more than £4000 per annum. The suggestibility of the mentally handicapped is highlighted by the Confait case and is intended to be covered by recent extensions to the Home Office regulations on interrogation of suspected criminals, with which this chapter appropriately ends.

Confait was a transvestite prostitute whose dead body was discovered by the police in his burning flatlet in South London in 1976. Three local youths thought by the police to know Confait, were arrested, interrogated in detail and confessed. Lattimore, then 18, was found to be mentally handicapped and sent to Rampton: Leighton, aged 15, was imprisoned and Salih, aged 14, was sent to Approved School. Later, two other men confessed to the murder, and the three were cleared. However, as late as 1977 the Fisher enquiry was puzzled as to the detail and comprehensiveness of the confessions and refused to accept police impropriety. Since then the Royal Commission on Criminal Procedure (1981) has accepted that mentally handicapped persons might be unduly suggestible to police interrogation and thus sign their names or a mark to a confession which was not wholly true, and there have been changes to the regulations on interrogation of suspected criminals. Paragraph 93 says, 'In the last few years, partly as a result of one or two individual cases, concern has been expressed about the position of mentally handicapped persons in police custody. The substance of a circular issued by the Home Office in 1976 is now consolidated in Administrative Direction 4A to the Judges' rules. This advises that officers should take particular care in putting questions to and accepting the reliability of answers from a person who appears to have a mental handicap. As far as is practicable, such persons should be interviewed only in the presence of a parent or other independent person.'

In 1971 the United Nations adopted the *Declaration of the General and Specific Rights of the Mentally Handicapped*, which states, 'The mentally retarded person has the right to protection from exploitation, abuse and degrading treatment. If prosecuted for any offence he shall have the right to due process of the law with full recognition being given to his degree of mental responsibility.' This latter is the nub of the issue and the Royal Commission on Criminal Procedure recommended that action should be taken to improve the training given to the police to enable them to recognise mentally handicapped persons more readily, so that safeguard procedures could be implemented at the early stages of investigations and expert guidance sought. This is particularly important because doubt has been expressed, both in the UK and USA, as to whether a person with a mental handicap can readily comprehend the phrases used to caution those about to be questioned (Hewitt, 1983).

In the author's experience Crown Court judges have ruled inadmissible evidence where:

1   A mentally handicapped person is arrested at midnight and interrogated alone through the small hours;
2   The mentally handicapped person was illiterate, yet in the confession, words were used beyond his proven ability;
3   A signature was appended whereas the mentally handicapped person could not write.

This has led to cases being dismissed.

In summary, research reports both in the United States and in the United Kingdom continue to show little support for a direct relationship between intellectual retardation and criminality. With increasing refinement of intelligence testing and control of relevant variables, it has been shown that retardates under IQ 70 have the same prevalence (2.4 per cent in one excellent study) as the general population. Because in the past the mentally handicapped have been shown to be unduly suggestible and prone to unreliable confessions, UK police procedure in obtaining statements from individuals known to be mentally handicapped is carefully regulated.

Early reports suggested an undue proportion of sex offenders and arsonists among the mentally handicapped under IQ 70. Since much of the research failed to control for intelligence tests, it is uncertain how reliable the results are today.

However, it is clear that the mentally handicapped are at least as ignorant of successful sexual practice as their peer group, and are likely to be more ignorant. Their sexual experimentation is often more visible and more upsetting (Craft and Craft, 1978).

In any discussion of criminality among the dull, two populations need to be disentangled. Firstly, in developed countries among fully educated adults the incidence of criminality among those scoring under IQ 70 on a reputable test is, at 2.4 per cent, similar to the parent population.

Secondly, there are social and personality misfits abounding among those scoring above IQ 70 in adult life, many of whom have been labelled 'subnormal' and 'defective' in the past, or now 'impaired', and rehabilitated in psychiatric hospitals. This population will continue to need help and aid, if not treatment. If, as a result of currently state-recommended closure of such units, this population is not cared for in mental handicap hospitals, it is likely they will be returned to the prison system where they were in the days of Dickens and Alfred Binet. It is not likely that the already overcrowded small group home system being developed by social service departments will give them any priority. Where best this considerable population can be cared for needs to be borne in mind in the discussions of forensic psychiatry in the chapters ahead.

REFERENCES

Brown, B.S. & Courtless, T.F. (1968) The mentally retarded offender. In *Readings in Law and Psychiatry*. Allen, R.C., Ferster, E.Z. & Rubin, J.G. (eds.). Baltimore: Johns Hopkins.

Craft, M.J. (1958) *Mental Disorder in the Defective*. Starcross: Royal Institution.

Craft, M. & Craft, A. (1978) *Sex and the Mentally Handicapped*. London: Routledge and Kegan Paul.

Fowles, M.W. (1977) Sexual offenders in Rampton. In *Sex Offenders, a Symposium*. Gunn, J. (ed.). Special Hospitals Research Report No. 14.

Gittins, J. (1952) *Approved School Boys*. London: HMSO.

Glueck, E.T. (1935) Mental retardation and juvenile delinquency. *Med. Hyg.*, **19,** 549–572.

Hewitt, S.E.K. (1983) Interviewing mentally handicapped persons. *Mental Handicap*, **11,** 1, 38–39.

MacEachron, A.E. (1979) Mentally retarded offenders: prevalence and characteristics. *Am. J. Ment. Defic.*, **84,** 165–176.

Parker, E. (1974) *Survey of Incapacity Associated with Mental Handicap at Rampton and Moss Side Special Hospitals*. Special Hospitals Research Unit No. 11.

Robertson, G. (1981) The extent and pattern of crime amongst mentally handicapped offenders. *Apex*, **9,** 100–103. *J. Brit. Inst. Ment. Hand.*

Tarjan, C., Wright, S.W., Eyman, R.K. & Keeran, C.W. (1973) Natural history of mental retardation: some aspects of epidemiology. *Am. J. Ment. Defic.*, **77,** 369–379.

Terman, L. (1916) *The Measurement of Intelligence*. Boston: Houghton Mifflin.

Walker, N. & McCabe, S. (1973) *Crime and Insanity in England*, Vol. 2. Edinburgh: Edinburgh University Press.

Woodward, M. (1954) The role of low intelligence in delinquency. *Brit. J. Delinq.*, **5,** 281–303.

13

Epilepsy, Mental Abnormality and Criminal Behaviour

George Fenton

Epilepsy, derived from the Greek word meaning 'to take hold of', is a disorder of the brain characterised by recurring fits. The essence of an epileptic seizure is an abnormal and excessive electrical discharge of nerve cells within the brain. The manner in which the epileptic discharge expresses itself clinically depends on the part of the brain in which the excessive discharge begins and the parts through which it spreads, as well as the number and location of the discharging neurones. For example, when relatively few motor cortex neurones discharge there may be only jerking of limb on the opposite side of the body without loss of consciousness. When millions of neurones throughout the cerebral cortex discharge, unconsciousness is accompanied by a tonic–clonic convulsion. Between these two extremes are many different types of seizure.

CLASSIFICATION OF EPILEPSY

It is customary to classify epilepsy according to the presumed site of origin within the brain of the seizure discharge.

Generalised Epilepsy

Generalised epilepsies are those in which the seizure discharge is generalised from the onset, involving all neurones in both hemispheres sychronously and simultaneously. Sudden unconsciousness is the usual first feature of seizure onset and this may or may not be followed by other motor phenomena. No aura or warning is reported since an aura is a manifestation of the local brain area where the seizure discharge commences to spread; consequently no aura can occur when the electrical discharge commences in all neurones of the cortex simultaneously. Further, early in the course of generalised seizure onset the reticular formation, a core of neurones located centrally in the upper brain stem that is responsible for maintaining consciousness, is involved and disabled.

The common types of generalised attack are the tonic–clonic convulsion or grand-mal attack, and the petit-mal absence. The grand-mal attack consists of a generalised convulsion. There is initial spasm of all muscle groups, often with tongue biting and incontinence of urine due to spasm of the jaw and bladder muscles respectively. This is known as the tonic phase and lasts a number of seconds. It is followed by the clonic phase lasting several minutes. There is rhythmic contraction and relaxation of all muscle groups causing convulsive jerking of the head, face and limbs. After the clonic phase fades away the patient remains flaccid but unconscious for a variable length of time; usually 5 to 10 minutes. Then there is gradual recovery of consciousness, sometimes accompanied by disorientation in time and place and amnesia for the events of the seizure. In contrast to the dramatic events of the grand-mal fit, the petit-mal absence takes the form of a momentary lapse of consciousness, the patient's activity and conscious awareness being merely interrupted, with immediate resumption of normal activity on cessation of the seizure. During the absence the only apparent change may be transient blankness of facial expression. Sometimes there may be brief flickering of the eyelids or twitching of the arms and hands. Absences frequently pass unnoticed and may occur many times a day. Photosensitive seizures may also occur. These consist of major fits or absences triggered reflexly by flickering light. Myoclonus, sudden involuntary jerking of a muscle or group of muscles, is an exception to the rule that there is initial unconsciousness in generalised seizures. Retention of consciousness occurs because the epileptic discharge in myoclonic jerks occurs in clear consciousness due to descending spread of the epileptic discharge to the spinal cord.

Generalised epilepsies are subdivided into *primary* and *secondary* generalised forms. The former are not a result of cerebral disease, being largely due to genetic factors. The secondary generalised epilepsies are associated with acquired brain disease. This is usually widespread, involving all areas of the cerebral cortex; it may occasionally be due to secondary spread of a cortical focus, usually located in the mesial surface or the orbital frontal regions of one or other hemisphere.

Partial Epilepsy

In partial epilepsy the attacks are known as partial seizures because they begin in a local area (part) of the cerebral cortex or related sub-cortical structures. Most are considered to have an acquired cause due to focal brain damage and a local epileptogenic lesion manifest by focal EEG spikes and sharp wave EEG discharges.

When the abnormal neuronal discharge remains localised, and involves one hemisphere only, it may elicit a conscious sensation or series of sensations that the patient learns to recognise as a warning or aura. The character of the aura is determined by the function of the part of the brain involved. Hence it is not a warning, but the initial event of the seizure. Motor phenomena may also occur as the initial event of the partial seizure. The epileptic discharge causing a partial seizure may develop into a generalised seizure (secondary generalisation). Such generalisation is a common occurrence. Therefore, patients with partial epilepsy commonly have a mixture of partial seizures, that are manifestations of the epileptic discharge remaining localised to its site of origin; and secondary generalised seizures, where the local discharge has spread to involve both hemispheres with secondary generalisation. The generalisation may occur so rapidly that focal features are not observed and no aura will be experienced. Partial seizures with onset in 'silent' areas of cortex like the frontal lobe usually have no aura. One in five people with temporal lobe epilepsy present with grand-mal fits without aura. Partial seizures are subdivided into the following two groups according to the type of clinical features manifest:

1   Partial seizures with elementary symptomatology (simple partial seizures). These are partial attacks without impairment of consciousness accompanied by simple motor or sensory symptoms due to involvement of one or more primary cortical or special sense areas of one hemisphere. Such seizure manifestations reflect the function of the area involved, for example an epileptic discharge localised to the motor cortex produces jerking of the opposite limb.

2   Partial seizure with complex symptomatology (complex partial seizures); attacks with disturbance of the highest level of function of one or more cortical areas, with impairment of consciousness. The types of disturbance include certain disorders in awareness of body sensation, for example a sensation of 'butterflies' in the stomach, altered perceptions of limb size, shape or distance of objects, hallucinations involving the sense of smell, taste, sight or hearing, disorders of memory, for example *déjà-vu* phenomena, disorders of affect, for example fear, and automatic behaviour. Most complex partial seizures are of temporal lobe origin, with the exception of the phenomenon of forced thinking, where a thought forces itself into the patient's mind; in such cases the seizure discharge originates in the posterior part of the frontal lobe.

CAUSES OF EPILEPSY

The causes of epilepsy are as complex as the manifestations. In the past, epilepsy has been divided into two broad categories: symptomatic epilepsy, where the condition results from a brain lesion such as injury or infection, and idiopathic epilepsy, where there is no demonstrable underlying brain disease associated with the condition. However, the validity of the concept of idiopathic epilepsy has been increasingly challenged as each advance in knowledge explains more and more epilepsies, hitherto diagnosed as idiopathic, in terms of known causes. There are three main groups of causative factors that interact to produce epilepsy. The first is the individual's predisposition to fits, which is inherited. The second is the presence of a lesion of the brain. The third group of factors are the electrical changes at cell level that generate the abnormal electrical discharge which precipitates the fit. This process seems to involve increased cell membrane permeability to certain ions and heightened cell membrane electrical excitability. The more powerful the influence of one of these groups of factors, the less is required of the others to cause recurring seizures. For example, the patient with a strong genetic tendency towards epilepsy can readily have seizures precipitated by fever, flickering lights, television or even sleep deprivation. A person who has developed a lesion of the brain is more likely to have seizures if there is a strong genetic background.

The known causes of epilepsy can be summarised as follows:

1 Genetic factors can increase the predisposition to epilepsy.

2 Heredofamilial diseases of the brain, such as tuberose sclerosis and phenyl-ketonuria, are frequently accompanied by recurrent fits.

3 Antenatal and birth factors including congenital abnormalities can lead to brain dysfunction which manifests itself in recurrent epileptic fits. Maternal bleeding, infections and toxaemia are suspected of causal involvement in the early epilepsies. Prematurity, prolonged labour, forceps delivery, lack of oxygen during the perinatal period and low birth weight have all been mentioned as possible perinatal causative factors. Studies have demonstrated that sudden alterations in the brain metabolism during the perinatal period, for example hypoglycaemia, may lead to brain damage and epilepsy.

4 Acute infections of the brain; convulsions may accompany an acute infection of the brain such as meningitis or encephalitis. Alternatively, fits may be a consequence of damage done to the brain by the infection.

5 Prolonged febrile convulsions, or status epilepticus, in children; otherwise quite healthy children may suffer convulsions during pyrexial illnesses. These convulsions usually do not cause any harm. However, if they are particularly prolonged or recurrent over a few hours, damage to the temporal lobe structures may occur. Over the course of a number of years the damaged area may become 'epileptic'. Such changes are thought to be the cause of temporal lobe epilepsy in about half the patients seen.

6 Accidents involving cerebral injury constitute one of the primary causes of symptomatic epilepsy, especially if the brain substance is penetrated during the impact. As many as 40 per cent of patients with missile wounds to the head develop fits. Indeed trauma is more likely to cause partial epilepsy than general-ised, and may be responsible for about 5 to 15 per cent of all causes of epilepsy.

7 Metabolic and endocrine disorders involving the brain; disturbances of meta-bolism of the brain due to vitamin deficiencies, for example pyridoxine de-ficiency, alteration in the electrolyte concentrations of the brain, and so on, may cause fits.

8 Cerebrovascular disease, brain tumours and neuronal degenerations can also be responsible for brain lesions leading to epilepsy.

9 Toxic factors can precipitate convulsions as in the case of alcohol, or lead to residual epilepsy as in the case of lead poisoning. Alterations in brain excitability due to sudden withdrawal of alcohol, narcotic or hypnotic drugs in people dependent on (addicted to) these agents can cause fits, known as withdrawal fits.

In addition there are a number of precipitating factors that bring on an attack in susceptible people; for example, high fever, anoxia, lack of sleep, overbreath-ing, emotional stress, and reflex epilepsies, where the individual has fits in response to certain environmental stimuli such as rapidly flashing light, music, and the like.

At present, between 70 and 75 per cent of patients with seizures do not have evidence of underlying brain disease. Of the remainder, whose epilepsy can be related to a definite or presumed brain lesion, the reported nature of the disease process varies widely in different surveys; this is doubtless a reflection of the amount of detailed case record information available and the variability of diagnostic criteria. However, the prevalence study in Rochester, Minnesota, between 1935 and 1967, is noteworthy for the thoroughness of case finding and length of follow-up (Hauser and Kurland 1975). Their findings are therefore of special interest. Twenty-three per cent of their sample of 156 patients had epilepsy of known cause; 2 per cent birth injury, 4 per cent congenital abnormalities of the brain, 4 per cent post-natal injuries, 3 per cent infections, 5 per cent cerebral vascular disease, 4 per cent cerebral tumours, 0.6 per cent degenerative disorders of the cerebral neurones.

Probably one person in 20 has a fit of some sort during the course of his lifetime. However, only one in eight of those who have had such an isolated fit will develop chronic epilepsy, that is, recurrent fits. In the latter, the onset of epilepsy occurs before the age of 5 in nearly one quarter, and before school leaving age in more than half. The majority of epileptic seizures are likely to recur intermittently over the years, though only a minority of patients will be seriously handicapped by frequent fits. These will tend to be those with an onset of fits in early childhood, a long duration of illness, a combination of different seizure types and evidence of widespread brain damage.

The diagnosis of epilepsy should be made predominantly on clinical grounds from the description of the seizure pattern. This can be supplemented by EEG investigation; though it is important to emphasise that a diagnosis of epilepsy should never be made on EEG grounds alone. A number of quite healthy people have bursts of generalised spike wave activity during EEG recordings while some patients with epilepsy have relatively normal EEGs.

An isolated seizure can be the result of drug or alcohol withdrawal, of medication with certain epileptogenic drugs such as the tricyclic antidepressants and phenothiazine drugs, acute changes in the metabolic state of the brain, cerebral oedema due to acute fluid retention, structural brain disease, or it may be the outcome of interaction between a genetically low convulsive threshold and certain provoking factors such as sleep deprivation, hypoglycaemia, high fever in infants, etc. The occurrence of an isolated seizure is an indication for further investigation to exclude such possible causes. However, a diagnosis of epilepsy should not be made unless there are recurrent seizures, that is, two or more separated by an interval of weeks or months. Only then should the diagnosis of epilepsy be made, since the label 'epilepsy' has social consequences as well as being a medical diagnosis. Being diagnosed epileptic may threaten the person's job and will inevitably lead to loss of driving licence.

When the diagnosis is made, full neurological investigation is required. This will include a detailed physical examination with special reference to the nervous system, a skull X-ray and EEG. If a diagnosis of partial epilepsy is made on clinical or EEG grounds, a CAT scan should be carried out.

Treatment of Epilepsy

After completion of the neurological assessment, anticonvulsant medication should be commenced, the aim being to obtain the best control of seizures without producing unwanted toxic effects. It has been estimated that current drugs now completely control seizures in more than half of patients with epilepsy; another 30 to 40 per cent gain a varying degree of improvement. Treatment usually must continue for many years because the anticonvulsant medication merely raises the seizure threshold and does not cure the disease. The indications for cessation of treatment are three years of freedom from attacks while still on treatment. However, it is well to remember that even after three years of freedom, up to half of the patients have recurrence of seizures when the treatment is stopped.

The selection of the drug to be used depends on the type of seizure and EEG finding. Grand-mal seizures of generalised origin respond best to phenytoin or carbamazepine. In resistant cases, both may be used together. When control is still not possible with these drugs, it may be necessary to resort to phenobarbitone or primidone in combination with either phenytoin or carbamazepine. It is important to remember that phenobarbitone and primidone tend to cause irritability and restlessness and aggravate behaviour problems, especially in children. Partial seizures will tend to respond to the drugs of choice for generalised seizures. However, carbamazepine is now the drug of first choice for the treatment of temporal lobe epilepsy, one of the most difficult types to treat. This drug does not have the same degree of sedative effect as the barbiturates. When the only type of seizure is absence attacks, the patient should be treated with ethosuximide or sodium valproate. Seizures due to secondary generalised epilepsy and the myoclonic epilepsies are notoriously resistant to treatment: sodium valproate is the drug of choice.

An important principle of anticonvulsant treatment is to avoid polytherapy and to use a single drug at one time if possible. Monotherapy is preferred because drug interaction is common with combinations of many antiepileptic drugs: this can lead to unpredictable side effects. It is best to administer a single drug, the dose being adjusted to keep the serum concentration of the drug within the range demonstrated to be the most therapeutically effective. Exceeding this level will only lead to toxic effects. If satisfactory control cannot be obtained with monotherapy, then it is permissible to try two drugs simultaneously. The therapist should always avoid getting into a position of using more than two drugs at any one time because of the problem of drug interaction and its consequent side effects. Chronic patients who have been taking a number of drugs concurrently for many years are difficult to manage; only a few are likely to be free of both fits and unwanted side effects. Such patients are frequently amongst those presenting with psychiatric problems.

The presence of a focal cortical lesion raises the possibility of surgical excision of the local area of epileptogenic cortex. Surgery is considered if the following criteria are fulfilled:

1   the patient is seriously handicapped by frequent seizures;
2   an adequate trial of drug treatment over 3–5 years has failed;
3   there is clinical and EEG evidence that the seizures arise consistently from a localised area of cortex that can be excised without causing the patient disability.

Temporal lobectomy, surgical removal of the anterior six centimetres of one temporal lobe, is the most commonly used surgical treatment and is very effective in some patients with drug resistant temporal lobe seizures. About two-thirds of such patients are markedly improved after surgery; half the total becoming seizure free. Surgical treatment can only be aimed at control of the fits. It usually has little effect on the person's behaviour disturbance. The only exception to this rule is aggressiveness in young men with temporal lobe seizures due to unilateral temporal lobe pathology. The aggressiveness often responds to the temporal lobectomy, but only if there is control of the seizures. It should be stressed that interictal aggressive behaviour in the absence of frequent seizures does not respond to surgery.

Once the initial diagnosis of epilepsy has been made, treatment commenced and any necessary social rehabilitation measures put into effect, the patient should be reviewed at regular intervals to make sure that he is taking his drugs and that they are effective; to sustain him in handling his life while the fits continue; to minimise the side effects and toxic effects of the drugs and to ensure that he benefits from advances in treatment.

EPILEPSY, PERSONALITY AND BEHAVIOUR DISORDER

Classification

The psychiatric disorders of epilepsy can be classified into the following three main categories.

Disorders due to the brain disease causing the fits

Disturbed behaviour may occur as a symptom of the brain disease that is causing the fits. This may be due to local (focal) damage especially involving the frontal or temporal lobes, or may be widespread throughout the cerebral cortex of both hemispheres. In the latter case, it is probable that the patient will manifest intellectual impairment as well as behaviour disorders. Mental handicap is an example where both the seizures and the intellectual deficit are a reflection of underlying diffuse brain damage. Between one-fifth and a half of severely mentally retarded patients have epilepsy, its prevalence increasing with the profundity of mental handicap. There is also a number of diffuse progressive brain diseases, usually developing in childhood, in which fits and progressive intellectual impairment are both symptoms of the underlying disease process.

Disorders related in time to seizure occurrence

(a) *Preictal.* Prodromal mood changes, particularly irritability and moodiness, can develop hours or days before the onset of a fit and be relieved by the occurrence of the seizure. Little is known about the prevalence of such prodromal changes nor indeed of their pathogenesis.

(b) *Ictal.* Disorders directly due to the seizure discharge can include complex partial seizures, absence status and complex partial status. The behavioural manifestations of these three conditions will be discussed in more detail later. (c) *Postictal.* Disorders can follow one or more seizures, usually generalised convulsions, the common feature being clouding of consciousness seizure with depression of cortical function.

Interictal disorders unrelated in time to the seizures

In the interictal disorders the behavioural abnormalities are present between attacks and persist even in the absence of seizures. In such patients it is assumed that the epileptic and/or the cerebral lesion causing the epilepsy have played a role in the genesis of the behaviour disturbance.

It is now appropriate to review in some detail those aspects of epilepsy, personality and behaviour that contribute to the understanding of the complex interaction between fits and abnormal behaviour. Special attention will be paid to those of forensic relevance.

Epilepsy and Automatism

Automatism is perhaps the most important aspect of epilepsy from the forensic point of view. Epileptic automatism may be defined as a state of clouding of consciousness which occurs during or immediately after a seizure and during which the individual retains control of posture and muscle tone without being aware of what is happening around him. It can occur either as the direct result of a seizure discharge or immediately after termination of such a seizure discharge, especially a generalised one.

If the automatic behaviour occurs as the result of a seizure discharge it must be a manifestation of seizure activity which does not interfere with the person's capacity to maintain normal posture and carry out simple movements, though of course it does affect the patient's comprehension of what is happening.

Ictal automatism is most commonly the result of temporal lobe epilepsy, due to abnormal electrical discharge commencing in the mesial temporal lobe structures in the region of the amygdaloid nucleus. It has been demonstrated that the degree of spread of the electrical disturbance from the periamygdaloid region is important in determining whether or not the seizure discharge leads to automatic behaviour. For automatism to develop there must be a spread to the same areas of the opposite hemisphere and to the upper brainstem structures. Indeed automatic behaviour in some patients results from lesions on sites other than the mesial temporal lobe structures, namely the frontal and parietal regions or the mesial surfaces of both hemispheres. In such cases the abnormal electrical discharge has spread to cause secondary involvement of the peramygdaloid structures of both temporal lobes.

A less common form of epileptic automatism is that due to prolonged generalised spike wave discharges (absence or petit-mal automatisms). As well as being a manifestation of seizure discharge (ictal automatism), automatic behaviour can occur during the clouding of consciousness that commonly follows one or more generalised convulsions (postictal automatism): automatism is especially probable if the clouding persists for a number of minutes. In this situation, the clouded state is due to residual inhibition of cortical function as the result of nerve cell fatigue following the period of intense neuronal activation by the seizure discharge. This impairment of function of the cortex is reflected in the appearance of diffuse EEG slow waves. If the clouding of consciousness lasts for hours, days or weeks, the condition is known as a post-epileptic confusional state with symptoms identical to those of any organic confusional state.

Behaviour during epileptic automatism varies greatly from patient to patient and in the same individual on different occasions. The person's actions often have a pseudo-purposeful quality, but are usually inappropriate to his environment. Impairment of awareness and lack of responsiveness are usual. Brief attacks, where the seizure discharge lasts ten seconds or less, merely cause cessation of whatever the patient was doing. More prolonged episodes of discharge of 20 to 30 seconds' duration produce stereotyped repetitive movements – for example, chewing, swallowing, clenching of fists. When the discharge lasts several minutes or longer, there is more complex, variable and pseudo-purposeful behaviour – for example undressing, wandering away, etc. This involves an interplay with the environment and gradually merges into normal behaviour. The earlier stereotyped phenomena are a direct manifestation of the seizure discharge. In contrast the later complex behaviour continues after electrical discharge has ceased and is a manifestation of clouding of consciousness owing to temporary inhibition of function of cerebral neurones following the intense activation of the same neurones by the seizure discharge. The majority of automatisms are brief, 5 minutes or less on 80 per cent of occasions, and never lasting more than an hour.

The inevitable clouding of consciousness that is part of the epileptic automatism means that well-structured goal-directed behaviour is impossible to initiate and continue. Hence, serious violence during epileptic automatism is rare. In one series of 43 patients, no aggressive conduct was observed in 36 (84 per cent). The remaining 7 tended to resist attempts to interfere with or restrict their activities during the period of automatism. Behaviour of only one of these patients was considered dangerous. This sample of 43 patients with automatism was taken from a total epileptic population of 434 patients attending a hospital for neurological diseases (Knox, 1968).

A survey of epileptic offenders in prisons and borstal institutions in England and Wales found only two cases out of a total of 158 epileptic offenders, where the crime was probably committed during or shortly after a seizure; one during the post-epileptic phase and the other during a possible epileptic automatism. A parallel study of epileptic population of Broadmoor Hospital, one of the special hospitals in England and Wales for mentally ill offenders and patients displaying dangerous antisocial behaviour, identified 29 male patients with epilepsy who had committed offences. In only two of these patients could a definite relationship be established between their crimes and the occurrence of seizures; both behaved violently during a postictal confusion state (Gunn and Fenton, 1969, 1971).

An international workshop on aggression and epilepsy was held at Bethesda, Maryland in March 1980 (Delgado-Escueta et al, 1981). A number of distinguished neurologists from USA, Canada, Germany, Italy and Japan, studied videotape recorded attacks of 13 patients, selected because they were believed to show aggressive behaviour during seizures. These patients were taken from a total population of 5400 people with epilepsy from a number of different countries. Seven patients were rated as exhibiting significant aggression during their seizures. The aggression varied from shouting insults and spitting to karate postures and chops and smashing of furniture. Five of the 7 patients were rated as showing an angry mood during the seizure. Of the 7 who did exhibit aggression, 4 were rated as displaying violence to property only, 2 made threats of violence to a person (including gestures, shouting and spitting) and one was rated as displaying mild violence only (the use of force against another person without inflicting serious harm, for example pushing or shoving). In all 7 patients, the aggressive behaviour appeared suddenly, without any evidence of planning, and lasted an average of 29 seconds during the seizures. All patients could be easily restrained. The automatic behaviour (for example, kicking and boxing, attempts at grabbing an intended target and face-scratching) were short-lived, fragmentary and non-sustained. This study confirms the previous observations that seriously aggressive behaviour is rare during epileptic seizures.

Nevertheless, despite the rarity of epileptic automatism as a cause of antisocial behaviour, there are more epileptic prisoners in gaols than would be expected by chance: 7.2 per thousand prisoners in England and Wales (Gunn, 1977). When a random sample of non-epileptic prisoners was campared with the epileptic prisoners, no differences in terms of clinical state or criminal behaviour could be discerned, nor was there any relation between temporal lobe epilepsy and violent offences apparent. Gunn (1977) has presented the following hypothesis to explain the higher prevalence of epilepsy in prisoners.

1   In some, the brain damage causes fits and uninhibited antisocial behaviour.

2   Some epileptics with psychosocial problems feel stigmatised by their fits and hit back at society by behaving in an antisocial manner.

3   A deprived early environment may provide the milieu both for acquiring brain damage and for learning an aggressive behavioural repertoire.

4   Finally, brain damage and the resulting epilepsy may be the consequence of the person's basically disorganised and impetuous life-style that accompanied the criminality. For example, Gunn (1977) quotes the case of the juvenile thief and lorry stealer who recklessly smashed up an army lorry and sustained a severe head injury and post-traumatic epilepsy.

Medico-Legal Aspects of Automatism

Fenton (1972) presented guidelines to help the physician in assessing the probability of a crime having been committed during an episode of epileptic automatism. These are as follows.

1   The patient should have a past history of definite epileptic attacks. It is probable that enquiry into his past history will reveal the occurrence of grand-mal attacks or other types of seizure as well as the alleged attacks of automatic behaviour. A study of vague perceptual disturbance such as *déjà-va* sensations or feelings of depersonalisation should not be accepted as evidence of temporal lobe epilepsy in the absence of other features. Neurotic patients frequently experience such symptoms in the absence of epilepsy. Indeed these phenomena can occasionally be a feature of schizophrenic symptomatology. Further, they can sometimes be elicited on enquiry from quite healthy people. In epilepsy such phenomena occur as transient, paroxysmal, stereotyped events, often in association with other temporal lobe symptoms and frequently accompanied by a brief alteration in the level of consciousness. Automatism need not be an invariable feature of the epileptic fits, nor does there have to be any previous history of automatism. The diagnosis of automatism must always be made on clinical grounds, for epilepsy can occur in the presence of normal routine EEG records. Conversely epileptic discharges, especially brief generalised spike and wave complexes, can be recorded from people who have never had an epileptic attack.
2   The abnormal behaviour will always appear suddenly, will usually be of short duration – minutes rather than hours – and will never be entirely appropriate for the circumstances. There should be no evidence of planning or premeditation. Amnesia for the events of the attack is the rule. However, one should regard with suspicion any complaint of amnesia preceding the attacks that last longer than a few minutes. The same applies to prolonged periods of amnesia following the attacks. In the unlikely event of the seizure being witnessed by bystanders, some evidence of clouding of consciousness will usually be noticed, for example, inappropriate actions or gestures, stereotyped movements of the face, lips and limbs, unresponsiveness or irrelevant replies to questions, aimless wandering around or a dazed vacant facial expression. However, these features may not be apparent to the untrained eye, but nevertheless, any witnesses should be subjected to careful enquiry about the presence of such features. There will often be little attempt to conceal the crime, though this is not invariably the case.

A recent House of Lords decision (*R. v. Sullivan*, 23 June 1983) has clearly defined the status of epileptic automatism in English law. The learned judges rejected the plea of non-insane automatism (automatism simpliciter). This latter concept implies that the unconscious, involuntary behaviour characteristic of the epileptic automatism is not insane in the sense used in English law, since the cause is a disturbance of brain function that is transient, with complete recovery between attacks. The judges argued that neither the cause of the disease impairing the mental faculties of reason, memory and understanding (the legal concept of 'mind') nor the transient duration of the fits were relevant to the question of whether or not the person was insane at the time of the automatic behaviour. They ruled that epileptic automatism is a disease of the mind within the law. Hence, criminal activity of an unconscious, involuntary nature due to psychomotor epilepsy must be interpreted using the McNaughton Rules. If the defence can prove that these apply, a verdict of not guilty by reason of insanity can be brought in. This judgment is discussed in more detail in the *Lancet*, 9 July 1983 (pp. 116–117). Though the legal arguments of the Law Lords have a convincing logic, the implications are unfortunate. Within the law, all people who have transient episodes of impaired awareness are, at least temporarily, insane.

Differentiation of Epileptic Automatism From Other Types of Automatic Behaviour

The diagnosis depends esssentially on the clinical assessment of the pattern of behaviour manifest during the attacks. Eye-witness accounts should be obtained whenever possible. It is also essential to elicit a description of the person's current life situation and personality as well as a history of his past life from a relative or close friend. Careful enquiries should be made about the occurrence of other types of epileptic seizure, either in the past or present. The possibility of alcohol and drug intoxication should always be borne in mind when the history is being taken. Care should also be taken to exclude medical and iatrogenic causes of clouding of consciousness, for example, hypoglycaemia due to an islet cell tumour of the pancreas or an overdose of insulin in a diabetic subject.

Epileptic automatism must be at first distinguished on clinical grounds from the following types of disturbed behaviour.

Episodes of co-ordinated well-integrated behaviour accompanied by a complaint of amnesia

1 Hysterical dissociation with amnesia and a fugue state is perhaps the most common. Usually this occurs at a time of crisis in the person's life. His behaviour will be purposeful and directed towards escaping from the situation of intolerable stress, for example travelling to another part of the country and arriving without knowledge of his identity or memory of the past. The person's memory will gradually return spontaneously. The amnesia may last hours, days or even weeks in contrast to the brief situation of an epileptic automatism. The amnesia also tends to be selective for the events of personal significance for the patient. The behaviour displayed will show no evidence of loss of awareness of the environment.

2 The syndrome of transient global amnesia occurs in middle-aged people and consists of periods of recurrent amnesia, usually lasting a few hours at a time. Though the patients have no recollection of events that have taken place during the episodes of transient global amnesia, knowledge of personal identity throughout the attacks is intact. The person's performance of his or her repertoire of everyday activities is not impaired, though the patients during these episodes describe themselves as feeling strange. In contrast to hysterical amnesia, which usually affects individuals in the third or fourth decade, these patients tend to be middle-aged or elderly, and often have a history of hypertension or atherosclerosis. Though they do not lose knowledge of their identity they cannot retain new information during the episodes. It is hypothesised that the episodes

result from transient ischaemia involving the mamillary-hippocampal complex of the brain. Obvious psychological precipitants do not come to light.

Most patients are said to be of normal personality and good premorbid stability. The structure of the memory deficit itself, with demonstrably faulty new learning and a time-related retrograde gap is entirely consistent with an organic origin. Knowledge of personal identity throughout the attack is intact. In contrast to hysterical amnesia, the memory difficulties are not restricted to matters of personal concern nor specific themes calculated to elicit psychological discomfort in the individual, nor are there any inconsistencies of performance.

The episodes of transient global amnesia can be readily distinguished from epileptic automatism. Automatic behaviour of epileptic origin is of brief duration, lasting minutes rather than hours. An aura may precede the attack, if the automatic behaviour is a manifestation of a complex partial seizure (usually of temporal origin). During the epileptic automatism subjects' behaviour manifests evidence of clouding of consciousness, poor appreciation of the environment and purposeless or automatic behaviour inappropriate to the circumstances of the moment.

3 Amnesia for criminal activity or behaviour that he would prefer to forget, may be feigned by an individual in order to protect himself from the legal consequences of his actions or the esteem with which he is held in the eyes of others. Detailed investigation of the circumstances of the behaviour concerned will usually reveal discrepancies in the person's story.

4 Occasionally, patients present with episodic outbursts of aggressive, uninhibited but well-structured behaviour. These episodes are variable in duration, from minutes only to several hours, and are not associated with any definite clinical manifestations of epilepsy. There is often a histrionic quality to the outbursts. Despite the well-integrated nature of the individual's actions, it is rare for the subject to do himself or others any injury. Environmental precipitating factors may or may not be apparent. Because of the impulsive and paroxysmal nature of the behaviour, a diagnosis of temporal lobe automatism is often erroneously made. EEG investigation is invariably negative. The patient tends to be an emotionally inhibited individual with difficulty in expressing his feelings and in tolerating any mental pain. His habitual defence against emotional conflict is to deny the existence of any such difficulty. Patient and sympathetic enquiry will often reveal an underlying depressive state related to stresses in his life situation. Similar episodes of explosive, aggressive behaviour with amnesia may occur in psychopaths, whose ability to tolerate provocation or frustration is often low.

5 Posturing or stereotyped movements in catatonic schizophrenia may sometimes be mistaken for epileptic automatisms but the other characteristic features of the psychotic process are invariably present. If rapport with the patient can be established it is usually possible to determine that the behaviour occurs in a setting of clear consciousness.

Other causes of automatic behaviour with clouding of consciousness

Intoxication with alcohol or other drugs must be excluded as well as clouding of consciousness due to toxic, metabolic or infective agents such as hypoglycaemia, post-infectious confusional states, encephalitis, etc. Automatic behaviour may also occur in clouding of consciousness due to cerebral ischaemia or degenerative pathology of the brain such as Alzheimer's disease. However, confusional states of toxic, metabolic, or inflammatory origin, or a result of widespread nerve cell damage, are usually prolonged, lasting days or weeks; neither are they often recurrent events.

Finally, epileptic automatisms confined to sleep may be confused with somnambulism or sleep-walking, a phenomenon which occurs in some healthy people. The sleep-walking episodes are usually longer in duration and the behaviour of the subject tends to be better integrated. Repetitive stereotyped behaviour is rare in sleep-walking. Somnambulism occurs during deep (stage 4) sleep. Epileptic automatisms occurring in sleep are a feature of light (stage 1) sleep. If waking occurs after such an event, rapid return to clear consciousness is usual in sleep-walkers while a varying degree of metal confusion may persist for some time afterwards in the case of an epileptic automatism. EEG studies during sleep may be necessary to distinguish between these two types of attack.

Episodic Dyscontrol Syndrome

A number of research workers have suggested that, after excluding patients who have demonstrable epilepsy, brain damage or psychotic illness as the basis of their aggressive acts (also those pursuing a motivated career of premeditated crime for gain), one is left with a number of persons who display explosively violent behaviour provoked by minimal stimuli. The group is largely composed of young men from disrupted families who often have an unusual susceptibility to alcohol and frequently have anomalous EEGs in the absence of demonstrable brain damage.

The propensity for violence begins in early childhood, lasts through adolescence and the third decade, but declines in at least 40 per cent of cases in the fourth decade. The patients' personal situations are mostly chaotic, with frequent histories of divorce, arrest, repeated dismissal from work, alcohol and/or drug abuse. Indeed, there may be evidence of behavioural maladjustment since childhood. Such patients may also report quasi-epileptic experiences preceding the outbursts of violence. These usually involve either transient changes in the patients' perception of the environment, for example, intensity of sounds is augmented, people around seem unreal, they experience a sensation of numbness in their hands and feet, changes in mood state such as a feeling of mounting inner tension, irritability and/or depression. These mood changes may be accompanied by the somatic manifestations of anxiety. Headache and drowsiness may follow the outbursts. Amnesia for the behaviour during and sometimes immediately preceding the episodes may be claimed.

Some display soft neurological signs in the form of minor ataxia of gait, incoordination of movement or some degree of left–right uncertainty. Anomalous EEGs are common, usually consisting of an excess of rhythms slower in frequency than the alpha rhythms (less than 8 Hz). These are present over both hemispheres, most markedly over the posterior parts, especially in the posterior temporal regions. In the latter site, these phenomena are known as posterior temporal slow waves. They are more prominent over the right hemisphere and often have a sharpened waveform.

Such sharply formed posterior temporal slow activity can be mistaken for the EEG sharp waves of temporal lobe epilepsy. This can lead to an erroneous clinical diagnosis of temporal lobe epilepsy (TLE) being made. Fortunately there are important differences in the location and physiological behaviour of the two waveforms that make them easily distinguishable. The posterior temporal slow waves are posterior in location and are seen best during relaxed wakefulness with the eyes closed. They are markedly attenuated by eye opening and disappear completely during sleep. A 3-minute period of overbreathing markedly augments them. In contrast, TLE sharp waves or spikes are located over the anterior part of the temporal lobe. They are not prominent or may even be absent in the waking state. Moreover, they are markedly augmented during light sleep but not influenced by the overbreathing procedure.

The association of episodic, explosive, aggressive episodes with little or no provocation sometimes heralded by transient perceptual or affective changes and followed by amnesia for the events of the episode, tolerance to alcohol, soft neurological signs and anomalous EEGs has led some research workers to propose that this behavioural pattern has an epileptic basis. It has been called the episodic dyscontrol syndrome.

The evidence for such a claim is not substantial. The behaviour of such patients though explosively violent is usually well structured, integrated and goal directed, differing markedly from that found in frank epileptic automatism. Consciousness is often clear and amnesia is by no means invariable. The behaviour manifested is more in keeping with loss of impulse control than of clouding of consciousness such as is seen in epileptic automatism.

The EEG changes are different from those found in temporal lobe epilepsy, being usually a generalised excess of slower background frequencies, most marked over the posterior quadrants of both hemispheres, especially in the posterior temporal region. Such anomalous EEGs are common in populations of patients manifesting antisocial behaviour but are not specially found in people with epilepsy. Indeed, their prevalence in any population increases with the degree of social maladjustment of the population being studied; highest in aggressive psychopaths (50 per cent) and lowest in people specially selected for stability of personality, for example, service personnel selected for air crew duties (5 per cent).

They do occur in a minority of quite healthy people (about 10 per cent). Their significance remains uncertain. Their prevalence is at its peak in adolescence and the early twenties and declines dramatically in the over thirties. The close relationship to age and the fact that such changes, anomalous in the EEG of the adult, are part of the normal developmental EEG pattern of children, has led to the hypothesis that their persistence into adult life is a reflection of failure of maturation of brain function. Such a view is attractive since much of the behaviour of such individuals is 'immature'. Unfortunately for this hypothesis the relation between EEG and behavioural immaturity is by no means a consistent one in an individual. Further, genetic factors have been shown to be important in the genesis of these EEG anomalies. There is also a little evidence linking them to early brain damage acquired around the perinatal period. It may well be that their common finding in psychopaths is a reflection of an interaction between genetic factors and the presence of early brain damage that interferes with the normal processes of maturation of brain activity, the outcome of which is immature EEG patterns.

People displaying the episodic dyscontrol syndrome frequently come from a socially disadvantaged background, where poor socio-economic conditions prevail; this is often accompanied by poor standards of medical care. Disrupted family life is almost the rule. Absence or loss of one or both parents is common as is parental emotional disturbance and/or alcoholism, marital discord, child abuse and other types of family problem. Such is the milieu that breeds delinquency and psychopathic behaviour. The poor social circumstances and inadequate parental supervision may also increase the risk of early brain damage due either to the complications of pregnancy and childbirth (higher in this socio-economic sector of the community) or to brain trauma or infection acquired in early childhood as the result of parental abuse or neglect. Such early brain damage, if relatively mild, will retard the processes of cerebral maturation and result in the immature EEG patterns common in psychopaths. More severe early brain damage will tend to lead to organic EEG changes and/or epilepsy. Hence the antisocial behaviour and the immature EEG changes can be viewed as a direct result of the pathogenic environments the patients were exposed to during the early formative years of their lives. Of course, genetic predisposition may also play a part in shaping both the behaviour and the EEG changes.

Indeed much of the behaviour of patients displaying the so-called episodic dyscontrol syndrome resembles that manifested by psychopaths due to low impulse control. Their previous history has also much in common with that found in psychopathy as have the EEG changes. Hence, a plausible explanation is that the episodic dyscontrol syndrome is merely a clinical label for the explosive episodes of behaviour disorder found in some psychopaths, secondary to their poor impulse control. Similar explosive behaviour is also found in a small number of emotionally inhibited people, who habitually exercise tight control over their aggressive feeling: overcontrolled (too much impulse control). Such people have led blameless lives in the past. However, if exposed to prolonged and intolerable provocation, especially from a person with whom they have a close emotional involvement, they may react with explosive aggressive behaviour, for which they have much remorse afterwards. Some such emotionally inhibited people may respond in a similar fashion to an underlying depressive mood state, since they often have little capacity to endure the psychic pain of depression.

This view of the episodic dyscontrol syndrome is supported by a recent neurological study of such patients that revealed that most of the disturbed behaviour reported had a psychological explanation. None had any evidence of epilepsy (Leicester, 1982).

From the point of view of practical management it is important not to be misled into diagnosing epilepsy. This diagnosis has serious social consequences for the patients and implies the need for long-term anticonvulsant drug treatment. Anticonvulsant drugs will not benefit the patient's behaviour. Indeed certain anticonvulsants such as phenobarbitone or primidone may aggravate the irritability. Further, long-term anticonvulsant medication is not without serious side effects on both bodily and mental function.

The presence of immature EEG patterns in such patients should be ignored. They have no specific diagnostic significance and do not have any bearing on management or outcome. However, though the EEG is only useful in the negative sense of excluding organic brain disease or epilepsy, it has immense theoretical potential in the investigation of patients with persistently antisocial behaviour. The contingent negative variation (CNV) is a slow negative voltage change developing in the cortex during an experimental situation that requires a person to process a pair of time-related signals, the first of which is a warning that the subject should perform a certain course of action in response to the second signal. The CNV develops in the interval between the two signals while the subject prepares to respond to the second one. It rapidly resolves when the subject carries out the required response.

Early claims that the CNV is absent or very small in psychopathic patients have not been confirmed. However, recent research has compared the CNV amplitude when an active response to the second signal is required, for example, a button press (GO response), with that generated when the response to the second signal has to be inhibited, for example, stop pressing the button (NO GO response). This experimental situation is not dissimilar to that of a motorist at traffic lights (green = GO; red = NO GO). The GO CNV is much larger. Of greater importance, however, is the observation that the difference between the GO and NO GO CNVs (degree of GO/NO GO differentiation) correlates with impulsivity. Poor differentiation is related to high impulsivity scores (Howard et al, 1982). This finding suggests a neural correlate for low impulse control. It is hypothesised that the brain system involved is the frontal-septal-hippocampal (brain inhibitory) system and that this system is modulated by the level of cerebral noradrenergic activity (Fenwick et al, 1983).

Epilepsy, Personality and Behaviour: Interictal Disturbances

The abnormal behaviour of people with epilepsy may show no direct time-relationship to seizure occurrence, often being manifest whether the patient is having seizures or not. In such cases it is assumed that the epilepsy (and/or the brain lesion causing the fits) plays a role in the genesis of the behaviour disturbance. Though the disorder is unrelated in time to seizure occurrence, the onset, intensity and course may be influenced by the fit frequency; more commonly by an exacerbation of fits; less often and more controversially by a reduction in fit frequency so that there is an inverse relation between fits and mental state.

There is much evidence that both children and adults with epilepsy have a greater prevalence of behaviour disorder of a nature that cannot be directly related to seizure occurrence. Rutter et al (1970) have demonstrated that in children at least this is not simply due to a reaction to the stress of coping with a chronic handicap. In a survey of Isle of Wight schoolchildren, Rutter and his colleagues found that epileptic children were 5 times more likely to have psychiatric disability than the general population. They were 3 times more likely than children with chronic handicaps not affecting the brain. Children with epilepsy due to damage affecting the higher brain centres had the maximum prevalence (more than 8 times that of the controls). This study also demonstrated that multiple factors interact to cause psychiatric disturbance in people with epilepsy. Organic brain dysfunction, temporal lobe disorder as manifested by complex partial seizures and adverse familial influences were found to be predisposing factors. The types of psychological symptom and behaviour disorder displayed by epileptic children did not differ from those of other children in the same community suffering from psychiatric disorder. Antisocial and mixed neurotic/antisocial disorders were the most common.

However, when disturbed children with epilepsy are selected by EEG criteria, the site of the origin of the epileptogenic process does influence the symptom profile. Nuffield (1961) showed that children with temporal lobe spikes (indicating temporal lobe epileptogenic activity) showed significantly more aggressive behaviour, while those with generalised spike and wave complexes tended to be non-aggressive and to manifest neurotic symptoms such as phobias, bed-wetting, and so on. Stores (1978) has reported that boys with fits and epileptic children of either sex with left temporal lobe dysfunction are especially vulnerable to a wide range of behavioural difficulty.

Surveys of adult epilepsies are less reliable because of sample bias. Pond and Bidwell (1960) in a general practice survey found that nearly one-third had psychological difficulties, mainly neuroses in adults and conduct disorders in children. Only 4 per cent showed features of the epileptic personality. Seven per cent had been mental hospital patients, half of whom had temporal lobe epilepsy. Indeed, temporal lobe dysfunction, low intelligence and adverse environmental circumstances were factors that seemed to predispose to psychiatric breakdown, especially behaviour and personality disorders. As in children, no specific symptom or behavioural profiles could be identified.

There is little doubt that the clinical features the patient develops are strongly influenced by age. Children in adolescence present with behaviour difficulties: antisocial/neurotic disorder. In contrast adults tend to develop affective symptoms, especially those with late onset epilepsy. Suicide is five times more common among people with epilepsy than in the general population.

Personality disorder, unless a direct result of a focal brain lesion, is usually a reflection of life-long disturbance with early onset of fits and a history of maladjustment with behaviour and/or neurotic problems during childhood. The depressant effects of anticonvulsant drugs on cognitive function and emotional control also aggravate behaviour difficulties or mood disorder in both children and adults. Indeed, phenobarbitone may have a paradoxical exciting effect on children and can lead to an increase in irritability and overactive behaviour.

Is There a Specific Epileptic Personality?

There is an abundance of literature on the concept that people with epilepsy have a specific constellation of personality traits (reviewed by Guerrant et al, 1962). The term 'epileptic character' was first used by the French psychiatrist Morel during the last century. However, by 1900 it came to be widely used. Epilepsy was regarded at that time as an inherited disorder, specific personality change being as prominent a feature as the fits. People with epilepsy were rarely considered mentally normal. Profound disturbances of mood, attitude and behaviour followed by inevitable mental deterioration were thought to be the rule. The character changes were considered so characteristic that a diagnosis of epilepsy could be made from assessing the personality of the person even in the absence of fits. The personality traits thought specific to the epileptic personality included egocentricity, eccentricity, irritability, circumstantiality, religiosity, impulsiveness, emotional instability, hypersensitivity, paranoid attitudes. Their speech was considered to be slow and perseverative and thought processes stereotyped and sticky. In both thought and affect they were regarded as being adhesive, sticky or viscous.

Both the fits and the abnormal personality were considered a reflection of a genetically determined disorder with a deteriorating course. The constitutional defect causing the personality changes and fits was also reflected in the facial characteristics. Some authors described the characteristic epileptic facies: broad forehead, broad and prominent nose, prominent jaw, thick lips and staring eyes.

There is little doubt that the epileptic personality evolved as the result of observations made on institutionalised patients, where intoxication with the bromide used to treat the fits was common and disturbed behaviour a frequent reason for admission. Hence the epileptic personality syndrome developed, as the result of generalisation to all people with epilepsy of observations made on a minority of people with epilepsy, whose disorder was so severe that they required long-term institutional care. Surveys of patients representative of people with epilepsy living in the general population indicate that, though epileptic personality traits do occur occasionally, they are rarely found in pure culture. For example, in Pond and Bidwell's (1960) survey of 14 general practices selected to be representative of the general population of England and Wales there were only 11 patients with prominent epileptic personality traits out of a total of 255 epileptic patients identified (just over 4 per cent of the total).

Further, there is no evidence that these personality traits have a genetic basis. It is more probable that their development results from multiple handicaps: biological, social and psychological. Brain damage, diffuse and focal, especially that involving the temporal lobe, childhood deprivation, the disrupting effects of early onset epilepsy and frequent seizures on the personality development of the maturing child and adolescent, the chronic effects of drug therapy and the psychological problems of living with severe epilepsy, all play a contributory role.

Though the specific epilepsy personality concept has been largely discredited, over recent years the idea that a specific temporal lobe behavioural syndrome exists has been formulated. This syndrome includes the following features, many of which were previously regarded as part of the epileptic personality: irritability and deepened emotionality, decreased sexual interest and arousal, an excessive tendency to adhere to each thought, feeling and action (viscosity) and an increased concern with philosophical, moral or religious issues, often in striking contrast to the person's education and social background. It has been proposed that this constellation of behavioural traits results from a change in functioning of the nervous connections between primary receiving areas of the cortex and the mesial temporal lobe limbic system structures. The function of these neural connections is to give emotional significance to in stimuli processed by the primary receiving areas of the cortex. Experimental work has demonstrated that structural lesions within the temporal lobe of primates may act to disconnect the emotion-mediating limbic structures, such as the amygdaloid complex and hippocampus, from the sensory association cortices of the visual and auditory system. An extreme example of this destructive process is the Klüver-Bucy syndrome caused by bilateral temporal excision. It has been suggested that abnormal electrical activity due to the epileptogenic process in the temporal lobe has a kindling effect on the medial limbic structures. The epileptic focus, as well as causing fits, acts as an electrode discharging from time to time into the limbic structures, increasing their reactivity. This leads to the growth of new synaptic connections between the limbic system and the association cortices. Hence, previously neutral stimuli, events or concepts are given an emotional labelling. According to this view, such a process leads to the development of many of the features of the temporal lobe behavioural syndrome. For example, continuously to experience events and objects with an unduly affective colouring will tend to lead to more intense emotionality and engender a mystically religious view of the world. If the person's immediate actions and thoughts are so coloured, the outcome may be an augmented sense of personal destiny and importance. Sensing emotional importance in even the most trivial of events or acts will lead to these being performed ritualistically and repetitively, with lengthy circumstantial speech or writing (Bear, 1979).

Bear and Fedio (1977) have developed a self-rating questionnaire to study the distribution of these behavioural traits in patients with epilepsy, and have published evidence claiming support for the above hypothesis. However, the amount of research data available from non-controlled, non-biased samples of epileptic patients is still limited and we must wait the results of more extensive surveys of patients representative of the general population of epileptic patients living in the community.

EPILEPSY AND VIOLENCE

Explosive aggressiveness, moodiness and irritability not related in time to the occurrence of fits has long been considered part of the epileptic personality. During the last few decades, such behaviour has come to be regarded as a specific manifestation of temporal lobe epilepsy. However, critical review of the published literature relating aggression to temporal lobe epilepsy (TLE) reveals that the relationship is far from proven. The definitions of aggression used by different research workers have varied widely. Some have restricted their attention to outright physical abuse. Others have included verbal abuse, bullying, stubbornness and assertiveness.

Kligman and Goldberg (1975) have carried out a comprehensive review of the possible connections between TLE and aggression. They critically reviewed the eight published studies that had used epileptic subjects not exhibiting aggression as controls. All were open to question because of sampling bias and only two produced definite evidence of a positive association between temporal lobe epilepsy and aggression. Indeed, only the study by Nuffield (1961) showing that children with temporal lobe epilepsy displayed significantly more aggressive traits was regarded as being methodologically sound. Though Nuffield's study does offer support for the association between temporal lobe epilepsy and aggression in children, Kligman and Goldberg hold the view that it will be necessary to have this study replicated and also caried out on an adult population before a definitive conclusion can be reached. In their review they conclude that TLE is a too heterogeneous and ill-defined clinical syndrome and human aggression too complex to allow definite interpretations of correlations between them at present.

Aggressiveness has been a not uncommon finding in those temporal lobe patients referred for anterior temporal lobectomy. About one-third of a large series of TLE patients operated on by Mr Murray Falconer at the Maudsley Hospital, were noted to have displayed overtly aggressive behaviour (Falconer, 1973). This behaviour was much more common in males, especially those in their teens. It tended to be associated with left temporal lobe lesions, a pathological diagnosis of mesial temporal sclerosis (nerve cell loss involving the mesial temporal lobe structures) and a favourable outcome in terms of successful rehabilitation after the operation and cessation of fits.

It may well be that temporal lobe epileptic patients with drug resistant fits complicated by aggressive behaviour are more likely to be referred and selected for surgical treatment. The presence of much aggressive behaviour undoubtedly causes greater management and social adjustment problems. Indeed comparison of temporal lobe epileptic patients treated medically, with those treated surgically, shows that the surgically treated group have an early mean age of onset and a much higher prevalence of personality and behaviour disturbance (Currie et al, 1971). This early age of onset, within the first decade of life, tends to be associated with mesial temporal sclerosis and may account for the relation between TLE, aggression and mesial temporal sclerosis in the surgically treated patients.

The occurrence of frequent fits throughout childhood may have adverse effects on parental and peer group attitudes, the processes of social learning and personality maturation. A cluster of other environmental factors may interact to produce a coincidental association between TLE and aggression leading to a high incidence of both in the same people. These include low socio-economic status, parental psychopathology, and child abuse. Antisocial children are more likely to have a low socio-economic background than neurotic children. The same background may expose children to poor parental and medical care with greater risks of acquiring brain damage due to inadequate obstetric care, head injury due to parental neglect or abuse, and infections that may provoke febrile convulsions. Temporal lobe damage may occur during such convulsions with, especially if they are multiple, consequent development of mesial temporal sclerosis. Unfortunately, little attention has been paid to controlling for socio-economic status in the many studies of TLE and aggression.

EPILEPSY AND SEXUAL DYSFUNCTION

Complaints of low libido and impotence are common in male patients with epilepsy. As with other associations between epilepsy and behaviour, the relationship between sexual function and epilepsy is complex. In many cases, the poor sexual skills are a reflection of poor social skills in immature, dependent persons, who have led sheltered and restricted lives with little opportunity to relate to the opposite sex because of frequent fits, parental over-protection and/ or heavy medication. An additional factor that requires more detailed evaluation is that most of the drugs used for the treatment of epilepsy increase the activity of certain liver enzymes, a process known as liver enzyme induction. This increased enzyme activity leads to more rapid breakdown of testosterone in male epileptics on long-term anticonvulsant treatment. Theoretically, such low free testosterone levels in the blood should influence sexual feelings and performance. There is now some research data available to support this hypothesis. An association between sexual deviation (fetishism and transvestism) and temporal lobe epilepsy has been reported in a number of patients. It is tempting to speculate on a relationship between the sexual abnormalities and limbic system dysfunction. However, it is difficult to draw firm conclusions from such a small and highly-selected group of patients. In any event temporal lobe dysfunction is rare among sexual deviants. The subject of sexual problems in epilepsy is reviewed by Scott (1978).

EPILEPSY AND PSYCHOSIS

As with other psychiatric disorders of epilepsy, psychoses may be closely related in time to the seizure occurrence (ictal-related) or there may be no apparent direct relationship (interictal). The ictal psychoses are usually brief in duration and accompanied by clouding of consciousness, and there is rapid resolution of the psychoses with complete recovery being the rule. The underlying cause can be continuous seizure discharge lasting hours or days and causing the patient's consciousness to be clouded. This is due to either prolonged spike wave activity of generalised origin or continuous temporal lobe spike discharges. The former state is known as absence (petit mal) status and is not uncommon in children with epilepsy. The latter is known as complex partial status and is a rare event. As well as clouding of consciousness, complex partial status may cause prolonged affective disturbance (anxiety or fear), hallucinosis or frequently recurring automatism. The other form of ictal-related psychosis is the postictal clouded state (confusional state): clouding of consciousness, which follows one or more generalised convulsions. The clouding of consciousness is due to post-seizure depression of the cortical function following the intense activation of the cortical neurones by the seizure discharge. Such clouded consciousness is the rule during the recovery phase following a generalised convulsion and is manifested by the patient being often disorientated in time and place for a few seconds or minutes after a major seizure. Usually recovery is rapid. If the clouded consciousness lasts between 5 and 15 minutes automatic behaviour may occur. If the duration of clouding continues for hours, days or even a few weeks, the clinical manifestation is that of a postictal confusional state. The difference is merely a matter of duration of time.

In contrast to the ictal-related psychosis, the interictal psychoses occur in a setting of clear consciousness. In symptomatology they resemble affective, schizo-affective or schizophrenic psychoses and are thought to have a special relationship to temporal lobe dysfunction (Flor-Henry, 1976). Such interictal psychotic states in clear consciousness take the following forms.

1   Very transient schizophrenia-like psychoses lasting a few days only, preceded by an exacerbation of seizures. Such brief psychoses remit quickly and are presumably due to sub-clinical electrical disturbance of limbic system function.

2   Affective or schizo-affective states lasting weeks or months. Complete remission is usual but, like classical depressive illness, relapses and further episodes are not uncommon. In contrast to the clouded states, the onset of these psychotic states is rarely heralded by clinical seizures but is occasionally terminated by a generalised convulsion. Indeed there may be a reduction in seizure frequency immediately before the onset of the psychosis.

3   Chronic schizophrenia-like psychoses may occur, the psychoses developing on average 14 years after the onset of fits. The most characteristic clinical presentation is that of a paranoid schizophrenia-like state. Though the symptomatology is generally similar to patients with non-epileptic schizophrenia, a number of differences have been noted.

Paranoid delusions are unduly uncommon, mystical delusional experiences being especially frequent, the patient feeling in communication with God or endowed with supernatural powers, or experiencing passivity phenomena with a mystical content. Visual hallucinations are more common than in typical schizophrenia, being often experienced during dreamlike states in the absence of confusion. Again, a mystical content to the hallucinations is common. The patient's affect is warmer and better retained than is usual in schizophrenia. The progress of the disorder is also more benign with less personality and social deterioration than commonly seen in non-epileptic schizophrenia.

These patients show no genetic loading for schizophrenia or any excess of schizoid premorbid personality traits. This contrasts with non-epileptic schizophrenic patients where a family history is common and schizoid premorbid personality traits frequent. Further, there is some epidemiological evidence that suggests that the occurrence of the two conditions, schizophrenia and temporal lobe epilepsy, is not a coincidental finding. All these observations have led to the view that the schizophrenia-like psychoses associated with temporal lobe epilepsy are the result of the temporal lobe dysfunction. In other words they are yet another symptom of the temporal lobe lesion.

The site and extent of the epileptogenic lesion in the brain and its role in the causation of such schizophrenia-like psychoses is the subject of much dispute. Both bilateral damage to the mesial temporal limbic structures and dysfunction of the dominant temporal lobe have been reported as predisposing to psychoses (Toone, 1981). The influence of changes in seizure frequency is also a disputed one. A change in seizure frequency, either a reduction or an exacerbation, has been described as the precipitating factor. The respective contributions of such changes in attack frequency remain to be clarified. It may be that both mechanisms can operate independently of each other in different patients. The increased seizure frequency may cause limbic system and/or global cortical dysfunction due to neuronal inhibition following the intense seizure activation. The phenomenon of a reduced fit frequency leading to psychoses may reflect underlying neurotransmitter changes, that cause both events. For example, increased brain levels of dopamine are both anti-epileptic and schizophrenogenic. Blocking dopamine activity increases the seizure activity but has a beneficial effect on the psychosis.

It should be noted, however, that interictal psychoses in clear consciousness are a relatively rare complication of temporal lobe epilepsy (2 per cent in the series of Currie et al, 1971).

SUMMARY

Though epilepsy is more common in prison populations than might be expected, antisocial behaviour as a direct consequence of epileptic automatism is rare. The relation between the offences and the fits is indirect and multifactorial. Organic and environmental causative factors play a role, their relative importance varying between individuals. Psychosis is a relatively rare consequence of epilepsy; psychotic patients may act dangerously in response to delusions or hallucinations. Such antisocial behaviour is rare.

REFERENCES

Bear, D.M. (1979) Temporal lobe epilepsy. A syndrome of sensory-limbic hyperconnection. *Cortex*, **15**, 357–384.

Bear, D.M. & Fedio, P. (1977) Quantitative analysis of interictal behaviour in temporal lobe epilepsy. *Arch. Neurol.*, **34**, 454–467.

Currie, S., Heathfield, K.W., Henson, R.A. & Scott, D.F. (1971) Clinical course and prognosis of temporal lobe epilepsy. *Brain*, **94**, 173–190.

Delgado-Escueta, A.V., Mattson, R.H., King, L., Goldensohn, E.S., Spiegel, H., Madsen, J., Crandall, P., Drieffus, F. & Porter, R.J. (1981) The nature of aggression during epileptic seizures. *New Eng. J. Med.*, **305**, 711–716.

Falconer, M.A. (1973) Reversibility by temporal lobe behavioural resection of the behavioural abnormalities of temporal lobe epilepsy. *New Eng. J. of Med.*, **289**, 450–455.

Fenton, G.W. (1972) Epilepsy and automatism. *Brit. J. Hosp. Med.*, **7**, 57–64.

Fenwick, P.B.C., Howard, R.C. & Fenton, G.W. (1983) Review of cortical excitability, neuro-humoral transmission and the dyscontrol syndrome. In *Advances in Epileptology: XIVth Epilepsy International Symposium*. Parsonage, M., Grant, R.H.E., Craig, A.G. & Ward, A.A. Jr (eds.) New York: Raven Press. pp. 181–191.

Flor-Henry, P. (1976) Epilepsy and psychopathology. In *Recent Advances in Clinical Psychiatry*. Granville-Grossman, K. (ed.). Edinburgh: Churchill Livingstone.

Guerrant, J., Anderson, W.W., Fischer, A., Weinstern, M.R., Jaros, R. & Deskins, A. (1962) *Personality in Epilepsy*. Springfield, Illinois: Charles C. Thomas.

Gunn, J. (1977) *Epileptics in Prison*. New York: Academic Press.

Gunn, J. & Fenton, G. (1969) Epilepsy in prisons: a diagnostic survey. *Brit. Med. J.*, **4**, 326–328.

Gunn, J. & Fenton, G. (1971) Epilepsy, automatism and crime. *Lancet*, **ii**, 1173–1176.

Hauser, W.A. & Kurland, L.T. (1975) The epidemiology of epilepsy in Rochester Minnesota, 1935 through 1967. *Epilepsia*, **16**, 1–16.

Howard, R.C., Fenton, G.W. & Fenwick, P.B.C. (1982) *Event-related Brain Potentials in Personality and Psychopathology: A Pavlovian Approach*. Chichester: Research Studies Press.

Kligman, D. & Goldberg, D.A. (1975) Temporal lobe epilepsy and aggression. *J. Nerv. Ment. Dis.* **160**, 324–341.

Knox, S.J. (1968) Epilepsy automatisms and violence. *Med., Sci. L.*, **8**, 96–104.

Leicester, J. (1982) Temper tantrums, epilepsy and episodic control. *Brit. J. Psychiat.*, **141**, 262–266.

Nuffield, E.J.A. (1961) Neurophysiology and behaviour disorders in epileptic children. *J. Ment. Sci.*, **107**, 438–458.

Pond, D.A. & Bidwell, B.H. (1960) A survey of fourteen general practices. II: social and psychological aspects. *Epilepsia*, **1**, 285–299.

Rutter, M., Graham, P.J. & Yule, W. (1970) *A Neuropsychiatric Study in Childhood*. London: Heinemann.

Scott, D.G. (1978) Psychiatric aspects of sexual medicine. In *Epilepsy 1978*. Wokingham, England: British Epilepsy Association.

Stores, G. (1978) School children with epilepsy at risk for learning and behaviour problems. *Dev. Med. Child Neur.*, **20**, 502–508.

Toone, B.K. (1981) Psychoses of epilepsy. In *Epilepsy and Psychiatry*. Reynolds, E.H., Trimble, M.R. (eds.). Edinburgh: Churchill Livingstone.

14

Predicting Dangerousness and Future Convictions Among the Mentally Abnormal

Michael Craft

The first recorded use of the word 'danger' was in 1523, and it was in use in the civil codes of justice of France and Imperial Russia by 1838 and 1876 respectively (Harding and Montandon, 1982). Of recent years the legal concept of dangerousness has been most ventilated in Anglo-American literature. A recent World Health Organization survey into 47 state jurisdictions showed how the more sophisticated (and wealthy) the state, the more attempt there has been to define the concept in an attempt to avoid lengthy prison or hospital care (Harding, 1980). This chapter reviews studies on prediction of dangerousness and its assessment by lawyers, psychiatrists and other professionals.[1]

DEFINITIONS

Defining one's terms is of first importance. Danger is defined in the Concise Oxford Dictionary as 'liability or exposure to harm, risks or peril'. The Butler Report favoured 'a propensity to cause serious physical injury or lasting psychological harm'. The Scottish Council on Crime suggested a 'probability that he will inflict serious and irremediable personal injury in the future'. Yet in the last resort, it is a subjective judgement, particularly in the field of psychological harm. Thus, to some, spiders cause lasting psychological harm, and to others, none. Similarly, in the field of dangerous offenders, where some jurisdictions regard repeated property offenders as dangerous and others not, the difference of opinion becomes crucial to the individual whose offence may or may not entitle him to an indeterminate sentence.

In the last resort, prediction is about individuals, yet studies on dangerousness are mainly concerned with definition and prediction of groups. There are a large number of papers on personal viewpoint, and a much smaller number analysing groups of people once thought to be dangerous. It is with groups that predictive power is most accurate. For instance, one can predict with consider-

---

[1] As manager of the country's four maximum security hospitals, the DHSS has a special interest in the dangerousness of psychiatric patients. In 1979 it financed a seminar on current research and practice in this field, and the updated papers were published by the Royal College of Psychiatrists in 1982 (ed. Hamilton and Freeman). This chapter summarises current research in the field, and draws heavily on the studies reviewed in the booklet.

able accuracy the numbers of people who will die this year, or who will be convicted of a particular crime, but it is far harder to say *which* individual will die or be convicted, because it then becomes a matter of probabilities. Yet professionals cannot escape responsibility for prediction, not least because consideration for prison parole or hospital release and court reports necessarily requires estimation of the risk element to the community at large and to the individual himself.

THE ROLE OF THE PSYCHIATRIST

It is an irony that with the increase in actual research data for prediction over the last two decades, there has been a decreasing confidence on the part of psychiatrists in advancing their predictions. In part this has been due to the waning enthusiasm for the concept of the universal efficacy of treatment for the personality disordered, in part to judges' expectations of increasingly sophisticated data to help them in their deliberations.

The offender who kills his wife in a depressive psychosis, or the schizophrenic who kills the subject of his delusions, may be cured of this present illness by new drugs. Treatment for the patient who is paranoid, psychopathic or mentally handicapped is not so clear-cut. With these latter groups, a continuing fault in reasoning has played a more or less important part in the offence and the psychiatrist has the responsibility of explanation of the options available, to patient, as to court.

The psychiatrist must be clear where his responsibility lies. If he appears for the prosecution, the prison, the Home Office or employer, he should explain this to his client and be chary of using unsubstantiated hearsay evidence in his report. Many a trusting patient has had a longer sentence because he confessed to the court psychiatrist about other willing boys he seduced. In Britain, with its adversarial system, the defence psychiatrist is on a surer footing with advice to his client, now probably a prospective patient, so that if the prosecution dislike the evidence they can get their own second opinion. In a conflict of opinion, both points of view can be aired. The responsibility for public protection and thus institutionalisation is that of the judge. The psychiatrist may present a useful report on the factors behind a behaviour-disordered offender and his dangerousness, but his opinion concerning treatment for such people is here on less sure ground than with the acutely depressed or schizophrenic patient. The evidence for the psychiatrist being better at predicting dangerousness than others is reviewed later; suffice it to say that predictions depend on individual judgements, and some judges are more fallible than others.

THE EVIDENCE FOR PREDICTION OF DANGEROUSNESS

Discussing, first, violent crime, research is unanimous only in showing that the best predictor of it is a previous conviction for violent crime. Each conviction increases the probability of a further conviction, and the expressed intention of further violence much increases likelihood – here on an individual and not a group basis. In comparing the studies that follow, one must remember the sixteen times greater homicide rate in the US than in England; the freer availability of firearms in the US and Australia than in Britain; and the degree of violence necessary to survive in communities; ranging from places such as Colombia, where sporadic civil war makes armed defence of life normal, to tough urban areas such as Glasgow, where the Saturday night brawl occasioning grievous bodily harm is a common occurrence.

As Walker (1982) says, 'It is very difficult to locate a study which reliably defines a group of violent males with a probability of further violence approaching even 50 per cent. Some of the samples taken by McClintock show 35 per cent or 40 per cent, within a five year follow-up; but that is differentiating only between those who have no previous conviction and those with one. What Steer and I did was to take violent Glasgow first offenders and follow them up; by the time they had reached their third and subsequent conviction, the probability of their being involved in another one had gone up to about 60 per cent.' Yet for most violent offenders 'an extension of custody imposed solely to protect others against violence will be unnecessarily imposed in the majority of cases. Put more strongly, it means detaining three individuals in order to prevent only one of them (and you do not know which) from committing further violence.' Further research on the convicted will probably define small sub-groups with a greater than 50 per cent likelihood of violence, but continuing custody would be at the expense of including a minority of those who would not commit a further offence.

Prior conviction as a predictor of future offence is at its most accurate in the field of theft. After four such convictions, the likelihood of a fifth within five years approached 70 per cent, although few thefts are dangerous (Walker, 1982). Walker also points out that a further excellent predictor for offence and dangerousness is that of declared intent. This has to be divided into two parts, those who voluntarily intend to commit, or go in search of the declared offence, and those 'unable to resist'. With the latter, residence in a place far from provocation helps. However, with the exception of terrorists, both groups are rare, and one is not suggesting monasteries for every pederast 'unable to resist'. Untreated psychotic patients, the subnormal and the senile provide members of the group 'unable to resist'.

American studies of predicting violence have reached a similar conclusion. After 'gross overcrowding' in the Alabama penitentiary, the state turned over assessment of dangerousness and release of once violent inmates to the State University Department of Corrective Psychology (see Pfohl, 1978). The 4000 penal inmates were interviewed by 12 teams of psychiatric professionals in 130 diagnostic sessions to set up predictive models. Unfortunately, the results showed that for 'each correct identification of a potentially aggressive individual, there were 326 incorrect identifications'. Even using the best predictor for future violence, that of conviction for past violence, there were 19 false positives in every 20 predictions. Similar results occurred in a study in Ohio (Pfohl, 1978), and in Missouri (Hedlund et al, 1973).

Surveys of discharged mental hospital patients have provided a happy hunting ground for studies of prediction of future conviction (but not necessarily of dangerousness). Their value is sometimes limited by the lack of control studies on relevant and coincident general populations and lack of information on convictions or offence prior to hospitalisation.

In his excellent review, Tidmarsh (1982) shows that early surveys of convictions among discharged mental hospital populations show a very low rate. Ashley (1922) found an annual arrest rate of 2.4 among 1000 parolees from Middletown State Homeopathic Hospital and no serious violence. Pollock (1938) found an 8.8 annual arrest rate for misdemeanour and 3.8 for felonies per 1000 male parolees from New York hospitals, and my research from Devon hospitals shows a similarly low rate, but in all three instances the patients had been carefully selected, found accommodation if not occupation, and were supervised (Craft, 1958, 1965).

Other studies were similar prior to the emptying of hospitals in the USA, UK and Australia circa 1960. Cohen and Freeman (1945) covered 1676 paroled patients, again with a lower arrest rate than the general population and minimal violence, whilst Brill and Malzberg (1962) found their discharged New York patients had a quarter of the current public arrest rate. By 1967 the situation had changed. Compared with the general population, Giovannoni and Gurel (1967) found higher arrest rates for offences against the person, but lower property offence rates among their 1142 discharged Veterans Administration hospital patients.

Following the 1969 Californian Mental Health Service Act – or Magna Carta for mentally ill (Chase, 1973) – the situation in this state changed even further. 'Where have all the patients gone?' asks Chase, for an inpatient population of 50 000 in 1955 had fallen to 7000 in 1973. Once discharged the patient had the right to refuse after-care. There are few useful follow-up studies. As an indication as to whether more potentially violent people were at large in New York, Zitrin et al (1976) analysed 867 admissions to Bellevue from Manhattan and found 9.8 per cent had been arrested for a violent offence during the two years prior to the key admission, much higher than the general population at this time.

Durbin et al (1977) analysed discharged inpatients in Wyoming. Among 268 patients followed up, 88 had been convicted of criminal offences, with one murder, seven assaults on persons, one rape. Similar results came from Sosowsky (1978) from the NAPA State Hospital, California. Steadman et al (1977) in their review of arrest rates among discharged mental hospital patients throughout New York State from 1957 to 1968 provide some of the background. Although the arrest rate among ex-hospital patients rose steadily throughout the decades over the period, this was coincident with shortening lengths of inpatient treatment, less and less supervision after discharge and an increasing number of young admissions, especially with personality disorders. This comprehensive study showed that the personality-disordered had far higher arrest rates than the general population, whilst the arrest rate for the psychotic (schizophrenic and depressed) and the brain damaged (mentally handicapped) were not greatly higher. Overall the arrest rate for discharged patients was 98.5 per thousand compared with 32.5 per thousand for the general population. In this very comprehensive state-wide review Steadman et al concluded that previous conviction, not mental illness, appeared to be the major predictor for higher arrest rates among discharged patients.

Greenland (1978) quotes a detailed survey of Boker and Hofner (1973) in West Germany which yielded similar results. Among names on the criminal register between 1955 and 1964 there were 533 ex-patients representing 3 per cent of all criminals. Offences were homicide, attempted homicide, serious assault and battery. Of these 533, 53 per cent were schizophrenic, 13 per cent mentally retarded; 7 per cent suffered from manic depressive illnesses; 6 per cent senile dementias; 6 per cent brain syndromes; 5 per cent epileptic, others 10 per cent. Boker and Hofner concluded:

1   Crimes of violence committed by mentally ill and mentally retarded are quantitatively proportional to the number of crimes of violence committed by the total population.
2   In affective illnesses and mental retardation, the risk of committing violence is 60 per million, in schizophrenia 500.
3   Depressive acts of violence are commonly self-inflicted.
4   Premorbid sociopathic (i.e. convicted) personality was a better predictor of crime than mental illness or mental retardation. The more sociopathic, the more crimes were committed.
5   100 per cent of the victims were close relatives or partners of depressed patients, but only 50 per cent in other categories of mental disorder.

Guze et al (1974) carried out a study in reverse to the above by following up 500 ex-psychiatric patients for a lengthy time (years not given). They found a felony conviction was reported for 37 per cent of the 35 sociopaths, 13 per cent of the 70 alcoholics, 23 per cent of the 13 drug dependants, 2 per cent of the 62 anxiety neurotics, and 1 per cent of the others. Only the sociopathic subject among 14 mental retardates was convicted, and none of the 200 schizophrenics.

The changing pattern in conviction rate for ex-psychiatric patients over the decade must reflect changing attitudes towards 'medical custody by the community'. Another of Steadman and Cocozza's (1975) surveys illustrates this: 'Five (US) studies done between 1922 and 1947 showed that ex mental patients were less likely to be arrested than members of the general population. A two year study of arrests in Connecticut showed that the annual felony arrest rate of 1676 ex mental patients was 42 per 10 000. In a study of more than 10 000 released patients in New York the annual arrest rate was 122 per 10 000 versus 491 per 10 000 for the general population.' By 1975, however, the situation had changed, and more recent follow-up studies found a greater arrest rate for ex-mental hospital patients than general, but Steadman and Cocozza conclude that this is more likely to be due to the greater numbers of sociopaths and personality disorders sent to the hospital by courts rather than to prison as in former decades. The better aftercare and supervision available in earlier years is relevant. Pre-war discharges were usually on 'licence' or parole.

Kozol et al (1972) are optimistic about psychiatric prediction, based on their study of 592 court referrals mainly for sex offences to the new Center for Treatment of Dangerous Persons in Massachusetts. After assessment 304 were thought non-dangerous after discharge from gaol: 26 (8.6 per cent) of these committed further serious offences; 226 were thought dangerous and sent to an indeterminate 'treatment' facility; of 82 later discharged 5 (6.1 per cent) committed a further serious offence; 49 were thought dangerous, but released nevertheless by courts; of these, 17 (34.7 per cent) repeated serious assaultive crimes, including two murders. From Ontario, Quinsey et al (1975) reported on 91 inpatients discharged from their state Broadmoor-type hospital by a local review tribunal: 16 per cent committed violent crime against the person in the year of follow-up. These patients had a mean age of 32 with 2.2 years of inpatient treatment. This compares with 56 patients from the same hospital, 59 per cent of whom had committed homicide and transferred on average after eight years' treatment to appropriate accommodation and work; only 5 per cent were reconvicted.

In 1966 the US Supreme Court released Johnnie Baxstrom from Dannemora State Hospital on the grounds he had been denied equal protection of the law. He was an epileptic transferred to a security hospital after expiration of his prison sentence. Following this judgment 920 men and 47 women were transferred from New York security hospital to ordinary psychiatric hospitals, from which most proceeded into the community. This was a splendid research opportunity to assess the dangerousness of patients alleged to need security care. Only 25 per cent of these patients' original offences had been serious (homicide, multiple assault, rape, robbery, arson); 42 per cent had *not* been convicted of violent crime. At admission the average age was 28. Eighteen years later, with an average age of 46, they were transferred to open psychiatric units, half being released into the community over the next four years. A one-in-five sample was followed up. Out of 98 men sampled, 20 were arrested and 11 convicted; only two offences were considered dangerous, an assault and a robbery. Cocozza and Steadman comment, 'The Baxstrom patients are a group of middle-aged people who had been continuously institutionalised in hospitals . . . for an average of 14 years . . . they are not typical of many of the patients now entering mental hospitals through criminal procedures.' Cocozza and Steadman constructed a Legal Dangerousness Score and found that for those aged under 50 they could retrospectively predict dangerous behaviour in 11 out of 14 patients, although a further 25 were falsely identified as positive. The sort of predictors of dangerousness identified by Cocozza and Steadman (1974) and others are:

1 Youth
2 A diagnosis of personality disorder
3 A history of violence
4 Short stay in hospital
5 Abrupt discharge without supervision or planned community integration

Tennent (1983) followed 617 English special hospital discharges for 12 to 17 years. He divided them into: 129 who, after discharge, committed a violent offence; 211 who committed a non-violent offence; and 277 who committed no offence. Five of the six men who committed homicide did so as their first serious offence. Of the 129, records were examined for earlier offences; 34 had previously committed a serious offence; 95 had not. Comparing the discharge career of those later convicted for violent crime (129) they had more court convictions of all kinds than other groups (P. <0.01). The more reconvictions for any crime the more significant the association with later violent offence. Repeated convictions for violence was the best of all predictors for subsequent convictions for violence. Abrupt discharge by tribunal (which had occurred in 43 per cent of 129 violent offenders) was also a good predictor for violence.

Tidmarsh (1982) who analysed Western predictor studies in great depth, comments that the yield was meagre. He points out that many of the populations reviewed were not particularly dangerous, and that Broadmoor 'with its 1 per cent post-discharge homicides, clearly takes in more dangerous patients than the Baxstrom hospitals did, and discharges them much more quickly'. A clear expression of personal view! Other studies predicting dangerousness have used a wide variety of tools.

Statistical prediction indices depend on an assessment of probabilities, and are best with groups, not individuals. The prediction tables reported by Mannheim and Wilkins (1955) and Craft (1965) are splendid creations of sophistry, but do rather worse for the individuals than groups, for to be certain of keeping one dangerous client from being convicted of violence in a particular time interval, at least two others like him will have to be locked up.

Psychological tests to predict dangerousness have been reviewed by Black (1982): 'The culmination of this work [at Broadmoor] has been two main branches of treatment; firstly, programmes based on the individual problems that patients pose, and secondly, training programmes for groups of individuals who seem to share a common lack of strategies for dealing with their life situations, or who have the wrong kind of strategies.' It is possible by psychological testing to identify two types of personality who have become dangerous as a result of provocative factors, the 'under-controlled' and the 'over-controlled' (Figure 23.1). The first is the commonly young, self-centred and aggressive psychopath, who impulsively hits out on slight provocation. The second is often a shy middle-aged man of otherwise impeccable character, perhaps henpecked by his wife, who unexpectedly murders her on a 'last straw' provocation. Black comments that there are a number of personality questionnaires, stress-sensitive physiological tests of pulse, respiration etc., even instruments to measure penile engorgement, all of which can readily pick out the types of personality described above – after the event. What cannot be so easily measured are the provocative circumstances which may 'fire' a particular individual. One can identify the young impulsive aggressive psychopath and predict a number of provocations. One can also identify the commonly over-controlled man, but not so easily identify when he 'breaks' on that 'last straw' (see Figure 23.2). However, as Black says, once the conviction has occurred then research now being pursued identifies the most successful treatment strategies.

The results of psychological testing still leave one with a series of probabilities, and the knowledge that with individuals such as the over-controlled, the 'final straw' may need to be very specific indeed. Yet, lest one deduce that the over-controlled wife-killer, once released, is unlikely to arrive in such a specific situation again, it can happen. One ex-Broadmoor patient killed three wives in this way!

X-ray and electroencephalographic tests are reviewed in Chapter 23. Once more, it is possible to record brain wave abnormalities in a person, but one has then to give a description of the degree of abnormality for each individual, and it still depends upon the occurrence of chance factors as to whether an individual will react with violence. The common instance of a brain-damaged young man being dangerous usually depends upon whether he also drinks to excess and likes to pick pub quarrels, or whether he has parents or wife strong enough to keep him from, or out of trouble, or will take Antabuse, and so on.

RESEARCH INTO OFFENCE TYPES

This has been a recent line of advance. For instance, many youths make threats to kill, but few do. MacDonald (1963) followed up those patients admitted to hospital after *making a threat to kill*. Only about 1 per cent actually did so after discharge. Research into sex offenders is reported in detail in Chapter 6. One interesting finding is the low but persistent re-offence rate of sex offenders over time, a quantitative difference from property offenders (Gibbens, 1981).

Arsonists are surveyed by Faulk (1982). He divides them into the group who fire with motive: these include the adolescent pleasure seeker, the deluded, even the would-be fireman; and the 'irresistible impulse group'; these include the inarticulate, the sexually excited, those whose tension is relieved by fire. The latter group re-offend most. The largest survey is by Lewis and Yarnell (1951) over a 15-year period; 30 per cent re-offended. They show arsonists to be a singularly handicapped group and say all 'normal people know fire is dangerous'. In contrast Soothill and Pope (1973) in a 20-year survey found a 4 per cent recidivism rate, although nearly 50 per cent committed other crimes. Sapford et al (1978) followed arsonist ex-prisoners over a five-year period. Short-term prisoners had a 2 per cent re-conviction rate for arson, long-termers a 20 per cent rate. Yet a quarter of the short-term and half the long-term re-offended in a destructive way. Only if property and theft offences are included, re-conviction rises to 43 and 80 per cent overall over five years. For the individual, the best indicators were previous convictions, their 'parole score' (unspecified), and length of previous sentences, which reflect the initial seriousness and determination of the original offence.

Dangerousness among adolescents has been the subject of a number of prediction studies. The best appear to be those analysing long-term follow-up of children and adolescents, 5, 10 or 30 years after first being seen. Initial characteristics can then be compared with final results.

West and Farrington (1977) followed up working class boys aged 8–9 years, attending ordinary primary schools in 1951 in a high delinquency area in London. At follow-up 10 years later, the following 11 factors were most predictive of repeated convictions (including violence and violent sex):

1   High anti-establishment attitude
2   Drug user
3   Immoderate smoker
4   Sexually very active
5   Heavy gambler
6   Drinks and drives
7   In antisocial group
8   Spends time lazing about
9   Unstable work record
10 High self-reported aggression
11 Tattooed

Recidivists were likely to have four or more factors.

Robins (1966) analysed the predictive factors behind the 90 who became adult sociopaths among 524 patients originally seen as child guidance patients (and 100 school controls) thirty years earlier. Many of the predictive factors are similar to the above. The best predictive factors in childhood for future sociopathy were :

1   For boys – antisocial behaviour (at follow-up 71 per cent were re-arrested, half frequently; half in prison).
2   For girls – antisocial behaviour (as adults 70 per cent divorced).

Half of these men and a third of these women were problem drinkers. Robins gives a further follow-up in 1978, reported in Chapter 24, p. 394–5.

TREATMENT VERSUS CUSTODY

Concerning *treatment* as opposed to *custody* for dangerous offender-patients, the main research data comprise statistics on the results of treatment and are reviewed in Chapter 28. The effects of treatment on any particular sub-group of offenders are heavily influenced by the social background (see in Denmark and Holland, Chapter 1), which unit is found for treatment (e.g. for the elderly pederast), the personal destruction wrought by care (e.g. child molesters in prison or security hospital) or indeed the chances of being treated constructively at all (e.g. the immature brutalised in custody). Most important, as many sections of this book testify, is the presence or absence of aftercare, and resources available to prevent relapse.

In general, psychiatric claims for successful treatment of mentally abnormal offenders are now far more modest than in earlier decades and readers should be suspicious of inflated claims for treatment success, especially from those practitioners without beds or not offering personal care. It is not only psychoanalysts, but some psychologists who overrate the long-term effects of behaviour conditioning, even hypnotherapists who overrate their hypnosis. It is of little use to use adversive conditioning to teach a compulsive car thief not to take cars, if next time he crashes a double-decker bus! The DHSS in its governmental green paper pointed out that if psychiatry could not produce marked benefit during the first six months of treatment, figures showed that such likelihood thereafter fell rapidly. The importance of this for care is that the remaining 4.5 years of a 5-year residential order have to be justified by protecting others against what the 1969 California Mental Health Service Act calls being 'imminently dangerous'.

Public opinion has its own viewpoint on what constitutes danger. The degree of dangerousness of the unconvicted wife-beater – even more so husband-beater – despite the physical violence, is much disputed by people, all swayed by their own emotions. Yet custodial sentences for the convicted, or continuation of indeterminate sentences, are far less disputed – such people are beyond the pale. The definition of danger is, as we have seen, a very personal one. Newspaper sensationalism helps to raise child molesters towards the top of most lay questionnaires on who are considered dangerous, yet as described in repeated recent research, many are mild shy men, lacking sex experience with women, who are as likely themselves to be seduced by predatory adolescents as to seduce. Public attitudes towards an immature adolescent will differ markedly before and after the parents of his 15-year-old regular bedfellow accuse him of what Americans call 'statutory rape'; such attitudes may even drive him out of town to do worse.

Finally, the emotional attitude of public parole board or probation officer differs very markedly with degree of identification with offender. As a convicted bank robber said to me of a cell-mate, 'He got half as long for twice as much as me, but his hand used a pen [for fraud]; mine thumped the counter.'

To conclude this evaluation of treatment and custody, governmental reports, research results and lawgivers are moving toward the view that if marked improvement is not seen as a result of six months' residential care, then increased length of care must be justified on other grounds, such as dangerousness, retribution, public safety, etc. This raises the question, who is to assess? Are psychiatrists better able to judge dangerousness than others? As Peter Scott pointed out in his classic paper in 1977, their training certainly helps them to pick up certain cues, but there have been many who questioned this, though without data to back their opinion. Apart from Kozol et al (1972) there is little follow-up evidence on the effectiveness of psychiatric assessment. Harding and Montandon (1982) report a WHO study covering six countries with 62 psychiatrists and 131 non-psychiatric raters to rate dangerousness, using 16 five-hundred-word case histories. Lay raters included judges, lawyers, health workers, police, teachers, politicians and priests. Dangerousness was rated on a four point scale from *no dangerousness* to *extreme dangerousness*; required care was rated on a four point scale: *community care without supervision, supervision, mental hospital* or *prison*. Of the 16 cases nine involved serious mental illness, the rest personality or neurotic disorders; eight involved serious personal violence. As might be expected, agreement between raters was best (over 60 per cent) in cases without violence, but three cases with mental illness and a violent outburst rated less than 35 per cent agreement, 'little better than the level of agreement expected from random ratings' say the authors. Psychiatrist readers of this chapter will be sorry to hear that there were no significant differences between the 62 psychiatrists and 131 non-psychiatrists in their ratings of dangerousness. As a group, psychiatrists did rate people more dangerous overall, and agreed among themselves better as to severity and where care should take place, especially where mental illness was an issue. This multicentre WHO study concludes that dangerousness could be assessed with a high degree of reliability in 25 per cent of cases (there was great variation in the other 75 per cent) and, if the concept is to be used, there is need for careful definition of operational practice.

This is not so far off the prediction rate quoted earlier for violent offenders – that to prevent one further offence by an individual among a violent group, two more would have to be locked up – it being impossible as yet to predict which of the three will commit an offence, because this will often depend on chance factors in the pub or the home.

AFTERCARE

All studies have shown the importance of aftercare and supervision in preventing recurrence in released once-dangerous residents. Abrupt departure, as for example by tribunal from security hospital, or sudden release from prison, is associated with high relapse rate. Alternatively, among serious assaultive patients, careful aftercare supervision and parole conditions give surprisingly good results. In McGrath's (1968) study of 293 murderers released from Broadmoor receiving structured aftercare, not one killed again, but this success rate was not maintained in the 1970s. Stürüp's study (1968) of releases from Herstedvester (Denmark's equivalent to Broadmoor) showed similar results at that time. He commented that follow-up was considerably easier in a small state with centralised crime registers.

There is no one characteristic of dangerousness. Among ex-psychiatric in-patients, those diagnosed as sociopaths are more likely to be convicted during a period of follow-up than the general population. The mentally ill and the mentally retarded ex-hospital inpatient is only slightly more likely to be convicted than the general population. However, the sociopath is usually defined in terms of his antisocial behaviour, so this is to some extent a circular argument, for the best predictor of all for future conviction is the number of past convictions, whether for property or for violent offences. In Britain, USA and Australia dangerousness is conceived of in terms of violence to the individual: in the USA and Australia there is also emphasis on further sexual offence, particularly involving children. When the issue is that of continued institutionalisation for a convicted patient, the best indicator for future violence or sexual offences is still the number and frequency of past offences. Other important factors are: expressed intent to repeat the offence, the availability of after-care, daytime occupation and home support.

In predicting dangerousness one is left eventually with an assessment of probabilities. Some of these are intrinsic to the individual, some extrinsic, some the result of pure chance. All estimations depend on a number of variables, only a few of which can be accurately assessed. In the last event the indication of continued liability to dangerousness seems to depend on exposure of the individual to the type of provocations that precipitated the key dangerous reaction. Some half of these key events of assault occur in pubs, clubs, homes or places of entertainment. Such provocations can be graduated by means of partial, supervised, or complete exposure, to community stresses. This has implications for type of supervision, after-care, daytime occupation and teaching of coping strategies needed. Estimation of dangerousness, particularly in the institutionalised, is intimately involved in quality of after-care available following discharge.

REFERENCES

Ashley, M.C. (1922) Outcome of 1000 cases paroled from Middletown State Homeopathic Hospital. *New York State Hospital Quarterly*, **8**, 64–70.

Black, T. (1982) The Contribution of the Clinical Psychologist. In *Dangerousness: Psychiatric Assessment and Management*. Hamilton, J.R. & Freeman, H. (eds.). Royal College of Psychiatrists Special Publication 2. London: Gaskell.

Boker, W. & Hofner, M. (1973) *Gewalttaten Geistesgestorter*. Berlin: Springer Verlag.

Brill, H. & Malzberg, B. (1962) Statistical report based on the arrest records of 5354 male ex-patients released from New York State Mental Hospitals during the period 1946–1948. *Mental Hospital Service Supplement 153*. Washington DC: American Psychiatric Association.

Chase, J. (1973) Where have all the patients gone? *Human Behaviour*, October, 14–21.

Cocozza, J.J. & Steadman, H.J. (1974) Some refinements in the measurement and prediction of dangerous behavior. *Am. J. Psychiat.*, **131**, 1012–14.

Cohen, L.H. & Freeman, H. (1945) How dangerous to the community are State Hospital patients? *Connecticut State Medical Journal*, **9**, 697–700.

Craft, M.J. (1958) *Mental Disorder in the Defective*. Devon: Royal Institute Starcross.

Craft, M.J. (1965) *Ten Studies into Psychopathic Personality*. Bristol: John Wright.

Durbin, J.R., Pasenark, R.A. & Albers, D. (1977) Criminality and mental illness: a study of arrest rates in a rural state. *Am. J. Psychiat.*, **134**, 80–2.

Faulk, M. (1982) Assessing dangerousness in arsonists. In: *Dangerousness: Psychiatric Assessment and Management*. Hamilton, J.R. & Freeman, H. (eds.). Royal College of Psychiatrists Special Publication 2. London: Gaskell.

Gibbens, T.C.N. (1981) Incest and sexual abuse of children. *Brit. J. Sexual Medicine*, **8**, 81, 23–6.

Giovannoni, J.M. & Gurel, L. (1967) Socially disruptive behavior of ex-mental patients. *Arch. Gen. Psychiat.*, **17**, 146–53.

Greenland, C. (1978) Prediction and management of dangerous behavior; social policy issues. *Int. J. Law Psychiat*, **1**, 205–22.

Guze, S.B., Woodruff, R.A. & Clayton, P.J. (1974) Psychiatric disorders and criminality. *J.A.M.A.*, **227**, 641–2.

Hamilton, J.R. & Freeman, H. (eds.) (1982) *Dangerousness: Psychiatric Assessment and Management*. London: Gaskell.

Harding, T.W. (1980) Du danger, de la dangerosité et de l'usage medical de termes affectivement chargés. *Déviance et Société*, **4**, 331–48.

Harding, T. & Montandon, C. (1982) Does dangerousness travel well? In *Dangerousness: Psychiatric Assessment and Management*. Hamilton, J. R. & Freeman, H. (eds.). Royal College of Psychiatrists Special Publication 2. London: Gaskell.

Hedlund, J.L., Slatten, I.W., Altman, H. & Everson, R.C. (1973) Prediction of patients who are dangerous to others. *J. Clin. Psychol.* **29**, 443–7.

Kozol, H.L., Boucher, R.J. & Garofalo, R.F. (1972) The diagnosis and treatment of dangerousness. *Crime and Delinquency*, **18**, 371–92.

Lewis, N.D.C. & Yarnell, H. (1951) *Pathological Fire-setting*. Nervous and Mental Disease Monographs, No. 81. New York.

Macdonald, J.M. (1963) The threat to kill. *Am. J. Psychiat.*, **120**, 125–30.

McGrath, P. (1968) Psychopath as a long stay patient. In *Psychopathic Offenders*, West, D.J. (ed.). Papers presented to the Cropwood Round-Table Conference. Cambridge: Institute of Criminology.

Mannheim, H. & Wilkins, L.T. (1955) *Prediction Methods in Relation to Borstal Training*. London: HMSO.

Pfohl, S.J. (1978) *Predicting Dangerousness. The Social Construction of Psychiatric Reality*. Lexington: Lexington Books.

Pollock, H.M. (1938) Is the paroled patient a menace to the community? *Psychiatric Quarterly*, **12**, 236–44.

Quinsey, V.L., Pruesse, M. & Fernley, R. (1975) Oak Ridge patients: pre-release characteristics and post-release adjustment. *J. Psychiat. Law*, **3**, 63–77.

Robins, L.N. (1966) *Deviant Children Grown Up*. Baltimore: Williams and Wilkins.

Sapford, R.J., Banks, C. & Smith, D.D. (1978) Arsonists in prison. *Medicine, Science and the Law*, **18**, 247–54.

Scott, P.D. (1977) Assessing dangerousness in criminals. *Brit. J. Psychiat.*, **131**, 127–42.

Soothill, K.L. & Pope, P.J. (1973) Arson: a twenty years cohort study. *Med. Sci. L.* **13**, 127–38.

Sosowsky, L. (1978) Crime and violence among mental patients reconsidered in view of the new legal relationship *Am. J. Psychiat*, **135**, 33–42.

Steadman, H.J. & Cocozza, W. (1975) We can't predict who is dangerous. *Psychology Today*, **8**, 32–35.

Steadman, H.J., Melick, M.E. & Cocozza, J.J. (1977) Criminality and mental illness. *Psych. News*, Oct. 21, p. 36.

Stürup, G. (1968) *Treating the 'Untreatable'*. Baltimore: Johns Hopkins Press.

Tennent, G. (1983) The English Special Hospital: a 12–17 follow-up study and comparison of violent and non-violent re-offenders and non-offenders (in press).

Tidmarsh, D. (1982) Implications from research studies. In *Dangerousness: Psychiatric Assessment and Management*. Hamilton, J.R. & Freeman, H. (eds.). Royal College of Psychiatrists Special Publication 2. London: Gaskell.

Walker, N. (1982) Ethical aspects of detaining dangerous people. In *Dangerousness: Psychiatric Assessment and Management*. Hamilton, J.R. & Freeman, H. (eds.). Royal College of Psychiatrists Special Publication 2. London: Gaskell.

West, D.J. & Farrington, D.P. (1977) *The Delinquent Way of Life*. London: Heinemann.

Zitrin, A., Hardesty, A.S., Burdock, E.I. & Drossman, A.K. (1976) Crime and violence among mental patients. *Am. J. Psychiat.*, **133**, 142–9.

15

Towards the Development of Principles for Sentencing and Detaining Mentally Abnormal Offenders

Larry Gostin

In this chapter I will try to construct a set of principles which can be used for developing a rational legislative structure for admission to hospital and treatment of offender-patients. The central issues to be considered are: which offender should be diverted from the criminal justice to the mental health system; how long a person should remain in one form of confinement or the other; and what principles should govern the length of confinement. Finally, I will examine some conceptual issues in forensic psychiatry relating to the prediction of dangerousness and preventive confinement. Before doing so, it will be helpful to examine critically some traditional assumptions behind the use of therapeutic confinement of mentally abnormal offenders.

LABELLING THE PROBLEM: PUNISHMENT OR TREATMENT?

The reason often given for treating mentally abnormal and ordinary offenders differently is that the former are receiving 'therapy', while the latter are receiving punishment. This traditional assumption has caused both the psychiatrist and lawyer to stop at the hospital door, and not really consider the comparative effects of a hospital order and a prison sentence.

The assumption that hospital admission is based exclusively upon therapeutic, and not punitive, principles has persistently been used to insulate 'therapeutic' confinement from critical analysis. The relevance of ordinary principles of criminal justice to 'therapeutic' confinement cannot be examined dispassionately so long as the observer rigidly labels the process as beneficial. Once a measure is considered to be entirely in the individual's best interests, legal safeguards become inapposite. This simplistic labelling should not, therefore, be used as a justification for the confinement regardless of the real intentions which lie behind it.

The psychiatrist's objectives are indeed therapeutic and not punitive. However, this should not obscure the fact that there is also an element of punishment in any judicial decision to confine an involuntary individual. Although a hospital has an essentially caring function, compulsory admission is often just as much a deprivation of liberty as a prison sentence. This is particularly so when one compares a secure hospital with an open prison.

It is over-simplistic to suggest that therapy is the only rationale for detaining

224

a mentally abnormal offender. The detention does not flow solely from the need for treatment, nor is the length of confinement measured according to medical grounds alone, but relates also to the seriousness of the offence and the probability of future dangerousness. It must be recalled that the confinement usually follows a determination by a criminal court that the accused has committed a dangerous act; decisions concerning the person's release inevitably refer back to the gravity of the original offence. Therapeutic confinement, then, appears to be justified on a number of overlapping grounds including treatment, punishment and public protection. These elements are relevant to confinement of ordinary offenders. Any differences are in emphasis, not in kind, and do not justify the adoption of entirely different assumptions and principles of fairness between the two groups. It has been increasingly recognised in a number of social contexts that a 'best interests' rationale cannot justify withdrawal of substantive and procedural rights which are afforded to those who are deprived of their liberty. It is true that technical legal procedures should not unnecessarily interfere with therapeutic objectives. The balance in the law should be to enable people suffering from mental distress to be admitted to hospital instead of prison, while ensuring that the need for treatment does not serve as a justification for depriving them of their liberty without due process of law.

THE INSANITY DEFENCE: COMPASSION OR RETRIBUTION?

The law has traditionally been founded upon the principle of responsibility. If a person intentionally engages in certain criminal behaviour the court is entitled to pass a sentence of imprisonment. The ancient jurisprudential basis for absolving the offender from punishment is rooted in the concept of involuntariness of action. A person is not culpable and cannot be held criminally responsible if he had no control over his behaviour.

The insanity defence developed within this system of 'fault' and responsibility. Punishment was administered according to a framework of moral disapproval of specified human activity, and the only means by which a mentally ill person could avoid penal consequences was if he could show some casual association between the offence and his mental abnormality. He had to show, under the McNaughton Rules, that by reason of a defect of mind, he did not know the nature and quality of his act or that it was wrong.

The insanity defence is difficult for us to accept because it says nothing about the performance of the act itself and its attendant circumstances. Rather, it is justified by the state of awareness and cognition of the actor. The determination is whether the actor has sufficient inner understanding of the act and its consequences to justify him being held responsible. The defence is thus inherently difficult to observe or to identify reliably. It has a unique combination of factors – none of which is subject to observation or validation: the justification for the defence originates and remains wholly within the character or psyche of the actor; there is no cognisable aetiology or measurable physiological process; and clinical assessment in respect of nosology and classification, and the degree of separation of consciousness and action (particularly where judgements are made retrospectively), lack scientific reliability and validity. It is for these reasons that we have had the greatest difficulty in defining the boundaries of this defence or even in justifying it. The defence of insanity has thus historically been a principal point of friction at the intersection of law, psychiatry and morals (Gostin, 1981).

The insanity defence has troubled psychiatrists because it has been the sole means by which an offender could be admitted to hospital instead of prison. Yet, if the McNaughton Rules were strictly construed, they would provide a very limited defence. Insanity seldom wholly deprives the actor of reason. A psychotic actor will comprehend the nature and quality of his act (e.g. he will know he is killing or setting fire to a building) and that it is wrong (e.g. he will know that murder and arson are imprisonable offences). Yet, alterations in mood and thought may diminish a person's freedom of choice. A person may kill another because of a persecution complex or a psychotic jealousy; volition may be sufficiently impaired so that he could not reasonably be regarded as a free agent. Nevertheless, the actor will know that his own feelings of persecution or jealousy do not provide a defence in respect of murder. Under the McNaughton Rules, he would be criminally responsible.

Thus, a conceptual problem arises from the insanity defence. Compassion requires that people who are suffering from severe mental distress should not be sentenced to imprisonment. Sensible policy also requires an outcome which flows from a rational assessment of the offender's state of mind, need for care and treatment, and propensity toward violence. The insanity defence is concerned with the moral blame which should, or should not, be attributed to the accused; the investigation of state of mind is exceedingly narrow and backward-looking to the time when the behaviour occurred.

The defence, then, is inherently unable to provide an assessment of current psychological and behavioural characteristics necessary for logical sentencing; it was never intended as a device for rational differentiation among offenders according to their need for hospital care and treatment. Yet, in the absence of any other method, the insanity defence was used to divert mentally ill people from the penal to the mental health system. The insanity defence has been stretched and distorted to achieve a purpose for which it was never intended and subjected to criticism for its failure to do more than it inherently could.

The principle I am putting forward for consideration is not that the insanity defence should be abolished. Rather, I am suggesting that this defence should not be regarded as a virtually exclusive agency for differentiation of offenders who should, or should not, be admitted to hospital. The defence is far too occasional and inconsistent a device for determining the social policy question of *which* offenders should be diverted from the penal to the mental health system. The narrow remit of the insanity defence (relating to cognitive awareness of the act and its lawfulness) is consonant with the objective of the defence – namely, to excuse an actor from responsibility and punishment where he is unable to comply with the law's dictates. Its continuance would not undermine any interest of the accused so long as there were alternative and more direct methods of achieving a therapeutic disposition. Maintaining the defence for rare occasions where the accused chooses to place his state of mind in issue provides a means for the insane defendant to ask to be excused from the formal statement of societal condemnation represented by a conviction.

The Mental Health Act, 1959 made it possible for the first time in England and Wales for the courts to assess rationally the need for hospital care on the basis of current medical and social advice. The governing consideration under the 1959 Act is not whether mental disorder negates culpability, but whether the individual could benefit from treatment in hospital (see Chapter 24). The utilitarian approach introduced by the 1959 Act represents a significant advance over traditional legal procedures for achieving the sensible policy objective of making rational differentiations among offenders in respect of the need for hospital care. Indeed, the utilitarian measures of the Act are so highly regarded that they have virtually supplanted the traditional procedures; offenders found not guilty by reason of insanity or unfit to plead constituted only 1.9 per cent of the total number of mentally abnormal offenders admitted to hospitals in 1979.

The United States, which largely inherited its jurisprudence on the insanity defence from the English common law, continues to follow essentially a traditional approach. Alteration of the law to adopt more humanitarian and sensitive measures for diverting mentally disordered persons from the penal system should be focused at the point of disposal. Traditional concepts within the insanity defence, however expanded by the legislature or by judicial construction, cannot be a satisfactory method of achieving compassionate objectives. The approach of the 1959 Act represents one way of assessing the need for care at the dispositional stage, without any formal consideration of blame. Adoption of similar measures in the United States would not pose constitutional problems, as it still authorises the defendant to place his mental state in issue at the trial stage.

Further Contradictions in the Insanity Defence

It is, on the face of it, curious that the insanity defence absolves the accused from blame but, at the same time, results in his confinement for an indefinite period of time. Traditionally, the legal and moral view is that a person who commits a dangerous act because of a mental illness is not culpable and should not be exposed to criminal sanctions. Our emotional and utilitarian feeling, however, is apprehension concerning his future possibly dangerous behaviour and a desire to prevent it. The fear is that the same mental process which deprived the actor of choice, and triggered the charged offence, will repeat itself. The defendant acquitted by virtue of insanity has demonstrated his inability to conform; the mental incapacity which has in the recent past been legally related to criminality is said to justify the prediction that the disease may render the offender unable to conform in the future. The insanity defence thus established marks the insane offender as someone who must be confined.

In Anglo-American jurisprudence, the defence of insanity is one in name alone because the acquitted defendant is invariably the subject of mandatory or discretionary commitment to hospital. Although, as suggested previously, the ostensible rationale is 'therapeutic', this can only be regarded as a conceptualisation and not a justification. It does not matter how one characterises the confinement so long as it is recognised that involuntary confinement by order of a court exercising criminal jurisdiction is inherently incompatible with the decision to exonerate from criminal responsibility.

If one examines the insanity defence carefully, it becomes clear that its purpose is not to absolve mentally ill people from penal consequences but rather to authorise confinement in cases where the law would not ordinarily allow such confinement. An offence in law has two elements: an unlawful act (*actus reus*) and the intent behind the act (*mens rea*). Absence of the mental element necessary for a particular offence (as would occur if the person did not know the nature and quality of his act under the McNaughton Rules) would ordinarily result in acquittal; the court would have no authority to impose a custodial sentence. The special verdict of insanity is, therefore, special only to the extent that it will result in mandatory confinement in cases where, under ordinary legal principles, the accused would simply be acquitted.

This suggests that if the law is to continue to use the insanity defence, it should not require or authorise the court to impose a sentence involving involuntary confinement. This result occurs in England and Wales where the court is obliged to make a hospital order with restrictions on discharge without limit of time (see Chapter 16). American jurisprudence has severely limited the extent to which a person acquitted by reason of insanity can be confined and, in some jurisdictions, it is permissible only to use civil powers for admission to hospital. The American model appears to be the most sensible outcome following the successful use of the insanity defence. The insanity acquittee should have the same substantive and procedural protections in respect of therapeutic confinement as individuals so confined under civil processes.

The principles I have tried to put forward thus far are that the law should, wherever possible, authorise the admission to hospital of mentally abnormal offenders who clearly require treatment and care. In doing so the law should enable a current assessment of the offender's state of mind and need for hospital treatment to be made. This direct medical assessment should govern the decision as to *who* should be diverted from the penal to the mental health system; legal considerations of *causality* between the insanity and the offence should not be a prominent factor in making this social and utilitarian choice.

THE TREATABILITY CRITERION

Another factor needs to be considered in developing a system for accurately assessing the individuals who should be admitted to hospital as opposed to prison. This is the question of 'treatability'. Mental disorder in itself is not a sufficient justification for admission to hospital. It must also be reasonably certain that the individual will not simply receive custodial care in hospital. It is important for the mental health services that hospitals are not used for the purpose of preventive or benign confinement, nor that scarce medical resources are allocated to people who cannot benefit from treatment (Stone, 1975). More importantly, it is not in the interest of the offender to be admitted to hospital if he cannot be treated, particularly if his confinement is to be of an indefinite duration. Since the offender cannot receive substantial benefit from the treatment, and thus meet clinical and social criteria of improvement, he may be confined for much longer than the period of imprisonment he would expect to receive if he were to be 'punished' instead of treated. The uncertainty in terms of length of confinement and as to the changes in character and affect needed to satisfy others that he is fit to take his place in society may result in a deep sense of unfairness and may ultimately be counter-therapeutic.

Surprisingly, most legislation, and even international guidelines (United Nations, 1981; Curran and Harding, 1978), do not specify that an offender must have a 'good prospect of benefit from treatment' as a basis for a hospital order to be made. The Mental Health Act, 1959 of England and Wales has been followed in many Commonwealth and North American jurisdictions. The 1959 Act had an implicit treatability criterion for psychopathy and subnormality; the Mental Health Act 1983 makes the treatability criterion much more explicit (see Chapter 16). Many American statutes focus on the concept of 'dangerous' behaviour and do not have a clearly stated 'treatability' test. The principle put forward here is that hospital admission should be based upon *severe mental illness* for which there is a *good prospect of benefit from treatment*. This would maximise the therapeutic nature of hospitals and help to prevent society from using psychiatry as a form of benign or preventive confinement – that is, detention which is based, not on what a person has done, but what he may do in the future. It asks the law to ensure that, if the rationale for confinement is therapeutic, treatment must be available which can alleviate the person's mental distress and help him to return to the community.

It is, of course, important to seek to provide care for people suffering from mental distress even if there is not a good prospect of benefit from conventional psychiatric treatment. However, it is preferable that that care should be provided, whenever possible, within the prison system where the offender can be assured that his length of detention will be based upon ordinary principles of criminal justice.

There is one further issue which does not have a place in current legislation but which is worthy of careful consideration. That is the *choice of the offender* as to whether he would consent to a hospital order being made. If there is uncertainty about whether psychiatric treatment would alleviate the offender's condition, it should be permissible for a court to make a hospital order only in respect of those who have expressed a preference for admission to hospital rather than prison. There can be little benefit which a patient would receive if he is clearly not prepared to co-operate with treatment (Gunn, 1979). The two categories of mental disorder where there are the most persistent doubts about 'treatability' are psychopathic disorder and mental handicap.

Psychopathic Disorder

One of the great dilemmas in forensic psychiatry is whether it is proper to use compulsory mental health powers over certain repetitive offenders who may be characterised as suffering from psychopathic disorder or other personality disorder. In order to justify the use of such powers it must be shown that psychopathy is a meaningful clinical entity which serves as a valid description of some underlying physiological or psychological disorder; that the disorder can be diagnosed with at least some reliability and objectivity; and that those suffering from the disorder can benefit from psychiatric treatment. The evidence to support each of these assumptions is highly equivocal.

It is clear from the literature that the concept of psychopathy is thought of in psychiatry as a meaningful concept. There is considerable agreement as to the characteristics of the label, including not being able to profit from experience, lack of control over impulses, recurrent anti-social behaviour and inability to experience guilt (Cleckley, 1964; Albert et al, 1959; Gray and Hutchison, 1964). There are, however, considerable difficulties associated with the use of listed signs or symptoms in determining whether psychopathy is a useful concept. The signs identified by psychiatrists have been numerous and highly diverse. It has been observed that psychopathy is a label which may be attached to a person for a variety of reasons, and that subsequently a large number of signs may be drawn upon to substantiate the application of the label (Davies and Feldman, 1981). Although there are a number of signs used to justify the label, there is no agreement on which, if any, are the crucial ones.

In referring to the concept of psychopathic disorder, it must be observed that there has never been any evidence that psychiatrists can objectively identify the characteristics of psychopathic disorder in offenders and make a reliable diagnosis; there does not appear to be any clear distinction between the behaviour of ordinary offenders and those diagnosed as psychopaths. The features of psychopathy listed in the journals appear highly subjective and would require fine judgements to be made. What are the objective indicators, for example, of the sign 'not profiting from experience', 'emotionally immature' or 'lack of moral sense'? More importantly, there does not appear to be any homogeneity in the features of psychopathy which range from recurrent anti-social behaviour (the gravity of the behaviour not being specified) to irresponsible sexual behaviour, excessive alcohol consumption, greater than average intelligence, occupational instability and homosexuality.

There could be other indicators of a valid clinical entity, such as the existence of a demonstrable aetiology or that some objective improvement could be measured from psychiatric intervention. Yet, there is also a multiplicity of opinions as to the cause and treatment of psychopathy; psychopathic disorder is a concept which appears to be understood, if at all, only by reference to the particular sense in which it is being employed by the individual practitioner. Treatment theories in respect of psychopathic disorder have included such diverse areas as physical or drug treatments, usually reporting short-term success and lacking in both control and long-term follow-up; open or therapeutic communities; and the use of strict supervision and control. There have not been any properly controlled studies which have shown any one method of treatment to be clearly more effective than any other. It appears that there are no agreed criteria for assessing the 'treatability' of psychopaths and no agreed combination or sequence of therapeutic procedures (see the Butler Committee, Home Office and DHSS, 1975).

The Mental Health Act 1983 in England and Wales is one of the few major mental health statutes which continues to employ the term 'psychopathic disorder'; the classification is not used in the legislation of Scotland or Northern Ireland. Psychopathic disorder as such is not part of the World Health Organization's International Classification of Diseases, although it is referred to in definitions of personality disorders. The WHO has referred to the compulsory admission of psychopathic patients as one of 'the most serious problems in the British mental health system' (Curran and Harding, 1978).

The Consultative Document (DHSS, 1976) and White Paper (DHSS *et al*, 1978) on the Mental Health Act, 1959 said that the Health Service could not at present offer effective treatment for people classified as psychopathic. However, the Government did not recommend the removal of the classification from the Act because one could not rule out the possibility of a future advance in treatment for this disorder. This reasoning is flawed, for it is difficult to justify the use of compulsory powers at present because of the anticipation of some benefit which may be possible in the future. The Mental Health Act 1983 did not alter the definition of psychopathic disorder but has required that there be some prospect that treatment can alleviate or prevent deterioration in the condition; it has not removed psychopathy as a condition which may render the person liable to compulsory admission.

Even if it were possible to conclude from the evidence that psychopathic disorder was a single and recognisable clinical entity, it would still be difficult to maintain the classification for legally relevant purposes. If the rationale for detention was psychopathic disorder alone it would be reasonable to insist that it was necessary to show that the offender would benefit; there would be no convincing rationale for admission to hospital instead of prison, except if the offender himself expressly chose a therapeutic alternative.

In sum, psychopathic disorder appears to be a most elusive concept: psychiatrists disagree on the meaning of the term and over its diagnosis in particular cases. Some would limit it to a narrow group of dangerously anti-social individuals, while others extend it to cover inadequates of various descriptions, including those with social, sexual, drug or alcoholic deviances (Gibbens, 1961); the concept is intractable and the behaviour of those so classified overlaps with ordinary offenders; there is no demonstrably effective therapy; and the label has proved stigmatic, harmful and indelible. Psychopathic disorder is defined in the Mental Health Act 1983 (Section 1 [2]) as amended, as a persistent disability of mind which results in abnormally aggressive or seriously irresponsible conduct. (Would serious irresponsibility include, for example, excessive gambling or unwise spending?) It appears that the most important aspect of the term is not the presence of a specific mental condition but its expression in some form of anti-social behaviour. This suggests a rather tautological definition in that it infers a disease from anti-social behaviour, while purporting to explain that behaviour by a disease. The concept of 'personality disorder' may in future present some interesting possible factors in influencing a person's behaviour and, to this end, further research is of some intrinsic value. The concept does not, however, aid us in making sensible choices about who should be confined, where, and for how long. A person's future liberty should be based upon his past behaviour. This method of determining the length of confinement is fair because it holds a person accountable for his own acts. It thus puts him in a position similar to others in society who are judged, not because of what they are (or rather how they are perceived by 'experts'), but because of what they have done. Agency, volition and social determination are all important aspects of human behaviour, which is not mechanistic and cannot be predicted purely on a biochemical, clinical or scientific basis.

The guiding principle put forward in this section has been that, if the classification of psychopathy is to have any relevance in law at all, it should be based upon the clear preference of the offender for hospital as opposed to prison. There should still be some prospect of benefit from treatment and the offender should receive a finite sentence based upon the gravity of the offence. This puts into effect the overriding principle in forensic psychiatry – which is, the level of responsibility that the offender is capable of exercising. The concept of choice in respect of sentencing would say to the offender 'you have offended against the criminal law, you are not entirely responsible for your actions, but you are responsible enough to be given a choice; either you accept ordinary punishment for this offence or you accept a course of medical treatment' (Gunn, 1979).

Mental Handicap

The case of mental handicap is in many respects quite different from psychopathic disorder and certainly more complex. As with psychopathic disorder, it is difficult to accept that direct benefit from treatment should not be an important condition for a hospital order to be made in respect of a mentally handicapped person. It is increasingly recognised that mental handicap is not essentially a medical condition which is subject to conventional psychiatric treatment in hospital (Gostin, 1978, 1979). If the *condition* of being handicapped were to be the exclusive basis for confinement in hospital then there would be no reasonably defined period after which that hospital confinement could be expected to cease; the condition itself would be unlikely to be alleviated. The needs of mentally handicapped people are more likely to be social and educational than psychiatric. Accordingly, if exoneration from punishment was to be on the basis of the person's best interests, the alternative to prison would more likely be a guardianship or probation order. This would allow supervised care in the community.

The Mental Health Act 1983 replaces the definition and terminology of mental subnormality with 'mental impairment'. This term, described on p. 178, is an amalgamation of the definitions of subnormality and psychopathic disorder. Accordingly no mentally handicapped person whose condition does not satisfy the definition of mental impairment with the attendent treatability criterion may be the subject of a hospital order or received into guardianship.

The difficulty with the treatability criterion in the case of mental handicap is the fact that there are often serious problems with sentencing such a person to a term of imprisonment. Mentally handicapped people, particularly if they function in the lower ranges of intelligence and social competence, would have difficulty in coping with a prison environment. The discipline and rigidity of such an environment often makes it an unacceptable alternative for reasons of compassion. It could reasonably be argued that a local mental handicap hospital would be more humane from the patient's perspective than a sentence of imprisonment. This dilemma needs to be carefully considered in each individual case. Certainly, a mentally handicapped person's choice of a hospital order instead of imprisonment should not prejudice the offender in terms of his length of confinement and right to a periodic review of the need for his detention.

The issue of offender-preference is also more complex in the case of mental handicap. It is wrong to suggest that all mentally handicapped people cannot make a reasonable choice between prison and hospital; many patients have very strong views which should be respected. There will be cases of severely mentally handicapped people where the ability to choose will be restricted and this problem must be recognised. The principle, however, still stands that a person's choice, whenever possible, should be respected.

In sum, in the case of psychopathic disorder and mental handicap, two principles should be particularly respected: the prospect of their benefit from treatment in hospital, and their own choice. In either case, where an offender chooses hospital care, it should not prejudice his rights as an ordinary offender. Accordingly, the duration of the hospital order should be proportionate to the gravity of the offence, and should not be greater than the period the offender would have received in prison.

THE 'TARIFF' PRINCIPLE

The principle I will put forward in this section is that if a person is sentenced by a court exercising criminal jurisdiction, the basic principles of sentencing applicable to ordinary offenders should apply also to mentally abnormal offenders (Gostin, 1977). These principles are used in law as a counterbalance and safeguard in respect of the sentencing powers of the court. If the principles are not correctly applied the offender is entitled to appeal and to have the sentence modified. There are two basic principles sometimes referred to as the 'tariff' principle and the principle of 'equality'. The tariff principle operates on the basis that an offender's length of confinement should not be disproportionate to the gravity of the offence. The equality principle operates on the basis that similarly situated offenders (e.g., with equivalent immediate offences and criminal records) should be dealt with similarly.

It has been suggested that these safeguards should not apply to the mentally abnormal offender for a number of reasons: his offence is not the reason for confinement but has called attention to his general need for hospital care; he is detained for treatment not punishment, and it is impossible to envisage at the time of sentencing the length of time it will take to alleviate his condition and return him to the community.

In discussing the issue of *how long* a mentally ill person should be confined in hospital, it is important to differentiate between detention on criminal grounds and detention justified on other grounds. Therapeutic confinement following the conviction of a criminal offence is qualitatively different from civil confinement. The actual mechanism for release may be different for offender-patients than for civilly detained patients. In England and Wales, mentally abnormal offenders may be given a *restriction* order without limit of time, which means that the patient cannot be discharged by his doctor without the consent of the Home Secretary (see Chapter 16). Further, discharges from hospital are usually conditional, and the patient can be recalled at any time. The restricted patient does have a periodic right to appeal to a mental health review tribunal with decision making powers. Nevertheless this places him in a markedly different legal situation from all other detained patients who, as well as being entitled to be discharged by a mental health review tribunal, may be discharged by their hospital managers and, in certain circumstances, their nearest relatives. The restricted patient, therefore, is detained on an entirely different basis than other patients; the former may be detained by a member of the executive, at least partly on the grounds of societal protection, while the latter are detained on medical grounds.

When it is said that a restriction order is not intended as punishment and cannot be governed by penal considerations (Home Office and DHSS, 1975), the implication is that it is made for the purpose of treatment. Yet, although it is a hospital order that is made for the purpose of therapy, the accompanying restriction order is made purely for custodial purposes. The Home Secretary's first duty is to protect the public, and he is not legally obliged to discharge a potentially dangerous offender even if there is little evidence that the person would benefit from continued hospital care. In *Kynaston*'s case (1981), a patient was determined by a unanimous recommendation of the therapeutic team not to be mentally disordered or in need of treatment. The Court of Appeal, however, did not grant him leave to bring an action against the Home Secretary for wrongful detention, as it was within his powers to disregard medical advice in this instance and to continue to detain the patient.

Apart from the formal legal differences between restricted patients and non-restricted patients, there is also the practical difference that discharge considerations in the former case inevitably are referred back to the original offence. So long as detention is seen to flow from a conviction it would be impossible not to consider the offence in the discharge decision, regardless of the length of time which has transpired.

One should observe, finally, that an offender-patient in England and Wales is much more likely to be detained in a high security hospital. In the United States there is a still more formal division between institutions in respect of whether they house offenders or non-offenders. Indeed there is jurisprudence to suggest that an offender-patient is entitled to be transferred to an ordinary hospital after a period which is governed by the gravity of the offence (*Baxstrom* v. *Herold*, 1966).

Thus, although it may be true that an offence may only call attention to the more general need for care, it is not solely that need for care which governs the place of duration of confinement. Accordingly, it would be improper to deprive the offender-patient of the traditional safeguards afforded by a finite sentence based upon the 'tariff' and 'equality' principles. This does not necessarily mean that the patient cannot be detained for a longer period on the basis of his need for care. However, it does mean that detention which is justified only by the need for care, and not by the offence, should be achieved through ordinary civil admission with all of the attendant safeguards.

In summary, when a mentally ill person has been convicted of a criminal offence society is justified in protecting itself by holding him in custody as it would any other offender – that is, for a period of time proportionate to the gravity of the offence. During that period society should do all that it can to rehabilitate him by offering treatment in a psychiatric hospital. Society should not, however, use the fact that the person is receiving treatment as a justification for holding him for an indefinite period without adequate safeguards.

It should be emphasised again that we cannot change the character of a compulsory measure merely by affixing a label. When a person is to be deprived of liberty it is imperative that we understand the objective, and that the consequences are consonant with the objective; further there should not be any gross anomalies. If an offender-patient is to be detained *because of his need for treatment*, then he should be entitled to the same rights and safeguards as a civilly detained patient, including the right to be discharged by his doctor and a mental health review tribunal. If, on the other hand, the reason is preventive, then he should have the same safeguards as ordinary offenders including adherence to the tariff principle. Yet, traditionally the offender-patient has received neither the safeguards which apply to offenders, nor those which apply to patients. Society feels certain that this is because we are acting compassionately towards the offender-patient. However, the dual characterisation of offender *and* patient serves only to diminish the individual's status in law and to increase the opprobrium in society.

DECISION-MAKING: A QUESTION OF INTERNATIONAL HUMAN RIGHTS

The foregoing analysis has been accepted in broad terms by the European Court of Human Rights. The Court's jurisprudence suggests that the rationale for detention must be established at the time of sentencing: if that rationale is the commission of an offence then the sentencing court makes the decision as to the length of confinement; if the rationale is therapeutic then the confinement should be subject to equivalent safeguards as for civil detention, including the right to a periodic review by a court. Article 5 of the European Convention of Human Rights states that both a substantive and procedural standard needs to be complied with in respect of any deprivation of liberty. A person cannot be deprived of liberty except on a number of specified substantive criteria. Included in these are Article 5(1) (a), following conviction by a competent court; and 5(1) (e), a person of unsound mind. The Court has laid down a rather arbitrary division so that a detention can be justified either by sub-paragraph (a) or (e), but not both. Thus, if a finite prison sentence is passed, sub-paragraph (a) is invoked even if subsequently the person is transferred to hospital. Contrariwise, if a hospital order is made, sub-paragraph (e) is invoked. This division has more than theoretical consequences. If the rationale for a detention is conviction of an offence the sentencing court is expected to broadly take account of the 'tariff' and 'equality' principles; any gross deviation from these norms could result in the sentence being regarded as inhuman and degrading under Article 3 (Jacobs, 1975). In this case the offender would have no right to a periodic review of his confinement because the original court determination is deemed to have fulfilled this obligation. However, if 'unsoundness of mind' is the justification for confinement, the European Court has ruled that the original court hearing does not satisfy the Convention and that there must be a meaningful periodic review by a court under Article 5(4).

Clearly, a hospital order, with or without restrictions on discharge, in the English context is justified only on grounds of unsoundness of mind. The question arises as to which decision-maker can determine when the patient is released and under what criteria?

The European Court of Human Rights in *Winterwerp* v. *The Netherlands* (1979) laid down standards which had to be complied with under Article 5(1) (e): 'the individual concerned should not be deprived of his liberty unless he has been reliably shown to be of "unsound mind". The very nature of what has to be established before the competent national authority – that is, a true mental disorder – calls for objective medical expertise. Further, the mental disorder must be of a kind or degree warranting compulsory confinement. What is more, the validity of continued confinement depends upon the persistence of such a disorder.'

The Mental Health Act, 1959 does comply with these standards at the time of admission. However, there has been some doubt whether it complied with those standards throughout the period of detention. In *X* v. *The United Kingdom* (1981) the Home Secretary recalled a restricted patient to hospital following a matrimonial dispute. The patient at all times complied with the conditions of his discharge; he had not behaved violently or committed an offence; and he was not seen by a doctor before his recall. The Court found that Article 5(1) (e) had not been violated because medical evidence was obtained *after* his recall. This decision, in my view, renders the Court's three criteria stated above as meaningless; it should be observed that the Court has never found a violation of Article 5(1) (e). Nevertheless, the issue of whether the Home Secretary needs to take account of medical evidence throughout the period of confinement has never been examined by the Court. An application has been made to the European Commission of Human Rights in *Kynaston*'s case (see above) to test this and other issues.

Article 5(4) of the Convention has always been most relied upon by the European Court. Article 5(4) provides that 'everyone who is deprived of his liberty by arrest or detention shall be entitled to take proceedings by which the lawfulness of his detention shall be decided speedily by a court and his release ordered if detention is not lawful'. As stated previously, this provision requires, in the case of a hospital order, a periodic review by a court of the need for detention. Minimally, the court must have regard to the three conditions of paragraph 5(1) (e) set out in *Winterwerp*'s case. The European Court found a violation of Article 5(4) because restricted patients did not have access to a court (Gostin, 1982).

What are the possible decision-makers in English law and why did the Mental Health Act, 1959 fail to comply with the European Convention? The Home Secretary was charged with ultimate decision-making powers but he is a member of the executive and, as the detaining authority, he is also one of the parties to the case; the Home Secretary acts in secret and does not give reasons for his decisions. Clearly, this form of decision-making does not meet the *Neumeister* test of being a 'court' (Jacobs, 1975). It is true that any person deprived of liberty in England can issue a writ of habeas corpus. However, the case of *X* v. *The United Kingdom* cast a cloud over the ancient English writ, except in emergency cases. Habeas corpus can be used to obtain the discharge of a person who is *unlawfully* detained but not if he is *unjustifiably* detained (see Gostin, 1982, for a further discussion of these issues). Since the Home Secretary had unfettered discretion under the 1959 Act his powers to detain patients are lawful and virtually unreviewable. The final possible decision-maker is a mental health review tribunal. However, the tribunal under the 1959 Act was empowered only to advise the Home Secretary in respect of a patient's discharge. The Home Secretary rejected approximately 40 to 50 per cent of all recommendations for discharge made by tribunals. Only during the passage of the Mental Health (Amendment) Act did the government introduce provisions to comply with the decision of the European Court. The Mental Health (Amendment) Act 1982 gave restricted patients the right to a mental health review tribunal with binding powers (see Chapter 16).

Therefore, the European Court has provided reasonable principles to abide by in respect of the detention of offender-patients. These are that detention must be based upon reasonable medical and social evidence of mental illness and the need for treatment and care in hospital. More importantly, if the justification for detention is mental illness, the offender-patient should be entitled to safe-guards which are similar to those granted to civil patients. This includes – but is not limited to – the right to a periodic review by a court of law concerning the need for detention.

SOME CONCLUSIONS CONCERNING THE LIMITS OF PSYCHIATRIC COMPETENCE AND THE CONCEPT OF DANGEROUSNESS

Psychiatry as a profession has suffered from unrealistic public expectations of its competence. Psychiatry is part of the fabric of medicine and its functions are governed by wider medical ethics. Psychiatry is not unique in the field of medicine by virtue of its inability to specify the aetiology of certain illnesses or to understand the reason for the efficacy of some of its treatments. Psychiatry, none the less, is criticised for these deficiencies, probably because society expects that if compulsory powers are to be used, minimal standards of knowledge must be attained. It is discomforting that, although mental illness itself may justify deprivation of liberty, diagnostic abilities of psychiatrists have been shown to be unreliable under normal clinical conditions (Gostin, 1983).

Psychiatry is a profession whose objective is to treat people suffering from mental distress. It thus forms a binary relationship with the patient. However, public expectations are often much greater than are applicable to other branches of medicine; there are formal and more subtle pressures on psychiatrists to act as representatives of society and not of the patient. Psychiatry is often perceived, along with the criminal law, as one of the guardians for the protection of the public. There is a deep public feeling that dangerousness and mental illness will lead to offending behaviour; and that psychiatrists have efficacious treatments which can significantly reduce the propensity of patients to re-offend.

The fact is that mental illness is not usually associated with dangerousness in a causal relationship. Offences of mentally abnormal offenders are often attributable to identifiable and normal motives such as greed, jealousy and hunger (Walker and McCabe, 1973). There are many aspects of a person's background, environment and character which may influence his behaviour. It is usually impossible to say with any degree of confidence that any one element (such as mental illness) *caused* a person to behave in the way he did. Thus although society presumes that psychiatrists can accurately examine and understand the interaction between mental abnormality and dangerousness, the fact is that there is very little expertise in this area at present.

It is also assumed, particularly by legislators and judges, that psychiatrists can accurately predict future behaviour and that these predictions can reasonably form the major justification for preventive confinement. The judge will ask, 'is he mentally ill or psychopathic?', 'has the disease *caused* the offence?', 'does he pose a danger to the public?' Every psychiatrist will know that mental illness is not equivalent to a discrete disease which either exists or entirely fails to exist. Rather, it is a continuum and is based upon symptomatology, which manifests itself in different ways and at different times; unsoundness of mind is not all-encompassing and there will be attributes as well as deficiencies in respect of the cognition and affect of most individuals. So too, it is difficult to identify a 'dangerous person'. The behaviour of individuals is complex and is governed as much by circumstances as by anything intrinsic within the person. A person driving a car while intoxicated or smoking while on a tanker may be dangerous.

On the other hand, a mentally abnormal offender who, suffering from a persecution complex, has killed his wife is not likely to kill again, particularly if equivalent circumstances do not arise and there is sufficient support and supervision in the community.

There have been a great number of studies which examine the ability of psychiatrists and others to predict future dangerous behaviour (see Chapter 14); many of these studies have focused upon 'high risk' patients where it would be expected that higher levels of prediction could be attained. Yet the studies have consistently shown that psychiatrists are not accurate predictors of future dangerous behaviour and are particularly prone to over-prediction. They tend to predict anti-social behaviour in instances where it would not, in fact, occur; a range of false-positive predictions between 50 and 95 per cent is indicated by the studies (National Institute of Mental Health, 1978; Steadman, 1979; Gostin, 1977; Levinson and Ramsay, 1979). What is noteworthy is that in the limited number of instances where dangerous behaviour is predicted better than chance, two characteristics are invariably present. First, all such studies deal with individuals who have previously engaged in the type of conduct which is being predicted. Second, the studies base their predictions upon a large quantity of detailed information about the groups studied. There has been no reliable evidence to suggest that psychiatrists, based on clinical assessment alone, can predict future dangerous behaviour. This is neither a surprising observation nor one which is critical of psychiatry; dangerousness is not a clinical entity or a personality characteristic but, rather, is an estimated probability based upon highly complex and diverse variables.

Given the fact that dangerousness is neither a psychiatric nor a medical standard (American Psychiatric Association, 1974) it is unsurprising that there are few, if any, demonstrated treatments to diminish the likelihood of future serious harm to others. Indeed, most conventional psychiatric treatments are intended to reduce the symptomatology of mental illness and are not directed toward future dangerousness. There may be instances where reduction in symptomatology may reduce the propensity for violence, but this is only an occasional by-product of psychiatric treatment and could not be relied upon for any legally relevant purpose.

The objective of this chapter, then, has been to show that 'dangerousness' is principally a legal and not a medical concept. Detention based upon a person's dangerousness should be governed by jurisprudential standards. These standards are well developed in the criminal law and include the principles of 'equality' and proportionality between the length of confinement and the gravity of the offence. These principles should govern the length of confinement so long as the rationale for that confinement is the commission of an offence. Any further detention would be governed on therapeutic principles and based upon civil legislation. The need for treatment, on the other hand, is essentially a medical concept and should be governed by psychiatric and humane principles. Assessment of the need for hospital admission should be made by medical and other relevant caring professions. In marginal cases, such as with psychopathic disorder or mental handicap, the decision should be on the basis of a person's prospect of benefit from treatment *and* his own preference for hospital care. Confusion in law and psychiatry has resulted from persistent false assumptions of a considerable overlap between the legal concept of dangerousness and the medical concept of treatability.

CASES

Baxstrom *v*. Herold (1966) 383 US 107.
R. *v*. Kynaston, *The Times Law Report*, February 1981.
Winterwerp *v*. The Netherlands, Application No. 6301/73. Report of the Commission adopted on 15 December 1977. Judgment of the Court given on 24 October 1979.
X. *v*. The United Kingdom, Application No. 6998/75. Report of the Commission adopted on 18 July 1980. Judgment of the Court given on 5 November 1981.

REFERENCES

Albert, R.S., Brigante, T.R. & Chase, M. (1959) The psychopathic personality: a content analysis of the concept. *J. Gen. Psychol.*, **60**, 17.
American Psychiatric Association (1974) *Clinical aspects of the violent individual*, New York: APA.
Cleckley, H. (1964) *The Mask of Sanity*, 4th edition. St Louis: C.V. Mosby.
Curran, W.J. & Harding, T.W. (1978) *The Law and Mental Health: Harmonizing Objectives*. Geneva: World Health Organization.
Davies, W. & Feldman, P. (1981) The diagnosis of psychopathy by forensic specialists. *Brit. J. Psychiat.*, **138**, 329-31.
Department of Health and Social Security (1976) *A Review of the Mental Health Act 1959*. London: HMSO.
DHSS, Home Office, Welsh Office & Lord Chancellor's Dept. (1978) *Review of the Mental Health Act 1959* Cmnd. 7320. London: HMSO.
Gibbens, T.C.N. (1961) Treatment of psychopaths. *J. Ment. Sci*, **107**, 181-6.
Gostin, L. (1977) *A Human Condition: The Law Relating to Mentally Abnormal Offenders - Observations Analysis and Proposals for Reform*, Vol. 2. London: MIND (National Association for Mental Health).
Gostin, L. (1978) The right of a mentally handicapped person to a home, education, and to socialisation: a case for exclusion from the Mental Health Act 1959. *APEX: J. Inst. Mental. Sub.*, **6**, 2, 28-31.
Gostin, L. (1979) The law relating to mental handicap in England and Wales. In *Tregold's Mental Retardation*, 12th edition. Craft, M. (ed.). London: Baillière Tindall.
Gostin, L. (1981) Justification for the insanity defence in Great Britain and the United States: the conflicting rationales of morality and compassion. *Bull. Am. Academy of Psych. and the Law*, **9**, 2, 100-15.
Gostin, L. (1982) Human rights, judicial review and the mentally disordered offender. *Criminal Law Review*, 779-94, Dec. 1982.
Gostin, L. (1983) The ideology of entitlement: the application of contemporary legal approaches to psychiatry. In *Mental Illness: Changes and Trends*. Bean, P. (ed.).
Gray, K.C. & Hutchison, H.C. (1964) The psychopathic personality: a survey of Canadian psychiatrists' opinions. *Can. Psychiatric Assn. J.*, **9**, 452-61.
Gunn, J. (1979) The law and the mentally abnormal offender in England and Wales. *Intl. J. Law and Psychiat.*, **2**, 2, 199-214.
Home Office & DHSS (1975) *Report of the Committee on Mentally Abnormal Offenders (Butler Committee)* Cmnd. 6244. London: HMSO.
Jacobs, F. (1975) *The European Convention of Human Rights*. London: Oxford University Press.
Levinson, R.M. & Ramsey, G. (1979) Dangerousness, stress and mental health evaluations. *J. Health Soc. Behav.*, **20**, 78.
National Institute of Mental Health (1978) *Dangerous Behavior: A Problem in Law and Mental Health*. Washington: US Department of Health, Education and Welfare.
Steadman, H.J. (1979) Attempting to protect patients' rights under a medical model. *Intl. J. Law and Psychiat.*, **2**, 2, 185-98.

Stone, A. (1975) *Mental Health and Law: A System in Transition*. Washington: National Institute for Mental Health.

United Nations (1981) *The Protection of Persons Suffering from Mental Disorder*. Siracusa, Sicily: Association Internationale De Droit Penal.

Walker, N. & McCabe, S. (1973) *Crime and Insanity in England*, Vol. 2, Edinburgh: University Press.

16

Mental Health Law in England and Wales 1983: An Exposition and Leads for the Future[1]

Larry Gostin

Traditionally, mentally abnormal offenders have been exempt from ordinary penal measures on the grounds that they are not criminally responsible for their behaviour. It is maintained in law that a person who does not have full comprehension when committing a criminal act cannot be held legally responsible for it. Thus, if medical evidence establishes that he was unable to appreciate the nature and quality of the criminal act (or did not know it was wrong), then the special verdict of 'not guilty by reason of insanity' is applicable. The court then has no choice but to make a hospital order with special restrictions and without limit of time.

Another traditional justification for exempting the abnormal offender from ordinary penal measures is that he is too mentally disordered to stand trial for the offence charged. Thus, if the defendant is unable to understand the course of the proceedings at the trial, he may be found unfit to plead. The result of such a finding is that the defendant will not stand trial, instead, a hospital order will be made, together with a restriction order without limit of time. In deciding whether the accused is fit to plead, the concept of criminal responsibility is not relevant: the medical evidence adduced must relate to his mental state at the time of the trial.

Offenders found not guilty by reason of insanity, or unfit to plead, accounted for only a small percentage of the total number of mentally abnormal offenders admitted into hospital. These traditional legal procedures have largely been supplanted by a 'utilitarian' approach, introduced by the Mental Health Act, 1959 and continued under the Mental Health Act 1983. Under section 37 of the 1983 Act, a magistrates' or Crown Court may make a hospital order if it finds (on the basis of two medical opinions) that the offender is suffering from a mental disorder of a nature or degree that warrants his detention in hospital for treatment.

A hospital order has a similar effect to an admission for treatment under Section 3 of the 1983 Act. This means that the patient can be detained in hospital

[1] *Note from the editors:* This chapter is taken from volume 2 of *A Human Condition* (Gostin, 1977). Some two-thirds of the provisions in the Mental Health (Amendment) Act 1982 derive from that publication. Account has been taken of the Mental Health Act 1983. The author wishes to thank Laura Jacobs for updating the chapter in light of the Mental Health (Amendment) Act 1982. For a full account, see Grostin (1984).

for six months; the authority for detention can be renewed for six further months and then for intervals of one year at a time. The patient can be discharged at any time by the responsible medical officer, a mental health review tribunal or the hospital managers. A Crown Court can make a hospital order subject to the special restrictions on discharge contained in Section 41 of the Act. This means that the patient can be discharged by a mental health review tribunal, or otherwise only with the consent of the Home Secretary. The order can be made for a fixed period or without limit of time; in recent years, virtually all restriction orders have been for unlimited periods.

In making a hospital order, with or without restrictions, the court is not concerned with the criminal responsibility of the offender, or whether he is capable of understanding the proceedings of the trial (he has already been tried and convicted); the only relevant considerations are his mental condition and his suitability for psychiatric treatment at the time of sentencing.

Thus, contrary to popular belief, no causal relationship has to be established between the mental disorder and the criminal behaviour. Moreover, partial or complete recovery from the disorder will not necessarily reduce the offender's criminal propensity. A person may be cured of his mental disorder, but still be disposed to commit a crime.

In several cases which have come before the Court of Appeal, the offender objected to a hospital order on the grounds that there was no connection between his illness and the offence committed. The court ruled that there need be no connection, and that the offender's consent to the order was not required (*R.* v. *McBride*, 1972; *R.* v. *Hatt*, 1962; *R.* v. *Gunnee*, 1972).

A prisoner may develop a mental disorder after he has been sentenced to a term of imprisonment. Alternatively, he may have been mentally disordered at the time of sentencing, but it was not detected and he was therefore dealt with as an ordinary offender. If a person serving a sentence of imprisonment is found to be 'mentally abnormal' he can be transferred to a hospital. The Home Secretary must find, on the basis of two medical reports, that the offender is suffering from a mental disorder of a nature or degree which warrants his detention in a hospital for medical treatment. He must also be of opinion, having regard to the public interest and to all the circumstances, that it is expedient to make a transfer direction. A transfer direction has the same effect as a hospital order. It can be made with or without restrictions on discharge. If it is made without restrictions, the offender is no longer subject to the prison sentence. He can therefore be unconditionally discharged from the hospital by the Responsible Medical Officer (RMO), a tribunal, or the hospital managers. But if it is made with restrictions the Home Secretary, if he is notified by the RMO, any other medical practitioner or a mental health review tribunal, that the offender no longer requires treatment in hospital for mental disorder, has two options: (i) to discharge the offender if he would have been eligible for release on parole or (ii) to direct the offender's remission to prison to serve the remainder of his sentence. However, the restrictions on discharge automatically lapse after the expiry of the earliest date of release with remission of the sentence.

The reader will notice from the short exposition of the relevant legislation presented above that the offender-patient is dealt with in different ways, depending on when his mental disorder arises (or else when it is detected). Table 16.1 presents a summary of the legislation in chart form; it includes also the relevant provisions in the Mental Health (Amendment) Act 1982.

Table 16.1 Mental disorder and the offender.

Legislation	Criteria and evidence	Decision-maker (and burden of proof)	Effect
A *Mental disorder present at the time of the offence*			
1 Special verdict of not guilty by reason of insanity Criminal Procedure (Insanity) Act 1964, S.2	McNaughton Rules: the offender did not know the nature and quality of the act or did not know that it was wrong No formal requirements – generally two medical opinions	Jury (Defence raises evidence and bears the burden of proof to 'a balance of probabilities')	Hospital order made with restrictions and without limit of time (mandatory) See C(2) below
2 Diminished responsibility, which is a plea in mitigation of sentence Homicide Act, 1957, S.2	The offender suffers an abnormality of mind that impairs his mental responsibility	Jury As A(1) above	Reduces charge of murder to one of manslaughter; thus it avoids the mandatory life sentence and allows the court a wide range of disposals
B *Mental disorder present at the time of the trial*			
1 Transfer direction before trial Mental Health Act 1983, S.48	The defendant must be suffering from mental illness or severe mental impairment which makes it appropriate for him to be detained in a hospital for medical treatment; and the patient is in urgent need of such treatment Two medical opinions required	Home Secretary	Hospital order with restrictions and without limit of time (mandatory) See C(2) below
2 Unfit to plead Criminal Procedure (Insanity) Act 1964, S.4	The offender is unable to understand the proceedings so as to make a proper defence, to challenge a juror, and to understand the evidence As A(1) above, except that in some cases only one medical opinion is put before the court	Jury (If the defence raises the issue it has the burden of proof to the balance of probabilities. If the prosecution raises the issue, it has the burden, beyond a reasonable doubt)	The facts of the original charge are not examined if the issue is raised at the outset of the trial; if trial proceedings have already started, they are abandoned when the issue is raised The defendant must be detained in hospital, with restrictions on discharge imposed without limit of time – see C(2) below. The defendant may be remitted for trial at a *(cont.)*

Legislation	Criteria and evidence	Decision-maker (and burden of proof)	Effect
			later date. The patient may apply for a Mental Health Review Tribunal within the first six months of detention. If this right is not exercised then the patient will be automatically referred to a tribunal after the expiration of six months

C *Mental disorder present at the time of sentencing*

Legislation	Criteria and evidence	Decision-maker (and burden of proof)	Effect
1 Hospital order Mental Health Act 1983, S.37	The defendant is suffering from mental illness, psychopathic disorder, mental impairment or severe mental impairment which warrants his detention in a mental hospital. In the case of psychopathic disorder or mental impairment such treatment is likely to alleviate or prevent a deterioration of his condition Two medical opinions are required. The court must be satisfied on the written or oral evidence of the medical practitioner who would be in charge of the patient's treatment or some other person representing the hospital managers The Regional Health Authority must, at the request of the court, provide information on available hospital facilities	Court	A hospital order has a similar effect to an admission for treatment under S.3 of the 1983 Act, as amended, i.e., detention is initially for a period of six months, and the order may be renewed for six months and then for periods of one year at a time. The patient may be discharged at any time by the RMO, the hospital managers, or by a Mental Health Review Tribunal
2 Hospital order with restrictions on discharge with or without limit of time Mental Health Act 1983, S.41	As C(1) above The court must also consider that restrictions on discharge are necessary for the protection of the public from serious harm Magistrates' courts must remit to the Crown Court for a restriction order to be made	Crown Court	Patients may be discharged by a Mental Health Review Tribunal, or otherwise only by or with the consent of the Home Secretary. A restriction order may be made for a fixed period or without limit of time

Legislation	Criteria and evidence	Decision-maker (and burden of proof)	Effect
	Opinions of two medical practitioners are required, and one must give oral evidence to the court		A requirement to provide an annual report on the patient's progress to the Home Office
3 Probation order with a condition of psychiatric treatment Powers of Criminal Courts Act 1973, S.3	The condition of the defendant must be such as requires and may be susceptible to treatment, but does not warrant his detention in a hospital The defendant must consent to the making of this order Two medical opinions are required	Court	The patient must attend hospital for psychiatric treatment as an informal in- or out-patient
D *Mental disorder present after sentencing*			
1 Transfer to hospital of a person serving sentence Mental Health Act 1983, S.47	As C(1) above As C(1) above, but the Home Secretary must consider, having regard to the public interest, that the transfer of the prisoner to a mental hospital is expedient.	Home Secretary	The prisoner is transferred from prison to hospital; an order made under S.47 has the same effect as a hospital order under S.37 As C(1) above
2 Transfer from prison to hospital with restrictions on discharge Mental Health Act 1983, S.49	As C(2) above As C(2) above	Home Secretary	As C(2) above The patient may be returned to prison if the Home Secretary is notified by the RMO, any medical practitioner or a MHR tribunal that he no longer requires treatment; or he may be released on licence if he would have been so released on return to prison The restrictions on discharge cease to have effect on the expiration of what would have been the earliest date of release from prison. He is thereafter liable to detention as in D(1)
E *New provisions introduced in the Mental Health Act 1983*			
1 Remand to hospital for report on accused's mental condition	The defendant is suffering from mental illness, psychopathic disorder, mental (*cont.*)	Court	Duration of remand is not more than 28 days at a time or 12 weeks in all

	Legislation	Criteria and evidence	Decision-maker (and burden of proof)	Effect
	Mental Health Act, 1983, S.35	impairment or severe mental impairment, and it would be impracticable for a report on his mental condition to be made if he were remanded on bail Opinion of one medical practitioner required		Person remanded in hospital for a medical report cannot be given treatment without his consent
2	Remand of accused person in hospital for treatment Mental Health Act 1983, S.36	If the accused is suffering from mental illness or severe mental impairment of a nature or degree which makes it appropriate for him to be detained in hospital Opinion of two medical practitioners needed	Court	Duration of remand as in E(1) above. However, person can be treated without consent in certain circumstances in accordance with the provisions of consent to treatment in Part VI of the Mental Health (Amendment) Act
3	Interim hospital order Mental Health Act 1983, S.38	If the offender is suffering from mental illness, severe mental impairment, psychopathic disorder or mental impairment and there is reason to suppose that the mental disorder makes a hospital order appropriate. Thus the person can be admitted on an interim hospital order to assess suitability for hospital treatment Opinion of two medical practitioners needed	Court	The detention is for a period not exceeding 12 weeks and may be continued for further periods of not more than 28 days at a time up to a maximum total period of six months

MENTAL DISORDER AT THE TIME OF THE OFFENCE[1]

There are five instances where the mental state of the accused at the time of the offence is material. These are the special verdict, diminished responsibility, drunkenness, non-insane automatism and infanticide. Strictly speaking, the last four categories stand outside the scope of this chapter since the courts do not necessarily make a treatment order on conviction in these cases. Readers interested in these areas of law are referred to other texts (Home Office and DHSS, 1975; Williams, 1978; Bluglass, 1980).

[1] For a more complete examination of the insanity defence see Gostin (1981).

The Existing Law

The law relating to criminal responsibility in England rests upon the unadorned McNaughton Rules. The Rules were formulated by the judges in 1844 in answer to questions submitted by the House of Lords following the acquittal of murder of Daniel McNaughton on the grounds of insanity. The proper charge to the jury was stated in the Rules:

> . . . to establish a defence on the grounds of insanity, it must be clearly proved that, at the time of the committing of the act, the party accused was labouring under such a defect of reason, from disease of the mind, as not to know the nature and quality of the act he was doing; or, if he did know it, that he did not know he was doing what was wrong.

There follows an examination of each of the elements of the McNaughton Rules.

Disease of Mind

The determination of whether the accused was suffering at the time of the act from a 'disease of the mind' is a legal, not a medical question, to be decided by the judge (*Bratty* v. *Attorney General for Northern Ireland*, 1963). The term has been construed widely by the courts, and this has acted to the disadvantage of defendants: involuntary behaviour as a consequence of disease of the mind results in the special verdict which requires a disposition of indefinite psychiatric confinement, while the same involuntary behaviour from most other causes results in an ordinary acquittal. Devlin, J. (now Lord Devlin) established the standard in *Kemp*'s case. A malfunction of mind, however caused, constitutes a 'disease of the mind' under McNaughton. 'It does not matter, for the purposes of the law, whether the defect of reason is due to a degeneration of the brain or to some other form of mental derangement ... The law merely has to consider the state of mind in which the accused is, not how he got there.' Accordingly, physical malfunction of the brain – for example, associated with epilepsy, arteriosclerosis, cerebral tumour, diabetes – may amount in law to a disease of the mind if it produces the required defect of reason. Devlin's expansive view of 'disease of the mind' was supported by the House of Lords (per Lord Denning) in *Bratty*'s case: 'any mental disorder which manifests itself in violence and is prone to recur is a disease of the mind. At any rate it is the sort of disease for which a person should be detained in hospital rather than be given an unqualified acquittal.'

In *R.* v. *Sullivan* (1983) the House of Lords upheld this view. The Lords considered that it did not matter whether the mental impairment (in this case if epilepsy) was organic or functional, or whether the impairment itself was permanent or was transient and intermittent, provided it subsisted at the time of the commission of the act. If the occurrence of an epileptic fit brought about a temporary suspension of the mental faculties of reason, memory and understanding during the course of which the offence was committed, the special verdict of not guilty by reason of insanity was appropriate.

The term 'disease of mind' as established in *Sullivan* would have inappropriate results if applied without identifiable boundaries. An involuntary act as a consequence of a blow on the head causing concussion, the administration of an anaesthetic, the consumption of an intoxicant, or the influence of hypnosis would be regarded as a disease of the mind within the parameters of the insanity defence. The preferred position was stated by Bridge, J. in *Quick*'s case (see also *R. v. Rabey*, 1977). Disease of the mind within McNaughton does not include 'malfunctioning of the mind of a transitory effect caused by the application to the body of some external factor'.

The House of Lords in *Sullivan*'s case alluded to this position and said in *obiter dictum*, that the courts have not excluded the possibility of non-insane automatism in cases where temporary impairment results from some external factor.

A principal difficulty with the *Kemp–Bratty* position is that it belies the ostensible compassionate concern of the special verdict. Confinement in a mental hospital of a person suffering from diabetes, epilepsy, tumour, transient concussion or arteriosclerosis would be custodial and not therapeutic. Such involuntary confinement of persons not medically insane and not susceptible to psychiatric treatment is incompatible with the supposed rationale of compassion and exculpation from criminal punishment. None the less, Bridge, J. took Lord Devlin's view as to the correct state of English law: it matters 'not whether the condition of the mind is curable or incurable, transient or permanent ... There is no warranty for introducing these conditions into the definition of the McNaughton Rules.'

And in *Sullivan*, Lord Diplock candidly observed that the purpose of the special verdict was to protect society against recurrence of the dangerous state, no matter how temporary. (This appears to make the mandatory restriction order of unlimited duration inappropriate from a policy perspective.)

The reported cases which attempt to distinguish automatism from insanity are fraught with contradiction. In *Charlson* a devoted father suddenly struck his son with a hammer and threw him into a river. He had suffered, at the material time, from a cerebral tumour, and acted without knowledge or intent. The issue of automatism, but not insanity, was put to the jury and he was acquitted. In *Kemp*, a devoted husband made an equally motiveless and irrational attack upon his wife. He, too, struck her with a hammer while suffering from arteriosclerosis. Here, the issue of automatism, not insanity, was put to the jury and they returned the special verdict. In virtually identical circumstances Charlson was given unqualified freedom while Kemp was indefinitely confined in a psychiatric institution. It is now accepted judicially and by commentators that *Kemp* is to be preferred over *Charlson*.

Defect of Reason

In examining the phrase 'defect of reason' as a consequence of disease of the mind it must be shown that the accused was, at the material time, deprived of the power of reasoning. The McNaughton Rules do not apply to those who retain the power of reasoning but who fail to use their powers to the full, such as a shoplifter who took groceries forgetting to pay for them (*R.* v. *Clarke*, 1972; see also *R.* v. *Islitt*, 1978).

Where the defendant has established that, at the time of the offence, he was suffering from a defect of reason from disease of the mind, he must further establish that, as a consequence of this defect of reason, his knowledge was critically deficient in one of the following respects.

Knowledge of the nature and quality of the act: limb one

The statement in the McNaughton Rules, 'nature and quality of his act' refers to the physical nature and quality and not to the moral or legal quality. Thus, a defendant is excused from responsibility only if he had no comprehension of the physical act he performed; the classic illustration is a man who squeezed a person's throat in the belief that it was a lemon. This is a rather narrow test because usually a mentally ill person will know that he is committing an act which is unlawful, but he may not have complete control over his behaviour. In such instances he would not be considered insane under the McNaughton Rules.

Knowledge that the act was wrong: limb two

The McNaughton Rules provide that a person who knows the physical quality of his act will, nevertheless, be excluded from punishment if he did not know it was wrong. Knowledge of the wrongfulness of an act may be interpreted variously: understanding that it is contrary to law; contrary to the general morals of the community; or contrary to one's own moral standards. It can be envisaged that a person may recognise that an act is unlawful, but nevertheless believe that it is morally accepted by his fellow men; or he may know that an act is contrary to law and general morals, but feel himself that it is morally proper.

The modern authority in England is that wrongfulness refers solely to the legal understanding. In *Windle*'s case the defendant, suffering from a communicated mental illness known as folie à deux, murdered his wife in the belief that it was morally justified. He did know that murder was unlawful as evidenced by his statement to the police: 'I suppose they will hang me for this.' The Court of Appeal, upholding his conviction, stated: 'in the McNaughton Rules "wrong" means contrary to the law and not "wrong" according to the opinion of one man or a number of people on the question whether a particular act might or might not be justified.' The Court therefore rejected individual or general morality as a ground for acquittal by reason of insanity.

Insanity established under limb two – knowledge of the wrongfulness of an act – provides the only pragmatic rationale for the special verdict. It is on this limb alone that an insane defendant may be excused from responsibility in circumstances that would otherwise render him criminally liable. Knowledge by a sane actor of the wrongfulness of his act is not within the prosecution's case; accordingly, a deficiency in such knowledge would not be a ground for acquittal.

To the contrary, a sane actor cannot succeed in a defence which pleads ignorance of the law or good motive.

The law of England, then, is that criminal responsibility rests upon a finding of whether, as a consequence of defect of reason, the actor knew the physical quality of his act or, if he did, whether he knew the particular act to be unlawful.

The Special Verdict and the Mandatory Imposition of a Hospital Order With Restrictions

Prior to the Criminal Lunatics Act, 1800 there were no statutory or common law arrangements for the detention of persons acquitted by reason of insanity. Section 1 of the Act of 1800 provided for the mandatory confinement of such persons until the pleasure of His Majesty was made known. The form of verdict under Section 1 was of acquittal. The Trial of Lunatics Act, 1883, Section 2, altered the form of the special verdict to one of guilty but insane. The alteration resulted following the trial of Roderick Maclean for discharging a pistol at Queen Victoria. The Queen expressed disapproval of the form of the special verdict indicating an acquittal. Thereafter the new name of the verdict went through Parliament without opposition. The Atkin Committee (1923), the Gowers Commission (Royal Commission, 1953) and the Criminal Law Revision Committee (1963) all recommended a return to the former verdict of not guilty by reason of insanity. These proposals were enacted in the Criminal Procedure (Insanity) Act 1964, which is currently applicable in England and Wales. The 1964 Act requires the mandatory confinement of those acquitted by reason of insanity – referred to as the special verdict. The form of confinement is a hospital order with restrictions on discharge without limit of time which is referrable to Sections 37 and 41 of the Mental Health Act 1983. The legal effect of a hospital order with restrictions is examined below.

MENTAL DISORDER AT THE TIME OF THE TRIAL

Where a criminal defendant is suffering from a substantial mental incapacity such that it would be legally improper for him to stand trial, there are procedures under the Mental Health Acts and the Criminal Procedure (Insanity) Act 1964 which can prevent him from being tried. In such circumstances, the defendant is said to be 'unfit to plead' or, as suggested in the Butler Report, 'under disability in relation to the trial' or, more simply, 'under disability'.

A determination that a person is under disability prevents him from being tried at all. Therefore, it does not show that he is either innocent or guilty since there are no findings of fact.

The existing criteria for determining whether a defendant is under disability are: whether he can understand the course of proceedings at the trial in order to make a proper defence, challenge a juror to whom he might wish to object, and understand the substance of the evidence. The Butler Committee has proposed that the reference to capacity to challenge a juror should be omitted, and two criteria should be added: whether the defendant can give adequate instructions to his legal advisers, and can plead with understanding to the indictment.

The meaning of the term 'mental disorder' in this context is considerably different from its meaning as used in the Mental Health Acts. Even if the accused is the proper subject of a formal admission to hospital, he is not necessarily under a disability in relation to the trial; although he suffers from a medically classifiable mental disorder, he may still be able to follow the proceedings in court and therefore be fit to stand trial.

Nor do other forms of mental disability necessarily place the person under a legal disability in relation to the trial. For example, it has been held (*R. v. Podola*, 1960; *R. v. Robertson*, 1968) that neither hysterical amnesia (where the defendant has no recollection of the alleged crime) nor persecution mania (where the defendant is unable to act 'in his own best interest' at the trial) constitutes sufficient basis for a finding of unfitness to stand trial. The finding of disability apparently turns upon the capacity of the defendant to comprehend the deliberations of the court; the content of the defence, that is, whether or not the defendant can put up a good defence, is not relevant for this purpose.

If the question arises during the trial whether the accused is under a mental disability which constitutes a bar to his being tried, the procedural provisions of the Criminal Procedure (Insanity) Act 1964 (which was based upon the Third Report of the Criminal Law Revision Committee, 1963) have effect.

The issue of disability may be raised by the defence or the prosecution; or if neither party raises the issue, the judge should do so himself if he has doubts about the fitness of the accused. He may resolve his doubts by reading the medical reports, though it is not desirable that he should hear oral evidence.

The burden of proof in such enquiries lies with the party that alleges disability. If the defence raises the issue, then the standard of proof required is that on a balance of probabilities the accused is unfit to stand trial; but if the prosecution alleges unfitness, it must be proved beyond a reasonable doubt.

Section 4(3) of the Criminal Procedure (Insanity) Act 1964 requires that the question of disability be determined as soon as it arises; under Section 4(2) of the Act, however, the court (having regard 'to the nature of the supposed disability' and if satisfied that it is 'expedient so to do and in the interests of the accused') has discretion to postpone the inquiry until the case for the prosecution has been heard. This means that the court may require the prosecution to present its case, and the defendant may be acquitted if there is insufficient factual evidence to justify a conviction. If the jury acquits the defendant, the question of disability will not be determined. If, however, the prosecution does present a substantial case showing that the accused is guilty on the facts, the issue of disability will immediately be determined by the jury. Under Section 4(2) the judge may postpone the determination of disability until the case for the prosecution has been heard, only if it appears that the defence has a reasonable chance of success on the factual issues of the case. This is so even where the disability is such that, whatever the outcome of the trial, the accused is likely to be detained in hospital.

Effect of a Finding of Unfit to Plead

According to the Criminal Procedure (Insanity) Act 1964, if a defendant is found unfit to plead, the trial proceeds no further. The court must make an order admitting the defendant to a hospital named by the Home Secretary and he must be detained in accordance with Sections 37 and 41 of the Mental Health Act 1983 (under a hospital order with special restrictions on discharge, made without limit of time). A person in these circumstances has the right to apply to a mental health review tribunal within six months and if this right is not exercised, he will be automatically referred to a tribunal after the expiration of six months (Mental Health (Amendment) Act 1982, Schedule 1).

Remit for Trial

If the person's mental condition subsequently improves, the Home Secretary (after consultation with the responsible medical officer) is empowered by Section 5(4) of the Act to remit him for trial.

In a memorandum to the Butler Committee, the Home Office pointed out that there are practical difficulties in proceeding with the prosecution of a person who has been detained in hospital for a long time. Accordingly, the Home Secretary's power to remit the patient for trial is sparingly used, generally only in cases where the patient's mental condition has improved rapidly, and the desirability of reaching a formal decision on his guilt is not counterbalanced by other considerations.

Leads for the Future

In making a determination that the defendant is under a disability, the court's intent is that he should receive treatment at the earliest possible time. This saves the defendant from the stress of a court appearance; it is better for the dignity of the legal process; and it authorises detention in a therapeutic environment. Moreover, it is unjust to make a mentally disabled person the subject of a criminal trial if he is unable to comprehend the proceedings and contribute to his own defence. It would be unfair to convict such a person because, if he were capable, he might be able to exculpate himself. Mental disability may substantially diminish a defendant's capacity to testify, to recall exonerating circumstances or identify corroborative witnesses, to instruct his lawyer, and so forth. Similarly, he may be highly suggestible, even to the point of incriminating himself where he is not in fact guilty of the offence charged.

Taking Police Statements From Severely Mentally Disordered People

The Judges' Rules on Interrogation and Taking Statements by Police do not make special provision for mentally handicapped people, although on 21 July 1976 the Home Office issued to Chief Officers of Police a circular of guidance on this subject (No. 109/1976). The circular draws attention to the need for special care in the interrogation of such persons. It recognises that it may sometimes be difficult for police to decide if a person is mentally handicapped. However, if there is reason to believe that a person is a mentally handicapped adult, it recommends that, so far as practicable, he should be interviewed only in the presence of a parent or other person in whose care, custody or control he is, or some other person who is not a police officer (e.g. a social worker). The Judges' Rules already provide for the presence of a third party for mentally handicapped children. The provisions in the Judges' Rules and 1976 circular outlined here are not mandatory. However, evidence obtained in breach of these rules and the 1976 circular may be excluded by a judge in the exercise of his discretion. The Home Office has issued draft codes of practice on the treatment, questioning and identification of persons suspected of crime (Home Office, 1982). The codes will be laid before Parliament with the Police and Criminal Evidence Bill as an indication of how the Home Secretary would exercise the relevant powers in the Bill should Parliament decide to grant them. The codes build upon the guidance contained in the 1976 circular.

The Importance of Finding the Facts

The criminal process should, as far as possible, protect the mentally disordered defendant from being wrongly convicted; the adoption of mandatory legislation along the lines suggested in the 1976 circular would be appropriate. However, the inability of the accused to defend himself properly should not prevent an investigation of the offence; he may in fact have committed the criminal act with which he is charged, and may therefore have to be confined for the protection of society. On the other hand, a simple showing that the defendant is mentally disordered at the time of the trial does not justify his compulsory confinement for an indefinite period of time, unless there is also proof that he committed an imprisonable offence. For some defendants, such as those suffering from certain forms of organic psychiatric illness or from severe subnormality, there is little or no chance that their mental capabilities will significantly improve; they become subject to potentially life-long involuntary confinement.

Under the Criminal Procedure (Insanity) Act, the court can determine that the defendant is unfit to plead without making a full finding of the facts. Moreover, if disability is found, the court must make a hospital order, coupled with a restriction order without limit of time. The defendant is therefore subject to confinement in hospital until the Home Secretary either remits the case for trial – which very rarely occurs – or conditionally discharges the patient from hospital. In this regard, the Home Secretary must naturally assume that the patient committed the crime with which he was charged, and this may affect his estimation of when he can safely be released.

Given the severe consequences of a determination that the defendant is under a disability in relation to the trial, it is important that the facts of his case should be established by a court. It is usually unjustifiable to confine an individual indefinitely if he has not committed the offence charged against him. A mentally handicapped person may not be liable to long-term compulsory admission to hospital under the civil provisions of the Mental Health Act for two reasons: first, a mentally handicapped person can under no circumstances be compulsorily admitted under Section 3 of the Mental Health Act 1983 and second, mental disability alone is not a sufficient basis for compulsory detention. It must also be shown that the person is in need of hospital treatment and the detention is in the interests of the patient's health or safety or for the protection of others. The mere filing of criminal charges against a person should not be taken as grounds for affording him less protection against confinement in a mental institution than any others are given. Of course, if the person is actually dangerous he should be dealt with, if at all, under the provisions of Part II of the Mental Health Act 1983 which relate to non-criminals.

The Butler Committee made the following proposal: when the question is raised whether the defendant is under disability, it should be decided immediately. If disability is found but the medical evidence suggests that recovery is possible within a few months, the judge can adjourn the proceedings for a maximum of six months, during which time the defendant will undergo treatment. The trial may be reconvened at any point during this period on medical evidence that the accused is either recovered, or on the other hand has not responded to treatment. At the adjourned proceedings, the question of disability will be reopened. It may then be found that the defendant has become fit to stand trial. If he is found to be still under disability, a finding of facts will take place; the object of this is to enable the jury to return a verdict of not guilty where the evidence is not sufficient for a conviction. If the jury finds that the defendant actually committed the criminal act, he will not be found guilty, because his disability has made it impossible for him to contest his guilt fully. Instead the Butler Committee recommended the verdict that 'the defendant should be dealt with as a person under disability'.

Disposal

As has already been stated, when a person is found unfit to stand trial, the court has no choice but to make an order for his admission to hospital, with special restrictions imposed without limit of time. On the other hand, once a conviction has been registered, the court has a discretionary power under Sections 37 and 41 of the Mental Health Act to make a hospital order with or without restrictions, for whatever period it considers necessary; it may also pass a non-custodial sentence such as a psychiatric probation order. It is anomalous that the court has considerable discretion in dealing with a convicted person, but has none in dealing with a person who has not even stood trial for the crime charged.

Accordingly, the present law should be changed to give the court wide discretion in the matter of disposal. The Butler Committee recommended that the court should have the power to make any social or medical order, including an order for in-patient treatment in hospital with or without a restriction order; an order for hospital out-patient treatment; a guardianship order; and a discharge without any order.

Remands to Hospital and Interim Hospital Orders Under the Mental Health Act 1983

The Butler Committee recommended that courts should be given the power to remand a mentally disordered person to hospital in cases where a medical report is required; where medical care is required during a custodial remand; and where a short period in hospital is necessary to determine whether a hospital order would be a suitable disposal.

The Mental Health Act 1983 implements these recommendations in the following ways.

Section 35 – Remand to hospital for report on the accused person's mental condition

The Crown Court or magistrates' court can remand an accused person to hospital before sentence if it is satisfied on the evidence of a medical practitioner approved under Section 28 of the Mental Health Act, 1959 that there is reason to suspect that the accused is suffering from one of the forms of mental disorder and it would be impracticable for a report on his mental condition to be made if he were remanded on bail. The court cannot make a remand under this clause unless it is satisfied, on the evidence of the medical practitioner who would be responsible for the report, that arrangements have been made for the admission of the offender.

The court can make a *further* remand if it appears, on the evidence of the responsible medical practitioner, that it is necessary for completing the assessment of the person's mental condition. The further remand can be made without the accused appearing in court, although his representative must have the opportunity of being heard.

The accused can be remanded or further remanded for not more than twenty-eight days at a time and for not more than twelve weeks in all.

Section 36 – Remand of accused person to hospital for treatment

The Crown Court may, instead of remanding the accused person in custody, remand him to hospital for treatment. The court must be satisfied, on the evidence of two medical practitioners, that the person is suffering from mental illness or severe mental handicap of a nature or degree which makes it appropriate for him to be detained in hospital for medical treatment.

As with Section 35, arrangements have to be made for his admission to hospital before the remand can be implemented. There are also similar provisions for a further remand; the time limits for remand and further remand are identical (twenty-eight days at a time and twelve weeks in all).

Section 38 – Interim hospital orders

Where a person is convicted of an offence punishable with imprisonment, the court may make an interim hospital order. The court must be satisfied on the evidence of two medical practitioners that he is suffering from one of the forms of mental disorder and there is reason to suppose that the disorder is such that it may be appropriate for a hospital order to be made. As with Sections 35 and 36, arrangements for admission must be made before an interim hospital order can have effect.

An interim hospital order is in force for a specified period not exceeding twelve weeks. It may be renewed for further periods of twenty-eight days at a time if, on the evidence of the RMO, its continuation is warranted. No such order can continue in force for more than six months in all.

MENTAL DISORDER AT THE TIME OF SENTENCING

Hospital Orders Without Restrictions

In pursuance of Section 37 of the Mental Health Act 1983 a court may authorise a person's admission to, and detention in, a specified mental hospital, or place him under the guardianship of the social services department of a local authority, or a person approved by the authority.

The following conditions must be fulfilled if a hospital or guardianship order is to be made. First, the person must have been convicted of an offence punishable with imprisonment in the Crown Court, an offence other than one for which the sentence is fixed by law (i.e. murder); in a magistrates' court, an offence punishable on summary conviction with imprisonment.

A magistrates' court may make a hospital or guardianship order without recording a conviction if satisfied (where the accused suffers from mental illness or severe subnormality) that he committed the act or made the omission charged.

Secondly, the court must be satisfied, on the written or oral evidence of two medical practitioners, that the offender is suffering from either mental illness, severe mental impairment, psychopathic disorder, or mental impairment which is of a nature or degree that makes it appropriate for him to be detained in hospital for medical treatment, and in the case of psychopathic disorder or mental impairment, such treatment is likely to alleviate or prevent a deterioration in his condition.

Thirdly, the court must be of the opinion, considering all the circumstances, including the nature of the offence and the character and antecedents of the offender, and the other available methods of dealing with him, that the most suitable method of disposing of the case is a hospital order.

Finally, a hospital order under Section 37 cannot be made unless the court is satisfied, on the written or oral evidence of the medical practitioner who would be in charge of the treatment of the patient, or some other person representing the hospital managers, that arrangements have been made for the admission of the offender to a specified hospital within a period of 25 days from the making of the order. The order may specify a special hospital (Broadmoor, Rampton, Moss Side or Park Lane) if the offender is thought to be dangerous; otherwise he will normally be admitted to an ordinary psychiatric hospital in his home area.

Similarly, the court cannot make a guardianship order under Section 37 unless it is satisfied that the local authority is willing to receive the offender into guardianship.

The medical evidence must be given by two medical practitioners, at least one of whom must be approved by an Area Health Authority for the purposes of Section 36 of the Act as having special experience in the diagnosis or treatment of mental disorders. The evidence of a medical practitioner may be in the form of a signed report, in which case the court may also require that he be called to give oral evidence. Where the court has directed that a medical report be produced in evidence 'otherwise than by or on behalf of the accused', a copy must be given to counsel or the solicitor who represents the accused. If he is not legally represented he must be informed of the substance of the report; where he is a child or young person, his parent or guardian must be so informed. The Court of Appeal has also thought it advisable that the judge should hear evidence from the doctor who will be treating the offender.

The accused may require that the medical practitioner be called to give oral evidence, and evidence to rebut that contained in the medical report may be called by or on behalf of the accused.

The court may request the Regional Health Authority or the Secretary of State for Wales to provide information on available hospital facilities in its region or elsewhere at which arrangements could be made for the person's admission. This is a new provision (Mental Health Act 1983, Section 39) to assist the courts to find a hospital willing to accept the mentally disordered offender.

The effect of a hospital order is to place the person in hospital on a similar basis to a patient admitted for treatment under the civil provisions of Section 3 of the Act. However, if a patient is under a hospital order, the nearest relative cannot exercise the right provided in Section 47 to order his discharge. Instead the nearest relative has the right to apply to a mental health review tribunal in the period between six and twelve months beginning with the date of the order and in any subsequent period of twelve months.

Patients admitted to hospital under Section 37 may be detained for a period not exceeding six months. The authority for detention may be renewed for a further six months, and thereafter for one-year periods at a time. The renewal is made by the responsible medical officer: he must examine the patient within the two months before the day on which the authority for detention ceases. If it appears to him that 'it is necessary in the interests of the patient's health or safety or for the protection of other persons that the patient should continue to be liable to be detained' he reports this to the managers. The Mental Health Act 1983 specified further renewal criteria, namely that medical treatment in a hospital is likely to alleviate or prevent a deterioration of the patient's condition. An alternative to this treatability criterion in the case of mental illness or severe mental impairment is that the person would be unable to guard himself against serious exploitation or obtain the care he needs if the order were not to be renewed.

In making a hospital order, the court is placing the patient in the hands of doctors, and is nominally forgoing the imposition of punishment. Therefore (unless the order is coupled with a restriction order under Section 41), the court and the Home Office relinquish control over the patient; the responsible medical officer, a mental health review tribunal or the hospital managers can discharge the patient at any time.

A patient under a Section 37 order has the same right to apply to a mental health review tribunal as his nearest relative. This means that the patient may apply for a tribunal hearing after the expiry of six months following the making of the order. He may also apply at any time during each further period of renewal. The Mental Health Act 1983 removes the previous right of Section 37 patients to apply to a tribunal within the first six months (conferred by the 1959 Act). There were two reasons given in the Parliamentary debate for taking away the right of a hospital order patient to apply for a tribunal within the first six months of detention. Firstly, the Government felt that the European Convention of Human Rights required consistency between restricted and unrestricted patients; this construction of the jurisprudence of the Convention has been questioned (Gostin, letter to *The Times*, 28 January 1982). Secondly, the hospital order patient will have had the appropriateness of admission and detention in hospital recently decided by the sentencing court. The tribunal has the power to discharge the patient either immediately or at a specified future date but does not have any lesser powers – for example, to order a transfer to another hospital or to grant a conditional discharge.

The effect of a guardianship order

A guardianship order under Section 37 confers on the authority or person named as guardian the same powers as a guardianship application made and accepted under Sections 7 and 8 of the Mental Health Act 1983 except that the nearest relative has no power to discharge the patient from guardianship.

Guardianship can legally require a person to accept the help or advice of a local authority (or a person named in the order) on a range of issues limited to employment, residence, attendance for education, training and treatment. The 1982 Act curtailed the wide-ranging powers conferred by the 1959 Act on the local authority or person named as guardian to exercise control over the ward as if he were under 14 years of age and the guardian were his father.

Hospital Orders With Restrictions

When a hospital order is made by a Crown Court and it considers, having regard to the nature of the offence, the antecedents of the offender and the risk of his committing further offences if set at large, that it is necessary for the protection of the public from serious harm, the court may also make an order under Section 41 of the Act restricting his discharge from hospital. The restriction order may be either without limit of time or for a specified period. If it is for a fixed term, once that term expires or otherwise ceases to have effect, the patient will still be detained under a hospital order without restrictions.

A magistrates' court does not have the power to make a restriction order under Section 41; however, if the accused is 14 years of age or older and is convicted of an offence punishable on summary conviction with imprisonment, the magistrates' court may, if it thinks necessary and if the conditions under Section 41(1) are fulfilled, either commit the offender in custody to be dealt with by the Crown Court, or order that he be admitted to a specified hospital (under a restriction order without limit of time) until the case can be disposed of by the Crown Court (Mental Health Act 1983, Section 43). In these instances, however, the Crown Court is not obliged to make a hospital order, let alone a restriction order; it may deal with the offender in any of the ways open to the magistrates' court.

A Section 41 restriction order cannot be made unless at least one of the medical practitioners who gives evidence in pursuance of Section 37 has given evidence orally before the court. The practitioner who gives oral evidence need not be the one who has special experience in the diagnosis or treatment of mental disorder.

Effects of restriction orders

Criticism of the Home Secretary's Powers under the 1959 Act Prior to the amendment of the 1959 Act neither the responsible medical officer, the hospital managers nor a mental health review tribunal had the power to grant leave of absence, a transfer to another hospital or a discharge without the consent of the Home Secretary. A restricted patient had no right to apply to a mental health review tribunal, but could have his case referred by the Home Secretary to a tribunal for advice. The Home Secretary was not obliged to accept the tribunal's advice and need not give reasons for his decision. Between 40 and 50 per cent of tribunal recommendations for advice are rejected by the Home Secretary. MIND (the National Association for Mental Health) successfully brought a case, *X* v. *The United Kingdom*, before the European Court of Human Rights, who found the Government to be in breach of Article 5(2) and Article 5(4) of the European Convention on Human Rights.

X v. *The United Kingdom* In 1969, the applicant was sent to Broadmoor Hospital under Sections 60 and 65 of the Mental Health Act 1959, following a charge of wounding with intent. His condition improved and he was conditionally discharged by the Home Secretary in May 1971. The conditions were that he live with his wife, be supervised by his probation officer and attend a psychiatric out-patient clinic. In April 1974 he was arrested and recalled to Broadmoor. No reasons were given for his recall. In subsequent unsuccessful proceedings for a writ of habeas corpus the official reason given by the Home Secretary was that his 'condition was giving cause for concern'. The applicant claimed he was not mentally ill, that his recall was unjustified and he had no effective way to challenge the decision which rested entirely with the Home Secretary.

The applicant complained that he was not given reasons for his arrest, contrary to Article 5(2) of the Convention, and that there was no procedure by which he could have the lawfulness of his detention decided speedily by a court, contrary to Article 5(4).

The European Court of Human Rights endorsed the finding of the European Commission, in that failure to inform the applicant promptly of the reasons for his arrest amounted to a breach of Article 5(2). The Government was found in breach of Article 5(4), which states, 'Everyone who is deprived of his liberty by arrest or detention shall be entitled to take proceedings by which the lawfulness of his detention shall be decided speedily by a court and his release ordered if the detention is not lawful.' The Mental Health Act, 1959 delegates to the Home Secretary authority to discharge, or consent to the discharge of, restricted patients. The European Court held that this was not a judicial function within the meaning of the Convention because the Home Secretary is a member of the executive and, as the detaining authority, can be regarded as one of the parties to the case. The writ of habeas corpus was found not to satisfy the requirements of Article 5(4) in mental health cases as it only examines the procedural but not the substantive lawfulness of detention. Although the patient had the right to request a mental health review tribunal six months after his recall, this review does not satisfy the requirement of speed in Article 5(4). Moreover, as an advisory body to the Home Secretary the mental health review tribunal does not constitute a court under the Article. The impact of the European Jurisprudence is discussed further in Gostin (1982).

The judgment of the European Court was given on 5 November 1981 and during the passage of the Mental Health (Amendment) Act through Parliament, the Government tabled an amendment to comply with the European Court ruling. The effects of a restriction order following the amendment of the 1959 Act are as follows.

Home Secretary's powers: the effect of the Mental Health Act 1983

Apart from the new powers given to mental health review tribunals under the Amendment Act (see below) the effects of a restriction order remain essentially unchanged. Thus, the responsible medical officer or the hospital managers have no authority to grant the discharge, transfer or leave of absence of a restricted patient without the consent of the Home Secretary. The Home Secretary may, at any time, discharge a restricted patient from hospital either absolutely or subject to conditions. With a conditional discharge, he may, at any time during the continuance of the order, recall the patient by warrant to hospital; the patient will then be detained as if the original restriction order were still in effect. The European Commission of Human Rights found a violation of Article 5(2) of the Convention which provides that a person must be informed promptly of the reasons for his arrest. The Government accepted the criticism of the Commission and issued circulars to the police, the probation service and hospitals introducing a two-stage procedure for informing patients of their recall.

Annual medical review

The Act increases the monitoring of restricted patients by requiring the RMO to furnish a report to the Home Secretary at intervals not exceeding one year.

Mental Health Review Tribunals

Section 73 and Schedule 2 of the 1983 Act set out the new authority of mental health review tribunals in respect of restricted patients.

Composition of tribunals

In the Parliamentary debates on the Act the Government were concerned that the judiciary might not have confidence in the tribunal as a method of protecting the public interest; this might result in some reluctance in making a hospital order in respect of mentally disordered offenders convicted of serious offences. Accordingly, the Amendment Act enables rules to be made for restricting the persons qualified to serve as president of a mental health review tribunal (MHRT) exercising jurisdiction over a restricted patient. It is expected that the president in such cases will be a lawyer with substantial experience in the criminal courts. This would normally be a circuit judge, but could also be a recorder.

Applications and references to tribunals

A restricted patient detained in hospital can apply to an MHRT in the period between six and twelve months of the date of the relevant hospital order or transfer direction, and in any subsequent period of twelve months. For these purposes a conditionally discharged patient who is recalled to hospital is considered to have a fresh hospital order made at the time of recall.

For reasons explained earlier in relation to hospital orders, certain patients have not had the opportunity of a court review on the issue of the appropriateness of hospital admission and detention. Accordingly, patients who are treated as subject to a hospital order and a restriction order under Section 5(1) of the Criminal Procedure (Insanity) Act 1964 have the right to apply to an MHRT during the first six months of detention. If such a patient does not apply during that period, the Home Secretary must refer his case to an MHRT.

Tribunal's powers

Absolute discharge The tribunal *must* direct the *absolute* discharge of the patient if satisfied that: (a) he is not suffering from one of the four forms of mental disorder of a nature or degree which makes it appropriate for him to be liable to be detained in hospital for medical treatment or that it is not necessary for the health and safety of the patient or for the protection of other persons that he should receive such treatment; and (b) that it is not appropriate for him to remain liable to be recalled to hospital for further treatment. It is important to observe that the tribunal's power to discharge must be based upon the fulfilment of these criteria. A tribunal exercising jurisdiction over a restricted patient does not have a general discretion to discharge as in the case of tribunals in non-restricted cases.

Conditional discharge If the tribunal is satisfied that criterion (a) but not (b) above is fulfilled, it must direct the *conditional* discharge of the patient. Where a patient is conditionally discharged he must comply with such conditions (if any) as may be imposed at the time of discharge by the tribunal or at any subsequent time by the Home Secretary. A tribunal may defer a direction for conditional discharge until such arrangements as they may think necessary are arranged. If, by virtue of a deferment, no direction for conditional discharge has been made before the patient's case is next heard by the tribunal, the case will be treated as if no direction had been made. A conditionally discharged patient may apply to a mental health review tribunal in the period between one and two years after he was discharged and in any subsequent period of two years. The tribunal may, in respect of such an application, vary or amend the conditions of discharge or direct that the restriction order or direction should cease to have effect.

Recall The Home Secretary may, at any time, recall to hospital a patient who has been conditionally discharged. However, when a restricted patient is recalled, the Home Secretary must, within one month, refer his case to a mental health review tribunal.

Transfers The tribunal's powers in respect of a transferred patient subject to a restriction direction are generally limited to notifying the Home Secretary whether, in their opinion, the patient would, if subject to a restriction order, be entitled to be absolutely or conditionally discharged; if they notify him that conditional discharge is appropriate they may recommend whether, if he is not discharged, he should continue to be detained in hospital. The purpose of these arrangements is to give the Home Secretary the opportunity within ninety days of notifying the tribunal whether he may be discharged. If the Home Secretary does not give notice within ninety days, the hospital managers must, unless the tribunal made a recommendation that he should remain in hospital, transfer the patient to prison in another institution where he could have been detained.

Leads for the Future

As indicated in Chapter 15 there are a number of serious legal and policy objections to restriction orders as presently constituted. It is often assumed that a mentally abnormal offender is exempt from ordinary penal measures on the grounds that he is not responsible for his criminal behaviour. The person committed the offence because he was mentally ill at the time of the offence and suffering, for example, from a delusion which caused him to commit the offence. However, contrary to popular belief, no causal link between the mental disorder and the crime is necessary for the court to make a hospital order, with or without restrictions. The fact is that quite often mentally abnormal offenders are convicted of petty offences, which are committed without planning or skill, for food, small sums of money or saleable items. Each of these could be ascribed to a motive which we regard as normal: hunger, desire for money, need for sleep and shelter. In these cases it is impossible to say with confidence that the offender would not have committed the offence if he had not been disordered, for they are indistinguishable from the acts of a large number of ordinary, if incompetent, people (Walker and McCabe, 1973).

It follows that a person may be 'cured' of his mental disorder, but still be disposed to commit a crime. It is similarly evident that psychiatric diagnoses or prognoses are not particularly important factors in the prediction of future dangerous behaviour, and this has been empirically demonstrated.

What does it mean to say that a mentally abnormal offender is exempt from ordinary penal measures? A restriction order, while it nominally excuses the offender from retributive punishment, still subjects him to an indefinite period of control in a mental institution. In fact, most patients in special hospitals are detained for between five-and-a-half and eight years. This period of detention is considerably longer than those customary for ordinary offenders, regardless of the types of offence considered. The average prison sentence passed by Crown Courts for ordinary offenders is six to twelve months. Even for the more serious offences of manslaughter, arson and wounding, the average prison sentence is two to three years. This means that with good behaviour the ordinary offender can be assured of unconditional discharge with remission in 16 to 24 months (Gostin, 1977).

The usual answer to the inequality of treatment between the ordinary and abnormal offender is that, in the case of the latter, the criminal offence is only one incident which has called attention to his need for medical care, and that he would be liable in any case to compulsory admission to hospital on more general grounds apart from his offence. Indeed, the legal profession has blindly accepted the concept of indeterminate confinement in the name of 'therapy'. For example, in *R. v. Bennett* (1968), the Divisional Court held that a restriction order without limit of time ('which is designed to treat and cure') is no more severe than a prison sentence of whatever length.

It is wrong to suggest that a restriction order is made for the purpose of treatment. A hospital order authorises detention in hospital; the accompanying restriction order is made purely for custodial purposes by the Home Secretary, whose first duty is to protect the public. The position of the Home Secretary here is the same as in life imprisonment.

The White Paper reviewing the 1959 Act (DHSS et al, 1978) acknowledged that: 'There can be little doubt that restriction orders have been imposed on occasions where they are not really justified by the nature of the offence or by the offender's previous criminal and medical history and hence that the wording of section 65 does give courts a rather wider discretion than was originally envisaged by the Royal Commission.'

The White Paper, however, did not accept the proposal in *A Human Condition* (Gostin, 1977) for more fundamental reform. However, the recent decision

by the European Court of Human Rights (see above) against the United Kingdom Government was taken into account. The Government received the judgment of the European Court of Human Rights in the case of *X* v. *The United
Kingdom* just before it published the Mental Health (Amendment) Bill. One of
the principal issues in the case was the question of the right of a restricted patient
to have the substantive grounds for his detention considered by a 'court' with
power to order discharge if it finds that further detention is not justified. The
Government did not take account of the Court's decision when it introduced the
Bill; however, it later tabled an amendment in Committee during the passage of
the Bill through Parliament. The effects of restriction orders in accordance with
the provisions of the Mental Health (Amendment) Act are described above.

MENTAL DISORDER WHICH ARISES AFTER SENTENCING

Transfer to Hospital of Persons Serving Sentences of Imprisonment

Section 47 of the Mental Health Act authorises the Home Secretary to transfer
a person serving a sentence of imprisonment to a local National Health Service
(NHS) hospital or a special hospital. The Home Secretary must be satisfied, by
reports from at least two medical practitioners, that the person is suffering from
mental illness, psychopathic disorder, mental impairment or severe mental impairment of a nature or degree which makes it appropriate for him to be
detained, and in the case of psychopathic or mental impairment the treatment is
likely to alleviate or prevent a deterioration in his condition. The Home Secretary
must also consider, having regard to the public interest and all the circumstances,
that it is expedient to make a transfer direction. If the specified hospital does not
receive the person within fourteen days after the transfer direction is made, it
ceases to have effect.

A transfer direction has the same effect as a hospital order. The Home
Secretary can make the direction either with or without special restrictions on
discharge. If it is made without restrictions (Section 47), the person ceases to be
subject to his prison sentence; hence he may be unconditionally discharged by
his RMO, the hospital managers or a mental health review tribunal. But few
transfers are effected without restrictions, and in these cases the prison sentence
generally does not have long to run.

A prisoner who is transferred to hospital with restrictions (Sections 47/49) is
subject to the provisions of Section 41. However, it must be remembered that he
is still subject to his prison sentence and will not necessarily be discharged into
the community. Therefore, if the RMO, any other medical practitioner or a
mental health review tribunal, notifies the Home Secretary that the offender no
longer requires treatment for mental disorder, the Home Secretary has two
options: if the offender would have been eligible for release on parole or with
remission, the Home Secretary can discharge him; or the Home Secretary can
direct that he be remitted to prison to serve the remainder of his sentence. When
the Home Secretary exercises either option, the transfer direction ceases to have
effect, and the prisoner is treated like any ordinary offender.

If the offender is still in hospital when what would have been the earliest date of release had he remained in prison expires, the restrictions cease to have effect; but he remains detained as if he had been admitted on that date in pursuance of a hospital order without restrictions.

Leads for the Future

One of the major principles put forward in Chapter 15 is that once an offender has been detained for a period proportional to the gravity of his offence, he should not be detained further, except through civil procedures. (If treatment is the reason given for continued detention in hospital, then he should be subject to a civil 'admission for treatment' under Section 3 of the Act.) The principle is especially clear in the context of an ordinary offender who has been sentenced to a fixed term of imprisonment; when that term expires, he should have the same rights and freedoms of any other ex-offender. There is no apparent justification for distinguishing a person who is nearing the end of a penal term from all other citizens liable to detention in hospital due to mental disorder. Yet cases are known where prisoners nearing the end of a sentence have been transferred to hospital with an accompanying restriction order. As a result they have been detained long after they would have been released from prison.

An important problem with the 1959 Act was that the restriction order did not lapse until the full term of the prison sentence expired. Had the offender remained in prison, he would, with good behaviour, have been released with remission after two-thirds of his sentence. For prisoners serving a long sentence, this has more than theoretical significance: for example, a prisoner serving a nine-year sentence would be released with full remission after six years; but if he is transferred to hospital under Sections 47/49, the restriction order will not lapse until the full nine years have passed.

The Government implemented in Section 50(3) of the Mental Health Act the following recommendation made in volume 2 of *A Human Condition*: 'If a prisoner is transferred to hospital under Section 47/49, the restriction order should lapse at the earliest date when he would have been released had he remained in prison. He will then be liable to detention under a hospital order without restrictions' (Gostin, 1977).

CONCLUSION

This chapter has been concerned with examining each stage in the criminal process which may result in the making of a therapeutic order. The consequences of a finding of mental disorder vary considerably depending upon the stage in the process when the disorder first arises or is detected. There remain a great many inconsistencies among the various legal formulae and inadequacies in social policy terms. Some of these have been corrected in the Mental Health (Amendment) Act, but there are other areas in urgent need of reform which were identified in the Butler Report and *A Human Condition*, which are discussed in Chapter 15, and are yet to be considered by Parliament.

CASES

Bratty *v.* Attorney-General for Northern Ireland (1963) A.C. 386, 412 (per Lord Denning).
R. *v.* Bennett (1968) 1 W.L.R. 988, 2 All E.R. 753, 52 Cr. App. R. 514.
R. *v.* Charlson (1955) 1 W.L.R. 217.
R. *v.* Clarke (1972) 1 All E.R. 219.
R. *v.* Gunnee (1972) *Crim. L. Rev.* 261.
R. *v.* Hatt (1962) *Crim. L. Rev.* 647.
R. *v.* Islitt (1978) *Crim. L. Rev.* 159.
R. *v.* Kemp (1957) 1 Q.B. 399, 406 (per Devlin, J.).
R. *v.* McBride (1972) *Crim. L. Rev.* 322.
R. *v.* Podola (1960) 1 q.b. 325.
R. *v.* Quick (1973) 1 Q.B. 910.
R. *v.* Rabey (1977) 17 O.R. (2d) (C.A. Ontario).
R. *v.* Robertson (1968) 3 All E.R. 557.
R. *v.* Sullivan (1983) 2 All E.R. 673, H.L.
R. *v.* Windle (1952) 2 Q.B. 826; 2 All E.R. *Accord,* R. *v.* Codere (1916) 12 Cr. App. R. 21.
X *v.* The United Kingdom. Application No. 6998/75. Report of the Commission adopted on 18 July 1980. Judgment of the Court given on 5 November 1981.

REFERENCES

The Atkin Committee (1923) *Report of the Committee as to the Existing Law, Practice and Procedure Relating to Criminal Trials in which the Plea of Insanity is Raised.* Cmnd. 2005. London: HMSO.
Bluglass, R. (1980) *Psychiatry, the Law and the Offender – Present Dilemmas and Future Prospects.* Croydon: Institute for the Study and Treatment of Delinquency.
Criminal Law Revision Committee (1963) *Report,* Cmnd. 2149, London: HMSO.
DHSS, Home Office, Welsh Office & Lord Chancellor's Department (1978) *Review of the Mental Health Act 1959.* Cmnd. 7320. London: HMSO.
Gostin, L. (1977) *A Human Condition: The Law Relating to Mentally Abnormal Offenders – Observations, Analysis and Proposals for Reform,* vol. 2. London: MIND.
Gostin, L. (1981) Justifications for the insanity defence in Great Britain and the United States: the conflicting rationales of morality and compassion. *Bull. Am. Academy of Psych. and the Law,* **9,** 2, 100–115.
Gostin, L. (1982) Human rights, judicial review and the mentally disordered offender. *Crim. L. Rev.,* December 1982, pp. 779–793.
Gostin, L. (1984) *Mental Health Services and the Law* London: Shaw and Sons.
Home Office (1982) *Draft Codes of Practice for the Treatment, Questioning and Identification of Persons Suspected of Crime,* London: HMSO.
Home Office & DHSS (1975) *Report of the Committee on Mentally Abnormal Offenders. (Butler Report).* Cmnd. 6244. London: HMSO.
Royal Commission on Capital Punishment (1953) (the Gowers Commission). *Report,* Cmnd. 8932. London: HMSO.
Walker, N. & McCabe, S. (1973) *Crime and Insanity in England,* vol. 2. Edinburgh: University Press.
Williams, G. (1978) *Textbook of Criminal Law.* London: Stevens.

17

The Law and the Mentally Disabled Offender in the United States

Larry Gostin

Chapter 15 set out the general principles governing the admission to hospital and detention of mentally abnormal offenders. In particular, criteria were suggested under which a person could be diverted from the criminal justice to the mental health system, and which could help determine the length of confinement. It was proposed that the determination of *who* should be admitted to hospital instead of prison should be based predominantly on medical evidence relating to a person's mental disorder and need for treatment. The criteria of potential benefit from treatment and 'patient choice' were considered particularly important considerations.

It was also suggested that the question of *how long* a person should be detained should be based upon ordinary concepts of criminal justice relating to the gravity of the offence and broad equality among similarly situated offenders. Indefinite sentences were not favoured, particularly if they did not follow a conviction for a serious (life-carrying) offence against the person. If indefinite sentences were used, however, there was a need for periodic judicial review of the continued justification for the detention. This was the approach taken by the European Court of Human Rights (*X* v. *The United Kingdom*, 1981).

This chapter will review the jurisprudence in the United States which has a bearing on these issues. The law in the United States is not uniform as it is in Great Britain. The statute law may vary from state to state and is affected by judicial construction which often does not extend beyond the boundaries of the relevant jurisdiction. Accordingly, the law in America is highly diverse. It would not be possible to present a comprehensive analysis in a single chapter. However, certain judicial decisions have suggested broader constitutional principles and it will be these that will be used as a focus.

This chapter will, firstly, examine the various methods by which a person can be admitted to hospital through the criminal courts. It will become apparent that there are no uncomplicated means for such an admission which flow directly from a medical assessment of the person's needs; this is markedly dissimilar to the more 'utilitarian' approach adopted in Great Britain. Instead, the criteria for admission in America are integrally bound up in jurisprudential considerations and often demand that some causal relationship is adduced between the state of mind of the accused and some legally relevant event – e.g. the offence or the ability to participate in the trial.

The second general consideration in this chapter is the legal question of how long an offender-patient can be detained in hospital; the criteria and procedural safeguards associated with this issue will also be a central feature of the discussion. Here, there are a number of highly relevant and interesting decisions which have been rendered by the United States Supreme Court.

CRITERIA FOR ADMISSION OF MENTALLY DISABLED OFFENDERS TO HOSPITAL

There are a number of options in the United States for dealing with a mentally disabled offender: to excuse him from punishment because he was insane at the time of the offence; to find him incompetent to stand trial because he cannot understand the trial proceedings or aid in his own defence; and to transfer him from prison to hospital. Each of these methods can result in his being admitted to a hospital for treatment. In addition, certain classes of offenders, such as sex offenders, dangerous or repetitive offenders, can be admitted to hospital or to special institutions designed for such offenders. There is also a diminished responsibility doctrine which is developing in certain American jurisdictions which allows a mentally abnormal, but legally sane, defendant to have his abnormality taken into account in assessing criminal liability and in devising a sentence (Morse, 1980). Depending upon the jurisdiction, this doctrine operates partly to exonerate the person from criminal responsibility and/or to reduce the seriousness of the charge. Clearly, the diminished responsibility doctrine is important and can affect the person's sentence. However, since it has the effect principally of reducing a charge and/or subsequent prison sentence as opposed to expressly providing an avenue for hospital admission, it will not be considered in this chapter.

There follows an examination of broad jurisprudential trends in respect of the two principal means by which a person accused or convicted of an offence may be admitted to mental hospital – i.e. the insanity defence and the plea of incompetence. It should be observed at the outset that the sentencing court in the United States cannot ask itself the direct question – is this person mentally ill and in need of hospital care? Instead, the court is bound to apply technical legal criteria which seek to effectuate some legal principle such as to determine criminal responsibility or a person's capacity to participate meaningfully at the trial. Although the judiciary and legislature have sought to make these jurisprudential considerations more flexible and to take account of a person's current medical condition, there has not been a total break from legal standards. Regardless of the provision examined, there is some reference to a legally relevant causal relationship, i.e. that the state of mind of the accused caused him to behave in the way he did or that his mental state affects his ability to comprehend the trial proceedings and to contribute to his own defence.

Rationales for the Insanity Defence

The McNaughton Rules (see Chapter 16) were formulated by the judges in answer to questions submitted by the House of Lords in England and subsequently were adopted in many American jurisdictions. The Rules state that to establish the defence of insanity successfully it must be shown that, at the time of the offence, the accused was labouring under such a defect of reason, from disease of the mind, as not to know the nature and quality of his act, not to know it was wrong.

Since the McNaughton Rules were first introduced into American jurisprudence they have been the subject of criticism. The most basic questions which have been raised are – why an insanity defence and what is the objective of such a defence? To establish a rational response to these questions it is necessary to make a more detailed examination of the Rules.

The McNaughton Rules state that a person shall be acquitted of an offence if his state of mind prevented him from understanding the 'nature and quality of his act'. This, it should be observed, is merely a particular statement of the ordinary doctrine of *mens rea* which is applicable to most offences. An offence is committed only where the defendant has proceeded with intention or recklessness in respect of all the circumstances of the act which constitutes the *actus reus* of the crime. However, this statement of the requirement of a guilty mind is co-extensive with the provision in that the defendant did not know the nature and quality of the act; a person who is unable to comprehend the physical quality of his act could not have formed an intent in respect of that act. Critical impairment in comprehension of the physical act, therefore, excuses the actor from criminal responsibility irrespective of his underlying psychiatric condition.

The application of the doctrine of *mens rea* to sane and insane actors results in an apparent anomaly. Where it is established that a sane actor was conclusively deficient in his appreciation of the behaviour which constitutes the offence for which he is charged, he will receive an ordinary acquittal. Where one of the elements of an offence is not proved, there is no authority for conviction and subsequent confinement or control. Where the same impairment of cognition is established in respect of an insane actor, this may result in psychiatric confinement, sometimes for an indefinite duration. Accordingly, absence of the mental element necessary for a particular offence will result in freedom for the sane actor, but possible indefinite confinement for the insane actor; the insanity defence is special only to the extent that it will result in mandatory confinement in cases where, under ordinary legal principles, the accused would simply be acquitted. This is one factor which suggests that the insanity defence is not uniquely constructed to absolve the mentally ill offender from blame and punishment; there is no special doctrine which need be constructed to achieve this purpose. Rather, the construction of a special defence for the insane indicates a contrary purpose: to impose control, and perhaps punishment, where the law would not ordinarily tolerate this. Further, if the latter is accepted as at least a partial rationale for the insanity defence, it follows that any proposal to widen the special defence (insofar as this wider construction more closely approximates the defence of *mens rea*) would further limit the circumstances under which a mentally ill offender could be entirely exempted from judicially ordered confinement.

It has been argued, therefore, that the objective of the insanity defence is to increase the likelihood of confinement of a mentally abnormal offender and that the defence should be abolished (Goldstein and Katz, 1963).

Criticism of the McNaughton Rules

The McNaughton Rules are pre-eminently concerned with the ability to reason. A disease of the mind must affect the comprehension of the accused, not his emotion, will or volition. The Rules therefore separate cognition from other components of a man's personality. This simple statement of the McNaughton Rules forms the basis upon which they have been criticised almost since their inception (Livermore and Meehl, 1967). Modern science regards the personality as an integrated whole; in determining the psychological antecedents to behaviour one cannot divide the mind into different functional categories. Psychiatry is unable to explain behaviour except by examining variations in mood, thinking and volition. By requiring the physician to explain behaviour solely by what a man knows produces an inaccurate jurisprudential understanding of medical insanity and places an impediment to full and expert testimony.

If the Rules were strictly construed they would provide a very limited defence (see Chapter 16). A mentally ill person will generally know that he is committing an act and that it is contrary to the law. Yet, a mental illness may affect his thinking or emotion and, thus, affect his freedom of choice.

The foregoing criticisms of the McNaughton Rules are based upon an inaccurate view of the rationale for an insanity defence. The underlying assumption of the critics is that legal insanity should, as closely as possible, comply with modern psychiatric concepts of unsoundness of mind. This reflects the intuitive position that, for reasons of compassion, the severely mentally disordered person should not be dealt with as criminally responsible. However, diagnosis and assessment of need for care are medical issues which are not incorporated within the Rules. Legal insanity is determined by moral jurisprudential judgments; criminal responsibility and unsoundness of mind are not co-extensive. Seen in the context of the pure legal moralism of the defence, the Rules appear more rational. The judges in McNaughton were not professing to define mental disorder or to make sensible differentiations in respect of the need for treatment; rather they sought to define the degree of disorder that would negative *mens rea*. The legal test is thus logically directed to the intellectual or cognitive faculties and yet that it is so directed is the main ground of attack on the Rules. The responsibility that has to be destroyed under McNaughton is responsibility in respect of a particular act and its lawfulness. Knowledge of that act and of the proscription set by law is thus the relevant standard. Those who would support the legal moralism of McNaughton observe that if an accused man knew he was doing an act which he knew to be contrary to the law, he must be held accountable under the law (Devlin, 1954).

The 'Irresistible Impulse' Test

It will be observed that most of the criticism of the McNaughton Rules reflects the intuitive assumptions that (i) the Rules are too narrow and do not include all of those who are ill and should be treated, and (ii) the Rules should be expanded to provide a mechanism to divert mentally ill and retarded people from punishment which the law might otherwise require. This line of argument, although propounded in influential quarters in the United Kingdom (The Royal Commission on Capital Punishment, 1953), has not been accepted by parliament. This is largely because the insanity defence is no longer considered principally to be a method of diverting mentally disordered people from the prisons; other legislation has been enacted to achieve that objective (see Chapter 16). However, many jurisdictions in the United States have now rejected the McNaughton Rules in favour of doctrines based more closely on medical standards; a hallmark of American jurisprudence in this area is the expansion of the scope of the insanity defence to achieve a compassionate objective. The clearest example is the American Law Institute (ALI), 1962, provision to include a 'control' or 'irresistible impulse' component within the framework of the McNaughton Rules. Variations of this formula have been adopted widely in the United States. The ALI formulation absolves a person of criminal responsibility if, 'as a result of a mental disease or defect, he lacks substantial capacity either to appreciate the criminality (wrongfulness) of his conduct or to conform his conduct to the requirements of law'. The irresistible impulse doctrine allows the accused to plead that, strictly speaking, he knew the nature and quality of the offence and that it was wrong, but that, due to a mental illness, he could not control his behaviour. In effect, the accused is saying, 'I could not help myself'. English courts, however, do not recognise this defence (*R.* v. *Kopsch*, 1925) on the pragmatic ground that it would be impossible to distinguish between an impulse which could not be resisted and one which simply was not resisted.

The ALI considered that the insanity defence is solely a means of distinguishing those cases 'where a punitive-correctional disposition is appropriate and those in which a medical-custodial disposition is the only kind that the law should allow'. It is clear, therefore, that the ALI test, which has been highly influential in American jurisdictions, seeks to apply broadly medical standards to the insanity defence; its basic purpose is to allow more people to put their mental state in issue at the trial for the purpose of being admitted to hospital.

The 'Durham' Rule

In 1954 Judge Bazelon for the District of Columbia Court of Appeals implemented an entirely new approach to the insanity defence (*Durham* v. *United States*, 1954). The Durham formula departed from previous insanity tests in one major respect. In other tests such as McNaughton and ALI, it had to be shown that mental illness or defect caused an incapacitating condition (cognitive or volitional impairment). The Durham Rule, however, simply assumed that severe mental illness *would* necessarily result in an incapacitating condition and would always justify absolving the accused from criminal responsibility.

The Durham Rule states that 'an accused is not criminally responsible if his unlawful act was the product of mental disease or defect'. The Durham Rule, therefore, effectively made legal insanity co-extensive with mental disease. It went, as far as possible, to broaden the scope of the insanity defence and to exculpate mentally ill offenders; it met with the warm approval of psychiatrists who perceived it as the more humane formulation for the insanity defence.

The Durham experiment came to an end in America in 1972 (*United States* v. *Brawner*). During its eighteen years of operation it epitomised, more than any other legal test, the efforts made in America to alter the insanity defence for reasons of compassion. Indeed, to this day, discussions of various methods of reforming the insanity defence to more closely coincide with medical concepts and to allow more humane disposals, have literally pervaded American jurisprudence; a discussion of the effectiveness of such efforts is contained elsewhere (Gostin, 1981).

Competence to Stand Trial

In terms of the numbers of people affected, the determination that a person is incompetent to stand trial is much more important than the insanity defence. One study showed that for each defendant found not guilty by reason of insanity, at least one hundred were found incompetent to stand trial and sent to institutions for the criminally insane (Bacon, 1969).

There is sometimes confusion between the insanity defence and a plea of incompetency. The former is concerned with a person's ability to understand or to control his behaviour *at the time of the offence*. It is thus a defence which seeks to enquire into a person's mind at a material time in the past. If the defence is successful, it absolves the accused from criminal responsibility. An incompetency plea, on the other hand, refers to a person's state of mind *at the time of the trial*; a successful plea does not absolve the accused from criminal responsibility, but has the effect of preventing him from standing trial for the offence. The general test for establishing whether a person is fit to plead was laid down by the United States Supreme Court in *Dusky* v. *United States* (1960): 'the test must be whether he has sufficient present ability to consult with his lawyer with a reasonable degree of rational understanding and whether he has a rational, as well as factual, understanding of the proceedings against him.'

DISPOSITION OF THE MENTALLY ILL OFFENDER: CONSTITUTIONAL ASPECTS

Having examined the two most discussed doctrines by which an offender can be diverted from the criminal justice to the mental health system, this section will investigate the legal standards which determine how long the offender can be confined in a mental institution. Here, I will briefly describe the relevant constitutional principles and then apply these to specific areas of concern such as the insanity defence, the incompetency plea and transfer from prison to hospital.

Equal Protection of the Law

The Fifth and Fourteenth Amendments to the United States Constitution guarantee individuals equal protection and due process of law. Equal protection does not require that all persons be dealt with identically, but it does require that the purpose of any distinction must be reasonably related to a valid government objective. Thus, any distinction between psychiatric commitments under a criminal process and commitments under a civil process must have a rational justification.

The charter case in this area is *Baxstrom* v. *Herold* (1966). In that case a person was committed to a mental institution at the expiration of his prison sentence. He had no right to a hearing, although a civil commitment to a hospital would have required a jury hearing. The Supreme Court held that there was no rational reason for granting a hearing to people in the community who are to be civilly committed, but to deny a hearing for those offenders who are ending a term of imprisonment.

In America, unlike Britain and much of Europe, the courts draw an important distinction between 'criminal' institutions maintained by the Department of Correction and ordinary mental institutions for civil patients. The Supreme Court in *Baxstrom* held also that there was a denial of equal protection because the person ending his prison sentence went into a 'criminal' hospital without any judicial determination on that issue – i.e. whether he was *dangerously* mentally ill.

The Supreme Court recently has upheld the *Baxstrom* doctrine in the case of a prisoner transferred during the period of his sentence (*Vitek* v. *Jones*, 1980).

Due Process of Law

A mentally disabled offender is also entitled to due process of law. If a person is deprived of his liberty, regardless of whether the ostensible rationale for the deprivation is 'prevention' or 'treatment', he is entitled to due process of the law (or 'natural justice' as it is referred to in Europe). In *Specht* v. *Patterson* (1967) the Supreme Court examined the Colorado Sex Offenders Act. The Act allows the court to admit a person to a treatment centre for an indefinite period where it finds that a person convicted of specified sex offences would be a danger to others, or is an habitual offender and mentally ill. The Supreme Court found that the offender had a right to a full judicial hearing with the full panoply of procedural protections which due process guarantees, including the right to counsel, an opportunity to be heard and to present evidence, and the right to confront and cross-examine witnesses.

In sum, the broad approach taken by *Baxstrom*, *Vitek* and *Specht* is that a mentally abnormal offender is entitled to proceedings at which the substantive justification for his detention can be reviewed, i.e., the existence of a mental illness and the probability of future dangerous behaviour. This applies irrespectively of how the detention is labelled, whether it be 'therapy', 'prevention' or 'retribution'.

There is little question that the United States Constitution would require a hearing in respect of patients detained following a verdict of not guilty by reason of insanity or following a plea of unfitness to stand trial. The Supreme Court has yet to hear a case specifically involving an insanity verdict, but has made a major ruling in the case of a person found unfit to plead

Equal Protection and Due Process Applied to the Insanity Defence and the Plea of Incompetency

Jackson v. Indiana (1972) is one of the leading cases in American constitutional law relating to the mentally disabled offender. Theon Jackson was a mentally retarded person who was also deaf and mute; he was not able to communicate and was unlikely ever to be able to attain competence to stand trial. Mr Jackson was convicted of minor offences involving the theft of sums of money. He was found unfit to plead and committed to a mental institution for an indefinite period of time. The Supreme Court determined that he had been denied equal protection of the law because the fact that he had charges pending against him did not provide a justification for subjecting him to a more lenient commitment standard and a more stringent standard of release than those generally applicable to all others not charged with an offence. The state had denied him equal protection of the law also because it 'condemned him in effect to permanent institutionalisation without the showing required for commitment or the opportunity for release' afforded under Indiana law.

The Supreme Court also found a violation of due process of law. It reviewed the practice in the federal system and the states whereby a person found unfit to plead can be committed to hospital until he is found competent to stand trial; sometimes this detention is automatic and sometimes it is conditional upon a finding of dangerousness. The practice of automatic commitment, with release conditional only upon attainment of competence, has been decried on policy and constitutional grounds (Gostin, 1977). This criticism has been based upon the fact that a person found incompetent may never become competent to stand trial and may face an indefinite period in confinement without a determination of facts relating to the alleged offence.

The Supreme Court held in *Jackson* v. *Indiana* that a person charged with an offence who is committed to hospital solely due to his incapacity to proceed to trial cannot be held more than the reasonable period of time necessary to determine whether there is a substantial probability that he will attain that capacity in the foreseeable future. If it is determined that he will not attain the necessary mental capacity, the state must either institute customary civil commitment procedures or release the defendant. The Supreme Court, therefore, enunciated the principle that 'due process requires the nature and duration of commitment to bear some reasonable relation to the purpose for which the individual is committed'. (For a comparison with the British position see Home Office & DHSS 1975; Gostin, 1977.)

LENGTH OF CONFINEMENT

Indefinite Confinement Coupled With Periodic Judicial Review

Two positions regarding the length of confinement of persons acquitted by reason of insanity seem to be emerging in the United States: indefinite confinement and a fixed period of detention.

Most states still regard commitment following a successful insanity plea as similar to a civil confinement. Here, the patient appears to have the same right to automatic periodic review as persons civilly committed (*State* v. *Fields*, 1978). The Baxstrom principle (that the State cannot withhold from a few the procedural protections or substantive requirements for commitment that are available to others) has not been considered by the Supreme Court in the particular case of persons acquitted by reason of insanity. However, the Baxstrom principle has been extended by lower federal and state courts to the insanity defence (*Bolton* v. *Harris*, 1968; *People* v. *Lally*, 1966). In addition, the Supreme Court has extended the Baxstrom principle to commitment in lieu of sentence following conviction as an offender (*Humphrey* v. *Cady*, 1972).

There is a clearly discernible jurisprudence evolving in the United States Supreme Court concerning the continuing confinement of mental patients. *Jackson* v. *Indiana* and *O'Connor* v. *Donaldson* (1975) suggest that the authority to continue restrictions on the liberty of a person detained in hospital must terminate when the patient's condition no longer satisfies the legal criteria for imposing those restrictions in the first place. The authority for detention, therefore, is contingent upon establishing a continuing justification for detention. This justification for detention must be determined by a judicial process which periodically reviews a person's current mental state and propensity toward dangerousness.

It is interesting to compare the constitutional principles enunciated by the United States Supreme Court with the human rights principles laid down by the European Court of Human Rights. Each Court has promulgated remarkably similar principles, although they have arrived at their conclusions through different reasoning.

The European Convention of Human Rights posits that there must be a discrete ground upon which a deprivation of liberty can be predicated. Article 5(1) of the Convention states a number of such grounds including: '(a) the lawful detention of a person after conviction by a competent court'; and '(e) the lawful detention of . . . persons of unsound mind . . .'

Admission to hospital for the purpose of treatment following an appearance before a criminal court would come under (e); this is particularly so in the case of the incompetency plea or the insanity verdict, as, in these cases, there is no 'conviction' (*X* v. *The United Kingdom*, 1981).

Article 5(1) is referrable to Article 5(4) which requires a judicial review of the lawfulness of detention. The European Court of Human Rights has held that such review must not merely be established at the time of admission, but must be re-established periodically by a court of law. The purpose of such a review is to determine whether the minimal requirements for detention of a person of unsound mind are established: 'The very nature of what has to be established before the competent national authority – that is, a true mental disorder – calls for objective medical expertise. Further, the mental disorder must be of a kind or degree warranting compulsory confinement. What is more, the validity of continued confinement depends upon the persistence of such a disorder.' (*Winterwerp* v. *The Netherlands*, 1979.)

In sum, there has emerged in Europe and North America a common view of the minimal guarantees of a person admitted to hospital following an appearance before a criminal court. The court may authorise such an admission to hospital only after a determination as to a person's state of mind and whether he requires treatment in hospital. The court need not specify a determinate period in hospital. However, there is a constitutional obligation to provide a periodic review of the need for confinement in hospital, and the patient's release must be ordered if the minimal requirements for hospital admission applicable to all other persons are not fulfilled.

Sentencing Alternatives

A trend in the United States is to make commitments following an insanity verdict more like sentencing alternatives and less like civil commitments. Such statutes do not permit indefinite commitments to exceed the maximum penal sentence. This approach recognises that, regardless of the intention of admission to hospital, it does have punitive effects. Legislators have considered, therefore, that detention should not exceed that which would be permitted based upon the gravity of the offence (see Chapter 15). If detention is to be continued beyond this period, it should be under civil procedures.

SUMMARY AND CONCLUSION

This chapter has examined the two principal methods in the United States for diverting a defendent from the criminal justice to the mental health system – the insanity defence and the incompetency plea. The statutory position in America was compared with that which exists in Great Britain; the constitutional position in America was also compared with the broad principles laid down by the European Court of Human Rights and the policy proposals put forward in Chapter 15.

The United States, in its operation of the insanity defence, still appears bound by the narrow jurisprudential concern of criminal responsibility. Thus, some causal relationship must be shown between a person's mental state and the offence before a hospital admission can be made. Yet, the defence is difficult to establish or even to justify; psychiatry is not yet in a position to make a reliable retrospective assessment of a person's covert mental processes to say whether a discrete illness in fact *caused* a particular past behaviour. None the less, the continuing existence of the insanity defence would not undermine any interest of the accused so long as there were alternative and more direct methods of achieving a therapeutic disposition.

Much of the controversy surrounding the insanity defence in the United States has resulted from the persistent feeling that humanitarianism is its only valid justification. Proponents of this view have sought to stretch and distort the defence to achieve an objective for which it was never designed. The ethical and retributive concerns of the insanity defence suggest that, inherently, it could not provide a rational assessment of the need for care and treatment. Regardless of how it were altered, it would continue to remain an unsatisfactory instrument for determining the social policy question of *who* should be admitted to hospital. In order to achieve important compassionate objectives, it is suggested that the courts in the United States should be directly empowered to make a therapeutic order following conviction; this has already been the position in Great Britain for more than twenty years.

The United States Supreme Court has evolved a coherent set of principles governing the length of detention of mentally abnormal offenders. The Supreme Court has determined that the length of confinement must be reasonably related to a valid purpose for that confinement. Thus, for example, commitment following an incompetency plea must be limited for the purpose of retaining competence to stand trial. Further, where indefinite commitment is authorised the court has required, in a number of contexts, that there be a periodic review of the need for continued confinement. This review would go to the issue of a person's mental state, need for care and propensity toward violence.

It was observed that the constitutional position in the USA was markedly similar to the position in Europe and also corresponded with the broad policy objectives outlined in Chapter 15.

CASES

Baxstrom *v*. Herold, 383 U.S. 107 (1966).

Bolton *v*. Harris, 130 U.S. App. D.C.1, 395 F. 2d 642 (1968).

Durham *v*. US, 214 F. 2d 862 (D.C. Cir. 1954).

Dusky *v*. United States, 362 U.S. 402 (1960).

Humphrey *v*. Cady, 405 U.S. 504 (1972).

Jackson *v*. Indiana, 406 U.S. 715 (1972).

O'Connor *v*. Donaldson, 422 U.S. 563 (1975), discussed in Gostin, L. (1979). Current legal concepts in mental retardation in the United States: emerging constitutional issues. In: Craft, M. (ed.) *Tredgold's, Mental Retardation*, 12th edn., London; Baillière Tindall.

People *v*. Lally, 19 N.Y. 2d 27, 224 N.E. 2d 87 (1966).

R. *v*. Kopsch (1925), 19 Cr. App. R. 50.

Specht *v*. Patterson, 386 U.S. 605 (1967).

State *v*. Fields, No. A-129 (N.J. July 31, 1978), reported in: *Mental Disability Law Reporter*, May-June, 1978.

US *v*. Brawner, 471 F. 2d 969 (D.C. Cir. 1972).

Vitek *v*. Jones, 63 L. Ed. 2d 552 (1980).

Winterwerp *v*. The Netherlands. European Court of Human Rights. Judgment, 24 October 1979. Strasbourg: Council of Europe.

X *v*. the United Kingdom. European Court of Human Rights. Judgment, 5 November 1981. Strasbourg: Council of Europe.

REFERENCES

American Law Institute (1962) *Model Penal Code* (Proposed Official Draft).

Bacon (1969) Incompetency to stand trial: commitment to an inclusive test. *Calif. L. Rev.*, **42,** 444.

Devlin, L.J. (1954) Criminal responsibility and punishment: functions of judge and jury. *Crim. L. Rev.*, 1954, 661.

Goldstein, J. & Katz, J. (1963) Abolish the insanity defense – why not? *Yale L.J.*, **72,** 853.

Gostin, L. (1977) *A Human Condition: The Law Relating to Mentally Abnormal Offenders – Observations, Analysis and Proposals for Reform.* London: MIND.

Gostin, L. (1981) Justifications for the insanity defence in Great Britain and the United States: the conflicting rationales of morality and compassion. *Bull. Amer. Acad. Psychiat. and the Law*, **9,** 2, 100–15.

Home Office & DHSS (1975) *Report of the Committee on Mentally Abnormal Offenders* (*The Butler Committee*). Cmnd. 6244. London: HMSO.

Livermore and Meehl (1967) The Virtues of M'Naghten. *Minn. L. Rev.*, **51,** 789.

Morse (1980) Crazy behaviour, morals, and science: an analysis of mental health law. *S. Cal. L. Rev.*, **51,** 527–653.

Royal Commission on Capital Punishment (Gowers Commission) (1953) *Report*, Cmnd. 8932. London: HMSO.

18

Defining the Dangerousness of the Mentally Ill: Involuntary Civil Commitment

Alexander D. Brooks

In the United States, the legal determination that a mentally ill person is dangerous may have drastic consequences. A finding of dangerousness can result in an indeterminate and lengthy involuntary confinement in a civil mental hospital.[1] If the civilly committed person is found to be too dangerous for safe confinement in the hospital he may be transferred to a maximum security hospital for the so-called criminally insane, even though he has committed no crime.[2] In some states, a dangerous civil patient, though guilty of no offence, can actually be transferred to a prison.[3]

For the mentally ill offender the consequences of a dangerousness finding are likely to be harsher.[4] A defendant accused of crime but ruled incompetent to stand trial and found dangerous may be confined in a maximum security hospital, rather than in a civil hospital, regardless of whether the criminal charge was for a crime of violence or a non-violent property crime such as embezzlement.[5] If the mentally ill offender has been tried but acquitted because of insanity

---

[1] See generally Brooks (1974). Many jurisdictions provide for the involuntary civil commitment of mentally ill persons who are dangerous to themselves or others or who are unable to care for their physical needs. The most recent compilation of civil commitment statutes is to be found in McGarry et al (1981).

[2] See, for example, Ohio Rev. Code Ann. §5125.03 (Baldwin, 1971) which 'permits an administrative transfer of any patient in a State [civil] hospital who exhibits dangerous or homicidal tendencies, rendering his presence a source of danger to others in Lima State Hospital for the criminally insane'. Such transfers have been ruled unconstitutional in New York in *Kesselbrenner* v. *Anonymous*, 33 N.Y.2d 161, 305 N.E.3d, 350 N.Y.S.2d 889 (1973), but the constitutionality of a similar provision has been upheld in New Jersey in *Singer* v. *State*, 63 N.J. 319, 307 A.2d 94 (1973), where the Court said, 'Surely a hospital does not become a jail merely because convicts are admitted when they are ill.' 307 A.2d at 96. The difference between the New York and New Jersey cases seems to be that the New York institution was, at the time, within the correctional system and the New Jersey institution nominally within the mental health system. Both institutions in fact served identical functions.

[3] A Colorado statute permits the transfer of civil mental patients to the state penitentiary 'for safekeeping' if they 'cannot be safely confined in any institution for the care and treatment of the mentally ill or retarded'. This statute has been declared unconstitutional, but only because psychiatric treatment in the prison was considered substantially inferior to that provided in the civil mental hospital. See *Romero* v. *Schauer*, 386 F. Supp. 851 (D. Colo. 1974). See also *Craig* v. *Hocker*, 405 F. Supp. 656 (D.C.D. Nev. 1975), holding unconstitutional Nev. Rev. Stat. §433.315, which permitted confinement of the 'dangerous' civilly committed mentally ill in the death row cell block of Nevada State Prison.

[4] For valuable general descriptions see Wexler (1976) and German and Singer (1976).

[5] A number of states require a finding of dangerousness to support a commitment of an accused found incompetent to stand trial. See, e.g., Iowa Code §783.3 (Supp. 1972) and Okla. Stat. Tit. 22, §1167 (1958); S.D. Compiled Laws §23-38-6 (1967).

(is NGRI), he can in a number of states be further confined only if he is found to be dangerous, the mode of this confinement being affected by that finding.[1] Release will depend on a determination that he is no longer dangerous, a difficult proposition for an NGRI patient to establish.[2] In some states, the NGRI may be retained in a mental hospital if considered dangerous, even if he is not mentally ill.[3]

Patients in hospital who are otherwise able to withhold their consent to medication may be medicated against their will if found to be dangerous.[4] A prisoner who becomes mentally ill can be transferred to and retained in a correctional mental hospital if dangerous.[5] Even juvenile offenders, members of a generally protected class may, if confined, be subjected to invidious transfers if found to be mentally ill and dangerous.[6] In California, the confinement of an otherwise releasable juvenile may be extended for two-year periods, which are indefinitely extendable to what has been characterised as a life term if the juvenile is found to be '... physically dangerous to the public because of his mental ... deficiency, disorder or abnormality'.[7]

Some states provide long-term indeterminate confinement in special treatment programmes for particular types of dangerous offenders such as dangerous sex offenders, whose confinement is sometimes provided in lieu of, but often in addition to, regular prison terms.[8] Maryland until recently provided indeterminate confinement for so-called 'defective delinquents', who were defined as 'intellectually deficient, or emotionally unbalanced persons, who, because of their persistent anti-social or criminal behaviour, demonstrate that they are an "actual danger" to society'.[9]

---

[1] A number of statutes provide for the commitment of the NGRI (a defendant found not guilty by reason of insanity) if he is found to be not only still mentally ill, but also dangerous. A number of relatively recent cases have required a finding of dangerousness as a condition of an NGRI commitment. See, e.g., *State* v. *Krol*, 68 N.J. 236, 344 A.2d 289 (1975).
[2] For an illustration of how difficult it is for even a model patient to shed the label of dangerousness after ten years of trouble-free confinement see *Covington* v. *Harris*, 419 F.2d 617 (D.C. Cir. 1969).
[3] See, e.g., *State* v. *Gebarski*, 90 Wis.2d 754, 380 N.W.2d 672 (1979), analysed in 1980 Wis. L. Rev. 381, where the court held that an NGRI may be retained in a mental hospital if he is dangerous, even if not mentally ill. This proposition was, however, specifically rejected in a New York case, Matter of Torsney, 47 N.Y.2d 667, 420 N.Y.S.2d 192, 394 N.E.2d 363 (1979).
[4] See cases discussed in Brooks (1980a). Leading cases are *Rennie* v. *Klein*, 653 F.2d 836 (3d Cir. 1981) and *Rogers* v. *Okin*, 634 F.2d 650 (1st Cir. 1980).
[5] See, e.g., *Vitek* v. *Jones*, 445 U.S. 480 (1980) and United States ex rel. *Schuster* v. *Herold*, 410 F.2d 1071 (2d Cir. 1969).
[6] *Morales* v. *Turman*, 364 F. Supp. 166 (E.D. Tex. 1973), reversed, 535 F. Supp. 864 (5th Cir. 1976).
[7] Cal. Welf. and Inst. Code §1800 et seq. (West 1972), discussed in Note, A Dangerous Commitment, 2 Pepperdine L. Rev. 117 (1974). See also *In Re Gary W.*, 5 Cal. 3d 296, 486 P.2d 1201, 96 Cal. Rptr. 1 (1971).
[8] A typical sex offender statute is that of New Hampshire, which defines a sexual psychopath as 'any person suffering from such conditions of emotional instability or impulsiveness of behaviour, or lack of customary standards of good judgement, or failure to appreciate the consequences of his act, or a combination of any and such conditions, as to render such person irresponsible with respect to sexual matters and thereby dangerous to himself or to other persons'. N.H. Rev. Stat. Ann. §§173-A:2 (1977 & Supp. 1979).
[9] For the text of the new legislation see Art. 31 B of the Annotated Code of Maryland (1977) Cum Supp. The statute is also reprinted at *Bull. Amer. Acad. L. & Psychiatry*, **5**, 260 (1977).

The American Law Institute Model Penal Code proposes lengthier imprison-ment for mentally abnormal persons found to be dangerous.[1] The Model Sen-tencing Act provides for longer terms for convicted criminals suffering from severe personality disorder who are regarded as dangerous.[2] A federal statute provides for additional sentences for 'dangerous special offenders'.[3] A recent California Supreme Court decision has made a determination as to dangerous-ness critical by imposing a duty upon psychotherapists to warn a prospective victim of any potentially dangerous act threatened by a person who is in treat-ment for emotional and mental problems or to take other appropriate action to avoid violence. If a patient is considered dangerous, the usual confidentially of the doctor-patient relationship is breached.[4]

Finally, the state of Texas has enacted a statute which mandatorily imposes the death penalty on a person convicted of a capital offence if the jury finds him to be dangerous.[5]

This brief but incomplete list of onerous dispositions resulting from a finding of dangerousness suggests the importance of that concept in a rapidly evolving body of mental health law.[6] In the past decade the concept of dangerousness has emerged as a major factor in determining the disposition of mentally disabled persons. In this chapter, emphasis will be placed largely on the use of the dangerousness concept in involuntary civil commitments.

FROM PARENS PATRIAE TO DANGEROUSNESS

The use of the term 'dangerousness' as applicable to the mentally ill is not new in the United States.[7] But the current emphasis on dangerousness and the remarkable evolution of that concept within the last decade is the result of intense dissatisfaction with the older *parens patriae* medical model standard which prevailed in most states until the early 1970s. Until recently many state civil commitment statutes typically provided that mentally ill persons could be involuntarily hospitalised if they were simply found to be 'in need of treatment', without a dangerousness finding being required. Lawyers entering the mental health field in the early 1970s found that standard to be intolerably vague. It

---

[1] Model Penal Code §7.03(3) (Proposed Official Draft, 1962).
[2] National Council on Crime and Delinquency, Advisory Council of Judges, Model Sentencing Act §5 (with commentary 1963).
[3] See 18 U.S.C.A. §3575 (Supp. 1971) as discussed in *United States* v. *Duarti*, 384 F. Supp. 861 (W.D. Mo. 1973) and *United States* v. *Duarti*, 383 F. Supp. 874 (W.D. Mo. 1974).
[4] *Tarasoff* v. *Regents of Univ. of California*, 551 P.2d 334, 131 Cal. Rptr. 14 (1976), discussed in Brooks (1976). See also Stone (1976).
[5] The jury is required to answer three questions affirmatively or negatively. One of the questions is 'whether there is a probability that the defendant would commit criminal acts of violence that would constitute a continuing threat to society'. Tex. Code Crim. Proc., Art. 37.071 (b) (1), (2), & (3) (Vernon Supp. 1980). If the jury answers this question affirmatively, the judge must impose the death sentence. As the United States Supreme Court put it in *Estelle* v. *Smith*, 101 S. Ct. 1866 (1981), 'In other words, the jury must assess the defendant's future dangerousness.'
[6] An additional list is presented in Shah (1978).
[7] The history of the dangerousness concept is traced in Dershowitz (1974).

gave, and still gives, practically no guidance whatsoever to judges that aids them in discriminating among the mentally ill to determine which are appropriately committable, and which are not.[1] Indeed, it is arguable that if all mentally ill persons are in need of treatment – a position maintained by a significant proportion of psychiatrists – then all, not merely some, mentally ill persons are subject to involuntary hospitalisation, a position repudiated by the U.S. Supreme Court in *O'Connor* v. *Donaldson*.[2]

In the early 1970s, mental health lawyers began to persuade the courts that no mentally ill person should be involuntarily confined, even for a brief period of time, unless found by a court to be dangerous. Their legal take-off point was a 1972 U.S. Supreme Court Decision, *Humphrey* v. *Cady*,[3] in which the court issued an important dictum concerning Wisconsin's involuntary civil commitment statute, which at the time provided for commitment if the mentally ill person involved was diseased 'to such extent that a person so afflicted requires care and treatment for his own welfare, or the welfare of others, or of the community'.[4] The Supreme Court noted that the language of this definition indicated a 'social and legal judgment that (the person's) potential for doing harm to himself, or to others, is great enough to justify such a massive curtailment of liberty' as was involved in involuntary civil commitment.[5]

Shortly thereafter, the case of Alberta Lessard was brought before a federal court in Wisconsin and the Wisconsin statute attacked as unconstitutional. *Lessard* v. *Schmidt*,[6] decided in October 1972, became the first landmark case dealing with a newly formulated concept of dangerousness and ruling that it would be unconstitutional under the federal constitution to involuntarily confine a non-dangerous mentally ill person. The Lessard court took a quantum leap from the Supreme Court's dictum in *Humphrey* v. *Cady*, noting that earlier courts had not 'felt much concern for either a definition of "dangerousness", or the effects of deprivations of liberty upon those committed'.[7]

In commenting on the Supreme Court's dictum, the Lessard court said, '[T]he (Wisconsin) statute, itself, requires a finding of "dangerousness" to self or others in order to deprive an individual of his, or her, freedom'.[8] The Lessard court then went on to say that although the U.S. Supreme Court had not directly addressed itself to the degree of dangerousness that would be constitutionally required before a person could be involuntarily deprived of liberty, the Lessard court would undertake to provide such a definition.[9] In upholding the Wisconsin statute by interpreting it in such a fashion that it would conform with the Lessard court's interpretation of the Supreme Court's standard, the Lessard court defined dangerousness as a condition where 'there is an extreme likelihood that

---

[1] See, e.g., *Developments in the Law* (1974).
[2] 422 U.S. 563 (1975).
[3] 405 U.S. 504 (1972).
[4] Id. at 509, n. 4.
[5] Id. at 509.
[6] 349 F. Supp. 1078 (E.D. Wis. 1972).
[7] Id. at 1086.
[8] Id. at 1093.
[9] Id.

if the person is not confined, he will do immediate harm to himself or to others'.[1]

Although the Lessard court did not further define the words 'extreme likelihood' or 'immediate harm' it seemed clear from the context that the selection of such terms ruled out long-term 'self-harm', the type of self-harm which results from neglect of self, a condition which by 1972 had, for several years, been characterised as gravely disabled in California's statute.[2] In a later order the Lessard court modified its standard by removing the terms 'extreme' and 'immediate', substituting the language 'imminent dangerousness to self or others ... based, at minimum, upon a recent act, attempt, or threat to do substantial harm', a newly conceived test that has come to be known as the 'overt act' requirement.[3]

The Lessard constitutional requirement that an involuntary commitment be supported by a finding of dangerousness based on a minimal showing of a 'recent act, attempt, or threat' is not so much a further definition of dangerousness, but rather a requirement of a sufficient amount of evidence to justify a finding of dangerousness. The new overt act requirement was tailored out of whole cloth by the court. Based on a recently developed scepticism about the ability of psychiatrists to predict dangerousness, the newly invented standard was intended to prevent involuntary commitment on the basis of psychiatric testimony alone.

The new approach caught on and within several years was widely adopted by other states, becoming a standard feature of judicial opinions and legislative enactments. The Lessard case became a high-water mark in dangerousness law. Many civil libertarian mental health lawyers hoped that other courts would follow Lessard's lead in providing highly restrictive standards concerning commitments focusing on dangerousness, which would be narrowly defined to encompass only physical violence to self or others, thus substantially reducing the number of involuntary civil commitments. However, while a number of courts followed Lessard in providing for extensive procedural due process of law and other protections for the mentally ill, and while they struck down extremely vague standards, they were more cautious about defining dangerousness. Two significant cases immediately followed Lessard. They were State ex rel. *Hawks* v. *Lazaro*[4] and *Lynch* v. *Baxley*.[5] Hawks defined dangerousness in terms of 'violence' and 'physical injury' to self or others, but modified the Lessard approach by providing that the physical injury to the person need not be exclusively through overt acts, but could take place by means of the slow deterioration that may lead ultimately to death or severe injury resulting from bodily neglect. *Lynch* v. *Baxley* took the same approach, stating that a showing of 'actual violence' would not be necessary to establish dangerousness to self. Said the Lynch court, 'There is sufficient dangerousness if a mentally ill person's neglect or refusal to care for himself poses a real and present threat of substantial harm

---

[1] Id.
[2] Cal. Welf. & Inst'ns Code §5250 (1972).
[3] 379 F. Supp. 1376, 1379 (E.D. Wis., 1974).
[4] 302 S.E.2d 109 (W. Va. 1974).
[5] 386 F. Supp. 378 (M.D. Ala. 1974).

to his well-being'.[1] In other words, a person who in California's terms was gravely disabled was regarded as dangerous within the interpretation of these newer cases. Following Hawks and Lynch there were a number of important civil commitment cases, most of them federal cases.[2]

On the legislative front there developed a spate of new state legislation in the field of civil commitment. Most of the new statutes conformed to a common pattern. Typically, new legislation provided two categories of dangerousness: to others and to self. Dangerousness to others is commonly defined in terms of acts, threats, or inducing fear of 'violence' or 'physical harm' to a person. Ordinarily, harm to property is not included, although it is understood that certain acts against property, such as arson, are also acts against persons.

Massachusetts' statute, which had been adopted as early as 1970, became a model for many of the statutes adopted later. It provides for commitment where there is 'likelihood of serious harm', defined as including 'a substantial risk of physical harm to other persons as manifested by evidence of homicidal, or other violent behavior, or evidence that others are placed in reasonable fear of violent and serious physical harm to them . . .[3]

THE SUPREME COURT ON DANGEROUSNESS

Judicial sanctification of the trend toward requiring dangerousness as an exclusive or major standard for involuntary commitment was substantially enhanced when in 1975 the U.S. Supreme Court decided *O'Connor* v. *Donaldson*,[4] which dealt with a mentally ill but non-dangerous patient who had been involuntarily confined in a Florida state mental hospital for almost fifteen years despite his harmlessness and in the face of a continuing high probability that he could have lived in the community successfully during all that lengthy period of time.

In deciding Donaldson, the Supreme Court did not actually rule, as had Lessard and other federal courts, that dangerousness is a constitutional requirement for involuntary civil commitment. Indeed, the Court specifically reserved that crucial question by stating that it was not specifically deciding whether the State could compulsorily confine a mentally ill and non-dangerous person for the purpose of alleviating or curing his illness.[5]

But since the Court did discuss dangerousness extensively its holding has been interpreted by some as, in effect, requiring a constitutional dangerousness

---

[1] Id. at 391.
[2] See, e.g., *Bell* v. *Wayne County Gen. Hosp.*, 384 F. Supp. 1085 (E.D. Mich. 1974); In Re Fisher, 313 N.E.2d 851 (Ohio 1974); *People* v. *Sansone*, 18 Ill. App.3d 315, 309 N.E.2d 733 (1974), discussed in Beis, Rights of the Mentally Disabled – The Conflicting Steps Taken in Illinois, 24 De Paul L. Rev. 545 (1975); *Kendall* v. *True*, 391 F. Supp. 413 (W.D. Ky. 1975); *Lausche* v. *Commr.*, 225 N.W.2d 366 (Minn. 1974); *Doremus* v. *Farrell*, 407 F. Supp. 509 (D. Neb. 1975); *Coll* v. *Hyland*, 411 F. Supp. 905 (D. N.J. 1976); *Stamus* v. *Leonhardt*, 414 F. Supp. 439 (S.D. Iowa, 1976); *French* v. *Blackburn*, 429 F. Supp. 1351 (M.D. N.C. 1977); *Suzuki* v. *Quisenberry*, 411 F. Supp. 1113 (D.C.D. Hawaii 1976); *Wessel* v. *Pryor*, 461 F. Supp. 1144 (D. Ark. 1978); and *Colyar* v. *Third Judicial District Court for Salt Lake County*, 424 F. Supp. 469 (D. Utah 1979).
[3] *Mass. Gen. Laws Ann. Ch.* 123 §7 (1972).
[4] 422 U.S. 563, 45 L. Ed.2d 396, 95 S. Ct. 2488 (1975).
[5] 422 U.S. 563, at 574 (1975).

standard. At least one influential constitutional text (Nowak et al, 1978) and several appellate courts have interpreted Donaldson in that questionable manner.[1]

The language of the Supreme Court does indeed suggest such an interpretation. Said the Court, 'a mentally ill person may not be involuntarily confined if he is dangerous to no one and can live safely in freedom'. Moreover, said the Court, the state 'cannot constitutionally confine a non-dangerous individual who is capable of surviving safely in freedom by himself, or with the help of willing and responsible family members or friends'.[2] In a footnote[3] the Court expanded on this by pointing out that a mentally ill person, even if not actively suicidal or prone to self-injury, is 'literally dangerous to himself' if he cannot, on his own or with the help of friends or family, avoid the 'hazards of freedom'. As previously indicated, the Court did not further define the hazards, but it is reasonably clear that, at minimum, they include the hazards of starvation, freezing, and disease, which result from inability to clothe, shelter, or feed oneself, or to obtain medical care when needed, all circumstances which in current legislation give rise to the categorisation of being either dangerous or gravely disabled.

The Supreme Court did not define dangerousness further, although a host of definitional problems lay dormant behind a seemingly simple façade.

Nor did the Court further define dangerousness in a later case, *Addington* v. *Texas*[4] which cried out for a definition. In Addington the issue before the court was the standard of proof that should be applied under the federal constitution to a finding that a mentally ill person is sufficiently dangerous to be involuntarily committed to a mental hospital.

The state argued that the court should apply the traditional civil preponderance of evidence standard since commitments are civil proceedings and for the benefit of the individual. In quantitative terms, a preponderance would signify an increment of proof somewhat over 50 per cent, or equilibrium. The state further argued that for it to be required to establish dangerousness beyond a reasonable doubt would put too heavy a burden on the state, as a consequence of which too many untreated mentally ill and dangerous persons would not be hospitalised, but would remain in the community, potentially harmful to themselves and to others. Nor, said the state, would such a rigorous burden of proof be necessary for the protection of the civil liberties of the mentally ill, since a committed person would have a right to treatment, which would restore him to normality and would have periodic review of his condition with immediate release if and when no longer regarded as dangerous. Thus the risk of erroneous over-commitment involved in a lowered standard of proof would be lessened by the existence of other practices, procedures, and legal guarantees which would obviate prolonged and unnecessary commitment, the real concern.

---

[1] *Scopes* v. *Shah*, 59 A.D. 203, 398 N.Y.S.2.d 911 (1977); *Doremus* v. *Farrell*, 407 F. Supp. 509 (D. Neb. 1975); and State ex rel. *Doe* v. *Madonna*, 295 N.W.2d 356, 362 (Minn. 1980).
[2] 422 U.S. at 576.
[3] Id. at 574, n. 9.
[4] 441 U.S. 418 (1979).

Respondents' lawyers, in urging that the standard of proof should be the criminal law standard of beyond a reasonable doubt, drew an anology between a civil commitment and a criminal confinement, arguing that deprivation of liberty or stigmatisation is common to both. The respondent invoked the *Winship*[1] case, a juvenile court case in which the U.S. Supreme Court had ruled that notwithstanding its civil label, a juvenile delinquency proceeding is in actuality a quasi-criminal process in which deprivation of liberty and stigma justify invoking the highest standard of proof in order to avoid error. The respondent attempted to brush aside the state's argument about the difficulty of establishing dangerousness by such a rigorous standard. Indeed, it was a barely concealed objective of respondent's lawyers to significantly cut back on dangerousness commitments by persuading the Supreme Court to adopt the highest standard of proof.

Chief Justice Burger in writing for the U.S. Supreme Court, chose a middle path, ruling that dangerousness should be proved by clear and convincing evidence.[2] In doing so, the Court acknowledged the partial validity of arguments made by both parties. The potential risk to significant liberty interests was discussed as giving rise to a need for a standard higher than mere preponderance. On the other hand, respondent's criminal law analogy was decisively rejected, the Court taking the view that the initial inquiry in a civil commitment proceeding is 'very different from the central issue in either a delinquency proceedings or a criminal prosecution'. The Court added, though without sufficient elaboration, that 'given the lack of certainty and the fallibility of psychiatric diagnosis, there is a serious question as to whether a state could ever prove beyond a reasonable doubt that an individual is both mentally ill and likely to be dangerous'. The cases and articles cited by the Court to support this questionable assertion do not, in fact, illuminate the issue. Nor are all of the Court's citations to the literature in point.[3]

In any event, the Court rejected both the strict criminal standard and the mere preponderance civil standard in favour of the middle level standard of clear and convincing, which, in the Court's view, 'strikes a fair balance between the rights of the individual and the legitimate concerns of the state'.[4]

In commenting on the *Addington* case elsewhere (Brooks, 1980b), I have pointed out that the Addington decision leaves open a question of great significance. What is it that is to be proved by 'clear and convincing evidence'? The concept of dangerousness, however described in a statute, is subject to a large variety of definitions.

There are at least three models involved in applying a standard of proof to dangerousness. The first model was adopted in the Lessard case, where the court required only that all *facts* necessary to show that an individual is mentally ill and dangerous require proof beyond a reasonable doubt. This standard does

---

[1] *In Re Winship*, 397 U.S. 358 (1970).
[2] *Addington* v. *Texas*, 411 U.S. 418 (1979).
[3] The Supreme Court's invocation of the Monahan and Wexler article, 411 U.S. at 431, is distinctly inapposite.
[4] *Addington* v. *Texas*, 411 U.S. 418, at 431 (1979).

not require that dangerousness itself be established beyond a reasonable doubt, but only the facts from which an inference of future dangerousness is to be drawn. Thus the protection involved is not significant.

The second model simply requires a prediction that the mentally ill candidate for commitment will engage in the future in dangerous behaviour. But many studies tend to show that most such predictions cannot be made with a sufficient degree of accuracy to meet any traditional standards of proof (see, e.g., Cocozza and Steadman, 1976). The lowest standard, preponderance of evidence, requires at the very least a level of accuracy somewhat over 50 per cent. Clear and convincing has frequently been quantified as requiring approximately 60 to 75 per cent of accuracy. Beyond a reasonable doubt has often been quantified as requiring approximately 90 per cent of accuracy. (For a fuller description of quantification of standards of proof, see Simon and Cockerham, 1977.)

Empirical studies tend to show that predictions of dangerousness tend to fall well below 50 per cent in the extent of their accuracy. In cases where this second model is followed (and there is reason to believe that many judges follow it), a paradox is presented. How can one prove by a standard requiring well over 50 per cent of accuracy that which research indicates cannot be proved by as much as 50 per cent of accuracy?

The third model avoids the paradox by presenting a definition of dangerousness in which the prediction of future behaviour is but one of a number of factors. Depending on the gravity of the projected behaviour and on other factors, a court can determine that even a 20 per cent likelihood that violent behaviour will occur may be enough to justify a finding of dangerous.[1]

Thus, it is necessary that there be a discussion here of how dangerousness is to be defined in order that the standard of proof be meaningful. Before that is done, a discussion of current judicial and psychiatric practices in defining dangerousness is in order.

HOW COURTS AND LEGISLATURES HAVE DEFINED THE TERM DANGEROUSNESS

One would ordinarily expect that if significant deprivations flow from a finding of dangerousness, the term would be precisely defined so that it could be applied in an appropriate manner and with reasonable uniformity. It is the tradition of the criminal law that where the deprivation of an individual's liberty is at risk because of an application of the state's police power, rigorous specificity in defining offences is demanded. Such, however, has not been the history in dealing with the mentally ill, even though a substantial number of involuntary hospitalisations are implementations of the state's police power. Not that an involuntary civil hospitalisation is a criminal punishment. But when mentally ill persons are confined against their will because of their perceived dangerousness to themselves or others, it is clear that in most of these cases the deprivation of their

---

[1] This approach was first spelled out in Developments in the Law (1974) and later presented in Monahan and Wexler (1978).

liberty is primarily for the benefit of the state and not primarily for the benefit of the mentally ill.

Yet legislatures continue their failure to define the term beyond simply providing that a mentally ill person may be involuntarily committed if he is dangerous or is likely to injure or harm himself or others. But words like injury and harm are just as vague as the word dangerousness. Indeed, some legislatures have merged the concept of mental illness and dangerousness by defining mental illness as a condition that makes one dangerous.[1] Some statutes are circular. An amusing illustration is New York's since-repealed 1971 Criminal Procedure Law which defined a dangerously incapacitated person as '. . . an incapacitated person who is so mentally ill, or mentally defective, that his presence in an institution operated by the Department of Mental Hygiene, is dangerous to the safety of other patients therein, the staff of the institution, or the community'. (See, e.g., Steadman, 1973.)

It is not obvious why there should be such a lack of precision in our statutes. Some legislatures may not have been clear as to what they intended when they adopted the term. A review of legislative history reveals that the word dangerousness and its counterparts are often not defined adequately at the inception of the legislative process. Some legislators may have thought that words such as danger, harm, injury, and the like are sufficiently self-evident to require no further explication. One court, in rejecting a contention that the term injury was unconstitutionally vague remarked that, 'Webster has no difficulty giving a definition of these words which are in ordinary and common usage'. The court reasoned that while the word injury is 'not an absolute model of clarity', those charged with administering the law should have little difficulty in applying it.[2]

Still other legislators may have hoped that further definitional clarity would emanate from the courts. Some legislators may have intended that the term be defined in an *ad hoc* manner by mental health professionals, judges, and juries. This last approach seems to have been the case in California, where the term dangerousness was deliberately left undefined 'in order to allow some flexibility in the commitment standards'.[3] In any event, legislators have either failed to recognise the complexity of the concept or, having recognised it, have been unwilling to wrestle with definitional problems.

Nor have the courts filled the definitional gap, either in their rule-making or adjudicative functions. Trial judges, charged with adjudicating cases and con-

---

[1] A now superseded Washington statute had defined a mentally ill person as one 'found to be suffering from psychosis or other disease impairing his mental health, and the symptoms of such disease are of a suicidal, homicidal, or incendiary nature, or of such nature which would render such person dangerous to his own life or to the lives or property of others'. Wash. Rev. Code 71.02.010. A typical formulation is that of Montana, which defines a committable mentally ill person as one who is 'so far disordered in his mind as to endanger health, person, or property'. Mont. Rev. Codes Ann. §38–208 (Interim Supp. 1974).

[2] *In Re Alexander*, 336 F. Supp. 1305, 1307 (D.D.C. 1972). The court cited Webster's Unabridged New International Dictionary (1955) as defining 'injure' a person to mean 'to do harm to; to hurt; damage; impair; to hurt or wound'.

[3] See *Civil Commitment of the Mentally Ill in California* (1974). But see §5300, providing that a patient may be detained for a 90-day period if he has recently either threatened, attempted, or successfully inflicted physical harm upon another individual.

fronted with day-to-day decisional demands, have relied heavily on the conclusory testimony of psychiatrists, unhampered by rules of law. Trial judges in the exercise of their broad discretion have tended to rubber-stamp psychiatric opinions about dangerousness. Appellate courts have provided little guidance to the trial courts below. The reason for this may be in part that reviewing courts have not been asked for such definitions. Lawyers, whose function it is to test questionable legal practices, have tended not to present with sufficient zeal these questions for appellate review and have failed to challenge aggressively questionable applications of the term by trial judges.[1] Their performances have tended to be perfunctory. Until recently, few lawyers have been attentive to civil commitment cases, with little goad to the courts as a consequence.

Appellate courts, to the extent that they were occasionally called upon to consider what the word 'dangerousness' meant, commonly ducked the issue. When they did address themselves to the question, they originally defined the term with such sweeping broadness that it became stripped of any significant meaning. To illustrate: in 1960 the District of Columbia Circuit Court of Appeals defined the term dangerousness as including any criminal act, whether violent or not, such as passing a bad cheque.[2]

It had been argued that the term dangerousness should be limited to describing a likelihood that the patient would commit an act of violence. The Court rejected that position, however, saying, 'We think the danger to the public need not be possible physical violence, or a crime of violence. It is enough if there is competent evidence that [the respondent] may commit any criminal act, for any such act will injure others and will expose the person to arrest, trial and conviction. There is always the additional possible danger – not to be discounted even if remote – that a nonviolent criminal act may expose the perpetrator to a violent retaliatory act by the victim of the crime.'[3]

A year later, the court *en banc* reiterated its position, but in the face of a three-judge dissent which pointed out that the term 'dangerousness' had not been intended by Congress to apply to 'any kind of unlawful conduct, however minor', but had been designed to apply only to 'persons who have engaged in unlawful conduct of a dangerous character'. 'The language used', said the dissenters, 'conveys the idea of physical danger to persons, and, perhaps, to property.[4] In 1962 the same court ruled that the term dangerousness also encompassed emotional injury.[5]

Because legislatures and courts, during the early years of dangerousness jurisprudence, abdicated their responsibility, the burden devolved upon psy-

---

[1] In *Jackson* v. *Indiana*, 406 U.S. 715 (1972) the U.S. Supreme Court commented on this, saying, 'The bases [for the power exercised in involuntary civil commitments] that have been articulated include dangerousness to self, dangerousness to others, and the need for care or treatment or training. Considering the number of persons affected, it is perhaps remarkable that the substantive constitutional limitations on this power have not been more frequently litigated.' at 738.

[2] *Overholser* v. *Russell*, 283 F.2d 195 (D.C. Cir. 1960). The language of the statute required a finding that the 'person will not in the reasonable future be dangerous to himself or others'. D.C. Code §24-301(3) (Supp. VII, 1959).

[3] Id.

[4] *Overholser* v. *O'Beirne*, 302 F.2d 852 (D.C. Cir. 1961).

[5] *Overholser* v. *Lynch*, 288 F.2d 388 (D.C. Cir. 1961).

chiatrists and other mental health professionals to give meaning to the terms dangerousness, harm, and injury. Since in psychiatry and in other mental health circles there is no generally accepted legal, psychiatric, or medical meaning of such terms and since it is not a part of psychiatric training to evaluate dangerousness, each expert provided his own personal, subjective definition.[1] These definitions tended to implement the expert's idiosyncratic legal views, his personal set of values about the protection of persons and society, and his hidden agenda about appropriate dispositions for the mentally ill.

HOW PSYCHIATRISTS HAVE DEFINED THE TERM DANGEROUSNESS

For many psychiatrists dangerousness is an elastic concept that may include within its ambit any harm whatsoever to self or to others that is psychiatrically cognisable and for which hospitalisation and treatment may be an appropriate medical intervention. Indeed, for certain psychiatrists dangerousness is equated with illness and need for treatment, concepts which the dangerousness concept was originally intended to displace.

This is understandable in light of the fact that the psychiatrist is trained in a tradition in which he responds with treatment and applications of the medical model to even the most minor medical problems. The doctor's concern about or perception of deprivation of liberty or of autonomy is minimal, especially if perceived as temporary. Moreover, even onerous treatments are regarded as appropriate if they 'work'. Finally, the average psychiatrist has little awareness that he may be performing a social control function, at times masked as treatment, in which he is actually the agent of others including the state, and not necessarily acting on behalf of the person who is often euphemistically referred to as his 'patient'.[2]

For many psychiatrists the status of being dangerous to others is regarded as including even remote and suppositious harms, however trivial. The mere outside possibility of the occurrence of some minor harm may elicit a psychiatric prognosis that the person involved is dangerous. A leading psychiatrist has observed, 'When practicing psychiatrists are faced with a potentially dangerous patient, we may evaluate him, using vague and subjective criteria which do not distinguish among menace, nuisance, assaultiveness, and violence' (Panel Report, 1973). Such an approach would include within the concept of dangerousness not only any criminal activity, whether serious or trivial, but also such risks as that a manic person may deplete his family's financial resources and expose them to economic hardship, or that a paranoid schizophrenic might frighten another with bizarre behaviour, or that a hysterical person might regularly call people on the phone in the middle of the night, or that a sex deviant might expose.

---

[1] Kozol et al (1972) point out that, 'the terms used in standard psychiatric diagnosis are almost totally irrelevant to the determination of dangerousness'.

[2] Judge David Bazelon has recently addressed himself to the unacknowledged social control functions of the psychiatrist in a paper delivered at the New York University Law School, 'The Role of Psychiatry in Judicial Decisionmaking', April 23, 1981. See also Szasz (1982).

For the psychiatrist dangerous to self is a particularly malleable notion. Judicial reports, transcripts, and empirical studies are crowded with instances in which psychiatrists have characterised as dangerous persons who have engaged in the following: wandering; being a vagabond; 'eating out of maybe the trash cans, or something like that'; failing to take medicine; or wearing inadequate clothing. Left to their own devices, many psychiatrists are prepared to characterise virtually all deviant behaviour of the mentally ill as dangerous.

Since few mentally ill persons are presented for commitment unless their behaviour is regarded as deviant, the process of equating deviance with dangerousness renders the dangerousness standard meaningless. The term affords guidance neither to the testifying psychiatrist nor to the judge or jury. This has troubled psychiatrists as well as lawyers. A psychiatric director of a court clinic has remarked, 'Too often, in my experience, judges and attorneys have failed to challenge psychiatric testimony which is either incompetent, or clearly erroneous. ... The absence of any clear written criteria for such evaluations [has] two consequences. It leaves the examining physician with only the broadest concept of what is expected of him. It leaves the courts and the attorneys without the means of adequately measuring the quality of his evaluation' (Jacobs, 1974).

Some psychiatrists routinely equate dangerousness with the existence of mental disorder. For some, all paranoid schizophrenics are *ipso facto* dangerous.[1] One well-known psychiatrist, when asked on the witness stand whether an aggressive paranoid would be potentially dangerous, answered, 'We think that any paranoid schizophrenic is potentially dangerous, because one can never tell when the meekness and submissiveness may turn around and become aggressive. Ask me whether a paranoid schizophrenic is potentially dangerous and I would say, yes.'[2] Other psychiatrists carefully point out that not all paranoid schizophrenics are dangerous, only those who have certain kinds of delusions, such as negative delusions about law enforcement officers.[3]

Experienced observers have called attention to the fact that some psychiatrists are well aware that legal definitions of dangerousness are intended to be more restrictive in their application but ignore this and manipulate the dangerousness definition in order to accomplish treatment objectives. One psychiatrist, when asked why he had certified the respondent as a menace to himself and to others testified under oath in a commitment case that the respondent 'had certain paranoid delusions; feelings of persecution to the extent that he felt his life had been jeopardised on numerous occasions ... I felt there was a reasonable possibility that he would seek redress for his persecution and ... I had no assurance that such redress would be of an orderly or lawful type. Therefore, I felt that he might seek redress of a violent nature'. Later, when asked to explain his testi-

---

[1] See, e.g., Matter of Collins, 271 S.E.2d 72, 72 (N.C., 1980) where a psychiatrist testified that the respondent, diagnosed as paranoid schizophrenic, was dangerous because 'unpredictability is one of the hallmarks of paranoid schizophrenia'.

[2] *Hough* v. *United States*, 371 F.2d 458, 468–469 (D.C. Cir. 1959).

[3] *People* v. *Sansome*, 18 Ill. App.3d 315, 309 N.E.2d 733, 736 (1st Dist. 1974), leave to appeal denied, 56 Ill.2d 584 (1974).

mony the psychiatrist admitted, 'Actually, he need not have been much of a menace to himself and society. That is the current phrase used by anybody we feel needs hospital care, whether he wants it or not.'[1]

In a pioneering empirical study of Arizona civil commitment practices, Professor David Wexler observed, 'The literal meaning of dangerousness is admittedly ignored in favour of the best interest of the patient, i.e., whether he will benefit from treatment. Although it is recognised that such a determination is probably illegal, the psychiatrists feel it is more humanitarian to require treatment than to be thwarted statutorily in their attempt to prescribe it' (Wexler and Scoville, 1971). Judge David Bazelon, an eminent figure in mental health law, has pointed out, 'I have even been told that psychiatrists believe they are justified in fudging their testimony on "dangerousness", if they are convinced that an individual is too sick to know that he needs help'.[2]

Psychiatric testimony which overextends or distorts the concept of dangerousness is an amalgam of ignorance, zeal, and self-protectiveness. The ignorance stems from an unawareness that the concept of dangerousness either is, or should be, carefully conceptualised. The zeal reflects the willingness of the psychiatrist to offer the appropriate talismanic language to accomplish his psychiatric objectives, whether or not the words are strictly applicable. Self-protectiveness represents the understandable desire of a psychiatrist not to run unnecessary risks by testifying to the non-dangerousness of a mentally ill person who may later, if not hospitalised, commit suicide, assault others, or engage in other undesirable and highly publicised acts. Few are keen to take even slight risks.

In a perceptive analysis of the role of the psychiatrist in dangerousness cases, Saleem Shah (1975) has pointed out that 'Psychiatrists may find themselves placed in a social role in which society expects them to assist in the labeling and social control of persons who are perceived by the community as disturbing, discomforting, and threatening. The "experts" might be responding to what they perceive as socially expected of them rather than in response to the specific legal questions and processes designed to attain the desired societal objectives.' Shah points out further that while many psychiatrists who are asked to apply the dangerousness label 'might not actually be very knowledgeable in the sense of having demonstrable and reliable knowledge' about dangerousness, nevertheless such psychiatrists often find themselves 'in a social role (viz., of knowledgeable and skilled "experts") which requires that they not jeopardize this ascribed expertise – and, thus, the associated status, prestige, and power. ...' 'It is not surprising', says Shah, 'that psychiatrists and other experts turn to medical decision rules which state: "When in doubt, suspect illness"; "When in doubt, suspect dangerousness ...".'[3]

---

[1] *Brock* v. *Southern Pacific Co.*, 86 Cal. App.2d 182, 198, 200, 195 P.2d 66 (1948).

[2] Bazelon (1973) The Adversary Process in Psychiatry, Address, Southern California Psychiatric Society, April 21, 1973. As quoted in Shestack (1974).

[3] Shah (1975). See also *American Psychiatric Association Task Force Report 8, Clinical Aspects of the Violent Individual* (1974), which points out that 'Psychiatrists, in order to be safe, too often predict dangerousness, especially in the case of the mentally ill offenders.' At 25.

If judges actually wished a more careful definition of dangerousness they could insist on it. But trial judges have routinely accepted the conclusory opinions of psychiatrists in hearings that have tended to be superficial and brief. A 1966 study of civil commitment hearings in Texas reported that 40 patients were committed within 75 minutes, at a rate of less than two minutes per hearing (Cohen, 1966). Wexler and Scoville (1971) later reported that five years later, in 1971, the average duration of a commitment hearing in one Arizona county was 4.7 minutes. Zander (1976) reported three years later in 1974 that following the path-breaking *Lessard* decision the average duration of commitment proceedings in Milwaukee, Wisconsin was all of 13 minutes. In such a few minutes there is little opportunity for an adequate inquiry into the dangerousness of the respondent, and the hearings tend to be pro forma. Testimony tends to be conclusory and without support. A typical psychiatric statement is 'The patient suffers from a major psychiatric illness and would be dangerous to others' (Zander, 1976). Psychiatrists are often not asked for an explanation of any of the factors that go into the formulation of their opinions nor are they asked what they mean when they testify that a patient is dangerous. Nor, according to a recent study (Lelos, 1981), is there adequate cross-examination and testing by respondents' lawyers of psychiatric conclusions on the dangerousness issue.

A typical hearing on the need for confinement because of mental illness and dangerousness following an insanity acquittal in the District of Columbia can be cut and dried. The following is an example:

Examiner:　　Do you find that the defendant is still suffering from paranoid schizophrenia?
Psychiatrist:　Yes.
Examiner:　　Is he likely to be dangerous to himself or others in the foreseeable future, because of his illness?
Psychiatrist:　Yes.
Examiner:　　I hereby commit the defendant to Saint Elizabeths Hospital, until such time as this court is satisfied that he is no longer likely to be a danger to himself or others, in the foreseeable future, by reason of mental illness. Adjourned. (Pugh, 1973.)

There is a twofold reason for such abbreviated hearings. First, the term dangerousness has been stretched to such an extent that it has become practically meaningless. Second, judges have too often abdicated their decisional role to the psychiatrist in their deference to psychiatric judgement. Many judges are unwilling to reject a psychiatric opinion. Such deference brings the court into an uneasy connivance with the psychiatrist in bending the law. Wexler has reported the following characteristic judicial reaction: 'In one county ... the veteran judge freely expressed his own lack of knowledge ... to the end that he has exclusively followed the doctors' recommendations for the past 20 years. In another county, little concern was expressed about the statutory commitment standards, for the attitude prevailed that the state hospital was capable of correcting errors which might be made by the committing court.' (Wexler and Scoville, 1971.) Zander (1976) has reported a Milwaukee judge saying to the respondent's attorney, after the attorney had said he did not understand why full-time inpatient hospitalisation was necessary, 'My feelings are the same as yours, but I can't disregard the expert testimony.' (For a further discussion of judicial deference see Shuman and Hawkins, 1980.)

THE NEED FOR A DEFINITION OF DANGEROUSNESS

After more than ten years of active judicialising on the issue of dangerousness, American courts have not yet analysed its component elements in such a way as to ensure clarity and uniformity. Courts tend to dispose of cases by reaching conclusory decisions, as though the facts involved speak for themselves and as though dangerousness is a self-evident and self-defining proposition. In only a few cases has there been any attempt on the part of appellate courts to provide an analytical framework within which dangerousness can adequately be conceptualised.[1] The U.S. Supreme Court has compounded the confusion by establishing a burden of proof without clarifying what it is that should be proved.

Trial judges have little guidance. There is no uniformity in decision-making. What is dangerousness to one judge is not dangerousness to another. At least one judge who has been extensively involved in civil commitment cases has candidly acknowledged this. He reported that a judicial colleague of his had found only about 50 per cent of persons appearing before him to be dangerous, whereas he had found more than 95 per cent of them to be dangerous. Said the judge, 'I suspect that the marked difference in results comes from the fact that we are working with different concepts of dangerousness' (Stanton, 1975).

Given such a state of affairs, it appears that there is a great need for clarification. To meet that need, a model is offered here which is intended to clarify decision-making about the dangerousness of the mentally ill, especially for purposes of involuntary civil commitment.

A MODEL FOR DEFINING DANGEROUSNESS

In deciding whether an individual is dangerous, lawyers, judges, psychiatrists, and other mental health professionals should consider and weigh seven factors. These components are in fact often used implicitly by decision makers, but are seldom articulated either in judicial decisions or in legislative formulations.

The seven factors are as follows: (1) the nature of the harm involved; (2) its magnitude; (3) its imminence; (4) its frequency; (5) the likelihood or unlikelihood that it will occur; (6) situational circumstances and conditions that affect the likelihood of harm occurring; and (7) the substantive due process interest balancing between the alleged harm on one hand and the nature of society's intervention on the other.

It is not suggested here that these factors can at present be quantified in such a way that scores can be applied to different factors in the dangerousness evaluation and a mathematical conclusion about the dangerousness of a given individual reached. Rather, the purpose in identifying these factors is to call

---

[1] One notable exception is *Cross* v. *Harris*, 418 F.2d 1095 (D.C. Cir. 1969), one of the few cases that presents an elementary analysis of the factors involved in the dangerousness finding. See also *State* v. *Krol*, 67 N.J. 432, 344 A.2d 289 (1975).

attention to the generally ill-perceived complexity of the dangerousness decision and to alert decision makers as to what they should consider in each individual case.

The Nature of the Harm

We begin with the kind of harm involved. An anticipated harm may be either to persons or to property. Generally speaking, there tends to be more concern about potential harm to persons and less with respect to property. Some courts and legislatures, in fact, have gone so far as to rule that harm to property is not sufficiently significant under the federal constitution to be defined as dangerousness for purposes of civil commitment.[1] But a number of states do include harm to property in their statutes.[2] A few of these limit property harm to the property of others, not of oneself, and require evidence of already inflicted substantial loss or damage.[3] Some harm to property may also involve harm to persons, as in the arson of a house in which people are present. Moreover, some courts take the view that harm to property may lead to physically violent retaliations from those whose property is affected.[4] Thus, property harm is really physical harm.

---

[1] In *Suzuki* v. *Yuen*, 617 F.2d 173 (10th Cir. 1980) the court struck down as unconstitutional a statute which made a threat to property evidence of dangerousness. Said the court, under such a statute a 'person could be committed if he threatened to shoot a trespassing dog'. Such a criticism is not realistic in view of the analysis presented here. The reason is that in some cases such a threat would be trivial. In others it could be traumatic and ominous. See also Matter of Herman, 30 Wash. App. 321, 624 P.2d 310 (1981), where the court ruled that the vandalisation of a statue in a cemetery was not sufficient evidence of dangerousness to warrant retention in a mental hospital. In Matter of Arnold, 36 Or. App. 869, 586 P.2d 93 (1978) when the young respondent broke a window to get into his own house, his mother having locked him out on a stormy night, the court held that such an act of violence being against property was not dangerous.

[2] See, e.g., Wash. Rev. Code Ann. §71.05.020(3)(c) (1979).

[3] Wash. Rev. Code Ann. 71.05.020(3) (1979) provides that a person is dangerous where there is 'a substantial risk that [he will inflict] physical harm upon the property of others, as evidenced by behavior which has caused substantial loss or damage to the property of others'.

[4] An early example of this was the characterisation in 1960 by Judge (now Chief Justice) Burger of the act of passing a bad cheque as dangerous because, though itself non-violent, such an act 'might expose the perpetrator to violent retaliatory acts by the victim of the crime'. *Overholser* v. *Russell*, 283 F.2d 195 (D.C. Cir. 1960). This view has been echoed in 1978 in Matter of Arnold, 36 Or. App. 869, 586 P.2d 93 (1978), where the respondent had entered a neighbour's unoccupied apartment, believing he had been invited. The neighbour found the respondent in his apartment and became upset. The judge concluded that the respondent was dangerous, observing that a 'man who enters somebody else's apartment is apt to have his head blown off'.

In Matter of Nelson, 408 A.2d 1233, 1236 (D.C. 1979) the respondent appeared twice at the White House, asserting that he was Nelson Rockefeller, the 'President of the United States,' and demanding to be admitted. The court affirmed the commitment for the reason that respondent 'would be likely to place himself, because of the delusions he holds, in a position of danger and in a position where he would be likely to suffer harm'.

But *State* v *Rath*, 613 P.2d 60 (Ore. 1980) approached the issue otherwise. The respondent, found sleeping in an automobile, was charged with stealing it, but was acquitted by reason of insanity. At the commitment hearing he explained that because of feelings of persecution he had travelled extensively across the country, frequently sleeping in unlocked cars. The trial judge, in committing, ruled that respondent was dangerous, saying, 'I think that he does ... present a substantial danger to himself. If he keeps taking somebody else's property, somebody is going to get mad about it.'

The appellate court reversed, pointing out that the respondent was not 'inherently violent or even verbally abusive'. Said the court, 'Absent evidence of violent tendencies against others, the trial court's reasoning that defendant's sleeping in unlocked cars could eventually produce a confrontation with the owner of such vehicle does not support a finding that defendant would act in a manner dangerous to the owner or himself.'

But not all property is included. For example, harm to financial assets, which may result from an excessive and irrational spending of money, as by manics, or harm to present and future earning power, is considered by some courts not definable as dangerous.[1] Such a harm might serve as a basis for a determination that the person involved is incompetent to manage his property and should have a guardian, but would not, standing alone, be considered a type of harm warranting hospitalisation, unless other factors were involved. Trivial property harms, such as eating a meal and refusing to pay for it, are not regarded as dangerous behaviour, but as mere nuisances.

Emotional or Psychological Harm

The harm need not be physical. It can be emotional. A number of states regard some emotional or psychological harms as sufficiently dangerous to justify civil confinement.[2] An Iowa statute, for example, permits commitment where a person 'is likely to inflict emotional injury on members of his, or her, family, or others who lack reasonable opportunity to avoid contact with the afflicted person . . .'[3] The provision concerning lack of reasonable opportunity to avoid contact is an important one. Many persons psychologically threatened by a mentally ill person cannot move from their houses or leave their jobs. It seems rational to hospitalise the mentally ill individual rather than to disrupt the lives of others.

'Serious emotional injury' is often defined as 'an injury which does not necessarily exhibit any physical characteristics, but which can be recognised and diagnosed by a licensed physician or other qualified mental health professional, and which can be causally connected with the act or omission of a person who is, or is alleged to be, mentally ill'.[4] One commentator has pointed out that the Iowa statute provides that the injury 'need not be physically overt, but it must be medically overt, and susceptible of medical diagnosis . . .'[5]

Professor David Wexler (1978a), in disapproving of emotional injury as a basis for a dangerousness finding, has argued that its use establishes a 'precarious standard' because it 'requires a double prediction that the patient's behavior will emotionally injure another'. But, as the total analysis here indicates, all dangerousness definitions involve at least such a double finding and much more. It must be proved, first, that the respondent will do the act (the prediction) and, second, that the act will do a requisite harm (nature and magnitude). In that sense, the emotional injury standard is no different from the physical injury standard. Since many emotional or psychological harms are just as injurious as physical harms, their inclusion seems sensible. But it is true that it is less easy to prove an emotional harm than a physical harm.

---

[1] In Matter of Mendoza, 433 A.2d 1069 (D.C. 1981) the court repudiated an instruction to the jury to the effect that consideration should be given to injury to 'reputation, his chance for future employment, his chance for progress in the world and the like'.

[2] See, e.g., *Lynch* v. *Baxley*, 386 F. Supp. 378, 391 (D. Ala. 1975).

[3] Iowa Code Ann. §§1–82 (West 1969 & Supp. 1981).

[4] Id.

[5] This and other aspects of the 'emotional injury standard' are discussed in Bezanson (1975).

Threats

A significant form of emotional or psychological harm stems from threats made by mentally ill persons that they will do violence to themselves or others. Threats can be very frightening. To be put in fear is to be harmed, even if there is no physical harm. In fact, the criminal law recognises such a harm, defining it as an assault, a criminal offence which involves threatening behaviour that puts a person in fear.

Indeed, in the *Addington* case, already discussed,[1] the mentally ill respondent had originally been arrested on a misdemeanour charge of assault by threat against his mother, a charge which was dropped when commitment proceedings were successful.

A threat to do harm has two facets. First, the threat may be regarded as a verbal act which is inherently dangerous if it frightens and traumatises others to whom the threat is directed.[2] Second, even if the threat does not cause fright it can be an indicator of future behaviour. As such, it constitutes evidence of dangerousness. In this section, however, we deal with the threat as an inherent harm, not as evidence.

Passive harm: the gravely disabled

The harm need not be to others. It may be to oneself. Some harms are active ones: to one's life by suicide or to one's bodily integrity by self-maiming. These harms are easily identifiable.

Another type of harm which is more controversial is the type of harm resulting from the passivity of the mentally ill person. Within the past decade a new legal category of mentally ill persons has been established which has generally been described by use of the term 'gravely disabled'. A description of California's 'gravely disabled' statute is set forth in Morris (1978). These persons are passively dangerous to themselves in that they are unable by reason of their mental illness to provide adequately for their food, shelter, clothing, or medical care. For such persons, the nature of the harm that might befall them is that they might freeze or starve to death, die from disease, or become extremely ill because of inattention, unconcern, unawareness, or inability to act.

Originally it was thought that gravely disabled persons should not be characterised as dangerous. But in point of fact they can be regarded as dangerous to themselves due to their inability to attend to their critical life functions. The United States Supreme Court in a significant footnote in the Donaldson case pointed out that 'a person is literally "dangerous to himself" if for physical reasons he is helpless to avoid the hazards of freedom . . .'[3]

While the Supreme Court did not further define the hazards of freedom, at least one other influential federal court has pointed out that the 'problem of

---

[1] *Addington* v. *Texas*, 441 U.S. 418 (1979).
[2] See, e.g., Matter of Goedert, 591 P.2d 222 (Mont. 1979), defining a threat as a verbal act.
[3] *O'Connor* v. *Donaldson*, 422 U.S. 563, at 579, n. 9 (1975).

inability to care for one's self' which 'has been largely ignored' is in fact a problem of dangerousness.[1] Some states, in fact, include these persons in their statutory definitions of dangerousness.

Thus, the nature of the harm involved may very well place so-called gravely disabled persons within the dangerousness category, and make them appropriate candidates for involuntary commitment.

The Magnitude of the Harm

Harms can range from the trivial to the catastrophic. At one end of the spectrum are nuisances and such minor harms as cursing at people, scuffling with them, hitting them, exposing genitalia; urinating and defecating on a lawn, refusing to pay for a meal, and the like.[2] At the other end are suicide, homicide, mass murders, an assassination of a high governmental official like the president, etc. In between there is a host of harms of varying degrees of magnitude about which disagreement is often expressed as to seriousness or gravity.

Whether a person is regarded as sufficiently dangerous to commit will necessarily depend in large part on the magnitude of the anticipated harm. Those who curse, nudge, and telephone at three o'clock in the morning are ordinarily regarded as nuisances and are not usually thought of as dangerous. A homicide or suicide is an incontrovertibly dangerous act. But there is a wide range of harms about which there can be controversy. The social and political values of the judges tend to determine what is of sufficient magnitude to be regarded as dangerous. For example, how harmful to women, girls, or to little boys is the behaviour of an exhibitionist who exposes his genitals? In a fascinating case, two celebrated judges, Chief Justice Warren Burger and Judge David Bazelon, each of whom has dealt extensively with mental health issues, voiced diametrically opposed views about the dangerousness of a particular exhibitionist who was requesting release from a very lengthy commitment.[3]

Many legislatures and courts have attempted to define the magnitude of harm by the use of such adjectives as substantial or grave. These terms, however, apparently mean all things to all men. They are subject to uneven interpretation and even to 'outright misrepresentation' (Wexler, 1978b) and therefore tend to provide little additional precision.

It has been proposed that 'substantial bodily harm' be more fully defined in legislative enactments as unjustified physical harm of such a magnitude as to give rise to apprehension of danger to life, health, or limb.[4] Such a definition would include grave as opposed to trivial injuries but would not require that the injuries involved be such as could result in death. A more elaborate type of definition such as this has, however, not yet been adopted by any jurisdiction.[5]

---

[1] *Mathew* v. *Nelson*, 461 F. Supp. 707, at 712 (N.D. Ill. E.D. 1978).
[2] See, e.g., *Harris* v. *State*, 615 S.W.2d 330 (Tex. 1981), holding that scuffling and hitting slight blows is not dangerousness.
[3] *Cross* v. *Harris*, 418 F.2d 1095 (D.C. Cir. 1969).
[4] See H.R. 2326, 33d Legis., 1st Sess. §36–501(27) (Ariz. 1977).
[5] The current Arizona statute contains no definition of 'substantial', Ariz. Rev. Stat. Ann. §36–501(3) (1956 & Supp. 1980–81).

Imminence of the Harm

A number of states require for purposes of civil commitment that the harm involved be 'imminent'. It is currently being urged that the imminence concept be adopted by states that do not already have it (Comment, 1981).

Few statutes or cases define in a meaningful way what is meant by imminence. An imminent harm is sometimes described as a harm that is present, is fairly immediate, or one which will occur in the immediate future or at any moment.[1] An imminent harm is thought to be more dangerous than a more distant one because a non-imminent harm may be averted by a variety of interventions and therefore might not even occur. For example, a physically healthy person who refuses to eat may resume eating long before significant harm to his health occurs, especially if treatment takes place. A person who is decompensating because he has been given insufficient medication may be given more medication in time for him to be restored. There are many situations where an appropriate intervention short of confinement may prevent a non-imminent harm.[2]

On the other hand, imminence implies that the danger must occur momentarily rather than within a longer period of time. The application of such an interpretation might be particularly hazardous for passively dangerous persons whose potential harm may not be momentary, but who may be headed inexorably toward harm in the not-too-distant though non-imminent future. For that reason it has been suggested that a more satisfactory definition of imminence would be something like 'in the near future' or 'within 30 (or 60) days', etc. (Wexler, 1978c). Pennsylvania's statute provides that there be a reasonable probability that death, serious bodily injury, or serious physical debilitation ensue within 30 days unless adequate treatment is afforded.[3]

It is not clear whether a vague or specific definition of imminence is better. Some states that have had experience with the term, such as North Carolina, have eliminated the requirement altogether.[4] There is little recorded empirical experience on the issue.

Frequency of Harm

Some harms occur seldom and are tolerable, especially if modest. Other harms, even if modest in magnitude, may occur very often and become intolerable for that reason. For example, an occasional mild hitting may be acceptable but constant hitting may not be. A rare and infrequent exposure of genitalia may be tolerable, whereas frequent exposure of genitalia may become intolerable.

The Probability that the Harm Will Occur

The predictability factor is the most controversial of all the factors involved in

---

[1] These three definitions are drawn from Matter of F.B., 615 P.2d 867 (Mont. 1980).

[2] See, e.g., *Semler* v. *Psychiatric Institute*, 538 F.2d 131 (4th Cir. 1976).

[3] See Pa. Stat. Ann. tit. 50 §7301(b)(2)(i) (Purdon Supp. 1981–82), discussed in In Interest of Green, 417 A.2d 708, 710 (Pa. 1980).

[4] See, e.g., North Carolina's statute, Gen. Stat. §§122–58.1 & Gen. Stat. 122–58.7(i) (1981), discussed in Matter of Collins, 271 S.E.2d 72 (N.C. 1980).

an evaluation of dangerousness. Generalised experience and extensive empirical research have tended to show, although the findings are controversial, that it is extremely difficult in many cases to predict with accuracy that a given individual will commit an anticipated harm, especially if that person has not done so in the past.[1] Predictions tend to become far more accurate about individuals who have committed a particular harm on five or six occasions (Wolfgang, 1978; Petersilia et al, 1977). But other predictions are not.

There seems to have been in the past a relatively high rate of overprediction of dangerousness which has resulted in rates of confinement which could be regarded as excessive. Overprediction of dangerousness results in a high rate of confinement of 'false positives', persons who are predicted to do a harm but who would not do so if permitted to remain at liberty.

Efforts have been made to improve our ability to predict dangerous behaviour. Some researchers claim that short-term predictions tend to be more accurate than long-term predictions. Some psychiatrists believe that they can predict dangerousness with accuracy (Rofman et al, 1980), others no longer think so (American Psychiatric Association, 1974; Diamond, 1974), and the evidence is discussed further in Chapter 14.

Current legislation and judicial opinions reflect the concern that too many determinations about dangerousness have been based on questionable psychiatric testimony, without more. For that reason, several evidential approaches have been emerged which stress the need for more objective evidence.

The overt act requirement

A number of legal decisions and statutes now require that a finding of dangerousness be based on evidence, at minimum, that the respondent has engaged in a recent overt act, attempt, or threat.[2]

These enactments and judicial decisions tend not to define the term recent, thus leaving it up to judges to define it in an *ad hoc* manner. Some enactments provide a time limit, such as 30 days.[3] In such situations, that which may have occurred forty or fifty days earlier, however otherwise relevant and probative, would not be admissible in evidence for the purpose of establishing that the respondent is dangerous. But some courts regard acts which have occurred 75 days before the filing of a petition as sufficiently recent, especially where the acts are of great magnitude.[4]

---

[1] There is a substantial amount of research on this proposition, the most important of which is summarised and analysed in an outstanding monograph, Monahan (1981). Two important articles worth separate reference are Cocozza and Steadman (1976) and Ennis and Litwack (1974). The Ennis and Litwack article has become a bible for many lawyers in this field. On the difficulty of predicting where there is no previous history of acting out see, Rubin (1972) and Kozol et al (1972).

[2] For statutes, see, e.g., Mass. Gen. Laws Ann. ch. 123, §1 (1972); Neb. Rev. Stat. §83–1009 (1976 & Supp. 1980). For cases see, e.g., *Stamus* v. *Leonhardt*, 414 F. Supp. 439 (S.D. Iowa, 1976).

[3] Pa. Stat. Ann. tit. 50 §7301(b)(2)(ii) (Purdon Supp. 1981–82).

[4] In *In Re Prime*, 424 A.2d 804 (N.H., 1980) respondent threatened to slit his mother's throat with a knife and smashed a knife through a door she had locked behind her. Held, a two and a half month lapse was 'sufficiently recent'.

It is not always clear what kind of overt act, attempt, or threat is required. In one leading case an overt act was defined as an act or omission which physically injures the actor or another, or which constitutes a failure to care for one's self so as to guard against physical injury or provide for one's own physical needs.[1]

One thoughtful analysis of the overt act requirement has suggested that for a mentally ill person, in a fit of rage, to smash a platter on the floor, causing his spouse to fear that 'the next furious act will result in harm to her' would not meet the overt act requirement because 'by itself it presents no risk of physical harm to the spouse' (Note, 1977).

But other courts do not require that the overt act be itself injurious. They argue that the purpose of the overt act provision is to require the showing of an act from which a reasonable inference of future dangerousness may be shown. For example, in Matter of Gatson[2] the respondent was ruled dangerous because she was picked up by the police as she walked down the street nude. The police thought she might have been raped. She had gone out in cold weather without clothes or shoes, and did not eat properly. Her lawyer pointed out that the respondent had not physically hurt herself or others, but the appellate court rejected that argument on the basis that there was no need to show actual violence or physical harm, since the purpose of the statute was to provide treatment before physical harm did result.[3]

One problem with the overt act requirement is that because it is a part of the legislative definition of dangerousness, many courts treat it as an over-arching requirement which, once satisfied, justifies a finding of dangerousness and commitment. Case after case reveals a search for the overt act, without adequate consideration of its magnitude, the validity of the inference to be drawn from it as to future behaviour, the nature of the behaviour, and the like. Thus, ironically, the overt act requirement, designed to protect the mentally ill, too often becomes a vehicle facilitating their commitment, because the overt act is easy to find and identify.

Recently, a few courts have refused to make a constitutional requirement that the finding of dangerous be based on an overt act, taking the view that the showing of only one overt act, which is all that is required, does not add appreciably to the accuracy of a prediction of dangerousness. In *Mathew* v. *Nelson*,[4] the court heard testimony from four outstanding experts on the prediction of dangerousness, two selected by each of the parties. All four experts agreed that evidence of one overt act adds little. Thus, scepticism is now developing about the usefulness of the overt act requirement.

Though the overt act requirement may add little to accuracy, it could detract

---

[1] *Mathew* v. *Nelson*, 461 F. Supp. 707 (N.D. Ill. 1978).
[2] 3 Kan. App.2d 265, 593 P.2d 423 (1979). See also Matter of F.B., 615 P.2d 867 (Mont. 1980).
[3] Id.
[4] 461 F. Supp. 707 (N.D. Ill. 1978). The overt act issue is discussed in Note, Overt Dangerous Behavior as a Constitutional Requirement for Involuntary Civil Commitment of the Mentally Ill, 44 U. Chi. L. Rev. 562 (1977) and Note, 7 Loyola U. L. J. 507 (1976). See also *People* v. *Sansone*, 18 Ill. App. 3d 315, 309 N.E.2d 733 (1974) and *In Re Salem*, 228 S.E.2d 649 (N.C. Ct. App. 1976).

from rational decision-making if its implementation prevents the hospitalisation and treatment of dangerous persons whose behaviour has not reached the level of an overt act as defined by the courts. The courts and legislatures, in an effort to protect the mentally ill from the abuses of subjective and inaccurate psychiatric testimony, may have gone too far in the opposite direction by requiring objective evidence of spurious probative value. Yet, because of the absence of empirical evidence, we have no way of knowing how the overt act requirement has actually worked in those jurisdictions that have adopted it.

Situational Factors and Judicial Conditions

Mentally ill persons may be potentially harmful under certain circumstances yet not under others. An obvious illustration is that of the person who is not dangerous when he takes his antipsychotic medication regularly, but who may be potentially dangerous if he stops taking that medication and again becomes delusional.[1] This is what some judges mean when they say that a mentally ill person is dangerous because 'he won't take his medication'. On the face of it, such a statement may seem absurd. In fact, such a finding, without additional facts, is wholly inadequate, to the extent that it focuses on the factor of refusal of medication alone, without consideration of any of the other factors discussed in this model.

The importance of conditions is recognised in conditional releases from hospitalisation which emphasise the value of imposing limitations on the life situation of a mentally ill person, such as that he never carry a gun, that he report to a community mental health centre periodically, that he accept a certain form of treatment, that he not associate with certain persons, that he not drink or use drugs, and the like, all of these being environmental conditions which can either encourage or discourage potential harm.[2]

Substantive Due Process Interest Balancing

Finally, it should be recognised that a characterisation of a particular person as dangerous does not describe an absolute quality of that person. Rather, such a characterisation represents a balance on one hand between the first six factors described here and, on the other, the societal intervention involved. One must ask: in relation to what prospective societal intervention is this person to be regarded as 'dangerous'? Are we considering a short-term or a long-term hospitalisation? Are we considering enforced medication? A transfer from an open to a locked facility? The death penalty?

The United States Supreme Court in the Humphrey case has made the

---

[1] See, e.g., *Warren* v. *Harvey*, 632 F.2d 925 (2d Cir. 1980), where the court characterised as dangerous and unreleasable an NGRI patient who 'could not be trusted to take his medication, as was required'. To the same effect is Matter of Lee, 35 N.C. App. 655, 242 S.E.2d 211 (1978). But see *Cramer* v. *Tyars*, 151 Cal. Rptr. 653, 588 P.2d 793 (1979), which ruled that an inquiry into whether respondent would take his medication if released was to invite 'consideration of possible future behavior under hypothetical conditions'.
[2] See, e.g., Matter of Torsney, 47 N.Y.2d 667, 420 N.Y.S.2d 192, 394 N.E.2d 362 (1979) and Annot., Validity of Conditions Imposed when releasing person committed to institution as consequence of acquittal of crime on ground of insanity, 2 ALR 4th 934.

balancing principle clear. Said the Court, 'the dangerousness definition requires that a person's potential for doing harm to himself or to others should be great enough to justify a "massive curtailment" of liberty.'[1]

Thus, a determination that a person is dangerous must always be based on such a balance. For example, a combination of factors indicating a potential for behaviour of modest magnitude, type and imminence might justify a short-term confinement but not a longer-term commitment. In other words, the mentally ill person is dangerous enough to be kept in a hospital for a short time during which the prospects of recovery from the illness and from his dangerousness are encouraging. Such a curtailment of liberty is not 'massive' and the need for confinement may be great. On the other hand, a person may not be dangerous enough to be kept for a long time, if the likelihood of restoration has now become poor, and retention of that person in the hospital is merely preventive detention, where the feared dangerousness is relatively trivial or modest and its predictability poor. Here the curtailment can become massive and the need for confinement inadequate.

On the other hand, if the nature of the dangerousness is serious and highly predictable then a long-term retention of a mentally ill person in the hospital may become a sheer necessity. The type, magnitude, and probability of the potential conduct may justify prolonged retention even if treatment is of no avail. Some states, such as Wisconsin, appear to require prospects for treatment along with dangerousness as a basis for longer-term hospitalisation. Such a position does not seem rational where treatment prospects are dim and where the dangerousness to others is great.

It seems clear from this discussion of substantive due process interest balancing that contrary to Chief Justice Burger's statement in the Addington case, there should be little difficulty for a judge to find a mentally ill person to be dangerous by clear and convincing evidence or even beyond a reasonable doubt, if the facts so warrant. Dangerousness not being the product exclusively of a prediction, there is no necessity to confront the paradox of not being able to predict a future act by a measure well over 50 per cent. A person can be dangerous if there is a 5 or 10 per cent chance that he will kill himself or someone else. He may be considered dangerous if there is only a 1 per cent chance that he will kill the President. On the other hand, a 75–100 per cent likelihood that the mentally ill person will engage in a relatively trivial act of slight magnitude should not justify a lengthy confinement. The determination of dangerousness is not based exclusively on a prediction, but rather to a more complete balancing process that takes place in which the magnitude, imminence and other factors identified here must be weighed in with probability, then balanced against the particular intervention intended: a 72-hour hold, a two-week or six-month confinement, and the like.

This formulation raises as many questions as it answers. Even if we could measure the degree of probability with which a given act is likely to occur, we would still be left with the value question concerning how many false positives

---

[1] *Humphrey* v. *Cady*, 405 U.S. 504, 509 (1972).

we would tolerate in order to prevent a particular harm from occurring. Do we confine 99 persons who are not likely to commit a homicide in order to prevent the one in a hundred who surely will? These are currently unanswerable questions that confront the conscience of the judge who is sensitive to the dilemma. Most judges are not aware of this dilemma, however, and simply hospitalise if there is evidence of an overt act which merely suggests the bare possibility of violence.

What does emerge is that the standard of proof problem is largely a false issue. The judge who would commit under a preponderance standard has as much freedom to do so under the clear and convincing standard or, indeed, under even the reasonable doubt standard. Empirical studies, if done, would probably show that a *parens patriae* oriented judge would commit approximately the same number of persons regardless of which standard of proof prevails in his jurisdiction.

CONCLUSION

In this analysis I have not discussed arguments in favour of or against the use of the concept of dangerousness for purposes of involuntary civil commitment. Those who favour a libertarian position support the use of dangerousness as an exclusive standard for civil commitment. To protect the integrity of that approach they urge that definitions of dangerousness be stringent and limited. But in fact, the definitions of dangerousness are becoming broader and more inclusive, drawing into the net of dangerousness more and more mentally ill persons. One illustration of this is that the 'gravely disabled' are now regarded as dangerous and the U.S. Supreme Court has lent its imprimatur to that inclusion.

Those who favour the medical model of treatment oppose exclusive or major reliance on dangerousness as a basis of commitment, arguing that it is too limited and too ill-defined a concept. It prevents the hospitalisation of many mentally ill persons in need of such care. In fact, many mentally ill persons endure and cause much unnecessary human suffering which could be alleviated by a timely hospitalisation. They are permitted to deteriorate because they do not fit neatly enough into the dangerousness category. My analysis of danger-ousness here is, rather, intended to provide a model which, if used in good faith, should lend clarity to decision-making, whatever one's subjective approaches, biases, prejudices, values, socialisation, and experiences may be. In speaking of 'good faith' I have in mind the implementation by courts and other committing agencies of the policies that resulted in adoption of the dangerousness standard in the first place. These policies embody a rejection of the long-prevailing and still persistent position that the commitment of a mentally ill person 'for his own good' or for treatment to improve his condition, without more, is justified. This *parens patriae* approach is hard to shake off. Many judges continue to implement it, overtly or covertly, in the guise of applying a dangerousness standard. For such judges, a close analysis of the component elements of the dangerousness concept may be an act of gratuitous fatuity.

But to the extent that the law in many jurisdictions now requires a showing of dangerousness for the purpose of hospitalisation, application of the law should rationally reflect the policy considerations that have given rise to the dangerousness requirement. The term dangerousness should be defined in such a way as to effectuate the determinations made by appellate judges and legislators that mentally ill people should not be confined unless the cost of hospitalisation to that person is outweighed by the benefit to himself and the state in avoiding dangerousness. This cost-benefit analysis must be made in the context of a rigorous evaluation of all the facts in the light of clearly stated and understood factors. The analysis presented here is intended to enhance that process.

REFERENCES

American Psychiatric Association (1974) *Clinical Aspects of the Violent Individual.* The ability of psychiatrists or any other professionals to reliably predict future violence.

Bezanson (1975) Involuntary treatment of the mentally ill in Iowa: the 1974 legislation. *Iowa L. Rev.,* **61,** 261, 300–7.

Brooks (1974) *Law, Psychiatry and the Mental Health System.* pp. 677–717.

Brooks (1976) Mental health law. *Admin. in Mental Health,* **4,** 94.

Brooks (1980a) The constitutional right to refuse antipsychotic medications. *Bull. Am. Acad. Psychiatry & L.,* **8,** 179.

Brooks (1980b) *Law, Psychiatry and the Mental Health System.* pp. 127–9.

Civil Commitment of the Mentally Ill in California: The Lanterman-Petris-Short Act (1974) *Loyola of L.A. Rev.,* **7,** 93, 113.

Cocozza & Steadman (1976) The failure of psychiatric predictions of dangerous clear and convincing evidence. *Rutgers L. Rev.,* **29,** 1048.

Cohen (1966) The function of the attorney and the commitment of the mentally ill. *Tex. L. Rev.,* **44,** 424.

Comment (1981) Involuntary civil commitment: the inadequacy of existing procedural and substantive protections. *U.C.L.A. L. Rev.,* **28,** 906, 948.

Dershowitz (1974) The origins of preventive confinement in Anglo-American law. Part II: The American experience. *U. Cin. L. Rev.,* **43,** 781.

Developments in the Law (1974) Civil commitment of the mentally ill. *Harv. L. Rev.,* **87,** 1190, 1253–1258.

Diamond (1974) The psychiatric prediction of dangerousness. *U. Pa. L. Rev.,* **123,** 439.

Ennis & Litwack (1974) Psychiatry and the presumption of expertise: flipping coins in the courtroom. *Calif. L. Rev.,* **62,** 693.

German & Singer (1976) Punishing the not guilty: hospitalization of persons acquitted by reason of insanity. *Rutgers L. Rev.,* **29,** 1101.

Jacobs (1974) Psychiatric examinations in the determination of sexual dangerousness in Massachusetts. *N. E. L. Rev.,* **10,** 85.

Kozol, Boucher & Garafalo (1972) The diagnosis and treatment of dangerousness. *Crime & Delinquency,* **18,** 371, 383.

Lelos (1981) Courtroom observation study of civil commitment. In *Civil Commitment and Social Policy: An Evaluation of the Massachusetts Mental Health Reform Act of 1970.* McGarry, A. et al (eds.). p. 114.

McGarry, et al (1981) *Civil Commitment and Social Policy: An Evaluation of the Massachusetts Mental Health Reform Act of 1970.*

Monahan (1981) *The Clinical Prediction of Violent Behavior.* New York: Sage.

Monahan & Wexler (1978) A definitive maybe: proof and probability in civil commitment. *L. and Human Behav.,* **2,** 37.

Morris (1978) Conservatorship for the 'gravely disabled': California's nondeclaration of nonindependence. *San Diego L. Rev.,* **15,** 201.

Note (1977) Overt dangerous behaviour as a constitutional requirement for involuntary civil commitment of the mentally ill. *U. Chi. L. Rev.,* **44,** 562, 579–80.

Nowak, Rotunda & Young (1978) *Constitutional Law.* p. 484. New York: West.

Panel Report (1973) When is dangerous, dangerous? *J. Psychiat. & L.,* **1,** 427, 431.

Petersilia, Greenwoold & Lavin (1977) *Criminal Careers of Habitual Felons.*

Pugh (1973) The insanity defense in operation: a practicing psychiatrist views Durham and Brawner. *Wash. U.L.Q.,* **87,** 91.

Rofman, Askinazi & Fant (1980) The prediction of dangerous behavior in emergency civil commitment. *Am. J. Psychiatry*, **137,** 1061.

Rubin (1972) Predictions of dangerousness in mentally ill criminals. *Arch. Gen. Psychiatry*, **397,**
400.

Shah (1975) Some interactions of law and civil commitment of the mentally ill: some public policy
considerations. *Am. J. Psychiat.*, **132,** 501.

Shah (1978) Dangerousness: a paradigm for exploring some issues in law and psychology. *Am.
Psychologist*, **33,** 224, 225.

Shestack (1974) Psychiatry and the dilemmas of dual loyalties. In *Medical Moral and Legal Issues in
Mental Health Care*, *11*, no. 3. Ayol, F. (ed.).

Shuman & Hawkins (1980) The use of alternatives to instiutionalization of the mentally ill. *Sw. L.
J.*, **33,** 1181.

Simon & Cockerham (1977) Civil commitment, burden of proof, and dangerous acts: a comparison
of the perspective of judges and psychiatrists. *J. Psychiatry & L.*, **5,** 57.

Stanton (1975) Involuntary civil commitment proceeding: a trial judge's view. *N.J.L.J.*, **98,** 25.

Steadman (1973) Some evidence on the inadequacy of the concept and determination of dangerousness in law and psychiatry. *J. Psychiatr. & L.*, **1,** 409, 413.

Stone (1976) The Tarasoff decisions: suing psychotherapists to safeguard society. *Harv. L. Rev.*, **90,**
358.

Szasz (1982) The psychiatrist as moral agent. *Whittier L. Rev.*, **4,** 77.

West (1972) Discussed in 'Note, A Dangerous Commitment'. *Pepperdine L. Rev.*, **2,** 117, 1974.

Wexler (1976) *Criminal Commitments and Dangerous Mental Patients: Legal Issues of Confinement,
Treatment and Release.*

Wexler (1978) Comments and questions about mental health law in Hawaii. *Hawaii Bar*, **13,** (a) 3,
(b) 4, (c) 5.

Wexler & Scoville (1971) The administration of psychiatric justice: theory and practice in Arizona.
Ariz. L. Rev., **13,** 1, 100.

Wolfgang (1978) An Overview of Research into Violent Behavior. Testimony before the U.S. House
of Representatives Committee on Science and Technology.

Zander (1976) Civil commitment in Wisconsin: the impact of Lessard *v.* Schmidt. *Wis. L. Rev.*, **503,**
526.

POSTSCRIPT

This chapter was completed in May 1982. All judicial and statutory references are up-to-date only
as of that time, but two important cases have been more recently decided by the United States
Supreme Court that deserve special mention. The first is *Jones* v. *United States*, 103 S. Ct. 3043
(1983), which dealt with the rights of insanity acquittees. In that case, the Court, in defining
'dangerousness', said in dictum that, 'The fact that a person has been found, beyond a reasonable
doubt, to have committed a criminal act certainly indicates dangerousness.' The Court continued
with the statement that such a fact is 'at least as persuasive as any predictions about dangerousness
made in a civil-commitment proceeding.' Finally, the Court observed that it had never ruled that
violence, 'however that term is defined', is a prerequisite for a constitutional commitment. In saying
this the Court startled many mental health lawyers, who had assumed that non-violent crimes are,
per se, not indicators of dangerousness. In other words, the Court's dictum now suggests a broader
definition of dangerousness than had been anticipated.

The second case is *Barefoot* v. *Estelle*, 103 S. Ct. 3383 (1983), which deals with psychiatric
testimony that predicts the dangerousness of a convicted murderer in a death penalty case. The
petitioner, relying on empirical studies, argued that psychiatric predictions in testimony as to
dangerousness are too unreliable to be used for purposes of applying capital punishment.

The Court, by a 6–3 vote, rejected the empirical evidence as inadequate and affirmed the appropriateness of psychiatric testimony, even where the psychiatrist had not actually examined the felon
but had based his judgement on facts placed before him in a hypothetical question.

The Supreme Court decision is a powerful blow to libertarian lawyers who have long urged that
psychiatric predictions of dangerousness are too untrustworthy and too prejudicial to be used for
such a drastic purpose. The states are likely to follow the lead of the federal Supreme Court.
Moreover, at least one of the leading dangerousness theoreticians (John Monahan) now writes of a
'second generation of theory and policy' which is not as critical of all psychiatric predictions in all
contexts as in the past (*Am. J. Psychiat.*, **141,** 10 (1984)).

Thus, the latest developments in significant U.S. constitutional law are that both the definition of
dangerousness and the psychiatric data base for defining it are being expanded.

The concept of 'dangerousness' continues to move further away from the libertarian protectiveness
with which it was originally conceived.

19

Psychiatric Reports for the Courts

Michael Craft

Professionals who do not have the advantage of legal training are often unclear how the legal hierarchy is arranged, and what is required from them in court. This section therefore describes the English system of law courts. Much of the Australian and United States practice derived from this and is still similar. An outline is given as to what reports should contain, the pitfalls which may lie ahead, and how lawyers and doctors may assist – or destroy – each other.

English law is derived from the customs of the people over the ages – so-called common law – interpreted by law courts and called case law. This is changed year by year by parliamentary statutes or Acts. What was meant by the words in an Act is interpreted by judges, or by Appeal Courts, following either of which a judicial precedent is set. Courts usually follow precedents until they are reversed or changed by a new Act. However, since 1966, the House of Lords has no longer been bound by its own decisions, and the Court of Appeal (Criminal Division) need not follow a precedent where, not so to do, would work in favour of the Appellant (*R*. v. *Merriman*).

Law is generally concerned with offences against the majesty of the Queen, subsumed in criminal law; and the rights and duties of people to each other, which comes under civil law. This last has family law, *inter alia*, divisions for property, contract, inheritance and the law of tort which is a civil wrong remediable by action for damages. Trespass, defamation, nuisance and other wrong-doings are torts remediable at law.

Criminal acts may be tried in the following court venues.

1 *Juvenile*: for those between 10 and 16 years, by three lay magistrates without a jury.

2 *Magistrates' courts* deal with all summary prosecutions comprising nearly 99 per cent of all criminal prosecutions. Lay magistrates are appointed by the Lord Chancellor and advised by a clerk who is either a barrister or solicitor. There are also professional stipendary magistrates who are lawyers. Cases can be:

(a) non-criminal, for example licensing hours, extensions;

(b) criminal, but non-indictable (summary), for example road traffic offences;

(c) triable either way where defendant has elected summary trial, for example petty theft. Here, if the offender is found guilty, he can be committed to the Crown Court for sentence if, because of his character and previous convictions, the magistrates consider their powers of dealing with him to be inadequate, e.g. if he merits borstal training.

3   *Crown Courts* deal with all indictable offences and offences triable either way which are not tried in the magistrates' court. They also hear appeals from lower courts, except on points of law. Crown Courts are presided over by:

(a) a High Court Judge, a puisne Judge of the Queen's Bench;

(b) a Circuit Judge who is a barrister of ten years' experience, or Recorder of five years' practice, appointed by the Crown;

(c) a part-time Recorder serving for at least a month a year who must be a barrister or solicitor of ten years' practice.

A Recorder can try crimes or conspiracy to commit forgery, a robbery, burglary, wounding, death from reckless driving or offences, triable either way, committed from magistrates' courts.

A Circuit Judge can try the preceding, together with manslaughter, infanticide, child death, unlawful abortion, rape, unlawful sexual intercourse, sedition, mutiny or conspiracy to commit the above.

A High Court Judge can try the preceding together with treason, murder, Official Secrets Act offences, and conspiracy to commit the above.

4   The *Court of Appeal* (Criminal Division) hears appeals from Crown Courts.

5   The *House of Lords* is the highest court of appeal on points of law of general public importance.

All types of courts need reports. Civil courts need expert evidence to assess damages, criminal courts to assess mental state. Psychiatric reports are requested with increasing frequency in sophisticated societies keen to unravel the *mens rea* or intent behind the *actus reus* or act of crime. Thus, if a shopper walks out with goods unpaid there are many possible explanations of intent (discussed in Chapter 5), some of which may be elucidated by a psychiatrist. For more serious crimes, and when people are severely ill, the report may need psychiatric evaluation of fitness to plead, McNaughton insanity, diminished responsibility, presence or absence of mental abnormality before, during, after or as a result of the crime.

Ideally a professional report should consist of

1   The facts with their supporting evidence;

2   The professional's deductions from the facts, which amount to an opinion;

3   The recommendations for action.

THE ETHICS OF COURT REPORTS

Before seeing the client, the psychiatrist must be careful to determine where his duty lies. If he is asked by the Crown prosecution or prison to attend, he is ethically bound to state the position to the defendant, and should make available a copy of his report to the defending lawyer. The question of malpractice here is examined later in this chapter. If the defence lawyer commissions a written report, the ethical position is simple, anything which is contrary to the client's interest can be withheld. However, if a psychiatrist gives verbal evidence he is obliged to tell the whole truth, even if this means giving evidence detrimental to his patient's interests.

In English law, privilege attaches to a lawyer and his client, but this may not apply to other professional communications. Lord Denning, Senior Law Lord and Master of the Rolls, summarised the position in 1963 by saying:

The only profession that I know which is given privilege from disclosing information to a court of law is the legal profession, and then it is not the privilege of the lawyer, but of his client. Take the clergyman, the banker or the medical man. None of these is entitled to refuse to answer when directed to by a judge. Let me not be mistaken. The judge will respect the confidences which each member of these honourable professions receives in the course of it, and will not direct him to answer unless not only it is relevant but also it is a proper and, indeed, necessary question in the course of justice, to be put and answered. A judge is the person entrusted, on behalf of the community, to weigh these conflicting interests – to weigh on the one hand the respect due to confidence in the profession and on the other the ultimate interest of the community and justice being done ... [Discussed in detail in Palmer, 1980.]

Thus, matter passing between a lawyer and his client is privileged. This extends to medical and other reports prepared for the purpose of litigation for either party. The doctor would be expected to keep his records confidential, but the lawyer can decide himself whether the whole or part should be disclosed in open court. If the doctor considers that reports he wishes to be kept confidential are covered by legal privilege as being prepared for the sole purpose of litigation, he may refuse disclosure until it is ordered by a judge. Any such order could be appealed if wrong in law.

A separate area of confidentiality is where disclosure of matters adverse to the patient is required by the law itself. This covers disclosure of infectious illnesses such as tuberculosis, fitness for driving licence such as epilepsy, police surgeons' reports and those carrying out life insurance examinations (Parkes, 1982).

A third area, that of doctors employed by an authority carrying out a report for that authority, is contentious. It has been held that such a report commissioned by the employing authority is the property of the employing authority, and in the field of mentally abnormal offenders, this particularly attaches to prison officers' reports. For instance, suicidal attempts, verbal threats of arson, or violence within a prison, reported by the prison medical officer to the court may be extremely damaging to the client's prospects, and may even go towards an indeterminate sentence in a special hospital rather than the finite prison sentence. It is sometimes worthwhile for defence lawyers to remind their clients of the danger in this state of affairs. If psychiatric reports are for the defence, they will be covered by privilege. The defence may withhold matters which are damaging to the client. The psychiatrist should forward a report couched in such a way that facts are clarified, and opinions clearly stated as such. A highly damaging phrase such as 'the prisoner attempted arson in his cell and the suicide of himself' would be separated out, as in any case a good report should be, into hard facts, hearsay evidence and opinion. Many psychiatric reports are an inextricable mixture of concrete fact, patient's statements, hearsay evidence and opinionative utterances which make them very susceptible to destructive cross-examination in the witness box (see Epilogue). Ideally all such reports should first give the facts behind the issues, hearsay evidence and its weighting if any, and opinions with their pros and cons. If the issue is known to be coming to court, and a cross-examination is likely, there is much to be said for allowing one's final weighted opinion to be brought out under circumstances where it can have the weighting for and against it displayed for judge and jury to decide. Not only is a decision on guilt a matter for the court alone, so that prior to this finding some medical opinions on disposal could be presumptuous, but further evidence later to appear in court may make an early opinion appear unwise.

THE SEVEN ELEMENTS OF THE IDEAL COURT REPORT

While the psychiatrist may be used to writing letters or reports during the course of his work, there is much to be said for training himself in a discipline of writing a court report. If he has left out part of the following, it is embarrassing to be asked in a court cross-examination whether this area has been covered, and if so, why it was omitted.

First Part: Orientation

This consists of a brief headpiece, identifying the patient, his age, address, for whom the examination was made, where it was made, even the time taken in so doing. Apart from orientating the reader, it may also orientate the professional as to whether he is giving a view for the prosecution or for the defence, or for his own hospital or clinic.

Second Part: Presenting the Situation

Here the factual details of the offence are given with relevant data and background. If a 'not guilty' plea is entered, the circumstances of the alleged offence are a matter for trial. Only if a 'guilty' plea is entered can one legitimately discuss the offence, motivation and factual background. The patient's own account (described as such) of how it occurred and the reasons for it are needed. There is no point in the professional passing an opinion, for it comes better at the end of the report when it can be seen that he has assessed all the data and has taken due weight of each part. Amongst the factual data at this point should be a description of how the patient told his story, his observed emotional reactions, type of smoking, hand wringing, eye contact and so on.

Third Part: Relevant Life History

More hard facts are given here. Where the patient is giving the history and details of his past illnesses and treatment this can be shown as his account in brackets on the right hand side. The professional is on much safer ground under cross-examination when he has noted the source of his data so that if the patient is later shown to be a pathological liar the professional can allow later facts to speak for themselves. A good deal of hard data may be available in third party hospital and social reports so that again if the sources are given, the professional can refer to them, and not be obliged to defend himself. Obviously, one has to be selective and this introduces an element of personal bias. It is the art of report writing that relevant matter is included and irrelevant matter left out.

Fourth Part: Professional Examination

The writer divides his professional examination into five parts: observed behaviour during the entire interview; psychological testing, for instance reading, memory recall, concentration; intelligence and mental ability level, including the level of intellectual performance as opposed to testing of quotient; some doctors include a brief physical examination, which may indicate need for further specialist reports; a fifth part immediately following the deduction after the examinations of the patient's neurological and psychiatric state, since at this point of the report an opinion logically follows.

Fifth Part: Further Investigations and Reports

These may be numerous. A number of medical investigations might be indicated, such as skull X-rays, blood analyses or psychological tests, but there may also be indicated interviews with wife, parents or children in order to attest to change in behaviour, personality or mental state over a period of time. Brain investigation such as electroencephalography or computer axial tomography may be required with their reports and attendant opinions. If the opinion of fellow professionals is involved at this point, their permission may be required, and their fees paid. A social work or probation report may need to be requested.

Sixth Part: Final Diagnosis and Opinion

This is necessarily an opinionative part of the report, and may be more or less detailed, depending on the professional weight of the writer. For instance, a social worker without the ability to offer a hostel placement or any supporting service by his authority, may have a very short opinion indeed.

Seventh Part: Recommendation, Prognosis and Options

The weighting of this part of the report is crucial. Not only is it opinionative, the writer is hazarding guesses as to the future. It behoves him to make allowances for the chances of fate. Most courts are keen on an assessment of dangerousness, and this is most open to the elements of chance. Clearly a mentally abnormal offender convicted for murder is quite safe by himself on a desert island, at least so far as others are concerned, but like rats in a crowded cage, potentially lethal in a Glasgow tenement. Where the vicissitudes of human fortune are concerned it behoves the writer to be circumspect. What is needed is a description of possible treatment options and their likely effect on improvement of behaviour and future avoidance of law-breaking. If treatment is offered the availability of a bed or out-patient course should be clearly indicated. The psychiatrist who talks in vague generalities without individual commitment is poorly received at court. Following a written report, the psychiatrist may be asked to attend court for verbal cross-examination. This allows for further observation of the patient whose abnormal behaviour in court, also observed by the jury, may be used to convince the jury of the logic of the psychiatric diagnosis (see also Chapter 7).

THE PSYCHIATRIST AND HIS PATIENT

Referral for possible treatment is often high on the list of reasons that psychiatric reports are requested by courts. When this is the issue, psychiatrists evolve their own presentation to the patient. I think of this as a package deal for my prospective patient, often as a condition of probation, and always requiring provisos the client must fulfil.

One enters the patient's presence against a background of past crisis. One is conscious of a short time interval against which one personally has to work, while the patient will be aware of the past offence, guilt or tension as a result, and his own feelings and possibly those of his relatives or loved ones, hanging over his head. Before I speak I evaluate the patient's body expression, the lay of his hands upon the table, the state of his facial expression and any nervous twitchings that may be visible. This allows one's opening gambit to get to the heart of the matter: 'You must have many worries.' 'You must be very upset.' Or for a young recidivist who clearly doesn't care a damn, 'Do you think you'll be found guilty?' Receipt of all available documents from the defence lawyer allows one to have in one's possession the factual basis before one sees the offender/patient. This allows for a proper expression of concern when one listens to a patient's story, and the marking out of the subject's fears and worries which serve as the basis of the therapeutic contract with him. As a result of a physical and mental examination, further items of concern are clarified by the patient, and although there might be a need for further investigation to throw light upon the clinical picture, it should be possible at the end of the first interview to arrive at a formulation which makes sense both to the patient and to the court.

Therapeutic Contract (Section 37 Version)

The first stage of a therapeutic contract is to outline to the offender/patient the picture as one sees it, with an analysis in simple terms of the diagnosis and what this means to the offender, and a statement of what psychiatric and/or medical treatment can do. The medical treatment element is important, since many younger patients have alcohol abuse as an extra complication, which can respond impressively to medical and nursing care. As an example of psychiatric treatment under a hospital Section 37 Order, the seducer of small boys may wish both his tension anxiety to be relieved by psychiatric treatment and/or his sexual desires clarified. He is then left with a clear picture that permanent relief of his worries and tension can be achieved only after he co-operates and needs to change the direction of his sexual desire.

The second stage of treatment is to arouse motivation. If initially a prisoner is remanded back to prison, and later to the hospital concerned, his motivation for treatment may be assisted to the point where he is prepared to welcome treatment on a hospital order in place of the likely prison sentence.

Stage three follows the arrival in hospital and concomitant relief from worry and tension. There may be disinclination to work through the psychotherapy plan. Enthusiasm often evaporates after a month, a dislike of fellow patients may take its place, and the wish to get away from hospital may bring extra tension and treatment need. At this stage of treatment the patient may realise that the hospital has no locked ward in which to keep him and should he decide not to stay in hospital, the court cannot re-sentence him as sentence (Section 37) is already passed. Thus, if he absconds, and refuses to return to the unlocked hospital under this 'compulsory' order, the hospital commonly has no means of detaining him effectively, without recourse to heavy medication. The new interim hospital orders offer the possibility of a trial period for both hospital and offender.

Stage four is the designation of a date for the end of inpatient psychiatric treatment, and working towards return to the community, together with its advantages and disadvantages.

Stage five is the hospital discharge, solution of practical problems such as satisfactory residence, day occupation, financial income and occupation of leisure hours in such a way that they are constructive for the patient and not destructive for relatives. For some patients, groups such as Alcoholics Anonymous organise leisure time groups and discussions which can constructively take up time, but mentally abnormal offenders are often lonely people who have surprisingly little in common with each other.

The Therapeutic Contract (Voluntary Version on Probation)

For most offender/patients, this means a condition of psychiatric treatment under a probation order, whether for inpatient or outpatient purposes. Stages are similar to the outline detailed immediately above, with the difference that throughout treatment a court representative in the shape of a probation officer has a significant part to play. Probation officers themselves differ in the way they regard their role in the psychiatric probation order, with some anxious to take part in the therapeutic process by way of their own contribution to psychotherapy, and others preferring to stay out of the treatment process with only occasional visits to keep in contact.

The main difference with a psychiatric probation order is that should the patient change his mind and wish to discontinue treatment, an absconsion or self-discharge itself constitutes a breach of the probation order for which the offender/patient can be brought to the local court for further sentence. Thus instead of a possible transfer to the locked ward which is no longer available in many psychiatric hospitals, the very real possibility may exist of a transfer to a locked prison, either on remand for the breach of probation, or as an alternative to the probation order itself by way of final sentence.

Most psychiatrists working in unlocked psychiatric hospitals are happy to work with a probation order containing a condition of inpatient or outpatient psychiatric treatment. The length of the inpatient residence is commonly left open by the initiating court, for under the recent Criminal Justice Act, there is no longer any need to specify the length of inpatient residence on the initial probation order. As a result, all the psychiatrist has to do at the end of his inpatient treatment period is to recommend to the court that this condition be deleted from the probation order, and he is then able to arrange the time of discharge convenient to both himself and his patient, and thereafter to continue outpatient treatment with the probation component of aftercare being extremely valuable.

CONCLUSION

The courts expect more than the fundamental examination of mental state from the psychiatrist. As a highly trained professional he is expected to take a deal of time and trouble to sift through relevant issues from the mass of background, present them cogently to the court and explain their relative importance. With many of the cases in local court practice the interests of the patient and the court coincide so that a constructive plan of treatment can be arranged if the court accepts the psychiatric recommendations. Ideally the psychiatrist should also furnish a prognosis, or estimation of the effect of suggested treatment on future behaviour and likely reconviction.

CASES

Lord Denning, M. R., (1963) In: A-G Mulholland and Foster 1 ALLER 767.
Merriman, R. V. (1973) A.C. 584.

REFERENCES

Palmer, R. N. (1980) Defamation, assault and confidentiality. In *Medical Malpractice*. Taylor, J. L. (ed.). Bristol: John Wright.
Parkes, R. (1982) The duty of confidence. *Brit. Med. J.*, **285**, 1442–3.

FURTHER READING

British Medical Association (1981) *Medical Evidence. The report of a Joint Committee of the British Medical Association. The Senate of the Inns of Court and the Bar and the Law Society*. Tavistock Square, London.

20

Drugs, Alcohol and Addiction

Michael Craft

The law on self-induced intoxication is quite clear. Self-induced intoxication, whether by drink or drugs, does not absolve the accused from liability in cases of 'basic intent' by reason of lack of *mens rea*. In *R.* v. *Majewski* the House of Lords unanimously agreed that a defendant may properly be convicted of assault notwithstanding that, by reason of self-induced intoxication, he did not intend to do the act alleged to constitute the assault. Crimes of 'basic intent' are generally those where the accused may be guilty if he did the act in question recklessly as opposed to crimes of specific intent where the prosecution has to prove a particular intent of knowledge. Important examples of offences where recklessness is sufficient *mens rea* are manslaughter, arson and rape (see Mitchell, 1982, p. 1032). An increasing proportion of the general population take self-prescribed agents affecting the mind, such as alcohol, or medically prescribed agents such as Valium or antidepressants. Any or all of these may be causal coincidental or combined agents in relationship to timing of mental abnormality and crime. This chapter starts with a brief introduction to the major antipsychotic and antidepressant drugs, reviews antimanic and mood stabilising drugs, comments on anti-epileptic drugs, and ends with a final short review on alcohol and addiction.

ANTIPSYCHOTIC DRUGS

Schizophrenia affects at one time or another up to one in a hundred of the general population. As outlined in Chapter 9 its association with offence is probably more coincidental than cause and effect, yet since a substantial proportion of the population are reared under deprivative or delinquent-prone conditions, and the illness itself leads to disorder of thought and planning, it is not surprising that a small but persistent minority of criminals are also schizophrenics. Both the leading symptoms of schizophrenia, and their response to the powerful new antipsychotic agents can best be laid out in tabular form so that the non-medical reader can evaluate which parts of his client's schizophrenic illness might respond best to drug treatment (see Table 20.1).

The major symptoms of schizophrenia are described in Table 20.1; the common term 'splitting of personality' is better expressed as 'marked change in personality'.

Table 20.1 Main schizophrenic symptoms and their response to drug treatment.

Symptom	Drug Effect
Disorder of thought	Very good
Withdrawal from company	Good
Self-preoccupation	Good
Overactivity	Very good
Resistance to help	Good
Aggressiveness	Good
Hallucination[a]	Good
Suspicion and paranoia	Good
Twitching of hands and face	Good
Emotional coldness	Fair
Delusions[b]	Fair
Inactivity, laziness	Little effect
Preoccupation with bodily functions	Little effect
Lack of insight	Little effect

[a] Hallucinations are perceptual experiences in the absence of actual sensory cues; an example is the flickering lights commonly seen in migraine.
[b] Delusions are false beliefs firmly held despite community contradictions. An example is of the old lady who believes burglars are under her bed despite being shown to the contrary.

The patient with acute schizophrenia is unlikely to come the way of a lawyer or probation officer, because he is so obviously 'mad' that he first goes to hospital. Here about a third completely recover and do not have another episode for many years, if at all. Another third predominantly recover, but have relapses on occasion, often at an interval of years. About a third only make a partial recovery from the first episode or other acute relapses and may display the hallmark of more and more damage to the personality, although medication (see Table 20.1) alleviates many symptoms. These are the people liable to turn up in the office or consulting room with oddities of history, or behaviour, even of deep-rooted suspicions or paranoia quite resistant to reason. Others continue with repetitive behaviour which, since the lawyer or probation officer does not usually take a full clinical history with admissions to hospital, defy understanding until the 'penny drops' or a medical report arrives on the desk. After all schizophrenia is a very common affliction affecting one in a hundred of the population, as common as diabetes or alcoholism, each having an incidence of half a million in the UK population of fifty-six million.

Barbiturates and alcohol blunt both the stress and the tension of schizophrenic symptoms. Being sedative drugs themselves they increase the withdrawal, emotional flatness and inactivity which are cardinal features of the long-standing condition. The unfortunate paranoid schizophrenic who is suspicious of a doctor's drugs, may find out the beneficial effect of alcohol and dose himself.

Chlorpromazine (trade name Largactil) was introduced in the early 1950s coincident with an increase in discharge of mental hospital inpatients since that date, which is so evident in practice today. A low dose of 25 mg of chlorpromazine lasts for some eight hours, so that three times a day medication is effective, although it has a wide range of safety and up to 1000 mg can be given in hospital.

Its breakdown in the body is highly idiosyncratic. At least 167 different enzymes are known to contribute to breakdown in the gut or liver. Enzymes are by genetic endowment present or absent in an individual; if he has most of the 167 he breaks down chlorpromazines so fast that even a large dose is relatively ineffective; if he has only a few of these enzymes, the same dosage obviously lasts much longer. The same principles also apply to other drugs, which is one of the reasons why some people are genetically more tolerant to drugs than others. A more common reason for non-response to drugs is of course failure to take, due to forgetfulness, or dislike.

Since the advent of chlorpromazine, literally hundreds of potent anti-psychotic drugs have been evolved, varying in their anti-psychotic effect, and each with different side effects. For instance, chlorpromazine has a degree of sedation which is useful, but it may also cause jaundice, sensitivity to sunlight with sunburn, or a general tremulousness, technically called Parkinsonism. Other drugs such as trifluoperazine (trade name Stelazine) have a slightly stimulant quality, whilst yet others such as the butyrophenones, e.g. haloperidol (trade names Serenace or Haldol) have a mood calming effect which means they are useful in other emotional states. For the erratic drug-taking patient, some preparations are supplied as intramuscular injections in sesame oil, so that given once a month, they are slowly absorbed over some weeks. This avoids the need for daily drug dosage.

Effective medication is not the only variable causing improvement in schizophrenia although like insulin and diabetes, it plays a substantial part. Figure 20.1 depicts a well-known research experiment showing daily drug dosage. It summarises the results of 25 patients admitted to a London teaching hospital for the first time suffering from schizophrenia. Nine months after discharge, they were followed up and as a result of a social worker visit to their homes, divided into 69 discharged to emotionally low-key relatives and 56 discharged to highly emotional relatives. For those discharged to low-key acceptant relatives, there was only a slight difference in relapse between those who continued to take their drugs (only 12 per cent relapsed) and those who stopped taking their drugs, of whom 15 per cent relapsed. A further variable, which was very important among those who were discharged to highly emotional and complaining relatives was how much time they had to spend in their company. Of the quarter who attended day hospital each week, and took drugs, 42 per cent relapsed and of those who did not take drugs, 55 per cent relapsed. However, among the three-quarters who did not attend day hospital, the influence of drugs was much more impressive. Fifteen per cent relapsed who took drugs and 92 per cent relapsed who stopped taking drugs. This research project shows in elegant form the influence of medication upon relapse of illness, the influence of highly emotional relatives compared with those who are acceptant, and the importance of day occupation in influencing relapse of illness. Drugs are obviously important, but by no means the most important variable.

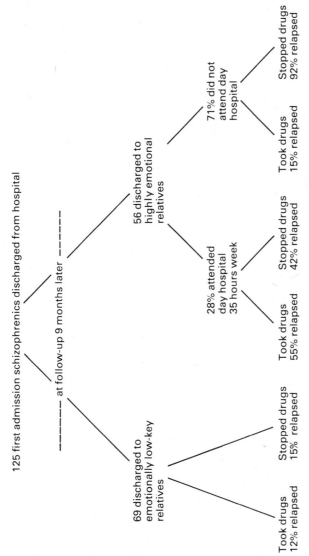

Figure 20.1 Outcome with drugs in schizophrenia. (From Leff, 1976, with kind permission.)

ANTIDEPRESSANT MEDICATION

Sadness in response to upset is normal, but consistent depressive episodes lasting longer than a few weeks may merit treatment. Depressive downswings of a month either after tragedies such as bereavement (reactive depression) or out of a clear blue sky (called endogenous depression) are more frequent than schizophrenia. Population surveys suggest that between two and three per cent of a population will have severe depressive episodes lasting longer than a month at one or more times during their lives. Some people also have manic upswings, lasting over a month, as well as depressive downswings.

These people are called constitutional cyclothymes in temperament and the illness is termed bipolar. Much more common is the woman with repeated depressive downswings over a month in duration, either reactive or endogenous, who is said to suffer from a unipolar illness, that is an illness in one direction only. These illnesses constitute the most common psychiatric treatable entities and account for a large proportion of the one in six women and one in nine men who are calculated to enter a psychiatric unit at some time in their lives. Other types of mental ill-health involve anxiety states, bodily worries and personality problems. Together these mental illnesses make up the 30 per cent of patients in a general practitioner's surgery who have psychiatric ill-health. As Chapter 10 describes, depression and crime are commonly associated, not only for coincidental reasons, but also because the consequences of crime are depressing in themselves. As Dr Lawson says in that chapter, a reactive episode of depression is very common following imprisonment on remand, and when it reaches suicidal proportions may well be treated more safely in a locked remand unit, than the patient's home. Such depressive episodes have the classic triad of symptoms: firstly, concerned with sleeplessness, difficulty in sleeping, light sleep with nightmares, early waking in the morning; secondly, the daytime depressive symptoms such as weeping, being worse in the morning and getting better in company during the day, preoccupation with bodily bad feelings; and thirdly, weight loss, with loss of appetite, disinterest in food, loss of flesh. The depressed patient can be recognised across the office desk before he says anything, but most respond not only to sympathy and loving care but dramatically to medication. Safe moderately effective antidepressants such as the tricyclic (named from its chemical composition) Imipramine (trade name Tofranil) and amitriptyline (trade name Tryptizol) are widely prescribed by general practitioners. The risky stronger monoamine oxidases, of which tranylcypromine (trade name Parnate) and phenelzine (trade name Nardil) are examples, are widely used in reactive depression. They have the serious side effect of hypertensive crisis on consumption of amine-rich foods such as cheese, beans and Marmite. Other side effects occur with both drugs, such as indigestion and agitation. In Britain (see p. 333) a court action brought against a physician following the death of a depressed patient prescribed a monoamine oxidase inhibitor drug resulted in a finding for the defendant on the grounds that the patient had ignored verbal instructions to avoid amine-rich foods such as beans, cheese and Marmite. It is now usual practice for doctors to give patients a written list of such foods when prescribing

monoamine oxidase inhibitors (MAOIs). Depressive episodes are usually alleviated within one month on an ordinary dose of either of these groups of drugs,
although resistant depressive illnesses are responsible for a smaller proportion
of patients needing admission to the psychiatric inpatient unit. Indications for
admission are now more often social than medical, for instance elderly people,
those living alone, those making suicidal threats who cannot be cared for by
relatives, and those on remand for an offence.

Two varieties of depressive illness are more often associated with offences
than others. The first consists of the depressive illnesses of old age with clouded
consciousness which are associated with shoplifting offences. The second type of
illness has features of severe agitation, so that the individual becomes markedly
mentally abnormal, draws attention to himself round the district, and attacks
others or commits episodes of malicious damage, such as throwing or breaking
articles, which might be construed as calling attention to his condition and
asking for treatment. Panic anxiety states during which individuals have a degree
of fearfulness, either in response to specific persons or specific objects or places,
may also lead people into the law courts, either because of violence when the
person feels he is trapped or by way of the divorce courts when the other partner
is unable to cope with the mentally abnormal individual any further. In both
these types of illness, antidepressant drugs can be advantageous.

ANTIMANIC AND MOOD STABILISING DRUGS

Mania or hypomania are names given to overactive agitated sleepless episodes
longer than a month in duration, which constitute the opposite polar illness to
depression, in the bipolar cyclothymic personality. Hypomania is not the happy
illness a layman might think. A recent example in the writer's clinic was a
landlady who by overactivity, overcleanliness and overcooking during the day
and by sleepless agitation at night terrorised her 'guests' most of whom could
not defend themselves. Her daughter was scared of the many bills that lay
unpaid, her bank manager furious at the mounting overdraft, her lawyer at his
wits' end because of her non-appearance at court, her dogs fearful because if
they did not eat her overplentiful provision of food, she kicked them unmerci-
fully. Even they ran howling from her house.

Lithium is effective in both the acute and long-term cyclothymic patient.
This is not a drug, it is a member of the ionic family of which fluorine (useful for
teeth) and chlorine (essential for life) are other members. Whether lithium is
essential to stability of mood may well depend on genetic endowment, or other
factors, as is susceptibility to fluorine and chlorine. Other tranquillisers, as noted
under schizophrenia above, are also effective in mania or hypomania, whilst in
an extreme excited episode, sedative drugs in anaesthetic dosage are occasionally
needed. The patient usually has to be admitted to an inpatient psychiatric unit,
as much to protect his relatives and friends as to care for himself. Stabilisation
of mood for the cyclothymic personality may be accomplished with effectiveness

by the daily use of lithium. Offences can occur as a result of hypomanic upswings or depressive downswings; both may be amenable to lithium. However, this substance is prone to toxic side effects and needs frequent monitoring by blood samples.

ANTI-EPILEPTIC DRUGS

The contribution of epilepsy to offence and the so-called epileptic personality are reviewed in Chapter 13. Epileptic fits may be reactive in the sense that they follow previous infection or brain injury, but are usually endogenous in the sense that some brains appear genetically to react with a fit more commonly than others to excessive electrical wave patterns. Both types can now be very effectively treated with drugs, of which the older members are barbiturates and the newer are more specific to the type of epilepsy.

Epilepsy is now classified into *generalised seizures* such as grand mal and petit mal, and *focal seizures*. A *grand-mal* starts with an odd feeling, peculiar to the individual by which he recognises the onset of a fit. This is followed by loss of consciousness with a fall and brisk muscular movements during which the tongue may be bitten and urine passed, followed by a period of coma and loss of memory for the incident. In a *petit-mal* the patient has a momentary absence of consciousness, not long enough to cause him to fall to the ground. To the observer it often looks like a passing spasm of inattention. Approximately one in 300 of the general population have grand mal or petit mal attacks, although all of them can now be controlled to a complete or lesser extent by drugs, so that most do not suffer a fit during the course of any particular year. When *focal fits* arise in a temporal lobe of the brain they may consist wholly or in part of automatic movements such as little dances, biting movements or dressing. They are rarely associated with an offence (also considered in Chapter 13) because the resulting partial consciousness and glazed look rarely allows other than a simple movement sequence such as picking something up and looking at it. Other types of *focal fits* occur as a result of a developing abscess or brain tumour, when, depending where it starts, there may be irritation causing twitching in a thumb or great toe. If the irritation spreads across to the other half of the brain a general epileptic grand mal fit results.

All types of epilepsy can be influenced by drugs and the newer the drug the more specific in its action on a particular part of the brain. It is a nice piece of clinical judgement to determine the right drug or drugs for the person, with the least number of side effects.

PERSONALITY DISORDERS AND DRUG RESPONSE

By nature personality disorders are long-standing phenomena, least likely to be responsive to the drugs described above. An exception is the cyclothymic personality, where there may be a genetic sensitivity to lithium. None of the personality disorders likely to be associated with offences responds more than on a short-term basis to tranquillisers, antidepressants or mood drugs. Nevertheless, the anxious personality with short-lived panic or anxiety states of disabling severity can be helped in the short term by anti-anxiety drugs such as diazepam (trade name Valium).

Unfortunately tolerance to these drugs is rapidly established, and unless a long-term treatment plan or behaviour conditioning programme is set in motion, the short-term benefit of these drugs is often lost, and a long term addiction acquired in its stead.

In the field of sex deviations, there are a few specific antihormonal preparations which are of use. Drugs like cyproterone acetate by competition at target organs for the naturally-produced hormone testosterone can reduce the level of the normally circulating hormone in the blood and thus reduce the degree of sex drive, and aggression. It cannot change the *direction* of sex need, which may be male and/or female. This drug, therefore, has a limited use in the treatment of sex deviation, for instance those with a predilection for small boys and small girls.

Other personality disorders find consolation for their mood state by experimenting with drugs of different sorts. Since time immemorial mankind has attempted to improve his mood state, or whet his appetite by the use of active medicaments, and again and again has discovered that the fleeting solace of such drugs has turned into a long nightmare if dependence develops. Personality disorders associated with immaturity, emotional instability, inadequacy, even cyclothymia, can respond in the short term to a wide variety of therapeutically active agents varying from coffee and tea, to alcohol, cannabis and LSD. The most commonly used drug of this sort is, of course, alcohol, and addiction to this and other mind-bending drugs is discussed in the next section.

ALCOHOL AND DRUG DEPENDENCE

There is an accepted distinction between medical and social use of psychotropic drugs, in that the first are taken on the direction of a doctor ostensibly for the relief of mental abnormality or illness on the part of the user, whilst the latter are self-prescribed with the intention of inducing well-being or improvement of the mental state of those who are generally thought to be in their 'normal' state of mind. This distinction hangs more upon the social circumstances of the use of these drugs acting on the psyche than on criteria of action.

Alcohol and tobacco are by far the most potent and most widespread self-administered drugs, the one being a sedative, and the other a central nervous system stimulant. The nicotine from tobacco is very rapidly absorbed from the lungs direct to the brain, constituting a very rapid 'reward' and behaviour modification of the user in favour of its further use. Amongst the enormous literature and useless facts available for the interested professional, it is recorded that so long ago as 2285 BC a man was evicted from Imperial China for fermenting rice into an intoxicating drink, whilst in seventeenth century England an early smoker was similarly banished from the court of St James. Neither banishment, torture, imprisonment or death stayed the steady march of users. Recent awareness of evidence of dangers attendant on the use of these drugs has led to a decrease in the customary usage.

In the UK it has been estimated that nearly 500 000 people are alcohol-dependent, that is to say they need a drink in the morning to 'steady their nerves', whilst some 100 000 show obvious deterioration and constitute chronic alcoholics. In the UK, tobacco and alcohol consumption represents 15 per cent of total consumer expenditure in any one year. In the mid-1970s it was estimated that 50 000 died from smoking-related conditions each year, with a further 2000 from cirrhosis of the liver or other alcohol-related poisoning incidents (this excludes alcohol-related road accidents and suicide). In the USA it has been estimated that there are 9 000 000 alcoholic persons of whom only some five per cent are the obvious 'skid row' types. A government working party estimated that five per cent of the country's work force were alcoholics within the definition given above, but another five per cent were serious abusers to the extent that it interfered substantially with their work output. Other working parties have estimated that one-third of the arrests each year in the USA are for public intoxication, and that if drunken driving, disorderly conduct, vagrancy and other alcohol-related offences were added, the proportion would rise to 40 to 49 per cent. Still in the USA, American Indians have the highest alcoholism rate up to 50 per cent on some reservations. There used to be a ratio of five males to one female but recent reports both in the USA and in the UK show a substantial shift towards parity. An American Medical Association working party showed a distinct bias by physicians in diagnosis. The incidence of alcoholism among physicians has been shown to be higher than in the general population, and the working party showed that physicians were loath to diagnose those who were drinking as much as themselves as alcoholic, but were quite happy to label those drinking more than themselves as sufferers! With the known bias of alcoholics to attend physicians who were in sympathy with their cause, the influence on reported figures is clear. Although tobacco has fairly lethal consequences long-term the short-term stimulant effects of 'over-dosage' do not lead to any substantial fall-off in working ability. This is not so for alcohol, where the short-term consequences of excess dosage by way of spirits can lead to acute alcoholic poisoning and death. With both there is a considerable degree of genetically endowed susceptibility, so that with tobacco, some smokers of 40 or more cigarettes a day can do so for decades without lethal consequences, whilst others have died in their early teens from coronary thrombosis or lung cancer. The youngest death so far reported as a direct consequence of excess smoking is of a boy of 14 who started when he was four. Tolerance to the effect of alcohol on the various systems of the body is also in part genetically determined, although like other drugs, tolerance to the mental effects builds up over a period of usage. Anecdotes such as the heavy drinking Anglo-Indian colonel given the standard dose of anaesthetic for an appendicitis operation, who yet removed the tower clips during the operation, are well known. A blood alcohol concentration of 80 mg per 100 ml has been regarded as standard in many countries as a limit beyond which it is illegal to drive a car. Addicts function well on higher levels: The *British Medical Journal* (1981) reported that:

Some medical experts have collected egg on their faces: they persuaded the courts in New South Wales that a blood alcohol concentration of 260 mg/100 ml was *prima facie* evidence that an individual would be too drunk to be able to drive at all. A forensic pathologist (*Medical Journal of Australia*, 1981, **68**, 226–7) has now reported that in Western Australia higher levels were recorded in 300 convicted motorists and concentrations as high as 520 mg/100 ml have been found in fatally injured drivers.

Treatment for addiction to tobacco is generally on an outpatient basis using placebo sucking, inhaling or nicotine-like agents in chewing gum as a substitute. Hypnosis and acupuncture are also employed. Short-term success rates of 30 to 50 per cent have been reported, depending very highly on the enthusiasm of the treatment leader, the length of follow-up, and the motivation of the client.

Most regional authorities, states and cities now have alcohol and addiction treatment services, led by full-time professionals with varying degrees of enthusiasm and dependent on well staffed inpatient units. The success rate of these units in short-term treatment of crises, and weaning of those temporarily highly motivated is high; figures of 60 to 80 per cent who become non-alcoholic have been quoted. Unfortunately the fall-out rate is also high, and long-term success rates have much to do with the motivation of client, the efficiency of the follow-up treatment agency, the degree to which the family can be motivated to fill in daytime gaps, particularly for housewives, and the replacement of the public house as the main location for social interaction. Perhaps the saddest commentary on the recovering alcoholic is that he loses most of his friends in having to avoid the previous inns, cocktail parties and socials. Alcoholics Anonymous has been very successful in providing alternative social groups, often dedicated to the point of fanaticism, which replace those groups lost.

Thus the professional trying to secure the best agency for the treatment of his client should look beyond the immediate court appearance, and investigate the strengths and weaknesses of treatment agencies in his area or beyond. If the client has substantial financial resources, a distant rehabilitative agency may be more efficient than a local one, whilst with the death and disablement rate so high with this illness, there may be much to be said for a geographical re-location of patient, family or both.

OTHER ADDICTIONS

Drug addiction, drug habituation and drug dependence are all phrases with a variety of meanings with some degree of practical differentiation. In 1950 the World Health Organisation (WHO) described addiction as 'a state of periodic or chronic intoxication detrimental to the individual in society, produced by the repeated consumption of a drug, natural or synthetic'. By 1956, they described habituation as a 'state creating a desire, but not a compulsion, to continue taking the drug for the sense of improved well-being it engendered'. Any detrimental effect fell primarily on the individual or his pocket. By 1964 the WHO was recommending that the term 'drug dependence' be submitted for the previous terms. 'Such drugs created a drive requiring a periodic or continuous administration of the drug for pleasure or to avoid discomfort. Abuse of a drug occurs when the results of the drug dependence has an obvious detrimental effect on individual society.' (Full quotation given in the OHE booklet: *Alcohol*.)

Until the 1940s most UK addicts were either medical men or pharmacists who had learned to use drugs in their work, or immigrants such as the Chinese, who had brought their drug usage with them into the country. There is a distinction between 'hard' drugs such as the *depressant* group of opium, morphine (manufactured 1805), heroin (1889), barbiturates (1903); the *stimulant* group, amphetamines (1887), benzedrine (1936), dexedrine (1944); *hallucinogenics* such as peyotl (used by Incas), psilocybin (purified from mushrooms (1953) LSD (1938); and 'soft' drugs such as cannibis or mescaline (1898). 'Hard' drugs were once believed to be more addictive and damaging than 'soft'. The incidence of drug dependence with all these drugs has increased substantially since the 1940s, particularly in the United States. In the United Kingdom there was a steep increase in the 1960s of those addicted to drugs covered by the Dangerous Drugs Act of 1920 with its revisions. Such addicts are reported to the Home Office and by the 1970s the principal drug concerned was heroin. By the early 1970s Britain had a rate of known narcotic addicts of 25 per million, compared with 290 per million in the United States. These are certainly underestimates, the figures applying only to registered addicts in both countries. In the United States the pushing of addictive drugs has created a sizeable industry. It is said that in the mid-1970s the rate per million was 3000 in Hong Kong and 7000 in Iran with consumption mainly of opium. These figures do not apply to cannabis smoking, which is said to be less addictive and more common. A recent research project among Oxford University students suggested that 5 per cent were regularly using cannabis, and three times this number had tried the drug at least once. Addiction to barbiturates has decreased recently, following a doctor-supported campaign for the replacement of barbiturates by the new generation of benzodiazepine drugs. As a result the number of addicts has fallen steeply.

Glue-sniffing and the abuse of solvents is a recent addition to abuse of inhalants. Nitrous oxide (laughing gas) was so used after its discovery by Priestley in 1776 – 'ether frolics' in the nineteenth century. Glue-sniffing among adolescents was first reported in the USA in the 1950s.

Many industrial products containing volatile solvents are easily bought. Organic solvents such as toluene, benzene, amyl acetate, and butane are widely used as paint thinners, lighter fuel, dry cleaners, hair spray, nail varnish removers and polystyrene cement solvents. They have in common an ability to be absorbed rapidly from the lungs, to dissolve in fatty tissues, to be cerebral depressants, and have chemical side chains which may cause toxic effects on the liver, kidney, brain or heart. Accidental death from cardiac toxicity, or inhalation of vomit whilst stuporose, are hazards. One hundred and seventeen deaths associated with abuse of volatile substances occurred in the UK from 1970–81.

The substance is usually inhaled from a saturated rag or plastic bag such as a crisp bag, or direct spraying on to the mouth or nose. Boys aged 13–16 are common group users, usually casually from curiosity, peer group pressure, or boredom. School epidemics occur. Scottish reports suggest association with social deprivation and alcohol-abusing families. Most casual and group users pass on to other interests, but the solitary and persistent user may become addicted, usually because of other intractable social or personality problems. Mild intoxication occurs in a few minutes and may last up to half an hour, but the experienced user or addict may prolong this to 12 hours' judicious sniffing. The initial euphoria may pass into a confusional state as a result of which offences occur. Treatment suggested has been health education, group activities for bored adolescents, occasionally hospital admission for addicts (Black, 1982).

Mental abnormality, crime and addiction are closely linked with usage of harder drugs. With addiction, the decreasing inclination to work, the increasing cost of the increasing need to get over the tolerance developed, means that money becomes a pressing problem under circumstances of deteriorating ability to gain it. It seems unlikely that the drugs themselves lead addicts to crime, acts of violence or sexual molestation, because whilst taking these drugs, the user's attention is focused inwards rather than outwards. It is his desperation between peaks of mood 'highs', which drives him to crime and makes him a prey to the directions of peddlers.

Treatment of hard drug addicts is not successful over the long term. The main method of treatment is slow withdrawal from the drug over a period of time, in a well-staffed psychiatric treatment unit. There are often unpleasant physical sequelae, such as epileptic fits, the 'cold turkey' syndrome, bodily collapse. A recent research investigation in Britain found that over 80 per cent of addicts over a ten-year period remained addicted or had died as a result of the drug. Other writers have given a long-term success rate of between 10 and 20 per cent. While some good results have been obtained by residential care in supportive or religious communities, departure is associated with relapse.

SYMPATHIN AND THE 'BRAVE NEW WORLD'

Aldous Huxley in his novel *Brave New World* gave one of the best descriptions of a future society able to dose itself with mental stimulants for reward, and solace for frustration. Research has advanced since that time to the point where it is very likely that such drugs will become universally available. Research currently focuses on neurotransmitters with an increased specificity of effect, that is to say the isolation or creation of substances able to stimulate a narrow range of cells or receptors in particular parts of the brain. Centres for well-being and pleasure have been shown to exist in the human brain, whilst in monkeys and chimpanzees, electrodes placed in appropriate parts can be used to create apparent happiness, enjoyment and pleasure.

Most recently the isolation of a substance in the human brain which appears to act as an endogenously produced endomorphin seems to explain some well-recorded instances of pain-free individuals, or those able to carry on fighting despite extensive injury. Synthetic production of endogenous opiate substances may be useful for the future control of pain or some forms of mental abnormality.

Control by drugs can be a personal or a community matter. Some wish to avoid medication, the hypomanic to enjoy his 'highs', or the schizophrenic his visions. Some need drugs to boost feelings of personal inadequacy or to rise from feelings of depression. From the Soviet Union there comes evidence that the state uses antipsychotic drugs to tranquillise 'deviants'. It is an ethical matter how far any court can go in requiring drug-taking by mentally abnormal offenders.

CASE

R. *v.* Majewski (1977) A.C. 443.

REFERENCES

Black, D. (1982) Misuse of solvents. *Health Trends*, **14,** 27–28. DHSS: London.
British Medical Journal (1981) *Views.* **282,** 1082.
Leff, J. (1976) Assessment of psychiatric and social state. *Brit. J. Clin. Pharmacol.*, **3** (3/Suppl. 2).
Mitchell, S. (1982) *Archbold Pleading Evidence and Practice in Criminal Cases.* London: Sweet and Maxwell.

FURTHER READING

The following small booklets on the subject are published by, and obtainable direct from, the Office of Health Economics, 162 Regent Street, London W1. The OHE is an independent organisation founded by the British Pharmaceutical Industry.
No. 25, *Drug Addiction,* 32 pp.
No. 53, *The Health Care Dilemma,* 24 pp.
No. 54, *Medicines which Affect the Mind,* 44 pp.
No. 69, *Suicide and Deliberate Self Harm,* 50 pp.
No. 70, *Alcohol,* 60 pp.

21

Professional Malpractice: Current Risks and Future Nightmares

Michael Craft

Mentally abnormal offenders pose risks for the professional himself. First, it is worth discussing the general field of professional risks with patients. As Parkes (1981) states, 'Professional negligence is one of the great growth areas of the law. Old habits of deference to the judgment and ability of the professional man may die hard, but they are dying none the less; and the wish of the courts both to devise a remedy for the injured and to fix liability on the broadest available shoulders, has tended to expand the frontiers of legal responsibility as well as encourage aggrieved clients to sue the well-insured professional.' In 1980 the then Health Minister, Sir George Young, put it equally clearly when he reminded doctors that each clinical judgement had to be substantiated now that an increasing wealth of knowledge was becoming available to laymen. The recent case of *Whitehouse* v. *Jordan* (1980) caused considerable fright to the medical profession. Here an obstetrician first used trial labour for a delivery in which the fetus had a poor lie, then forceps. The result of the birth was a brain-damaged infant. Although standard practices were used, substantial damages were awarded against the obstetrician in lower courts on the grounds that although the judgements used were standard procedure, yet had caesarian section been used in the first instance, the baby would probably not have been born brain-damaged. The damages, and by inference negligence, were set aside on appeal (*Whitehouse* v. *Jordan* 1981) by the House of Lords which laid down criteria of negligence.

Why is malpractice so important for the practitioner in the field of mentally abnormal offenders? Here law and medicine are already very closely involved, and issues of medical judgement are increasingly challenged by lawyers, whilst clinical assessments of dangerousness look very likely to become court issues in the near future.

How does negligence arise? Once more Parkes (1981), a barrister writer, comments:

It is impossible to catalogue the ways in which negligence may arise, for they are infinite: but a few examples might include failing to prescribe the appropriate drug, failing to respond to a patient's request for urgent treatment, failing to diagnose a patient's condition, failing to warn a patient of the dangers of a course of treatment, failing to make proper inquiries to find out what treatment, if any, the patient has received from his previous doctor, and failing to tell those responsible for continuing a patient's treatment of one's own findings. In each case no damage may be caused, in which case the patient has no claim, or on the particular facts of the case there may be a good defence. For instance, the patient who telephones an urgent request for treatment, may have cried 'wolf' so often in the past that it may be reasonable to treat the 'urgency' with a pinch of salt; or the correct diagnosis may not be one that the ordinary competent practitioner could be expected

329

to reach without the help of specialised equipment not available to doctor or patient. In neither case would there be a failure to meet the proper standard of care. Each case must be examined in the light of the circumstances to see if, on the particular facts, there has been a failure to meet that standard.

And later:

That is not the end of the doctor's responsibility. He is also liable by the principles of vicarious liability for the negligence of an assistant employed by him, and there is no reason why the liability should stop at medically qualified employees; if a receptionist is negligent in, for instance, failing to transmit to the doctor the symptoms described by a patient over the telephone, so that the doctor is unaware of the need to respond properly to the urgency of the situation, the doctor will be vicariously liable for that negligence.

It is clear the field for claim is great. The description given above has been the same for the last century or so in Britain, the United States, Canada and Australia, each having a common heritage of law. What has changed over recent years, is not the wide area available to dispute medical judgement, but particularly in the United States, for 'courts both to devise a remedy for the injured and to fix liability on the broadest shoulders'.

For the British or Australian professional, the results of malpractice can be less serious than for an American because of the more limited financial damage which might be claimed at law, for most professionals will be fully covered against this by their medical insurance companies. Often, the greater loss is in the field of personal health during trials which may be lengthy, or the loss of home, even family, following adverse result. Alternatively, as a result of the increasingly common procedure whereby a tribunal of peers is established within one's speciality to assess whether there has been a lack of judgement or negligence, loss of certification and job may be far more serious than damages, mitigated by insurance. For example, there is the British practice of dealing with doctors whose judgement in employment is questioned, by the 'three wise men' procedure, whereby the employing authority is entitled to ask the medical advisory committee of that authority to nominate three 'wise men' (usually the three most senior specialists) to assess the situation on hand. It was originally devised to deal with doctors whose obvious alcoholism was affecting their work, or specialists who appeared to be mentally ill or abnormal, and who had refused treatment. More recently, it has been extended to practitioners who might have a personality problem, who appeared 'mentally abnormal', as a result of pressure of work, or family, or other reasons, and who committed an offence at law, however trivial. In the context of this book, this type of 'mentally abnormal offender' is in the minority, but as the following case indicates, it behoves us all to take stock once in a while!

Case History
Dr A, 25 years a consultant and chairman of the psychiatric division of his Area Health Authority, was appointed by virtue of his long experience and prowess to head the new (Butler) interim secure unit of his hospital. Although much needed, there was a shortage of funds and staff, but Dr A's pushfulness, determination and briskness gained resources and facilities for his unit that might well have gone elsewhere. Court hearings, staff shortage and colleagues' fury came to worry him. He became stressed, overworked and sleepless; his family doctor prescribed medication to aid his insomnia, and amphetamines to keep him wakeful during the day. Dr A believed there was only another year to keep things going until the promised appointment of an additional psychiatrist. However, his colleagues had had enough of his over-activity and didactic approach. He was seen by

three of them at the end of the year preceding suspension. This was concerning crisp comments to the Regional Hospital Board concerning a colleague. During the interview the colleagues identified themselves as the 'three wise men' appointed by the Regional Health Authority to discuss complaints regarding his over-activity. Dr A said he felt caught in a 'Catch 22' situation. Four months later he was arrested by a policeman for a minor traffic offence and then drove off in a manner which suggested he was not in full control of the vehicle. This was the first motoring offence he had had; there were no previous convictions. At court the policeman gave evidence that Dr A appeared unwell, and his blood and urine showed traces of the two drugs prescribed above by his family doctor. He was fined and the matter reported to the General Medical Council, who later cautioned him as to the consequences of pleading guilty in a police court, but took no other action. He heard nothing further until his return from summer holiday when he received a notice from the Regional Health Authority suspending him. The Regional Tribunal of Inquiry did not meet until the following summer to hear evidence for dismissal. They found only a few of the original charges proved to their satisfaction; namely, misuse of drugs; a bending of administrative rules to gain staff positions for his unit; an altercation with an excited forensic patient which resulted in an exchange of blows. On the grounds that this was behaviour in a manner inconsistent with being a consultant he was dismissed. He did not appeal, deciding that his regional hospital colleagues clearly did not like him, and he would do better to gain a job elsewhere. This was very much more difficult than he expected, since even in a country the size of Britain news of colleagues' behaviour travels fast.

What are the morals of this story? Clearly, over-activity can be construed as hypomania, and if one gains resources at colleagues' expense, this mental abnormality will not make one popular, although it probably needs a conviction for a 'mentally abnormal' staff 'offender' to be dismissed. The use of drugs or alcohol by overworked professionals is extremely common, and it is a risky business for any senior professional who drives a car, to carry quantities of drugs even when the drugs are prescribed by one's family practitioner. In this case, following a police search, no evidence could be found of patients' prescriptions being abused. In the last event, one is subject to judgement by one's peers, and it may be a narrow thing as to whether one is rewarded for getting ahead of them or derogated for succeeding at their expense. This story is recounted to remind readers that so-called mentally abnormal offenders may on occasion be found among colleagues. At peer group review in a competitive practice situation, the review may become personal. A different type of anecdote follows, to describe an alleged shortfall in forensic evidence.

NEGLIGENCE IN EVIDENCE

Evidence at court can be divided into that of fact, and that of opinion. Psychiatric evidence on the degree of mental abnormality of offenders is particularly open to differences of opinion. Where the professional is giving evidence as an expert witness, and his opinion is sought, he should first present the facts, then the deductions that flow from them, finally how he arrives at his own opinion. This allows others to weigh it all in the light of other evidence. It is not only important to be fair, and to summarise the likelihood attached to each deduction, but to so set out one's opinion that judge and jury can decide in the light of cross-examination, whether the opinion is still valid or not.

The case of Dr Alan Clift, a Home Office forensic pathologist, illustrates some of the pitfalls. It is taken from the UK *Sunday Times* (5 July 1981):

Dr Clift's evidence was dismissed as 'discredited' by Scottish Appeal judges last month when they freed John Preece, the lorry driver who served eight years of a life sentence for a murder he did not commit. Since 1977 Clift has been suspended by the Home Office because of concern about his work. At the appeal hearing of the Preece case, Dr Clift was strongly criticised for failing to make it known that Preece and the murdered woman shared the same blood group.

Professor Gilbert Forbes, the forensic expert originally retained by the Preece legal team said last week, 'I was only dealing with one part of the scientific evidence – the hairs found on the murdered woman. I wasn't asked to deal with the blood grouping or anything else. The key thing about the blood group evidence was that *although Clift didn't tell the court about the similarities between the victim and the accused, neither was he asked about it. The defence didn't pick it up, and because of the way evidence is given, he couldn't then volunteer it.*' [my italics] Dr Kenyon Mason, professor of forensic medicine at Edinburgh University said, 'The central issue is are juries capable of understanding modern forensic evidence? Although judges will guide them, judges don't always understand the issues either. The adversary system may not be the best way of dealing with complex scientific details. The Scandinavians have a system with many advantages over ours – their experts argue over a case before it gets into court.

The Sutcliffe case described at the end of Chapter 7 is an example of British practices before and during trial. In fact, because Dr Clift was pronounced as 'discredited' by Scottish Appeal judges, he was suspended on full pay by the Home Office, and the situation was assessed. For Dr Clift the position was particularly invidious, because being *sub judice* he was unable to respond to accusations. As a result of the uncertainty, the government re-examined every case involving his evidence and a number of people convicted as a result of his evidence were freed and compensated. (From the *Daily Telegraph* 22 June 1981.)

In this case, what was at issue was the weighting of evidence. Dr Clift was believed to have given one set of facts, whereas if the existence of other facts had been known to the judge and jury, they might not have proceeded to the convictions that took place. In the event, Dr Clift was eventually subjected to a compulsory peer review, who decided on early retirement for him.

The assessment of opinion in evidence has become more important now that plaintiff's solicitors in respect of a claim for personal injuries or in respect of a person's death, may require the production of all relevant documents. This constitutes the extension of Section 32 of the Administration of Justice Act 1970, following the case of of *McIvor* (1978).

Although solicitors are asked explicitly not to go on 'fishing' expeditions for the pursuit of any medical evidence which may support a claim for personal injury, in practice it is difficult to prevent them doing so, especially when the interpretation of brief comments in hospital casenotes may itself be very much a matter of opinion. Even more than before, it now behoves the professional, after he has separated fact from opinion, to arrange his opinions in the order of probability, so that judge and jury can assess the likelihoods. It also behoves the professional, particularly in the case of personal injury or death, to ensure that inpatient hospital notes are not ambiguous.

In the field of psychiatry (laboratory reports on mental abnormality are less commonly available than in general medicine or surgery!) the number of actions in Britain for negligence or malpractice have been very few, even after the *McIvor* judgments. In a recent survey of the field of medical negligence written in 1980 by Leahy Taylor, Secretary of the London Medical Protection Society, only four out of the 45 cases quoted were to do with mental health. These recent cases are of interest to show the direction of current legal thought.

Case A
In the case of *Bolam* v. *Friern Hospital Management Committee* (1957, 2 Aller 118: 1 WLR 582) the plaintiff claimed damages for fractures received whilst having unmodified ECT with neither relaxant nor anaesthetic. Negligence was denied in respect of danger of possible injury from this treatment. The judge found for the defendant, stating that the plaintiff would have had to have shown that treatment would have been refused if warned of the consequences, and that expert evidence showed that (in 1957) unmodified ECT was in accordance with a practice which had the support of a responsible body of medical men.

Case B
In *Buckle* v. *Delauney* the family doctor prescribed a depressed patient a monoamine oxidase inhibitor drug, verbally giving advice as to which foods to avoid. However, two days afterwards, the client ate a large amount of cheese and on the fourth day died of brain haemorrhage. The court once more found for the defendant on the grounds that the family practitioner had warned the patient and the patient had chosen to neglect his advice.

Case C
In *Landau* v. *Werner* a psychiatrist admitted 'dating' his female patient outside the consulting room. The latter alleged that such action amounted to negligence, and had caused her emotional damage. The Court of Appeal held that contacts outside the consulting room were not condoned by 'the majority of medical men' and thus the defendant would have to show this was warranted by this particular case. This was not done to the satisfaction of the Court of Appeal, who upheld a finding for the plaintiff, saying that the treatment appeared to be wrong.

Case D
The case of *Thorne* v. *Northern Group Hospital Group Management Committee* turned upon suicidal risk. In this area, both professional practice and current opinion has changed over the years. In 1960 Mrs Thorne was being treated on an informal legal basis in an unlocked ward for a depressive illness. She took clothes from a ward wardrobe, returned to her own home, gassed herself and died. The inquest established that she had been treated for mental illness, but was not insane on the day in question. The court held that whilst increased care and attention might reasonably be expected to be given to a person declaring suicidal intent or action, there was factual evidence that on the day in question Mrs Thorne was thought so far improved that she was due to transfer from a highly staffed ward to a lesser staffed one. The court decided that Mrs Thorne appeared to have been determined to escape and commit suicide and appeared to have kept an eye on the staff for this purpose. They therefore found against the plaintiff on the grounds that negligence had not been proved.

In a much later case a Mr Hyde sued the Thameside Area Health Authority in 1981 for alleged negligence of hospital staff in failing to detect and treat his depression to prevent him jumping out of the third floor ward window in the middle of the night, breaking his back and receiving injuries which caused him tetraplegia. The High Court relied heavily upon a fellow patient's evidence that Mr Hyde had been very depressed and had repeatedly said so, and should have been treated more effectively, that nursing staff had not fully informed doctors of the suicidal risk, and awarded £200 000 damages, saying, 'Although Mr Hyde inflicted the injuries on himself, he did so whilst under the influence of a serious depression which would never have come about if the staff had fulfilled their duty.' The Court of Appeal reversed this judgment – Lord Denning holding that close scrutiny of the contemporary hospital notes of the doctors showed that Mr Hyde had been treated with the utmost care and consideration, and no blame attached. The court noted the conclusion of the High Court Judge that the nursing staff had made an error of 'clinical judgement', but stated that this might be negligent and it might not. The question was whether error would have been made by a reasonably competent nurse acting with ordinary care. There were several such qualified and experienced nurses, none of whom had observed suicidal depth in this depression, and failure did not amount to negligence. The sequence of events was a series of possibilities. If the nurses had reported the condition to the doctors, the doctors might have called in a consultant psychiatrist, who might have ordered treatment which might have affected the depression, thus preventing the suicidal attempt, but these were hypotheses. The Court of Appeal also noted a consideration of public policy in that suicide, whilst no longer an offence, was still unlawful, Lord Denning holding that one attempting suicide should not be in a better position than one who succeeded. 'In the end, Mr Hyde's claim failed on the facts; an error of clinical judgement was not necessarily negligence, and the Court of Appeal found nothing negligent about the treatment which he received. But in principle the claim was legally sound, and Lord Denning's strictures on public policy considerations, which carry echoes of a rather sterner and more old-fashioned view of causation and personal responsibility than is generally accepted today, are for once unlikely to be influential' (*Brit. Med. J.*, 1981). Since the quoted passage was written the judgment of Lord Denning has been superseded by that of the House of Lords in *Whitehouse* v. *Jordan* (1981) above. In this important area, a senior Law Lord and Master of the Rolls in 1981 seems not to have shifted as far as public opinion probably has. For patients who clearly and frequently express suicidal intent, most people would say nursing staff should give extra care and observation.

NEGLIGENCE IN AUSTRALIA

What follows is written from the standpoint of personal practice in Queensland, one of six Australian states sharing a common heritage of English law from the time of the foundation of the colonies. These states were federated in 1901, but as late as 1943 the Chief Justice of the Commonwealth High Court ruled that Australian courts as a geneal rule should follow decisions of the House of Lords. However, by 1977, the High Court decided that since there was no longer an appeal to the Privy Council in London, it was no longer bound by the House of Lords' rulings. Nevertheless, in Queensland, as in other states, what would be described as English rulings are given considerable weight in local practice. For instance, a Queensland judge recently commented that the determination of negligence as in other matters is now likely to diverge in the Australian states from that in England, but at present the standard of proof required in cases of negligence is probably higher than in England, and consequently successful prosecutions are few.

As in England, the onus of proof is on the plaintiff, and it is necessary for the plaintiff accusing a doctor of negligence to show that he breached a duty to his patient, or failed to diagnose or treat with reasonable care and skill, and that the breach has resulted in damage to the plaintiff. However, it has been held that a doctor will not be held negligent for the type of treatment prescribed, if that treatment is in agreement with the responsible body of local medical opinion, and thus in any one state a 'responsible group' of local men can be called to support the defendant, and are often successfully so called. In the scattered state capitals of Australia, there is a very close knit accord among local medical practitioners, most of whom know each other closely at a social level. The results are very different from practice in the United States, where among 400 000 medical practitioners, some out-of-state doctor can usually be found to give evidence either for or against a particular point of view. Whilst there are occasional Australian instances of patients receiving compensation or settlement of threatened actions, it has been difficult to prove negligence, and awards of damages in Australian courts are by American standards very modest.

At disciplinary level, the peer group review instanced by the 'three wise men' system in England, has no exact counterpart. In the field of psychiatry, most doctors granted specialist psychiatric status are in private practice, practising one of the varieties of psychotherapy with additional medication as deemed necessary. For the few in state hospital full time employment, disciplinary machinery is essentially hierarchical, and in some states political pressures are high.

Each of the six states has a state licensing board for specialist practice, whose sittings are usually in private. In Queensland, the Medical Board is constituted under the Medical Acts from 1939 to 1976. The disciplinary provisions are more comprehensive than other states, and for that matter England, and can be more formal. Not only may the board make up its mind before hearing the case of a practitioner who has been convicted of indictable offence, but that practitioner does not necessarily have the right to be heard before it formulates its opinion. The Board also has wide discretion in its penalties, fining up to A$1500, issuing a reprimand, allowing the case to lie *sine die* for either twelve months or an unstipulated period of time, or erasing the practitioner's name. Appeal is by way of a Supreme State Court.

In addition to the common offence of drunkenness, other charges can relate to untrue or improper certification, failure to properly report this to the police, and a fairly wide interpretation of 'infamous conduct', which elsewhere might be described as 'misconduct in a professional respect'. For instance the High Court of Victoria (*Hoile* v. *Medical Board South Australia* 1960 104 CLR 157) held that a doctor's name should be erased following a proof that he had indulged in sexual relations with a nurse at his hospital with her willing consent. The circumstances were that the doctor concerned was Medical Superintendent of the County Hospital, the nurse the only duty nurse at this isolated hospital.

Not unexpectedly, many of the cases before Medical Board Tribunals relate to alcohol or sexual matters. Some of these instances relate to doctors indulging in sexual intercourse with patients under treatment, but even when the relationship occurs after treatment has ceased for some years, the Boards have held erasure still to be warranted. More recently malpractice cases in Australia have centred on the Medibank system, with a fraud and overservicing detection system.

The Commonwealth courts are the third tier of the disciplinary machinery relating to psychiatric and other professionals. Under the National Health Acts of 1953 to 1978, patients may receive drugs without other than a nominal charge under Section 87. Section 95 of this Act allows a local Committee of Enquiry to investigate medical practitioners who exceed their authority with regard to these drugs. The local committees of enquiry meet in private, and a practitioner is entitled to be called to give evidence, examine witnesses, call his own witnesses, and address the committee. The Health Insurance Acts of 1973 to 1978 set up the Medibank Health Scheme and allow various medical benefits and payments to be made to practitioners and others. Once more, local committees of enquiry, consisting of some five medical practitioners, may be set up under this Act. Most prosecutions under these Acts have related to excessive prescribing either of drugs, or of pathological examinations, and have been in private.

Recent successful prosecutions have mainly been to establish excessive fee for service, excessive pathology services or excessive prescription of drugs. The panel has been empowered to suspend or revoke authorities to write prescriptions. Although proceedings can be reviewed by a tribunal, the right of appeal is only on a question of law to the Federal Court.

PROFESSIONAL MALPRACTICE IN THE UNITED STATES

Whilst professional malpractice suits may rarely succeed in Australia, and damages are relatively modest, in the United States malpractice suits fuel a sizeable industry. The matter reached crisis proportions in the years of 1975 and 1976. For fear of rapidly mounting claims, escalating insurance premiums and numerous court cases, some hospitals declared they would refuse to admit cases other than emergencies, doctors in one hospital went on strike, elsewhere people feared to treat accidents. Guided by the bellwether state of California, all states rushed laws through their legislatures. It was an almost unique occurrence in the US where fifty states are rarely unanimous about anything. Law in most states is founded on English common law and negligence is defined in much the same way as in England. As the 1973 report of the Secretary's Commission on Medical Malpractice states:

During the nineteenth century and the first two or three decades of the twentieth there was essentially no such thing as a malpractice 'problem' in the United States. On the whole, sickness was accepted as a usual and expected thing. The first significant change began in the 1930s. California suddenly surpassed all other states in the number of malpractice suits. Similar jumps were soon noted in Ohio, Texas, Minnesota and the District of Columbia. Thereafter the number of malpractice suits continued to grow until World War II, when the number of cases temporarily declined. In the 1950s, litigation increased in part because of the increasing availability of medical care for all Americans and rapid increase in the complexity of new medical knowledge. New diagnostic techniques, therapeutic procedures, and powerful drugs were developed, all of which were accompanied by new risks to the patient and new challenges for the physicians.

The Commission spent September 1971 to December 1972 reviewing malpractice in medicine throughout the country, and apart from giving a very comprehensive report also detailed its research in an 870-page appendix. Yet by 1975 the situation had changed. Some insurance companies discontinued business in the field of malpractice, other companies refused to renew premiums, most increased premiums considerably, resulting in physicians in many states threatening to 'go bare', a nice expression for refusing to insure themselves, and when sued, decamp or go bankrupt. Other doctors refused to admit any except emergencies, others threatened to strike. The popular press proclaimed there was a nationwide crisis, highlighted in July 1975 by New York surgeons and anaesthetists declaring emergency service only thereafter. A number of federal solutions were suggested, whilst physicians in all 50 states pressurised their legislators to pass emergency laws which were completed in the winter of 1975 and 1976.

The legislation calmed the air of crisis, but only modified the basis for actions of negligence. Some states enacted a statute of limitations, so that the valid claims would have to be pursued within a shorter period of time. Other states provided a ceiling of damages to modify the previous practice of claiming millions whilst expecting damages in the thousands. A number of legislatures allowed payment of damage to be in annual payments over a period of time, which reduced the element of crisis for individual insurance companies. A number of states followed the Australian practice enumerated above, requiring the 'type of treatment' claimed to be that of the standard of care of local practitioners, rather than out of state, where as noted earlier, one doctor among half a million can readily be found to testify to any point of view. In a rather neat comment upon those doctors who made it their business to appear predominantly or solely at law courts, some states specified that in the case of an expert witness, he must spend three-quarters of his time seeing patients in the speciality concerned.

It was thought that practitioners' oral reassurances to clients could be the cause of misunderstandings which might later proceed to court, so written statements of the effects of treatment were recommended. This meant a typewritten schedule, explaining the treatment, its consequences and its probability of cure, signed by the patient and a witness, to be filed against a possible suit. In a number of states, it was felt that the contingency fee rewarding plaintiff advocates was at the seat of the crisis. Normally, in the USA, the advocate receives at least a third of the court award as his fee after expenses, getting virtually nothing if the case is lost. This practice is justified as being in the interests of the disadvantaged who would otherwise never be able to afford to sue for their rights. It has been said that this system results in greatly inflated claims, 'fishing' for any damage, however tenuous in nature, and the development of 'super experts', a type of doctor who makes a profession of the business. Some legislatures enacted sliding scales of compensation. Other states recommended arbitration, pre-trial assessment tribunals and informal hearings. Only formal tribunals were required to use the rules of evidence. Finally, one state specifically enacted laws to enable easier counter-claiming by aggrieved doctors.

Perhaps more to the point, after the 1975 crises, was a rearrangement of insurance for malpractice. Coincident with the phasing out of some commercial companies, groups of doctors and other professionals began to arrange their own insurance models on the tax profitable, charitable system, whilst 'captive' insurance companies, for instance in the Bahamas, proved very effective. The two latter usually used Lloyds of London by way of a re-insurance system. What was the result of what appeared to be a crisis year? The definition of malpractice as 'professional misconduct, unreasonable lack of skill or fidelity in professional or judicial duties, evil practice or illegal or immoral conduct' (Oxford English Dictionary) has in law three essential elements, viz.: (1) the defendant owes the plaintiff a duty not completed, (2) resulting in damage, (3) which can be proved.

Claims in the United States continue to rise. The Attorney General commented in 1978 that claims had increased sixfold over the previous five years, and increased hospital inpatient cost considerably. The federal government has pressed states to discipline professionals. Every state now has a peer review system and the American Medical Association reported that the number of cancellations of licences to practise rose from 45 in 1971 to 130 in 1976, whilst disciplinary actions tripled during the same period of time. They also estimated that some five per cent of physicians in the USA had alcohol-impaired judgement.

Disciplinary review by way of peer group oversight in the United States centres on required reporting and investigation of one doctor by another in the state, under cover of a legislated immunity from consequence of legal action. The various reports noted above have made it clear that there had been a considerable laxity in reporting of alcoholic addiction by both hospitals and government clinics, whilst the difficulties of dealing with physicians in private practice in competition with their peers in the locality, need no remark. As a result, the confidentiality of patients' records has also become an issue in such peer group reviews, but most legislatures have found no difficulty in ensuring access to these by disciplinary tribunals.

The literature on the subject is now vast, and references for further reading are given at the end of this chapter. By 1980 it was possible for Dunea of Chicago to say, 'The insurance premiums paid by hospitals amount to 1.2 billion dollars and add about five dollars a day to every patient's bill. Although plaintiffs lose nine out of ten cases coming to trial, the total number of suits is increasing by 10 per cent a year, and awards of over $1 000 000 may reward the successful attorney with a fine reputation, a handsome contingency fee up to one third of the award, and admission to an exclusive club limited to the select 95 who have hit the $1 000 000 mark. About 1 per cent of America's 500 000 lawyers specialise in medical malpractice; and for some who could not afford to become doctors, this provides an opportunity to practise medicine once removed. The cases brought before the courts are often surgical, but some are even metabolic, such as when a chloride deficient soya bean artificial milk formula caused an outbreak of metabolic alkalosis in infants.' Fuelling fears for the future he goes on: 'The Federal Drug Authority meanwhile warns pregnant women to eschew the pleasures of coffee and coca cola; refuses to release the promising new drug Isoprinosine for patients with sub-acute sclerosing encephalitis; delays the release of the artificial sweetener Aspartame; fabricates letters to frighten juveniles on the dangers of saccharine; recalls some brands of vaginal tampons, and requires others to label warning of the dangers of the toxic shock syndrome; is upset because farmers still fatten their cattle with stilboestrol; wants drug companies to conduct post marketing drug surveys; will require patient information leaflets for 120 000 000 prescriptions a year at a cost of millions of dollars; and may kill the goose that lays the golden egg, because already it takes ten years and costs $50 000 000 to market a new drug; which suggests too high a price for safety in these days of cost benefit analysis; especially if manufacturers can be held liable for adverse effects that could not have been foreseen 30 years earlier, such as vaginal cancer in the daughters of women who had taken stilboestrol while pregnant.'

In the 1966 edition of the prestigious *American Handbook of Psychiatry* edited by Dr Arieti, it was possible for a leading expert to report only 28 appellant court cases to date in which psychiatrists have been successfully pursued for malpractice. By the next edition of the book in 1975, the numbers were so considerably greater that the areas of malpractice had to be itemised. Although treatment views of 'responsible bodies of medical men' had changed in the meanwhile, so that it was felt unnecessary for instance for suicidal patients to be securely locked in maximum security wards, fresh areas of risk had been uncovered, with psychiatrists being held responsible for the untoward effects of drugs prescribed when their instructions for those drugs had not been issued in sufficient detail. Changes in individual psychiatric practice had occurred. This was partly the result of Medicare schemes and partly because the 'warehousing' of patients in the state mental hospital system was being rapidly phased out. In California treatment is now available for the insured patient privately or at federally subsidised mental health clinics. For the uninsured, unemployed, disadvantaged, or 'skid row' clients there may be little or no treatment. Critics say that the mentally ill now sometimes die untreated in prison with their 'civil rights boots' still on.

The field of negligence is rapidly expanding. In the USA the niceties of medical opinion fuel a sizeable legal industry. In Britain and Australia the degree of mental abnormality among offenders can still be presented to a judge as a matter of opinion and has so far rarely been the subject of later action by the defendant. The case of Dr Clift shows the way the wind could blow in years to come. Following the case of McIvor, the right to examine case histories afforded to solicitors might even allow an aggrieved plaintiff to sue for damages if described as 'psychopathic' without adequate supporting evidence.

CASES

Bolam *v*. Friern Hospital Management committee (1957) 2 Aller 118 1 WLR 582.
Buckle *v*. Delauney Medical Defence Union Annual Report (1971) p. 47.
Hoile *v*. Medical Board South Australia (1960) 104 CLR 157.
Hyde *v*. Thameside Area Health Authority (1981) *Brit. Med. J.*, **282**, 1716–1717.
Landau *v*. Werner (1961) CA 395A 105 SJ, 1008 (The Times 31 Jan. 1961).
McIvor and another *v*. Southern Health and Social Services Board, Northern Ireland (1978). House of Lords Appeal Aller 2 65.
Thorne *v*. Northern Group HMC, The Times, 6 June 1964.
Whitehouse *v*. Jordan (1980) Aller 650 80, 658 E.
    (1981) Aller 287.

REFERENCES

Arieti, S. (ed.) (1966 and 1975) *American Handbook of Psychiatry.* (1st & 2nd edns.) New York: Basic Books.
British Medical Journal (1981) Editorial, **282,** 1717.
Department of Health, Education and Welfare (1973) *Report of the Secretary's Commission on Medical Malpractice.* Washington DC: Department of Health, Education and Welfare (DS), 73, 88.
Dunea, G. (1980) Clandestine clippings. *Brit. Med J., ***281,** 1551–2.
Parkes, R. (1981) Negligence. *Brit. Med. J.,* **283,** 113.
Taylor, J.L. (1980) *Medical Malpractice.* Bristol: John Wright.

22

The Regional Secure Unit

James Higgins

EVOLUTION

The notion of the Regional Secure Unit was conceived in two reports published in the early 1970s: the report of the Committee of Mentally Abnormal Offenders (Home Office & DHSS, 1975) and a Working Party on Security in National Health Service Psychiatric Hospitals (DHSS, 1974), commonly known as the Butler and Glancy reports. Both these reports saw a regional secure unit as essential in solving the acute management and placement problems of the mentally abnormal offender. The remits of the two committees were different, the Butler Committee dealing in a comprehensive way with mentally abnormal offenders as a whole, the Glancy Committee solely with disturbed patients already within the National Health Service, requiring secure provisions. Thus the emphasis of the reports and the estimates of the size of the problem were quite different. The Butler Committee drew attention to the plight of the mentally disordered in prison, the vagrant in the community or under the care of the probation service, in addition to those unable to find a suitably secure place in a psychiatric hospital. The Glancy Committee limited its observations to those misplaced in special hospitals and ordinary NHS psychiatric facilities. The Butler Committee suggested that 40 beds per million of the population were required to solve the problems, the Glancy Report, 20 beds per million. Little research was done to evaluate these estimates, short of asking some of those who were looking after the potential clientele how many patients they had under their care who needed such a hypothetical facility and whom they wanted to be rid of, surely a hazardous and inaccurate exercise. Hazardous because it would raise expectations, and inaccurate because it could lead to quite inflated figures.

No criteria to justify admission to these proposed units were laid down but criteria for exclusion were listed. In brief these exclusions were: the acutely and very transiently mentally ill; the aggressive psychopath immediately dangerous on escape; the severely mentally handicapped; the wandering senile patient. The lack of criteria for admission was difficult to rebut and was undoubtedly seen by many as evasive and possibly treacherous, but uncertainty was inevitable in view of the political and practical necessity of producing some solution even without careful research of need.

As a magical solution the concept of the units was popular as they could be seen as all things to all men, but when costing, staffing and particularly siting were discussed, general enthusiasm quickly evaporated and strident opposition often arose. Nobody wanted such a unit in his hospital, in his locality or next to

341

his patients who would be stigmatised by association. The units, if designed to provide an active, humane and therapeutic environment, would be expensive to build and extremely expensive to run. Their advent unfortunately coincided with the financial stringencies of the mid 1970s. Most regional health authorities, lacking the impetus from medical and nursing staff, refused to find the necessary funds. The hope of the national health authorities that most regional secure units would be operational by 1977-78 became increasingly forlorn. Even the suggestion that small, cheap, flexible and experimental interim arrangements be made was not generally well received, though a few were set up notably in Manchester, Wessex (Faulk, 1979) and Liverpool (Higgins, 1979) in 1976 and 1977.

The first interim secure units were adaptations of old lockable wards in mental hospitals. The security of some of the wards was increased by having prison-type perimeter wire fences; in others only an internal upgrading to improve supervision and control, with strengthened windows and special locks; one was run predominantly unlocked. Staffing levels were increased to an overall ratio of over one to one, which allowing for sickness and off duty allowed most patients to be under reasonable observation inside the unit and to have liberal amounts of escorted parole. Various styles of management evolved, reflecting local conditions and demands, though all had a strong multidisciplinary and therapeutic community emphasis. Despite the limited security provided, few patients were rejected on grounds of security alone. More usually those refused were thought not dangerous enough or because they were unlikely to respond and be discharged within a reasonable period of time.

The obvious success of these interim units and their diversity of emphasis, regime and clientele have highlighted how regional secure units will have to develop; not to a nationally imposed stereotyped plan but in response to local and regional demands and attitudes which can be quite different from region to region even in quite a small country. To stimulate building the government eventually agreed to provide all the capital monies for regional secure units and a regularly increasing proportion of the revenue costs. The first regional secure unit was opened in late 1980, and the second, third and fourth in 1983; two or three others will open in 1984 and the remainder in the next four or five years. Despite considerable political pressure, some regions have been most dilatory and one has even refused to have such a unit as it considers that it does not need one. Some of the units will be opened without extensive experience of running a small interim secure unit and as a result are unlikely to have developed a coherent philosophy, clear criteria for admission, a core of experienced and skilled staff, and the network of relationships and services necessary to make the proper arrangements for the admission and discharge of patients. The interim secure units already opened have shown that such issues take a long time to resolve to the satisfaction of most parties involved (Higgins, 1981).

It has come to be realised that the size of the units might be a most important variable. Most interim secure units have about fifteen beds whereas regional secure units are generally intended to have between forty and fifty beds, though one of eighty beds and one of a hundred beds is proposed. Geographical and demographical considerations are also highly important. How large is the region in area? How is the population distributed? Where are the other psychiatric services sited? How easy will it be to arrange the proper follow-up arrangements for discharged patients? Will the unit staff have to do a substantial proportion of these themselves? To deal with the issues of size and geography, different strategies have been adopted: two equally sized units near the ends of a region; one central more secure unit with two, three or four satellite 'interim-like' units; one central regional secure unit with no satellites but a network of intensive care facilities in large mental hospitals. The interface between the provisions for the troublesome mentally handicapped and the secure facilities for difficult mentally ill patients and mentally abnormal offenders, has also been differently interpreted. Some regions are building special units for the mentally handicapped, but some intend to cope with all but the severely subnormal in the regional secure unit, together with those of average intelligence. In short, the concept of one, large independent regional secure unit has been dispensed with in favour of more sophisticated and more expensive solutions emphasising a network of facilities and an integrated regional service. This heterogeneity, more attuned to local needs, has received the blessing of the Royal College of Psychiatrists.

In addition to the changes above, shifts have occurred in the basic philosophy of the units, their perceived client group, and their relationship to other services. This has probably been due to the fact that the main protagonists of the units have been forensic psychiatrists and not general psychiatrists. It is therefore not surprising that the units reflect the experiences, aspirations and perhaps fantasies of forensic psychiatrists. Forensic psychiatry as a full time speciality is quite new to England. In the 1960s there was difficulty recruiting prison medical officers with sufficient psychiatric expertise, and difficulty in finding psychiatrists in the health service with suitable experience of mentally abnormal offenders. To solve these problems unusual appointments were set up, jointly funded by the Health Service and the Home Office which runs the prisons. The holders were expected to work in and integrate the facilities of both. Each regional health authority was to have such a psychiatrist who, with his academic links, was to stimulate interest in forensic psychiatry and develop services. Eventually eight of the fourteen regions employed such a person. However, for diverse reasons, the number of such posts has declined in recent years, the joint appointments being replaced and even overtaken in number by forensic psychiatrists employed entirely by the Health Service. With the expected development of regional secure units and regional forensic psychiatry services this increase in number is to be praised but increasingly the benefits of contractual working in prisons and other Home Office facilities are being lost. This is of even more pressing concern because of the decline in numbers of senior prison medical officers skilled in forensic psychiatry. Forensic psychiatrists have encouraged a philosophy of care in regional secure units which resembles much more closely the aspirations of the Butler Committee than the Glancy Committee. This development was not generally expected and perhaps not wanted by the health authorities who fund the units and certainly not foreseen nor wanted by general psychiatrists who expected just to be rid of their 'not nice' patients, enabling them to continue towards an even more free and open door policy, preferably in a district general hospital.

As most forensic psychiatrists initially worked single-handed in a region, the regional secure unit plans and policies tend to reflect their particular psychiatric interests and their view of what forensic psychiatry is about. With this reservation there follows an account of developments in Merseyside which aim to provide a comprehensive, integrated regional forensic psychiatry service based on a regional secure unit of fifty beds, preceded by an interim secure unit of initially fourteen and then twenty-four beds.

THE MERSEYSIDE INTERIM SECURE UNIT

Merseyside has a population of 2.5 million divided between Liverpool and Cheshire. Liverpool and its suburbs form a large, urban, industrial conurbation with very high rates of unemployment, an ethnically mixed population and the highest national crime rate; Cheshire has in the main a rich, rural, agricultural population. Liverpool and the cities form a compact grouping with about 2 million of the population; Cheshire is a much larger but much less densely populated area. There are extensive psychiatric facilities usually based in district general hospitals though four mental hospitals remain, two of them very large. Only one of the mental hospitals retains traditional locked wards. Coincidentally, two of the four national special hospitals are sited in Merseyside.

The first interim secure unit was opened in Rainhill Hospital on Merseyside in August 1976. A team had already been set up to plan a definitive regional secure unit as quickly as possible. It was the initial intention to open an interim secure unit in each of the four mental hospitals, a unit which would be truly interim and which would close when the regional secure unit opened. Each interim secure unit was to operate solely within the catchment area of its parent hospital and foster the type of care best suited to local needs. Only the Rainhill Hospital unit, with a catchment population of 1 million, started to develop satisfactorily. The only other unit, sited in a hospital in a rural area, has always had difficulties in attracting sufficient numbers of patients and its function deteriorated because of staffing difficulties.

The interim secure unit at Rainhill consists of a very cheap conversion of a ground floor ward, chosen because it contained fourteen single rooms. It was agreed with one nursing trade union that the overall nursing staff: patient ratio should never be lower than 1.5:1. The other principal nursing union 'blacked' the unit from the outset and still does for ideological reasons. In practice, however, there is now no interference in the function of the unit. In view of the uncertainties in the Butler and Glancy reports, the absence of suitable models, and the inexperience of the medical and nursing staff in the expected type of work, only very vague operational policies were drawn up. Volunteer nursing staff were sought and although the unit has always enjoyed local and national attention, usually favourable, there has never been a surfeit of nurses. Two features became apparent very early on. First, the unit could not function in isolation but only as part of a forensic psychiatry service. Second, some of the patients, often those who had committed a more serious offence, could not be returned as planned to the local psychiatric services with the confidence of the unit staff, the patients or the receiving staff. The crucial importance of these developments was that while the health authority was funding a unit with staff and monies dependent solely on the number of beds in the unit and with the expectation that the discharged patients would return to the conventional psychiatric services, experience was showing that for a significant proportion of patients, separate community facilities and follow-up by medical and nursing staff of the unit were required. Not only did the patients benefit from the more extensive range of services, but the staff also benefited as their job was more interesting and less institution-based. Fortunately, a forensic psychiatry outpatient service had already started in Merseyside in 1975. There were links with the local prison and remand centre and an out-patient department where assessments on bail and follow-up treatment could be undertaken, expanding contacts with the local probation services had been instituted, and informal but very useful links with the local special hospitals had been set up.

Development of the Unit

The history of the development of the unit can be divided into three quite separate phases. The first phase lasted about two years, during which the philosophy of the unit changed as described above, the staff gained experience in running the unit and an appreciation was gained of who should be admitted, as opposed to who should not. In the first year only ten patients were referred for admission, the small number being due to the persisting industrial action. Of these, only six were admitted, three from a remand centre and one each from prison, special hospital, and from Rainhill Hospital itself. All had committed very serious offences, homicide or serious violence or arson, all were psychotic, and half were women. The second year, as the industrial action waned, saw a marked increase in referrals, particularly from within psychiatric hospitals. The increase of referrals from other sources was less marked and out of a total of 23 referrals only 9 were admitted. Again the majority were schizophrenics in their mid twenties and the proportion of women remained considerable. This was a crucial stage of development as, if the high threshold set for admissions in the first year had not been adhered to, the unit would have been swamped by admissions from the local hospitals. The nursing staff had gradually gained confidence and had developed a surprisingly open and free but nevertheless firmly structured and secure regime. Some senior nursing staff had had some initial training in special hospitals to orient them to security considerations but it was quickly appreciated that such experience for the rest of the staff would colour the regime too much with issues of security. The relatively high nursing staff ratio permitted individual treatment programmes with elements of a therapeutic community approach; it was never necessary to deter violence on the ward by sheer weight of numbers.

The second phase, the next three years, was a period of consolidation. The number of referrals rose, but only slowly, and the admission rate remained static at around twelve per year, with almost equal numbers coming from special hospitals, the penal system, psychiatric hospitals and the forensic psychiatry out-patient department. Fifty percent of the referrals were accepted and all had committed most serious offences or had shown most difficult behaviour; 25 per cent homicide, 40 per cent serious violence, 11 per cent arson, and 11 per cent homicidal threats. The length of stay was in general between nine and twelve months. Again, schizophrenia was much the most common diagnosis but the number of those with a primary or secondary personality disorder started to increase. This requires further explanation. It was the initial policy to resist the admission of psychopaths for a number of reasons; considerable theoretical reservations about the treatability of such patients in small psychiatric units, the inevitable political consequences of a serious mishap early on, and the inexperience of the medical and nursing staff in this type of work. The numbers of psychopaths, however, gradually increased principally by the transfer from special hospitals of patients for rehabilitation and resocialisation before their eventual discharge into the community. Such patients would not have been admitted to the unit for treatment after conviction, though perhaps they might have been admitted for a detailed pre-trial assessment.

Most patients have been of normal intellectual ability but a substantial number have been of borderline subnormal intelligence and some have even been classified as subnormal at some point in their career. No patient has been excluded solely on the grounds of limited intellectual ability, but in any event, most subnormal offenders' abilities lie at the upper end of the range. The patients being so small in number and so highly selected, it is not surprising that they are difficult to categorise; however, it is most striking how multiply handicapped they are, having various combinations of mental illness, organic brain disease or epilepsy, histories of early or more recent gross material or emotional deprivation, and considerable limitations of personality and of intellect.

A simple medical approach of drug treatment of illness is rarely all that is required. Social and personal re-training is crucial and this cannot be given solely within the unit if the patient is eventually to be safely discharged to the community. However, if such rehabilitation is attempted outside the unit, staffing levels must be adequate to allow for this. Extensive community activities have developed to the extent that visitors often observe that it is surprising, in a secure unit, to find few of the patients and staff actually on the ward (Parry, 1982).

The last two years have seen the start of a third phase. A second consultant psychiatrist has been appointed, an additional catchment area population of 0.7 million adopted, and ten additional beds in a contiguous ward have been utilised for expansion. The number of medical, nursing and psychology staff has gradually increased and the burden of community supervision of discharged patients and patients about to be discharged is now very great. More than twice the number of patients are now admitted annually. These changes are immediately obvious. There is more uncertainty and discussion amongst staff about the direction the service is taking and the way in which beds in the two wards of the unit should be used. Management structures and policies have become more involved and time consuming. The type of patient admitted has changed; more are being taken for pre-trial assessment, more of them are more actively disturbed, and the level of violence, in what was an almost violence-free ward, has increased. The increasing number of patients from special hospitals, usually with marked and long-standing personality difficulties, poses new problems. There is now a waiting list for admission. Surprisingly, the number of patients coming from psychiatric hospitals and prisons has not increased beyond the previous amount. The rise in the admission rate is accounted for principally by admissions for pre-trial assessment and from special hospitals for rehabilitation. Much time is now spent by staff assessing patients in other settings and arranging accommodation and occupational activities for discharged patients. As suitable accommodation is not easy to find, an attempt is being made, with some success, to obtain accommodation managed solely by the forensic psychiatry services.

Evaluation

What has been happening insidiously and is now clearly obvious is that the model of service proposed in the Glancy Report, that is, a service integrated with the rest of the psychiatric services, was tried initially and did not work effectively for all of the patients. What is now being provided for about half of our patients is a service in many respects parallel to the rest of the psychiatric services. Whether this is an inevitable development in view of the characteristics of the clientele, their source of referral and their needs, or is the whim or idiosyncrasy of the staff, is as yet difficult to decide.

An account of a highly specialised service development has limited value, particularly as the variables which have shaped the development of the service may be peculiar to the unit, its staff, and to Merseyside, in particular Rainhill Hospital and its catchment area. When detailed accounts of the development of similar units are published, the importance of these issues can be evaluated. Rainhill Hospital and other psychiatric units in Liverpool seem much more tolerant of difficult behaviour than seems to be the case in other parts of the country. This has resulted in a low referral rate from within the hospital system and the acceptance that the interim secure unit is not, and the regional secure unit will not be, just a dumping ground for difficult or unwanted patients. The unit was allowed to develop slowly, paradoxically aided rather than hindered by industrial action, and as a consequence it was not flooded with patients. Time was available for the development of practical policies of management, not the imposition of highly academic but untested theories.

These factors have been crucial in the development of the confidence of nursing staff but this confidence will not be fully tested until some serious incident occurs, which fortunately it has not in the last six years. The small size of the unit has been important, particularly as the recruitment of acceptable nursing staff has been so slow, much slower than most expected. Already with the expansion of facilities, the much increased number of patients and staff and the bureaucratic machinery to ensure the necessary consultations, new problems have arisen. These will probably be overcome but only because of a considerable history of successful relationships and success in coping with the problems of discharging very difficult patients. Large units, abruptly opened, will have none of these benefits. The existence of the unit within an existing regional forensic psychiatry service has been most important, indeed, as time has passed, it has become much more difficult to disentangle the skeins of each. One without the other would be a failure. The extensive but very expensive follow-up of discharged patients is probably the most important factor in the successful treatment programme of the unit. It has led to a healthy delegation of responsibility, a broader view for staff accustomed to working solely within the setting of an institution, and a better awareness of the many factors which can contribute to dangerous behaviour, its prediction and prevention. The further developments as a result of the purpose-built regional secure unit to be opened in mid 1983 are eagerly awaited.

THE ROLE OF THE REGIONAL SECURE UNIT

What will be the future of regional secure units and what will be their effects? I suspect many will have difficulties because insufficient attention has been paid to the issues above. Elegant and expensive buildings will be constructed but severe staffing difficulties are likely to arise in all disciplines. While the effects of the units on general psychiatric facilities is likely to be small, their effect on prison will be greater but their effect on special hospitals will be profound. There will be an alternative model of handling difficult psychiatric patients, a model with independence, flexibility, staffing and structural advantages, and essential local community contacts; in marked contrast to the more traditional, national, more isolated and recently much maligned special hospitals. If regional secure units with their higher security and better facilities take even more difficult patients than the existing interim secure units, most mentally abnormal offenders will be assessed in regional secure units, the treatable majority retained, and only the very chronic patients with poor rehabilitation prospects passed on to special hospitals. Dangerousness will cease to be the sole criterion for admission to special hospital. The numbers of patients in special hospitals will decline, short stay patients will cease to be admitted and the already low morale will decline further. Special hospitals could then become the 'back wards' of forensic psychiatry. This should be avoided, with benefit to both regional secure units and special hospitals, if links between them could be much closer, even in a formal way by special hospitals coming to serve geographically compact groups of regional secure units, with interchangeability of staff and expertise, and transfer of patients, even for short trial periods, with a degree of flexibility impossible at the present time. Regional secure units and their staff would then be unable to reject and ignore the intractable difficult patient and provide a comprehensive regional service for difficult mentally abnormal individuals. In short, the only point in having regional secure units is to ensure that the proper liberalisation of psychiatry can continue for the vast majority of patients while ensuring that the currently rejected minority are provided for by a network of services stimulated and serviced by the regional secure unit. Any development not closely inter-related in terms of staff and patients with all the other agencies looking after the client group is unlikely to prosper, and will probably be succeeded in twenty years or so by the need for another facility for the perpetually remaining rejected group.

REFERENCES

DHSS (1974) *Report of the Working Party on Security in NHS Psychiatric Hospitals.* London: DHSS.

Faulk, M. (1979) The Lyndhurst Unit at Knowle *Hospital. Bulletin of Royal College of Psychiatrists,* March.

Higgins, J. (1979) Rainford Ward, Rainhill Hospital. *Bulletin of Royal College of Psychiatrists,* March.

Higgins, J. (1981) Four years' experience of an interim secure unit. *Brit. Med., J.,* **282,** 889–893.

Home Office & DHSS (1975) *Report of the Committee on Mentally Abnormal Offenders* (Butler Committee). Cmnd 6244. London: HMSO.

Parry, J. (1972) A secure environment. *Nursing Mirror,* 22 September.

Royal College of Psychiatrists (1980) *Secure Facilities for Psychiatric Patients – A Comprehensive Policy.*

23

Treatment in Maximum Security Settings

Tony Black

This chapter looks at the various maximum security settings, particularly 'special hospitals', and describes their structures and the treatment environments they provide. It attempts to identify whether and why they work and whether they could work better.

Within this system the chapter also looks at the treatment problems posed by the group defined in the Mental Health Acts of 1959 and 1983[1] as suffering from psychopathic disorder. What is the nature of this disorder; is it really untreatable and, if not, what does effect change in these people?

This leads on to considerations of how one may assess and evaluate treatment success. What methods do we have available and where shall we look to improve them? What criteria of success should apply? This leads to a look at the assessment of treatment outcome and discussion of one particular study carried out by the writer at Broadmoor.

Finally, the chapter looks at implications for the committal, care and discharge of people who have behaved dangerously; for the socio-legal processes available and for the structure and functions of care settings. It examines the alternatives either in existence already or in the planning of future legal and care services.

THE SETTINGS

In General

Maximum security settings in which treatment takes place occur in both the penal and health service systems and, to some extent, within local authority services. Mentally disordered offenders as defined in the Mental Health Act are not appropriately placed in a penal or local authority setting and so are the responsibility of the National Health Service. Nevertheless, for completeness we should mention that many prisons have hospital wings for the care of psychiatric as well as physical disorders, and that some even make a speciality of this kind of work. And one prison, Grendon Underwood, provides psychiatric facilities for some offenders. Its main purpose, however, is to make provision for those time-serving prisoners who present personality or neurotic disturbances. Any prisoner meeting the definitions within the Mental Health Act should be transferred to a special hospital under Section 47 of the Act.

The Health Service's provisions for mentally abnormal offenders are, of

---

[1] References to 'the Act' in this chapter refer to the 1983 Act unless otherwise stated.

course, wide ranging and a court may make a disposal under a hospital order (for example, under Section 37 of the Mental Health Act) to any psychiatric facility which is willing to accept the offender. Figures quoted elsewhere in this book demonstrate, for instance, that almost as many such offenders may be found scattered throughout NHS institutions as are found within the special hospitals themselves.

Then there are the gradually developing services of the 'regional secure units' recommended by the Glancy Working Party in 1975 (DHSS, 1975) and vigorously endorsed by the Butler Report (Home Office & DHSS, 1975) which have received public and official criticism for their slow appearance. These units, however, are not intended to meet the criterion of 'maximum security' although a considerable degree of security is envisaged for many of them.

This is the context, then, in which to set the special hospitals, the topic of this chapter.

In Special Hospitals

There are now four such special hospitals in England and these also accept patients from Wales, Northern Ireland and those remaining colonial dependencies for which the British Government is still responsible. There is also one special hospital in Scotland at Carstairs, known as the 'State Hospital', which is administered by the Scottish Home and Health Department. The English special hospitals are: Broadmoor Hospital in Berkshire, at Crowthorne on the Surrey/Hampshire border; Rampton Hospital near Retford, in Nottinghamshire; Moss Side Hospital on Merseyside at Maghull, almost mid-way between Liverpool and Southport; and lastly the new Park Lane Hospital, adjacent to Moss Side Hospital. In terms of the categories of mental disorder defined in the Mental Health Act, all the special hospitals, and the State Hospital, Carstairs, accept the 'mentally ill' and those suffering from 'psychopathic disorders', whilst Rampton, Moss Side and the State Hospital in addition accept the mentally impaired and severely mentally impaired.[1] The English special hospitals accept patients from England, Wales and Northern Ireland (and the State Hospital similarly for Scotland).

Size and Population

As regards the size of the special hospitals and therefore the population for which they can cater, the numbers of patients they hold have, for many years, been greater than was originally intended. Broadmoor, for instance, was intended for no more than six hundred of which one hundred were women. This assumed that almost all accommodation was in single rooms. At its maximum, however, in the middle fifties the Broadmoor population topped 900. This meant that much day room accommodation had to be given over to dormitories making for considerable overcrowding with its resultant stress, and limiting the treatment which could be carried out. Broadmoor's population is now approximately back to its intended 600 as a result of the transfer of some of its male patients

---

[1] These terms replace 'subnormality' and 'severe subnormality', respectively, in the 1959 Act and connote, as with psychopathic disorder, the addition of a conduct element to the disorder for the purposes of the Act.

to the new Park Lane Hospital, and the closure of some wards to enable rebuilding and modernisation of the hospital that is to take place over the remaining years of this century. Rampton Hospital has always been the largest of the special hospitals, with a population at its maximum of some 1100 but this is considerably reduced today. Moss Side's population has been much nearer the intended 400 mark and a similar total is envisaged for Park Lane when it becomes fully operational.

Staffing

The staffing of the special hospitals, despite popular misconceptions and the impression often gained by visitors as a result of the uniforms worn, is, nevertheless, an almost exact parallel to the staff of psychiatric hospitals nationwide. The basic service, of course, is provided by the nursing staff. The majority of these are qualified mental or mental subnormality nurses and each of the hospitals has had its own nurse training school to prepare candidates for the qualification of RMN (Broadmoor and Park Lane), or RNMS (Rampton and Moss Side). Pupil nurses are also trained for the SEN qualification and, of course, some staff are recruited at the nursing assistant level. It is necessary here to dispose of any misconception that there are separate grades of staff for nursing and security duties. Unlike some other countries this distinction is not made. The maintenance of security rests solely with the staff, both nursing and other professions, who provide the care. The reasoning underlying this is that security is best maintained when staff are in regular contact with their patients and come to know them sufficiently well that they are able to observe and anticipate any hazards to security which a patient's changing condition may present. Of course, physical security is provided by each hospital's secure perimeter (either wall or fence), its buildings (units, wards, sections of the hospital) which are locked off one from another, barred windows and, of course, a rigorously specified system of security procedures which staff must observe. Compared with conventional psychiatric hospitals the staff: patient ratios in the special hospitals are high also for security reasons.

The medical staff complement of the special hospitals similarly replicates other psychiatric hospitals although there tends to be a disproportion towards the higher, that is, consultant grades. This reflects their additional responsibilities for recommending and preparing all movements of patients out of the hospitals and the added workload arising from the numerous applications to the mental health review tribunal. Such applications tend to be much more numerous amongst special hospital patients because the entire patient population is compulsorily detained. A further task now usually undertaken by consultant psychiatrists at special hospitals is the pre-admission visit to see a potential patient at another hospital or on remand in prison. Thus a complement of consultant psychiatrists ('responsible medical officers') of approximately one to every 60–80 patients is about the average ratio for special hospitals. Non-consultant medical staff include some who are senior registrars in psychiatry and others who are designated 'associate specialists'.

Local management is by a hospital management team, the most frequent composition for which is the medical director, the head of nursing services and the hospital administrator. The hospital management team (or HMT) is sometimes augmented with a member of one of the other professional disciplines and in any case usually relates with and works through a forum comprising heads of departments or disciplines.

The other professional disciplines again parallel conventional psychiatric settings and include social workers, clinical psychologists, teachers, psychotherapists, speech therapists, pharmacists, chaplains, librarians, etc. There is also a group which merits special mention because it has no exact equivalent in conventional psychiatric settings. This is the group of occupations officers. They merit such attention because they are the most numerous of the special hospitals staff after the nursing staff and because work activities are of particular importance in the long-stay settings of the special hospitals. Thus occupations officers are not the same as occupational therapists in other psychiatric settings. They are predominantly people with trade skill qualifications who function primarily as instructors rather than therapists. This is because of the tradition in the special hospitals of having workshops which occupy patients in economically productive work. Moreover, this is not only, or even principally, the sort of work that has become familiar in ITU or IRU settings, where work, often of a routine assembly nature, is undertaken on contract for outside firms. Instead it has historically been intended to be work geared more to the requirements of the institutional setting, such as the manufacture and repair of furniture and fittings, upholstery and bedding, footwear, clothing and so on. In certain of the hospitals there has been considerable expansion of this kind of work to include both arts and crafts and work reflecting the advancing technologies outside the institution, for example, electronics, radio and TV building and repair. The occupations officers supervising and teaching these skills, although basically qualified in such trade skills, often also have a mental nursing qualification (RMN or RMNS) and, in any case, inevitably come to function as therapists as well as instructors.

Aside from staff whose function is directly associated with the assessment and treatment of patients, there are other groups of supporting staff. The principal examples are the administrative and engineering staff. As special hospitals are administered by central government, such staff are civil servants in the administrative, executive and clerical grades. They have, in most cases, been recruited from similar grades elsewhere in the DHSS and on promotion are liable to move to other DHSS departments and offices. The hospital administrator is assisted by executive and clerical grades in the various offices to do with finance, pay, personnel, supplies, stores, the hospital estate, medical records, etc. The engineering and works staff are members of the Property Services Agencies (PSA) of the Department of the Environment.

WHO GETS SENT TO A SPECIAL HOSPITAL?

The choice of this heading is deliberate to avoid the preconception inherent in the alternative titles of 'The Patients', 'The Clients', 'Mentally Disordered Offenders' and so on. The title chosen allows discussion of some interesting issues.

As explained above when describing the particular hospitals, all those who arrive for care and treatment must have been subject to detention under the provisions of the Mental Health Act as suffering from one of the four categories of mental disorder, namely, mental illness, psychopathic disorder, mental impairment or severe mental impairment. This, however, does not differentiate those who might be sent to a special hospital from those who might instead go to a conventional psychiatric facility within a district health authority; the difference lies in their perceived dangerousness. The word 'perceived' is to be emphasised for, whilst there is no doubt about the existence of a propensity for dangerous behaviour in the patient's history, there may be doubt over whether this implies a likelihood of dangerous behaviour recurring in the future. At one time the issue was simple: any dangerous offender brought to the court and considered not responsible for his actions by reason of insanity would almost invariably be sent to what was then called a 'criminal lunatic asylum' instead of a prison, this being a humane form of detention for one who could not be held to blame and therefore should not be punished. Advancing knowledge and changes in legislation have blurred this concept, however. The McNaughton Rules and the term 'insanity' embody concepts which have been succeeded by new terms such as 'diminished responsibility' and 'mental disorder'; these mean that degrees of impaired responsibility are at issue instead of loss of capacity for reasonable thought and action. At the same time, secure hospital accommodation was neither intended nor required for 'insane' offenders who merely shoplifted or stole milk bottles from doorsteps. It was the combination of mental disorder and dangerous behaviour which warranted secure accommodation and this meant that the patients admitted to the special hospitals have tended to be those who constitute a serious public risk by having killed, wounded, sexually assaulted or set fires.

These sorts of seriously dangerous offender, accepted by the courts as suffering from mental disorder and therefore requiring care and treatment rather than punishment, comprise, therefore, the people who are sent to a special hospital together with people who have behaved in similarly dangerous ways whilst patients in conventional psychiatric hospitals.

This, then, might be thought to have sorted out the problem of who needs a special hospital place. However, even within these categories, not all are equally prone to repeat their dangerous behaviour or to be a danger to the community at large. Infanticide by a mother during the months following the birth is now recognised to be a quite specific act, usually carrying no implications of dangerousness to other babies, let alone people in general. Yet such women were at one time frequently admitted to special hospitals. It has now become widely recognised in the care professions that violent acts in the domestic setting are often the result of very specific interpersonal and family stresses and do not necessarily carry any implication of hazard to members of the public. Even some of these violent or homicidal offenders accepted by a court as suffering mental disorder may not need the secure provisions of a special hospital. A thorough documentation of the circumstances of the offence; a full medical, psychological and social history; and a thorough assessment of the degree and type of mental disorder presented should help to discern whether there is a need for a special hospital place. Unfortunately this is not always done; it may not be feasible; or it may be nullified by presumptions that all dangerous forms of behaviour must require secure containment.

Another interesting issue here is whether the offence and the mental disorder are linked. Clearly in many cases they are, as for instance the paranoid schizophrenic patient who harbours delusions of persecution by some person or persons and takes steps to eliminate the source of this persecution by violent means. Clearly if one can resolve the paranoid schizophrenia a recurrence of the violence is unlikely; at least while he remains in remission from his mental disorder. Again, there are psychopathic disorders (which will be discussed more fully later on) where offending behaviour is a direct result of the individual's propensity to react to threats and stresses with physical violence, and to do this frequently if stress tolerance is poor. However, there may be other situations where a person initially commits a violent crime for, say, gain or revenge, for which he receives a custodial sentence and then subsequently develops a mental disorder. The Mental Health Act makes provision for this under Section 47 whereby a time-serving prisoner can be transferred to a hospital (special hospital only if he needs special security) if he develops a mental illness. The alleviation of such an illness may enable the prisoner to return to prison but it does not then mean that the offending or violent behaviour will cease; the two are not necessarily connected.

Another, more subtle, situation arises in the case of jealousies and hatreds resulting from stresses within relationships which are neither abnormal nor uncommon and which most people would tolerate or deal with in non-violent fashion. If, in these circumstances, the individual develops a mental illness, suffers a head injury from an accident, or simply becomes disinhibited through excessive use of alcohol or drugs, then the stresses and resentments of the underlying interpersonal problems may well no longer be controlled but may give rise to a violent solution to the problem. It is perhaps this kind of case which highlights difficulties in deciding on placement in a special hospital. It also exemplifies one of the reasons for the introduction of such concepts as mental disorder and diminished responsibility in place of the old 'black-and-white' distinctions of insanity and the McNaughton Rules. By and large, however, the behaviour categories in the special hospitals mostly do comprise forms of extreme violence and public hazard such as some kinds of homicide, wounding and assaults, sexual offences and arson. These, and the mental disorders associated with them, will vary from one special hospital to another. Psychopathically disordered patients are to be found in all the special hospitals, sometimes with the addition of mental illness or mental handicap, and associated with all types of offence. Because of the pervasiveness of this much disputed disorder, and the arguments over its treatability, it will be useful to devote some discussion to it before going on to deal with the treatments available within the special hospitals.

Psychopathic Disorder

A recurrent problem for both the legal and care professions is to decide where disability ends and natural human perversity begins. Even though, psychologically, interventions ('treatments') are possible to change either condition (science and moral values are unconnected) it is the courts' business to regulate society through the socially derived legal concepts of justice and therefore to decide where the blame lies. The introduction of the concept of diminished responsibility is recognition of a human being's variable capacity for self-control. Not only does the obsolescence of the McNaughton Rules emphasise this, but also the recognition that factors other than injury, illness and disease impair such control. It is a matter of continuing debate, of course, once one relinquishes such concepts of injury, illness or disease as the sole impairers of responsibility, how far one then goes in recognising other character disabilities as reducing a person's responsibility for his actions. And if one begins to recognise such widely variable human qualities as impulse control and emotional responsiveness (which seem to be as widely variable as the physical characteristics of height and weight) then how far should one also recognise such other personal and environmental circumstances as, for instance, family relationships, poverty, housing or unemployment? Of course, all of these factors are assessed when compiling patients' case histories and are evaluated in arriving at psychiatric or psychological formulations.

The law, however, has only comparatively recently moved away from injury, disease and illness as the sole basis for judging responsibility to be impaired and has not yet moved as far as recognising social factors for the impairment of responsibility. It has encountered quite enough problems over the concept of various kinds of 'pathological personality'. (Unlike his height and weight, the individual is regarded as having greater power to alter his social circumstances.) Nevertheless, it is quite clear from the array of such personalities as are met in the special hospitals that no single cause can be blamed, such as heredity or an extra chromosome; malfunctioning neurological circuitry of malfunctioning metabolism. Mental disorders, whether they be of the psychotic mental illness type, or of the various neurotic and personality disorder types, probably all owe their pathology to a combination of these constitutional and developmental quirks of the human system. Whatever endowments they start with, whether they finally grow into healthy successful adults or helpless and troublesome ones probably depends on a whole range of environmental factors. The situation may be compared to the growing of crops. A single field of wheat or potatoes in the same soil and receiving the same amount of rainfall and sunshine will not grow into adult plants of the same size or quality. Genetic differences decree otherwise. On top of this, however, other seed from the same supplier but planted in other farms, other soils and under other skies will display additional variations in size and quality. The environment adds its influence to that of inheritance. The public, and sometimes magistrates, may comment when presented with a catalogue of woeful personal circumstances that others suffering similar disadvantages have, nevertheless, risen above them to become useful citizens. This only underlines the complexity of nature and nurture which shapes the lifestyles of each one of us. Within a legal philosophy which takes as its standard the 'reasonable man', it is particularly difficult, once one relinquishes an illness or injury concept for impairing responsibility, to arrive at an alternative set of rules which will adequately arbitrate for such impairment.

Psychopathy inhabits this uncertain world of legal, philosophical and psychiatric doubt and preconception. Nevertheless, an advanced and advancing civilisation has recognised that there are disadvantages other than illness and injury which are to a great extent beyond the control of some individuals and which require a public response which is more contructive than punishment and incarceration. Hence we must grapple with the concepts of psychopathy and 'personality disorder'.

The Mental Health Act defines psychopathic disorder (Section 1.2) as a 'persistent disorder or disability of mind (whether or not including significant impairment of intelligence) which results in abnormally aggressive or seriously irresponsible conduct on the part of the person concerned'. To this definition the 1959 Act added 'and requires or is susceptible to treatment'. The 1983 Act amplifies this phrase in respect of compulsory admissions for treatment under Section 3.2b with the following: 'in the case of psychopathic disorder ... such treatment is likely to alleviate or prevent a deterioration of his condition'. The additional phrase in the 1959 Act and the additional Section 3.2b in the new Act just quoted add a treatability requirement to a clinical concept for legal purposes. This creates two kinds of psychopath – treatable and non-treatable – out of a condition where clinically and certainly psychologically no such difference exists. There is no such distinction made between treatable and non-treatable mentally ill patients. This creates great difficulty for the clinician who, as a witness, has to say whether a particular person before the court, who may be clearly a psychopath in clinical terms, is also treatable for legal 'sentencing' (disposal) purposes.

Treatability in psychiatric settings is often very much a 'try-it-and-see' situation, especially with personality disorders. Another problem occurs if, after admission to hospital as treatable (upon which the court's decision has depended), the psychopath turns out not to be. Return to court is not possible under the terms of an interim hospital order (though could be if certain proposals of the Butler Committee were enacted); nor is transfer to prison, because the psychopath was not sentenced in the first place but was made the subject of a hospital order as a person not fully reponsible for his actions. Discharge would not usually be regarded as appropriate. The probable result is a continued hospital stay and the hope that a treatment will eventually be found that will work. Other problems and other consequences beset the treatability issue, but these examples illustrate the point for present purposes.

It is not only the treatability issue which gives rise to concern, however. To return to the first part of the definition of psychopathy, based on long-standing aggressive or otherwise irresponsible conduct, and attributed to mental disorder or disability, this could be applied to many patients in many diagnostic categories. For instance, there are paranoid schizophrenics whose condition is persistent and whose behaviour may be abnormally aggressive. They are not classified psychopathic because an alternative, more clinically satisfactory and comprehensive description is available for them. Clinical definitions are more specific and circumscribed than a legal categorisation can or is intended to be. Clinical definitions have an explanatory, a prescriptive and prognostic function as well as a diagnostic one instead of the socially regulating function of the legal definition. In the case of psychopathy they make use of such psychological qualities as 'failure to profit by and learn from experience'; 'failure to control impulses'; 'failure to acquire normally accepted social standards, resulting in antisocial behaviour and ultimately aggression'; 'emotional coldness and callousness, resulting in lack of sensitivity to the feelings and needs of others and an inability to maintain normally warm and enduring human relationships'. These elaborations by Cleckley (1955) have been repeatedly invoked by other workers in the field of psychopathy such as Albert et al (1959), Craft (1966) and Hare (1970). Such a clinical amplification, however, still attributes these characteristics to a 'defect or disability of "mind"' which, as many writers have pointed out, is a tautology because the only evidence forthcoming for such defect or disability has traditionally been the very collection of behaviours or traits which are supposed to have *resulted* from such defect or disability of mind. In the case of those psychopathic patients who have offended we thus have further confusion following from the legal–clinical ones: a condition which is considered to be beyond the individual's control, by reason of which he is partially absolved from responsibility for his actions and for which he is considered eligible for medical treatment, then turns out to be substantiable only by means of a description of a cluster of social defects which, in other words, constitute the charge on which he is brought to court.

Nevertheless, recent researches into the phenomenon of psychopathy do support the notions, firstly, that psychopathy is a distinct and valid entity and, secondly, that there are distinct personality differences and neurological mechanisms associated with the condition. This is not to say that the causes are necessarily known; but at least if a set of correlated characteristics can be consistently described, there may be a basis, firstly, for appropriate disposal by the courts and, secondly, for planning rational remedial programmes. Much of this, of course, still remains to be tested. So far, however, treatments have been based on the principles of behaviour change which seem to apply to all people, psychopaths being no exception. The observation that many psychopaths seem to fail to learn and profit from their experiences is relative. Investigation demonstrates not so much that they lack this capacity as that they are relatively slow to form certain categories of behavioural learning connections or that they are susceptible to different kinds of motivation.

The different definitions of psychopathy deriving from legal, medical and psychological practices may not be too much of a handicap in deciding disposal and treatment so long as the social, psychological and neurological components of the condition are distinguished and specified. This does not mean that there will be a standard treatment programme for all who are classified as psychopathic. Antisocial and aggressive behaviour in people identified as psychopathic may arise from a number of different causes and may require one or more of a number of different treatment approaches. For instance, an impulsive, extraverted, emotionally callous individual with poor stress tolerance who resolves threat to such tolerance by aggressive means may require a quite different treatment approach from a shy, ruminating, introspective and emotionally sensitive aggressor. Both can equally be found within the Mental Health Act definition of psychopathic disorder but their psychological descriptions and treatment requirements will be quite different. These differences will be illustrated later on when the range of available treatment processes in use in the special hospitals is discussed. However, it needs to be emphasised here that if psychopathy is seen as a socio-behavioural phenomenon resulting from a number of complex but critical mixtures of individual and environmental causes, then it must be regarded as potentially treatable; any such behaviour is, in principle, modifiable. Whether or not a neurological or biochemical basis which can be modified or controlled is eventually confirmed, the deviant social behaviour which comprises the outward and visible manifestation of psychopathy should be changeable according to the same principles which develop, maintain or change any other sort of behaviour. Whether a programme can be devised to effect this, however, is another matter. It may be that certain behaviours are so strongly formed by the time adulthood is reached that there is no treatment programme whose incentives are sufficiently powerful to achieve the required behaviour change whilst remaining at the same time ethically acceptable. At the moment, however, it does not look as though psychopathy comes into such a category. Even if, like deafness or thalidomide damage, no amount of treatment can restore the faculty, or lost growth, nevertheless training programmes look to be possible which can overcome, offset or minimise the dysfunction.

TREATMENTS

In General

Special hospitals, like any other hospitals for the mentally ill or handicapped, are provided with the staff and the equipment to carry out any of the standard treatments to be found elsewhere in the National Health Service. The history of the special hospitals demonstrates that most of the new discoveries and developments have at some time been tried within the special hospitals. Many of these have proved effective and they continue. Brain surgery, however, such as prefrontal leucotomy or temporal lobotomy, is generally regarded as inappropriate. One of the main reasons for this is that an effect of such neurosurgery is disinhibition. Indeed, this was one of the aims of such surgery in, for instance, cases of severe obsessional neurosis. Disinhibition in patients already lacking inhibition over their dangerous impulses is, however, quite contrary to the treatment needs of most special hospitals' patients. Over the years some previously leucotomised patients have been admitted to special hospitals. This has tended to confirm the view that such brain surgery is inappropriate for patients at the special hospitals.

The main treatment difference between the special hospitals and other hospitals for the mentally ill or handicapped is in the frequency with which the available treatment methods are used. Whilst it may be thought that the relatively long stay of patients in special hospitals might lend itself to the more time-consuming forms of psychotherapy and psychoanalysis, these have not tended to be extensively used, at least until lately, for reasons quite other than length of stay. These reasons are that, until the implementation of the 1959 Mental Health Act, levels of professional staff at the special hospitals were very much lower than in regional psychiatric settings. For instance, Broadmoor's second consultant psychiatrist (the first being the physician superintendent himself) was not appointed until 1956. Although a clinical psychologist was appointed at Rampton in 1953, there was none at Broadmoor until the end of 1959 and not until well into the sixties at Moss Side. Effective numbers of consultant psychiatrists, senior registrars in psychiatry, psychotherapists, clinical psychologists and social workers did not emerge until well into the seventies.

Thus, the main burden of psychiatric treatment has been borne by the advancing techniques of physical and particularly pharmacological medicine. Both electroconvulsive therapy (ECT) and a wide range of psychotropic drugs have carried, and look likely to carry, the brunt of the treatment burden. They are cost effective in terms of rapidity of result and minimal demands on staff time.

Where the emphasis is rather different from other psychiatric settings is in the proportionately greater investment in educational, occupational and recreational programmes. This is entirely appropriate in such long-stay settings, where residents need to be occupied. Many residents also possess considerable potential ability which, by virtue of the unstable and deprived backgrounds which have often contributed to their being in a special hospital, has never been developed or found expression. What more natural, then, than to make use of the long stay of the resident population by enabling them to make up such educational and occupational leeway. The bonus for such a programme might also be expected to be the enhanced chances of resettlement into the world outside if new skills have been gained or old ones improved.

Education

The special hospitals, therefore, have classroom facilities and a range of teaching staff. All the special hospitals make considerable use of local education authority teachers, although some teachers are directly employed. A wide range of education is provided, from the basic three Rs, through conventional secondary education, to 0 and A levels and even, in a few cases, to degree level via the Open University. At the same time, various trades, and business and secretarial skills are taught, often in conjunction with the occupations departments and directed towards City and Guilds, R.S.A. and similar qualifications. Another aspect of education is, of course recreation. This might range from the relatively academic, foreign languages, for example, to the artistic and creative, e.g., guitar playing, painting and so on.

Occupational Departments

A wide range of workshops exists at the special hospitals, as described when discussing staffing at the beginning of this chapter. These provide, at one extreme, the opportunity for an occupational pastime, such as art work or various handicrafts, through to a more 'production line' type of occupation such as printing, tailoring and carpentry. At one time such workshops provided considerable economic support to the hospitals in the way of staff uniforms, patients' clothing and the manufacture and repair of shoes, furniture, upholstery, bedding, etc. Considerable use is still made of these workshops for the internal economy of the hospitals, for instance in printing, bookbinding and the building and repair of furniture, radios and televsision sets. Two things, however, have only recently developed in the provision of occupational facilities, the first being occupational therapy and the second, which is to a great extent related to this, the integration of occupational programmes into the planning of individual patients' treatment needs. The reasons for this are that the occupational centres became established largely as ways of usefully filling patients' time, before the advances in all professions which characterise the sophistication of the modern clinical team. It is now recognised that the occupations officers of the special hospitals are well placed to incorporate the concepts of occupational therapy in the occupational programmes of patients so that they are planned in conjunction with overall therapeutic needs. The Boynton Report on Rampton (1980) has emphasised such opportunities.

Recreation

Because of the long-stay nature of the special hospitals, there has grown up a wide range of recreational activities which enable the patients to benefit from the experience of sharing the responsibility for running them. Thus sports are practised, including football, cricket, bowls, table tennis, athletics and swimming. Inter-ward competitions are arranged in addition to a regular programme of matches and competitions between the hospital teams and outside teams. This enables selected patients who become fit enough, to take on the organising and running of these recreations e.g., arranging the fixture lists, selecting the teams, entertaining the visitors, providing refreshments and even umpiring and refereeing. Similar therapeutically helpful opportunities can occur with other recreations, such as compiling and producing the hospital magazine, putting on plays and concerts, arranging arts and crafts exhibitions, discos, and Christmas parties.

The Milieu

All these three treatment provisions, educational, occupational, and recreational, may perhaps be loosely grouped under the heading of 'the milieu'. Milieu treatment is often referred to in disparaging terms and, indeed, its main criticism is that it deals with general social requirements rather than the specific problems of individual patients.

Nevertheless, it is probably unfair to dismiss the beneficial effects of the milieu and before passing on to the specific and individual treatment programmes that are available it is worth examining the milieu in a little more detail. For instance, to emphasise the occupational and educational centres at the hospitals is to ignore the fact that an equal or greater part of the patients' waking hours are spent in the ward, which is therefore an important part of the milieu. Thus all staff, whether in workshops or anywhere else, but particularly the staff on the wards, inevitably play a part in such treatment. The presence of people with knowledge and skills relevant to the treatment of psychiatric disabilities provides a constant stimulus, as well as a constant support and reference point, for patients, large numbers of whom have never experienced the presence and support of families and friends. For most of us, the latter not only provide support but a modifying influence upon our ideas and behaviour; in other words they give us feedback about what is acceptable and not acceptable. The case histories of special hospitals' patients are notorious not only for the enormity of the offences which have often brought them into hospital, but also for the catalogue of woe and disaster which seems to have punctuated their lives from birth. Desertion, neglect, maltreatment, or simply an emotional vacuum, often characterise the backgrounds of special hospital patients. One should not, therefore, belittle the beneficial effect of a constant environment within a setting which provides many of life's needs for patients, many of whom have never previously experienced them. A bed; three meals a day; a place to sit, talk, play cards, watch the TV; the regular habit-building facilities of work and recreation; the presence of staff who, whilst firm, are nevertheless fair and humane; all are part of a milieu which is beneficial to so many people whose chaotic past has lacked just these sorts of things.

Nevertheless, it is where the milieu of institutions is concerned that they have chiefly been criticised. There are several issues here. Firstly, there is the comparison to be drawn between a hospital (whether special or conventional) and a prison; then there is the distinction between a psychiatric institution and one in the field of general medicine; next there is the contrast between institution and community; and finally, within a treatment philosophy which deals with people's way of life rather than a topical or transient ailment, there is the issue of there being no such thing as leaving someone untreated. Where psychiatric and psychological problems are concerned 'doing nothing' may promote change just as much as 'doing something'; and both may move a patient forward or back. How do these several issues limit the special hospitals and what might be done to offset or overcome them?

Hospitals and prison compared

Where the comparison between a hospital and a prison is concerned, therapeutically the advantages are with the hospital and, indeed, prison staff would not claim to be in the treatment business although they acknowledge an obligation to rehabilitate offenders. The principal advantage of the hospital is that it does not represent public opprobrium as does a prison, although undoubtedly, in the case of the special hospital, it represents public control. The offender patient, however, is treated according to how he behaves and there is not the loss of personal identity and self-respect that tends to occur in prison, even though these personal qualities will be less easily maintained in a special than in a conventional hospital. Many a 'personality disordered' patient has arrived in a special hospital from long periods of solitary confinement in prison to find that he 'starts from scratch', is treated on his merits and his past is not held against him. His response is usually correspondingly normal and his former prison officers are often surprised at his new-found social conformity in response to encouragement and opportunity. A special hospital, however, occupies a less favourable position than a local psychiatric hospital in these respects. Because many of its residents are offenders something of the judgemental attitude of the prison characterises some of the staff most of the time, most of the staff some of the time. Then there are the security requirements of locked doors, barred windows, checks on incoming and outgoing goods and on the everyday implements of living (cutlery, workshop tools); the routine of counting, observation and supervision; the use of staff uniforms to 'provide ready recognition in an emergency' and all the other indicators that inevitably proclaim a lack of trust. Because treatment so often turns upon human relationships and problems of trust, such an environment cannot be otherwise than a handicap to the treatment needs of most patients.

Special hospital and prison compared

The comparison between a special hospital and a prison draws attention to a paradox which does not exist in the comparison between the conventional hospital and prison. Although some of the residents in conventional psychiatric hospitals are compulsorily detained under the provisions of the Mental Health Act, most are voluntary patients who are free to leave hospital if they wish to do so. They remain so long as they accept a need for treatment. All the residents of penal establishments, however, are there to serve sentences of imprisonment during which their lives are under conditions of total control. Special hospitals patients are similarly under conditions of control but in order to undergo treatment, not to serve sentences of imprisonment. The paradox of the special hospital, therefore, is that it is attempting to provide treatment, an essentially voluntary process, under conditions of control normally associated with the serving of a sentence.

Now the attainment of new means and new levels of self-control may be the appropriate therapeutic goal for some patients (especially many of the psychopathic ones) so that the controlling element of the special hospital may contribute to treatment. For others, however, the controlling environment may represent a therapeutic hindrance. Examples are the inhibited kinds of patient with inadequate repertoires of social and sexual behaviours. Less obvious examples are many kinds of patient who, on reaching the rehabilitative stage of their treatment (for example, many recovering from chronic psychoses), need to experience a wider range of more normal, less restricted environments. In both cases it is difficult to achieve the graded transition to an environment approximating the normal world outside hospital without jeopardising or relinquishing the control which is the second element of the special hospitals' purpose.

Another example is afforded by the common psychotherapeutic practice of exploring the conflicts and fantasies of psychiatric patients where usually freedom of expression and confidentiality is crucial to the therapist–patient relationship. If violent urges are revealed in these procedures however, the special hospital therapist is bound to make such preoccupations known in order to avoid risks to others and to observe the control function of the special hospital's dual role. The therapeutic process is thereby hindered and possibly even halted.

Yet another and quite different example is afforded by the need to carry out investigations into very personal and private areas of experience; such as the recording of levels of physiological arousal to emotionally exciting, frightening, frustrating, anger-provoking or sexually arousing situations depicted pictorially and/or in sound. Such recordings can only be carried out with the compliance of the patient, which is invariably confirmed by means of a signed consent form. Nevertheless, the paradox of the special hospital situation is again exemplified when one considers how far such consent can ever be said to be free of constraint. Most patients realise that their ultimate discharge from hospital depends on their agreement to undergo the treatment recommended and considered necessary by the staff of the hospital.

Hospital and special hospital compared

Even so, in some respects the special hospital milieu has advantages over the mainly open environment of the district psychiatric hospital. A community within a secure perimeter can organise many of the corporate activities described in earlier paragraphs (pp. 359–61) which would not be possible in the open situation of a local psychiatric hospital. One of the criticisms of the 'regional secure unit' concept has been that it would be too small in both space and numbers of residents to be able, for instance, to field a football team. Another advantage of a special hospital is the privacy it provides for the notorious offender whose name is a newspaper headline. Whereas a murderer would be a curiosity in a local hospital he is the 'norm' in a special hospital, faces similar problems to those around him and exchanges notoriety for ordinariness. The prospects for treatment are thereby improved.

Hospital and the community compared

Contrasting the hospital milieu with the community raises some issues which also arise in contrasting the psychiatric hospital with the general hospital. The community provides freedom and independence in a way that an institution cannot. The 'vegetable' or 'mindless automaton' effect of the institution is well known and this, like other institutional problems already described, is graphi-

cally illustrated in Erving Goffman's classic book *Asylums* (1961, 1968). However, a more subtle form of dependence is promoted by what may be termed the
'Florence Nightingale' effect of hospitals where the unavoidable helplessness of
the physically sick or injured person, which is usually short-term and which
most patients are thankful to leave behind them, is transferred to the practice of
psychiatric nursing care. This is an effect which is accentuated rather than
diminished by the shift of emphasis in psychiatric care from the former rural
mental hospital to the psychiatric department of a modern urban general hospital. It is usually for the best of motives and derives from the notion that mental
illnesses are like physical illnesses – visitations upon the sufferer of some ailment
essentially separate from the individual's 'self' and incapacitating him so that he
must be 'looked after'. Many psychiatric patients in the acute stage of their
'conditions' (some of which are true illnesses whilst others are dysfunctions of
processes integral with and defining 'self') are indeed helpless to the point of
needing things done for them. Feeding and toilet requirements are instances in
point. And all patients are in need of care, although with some it may be of the
'tender-loving' kind, with others the 'dutch uncle' or 'shot-in-the-arm' variety.
For several kinds of psychiatric patient, however, and for others at different stages
of their disorder, particularly during rehabilitation, it may be quite inappropriate
to perform for them the essential functions of life when they should be learning
or re-learning to do these for themselves. In this way does the institution, particularly the medically-oriented general hospital unit, effect its subtle stultification
of initiative, independence and progress towards total self-coping behaviour.
The admirable nursing traditions of Florence Nightingale, so appropriate for
the medical emergency, are quite counter-productive in many psychiatric settings
and it is only lately that psychiatric nurse training has begun to break away from
its general nursing roots to construct a philosophy and practice suited to the
needs of dependent, non-coping, crippled personalities. So the dangers of the
'mental institution' may not be offset and may even be perpetuated by the
movement into general hospitals.

The drawbacks of institutions of all kinds are by now well understood by
most planners and managers of care. But some of those who carry out the plans
and policies are not always so well informed nor is it always easy to carry them
out in practice. Inertia, apathy, or preocupation with keeping a 'medically tidy'
ward (sheets and towels in order, lists up to date, medicines dished out punc-
tually) can often prevail over the observation, intervention and prevention of
inappropriate coping behaviours, whilst emotional smothering or scolding can
all too often replace balanced emotional care.

There is, however, one advantage the institutional milieu has over the community which tends nowadays to be forgotten in the enthusiasm for community
care and maintaining the psychiatric casualty in the bosom of the family. This is
the respite or refuge factor (the original sense of the word 'asylum' which is now
such a pejorative term). Whether or not Laing and Esterton (1964) are right
when they see the patient as the victim of the family, both may require respite
from each other at some stage of the recovery process. For many distressed and
chaotic families it is a relief to be separated for a while from the stresses or just

sheer hard work of coping with an oppressive environment. It may be a relief for the patient to be away from the demands – material or emotional, work or family – that no longer can be met. For the family it may be a relief to be free for a while from the strain of propping up, cleaning up, chasing up, bailing out or just keeping awake in order to cope with a mentally disordered relative.

All milieux have both beneficial and malign influences and it is a legitimate demand upon the skills and knowledge of those who work in them to capitalise on the one and minimise the other. Care is a continuum, a dynamic process. As one medium of care is created it carries the seeds of its own obsolescence and must be changed for another. One way special hospitals attempt to offset institutionalisation and prepare patients for moving on to a different care environment is to organise outings. These may be leisure outings to seaside or country parks or they may be more functional like shopping trips or to see places of work and meet prospective employers. In this way new skills are generated, old ones revived or prevented from stagnating, within the restrictions of the institutional environment. The generation or regeneration of specific skills leads on to the next section on specific psychological and social treatments.

Psycho-Social Treatment

This brings us to the programmes devised specifically for individual needs. It is always difficult to find a title for this area of work, because of the involvement of several professional disciplines and orientations. What we are dealing with here is the work of psychiatrists, psychotherapists, psychologists, social workers, speech therapists and numerous nursing and occupational staff who treat patients individually or in small groups with a view to promoting increased knowledge, insight and emotional and social competence through psychotherapy, counselling and the behavioural approaches. Increasingly, nursing staff on the wards are involved in these treatments as nurse training programmes at the student and post-qualification level include greater coverage of the growing range of treatment methods. At the special hospitals, too, nursing staff are involved in group treatment processes on the wards.

The traditional and historical emphasis in these forms of treatments has been towards psychotherapy, usually of the more dynamic kind, and various forms of counselling. This is usually the extent of the average reader's knowledge of such approaches unless perhaps the term 'behaviour modification' has become familiar, in which case it is usually obscured by images of aversion therapy deriving from sensational stories of the 'Clockwork Orange' kind. Dynamic psychotherapy and counselling methods continue to have their place and are practised by some consultant psychiatrists at the special hospitals, but more often by specialist psychotherapists. The speech therapist also conducts individual and group treatment sessions designed not only to deal with specific speech problems but also related communication and similar social skills. It is in the area of behavioural therapies, however, that there has perhaps been the most noticeable and significant growth, hand in hand with the growth of psychological services at the special hospitals. The range of work undertaken needs to be described as it is both far removed from, and far more varied than the inhumane and mechanistic image often given to it in the media. Such psychological treatments embrace a range of methods which enable people to acquire new behaviours they have not previously possessed, or to rid themselves of unwanted or inappropriate behaviours. Aversion therapy (the 'Clockwork Orange' concept) was indeed one method of eliminating unwanted behaviours but it is relatively little used these days, not only because of its distasteful ethical overtones, but also because it has been generally found that encouraging new and more rewarding behaviours to take the place of unwanted ones is a more effective way of engendering long-lasting change.

How then are such behavioural changes promoted? With the more traditional psychotherapies the general principle is to try to uncover problems and difficulties which are hindering the individual from achieving a full and satisfying life.

For instance, it may be that individual or group psychotherapy is necessary to promote insight and uncover problems which then need a behavioural training programme to change them. Conversely, it may be that a basic social skills training is undertaken to provide a shy, anxious, withdrawn, socially inept individual with social interactional skills he has never before possessed. Having developed the ability to communicate and inter-relate, it may then be found that he has a need to explore personal problems and feelings with a small group of similarly placed people, and that in this way he can discover that he is not alone in his problem and gain support, confidence and a plan for the future from this therapist-guided interchange with his fellow patient.

Basic social skills training has been a feature of special hospitals work in recent years, as it has become clear that some offenders, contrary to the public image of a 'tearaway', are indeed shy, withdrawn, inept individuals whose offences represent a botched-up attempt to accomplish something they had never learned to do in an acceptable way (e.g., making a social and eventually a sexual relationship). Alternatively, the offence might represent the result of exasperation in such a frustrating situation, the victim being seen as the cause of this and therefore suffering the result of the offender's rage. Such socially fearful and inept individuals are frequent amongst the category of young sex offenders and not only turn out to need basic social skills training but also desensitisation to what amounts to a 'heterosexual phobia'. They often also need sex education because their shy and socially isolated lifestyle has kept them ignorant of this. A comprehensive programme combining several different sorts of treatment approach may be required for many kinds of offender (Crawford, 1979).

Desensitisation is an example of another behavioural approach in which the aim is to detach from a threatening, but normally tolerable, situation the excessive anxiety which is experienced by these people who reach the extreme condition of a phobia. Before desensitisation can be attempted, however, it is usually necessary to train the patient in ordinary relaxation techniques. Then the gradual buildup of tolerance towards the feared object or situation can be started. This usually takes the form of working through progressively more concentrated and realistic activities of the anxiety provoking kind.

Examples with general psychiatric patients would be fears of objects like spiders or sharp instruments, or fears of situations like crowded places (super-markets, the underground or escalators), heights, flying, isolation (e.g. high rise flats, hence maybe also fear of lifts) and the similar stresses of modern western culture. Special hospitals patients have usually reacted aggressively instead of fearfully in like situations to these or their fears may be of particular relationships such as the sexual one which, since it is associated with one of life's primary drives, cannot be avoided for ever; hence the often botched attempts to cope, frequently resulting in violence.

The alternative 'tearaway' approach to life's stresses, in which impulsive intolerance has resulted in success being achieved by dealing violently with aggravation, is also a frequent characteristic of special hospitals patients. In this situation a behavioural training programme requires to be instituted, seeking to replace with socially acceptable solutions to the patient's problems the existing socially unacceptable approach. Replacing one behaviour with another usually presents greater difficulties than simply instituting a behaviour that was never there. Nevertheless, work in the special hospitals has been undertaken to try to do this. As well as conventional 'behaviour modification' this sort of problem appears to be appropriate for the more recent development of 'cognitive behavioural psychotherapy'.

Cognitive behavioural psychotherapy entails, first of all, examining the thinking processes that accompany the antisocial behaviour in order to suggest changed interpretations of what is going on. This may remove the necessity for the patient to see the situation as one where he needs to be aggressive. Alternatively, however, it may enable the patient and therapist to devise an alternative method of meeting the problem which promotes success, and therefore satisfaction, for the patient without the catastrophic consequences of violence. Either way, it is of central importance for the therapist to make use of motivations which are more powerful in the new behaviour than the old, otherwise change will not occur. Towards this end, two resources can be helpful. The first is 'peer group pressure' where a small group of fellow patients may help provide the necessary motivation. Despite a fellow patient probably being just as inefficient or aggressive in his own way and his own situations, he can still often provide a powerful commentary upon his fellow patient's predicament and his effect on others.

Another potent reinforcer is the *video recording*. Not only does this allow examples to be demonstrated of the sorts of behaviour one wishes to help the patient adopt, but it also permits the patient to see the results of his own attempts to deal with social situations. Just as the audio tape recorder shocked many people into disbelief when they heard their own voice, when a patient sees his own social interaction on video tape he can often realise for the first time how off-putting, rude and hostile he appears. When persuaded to try alternative behaviour he can then also see how effective and acceptable this is. Video tape also provides that other requirement of rapid and efficient learning, namely, immediate feedback.

Behaviour modification. The special hospitals which provide treatment for significant numbers of mentally handicapped offenders (Rampton and Moss

Side) lay particular emphasis on behavioural training methods such as 'behaviour modification'. Patients whose intellectual and critical faculties are less well developed will often be helped by the setting up of automatic responses in many social and working situations, and these may either replace inappropriate behaviours or fill what may often have been vacuums of behavioural inactivity. Either way, the opportunity for inappropriate behaviour may be reduced and the satisfaction previously gained from such inappropriate behaviours outweighed by the greater satisfaction gained from the social approval that follows the new behaviours.

This is where the use of outside visits, as described earlier, can be a useful rehabilitation strategy. The novelty of places outside the institution, plus the discovery that one can successfully negotiate situations that were previously feared, shunned or attacked, act as powerful reinforcers to the new behaviours which one wants to see replace the old ones.

PRE- AND POST-TREATMENT EVALUATION

General and Historical Psychiatric Considerations

No treatment can take place until the individual's specific needs have been assessed and planned; similarly the outcome of treatment must be monitored and its effects evaluated. Unfortunately, neither of these procedures can always be assumed. The reasons are several. Firstly there is the well known phenomenon, applicable to many mental disorders just as much as to many physical injuries or illnesses, namely, that 'time is an effective healer'. And there is a great deal to be said for this as the survival of the human species owes much to its capacity, bred into successive generations, to solve its own problems and put itself right. This leads into the second reason, that historically our mental institutions have come to be built in what were at the time, and often still are, rural areas. The reason was probably that land was cheaper in the country. However, there was the added bonus that patients in the then new county asylums could benefit from the fresh air and healthy physical exercise of the outdoor life. To get away from the crowding, pressure and poverty of the growing industrial sprawls of our Victorian cities was beneficial to psychiatric treatment by comparison with chaining madmen to the walls in city institutions. And indeed, such developments often did promote tranquillity and a subsidence of troubled behaviour. To the extent that many mental disorders are stress related, removal from the stress will usually be beneficial. Thus the self-healing properties of the human system plus our inherited institutional traditions have often led to a minimum of attention being paid to the assessment of treatment needs. A third reason rests with the diagnostic process in psychiatric disorders and the available medical treatments. Despite the long lists of disorders in the psychiatric glossaries most of the names are variations of no more than probably half a dozen main psychiatric categories. Apart from psychopathic disorder and mental handicap, most of the patients, in special hospitals in particular, will be classified as some form of schizophrenic or depressive or else neurotic or para-

noid personality disorder. Thus, a relatively small number of diagnostic groupings are likely to arise for which to plan treatment. On top of this the available
medical treatments for such conditions are again limited. Despite the bewildering
array of listed drugs most of those applicable to psychiatric conditions are
derivatives of a relatively small number of groups of chemical compounds. Thus
the evaluation of what medical treatment is needed depends on a relatively brief
diagnostic and prescriptive process which can be carried out almost entirely by
one person, namely the psychiatrist.

Specific Assessment Needs

Yet this chapter has described special hospitals like other psychiatric hospitals,
as being provided with a wide range and growing number of professional staff of
several disciplines and as providing a similarly wide range of treatment facilities.
The tailoring of these facilities to the needs of individual patients does require a
full and careful history-taking and assessment of disabilities. This is why psychiatric assessment must be based on a thorough physical and mental examination with a full family and social history. Treatment specification as well as
diagnostic refinement depends upon this. Equally, however, the prescription of
some form of psycho-social treatment requires both these sets of information as
well as a number of other psychological and social observations. If one is
catering for impulsive, antisocial or aggressive behaviour which occurs only
intermittently and in certain specific circumstances, then a time schedule of
observations by nursing and occupational staff on the ward and in the workshop
needs to be obtained over a baseline period of days or weeks. A psychologist will
also need to take a 'behavioural history' aimed at discovering the frequency and
the precipitating circumstances for such impulsive antisocial or aggressive incidents over the patient's past lifetime. When the circumstances which give rise to
such undesirable behaviours are known, and the outcomes can be specified
which act as the reinforcers for the recurrence of such behaviours, then the
psychologist can begin to plan a programme for changing these. This will be
achieved either by providing more powerful incentives than were available for
the old behaviours or by blocking the unwanted behaviours with freshly substituted unsuccessful outcomes.

Psychological Assessment

As well as psychological or behavioural histories and current behavioural
observations, the psychologist has the assistance of various standardised techniques for describing and comparing patients' personality characteristics. Thus,
tasks in the laboratory or consulting room which simulate real life can often
indicate behavioural deficits or excesses, measured in relation to the responses
of large numbers of other people in a similar situation; these constitute the
'norms' upon which the assessment method is based. Similarly, questionnaires
which have been validated universally can form the basis of estimating how close
to various occupational, socioeconomic or diagnostic types an individual's re-

sponses bring him, again by comparison with norms. The expression 'norms' in this situation represents how far strategies for coping with stress, as shown by answers to the test items, are similar to the results from other known groups of 'stress copers', 'stress avoiders' or 'stress aggressors'. A considerable amount of work has been reported in the psychological, psychiatric and criminological literature with regard to these sorts of human capacities and failings. The clinical work of special hospitals' staff has also provided a steady flow of data which can be used in research. Much of this, too, has been reported in the scientific literature. One example may be quoted from the now quite widely known and replicated finding concerning the personality trait of 'impulsivity'. This trait, measurable from responses to questionnaires (amongst other methods) demonstrates at one extreme a group of highly impulsive individuals and at the other extreme a group of strongly controlled and inhibited individuals. Both extremes of this personality dimension are disproportionately over-represented amongst special hospitals' patients.

Whilst it is, perhaps, no surprise to find that at the impulsive end of the continuum are many of those classified as psychopathic, who have committed a variety of violent offences against the person, it probably will be some surprise to learn that homicides are relatively infrequent at this extreme of the impulsivity personality dimension. It is amongst those at the other extreme – the inhibited group – that the greater proportion of homicides are to be found. This is probably as surprising to most people as that there should be people of this personality type who commit offences at all: excessive inhibition and control might be expected to result in particularly law-abiding behaviour. This is not the place to discuss in detail this phenomenon which is well reported and discussed in the psychological literature (for example, Megargee, 1966, Blackburn, 1971). Figure 23.1, however, illustrates the impulse control phenomenon. The relevance here of this particular personality discrimination emphasises both the strides that psychological assessment has made and the need for such assessment in planning the treatment programmes of various kinds of offender. It should be obvious from this brief reference that a quite different psycho-social treatment

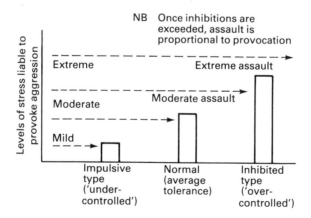

Figure 23.1 Impulse control types.

programme will be required for the excessively impulsive offender as will be required for the over-controlled and inhibited offender.

Additional pre-treatment evaluations need to be made however, not merely of the 'personal styles' of individuals, but also of the particular areas of their lives to which they are vulnerable. Almost by definition the impulsive 'psychopathic' type of person is likely to exhibit law-breaking behaviour across a wide spectrum of life situations. Such is the nature of the trait. With those, however, for whom impulsive or aggressive responses are not habitual, there is a need to specify just what situations prompt aggressive behaviour. Standardised techniques have been developed, in addition to the use of the usual interview, to discern and compare the provocative value for an individual of different life situations, such as relationships with parents, with spouse, with authority figures like the police or one's boss at work, situations where one's personal status and value is threatened, and sexual situations either general or specific to one person or partner. Figure 23.2 illustrates the numerous possibilities that these interactions of personality traits and areas of vulnerability may produce.

Co-ordinating Treatment and Assessment

When all this information has been obtained then an already available treatment programme may be selected or, more probably, a specific programme will have to be devised. It is likely to incorporate an input from a number of disciplines and resources within the hospital. For instance, it may be decided first to encourage movement away from inhibited behaviours by means of, say, a social skills training group. Progress towards more socially viable and effective behaviours may then need to be followed by, say, group psychotherapy in order that the patient's newly developed ability to relate and converse may be used to discover more about his worries and preoccupations. He may then be able to move forward into a more constructive way of thinking about these and planning his future way of life. On the other hand, it may turn out that there are sexual deviations which need modifying, so that a programme of desensitisation to

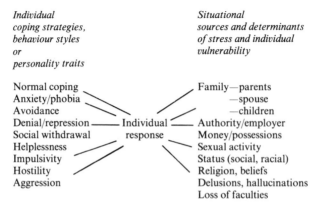

Figure 23.2   Examples of individual-situation interaction possibilities.

heterosexual phobia or aversion to deviant arousal has to be undertaken. In this case, pre-treatment evaluation will need to be carried out by means of laboratory equipment designed to monitor sexual and other physiological arousal to various kinds of sexual situations. This will provide a baseline measure prior to treatment which can then be repeated following treatment.

Post-treatment evaluations make use of the same procedures as have been described for pre-treatment assessment. The same time-scheduled observations of ward and workshop behaviour, such as reactions to other patients and staff, ability to cope with personal needs, all these require to be carried out both before and after treatment. Interviews, from which assessments may be made of the patient's confidence when discussing hitherto sensitive life situations, need to be carried out again. Sensitivities, uncertainties, embarrassments, defensiveness and even concealment are usually apparent to the skilled interviewer. Psychological assessments of the questionnaire type, the simulated task type (e.g. verbal and abstract reasoning, visuo-motor coordination), the physiological arousal type (e.g. pulse, breathing, muscle tension), and various others may also be repeated in order to discern what changes, if any, have taken place.

Evaluation Problems in Special Hospitals

There are particular problems which beset the special hospitals where the evaluation of treatment is concerned. One is the relative dearth of information on how patients in a closed institution respond to the various complex measures which have just been described. In any other setting, for instance, outward and apparent improvement, a feeling of relief from distress and a willingness to return to normal life will usually be sufficient basis for discharge from hospital. 'Norms' for the kinds of assessment described above are therefore rarely obtained after treatment is completed. At a special hospital, however, where discharge is usually a recommendation which has to be supported by the DHSS and endorsed by the Home Office, assurances are needed that therapeutic change is going to be followed by a cessation of the behaviour which brought the patient into a special hospital in the first place. This requires evidence from all the various procedures just described as to their predictive validity in such circumstances. This is difficult because of the rarity of the special hospital situation. Relatively little data will be available from patients discharged from other hospitals if, as has been said, the patient's willingness to leave hospital is regarded as sufficient for discharge to be effected. In any case, the circumstances of patients elsewhere will be different, so comparisons will be spurious. The numbers of patients, moreover, who leave special hospitals is small (300 in 1981) so that norms based on large samples accumulate very slowly. It is not possible to conduct an experiment in which a random sample of patients are discharged in order to see how they fare because of ethical and public safety considerations. Research into the effectiveness of post-treatment evaluations is therefore difficult to promote. Most commonly it is achieved by such methods as studying samples of those patients who are discharged as a result of the best means of assessment so far available and then analysing the differences between those who subsequently succeed and those who reoffend or relapse; or looking at populations of offenders whose offences are less serious than those of the special hospitals' patients but who present similar diagnostic and personality characteristics. Blackburn has reviewed studies of this kind (1980) and finds that the very variable level of success becomes less variable when treatment methods set out to match the problem or the person with the procedure, that is, make it specific rather than apply a 'blanket' treatment.

Conversely, success has been limited when treatment has been carried out in inappropriate settings or when an inappropriate model for change has been used. Success has also been limited when methods have focused on inappropriate targets, for instance, when the target or goal has been conformity to some institutional programme when the offence has been related to quite different behaviours and situations. The natural frequencies of offending behaviours are important here. When such behaviours are of low frequency in any case, and are even lower (or totally absent) within the institution, it is particularly important to identify and tackle the problems which are specifically associated with the offence. 'Institutionally useful' behaviours generated in treatment may be misleading where post-discharge success is concerned.

Thus, treatments that develop behaviours which are 'individual dependent' rather than 'institution dependent' are what the special hospitals should be aiming at. The pre-treatment assessment, therefore, should be identifying precisely the nature of the offending behaviour and the context in which it occurs, so that some kind of replication of this environment in which the treatment can take place, can be created within the hospital. If the patient can learn to generate a new behaviour specifically in the context, say, of being insulted for some humiliating inadequacy, and the new behaviour is then practised in some of the social events within the hospital which approximate social events outside, then, according to Blackburn's analysis, there is a better chance that this new behaviour will carry over into the outside world. Socially controlled behaviours in the setting of, say, the organising of a sports fixture within the hospital and stress imposed by, say, criticism of sporting prowess, valuable though this may be for engendering general control over impulsivity, cannot be expected necessarily to carry over into successful control of aggressive impulsiveness in the outside world in the context of, say, gibes about sexual inadequacy. Thus, treatment which generates behaviours to cope in a socially acceptable manner with sexual gibes is classifiable as 'individual dependent', whereas success at coping with an institutional sports fixture (unless this is the individual's particular problem) comes under the heading of 'institution dependent'.

Follow-up Research

A research study analysing the outcome of discharges from Broadmoor has been carried out by the present author (Black, 1982). A six-year consecutive group of 128 male patients discharged from Broadmoor during the sixties was followed up five years later (see Table 23.1).

Unfortunately, neither opportunity nor the available documentation en-

Table 23.1 Characteristics of the sample.

Number discharged (males only)		128	
During period		1960–65	
Followed-up for		5 years	
By means of		Hospital records	
		SHRU records	
		Mental Health Register	
Average age—	on admission	34.07 years	
	on discharge	41.54 years	
Average length of stay		7.48 years	
With previous—	convictions	77	(60%)
	psychiatric admissions	63	(49%)
	Broadmoor admissions	13 + 1 Rampton	(11%)
Diagnosis (not	schizophrenia	33	(26%)
mutually exclusive)	affective	41	(32%)
	psychopathic	54	(42%)
	organic	14	(11%)
	subnormal	5	(4%)
Offences	homicide	62	(48%)
	others against persons	33	(26%)
	property damage (+arson)	6	(5%)
	acquisitive	23	(18%)
	sexual	4	(3%)
Victims	wife/partner	32 ⎫ 76	(25%) ⎫ (59%)
	other family or known	44 ⎭	(34%) ⎭
	casual/stranger	20	(16%)

abled the success of discharge to be related to the particular treatment undergone by the patients during their hospital stay. Also, during their period in hospital, treatments were general rather than specific because of the very circumstances described earlier, namely, lack of professional staff able to carry out individually planned psychotherapy or behavioural therapy. So the results of the study are a commentary upon the effect of the 'milieu' together with the psychiatric (mostly pharmacological) treatments available at that time. Nevertheless, the sample was surprisingly successful (see Table 23.2). Of the 128 men half had originally been committed following homicide, another quarter for serious personal violence. During the five years after discharge 13 men committed offences involving violence against the person; 37 were convicted of offences more trivial than their original crime. None was involved in homicide during the follow-up period (although two were much later). Half of the sample remained in the community, free of either a hospital or penal admission, for the whole of the five years.

Whilst these results are fairly encouraging they can tell us little with regard to the treatment effectiveness of Broadmoor as it was not possible to relate outcome to the specific treatment a patient had undergone. The intention of the study was to discover, from the kind of data available, the relationship of the

Table 23.2 Outcome summary (based on the 125 members of the sample in Table 23.1 for which information was complete).

	No.	%
Hospital events		
Subsequent psychiatric readmission	24	19
Subsequent Broadmoor readmission	24	19
Both local and Broadmoor readmission	11	9
Neither local nor Broadmoor readmission	89	71
Offender events		
Subsequent court appearances	50	40
Subsequent imprisonment	29	23
Committed further assaults	13	10
(No homicides in the 5-year follow up but 2 later)		
No offender event	75	60
Other events		
Death/suicide	13	10
Success events		
Remained in the community for the entire period	64	51
No psychiatric readmission *and* no court appearance	63	50

Success (in months) of those who incurred 'fail' events

	No.	Range	Mean	SD
Total time spent in community of those readmitted or reconvicted	61	1–59	31	20
Time until first psychiatric or Broadmoor readmission	36	1–59	15	14
Time until first court appearance	50	1–57	21	14
Time until first imprisonment	29	2–53	21	15
Time spent in psychiatric hospital	24	1–59	9	14
Time spent in Broadmoor again	24	4–59	25	15
Time spent in prison	28	1–41	20	11

psychological and diagnostic characteristics of the patients to their eventual success or failure. The group characterised by high impulsiveness, extraversion and psychopathic traits was the least successful in terms of reconvictions, and the group characterised by the opposite trait, namely strong inhibitory controls, was the most successful. Those who had committed homicide, who came into the older age bracket, who had been diagnosed as depressed and whose personality was inhibited and highly controlled were the most successful group (see Table 23.3). Among the reoffenders, however, could be discerned a small subgroup of impulsive psychopathic types who additionally presented signs of emotional instability, that is, low threshold of stress tolerance. These tended to be the ones whose reoffending included violence. Another sub-group of the 'failure' category, comprising those who were readmitted for a recurrence of mental illness, showed more evidence of residual psychotic disabilities, that is to say, raised scores on measures of bizarre thoughts and sensations.

It is important in a study of this kind to take account of differences in the so called 'base rates' for the different kinds of offence. Homicide is well known, for instance, to be a non-repeating offence and not merely for the somewhat cynical reason that many who killed in the past have either been hanged or committed to prison for life. Sufficient numbers have returned to normal life to

Table 23.3 Success and failure tendencies.

Success	*Failure*
No previous history (offending or psychiatric)	Previous convictions
Current offence homicide	Currently property offender or non-homicidal violence
Victim family or well-known	Victim stranger or casual acquaintance
Older	Younger
Under indeterminate 'sentence' (hospital order now)	Under fixed sentence (Section 47 of the MHA now)
Been in Broadmoor longer	Been in Broadmoor shorter time
Diagnosed 'affective disorder'	Diagnosed 'psychopathic disorder'
On psychological assessment:	
Less emotionally disturbed	(a) Psychiatric readmissions: more sensory and thinking disturbance, more hostile attitudes
More socially conforming	(b) Re-offenders: more impulsive and extraverted
Greater impulse control	(c) Subsequent assaulters: more impulsive and emotionally disturbed

have established that their reoffending rates are negligible by comparison with non-fatal assaulters whose offending base rate is usually much higher. This latter group also tends to feature more past convictions for non-violent offences, which usually outnumber the violent ones. The relative success of homicides in the discharge study described again emphasises that little in the way of conclusions can be drawn about the treatment effectiveness of Broadmoor. However, the finding that psychological and psychiatric characteristics of the kind now used to specify treatment needs are significantly associated with success or failure of discharge, suggests that treatment programmes more closely related to the personality characteristics of the patient should augment the chances for post discharge success. It would be reasonable to extrapolate from this and say that taking additional account of specific problems and vulnerabilities, as well as general personality considerations, should further improve the chances of post-treatment and post-discharge success. However, this would indeed be an extrapolation, despite its logical appeal, and further investigation needs to be undertaken yet to corroborate such expectations. Data were not available from this study, but a new study (Norris, to appear), now nearing completion, should throw more light on such issues. This study is more sociological in scope and it aims, *inter alia*, to investigate the associations between the patient's perceptions of personal circumstances and the actual circumstances in which he is situated following discharge. Through a careful process of contact via the supervising doctor, social worker or probation officer, by which the ex-patient was able to decline to be contacted if he wished, but where the supervisor was unaware of his decision, a large proportion of discharged Broadmoor and other special hospitals patients in the community has been visited. The results when analysed will throw light on the particular relationships and influence exerted upon the patients' subsequent survival in the community by such factors as family and general practitioner support, type of domicile, and nature of employment.

IMPLICATIONS

Whether by reason of its treatment provisions or because it contains a more 'success prone' population than is to be found in most other therapeutic or penal institutions, or perhaps a bit of both, the Broadmoor part of the special hospital system would appear to enjoy a reasonably successful record. Because of the uncertain causes, however, this is no reason for complacency. Attention has been drawn in this chapter to fruitful areas for promoting improved treatment success in the future. Moreover, the well publicised disasters of the small proportion of discharged special hospitals' patients who have catastrophically reoffended effectively prevents complacency. Could the special hospitals work better?

Within the Hospital

The results of clinical practice and research do seem to emphasise the need for full, accurate and relevant assessments of patients' backgrounds and current state from the standpoint of all the different professional disciplines involved. If treatments are to be 'individual dependent' and not merely 'institution dependent' then this careful assessment at the outset is vital. One implication, however, is clear straight away from the description of groups of patients occupying opposite ends of the personality trait 'impulsivity–inhibition'. If the special hospitals' milieu provides an effectively consistent and reasonably benign setting in which to shape and control the pervasively impulsive behaviour of one extreme group, then it would seem to be providing precisely the opposite of what may be required for the excessively inhibited group. Yet a secure institution cannot afford to abandon its *raison d'être* for the sake of a group of its residents for whom a controlled environment is counter-therapeutic.

There would appear to be a need for a greater development of units, within the hospitals, providing a specifically tailored treatment regime for specifically selected groups of patients. The large numbers contained in the special hospitals should enable such small units to be created. Amongst these one would envisage a unit, for instance, staffed and organised to encourage emotional expression and the disclosure of feelings and problems by overcontrolled and inhibited patients within a structured daily routine. This would go some way to overcoming the present problem with such behaviour: when developed only within the scope of perhaps an hour's group therapy or assertiveness training, there is insufficient stimulation, practice and opportunity for behaviours to be reinforced and maintained throughout the day. Units organised to do this are as necessary for this kind of patient as a token economy unit would be for chronic psychotic patients. (In fact, such a token economy unit might well be appropriate for an early stage in the treatment of some special hospital patients of the chronic psychotic type.)

Then again, and despite the generally beneficial control provided by the 'milieu', one might also enhance and speed up the treatment response to specific kinds of stress and provocation. One of the counter arguments for this that is commonly raised within the special hospitals is the problem posed by concentrating too many patients of the psychopathic type in one unit. It has been generally accepted to be beneficial to mix psychopathic and psychotic patients. Perhaps, therefore, this kind of unit would be more appropriate for groups of psychopaths at a later stage of their stay in the special hospital when they have begun to show some ability to profit from the effects of the 'milieu'. This would be the time to move them to a unit where there are activities akin to those of the natural environment outside the hospital and where they can test out their acquired control in more realistic situations and learn strategies to deal with the specific threats which arise in the natural environment.

Both types of unit, i.e. for assertiveness and expressiveness in inhibited patients and for the control of impulsiveness in psychopathic patients (and one can envisage others for other kinds of violence-prone interaction as exemplified in Figure 23.2) require the ability on the part of the staff to vary their own patterns of behaviour, and in particular to adjust their values and expectations. The tendency at present is to run the special hospitals on similar lines within a general ethic of humane concern and control (although Park Lane is exploring interesting new possibilities). Explosions of physical violence or verbal abuse are regarded as indicators of failure in the therapeutic process. With many patients, of course, they may indeed be so but with others they may signal therapeutic advance. To facilitate both ward management philosophies on the part of the staff and the maximum effectiveness of the treatment milieu for the patient it would greatly assist if specific locations were set aside for cultivating and enhancing specific behaviours. To be effective such programmes need to be operative for 24 hours of the day and not merely one hour a week.

These sorts of implications are internal to the hospitals themselves and require considerable flexibility and willingness on the part of all professional disciplines if they are to be achieved. They also require new emphases in staff training curricula. It is gratifying to see changes in this direction in the General Nursing Council syllabus and examination papers. Perhaps, however, there need to be specific post-qualification training programmes for special hospitals and maybe something like the courses promoted by the Joint Board of Clinical Nursing Studies should be developed.

Before and After the Special Hospital

There are implications, too, for procedures prior to arrival in the special hospitals and for what happens after leaving. The first is for procedures at the committal stage. The report of the Butler Committee on Mentally Abnormal Offenders (Home Office & DHSS, 1975) has already referred to some of these. In general there needs to be a sharper focus on assessment services provided to the court for all cases of mental disorder, and especially where diminished responsibility is an issue. Alternatives other than a special hospital may be quite appropriate for an offender whose violent behaviour is not generalised but is specific to, say, a private relationship or domestic problem. Lack of understanding of this, however, often leads to considerable resistance to the proposal to admit to a local instead of a special hospital. The problem is especially frequent in the case of mentally handicapped non-offender patients.

At the other end of the process, that is to say where a patient leaves a special hospital, other difficulties arise in trying to arrange aftercare and, in the case of restricted patients, supervision. In these circumstances there again needs to be an awareness that not all mentally disordered offenders have been a general danger. Whilst some may have been, the hostility of others may be specific to one particular person or private situation. The degree of security and supervision following transfer or discharge should reflect this. Transfer from a special hospital is part of a gradual therapeutic learning and rehabilitative process which should replicate that of the ordinary psychiatric patient moving from institutional to community care. Careful assessment, better information to the courts, more precise treatment specification, rigorous post-treatment evaluation and precisely specified after-care provisions are all prerequisites for a more relevant and efficient committal, care and discharge system. Training programmes for all disciplines are, therefore, a top priority in the promotion of this continuing treatment process, extending as it does from secure institution, through an open institution, to supported community living and ultimately full independence.

The Problem of Continuity of Treatment

The continuous treatment process, in which patients move from one set of planned environmental conditions to the next ('reinforcement contingencies' as they are sometimes called), implies the opportunity to move to a new environment when ready. There is a limit to the number of these environments that can be created within a secure institution such as a special hospital. At some point the next treatment move will require an environment only available outside the secure institution. This is the step which is difficult to effect rapidly. Discharge or transfer out of a special hospital, even if only for a period of trial 'leave', inevitably takes time because of the various possibilities to be explored and arranged, precautions specified and authorisation obtained (involving both DHSS and Home Office in the case of restricted patients). This process can occupy not merely weeks or months but sometimes years (Dell, 1980). A delay of this length can set back and often undo the treatment progress up to that point. The result may be to jeopardise the success of the next phase of treatment.

Additionally, the therapist must at some level (although not usually alone, unless he also happens to be the responsible medical officer) be seen by the patient as involved in effecting or preventing discharge from the special hospital to the next stage of treatment or rehabilitation. This inevitably colours the therapeutic relationship and may again hinder progress through the patient's doubt, lack of trust or reluctance to disclose what he fears may hinder his discharge.

There are several possible solutions to the continuity predicament, though all are arguable and none without its drawbacks – otherwise one or other would have been adopted by now. The Butler Committee considered reviewable sentences and referred to the under-employed opportunity to use trial leave or to adjourn tribunal hearings so as to allow preparation for the intended outcome. Some countries and some states of the USA provide for a hospitalised offender-patient to return to court for consideration of discharge.

None of these procedures, however, entirely meets the need for prompt movement on to the next phase of treatment or rehabilitation when progress requires this. A procedure which would is the so-called 'tariff' system by which discharge or transfer to an ordinary psychiatric hospital, as appropriate, would occur at the expiry of a notional sentence or 'tariff' for the offence committed. Objections to such a system encompass philosophical, ethical and jurisprudential concepts: a sentence, however notional, is contrary to the concept of a mental disability court finding with its implication that the offender is not fully responsible for his actions; a codified sentencing procedure does not exist in Britain; the prognostic element is inadequately accommodated; the custodial aspect of the special hospital could be accentuated; and the 'tariff' for certain offences common among special hospitals patients may, in any case be 'life' (murder mandatorily, manslaughter, rape and others on occasion).

Nevertheless, if some way of overcoming or offsetting these objections could be found, the 'tariff' system is one that could provide for movement to an ordinary psychiatric setting after a certain length of time and would facilitate continuity of treatment in some cases. A spin-off advantage would be the removal of the 'gaoler' aspect of the therapist's double image and the removal also of some of the responsibility borne by the special hospital consultant for 'permitting' the discharge of a potentially dangerous person. Such a responsibility is not usually attributed to the person who releases a convict from prison at expiry of sentence or an informal patient on discharge from a conventional psychiatric hospital; these are automatic events on the one hand and self-determined on the other. Only in the case of a life sentenced murderer is there a similar responsibility laid upon the discharging or releasing agency. The Mental Health Act 1983 which has just come into force will effect improvements to some of the problems discussed in this section, principally procedures for trying to ensure the best and appropriate placement at the outset and for reviewing subsequent progress. The problem of treatment continuity, and hence efficacy, is still likely to be with us, however. In any case it is unlikely that all the required improvements will be achieved through statute. The Act's creation of a Mental Health Act Commission, however, may facilitate both the development of good multidisciplinary practice and the provision of appropriate treatment specification, assessment and continuity.

SUMMARY

In summary, this chapter has looked at the present treatment programmes of the special hospitals. In order properly to understand and critically examine these, it has been necessary first to describe the treatment settings which the special hospitals constitute and the rationale for their existence. Discussion of treatment requires also a discussion of associated assessment requirements, which leads in turn to a look at research into the outcome of treatment. Finally the chapter has considered some of the problems and implications.

Acknowledgement and Disclaimer

The author gratefully acknowledges the assistance of many colleagues in the day-to-day work which forms the basis for this chapter, and especially Dr Louis Warnants for help in drafting and with factual material on the special hospitals. Responsibility for opinions expressed is, however, entirely the author's and does not necessarily represent the official views of the managements of any of the special hospitals concerned nor of the DHSS.

REFERENCES

Albert, R.S., Brigante, T.R. & Chase, M. (1959) The psychopathic personality: a content analysis of the concept. *J. Gen. Psychol.*, **60**, 17–28.

Black, D.A. (1982) A five-year follow-up of male patients discharged from Broadmoor Hospital. In *Abnormal Offenders Delinquency and the Criminal Justice System*. Gunn, J. & Farrington, D. P. (eds.). Chichester: Wiley.

Blackburn, R. (1971) Personality types among abnormal homicides. *Brit. J. Criminology*, **11**, 14–31.

Blackburn, R. (1980) *Still Not Working? A Look at Recent Outcomes in Offender Rehabilitation. Paper to Scottish Branch of the British Psychological Society Conference on 'Deviance'*, University of Stirling.

Boynton Report (1980) *Report of the Review of Rampton Hospital*. Cmnd. 8073. London: HMSO.

Cleckley, H. (1955) *The Mask of Sanity* (3rd Edn). St Louis: Mosby.

Craft, M. J. (ed.) (1966) *Psychopathic Disorders and Their Assessment*. Oxford: Pergamon.

Crawford, D. A. (1979) Modification of deviant sexual behaviour: the need for a comprehensive approach. *Brit. J. Med. Psychol.*, **52**, 151–56.

Dell, S. (1980) The transfer of Special Hospitals patients to National Health Service Hospitals. *Special Hospitals Research Report No. 16* London: DHSS.

DHSS (1975) *Revised Report of the Working Party on Security in National Health Service Psychiatric Hospitals. (The Glancy Report.)* London: HMSO.

Goffman, E. (1968) *Asylums*. Harmondsworth: Pelican Books.

Hare, R. D. (1970) *Psychopathy: Theory and Research*. New York: Wiley.

Home Office & DHSS (1975) *Report of the Committee on Mentally Abnormal Offenders (Butler Committee)*. Cmnd. 6244. London: HMSO.

Laing, R. D. & Esterson, A. (1964) *Sanity, Madness and the Family*. London: Tavistock Publications (1970). Harmondsworth: Pelican.

Megargee, E.I. (1966) Undercontrolled and overcontrolled personality types in extreme anti-social aggression. *Psychological Monographs*, No. 611, **80.**

Norris, M. (to appear) *Social Factors Associated with the Re-integration of Ex Special Hospital Patients into the Community*. Report to DHSS.

FURTHER READING

For coping behaviour and behaviour change in connection with personality problems and neurotic reactions
Argyle, M. (1967) *The Psychology of Interpersonal Behaviour*. Harmondsworth: Pelican.
Beech, H.R. (1969) *Changing Man's Behaviour*. Harmondsworth: Pelican.
Kanfer, F.H. & Goldstein, A.P. (1980) *Helping People Change*. Oxford: Pergamon.
Lanyon, R.I. & Lanyon, B.P. (1978) *Behavior Therapy*. Reading, Mass: Addison Wesley.
Meyer, V. & Chesser, E.S. (1970) *Behaviour Therapy in Clinical Psychiatry*. Harmondsworth: Penguin.

Basic and background texts
Bellack, A.S. & Hersen, M. (1977) *Behavior Modification: An Introductory Textbook*. Baltimore: Williams and Wilkins.
Craighead, W.E., Kazdin, A.E. & Mahoney, M.J. (1976) *Behavior Modification: Principles, Issues and Applications* (2nd ed). Boston: Houghton Mifflin.
Stumphauzer, J.S. (1973) *Behavior Therapy with Delinquents*. Springfield, Illinois: Charles C. Thomas.
Ullman, L.P. & Krasner, L. (1975) *A Psychological Approach to Abnormal Behavior*. New Jersey: Prentice Hall.

General books on psychopathy and criminality, their treatment and management from a psychological standpoint
Ayllon, T. & Millan, M.A. *Correctional Rehabilitation and Management: A Psychological Approach*. London: Wiley.
Feldman, M.P. (1977) *Criminal Behaviour: A Psychological Analysis*. London: Wiley.
Hare, R.D. & Schalling, D. (eds.) (1978) *Psychopathic Behaviour: Approaches to Research*. London: Wiley.

24

Should One Treat or Gaol Psychopaths?

Michael Craft

This book earlier suggested that the terms psychopath and sociopath should be seen *quantitatively* as the visible tip of an iceberg of personality disorders, most of which function under a surface of community acceptability. *Qualitatively*, psychopaths have traits of committing repeated offences, lacking feeling for others (and careless as to themselves), being highly impulsive, often aggressive and sometimes vicious or wishing to hurt others. Tolerance, sympathy and community acceptability varies very much in time and place. In view of the lengthy maturation of the psychopath, should one rely on finite sentences, short-term treatment periods or hospital care 'without limit of time'?

From the judge's viewpoint the repeatedly convicted compulsive offender is an enigma because he does not respond to punishment, he gets little from his escapades and soon squanders his gains. He does not even appreciate the help people give him, often biting the hand that tries to feed him. What is one to do? The community has to be protected.

To the probation officer or social worker, this client can be a millstone round his neck. Like the girl in the nursery rhyme, when she is good she is very, very good, but when she is bad she may be impossible. She does great damage to her children and her sorrowing relatives, but always goes for the 'good time', never learns her lesson, weeps buckets of tears, but her suicidal gestures seem to be petulance, for two hours later she is as right as rain. To the client's sorrowing parent, the simplistic and incorrect hypothesis of 'bad seed' or faulty genetic endowment is of small comfort. No one wants to recognise the faulty rearing which is the common background. By the time the psychopath is diagnosed as such, his relatives will commonly have disavowed him, to limit damage to themselves.

To the solicitor, retained by legal aid because this client is penniless if not in debt, the tale of deprivative upbringing, bad luck and mistakes can be sad indeed. The good-looking, good time boy may not choose to remember the lapses of the past, but if the professional cares to elicit the factors pointing to what West and Farrington call *The Deliquent Way of Life* (1977), he can orientate himself (see pp. 218–19).

To psychiatrists, psychopaths are unrewarding and unthankful patients. Some doctors will not treat them at all; others avoid using the term since it negatively labels the patient; still others use them to mine court fees. Some, like

Dr Lawson in Chapter 11, accept them philosophically, or like Dr Black in Chapter 23 define their problems and try to teach 'coping strategies'.

A PERSONAL ACCOUNT OF WORK WITH PSYCHOPATHS

Personally, I have always been fascinated by their short-term hedonistic enjoyment of life, their Oscar Wilde-like yield to impulsive temptation, their extravagant hopes for the future, their crocodile tears for the past. As I started a psychiatric career, it seemed to me that they should respond like young children to affection as well as discipline.

Results from Royal Western Counties Hospital, Devon

Arriving in 1956 in a 2000-bed hospital system for mental defectives with many psychopaths certified from courts as 'morally defective' or 'feeble minded' under the 1913 Act, the first job seemed to be to study their characteristics. At this time many people thought psychopathy was the result of genetic misendowment or 'bad seed'. Indeed, an excellent contemporary Hollywood film, *The Bad Seed*, concerned the angelic looking daughter of a murderess adopted into a good family, who could not help killing her playmates. However, analysis of certified hospital patients showed a very different upbringing. Often illegitimate, usually unloved, they fell behind classmates at school, and were labelled defective. The aggressive became absconsive, delinquent and finally dangerously violent; the shy ones became inadequate, child molesters, drifters. From this 2000-bed hospital, some 50 'recovered' patients were placed each year in residential employment under licence of recall, and I followed up 315 of these, discharged on average 5.3 years earlier after seven years of treatment (Craft, 1958). Of the total 43 had been repeatedly convicted in the past, were affectionless, impulsive on admission, some had been in special hospitals for violence and seemed 'psychopathic'. Yet the follow-up of all these highly selected, well supervised patients showed good results. From an average admission IQ of 68, their intellectual ability had risen overall (one by 40 points). On the day of the follow-up 78 per cent were in open employment (48 per cent in regular work); 43 per cent had married; 27 per cent had children; only 14 per cent had been reconvicted, 5 per cent being imprisoned. These seemed to be quite reasonable results from a very unpromising group. I wondered if they could be improved upon.

The Balderton Adolescent Unit, Nottinghamshire

When I transferred to take charge of Balderton psychiatric hospital in 1958, the Home Office kindly supported a controlled trial of treatment of psychopaths (Craft, 1964). We opened a new ward to be run on a counselling group therapy model, whilst elsewhere in the hospital there was an older type ward run on authoritarian and disciplinary lines. New admissions from courts were placed on a psychiatric probation order: in addition the Home Office was happy to stream in unwanted 'psychopathic' young men from penal units all over the country. Admissions were alternately to the two units on a random basis to evaluate the effects of therapeutic community versus discipline as part of the controlled trial of treatment. The average age (of these 100) was 18.3 years (range 12–44), average IQ 83 (range 56–117), average prior convictions 3.1, average length of treatment at Balderton 11.1 months. At follow-up, an average of 15 months after discharge, 52 in all had been re-convicted, 44 were back in penal or hospital units, 14 were still under continuous treatment. Thirty-nine were employed, two still at school, one had died from a road accident whilst drunk. At a five year follow-up 58 were in open employment, one in sheltered employment, eight unemployed and 30 in penal or hospital units. Analysing statistics, we found the group receiving authoritarian discipline and work training had significantly improved their average scores on intelligence tests to 89.5, whilst the group therapy subjects changed from an initially higher average up to 90.5 which was not significant; individually 19 of the former had improved, compared with only 9 of the latter. On paper tests of impulsivity, the authoritarian group showed a highly significant decrease, while the group therapy subjects showed no change; whilst at follow-up one quarter of the first group and half of the second impressed either doctors, magistrates or both as still needing institutional care. In no test, either on paper or in the field, did the group therapy young men do significantly better than the authoritarian regime young men.

Despite their being a very disturbed group of young men, we found the work enjoyable and rewarding. On a wave of enthusiasm we took them to dances, goose fairs, horse racing and fishing. Over the two years we had no adverse community incidents. After I left the enthusiasm continued under Dr Hunter who persuaded the DHSS to build a new unit, the present Eastdale. I transferred to North Wales in charge of eight psychiatric hospitals. At transfer it certainly seemed that one type of treatment for these dull psychopaths was better than the other, but it was not clear how important were the variables of education and work training. A new controlled trial of treatment was planned and carried into effect, using the best features of results so far (Craft, 1968).

A Welsh Trial of Treatment

Among the eight Welsh hospitals a second trial of treatment was planned. This compared admissions of psychopathic young men throughout Wales, alternately to a group therapy regime in a ward at Oakwood Park Hospital, North Wales, in which the emphasis was on education and a reality testing type of counselling, and to a highly patriarchal system of work training under Mr T. A. Jones, superintendent of Garth Hospital, Dolgellau, Mid-Wales. Once more, among a group of 50 young men on the dull side of average intelligence, results of the Garth authoritarian discipline system of handling, with an emphasis on work training, proved superior. The Welsh Hospital Board ran both hospitals, and disapproved of probation orders, so most admissions were compulsory under

Sections 60 and 65 of the Mental Health Act under psychopathic or subnormality provisions.

In all, 100 young Welshmen were admitted to the two systems with similar clinical criteria as above. Their average age was 19.2 years (range 12–51), average IQ 82 (range 56–133), average convictions 2.8, average length of treatment 9.1 months, with 38 being on compulsory mental health orders (mainly Section 60 psychopaths). Both the Devon results and the Balderton results had shown the importance of statutory supervision, a job being found prior to hospital discharge, and constructive home backgrounds or landladies being involved. To compare results from the package treatment of discipline work training, careful discharge and supervision thereafter, the follow-up time of 15 months after inpatient discharge was chosen as similar to that of the Balderton group (Balderton figures given in brackets); 42 compared with the Balderton 41 were in jobs or in school at follow-up, 40 were still in hospital or prison (44), 13 were still in continuous treatment (14); however only 33 had been convicted (52). At the end of a three-year follow-up most of the Welsh are still on statutory supervision but more were in open or sheltered employment, 13 were unemployed, 31 were back in hospital or prison. Results seemed to show that the directive handling and work training of Garth was superior in results to the Oakwood Park method for dull normal psychopaths. For this, and other reasons, the Oakwood unit was closed, but Garth continued to admit. By 1979, 209 dull normal young men had been treated at Garth.

North Wales Follow-up of 209 Psychopaths Admitted to Garth 1961–79

These 209 admitted to Garth were all within the previous criteria for psychopathy. The Home Office kindly supplied yet another funding for follow-up which was completed in December 1981, the last of the 209 leaving Garth in February 1982 (Craft and Craft, to appear). Research results on the groups treated in Devon and in Nottinghamshire showed that the most effective treatment appeared to be work training with disciplinary background and a type of staff counselling then known as reality testing and now covered by the term 'cognitive therapy' (Meichenbaum, 1977). The most successful group in this series so far treated had been the Devon 43, an important feature of whose success had been five years under compulsory licence under the old Mental Deficiency Acts. The Aarvold Committee considering the most efficient way of discharging dangerous patients whilst safeguarding the public, came to a similar conclusion, namely that results appeared to be best among those who had had jobs and lodgings arranged before hospital discharge, long-term probation officer or social worker supervision thereafter, and return to hospital available in the event of breakdown (Home Office & DHSS, 1973). These principles were already apparent in 1961 from the Devon survey, and were compared with the lack of success beginning to be obvious from the Balderton group. The preferential use of the Mental Health Act (requested by the Welsh Hospital Board for these folk) and the enthusiasm of social workers and psychiatrists in North Wales, allowed similar provisions to be made for the 209 passing through Garth from 1961 onwards.

Looking back, it seems clear that part of the outstanding success of the Devon group of 43 was their careful supervision after discharge. These 43 represented the convicted group of a series of 315 mental defectives discharged from the Devon mental deficiency group over a ten-year period, themselves selected from a 2000-bed hospital. Thus the numbers actually discharged each year were very small in relation to the total patients available, the element of selection for placement was high, compulsory supervision made those on licence very wary of wrongdoing, and at that time in the early 1950s the labour requirements of unmechanised farms were high. It was a good deal easier to place young men in rural farming employment when they had already spent some years in exactly the same type of employment in the hospital farms and horticultural gardens. In contrast, the 209 admitted to Garth during 1961–79 and followed up were the entire admissions to a hospital set up for this purpose during this period of time, and not a highly selected group of discharges as in Devon.

Garth had been set up by the Welsh Hospital Board as a hospital for mental defectives in 1954. Remotely placed in mountains alongside a precipice, it was never intended for other than moral and feeble-minded defectives, sufficiently bright and physically able enough to avoid pitfalls. It specialised early in these, particularly from the slums of Newport, Swansea and Cardiff and the Glamorgan mining valleys, which in any case contain the majority of the Welsh population. By 1961 Garth was fully occupied with 74 inpatients and 12 nursing staff. The small number of staff meant that the most responsible patients were treated in the same way as 'trusties' in prisons. By contrast in 1982 after reorganisation as an interim remand and treatment Butler-style unit, 23 nursing staff cared for 19 inpatients.

The philosophy of care at Garth during 1961–1979 was patriarchal. Mr T.A. Jones, RMN, superintendent of Garth in 1961, was a disciplinarian in charge of a castellated mansion, 12 nurses and 74 able-bodied rascals, not all amiable, in 200 acres of mountain grazing pasture, forest and market garden. The estate was expected to feed itself and for many years had the lowest cost per patient of all Welsh psychiatric hospitals. It also had by far the lowest drug bill per patient. Mr Jones's philosophy was to provide a home, a refuge and an asylum for mentally disordered offenders, in a firmly religious setting, with grace before each meal. Patients and staff stood up when superintendent and doctor came in. The funding committee empowered him to teach inmates good work habits, good social habits, reality testing and further education. There was an obligation to protect society from further wrongdoing for years if necessary, but also to provide a home and refuge for either ex-patients returning voluntarily, sometimes for a holiday, or new admissions from court.

The result was an asylum in the oldfashioned sense, an asylum for residents from deprived backgrounds, unwanted by kith, kin or community, and an asylum for the community anxious to be rid of them for a long time, if not all time. The regime was paternalistic, the work ethic predominant, with emphasis on saving for holidays and for discharge. There was a right to holidays at home three times a year, providing the resident could persuade home to have him.

Otherwise camps and outings were organised: the fairgrounds of Rhyl were particularly popular. Admission was from court on Welsh Hospital Board request, usually without remand and commonly without being seen. Indeed, it was not possible for a single-handed psychiatrist in charge of 1000 other beds to see each applicant. Rather like an army unit or naval ship, orders and new patients were passed along without question, and just like an army unit, the best results were from staff using a sense of humour, all enjoying their work as much as possible, and frequent encouragement from visiting professionals. The first four weeks were the testing time (or assessment time) for each of the three parties concerned in therapeutic contract – nurses, patient and police. The admission motivation for patients was sometimes for 'treatment' or 'care' or sometimes because there was nowhere else to go and for a substantial minority because everywhere else was more hateful than Garth itself was hated.

Departure was easy, for Garth was always unlocked, there was no side room and no psychiatrist within 50 miles for emergency treatment. Miscreants, unwilling for further treatment, simply left. One travelled free on British trains up and down the country for a month, had a brief re-admission but departed unexpectedly because he had left his spare shirt in a railway locker in Edinburgh. Another left the country to visit the leaning tower of Pisa, without a passport or visas. He was picked up in Dijon, with sub-acute bacterial endocarditis, having been sleeping rough (he is among the early deaths to be reported). These two, and others, returned or were returned, and then settled and stayed for treatment.

Discharge was primarily at the request of the patient. The philosophy was to let an order – any order – simply run out, while the resident stayed on. Sooner or later most wanted discharge, often because their friends had found a job, and then the discharge and after-care machinery was set in motion. Some were able to make peace with their families and find jobs with relatives. Others – like present-day divorcees – wanted a clean break with the past and a fresh start in a new area. In North Wales this was arranged for South Walians by way of a 'package deal', North Welsh counties wanting admission for their own citizens resettled South Walians in exchange.

Thus the system worked. It often took a good deal of time. What sort of men did courts and other agencies certify as psychopathic under the Mental Health Act and send to Garth? Most candidates were recidivists in their teens and twenties with long histories of psychiatric disorder. They were not particularly physically handicapped, both because of the precipices and because the non-psychopathic with simple handicaps tended to be more acceptable and wanted by relatives to be in residential units near their home. They were not psychotic because in the early 1960s local mental hospitals still cared for mentally ill offenders in the traditional way. The detailed analysis of case notes of the 209 is noteworthy for several points: a lack of bonding to parents, or parent substitutes and resultant lovelessness of so many, the deprivation of emotional care and material circumstances in childhood; the numbers of school changes and general educational retardation reported among a group who, later in their twenties, had practical abilities and work capability quite close to average; the sheer numbers of illnesses and accidents which left their damage on body and brain;

the carelessness if not recklessness behind many of the offences, suggesting a wish by some to be caught and cared for, although a small and important minority destroyed or damaged property or hurt people in their wish to inflict harm; the sexual ignorance behind many of the sexual offences (this led to a separate programme to aid some of these into a happy marriage; Craft and Craft, 1979); the appreciation of many at being well-fed, warm, cared for and praised for work well done in Mr Jones's 'well run ship'. This represents the sad side of these deprived young men. There were plenty of statistics in the final Home Office report to bear the sadness out. Forty six per cent had had a prolonged, if not complete, separation from one or both parents whilst under the age of 15, while a further 18 per cent had a high degree of home disturbance reported, out of the 84 per cent of case notes that had any record of childhood at all. Only 17 per cent had had a normal state schooling without disruption, expulsion, relegation, or long periods of illness. Early admissions were all tested by a psychologist on admission, with an average of IQ 83 on the Wechsler Adult Scale, similar to the Balderton group, but by the 1970s psychologists had ceased to believe in or do such tests, on the grounds that they underestimated true ability. At Balderton, the average admission IQ was 84. Of the 209, for the 143 convicted the average number of previous court convictions was 3.8, more than the average for the convicted admitted to Balderton (3.1), and Oakwood Park (2.8). About one quarter of the 209 had committed property offences only, 12 per cent sexual offences only, a low number of arsonists were also admitted. It was known that a predominant reason for admission was aggression, particularly among those transferred from other psychiatric hospitals (47 per cent of admissions). Many of these were originally certified and admitted to mental hospitals for violence in the family and community, but had no convictions (see Case A, below).

Diagnostically, a unit set up for offender-patients would expect to have a large proportion of psychopaths and 'subnormals', and so it was. Of the 209, 11 per cent had schizophrenia or affective illness, 14 per cent had a history of brain damage and 9 per cent epilepsy both usually complicating previous personality disorder. The remainder were mixtures of psychopathic or 'subnormal' disorder, with 1 per cent being severely subnormal. A substantial minority (22 per cent) had a history of brain damage, with or without epilepsy, some with frontal lobe syndromes, and gross loss of judgement, forethought and emotional control – yet driving cars to admit themselves! Four had sex chromosome anomalies.

Serious violence to family or community is a trigger for action to be taken to secure asylum for a patient or community. In an analysis of case notes and criminal records it was found that almost two-thirds of the 209 (126 men) had pre-admission histories of physical and sexual violence involving actual damage to persons or property. One hundred and twelve had used violence against other persons, but only 31 had actually been convicted of such offences (12 of these came to Garth after spending time in special hospitals). Fourteen had been convicted of arson prior to admission (including 3 from special hospitals), one other young man had at 15 made a determined attempt to set fire to a bus, but was felt to be 'subnormal' and not charged. The one-third who did not have a history of violence were high social nuisance value and included petty and persistent thieves, men who sexually exposed themselves, and itinerants who stole to support themselves or dodged paying for goods and service.

There was a reversal of these proportions in Garth after admission, with two-thirds using no physical violence. This was thought to be due to the disciplined environment, the ready availability of work, particularly hard, exhausting physical work, and removal from the emotional upsets of a disturbed family life which had provoked them to violence at home. The level of violence during the 20-year period of follow-up after Garth was also lower, with 85 men known to have been violent. Of the remainder, 85 had not been violent, no records were available for 34 (although it is known that eleven of these had no convictions); this includes 16 who were sexually violent, eight who committed arson and nine who damaged property. Treatment at Garth was a median 12 months, mean 23 months,the longest being 14 years 5 months. Four died at Garth in 20 years.

Broadmoor, Rampton, Moss Side and Carstairs transfers made up 12 per cent of the 209 admissions. In the other direction, there were nine direct transfers from Garth to these maximum security hospitals, four for arson attempts, the last of which caused major damage to Garth in 1973. The other five transfers were for extreme violence at Garth, including attempted murder (see case vignettes below). During the 20 years it was found on follow-up that there had been 11 further admissions of ex-Garth patients to maximum security hospitals, 4 of whom had originally come to Garth from a special hospital.

The 324 re-convictions among ex-Garth patients during the 20-year follow-up, affecting 42 per cent, might have been less if over one third (36 per cent) had not been discharged back to their families. Those who did best in terms of lack of convictions and lack of violence were those who had been placed in sheltered housing or lodgings, found employment and assiduously supervised. Unfortunately, resources of housing, sheltered employment and social work were not sufficient to allow this for more than 18 per cent (37 men). This sheltered care group had a lower conviction rate (45.5 per cent) prior to admission than the parent group (68.4 per cent) so one factor here is probably perceived suitability for such care. Even so, 89 per cent had not re-offended (as opposed to 44 per cent unsupervised in the community) and most continued in sheltered work at the date of follow-up. Of the 324 convictions during the 20-year follow-up 12 were very serious offences – two murders (reduced to manslaughter), one grievous bodily harm, three rapes, six arson. In addition two others committed serious arson while still at Garth. The 324 offences were committed by 85 men, and were mainly property offences, although there were 21 convictions for violence against the person and 39 for sexual offences. Many of these re-convictions were used by the police to gain further hospital or community care for ex-patients, for police usually did not reprosecute if easy hospital readmission was available. Further asylum was provided by Garth for one-third of ex-residents at the request of police, social workers or ex-patients themselves on one or more occasions. No doubt many further convictions were thus avoided, judging from the tensions recorded on case notes at crisis readmissions. There is no meaningful way of estimating the cost evaluation of this type of community protection affording such asylum, in terms of property not stolen or burnt, women and children not assaulted and/or physically harmed. As examples of murders not committed, there follow two case pictures:

Case A

Six-year-old Paul was one of the youngest admissions to a psychiatric hospital elsewhere. He was strikingly beautiful, with his fair hair, blue eyes and polished veneer of good manners. He was a bonding failure, the third unwanted son of a career woman with a violent husband. As the family scapegoat, he had a history of vicious acts, tearing wings off flies, eyes out of animals, torturing other children. Ten years of hospital, children's home, residential school, care by a mother now divorced and remarried, only aggravated his personality twisting. At 15 he was the youngest-ever Garth admission and within the first year had had to be transferred to a special hospital, still unconvicted, for attempted murder. Having already threatened death to staff and other residents who looked at him too long, too accusingly or too unkindly, he first stunned an unwise paranoid schizophrenic, and tore out his eyes, saying later that he would have killed him if three patients and a staff member had not restrained him forcibly. The victim made a partial recovery. Ten further years later Paul returned to Garth, still beautiful, still well spoken, and a matured if still warped personality. He went home to his newly-divorced mother, and at the date of writing (1982) is still above average in intelligence, and is still inconvicted and unemployable. He dodges in and out of traffic in his Welsh market town and remains a vulnerable personality. The community is still at risk.

Case B

Ronald, aged 39 and average in intelligence, was an ex-hotel kitchen porter, transferred from special hospital to Garth with one conviction for pre-war murder of a boy during sexual panic. He was a small, mousy man, with a shy, ingratiating manner and weak smile below his sandy brown hair and light blue eyes. Within one year of transfer to Garth he had been returned to his special hospital for near-murder. Ronald's ready and willing sexual partners at Garth, often much bigger and stronger than him, allowed him to 'turn off their gas' by cord strangulation gaining, as one of them said to me afterwards, a 'real kick' from coincident sexual stimulation. Ronald's motives were different. As he said to me on examination, 'I hate people', and I had no doubt that the fate of his victims left him as cold as it might have left them.

The death rate among the 209 was surprisingly high at 31 (14.8 per cent). The analysis gives suicide, 2; alcohol behind road accident, 1; accidents, 2; natural causes such as coronary and carcinoma, 22; unknown, 4. The analysis led to a general impression that these were people who did not care for themselves very well.

In summary then, the follow-up of these 209 dull normal personality disordered recidivists over 20 years showed up the vulnerability of both community and ex-patient. They seemed unable to deal with the twists and changes of upbringing and fate. Apart from the risks to the community, the cost in personal unhappiness, lack of fulfilment and general instability among ex-patients is clear. Many have needed repeat hospital and/or penal care, in fact 73 men have spent most of the time since their discharge from Garth in hospitals (11 in special hospitals) or prison. Since discharge 42 per cent have been convicted of offences ranging in seriousness from minor misdemeanours to manslaughter. At the date of follow-up in December 1981 30 per cent were in institutional care. Only 2.3 per cent owned their own home, a further 12.4 were council tenants, 18.5 were living with their family of origin even though most were now well into their twenties and older. Only 16 men (9 per cent) were in open employment, 47 (26 per cent) were unemployed. Only 26 men (14.6 per cent) were or had been married, relatively few when it is considered that marriage is very much the norm in our society. The death rate was high (14.8 per cent). On reassessment at follow-up the main impression was how vulnerable many had become. Gone was the aggression, bluster and fiery stare of earlier years. These now were men that life had passed by, and they knew it. Many still offended in their set ways, pilfering, children, an occasional burglary, but most passed their time in front of the television, visiting friends or drinking.

What had been achieved by the 20 years of hard work at Garth? The public had certainly been protected, in a way humane for residents. There had been one local rape occurring in the earliest days of Garth, but no serious incidents occurred within the vicinity after 1961. Public service had been achieved humanely at small expense, for the cost of Garth during 1961–1978 was usually some two-thirds of the annual prison cost. Public service was done by an efficient aftercare placement service using North Wales landladies; this meant continuous availability of beds for admissions from courts. Beds were also available to acute psychiatric hospitals throughout Wales to provide placement for the many felt unsuitable for continued care.

For residents a better placement than prison was available: limited freedom, a personal cubicle or room, a constructive job to do, money saved, holidays at home or wherever wanted. Many residents lost their bitterness, some learnt a trade. At follow-up, a few expressed thanks, most had some happy memories.

For staff, there was also the comradeship of a well-run ship, with confidence in doing a job worth doing.

It was clear at follow-up that although this group had lost most of its aggression, it was now a very vulnerable group of middle-aged men without roots, without family, without prospects, without savings, without home, and without many friends. They were pathetically thankful both to see us, and to feel someone still cared, and also for any small help we might give.

Comparison of Results

How does this group compare with others? As might be expected, there are not many follow-ups of patients treated for psychopathic traits. Tidmarsh (1982) describes Walker's 15-year follow-up of 673 UK offender patients detained 1963–64 under the court provisions of the Mental Health Act, there being a very high death rate and continued recidivism. Other studies have found the same, and so did we.

Robins (1966) presents a 30-year follow-up of 524 predominantly white patients originally brought to attention as children for deviant behaviour. She compared 90 sociopaths among these with the remaining 434 and with 100 controls, these last being normal children in schools in the original locality. The death rate after age 25 among the 90 diagnosed as having a sociopathic personality (15 per cent) was higher than the rate in either the remaining 434 group (12 per cent) or in the 100 control subjects (8 per cent). She estimated that US death rates between the ages of 25 and 45 are 7 per cent for white men born in 1910, and 5 per cent for white women. As among Garth patients, hers were higher due to natural causes, war and accident (9 per cent) whilst 6 were consequences of their own behaviour problems; two shot by police in line of duty, one found murdered in an alley, two suicides and one death from acute alcoholism. Although no ex-patients were 'shot in line of duty', the Garth results were similar.

Robins asked psychiatrists to diagnose her population at follow-up. Ninety were found to be sociopathic as defined in the American Diagnostic and Statistical Manual, 1952. Follow-up results of these showed that subjects (compared with controls) were less likely to own their own home, 30 per cent (73 per cent); less likely to be in full time employment, 58 per cent (95 per cent); more likely to have records of aid from public funds, 63 per cent (8 per cent); to be in debt, 14 per cent (2 per cent); to be in prison, 12 per cent (0 per cent); to have a history of arrest, 94 per cent (17 per cent), for a major crime, 73 per cent (13 per cent); to have psychiatric symptoms, 8 per cent (3 per person); to have had past mental hospitalisation, 21 per cent (1 per cent). In Robins' study sociopaths had married, 91 per cent (91 per cent in controls), divorced 78 per cent (20 per cent); were living together 'now', 50 per cent (89 per cent); and been accepted for the Armed Forces 45 per cent (58 per cent). Their rate of child production, 75 per cent (83 per cent) was near normal. These last family statistics apply far less to the Garth patients who at admission averaged IQ 83 (Robins median 95.7 per cent) were duller and more damaged than the Robins group.

In a later analysis of the same group Robins (1978) looked at childhood factors predicting repeated antisocial behaviour in these adults. One cannot do better than quote the summary.

Results are compared in studies of four male cohorts – one all white, one all black and two racially representative of the population – growing up in different eras, followed through varying portions of their adult lives, living in different parts of the US. Despite sample differences and differences in sources of information and in the variables used to measure both childhood predictors and adult outcomes, some striking replications appear with respect to childhood predictors of adult antisocial behavior. *All* types of antisocial behavior in childhood predict a high level of antisocial behavior in adulthood and each kind of adult antisocial behaviors, indicating that adult and childhood antisocial behavior both form syndromes and that these syndromes are closely interconnected. Also confirmed across studies are:
(1) adult antisocial behavior virtually *requires* childhood antisocial behavior;
(2) most antisocial children do *not* become antisocial adults;
(3) the variety of antisocial behavior in childhood is a better predictor of adult antisocial behavior than is any particular behavior;
(4) adult antisocial behavior is better predicted by childhood *behavior* than by family background or social class or rearing;
(5) social class makes little contribution to the prediction of serious antisocial behavior.

One of the many interesting results from Robins' work is that social class did not play a part in the proportions developing sociopathy. Many writers have suggested that social class influences diagnosis, that because of professional identification fewer from the upper classes are labelled by professionals as sociopathic/psychopathic. Robins' analysis makes it clear that although there were more children from lower classes and deprived material backgrounds forwarded as being antisocial to the original child guidance clinics, a similar proportion of each social class group eventually became sociopathic.

Turning to the few other long-term studies the Gluecks' 15-year follow-up (1940) is of young delinquents whose arrest patterns are traced. The Cambridge Somerville Youth Project study (McCord and McCord, 1959) followed severely behaviour disordered predelinquent children matched and divided into treated and non-treated groups.

CONCLUSIONS

Should one treat psychopaths or gaol them? Our follow-up of 209 dull normal young men shows that with most, society is impelled to do something about them at the stage described. Like many recidivists in prison, of inadequate or vulnerable personality (West 1963), most of those initially admitted to Garth did not need maximum security: some were quite pleased to have a refuge, an asylum to care for them. Garth was cheaper than prison, probably more humane, and allowed free visiting, regular holidays, some degree of 'treatment' and work training. It was possible to identify and forward to special hospital those who needed maximum security. As part of the humane system of care it had its merits and it certainly protected the local public and forwarding publics from further danger.

As to treatment success, the results are debatable. At various times of follow-up, I am on record as saying there were good results with a substantial minority, and many who came in disturbed or mentally ill were alleviated and discharged. This is true and I still believe this part was worthwhile. Viewed against the lifetime need of many of these men, Garth should be seen as only one of the many niches needed by a humane society to care for an initially aggressive and dangerous group, whilst time for treatment/maturity/careful onward placement is allowed to reduce further danger to a minimum. Security hospitals are needed for the most aggressive and dangerous; Garth-type units for onward progress, and the many lesser dangers; hostels, group homes and residential complexes for better local placement. In addition are needed many caring people, boarding-house landladies, foster homes for difficult subjects and vulnerable personalities. As with Garth ex-patients, prodigious work is needed over many years by social workers and probation officers to keep these men afloat in the community. Otherwise, as John Wing makes clear in *Helping Destitute Men*, they end up as ship-wrecked middle-aged men adrift on the sea of life without help or hopes, in gutters, refuges or Salvation Army hostels. Others commit offences in order to earn admission to prison.

So one can indeed answer the original question for the 209 dull normal young psychopaths admitted to Garth and lengthily followed up. At the time of diagnosis, their families or communities had been impelled to act and some kind of treatment or gaol admission was required, either to protect society from them, or sometimes to protect their families (or themselves) from further harm. Prison, or maximum security hospitals, were certainly necessary for a small proportion. For most this isolated hospital, and its associated lodgings system, was a safe harbour, and cheaper than prison. Whether one believes in treatment or not, (and I believe skilled counselling and drugs can help) this follow-up and many other studies show that a careful system of job training, job replacement, sheltered housing of different types, and supervision with easy recall, is much safer for client and community than gaol. Reports show that the more violent or convicted the client is, the more likely is he to be further dangerous or reconvicted. Apart from continuous prison care, a flexible treatment/care system allows the greatest safety for all.

This conclusion leads on to the need for partnership between treatment agents and law enforcers in dealing with unstable recidivists. There are three models for this with serious offenders.

Initial prison, with parole available after the first few months of a long sentence, is the latest method to be tried in Britain. Parole can be made conditional on hospital admission; recall to prison or hospital or both is possible on relapse: conditions can be imposed to make the arrangement very flexible. Life sentences as currently practised, are another variation.

The restriction order 'without limit of time' is a hospital variant; the security hospitals of Rampton and Broadmoor are available where such transfer is needed.

The psychiatric probation order is a third variant. Provided all parties are prepared to make it work, this can be both flexible and safe; the probation officer component gives an effective social work contribution.

In the last resort, whether such people are helped or held is a political question – the disposition of resources. There are few hospitals like Garth specialising in care for such people, and few psychiatrists or treatment systems that care to work in what many feel is an unrewarding field.

REFERENCES

Aarvold Committee (1973) *Report on the Review Procedure for the Discharge and Supervision of Psychiatric Patients subject to Restriction.* Cmnd. 5191. London: HMSO.
Craft, A. & Craft, M. (1979) *Handicapped Married Couples.* London: Routledge and Kegan Paul.
Craft, A. & Craft, M. (to appear) A long term follow up of men with personality disorder.
Craft, M. (1958) Withdrawal from licence in mental deficiency. *Am J. Ment. Defic.,* **63,** 47.
Craft, M., Stephenson, G. & Granger, C. (1964) A controlled trial of authoritarian and self-governing regimes with adolescent psychopaths. *Am. J. Orthopsychiat.,* **34,** 543–48.
Craft, M. (1968) Psychopathic disorders: a second trial of treatment. *Brit. J. Psychiat.,* **114,** 813–20.
Glueck, S. & Glueck, A. (1940) *Juvenile Delinquents Grown Up.* New York: Commonwealth Fund.
McCord, W. & McCord, J. (1959) *Origins of Crime.* New York: Columbia University Press.
Meichenbaum, D.H. (1977) *Cognitive Behavior Modification.* New York: Plenum Press.
Robins, L.N. (1966) *Deviant Children Grown Up.* Baltimore: Williams & Wilkins.
Robins, L.N. (1978) Sturdy childhood predictors of adult antisocial behaviour: replications from longitudinal studies. *Psychological Medicine,* **8,** 611–22.
Tidmarsh, D. (1982) Implication from research studies. In *Dangerousness; Psychiatric Assessment and Management.* Hamilton, J.R. & Freeman, H. (eds.). London: Gaskell.
West, D.J. (1963) *The Habitual Prisoner.* London: Macmillan.
West, D.J. & Farrington, D.P. (1977) *The Delinquent Way of Life.* London: Heinemann.
Wing, J. (1972) *Helping Destitute Men.* London: Routledge and Kegan Paul.

25

The Function of a Forensic Assessment and Rehabilitation Unit

William B. Spry & Michael Craft

The 1975 Butler Report was a milestone in British psychiatric history (DHSS & Home Office, 1975). For the first time a major governmental commission recommended joint forensic psychiatric services between the Regional Health Authority and the Prison Medical Service. In recommending secure hospital units in each hospital region for forensic psychiatric (mentally abnormal offender) patients, they said (para 20.13):

These secure units will fulfill a need for non-offender patients while advancing the general cause of the 'open door' policy in psychiatric hospitals, by enabling the most difficult cases to be treated in more appropriate conditions; but by reason of our terms of reference, our main concern is that the units are crucial to the greater flexibility and placement which is needed for mentally abnormal offenders, and to the early relief of the prisons and special hospitals. We think it right that offenders and non-offenders should be treated together; they should share all the facilities of the unit without any distinction being made between them. At present the services dealing with the mentally abnormal offender are fragmented, and we have received a great deal of evidence urging closer co-operation among them, and the more effective use of the scarce professional resources. By focussing the activities and expertise of the various professions in these centres, much can be achieved towards these ends. The offender in need of treatment would be better served not least because of improved assessment, which will also be of immense benefit to the court in deciding what to do with him, and besides providing reference points to which the probation and after-care service will be able to turn to for advice, which they have often told us they often need, the centres will have an essential role in treatment, training and research, for which reason they should be closely associated with the universities.

Following considerable disruption of Garth Angharad Hospital in North Wales by arson in 1973, funds became available to re-use Garth as a 19-bed unit for the assessment and rehabilitation of mentally abnormal offenders in early 1979. Partly because of its remoteness and partly because of the philosophy of returning offenders to the community and training them in socially acceptable behaviour, there has been no need for locked doors, and the house and grounds are open to residents at all times of the day. The following analysis describes the results of research over the last three years.

The work of a forensic psychiatric unit, as the Butler Report suggested, should be at preventative as well as at remand and treatment levels. The geographical isolation of Garth, being over 100 miles from the main cities of South Wales, has meant that local psychiatrists using their own local facilities are better able to cope with crisis care as needed, but a network of outpatient facilities which are used both for assessment and follow-up purposes is being established in places such as Swansea, Cardiff and elsewhere. The majority of the initial referrals come from defence solicitors. Others are from various hospital psychiatrists and some are referred directly from the courts. Far fewer clients are referred by social service departments, who rarely come into contact with convicted mentally abnormal offenders.

The report advises that the principal task of the new semi-secure units and of units such as Garth Angharad should be to ameliorate the overcrowding of the special hospitals such as Moss Side, Rampton and Broadmoor. It is, therefore, anticipated that in the early years a high proportion of patients from these sources would be expected. The relief of prison overcrowding was a further recommendation of the report, and gradually a small but steady proportion of Garth referrals come from this source (Craft et al, to appear).

Our initial analysis of referrals from 1979–81 found that mixed diagnostic categories were frequent, for the deprived upbringing and current background suffered by many of the abnormal offenders was commonly reflected in their educational retardation and poor intellectual scoring on tests that were less than might be expected from good practical abilities. Abnormal personality development due to warping family influences, and the occasional concurrent development of frank psychotic illness in the face of severe stress were also seen. Diagnoses according to the International Classification of Disease (1978) were also both varied and multiple; a large range of personality disorders was covered in the referral group, with a high proportion of emotional instability, immature personalities and inadequate personalities. Most referrals accepted for treatment showed long-standing personality disorders and would have scored in the dull normal range of ability on standardised tests of intelligence, judging from the records of past tests in their case notes. Many would have ranked as candidates for the mental health category of psychopathic personality disorder, though the psychiatric probation order was the preferred method of therapeutic contract. Those transferred from the special hospitals were largely legally detained as suffering from psychopathic disorder of subnormality.

The age range of referrals tended towards the younger group, and annually in the general community some 50 per cent of all convictions are of those under the age of 21. In this age group, referrals were below 14 per cent but this more commonly reflects the concentration of the unit on developed personality disorders than the number of young people below the age of 21 who might have benefited from treatment. The substantial contribution made by the older age groups reflects the later arrival of special hospital patients, many of whom had been under treatment for a number of years. It seems probable that in later years the number of younger people will increase as the waiting list of people from special hospitals is relieved by units such as Garth.

THE WORK OF A FORENSIC ASSESSMENT AND
REHABILITATION UNIT

It is always difficult to present a current analysis of the reasons why some referrals are accepted for treatment and others rejected. The comparatively high proportion of rejects (59 per cent of those referred) was due to their being too severely disturbed for treatment at Garth and needing either short-term security provision or longer term care such as a special hospital might provide. Others might have benefited from a semi-secure Butler unit, and the provision of such a unit would complement the work undertaken at Garth Angharad. At present all female referrals for inpatient treatment have to be rejected as no facility currently exists for them. Others were rejected because of lack of accommodation.

A substantial group were outside the guidelines of care at Garth. For a variety of reasons, including the aggression and sexual deviancy of older men, it has been policy not to accept referrals under 16. Other referrals from elsewhere in Britain were rejected because of their lack of a Welsh connection. Others again were rejected because their degree of mental handicap was such that they would not be able to benefit from the type of care and training offered, although a mild degree of mental handicap is no bar. In addition, a degree of physical fitness is required in order to participate in the activities of Garth, and on occasion physical infirmity has precluded such admissions.

It is also necessary, in a unit offering a planned rehabilitation programme whose usual duration is approximately one year, to have available some form of onward placement at the conclusion of the treatment programme. One referral was rejected on the grounds that there appeared to be no such availability. A further candidate was rejected because it seemed that full-time remedial education was his main need, and two because their estimated period of treatment was seen to be in excess of the normal standard period at Garth. A further group presented various mental health problems which either could be relieved during a period of assessment on remand or were more appropriate for outpatient care while resident in the home area than for inpatient treatment. It is hoped that with increasing contact with the far distant areas involved, the numbers benefiting from such remand assessment may be increased.

The range of antecedent offences was also wide. As might be expected in a forensic psychiatric unit, the biggest groups for referral were those who caused agencies most concern, namely sexual misdemeanours and aggression to persons. A unit for males only is perhaps not the ideal place to treat sexual misdemeanours, of which a high proportion are concerned with offences against other males, but it does have the great advantage that, with a substantial minority of such people, a useful programme of hygiene, health and sex education can be set in progress. A surprising number of these dull normal, poorly educated and personality warped young men were sexually ignorant as to how to channel their sexual tensions and needs, or even how to approach a female in a way which might elicit a positive rather than a negative response. This type of elementary health and sex education is undertaken as a form of sex education in groups, boosted by individual counselling by all members of the staff, adopting a frank approach, so that residents may get personal guidance with their interests and problems when the time and opportunity move them.

Arson has been a particular problem at Garth, and the old fashioned construction of the building and the multiplicity of small rooms render it at high risk. During its previous career as a long term rehabilitation and assessment agency for personality disorder, eight deliberate fires had occurred, of which the last ones had gutted the main building and two outbuildings. An investigation of records at this earlier time had shown that over a third of these mentally abnormal offenders had documented or personal history of previous misbehaviour with fire. The dilemma of attempting to treat these young men in an old building is clear. One-third are so documented and it is likely that more are undocumented; if perhaps half of all referrals are avoided, there is no sure way of knowing that this is the 'right half' of a highly emotionally unstable group of young men. In the event, persistent arson offenders were refused and regarded as needing maximum security.

IMPLICATIONS FOR THE FUTURE

Clearly Garth Angharad can be only one unit in a series dealing with the forensic psychiatric needs of a scattered population of about 2.8 million. It serves a number of functions, both in its immediate locality and to Wales as a whole. It provides an effective venue for assessment, remand and treatment purposes on a short-term basis that is necessary for the considerable incoming numbers of patients. There are current disadvantages in the shape of its construction and geographical isolation, yet the latter may be counted as an advantage in that it allows for safe treatment under intensive care circumstances of staffing, whereas near a big city the same resident would need far more security to avoid absconsion. Treatment patterns take a long time to build up, and inpatient facilities are only one part of a system which needs to provide a long period of care for what is often a deeply-rooted personality abnormality.

At present the unit offers a short-term assessment period, usually of a month's duration, and subsequently takes a proportion of such people for an intensive period of rehabilitation based upon the development of group skills and group psychotherapy, lasting approximately a year. Others, as mentioned before, come from special hospitals, and a few directly from the prisons as a condition of parole. As the unit develops, it is anticipated that the assessment service will be more greatly utilised and the referrals from the special hospitals will gradually diminish. More emphasis may well be placed on taking parole patients from prison. However, the principal future developments must lie in the field of after-care and prevention. In this area, it will be necessary to develop and integrate community facilities, to offer support and supervision so as to minimise the risk of further offences, and as regards prevention, to develop assessment and treatment methods, probably in the community, for those people considered at risk, such as those with abnormally aggressive temperaments or aggressive sexual fantasy life.

There is, therefore, a very real need for the development of units similar to the one at Garth Angharad as an essential component of any comprehensive forensic psychiatric service. Other facilities are also needed, such as the regional secure unit (described in Chapter 22), but without the strong accent on rehabilitation and return to the community that can be offered by the open unit with good supervision, no service can be complete. To provide the reader with an outline of the way in which the service currently works, a few pen portraits of some of the recent residents are given below.

Case A

Joe was born in Cardiff in 1949 in a home described as deprived and which when the family broke up, this resulted in his being taken into care by the Children's Department at a young age.

As a child he was described as unhappy, unloving and ungrateful, with minor thieving, rudeness and some bullying of other children. He was assessed as educationally subnormal. In 1963 and 1964 Joe was convicted of minor larceny. In 1965 he was convicted on two counts of indecent assault on a female, and two of common assault. In 1966 he was convicted again of indecent assault and made subject to a hospital order to Garth Angharad Hospital, but failed to settle and absconded several times. He was also involved in further property offences. In 1967, after indecent assaults against both males and females, another hospital order was made under Section 60/65 of the Mental Health Act, 1959 without limit of time. He then went to a hospital in mid Wales where again he bullied, was violent to others and absconded. In 1970 he was transferred to Moss Side hospital where he remained until his transfer to Garth Angharad in September 1980. Whilst in Moss Side he was not violent and his sexual development appeared to mature in that he ceased previous homosexual activity.

Joe remained at Garth Angharad until February 1982, having various periods of extended leave in the Cardiff area prior to his discharge. During his stay at Garth he was co-operative, helpful, and showed no violence though he was of dull intellectual ability.

He was discharged to live in lodgings in Cardiff, where he has maintained good contact with his supervising probation officer. He is now self-reliant with quite reasonable insight into his past difficulties and has regular employment selling newspapers.

Case B

David was born in Maesteg in 1963 and was the younger of two brothers. He has an over-protective but caring mother and a father who was formerly a miner but who was prematurely retired on grounds of nervousness. At the age of three David was hit by a train, suffering severe head injuries, and was unconscious for a long period and in hospital for nine months. As a result of this accident he was blinded in his right eye, lost his sense of smell and developed post-traumatic epilepsy which is controlled by anti-convulsant therapy.

He was assessed as educationally subnormal as a result of his brain damage and attended a residential special school from the age of 10 to 16, where his behaviour was satisfactory but his academic achievement was limited to very elementary reading and writing.

On leaving school David spent much of his time at a local amusement arcade, and also smoked heavily. He appeared to have few friends and he did not abuse drugs or alcohol. However, he ran short of money for his activities and began thieving to obtain more. Various court appearances followed, in which he was ordered to pay compensation and placed on probation. He said, however, that he was bored and continued to act as before, with a number of other offences of burglary and breaking and entering and one of taking and driving away a dumper truck.

As a result of some of these last offences he was placed on probation with a condition of residence at Garth Angharad Hospital, where he was admitted in May 1981 and stayed until December 1981. During his time at Garth Angharad he made notable progress in his education and became more sociable and independent, although still inclined at times to be mischievous. Since David's discharge to live with his parents he has stayed away from the amusement arcades, and is smoking less heavily. He has a government training job on a building site and is managing his money well and has not got into debt or offended again. He attends a follow-up clinic regularly and keeps in good contact with his supervising probation officer.

Case C

Tony was born near Bridgend in 1947, and was the eldest of three children. As a child he was slow in walking and talking, and episodes of sleep-walking and night terrors occurred until the age of five. He was enuretic until the age of 14. He was, however, described as a happy child, but undistinguished at school, although not graded as educationally subnormal.

Tony's parents divorced in 1963 and his mother subsequently remarried. He first offended in 1961 at the age of 14 with an indecent assault on a young girl. Similar offences brought him before the courts again when aged 15, 16 and 17. As a result of the last offence he was made the subject of a hospital order under the Mental Health Act, 1959 and received several months' inpatient care for his personality disorder.

However, after his release in 1966 when aged 19, Tony again repeated the offence which involved inflicting corporal punishment to little girls' bare bottoms and was accompanied by considerable immature sexual fantasy life. An order under Section 60/65 of the Mental Health Act was then made and he was admitted to Broadmoor Hospital in 1966 where he remained until June 1981. During his stay there, intellectual tests showed him to be of average ability. He was never violent and psychometric assessment showed diminution of his abnormal interest in little girls.

Tony was transferred to Garth Angharad Hospital in June 1981 where he was found to be a pleasant but obese and mildly hypertensive man who functioned at good average level. His manner and behaviour were institutional, but he quite rapidly formed good relationships and developed a wide range of hobbies. He showed almost no sexual interest. He was discharged from Garth Angharad hospital in June 1982, and has since been living in lodgings in the Port Talbot area and keeps in contact with both his parents. He has not been able to find employment yet, but leads an active life and has become a keen supporter of local sporting activities. Tony attends a follow-up clinic regularly, and maintains good contact with his supervising probation officer. He now appears well settled, with no abnormal personality features.

REFERENCES

Craft, A., Craft, M. & Spry, W. B. The function of a Welsh Forensic Assessment and Rehabilitation Unit (to appear).

Home Office & DHSS (1975) *Report on the Committee on Mentally Abnormal Offenders (the Butler Committee)*. Cmnd. 6244. London: HMSO.

World Health Organisation (1978) *Mental Disorders: Glossary and Guide to their Classification in Accordance with the Ninth Revision of the International Classification of Diseases*. Geneva: WHO.

26

Treatment of Sexual Offenders

Ann & Michael Craft

There has been far more awareness in recent years of the complexities of human sexual behaviour and response. The studies of Kinsey and his associates and Masters and Johnson were landmarks in this respect (Kinsey et al, 1948, 1953; Masters and Johnson, 1966). With the increasing awareness of sexual function, came a better understanding of sexual dysfunction and the frequently accompanying psychological distress which is sometimes linked to relationship and behaviour disturbance.

Sexual disorder (either distress or deviation) may, although, of course, does not necessarily, lead people to commit offences. We have already seen that physiological and psychological sexual difficulties are often found in male sexual offenders (Chapter 6). While psychiatrists and others may disagree about the deviancy of homosexual activities, the law is quite clear that boys, young men and indeed the public at large, should be protected against 'unnatural acts'. Falling foul of the legal code in addition to other forms of societal disapproval, leads some homosexuals to seek treatment to alter their sexual preferences. Other common examples of sexual misconduct, such as child molestation and indecent exposure, provide numerous instances of men who appear to be driven by compulsive pressures and temptation they cannot resist, but which leave them guilty, ashamed and self-loathing. Both they and the courts look to psychiatrists for help and treatment.

Clinics treating sexual dysfunction are becoming more widespread and may offer some relief to the sexual offender with problems such as erectile impotence or ejaculatory failure for which there is a very reasonable treatment success rate (Masters and Johnson, 1970). One difficulty may be that the clinic will only treat the couple rather than the individual, and this may preclude the unmarried offender or the one with severe marital distress.

Masters and Johnson (1970) originally used surrogates in the treatment of those without sexual partners. Interesting accounts of the difficulties and responsibilities of such an intervention are given by Greene (1977) and Wolfe (1978). Cole (1982) claims that: 'Sexual skill training, the reduction of anxiety, the initiation of arousal or the application of a specific behavioural strategy, requires the participation of an involved partner without which behavioural change is virtually impossible.'

Surrogate therapy may have distinct advantages for certain sexual offenders precisely because the emotional content of the relationship is naturally limited.

The choice of surrogate is made almost entirely by the therapist, thus bypassing past failures in the area of relationship formation; and in the absence of a strong emotional bond, performance anxiety and fear of failure are much reduced. Cole (1982) reports on a series of 133 men and 17 women treated by surrogate therapy. The largest categories of presenting problems were male heterophobia, i.e., anxiety about heterosexual relationships sufficient to block socio-sexual behaviour very early on and prevent relationships forming (34 per cent); erectile dysfunction (32 per cent); and premature ejaculation (11 per cent). Subjects were rated by Cole on a 5-point performance scale. Behaviour changes before and after therapy were recorded as mean shifts in score and were all at the highly significant level. Unfortunately, follow-up difficulties make it hard to assess the maintenance of newly acquired behaviour accurately; only 30 of those taking part supplied follow-up data concerning performance six months or more later. Of these, 22 (73 per cent) showed a substantial degree of generalisation of their sexual skills with a new or existing partner.

West (1980) highlights some of the difficulties inherent in the treatment of sexual offenders, particularly those whose crimes warranted prison sentences, pointing out that a large percentage will have records of convictions for both sexual and non-sexual offences. They thus present similar problems to those evinced by the generality of offenders, but have added difficulties specifically relating to sexuality.

They tend to display many characteristics typical of the ordinary recidivist, notably an impulsive, hedonistic lifestyle, involving heavy drinking, erratic work record and scant attention to family responsibilities. In short, aggressive sexual misconduct often reflects a global defect of socialisation or ... an 'antisocial personality deviation' that shows itself in the sexual as in other aspects of life (West, 1980).

Sexual offenders with frank psychiatric illness which complicates, or even causes, sexual misconduct present very specialised therapeutic problems. West (1980) says that alcohol abuse is perhaps the commonest complication, with such men denying sexual problems and claiming they only offended because they were drunk. This denial is unusually unrealistic, but nevertheless, until the drinking problem is overcome, the likelihood of re-offence remains high. Cerebral deterioration, with its disinhibiting effects, can also give rise to problems where ageing men, cut off from their former sexual outlets, may begin to offend against children. Psychotic offenders, particularly confused schizophrenics, sometimes commit bizarre sexual crimes while in the grip of their delusions.

In short, because of the range of personality types, the plethora or problems they present and the negative aura surrounding sexual crime, the treatment of sexual offenders is a complex area of practice. It is one that has been receiving more and more attention in recent years. This chapter is given over to a discussion of treatment options.

TREATMENT VENUE

In many cases the treatment venue is imposed on therapist and offender alike by courts who decide that a custodial sentence is necessary to protect the public.

However, for less serious offences the offer of treatment by a psychiatrist in a specialised clinic may persuade the court to opt for probation. In Bluglass's clinical experience continuing community supervision (often over long periods of time) by a sympathetic and understanding therapist (whether psychiatrist, social worker or probation officer) is as valuable as any other form of treatment for minor offenders such as exposers, voyeurs, makers of indecent phone calls and fetishists who steal from clothes lines. He comments, 'What it is in the quality of this kind of relationship that keeps the patient out of trouble is unknown, but it is a practical method of management which produces results ...' (Bluglass, 1982).

Gunn (1976) argues that a probation order with a condition of treatment is an almost ideal disposal for the majority of sexual offenders, particularly now that the Criminal Justice Act 1972 has extended the period of treatment to up to three years. Living in the community a patient does not have his social life destroyed and the development of normal personal and sexual relationships is a real possibility. It has other positive features: (a) it requires consent by the patient; (b) the treatment can be as an inpatient or an outpatient, allowing the supervising medical practitioner both possibilities according to need; (c) a probation officer skilled in social work is involved, and can advise and assist with management; (d) the offender may be taken back to court for an alternative disposal if it becomes clear the original order is proving unsatisfactory.

Prison can be a bleak and destructive place for sexual offenders, even with the use of rule 43 which permits the segregation of a man from other prisoners if he is thought to be at risk. It may be particularly damaging for the recovery prospects of persistent exposers because of the disruption brought to relationships and job. 'For someone whose social and heterosexual adjustment is already precarious, a prison sentence is a major disaster.' (Rooth 1971.) Separation from the family may also be deleterious not only to the father who committed incest, but to the child also. Rosenfeld (1981) suggests she may suffer more from guilt feelings arising from the father's incarceration than from the incestuous relationship itself. This is particularly so when the father has been the more nurturant parent, so the child becomes an 'emotional orphan'. In such cases an intervention into the family dynamics, individualised to the family's lifestyle and emotional needs would be a preferable approach.

While much important work with sexual offenders has been done within closed institutions (and will continue to be) some comment on the restrictions such a milieu imposes on treatment needs to be made. A prison or secure hospital is an artificial setting. While there are still plenty of opportunities for the aggressive offender to display violence, the virtual absence of opportunities to offend means that sexual offenders are often model patients or prisoners. Exemplary behaviour may be a sign of improvement, but is far more likely to indicate only that he has been removed from temptation. As in secure hospitals, contact with female inmates is necessarily controlled and supervised, there is little opportunity of assessing whether a particular sex offender has learned to exercise self-control. The absence of children in hospital or prison makes reality testing impossible with paedophiles, and so on.

West (1980) comments on the dysfunction likely to occur with the release of a sex offender from prison. While therapy may be well begun, it cannot be successfully completed in a closed establishment. 'Therapy that ceases as a man walks out of the gate is unsatisfactory to the point of futility' (West 1980), but difficulties may arise in the referral of the offender to an outside clinic, both in terms of relating to new therapists and in the resources and time they can offer.

Therapists would naturally prefer prison release to coincide with an appropriate stage in treatment, but parole decisions are taken on different considerations by independent authorities. Indeed, while time of release is unpredictable and thus unrelated to treatment needs, there would be a danger in allowing therapists to influence parole dates. Clients would have strong motives either for pretence and concealment, or for non-participation in the programme if they felt their release would be delayed.

SOCIAL SKILLS TRAINING

As Crawford (1977) says, '. . . if any treatment is to stand a chance of long-term success it seems clear that appropriate social behaviour must be established in addition to modifying any deviant sexual arousal'. These appropriate social skills encompass not only the finer points of interpersonal behaviour, but also the ability to express emotions (assertiveness), to cope with aggressive confrontations and the general problems of living experienced by individuals.

While lack of requisite social skills is frequently mentioned in relation to sexual offenders, little research has been published to show the specific effect of a remedial programme. Becker et al (1978) incorporated social skills training in their overall treatment, but did not evaluate it independently. Serber and Keith (1974) set up a programme for paedophiles at Atascadero State Hospital, California which relied heavily on a social skills approach, but give no results. Crawford and Allen (1979) used a behaviourally orientated social skills training programme with six sexual offenders in Broadmoor special hospital. Three had committed offences against children, three against adults; four had histories of sexual offences and all six had long-standing social problems preventing the formation of satisfactory sexual relationships. A battery of assessment measures was employed and the programme used instruction, modelling, role-play and feedback with male and female co-therapists. The programme was effective in improving social skills, this being maintained on a two-year follow-up (Crawford, 1981), but no data are yet available to show whether the improvement in social skills will result in a decrease in sexual re-offending. Burgess et al (1980) describe a nine-session social skills programme for six sexual offenders in a local prison, all selected on the basis of social incompetence and previous solitary lifestyle. All improved in social skills and were keen that a similar course should be run again for others.

SEX EDUCATION

Particularly with young and dull men, inaccurate or inadequate knowledge about their own and others' sexuality may be a contributory factor in the offence. Crawford (1979) reports on the effectiveness of small sex education groups in Broadmoor special hospital, showing that it both increased levels of knowledge *and* that the patients expressed less anxiety towards the idea of sexual intercourse, reported less conflict associated with sex, and had improved their self-image. He concludes, 'By improving their sexual knowledge the programme had reduced their anxiety and increased their confidence in the area of sexual functioning.'

Both sex education and social skills training have an important part to play in an overall treatment strategy.

BEHAVIOUR THERAPY

See Crawford, Chapter 27 for a comprehensive description.

TREATMENT FOR HOMOSEXUALS

While recent years have seen the growth of homosexual rights movements and some evidence of a slight easing in the social climate, there are men who are desperately unhappy with their homosexual orientation, and who ask for treatment to help them change.

Various behavioural methods have been used, notably aversive techniques, but latterly a more comprehensive approach has been employed, so that besides the suppressing or decreasing of the undesired sexual orientation, a rewarding non-deviant sexual activity is substituted. Bancroft (1969) found that an increase in heterosexual response distinguished between successes and relapses at follow-up. Barlow and Agras (1973) increased heterosexual responsiveness in three homosexual subjects by superimposing a female slide on a male slide and as the subject became aroused the brightness of the female slide was increased and that of the male decreased. Herman et al (1974) found non-deviant arousal increased in their homosexual subjects simply by watching explicit heterosexual films.

As might be expected with such a complex behaviour, success rates vary. Feldman and MacCulloch (1971) reported that 57 per cent of their sample of homosexuals were improved at follow-up. Bancroft (1974) compared various studies with adequate follow-up and found a success rate of between 30 and 40 per cent more common. Masters and Johnson (1979) treated 54 men and 13 women who wanted to convert or revert to heterosexuality and had a failure rate of 35 per cent, which they do not expect to exceed 45 per cent when all five year follow-ups were complete. It is very likely that motivation for change is a significant factor.

SELF-CONTROL

Kanfer and Phillips (1970) define the process of self control as one in which a person alters the probability of behaviour occurring by changing the variables which have controlled its occurrence in the past. The development of self-control techniques has obvious potential in the treatment of sexual offenders. The general procedure involves self-monitoring, self-evaluation, self-reinforcing, intention statements and interpersonal contracting. For sexual offenders the emphasis lies in the modification of deviant sexual fantasy because such fantasy, particularly in masturbation and reinforced by orgasm, is considered to play a part in helping form and maintain deviant sexual behaviour. Substitution of more normal fantasies can be achieved by several behavioural methods, and can allow an individual to develop self-controlling responses whenever he begins to engage in deviant imagery.

Crawford (1981) described a treatment programme at the South Florida State Hospital which stressed the development of self-control. Patients became skilled at recognising 'early warning signals' in their own behaviour which they knew from past experience had resulted in a sexual offence. By taking early evasive action the patient can interrupt the chain of events before he re-offends.

DRUGS

'Sexual urges are peculiar in that they are, to a large extent, under chemical control. To be specific, male sexual drive, normal or deviant, seems dependent upon a considerable excess of circulating androgen over circulating oestrogen. Or, at least, if circulating androgen levels are decreased or circulating oestrogen levels increased in the male, then libido seems to decline' (Gunn, 1976). Yet analyses of androgen or testosterone levels in the population show a shaped curve of distribution varying from 3.6 to 15.4 ng/ml (mean 8.0). Unfortunately there is no simple correlation between testosterone level, type or degree of sex activity or degree of interest. Interest and activity depend on a complex interplay between all the sex hormones produced in brain, testes and elsewhere. For example, in one study men with a coital frequency up to 12 times a week had an average testosterone level well below the average given above (Brown et al, 1978). The administration of drugs to sexual offenders, however, is a complex issue, not only because of side effects, but also because of the degree of coercion which may implicitly colour the patient's consent ('If I accept this they will let me out sooner'), and ethical considerations of social control.

West (1980) points out that the use of chemical suppressants presupposes that an offender's sexuality is unwanted, whereas 'for all but the most hopeless cases' the aim should be to train and develop more appropriate sexual outlets. Brandon (1975) comments that in the case of indecent exposers, where the offence may reflect anxiety about potency, the effects of chemical reduction in libido need to be carefully considered.

Where offenders in hospitals or prison agree to start medication, the vital factor is that they continue with it, often for long periods of time, after they are released. Shaw (1978) makes the apt observation that the social situation in which many sex offenders find themselves is not conducive to regular medication or in some instances even a desire to change. 'Many offenders exist in a state of anomie and if this is not corrected there can be little expectation of their continuing in a self-imposed sexual vacuum by regular drug taking' (Shaw, 1978). Drug therapy is most likely to succeed when the offender is not a loner, but part of a supportive family.

Gunn (1976) suggests some ethical safeguards for the use of hormonal treatments.

1 The patient must be fully conversant with the risks involved before any treatment begins.

2 He must give signed consent after discussion.

3 No patient should be offered such drastic treatment unless he has a serious and dangerous perversion and is well motivated to undertake the treatment.

Oestrogen, the female hormone, was earlier used extensively to decrease libido in patients unable to control their sexual drive. (See Crawford (1981) for a survey of reporting studies.) However, all studies reported serious side effects – nausea and vomiting to a degree that makes treatment unacceptable to patients, feminisation (with growth of breast tissue often requiring surgical removal), testicular atrophy, a reduced sperm count, and occasionally carcinoma. The serious side effects of oestrogen prompted research into alternative anti-libidinal drugs.

Benperidol (a butyrophenone) has anti-libidinal properties but none of the steroidal side-effects of feminisation. It can, however, have extra pyramidal effects which may need to be controlled with anti-Parkinson drugs, and can also lead to feelings of drowsiness. In a carefully controlled double-blind trial comparing benperidol, chlorpromazine and a placebo, Tennent et al (1974) found evidence of only a weak libido-reducing effect for benperidol, mainly in the area of lower frequency of sexual thoughts. They concluded it was unlikely to control severe antisocial behaviour.

Cyproterone acetate is another widely-used anti-androgen drug, generally agreed to be effective in suppressing libido and reducing erectile and ejaculatory capacity. Side effects of tiredness, temporary or permanent breast growth and weight gain have been reported, but in most cases do not seem to be severe. Libido returns once the drug is stopped. Bancroft et al (1974) in a controlled study compared cyproterone acetate, oestrogen and no treatment as libidinal reducing agents on 12 sexual offenders in Broadmoor special hospital. Both drugs were equally effective in reducing frequncy of sexual thoughts and sexual activity, but only cyproterone acetate had an effect in reducing erectile and subjective response to erotic stimuli (the effect was weak). They concluded that cyproterone acetate is the most useful drug for controlling sexual behaviour, especially because of its lack of troublesome side-effects. Craft (1981) recommended that specialist clinics are the most appropriate agency for carrying out cyproterone acetate treatment.

The cautious use of a drug such as cyproterone acetate can be extremely valuable. Shaw (1978) suggests that a possible effect is the reduction in the amount of time a man spends actively thinking about sex, allowing him '... a period of "sexual calm", as a result of which the individual could be more receptive to psychotherapy, casework, group work and so forth'.

Gunn (1976) reminds us that the general problems of treating offenders are very apparent in the area of drug therapy.

Medicine is not a form of police work, nor a social control agency. Patients who come into conflict with the law are entitled to the same quality of service and ethical considerations as all other patients. Some courts are tempted to regard forensic psychiatrists as a useful state-control agency; doctors under such pressure should resist it.

As noted above, drugs may *control*, but they do not by themselves *cure* in this complex field of human sexual behaviour. The high sexual drive that drugs can reduce is not usually the main contributory factor in an offence; that may lie in quite other directions and may not be primarily or exclusively sexual. Drugs should be an adjunct to treatment, and not be used in isolation.

PSYCHOTHERAPY

Psychoanalysis has not generally been found to be an effective way of treating sexual offenders. Psychoanalytic theories may offer an explanation of sexual perversion (although basic concepts have been severely criticised by Eysenck and Wilson, 1973) among others, but no controlled attempt has been made to assess treatment outcomes. Psychoanalysis is in any case time-consuming and expensive and on practical grounds is outside the bounds of possibility for all but a few.

Individual psychotherapy also has drawbacks, for sexual offenders tend to deny guilt and to lack motivation for change. Social and educational differences between offender and therapist often make rapport hard to achieve. Field and Williams (1970), working with sexual offenders in a British prison, found psychotherapy 'disappointing'. Although the most intelligent and least psychopathic men were selected, it was found that many had neither the requisite level of intelligence nor the verbal facility to make psychotherapy meaningful. The authors reported: 'Too often the prisoner found the discussion embarrassing or felt compelled to constantly justify and rationalise his past behaviour.' The most damning criticism came from the prisoners themselves:

... even simple explanation along psychoanalytical lines was fraught with difficulties and often evoked from the offender the question of how, even if the explanation were understood and accepted, this knowledge alone would give him sufficient control over his impulses to avoid the next offence (Field and Williams, 1970).

Group psychotherapy has distinct advantages because, besides being more cost-effective, it can effectively bridge the socio-cultural gap between therapist and offender, and facilitate ventilation of problems by bringing together individuals who have experienced similar difficulties. Common background of like needs and experiences can be a powerful aid to the breakdown of the defence mechanisms of rationalisation, isolation and denial. Cox (1980) gives a graphic example from a Broadmoor therapeutic group.

For example, once one rapist has found at long last, that he is able to disclose to the other members of the group (half of whom are women) that he had always had doubts about his sexual orientation and the assault was to test himself out, it can be immensely reassuring to his fragile self-esteem that his disclosure did not result in a cynical giggle, but in a snowball effect of similar disclosures '... I used a knife because I was afraid my "hard" would not hold ... I wore a mask, not to escape recognition but because I've always been frightened of women looking at me in the face, I feel they can see right through me.'

Peters and Roether (1972) report from Philadelphia on a retrospective study of the effects of group therapy on sexual offenders. They found that although the original offences of the 92 men in therapy were more serious than the 75 controls on probation without therapy, the reconviction rate for both sexual and non-sexual crimes was far lower for the therapy group (two year follow-up).

Saylor (1980) describes a group psychotherapy programme for sexual offenders at a psychiatric hospital in Washington State. Here, in a group therapy setting, offenders treat other offenders under the guidance and supervision of a professional therapist. The groups are very intensive, meeting for a minimum of 25 hours each week, and the group members the arbitrators of individual progress. The intensiveness of the groups serves to break down the 'loner' lifestyle of the offender as he is constantly forced to be involved and share with his peers. Perhaps the most essential element is the insistence that an individual identifies himself as a sexual psychopath[1] *for life* and takes measures necessary to prevent himself from re-offending.

The programme is closely structured – once accepted, a man spends a minimum of 18 months as an inpatient (average stay 20 to 24 months); a minimum of three months working or going to classes outside but at first returning each night to the hospital, then winning longer and longer overnight leaves; the last phase is as an outpatient (minimum 18 months) required to attend weekly sessions back with his group in the hospital. This latter phase serves also to reinforce the group's inpatients' progress towards responsibility: '... it makes the statement that someone like himself, applying appropriate controls and maintaining a responsible lifestyle, can and has succeeded and, therefore, so may he' (Saylor, 1980).

At the time of Saylor's report (1980) some 402 men had progressed through the inpatient stage and had spent time at risk in the community over a span of 12 years. The recidivism rate was 22 per cent.

---

[1] The elements that seem to constitute sexual psychopathy under the legal statutes include compulsiveness, repetition and a certain bizarre or disconcerting quality in sexual behaviour. The term 'sexual psychopath' does not correspond to any particular psychiatric disease; rather it is a legal term which incidentally poses some of the same problems as the legal term 'insanity', which also does not correspond to any particular form of mental illness.

The weakness of group (or individual) psychotherapy is the importance of the continuing relationship with trusted therapist and/or group. It is rarely possible for such a relationship and the support it affords to be available for an indefinite period. This, of course, is a criticism that can be made of most treatment programmes.

SURGICAL INTERVENTION

In an attempt to control deviant sexual activity two methods have been employed – castration and hypothalamotomy.

In the Middle Ages *castration* was performed as a punishment for such crimes as rape or adultery according to the *jus talionis* (an eye for an eye and a tooth for a tooth). In modern Europe castration for sex offenders has been generally known since 1906. Denmark legalised it as a medical treatment in 1929, Germany in 1933, Norway in 1934 and other countries followed. However, it does not appear to have been used in predominantly Roman Catholic countries, nor in Britain (Heim and Hursch, 1979). Where castration was permitted, its use was enthusiastic. Heim (1981) reports that in the region of Zürich alone more than 10 000 inpatients have been castrated for various psychiatric problems since 1910. In Denmark about 1100 operations have been carried out, although it has not been used for several years (Stürup, 1977, in personal communication to Heim and Hursch, 1979). A reliable estimate for West Germany is said to be 800 sex offenders castrated during 1955–77. Initially, enthusiasm for its use was high, with Stürup (1968) concluding that '... the persons who are convinced that life before castration was terrible and burdensome and who have a great guilt complex concerning the terrible things they have done are nearly always very happy that they have been castrated.'

In a follow-up of 900 castrations in Denmark Sand et al (1964) found that more than 90 per cent were satisfied with the effects of the operation, with a 2.2 per cent recidivism rate for sexual criminals. (See, however, Heim and Hursch (1979) for a discussion on the pitfalls of analysing recidivism rates.) Since the 1970s the number of castrations has been considerably reduced, and in some countries, for example the Netherlands, it is now illegal for institutionalised patients. This decline is perhaps not surprising in the light of Heim and Hursch's comment that all the studies they reviewed were '... methodologically poor and allow few conclusions about the physical, psychiatric-psychological, social or geriatric side-effects of castration.'

In a later article Heim (1981) suggests that, 'In general, the findings do not justify recommending surgical castration as a reliable treatment for incarcerated sex offenders'. Looking at the sexual behaviour of offenders after the operation, Heim found that the data showed the sexual responsiveness of castrated males to be much more varied than had been supposed. Of the 39 men, 31 per cent were still able to engage in sexual intercourse, the rapists tending to be more sexually active after castration than homosexuals or paedophiles. There seemed to be a strong effect on sexual behaviour only when the operation was performed on males between the ages of 45 and 59. Heim writes: 'Using this physical method represents an atheoretical pragmatism and a gross misunderstanding of the nature and psychodynamics of sexual deviations.' He is raising a very fundamental point concerning the complexity of human sexual behaviour and our comprehension of its ramifications.

Another method of surgical intervention has been used in the past two decades, mainly in West Germany. This is a *stereotactic hypothalamotomy*, whereby about two-thirds of the nucleus ventromedialis is destroyed. In a highly critical article Schmidt and Schorsch (1981) report that three separate neurosurgical clinics used the procedure from 1962–79, mainly on patients who were not aggressive in their sexual behaviour, although some rapists were included. Very little reliable follow-up data are available, although the clinics involved assessed results of 65 of the operations and speak of 'improvement or cure of the sexual deviation' without giving details. The Hamburg clinic followed up ten such patients after three years. Three refused to be examined, one had died of pre-existing Addison's disease, three were 'normal in every respect', two had been surgically castrated after the hypothalomotomy as their sexual behaviour had not changed (one of these had committed suicide, but there were many pre-existing attempts), one paedophiliac with sadomasochistic fantasies received antiandrogens until he complained of impotence with his girl friend, and a few weeks after the discontinuation of the medication was accused of murdering a ten-year-old boy.

Schmidt and Schorsch's conclusion is scathing: 'The neurophysiological bases for hypothalomotomies on humans with deviant sexual behaviour are dubious. These operations have not been adequately legitimized *empirically* either as pragmatic or symptomatic therapy for sexually deviant behavior.' In fact it now appears that the psychosurgery has been discontinued by the surgeons themselves.

Both surgical methods have fallen out of favour.

CONCLUSION

As Cox (1980) reminds us, 'There are so many variables underlying that particular social encounter designated as a "sex offence", that it is unthinkable that there should be a standard therapeutic policy which would always be appropriate.' Most treatment programmes lump together sexual offenders as if they were a homogeneous group, yet even a cursory examination reveals categories of adult/child arousal, homosexual/heterosexual/bisexual preference, aggressive/non-aggressive action. Ideally, treatment programmes should not only differentiate between types of offenders, but also attend more closely to the needs of the individual. A necessary precursor to this is the development of more sophisticated assessment procedures. One method gaining acceptance is the measurement of penile response (plethysmography) to distinguish not only broad categories of sexual orientation, but specific arousal to aggressive components of sexual behaviour with both children and adults (Abel et al, 1978; Crawford, 1980).

Therapeutic provision for sex offenders needs to cover every stage at which such individuals may come to notice. As West (1980) points out, the earlier stages are the most important from the point of view of prevention (a rather unknown quantity in relation to sexual offences, but see Bancroft, 1978).

The existence of specialist treatment centres would make it possible for general practitioners, marriage counsellors, social workers, voluntary agencies and police, at a stage where discretion can be exercised, to refer individuals at risk of offending or re-offending. For those who get to the stage of prosecution, such a treatment centre would allow the court to make a constructive disposal by way of probation with a condition of treatment. The USA is rather better served in this area than Britain, with a number of specialist units attached to hospitals, community mental health facilities or correctional services (Brecher, 1978).

It appears that while we do have at our disposal a range of treatment possibilities which, either singly or, better, in combination, should aid many of the sexual offenders referred, we are still a long way from providing a comprehensive service, or from fully appreciating the long-term effectiveness of various therapeutic methods.

REFERENCES

Abel, G.G., Becker, J.V., Blanchard, E. B. & Djenderedjian, A. (1978) Differentiating sexual aggressiveness with penile measures. *Crim. Justice Behav.*, **5,** 315–32.

Bancroft, J. (1969) Aversion therapy of homosexuality. *Brit. J. Psychiat.*, **115,** 1417–31.

Bancroft, J. (1974) *Deviant Sexual Behaviour.* Oxford: Clarendon Press.

Bancroft, J. (1978) The prevention of sexual offenses. In *The Prevention of Sexual Disorders.* Qualls, C.B., Wincze, J.P. & Barlow, D.H. (eds.). New York: Plenum.

Bancroft, J., Tennent, G., Loucas, K. & Cass, J. (1974) The control of deviant sexual behaviour by drugs: 1. Behavioural changes following oestrogens and antiandrogens. *Brit. J. Psychiat.*, **125,** 310–15.

Barlow, D.H. & Agras, W.S. (1973) Fading to increase heterosexual responsiveness in homosexuals. *J. Appl. Behav. Anal.*, **6,** 355–66.

Becker, J.V., Abel, G.G., Blanchard, E.B., Murphy, W.D. & Coleman, E. (1978) Evaluating social skills of sexual aggressives. *Crim. Justice Behav.*, **5,** 357–68.

Bluglass, R. (1982) Assessing dangerousness in sex offenders. In *Dangerousness: Psychiatric Assessment and Management.* Hamilton, J.R. & Freeman, H. (eds.). The Royal College of Psychiatrists Special Publication 2. Gaskell.

Brandon, S. (1975) Management of sexual deviation. *Brit. Med. J.*, **iii,** 149–51.

Brecher, E.M. (1978) *Treatment Programs for Sex Offenders.* (No 027.000.00591.8) Washington, D.C., US Dept of Justice, Government Printing Office.

Brown, W.A., Monti, P.M. & Corriveau, D.P. (1978) Serum testosterone and sexual activity and interest in men. *Arch. Sex Behav.*, **7,** 2, 97–104.

Burgess, R., Jewitt, R., Sandham, J. & Hudson, B.L. (1980) Working with sex offenders: a social skills training group. *Brit. J. Social Wk.*, **10,** 133–42.

Cole, M. (1982) The use of surrogate sex partners in the treatment of sex dysfunctions and allied conditions. *Brit. J. Sexual Med.*, **9,** 82, 13–20.

Cox, M. (1980) Personal reflections upon 3000 hours in therapeutic groups with sex offenders. In *Sex Offenders in the Criminal Justice System.* West, D.J. (ed.). Papers presented to the 12th

Cropwood Round-Table Conference, Dec. 1979. Cropwood Conference Series No. 12. Cambridge.

Craft, M. (1981) Sex offences: the size of the problem and treatment. *Update, J. Postgrad. General Practice*, **23,** 1549–57.

Crawford, D.A. (1977) A social skills training programme. In *Sex Offenders – a Symposium*. Gunn, J. (ed.). Special Hospitals Research Report No. 14.

Crawford, D.A. (1979) Modification of deviant sexual behaviour: the need for a comprehensive approach. *Brit. J. Med. Psychol.*, **52,** 151–6.

Crawford, D.A. (1980) Applications of penile response monitoring to the assessment of sexual offenders. In *Sex Offenders in the Criminal Justice System*. West, D.J. (ed.). Papers presented to the 12th Cropwood Round-Table Conference, Dec 1979. Cropwood Conference Series No. 12. Cambridge.

Crawford, D.A. (1981) Treatment approach with paedophiles. In *Adult Sexual Interest in Children*. Cook, M. & Howells, K. (eds.). London: Academic Press.

Crawford, D.A. & Allen, J.V. (1979) A social skills training programme with sex offenders. In *Love and Attraction*. Cook, M. & Wilson, G. (eds.). Oxford: Pergamon.

Eysenck, H.J. & Wilson, G.D. (1973) *The Experimental Study of Freudian Theories*. London: Methuen.

Feldman, M.P. & McCulloch, M.J. (1971) *Homosexual Behaviour: Therapy and Assessments*. Oxford: Pergamon.

Field, L.H. & Williams, M. (1970) The hormonal treatment of sexual offenders. *Medicine, Science and the Law*, **10,** 27–34.

Greene, S. (1977) Resisting the pressure to become a surrogate: a case study. *J. Sex. Marital Ther.* **3,** 40–9.

Gunn, J. (1976) Sexual Offenders. *Brit. J. Hosp. Med.*, **15,** 1, 57–65.

Heim, H. (1981) Sexual behaviour of castrated sex offenders. *Arch. Sex Behav.*, **10,** 1, 11–19.

Heim, N. & Hursch, C.J. (1979) Castration for sex offenders: treatment or punishment? A review and critique of recent European literature. *Arch. Sex Behav.*, **8,** 3, 281–304.

Herman, F.H., Barlow, D.H. & Agras, W.S. (1974) An experimental analysis of exposure to 'explicit' heterosexual stimuli as an effective variable in changing arousal patterns of homosexuals. *Behav. Res. Ther.*, **12,** 335–45.

Kanfer, F.H. & Phillips, J.B. (1970) *Learning Foundations of Behavior Therapy*. New York: John Wiley.

Kinsey, A.C., Pomeroy, W.B. & Martin, C.E. (1948) *Sexual Behavior in the Human Male*. Philadelphia: W.B. Saunders.

Kinsey, A.C., Pomeroy, W.B., Martin, C.E. & Gebhard, C.H. (1953) *Sexual Behavior in the Human Female*. Philadelphia: W.B. Saunders.

Masters, W.H. & Johnson, V.E. (1966) *Human Sexual Response*. Boston: Little, Brown.

Masters, W.H. & Johnson, V.E. (1970) *Human Sexual Inadequacy*. Boston: Little, Brown.

Masters W.H. & Johnson, V.E. (1979) *Homosexuality in Perspective*. Boston: Little, Brown.

Peters, J.J. & Roether, H.A. (1972) Group psychotherapy for probationed sex offenders. In *Sexual Behaviors: Social, Clinical and Legal Aspects*. Resnick, H.L.P. and Wolfgang, M.E. (eds.). Boston: Little, Brown.

Rooth, F.G. (1971) Indecent exposure and exhibitionism. *Brit. J. Hosp. Med.* **5,** 4, 521–33.

Rosenfeld, A.A. (1981) Treating victims of incest. *Brit. J. Sexual Medicine*, **8,** 70, 5–10.

Sand, K., Dickmeis, P. & Schwalbe-Hansen, P. (1964) *Report on Sterilization and Castration*, Publication 353, Copenhagen. (In Danish.)

Saylor, M. (1980) A guided self-help approach to treatment of the habitual sexual offender. In *Sex Offenders in the Criminal Justice System*. West, D.J. (ed.). Papers presented to the 12th Cropwood Round-Table Conference, Dec 1979. Cropwood Conference Series No. 12. Cambridge.

Schmidt, G. & Schorsch, E. (1981) Psychosurgery of sexually deviant patients: review and analysis of new empirical findings. *Arch. Sex. Behav.*, **10,** 3, 301–23.

Serber, M. & Keith, C.G. (1974) The Atascadero project: model of a sexual re-training program for incarcerated homosexual paedophiles. *J. Homosexuality*, **1,** 87–97.

Shaw, R. (1978) The persistent sexual offender – control and rehabilitation. *Probation Journal*, **25,** 1, 9–13.

Stürup, G.K. (1968) *Treating the 'Untreatable'*. Baltimore: Johns Hopkins Press.

Tennent, G., Bancroft, J. & Cass, J. (1974) The control of deviant sexual behaviour by drugs: a double-blind controlled study of benperidol. chlorpromazine and placebo. *Archives of Sexual Behaviour*, **3,** 3, 261–71.

West, D.J. (1980) Treatment in theory and practice. In *Sex Offenders in the Criminal Justice*

System. West, D.J. (ed.). Papers presented to the 12th Cropwood Round-Table Conference, December 1979. Cropwood Conference Series No. 12. Cambridge.

Wolfe, L. (1978) The question of surrogates in sex therapy. In *Handbook of Sex Therapy*. Lo Piccolo, J. & Lo Piccolo, L. (eds.). New York: Plenum.

27

Behaviour Therapy

David Crawford

Behaviour therapy is an approach to treatment based on the principles of learning which have been derived from laboratories of experimental psychology. It is sometimes portrayed, and often practised, as a set of simple, some would say simplistic, techniques only loosely derived from theories of learning. This, however, is to do an injustice to the complexity of underlying research. To fully understand behaviour therapy it is necessary to appreciate that it is based on a science of human behaviour. Behaviour is seen, not as the product of spiritual or mental processes, but as the inevitable result of an interaction between genetic endowment, environmental history and current environmental situations. Even the most unusual or bizarre piece of behaviour is believed to be the lawful outcome of these complex interactions, and potentially amenable to the scientific processes of description, prediction and control. Behaviour therapy is the clinical application of these theoretical principles to problems of disordered behaviour.

Confusion often arises between a medical approach to abnormal behaviour and the behavioural approach, although in principle the distinction is clear. Disordered behaviour can arise from two, not mutually exclusive sources. There can be something physically wrong with the individual, such as organic damage, or a hormonal, biochemical or endocrinological disorder or a genetic defect, which produces abnormal behaviour. In such cases the problem is primarily one of medical concern. Alternatively, an individual may have nothing physically wrong with him but may have had a disturbed, unusual or disordered upbringing in which he has learned to behave abnormally. In this case the problem is primarily one for psychological therapies including behaviour therapy.

Too frequently unusual behaviour is tautologically attributed to a hypothesised illness with some phrase such as, 'He must be sick', when the only evidence of any sickness is the unusual behaviour it is intended to explain. The laws of learning do not differentiate between good and bad behaviour, and just as anyone can learn to excel in artistic, scientific or sporting fields so someone can learn to steal, to be aggressive or be sexually disturbed. In neither case do we need to posit any physical disorder.

Behaviour therapy provides a framework within which abnormal behaviour arising from disordered learning can be conceptualised, understood and sometimes changed. This is the essence of behaviour therapy, which is the subject of this chapter.

INTRODUCTION TO CLASSICAL AND OPERANT CONDITIONING

It is generally agreed that learning can usefully be divided into two types, known as classical and operant conditioning. In lay terms the former is concerned with involuntary or reflex behaviour and the latter with voluntary behaviour.

Classical Conditioning

Classical conditioning applies only to reflex behaviour and what is learned is not a new response, but instead how to produce an established reflex in response to a new stimulus. It is best illustrated by considering the famous experiments conducted by the Russian physiologist Pavlov. In his experiments he studied the reflex of salivation to the stimulus of meat powder in a dog's mouth. He then repeatedly preceded the presentation of the meat powder by the sounding of a bell, and in time the bell on its own came to elicit salvation. Thus, the previously neutral stimulus (the bell) now produced a conditioned reflex response (salivation). From this fairly simple finding Pavlov went on to develop his research with a series of sophisticated experiments which demonstrated a whole range of phenomena relating to the acquisition, extinction, generalisation and discrimination of conditioned responses.

The relevance of classical conditioning to behaviour therapy is primarily with neurotic disorders such as anxiety and phobias where harmless stimuli produce extreme fear. Classical conditioning provides a way of understanding how harmless stimuli, by association with fearful stimuli, could come to elicit such strong emotional reactions. It also provides the basis for treatments such as desensitisation, aversion therapy and the bell-and-pad for enuresis, though it must be acknowledged that there are theoretical arguments over some of these treatments. It has also been suggested that classical conditioning can account for fetishes, in which a neutral object comes to elicit sexual arousal, and other sexual deviations involving inappropriate sexual arousal.

Operant Conditioning

The second type of conditioning is concerned with voluntary rather than reflex behaviour, and with how new behaviours are learned. The foundations of operant conditioning were laid by Thorndike in 1898 with his Law of Effect which can be paraphrased as 'Behaviour is effected by its consequences'. The credit for building on these foundations goes to B.F. Skinner, probably the most influential living pyschologist, who in countless, carefully controlled experiments in numerous books and publications has developed a complex science of human behaviour based on the Law of Effect.

Like many good ideas, the basic principle of operant conditioning is disarmingly simple: behaviour is effected by what follows. If we do something and we get rewarded (or, more technically, reinforced) we are more likely to do it in the future. Conversely, if we do something and get punished we are less likely to do it again. Operant conditioning has elaborated these basic principles to include not only reinforcement and punishment, but also escape, avoidance, extinction, time-out, generalisation and discrimination, as well as many different schedules of reinforcement. Schedules of reinforcement refer to the frequency and timing of consequences rather than their magnitude. Schedules of reinforcement have been shown to be more important than the quantity of reinforcement and can help us to understand behaviour which otherwise appears inexplicable. For example, the inveterate gambler appears to be defying the Law of Effect because the net consequence of his behaviour is to lose money. The explanation lies in the fact that every so often he does indeed win, and although overall this does not cancel out his losses it is enough to maintain his behaviour, as has been repeatedly demonstrated in laboratory experiments using what is known technically as an intermittent reinforcement schedule.

A second example is the chronic alcoholic who has lost his job, wife, family, friends, money and self-respect as a consequence of his drinking. Surely this defies the Law of Effect, for all these aversive consequences should have stopped him drinking. A more detailed analysis of the problem however, reveals the answer. The immediate consequences of stopping drinking are withdrawal symptoms, a hangover and facing up to the loneliness, unemployment and social ostracism which have arisen because of drink. In other words, all the *immediate* consequences of stopping are aversive. Conversely, if he carries on drinking he escapes from the withdrawal symptoms, postpones the hangover and alleviates his social anxieties. So all the *immediate* consequences of continuing drinking are reinforcing. Operant conditioning would predict, therefore, what does indeed happen, that he will continue drinking. The fact that the *long-term* consequences of stopping would all be reinforcing is to little avail because it has been well established that immediate consequences have the most powerful effect.

Operant conditioning, therefore, provides a way of understanding human behaviour in terms of its environmental determinants. Our behaviour is determined by its consequences, not by free will or choice. If someone behaves badly we should not blame him, if someone behaves heroically we should not give him credit, and if we want to change someone's behaviour we should not try and change them but their environment. These are the basic beliefs of operant conditioning and they have aroused considerable controversy, particularly when Skinner has suggested how they might be applied to the widespread social problems of today's world.

In the clinical field, operant conditioning has been applied to a wide range of behavioural problems such as marital, sexual and relationship problems, rehabilitation and training, habit disorders and addictions, stealing and aggression, and in fact any behavioural disorder which is not a result of genetic or physical causes, and even in these latter cases operant conditioning might still have a role to play.

THE CONCEPT OF THE MENTALLY ABNORMAL OFFENDER

Before proceeding to applications of behaviour therapy with the mentally abnormal offender it is necessary to consider the concept from the viewpoint of a behaviourist. For whilst behaviour therapy techniques can be used with the mentally abnormal offender as much as with any other individual, the concept of the mentally abnormal offender lies uneasily within a behaviourist framework for two reasons. Firstly, because of its mentalistic connotations which contrast sharply with the behavioural emphasis on observable events. Secondly, because the concept is used to determine responsibility for behaviour, an idea which is incompatible with a deterministic science of human behaviour. Let us consider these two points in greater detail.

The official doctrine of the nature of man hails chiefly from the seventeenth-century philosopher René Descartes, who proposed that every human being has both a body and a mind. The body is public and exists in the physical world, while the mind is private and exists only in the mental world. This Cartesian dualistic philosophy of mind and body has had a profound influence on Western thinking to the present day, and is fundamental to the concept of mental abnormality, for if the mind is abnormal then a person cannot be held responsible, and therefore culpable, for his actions.

Behaviourists however, do not accept Descartes' doctrine of the separateness of mental and physical experiences. The arguments against the concept of mind have been most cogently espoused in the classic text of Gilbert Ryle (1949) but have been put forward equally forcibly by Skinner (1953, 1974). They argue that mind is a metaphorical abstraction having no physical location and no function. There is no need for a ghost in the machine. The reader who wishes to pursue these arguments in depth can refer to the original sources, but if the behaviourist view that the concept of mind is a seventeenth-century myth is accepted, then where does this leave the concept of mental abnormality? How can one detect abnormality in something having no physical existence and which is only accessible by private introspection? If the only evidence of mental abnormality is that the behaviour of an individual appears unnatural, irrational or unmotivated then the behaviourist would argue that one has a behavioural abnormality, not a mental abnormality.

The second problem with the concept of the mentally abnormal offender for the behaviourist is the implication it has for notions of freedom and responsibility. Existing law assumes that man is autonomous and exercises free will and choice, and therefore can be held justly responsible for what he does, and punished if he offends. Responsibility is synonymous with culpability, and only if responsibility is diminished in some way, such as by mental abnormality, is a person relieved of culpability for his actions.

However, behaviourism is based on a science of human behaviour and the concepts of free will and choice have no place in such a science. Our behaviour may be very complex and at present little understood, but we no more choose to behave than water chooses when to boil. A corollary of accepting that none of us is truly free to choose, is that talk of degrees of responsibility is meaningless.

Responsibility becomes an abstract term whereby people who behave in a responsible manner are simply those who act in accord with widely held rules and mores of social conduct. The problems this poses for the notion of criminal responsibility have been forcefully expressed for many years by Baroness Wootton (1963) and readers wishing to pursue the practical implications of this view of man would do well to read her books and also the evidence submitted by the British Psychological Society (1973) to the Butler Committee on mentally abnormal offenders.

Behaviour therapy is, therefore, concerned with the 'offence' component of the mentally abnormal offender rather than the 'mental abnormality'. If an offender is suffering from a recognised mental illness then that is a case for medical intervention. But if an offender's mental abnormality is of the type variously labelled as psychopathy, sociopathy, personality disorder, behaviour disorder or sexual deviation, then behaviour therapists would not see it as useful to distinguish him from a so-called mentally normal offender, or indeed from an individual with behaviour problems which are not illegal. The laws of learning, like all laws of nature, do not recognise legal or social classifications.

APPLICATIONS OF BEHAVIOUR THERAPY TO THE MENTALLY ABNORMAL OFFENDER

Behaviour therapy with offenders can usefully be divided into institutional management programmes and individual treatment programmes.

Institutional Management Programmes

These programmes, often termed behaviour modification, are based on principles of operant conditioning and are designed to structure the environment so as to reinforce appropriate behaviour and punish undesirable behaviour (Steffy et al, 1969). Most institutions would of course claim that they already adopt such a policy and might feel that behaviour therapy had nothing to offer. The difference is that a properly established behavioural management programme will have a degree of structure, specificity, consistency and monitoring that is invariably lacking in institutions that are not run along formal behavioural lines. Careful observation quickly reveals in most institutions that rewards and punishments are dispensed in a haphazard fashion and one can often witness examples of patients being inadvertently reinforced for inappropriate behaviour. Consider the situation where a mentally ill patient sits quietly on the ward all day and no-one pays him any attention because he is not causing any problems. He then breaks a window and immediately staff run up, ask him what is the matter and for the rest of the evening a nurse stays with him to ensure that he does not do it again. It is clear that the patient is learning: 'If you want staff attention, smash a window.'

By contrast, in a well-run behavioural programme the patient would have received staff attention at intervals throughout the day, all the time he was sitting quietly, as well as possibly receiving tangible reinforcers such as money, sweets or cigarettes. Under this benevolent regime it is unlikely that the window-breaking incident would have occurred.

One particular type of behavioural ward programme which has been developed is the token economy. This was originally developed by Ayllon and Azrin (1968) as a method for rehabilitating long-stay psychiatric patients, but has subsequently been used with a variety of clinical and behavioural problems. In a token economy some form of tangible tokens (e.g. poker chips) are dispensed to the patients contingent on appropriate behaviour. The tokens can subsequently be exchanged for back-up reinforcers such as cigarettes or sweets, but also outings, privileges, privacy, attendance at social events, and in some cases even meals and a bed for the night. All aspects of the patient's behaviour can be included in the token system and all aspects of institutional life can be included in the range of back-up reinforcers.

Token economy programmes have been used with delinquents, adult offenders and mentally abnormal offenders generally with successful results in terms of modifying institutional behaviour (e.g., Burchard, 1967; Tyler and Brown, 1968; Boren and Coleman, 1970; Karacki and Levinson, 1970; Cohen and Filipczak, 1971; Lawson et al, 1971; Mann and Moss, 1973). However, in spite of many theoretical advantages of token economy systems and the evidence that they can significantly modify institutional behaviour, they have not achieved widespread popularity because of practical and ethical problems. Because of the degree of organisation and monitoring required to dispense the tokens and subsequently reimburse them, many token economies fail to survive in the long term and the institution returns to its earlier methods of management (Hall and Baker, 1973; Laws, 1974).

Individual Treatment Programmes

For the reader unfamiliar with behaviour therapy details will first be given of the various techniques, and in the next part of this chapter their use with sex offenders will be described to illustrate how they can be applied to one particular group of offenders.

Desensitisation

This is an anxiety reduction technique originally developed by Wolpe (1958) based on principles of classical conditioning. The person undergoing desensitisation is first taught to relax deeply, and the anxiety provoking stimulus is then presented at low levels of intensity either in imagination or *in vivo*. Gradually the therapist works through a hierarchy of increasingly fearful stimuli until the most feared can be presented whilst the client remains calm and relaxed.

Anxiety is a serious problem for many of the more inadequate and insecure offenders and in such cases systematic desensitisation would probably be the behavioural treatment of choice (e.g. Rim et al, 1971).

Flooding

This is an alternative anxiety reduction technique (Baum, 1970) based on class-ical conditioning procedures, but which contrasts with desensitisation in that the feared stimulus is presented at full intensity right from the start. A client stays exposed to the stimulus for a lengthy period of time until all anxiety has dissipated. This procedure is much quicker than desensitisation but generally is less acceptable and requires a strong therapeutic relationship to prevent the client escaping from the situation in panic thus enhancing anxiety rather than decreasing it.

Aversion therapy

This is probably one of the best known behaviour therapy techniques and is designed to decrease the frequency of inappropriate behaviour, feelings or fan-tasies. It has been frequently used with sex offenders, alcoholics, disorders of appetite and a variety of behavioural problems such as shoplifting. (For useful reviews see Rachman and Teasedale, 1969 and Hallam and Rachman, 1976.) It can be conceptualised as a classical conditioning procedure whereby conditioned anxiety is produced in response to the previously pleasurable but undesirable behaviour, or as an operant conditioning procedure whereby undesirable be-haviour is punished. In either case an aversive stimulus, nowadays almost always an electric shock, but sometimes a nausea-inducing drug or a foul-smelling chemical, is presented contingent on the undesirable behaviour one wishes to eliminate. Considerable controversy surrounds its use on ethical, practical and theoretical grounds.

Covert sensitisation

This is an alternative to aversion therapy developed by Cautela (1967) which makes use of unpleasant imagery rather than physically aversive stimuli and is thus more ethically acceptable. It also has the advantage that the client can use it as a self-control technique by visualising the unpleasant image, whereas with traditional aversion therapy he knows that the shock is only ever delivered in the treatment setting. The technique involves the client imagining the problem behaviour and then switching to an extremely unpleasant, often noxious or nauseous, scene. It has shown considerable success with behavioural problems.

Operant conditioning

The theory of operant conditioning has given rise to a variety of behaviour therapy techniques. Some, such as reinforcement and punishment, are so widely used in a variety of treatments that it is inappropriate to consider them as individual techniques, but others can be usefully identified.

Extinction is the removal of reinforcement for an established behaviour, which results eventually in a decrease in the behaviour. In the short term, however, it can cause an increase in the behaviour as well as emotional responses such as aggression.

Time-out is the removal of an individual from a reinforcing environment to one in which reinforcers are not available. Often this entails a 'time-out room' which is empty and plain, in which an individual is placed for short periods of time as a way of eliminating disruptive behaviour.

Shaping is the building up of a new piece of behaviour by reinforcing successively closer approximations to the final desired performance. *Prompting* and *fading* are alternative ways of producing new behaviour by initially using a physical, verbal or gestural prompt to assist the client. Once the prompted behaviour has been produced it can be reinforced, and the prompt can then be gradually faded out until the client is able to emit behaviour entirely unprompted. This is useful for complex behaviour which it would be difficult to teach by the successive approximations method of shaping.

Chaining is a method for establishing lengthy repertoires of behaviour. The chain of behaviour is broken down into its component links, and each of them is then taught individually, starting contrary to normal expectations, with the last link in the chain and working backwards.

Satiation is a way of reducing the power of a reinforcer by providing it to excess. The opposite of satiation is *deprivation* which serves to enhance the power of a reinforcer.

   All of these operant techniques can usefully be applied to mentally abnormal offenders once a thorough behavioural assessment has identified the nature of the behavioural excesses and deficits presented by the individual.

Modelling

This is the name given to techniques based on principles of observational learning, developed primarily by Bandura (1971). Bandura's investigations have demonstrated the powerful effect of social imitation, with both good and bad results. As a treatment, modelling has been used to reduce anxiety and teach social skills by arranging for the client to observe a competent, coping model. However, modelling also provides us with clues to the development of problem behaviours. An anxious model can lead to an increase of anxiety in the observer, and the likelihood of aggressive behaviour is increased in people who have seen an aggressive model. The message from studies of modelling is that staff of institutions should attempt to behave appropriately at all times so as to provide suitable models for the residents.

Biofeedback

This is an approach, developed from innovative studies by Miller (1969), which has generated great interest over the past decade because of the possibilities it offers for exercising voluntary control over functions which were previously considered to be only under involuntary control. In biofeedback the client is given immediate feedback, usually by an auditory or visual stimulus, of the magnitude of a particular physiological response such as heart rate, and is then reinforced for alterations in the physiological state. Using biofeedback techniques a number of autonomic nervous system responses have come under voluntary control and clinical applications have included anxiety reduction, lowering of blood pressure, controlling epilepsy and altering sexual arousal. The clinical utility of biofeedback has, however, been questioned because the magnitude of the change which can be achieved is often of statistical rather than clinical significance.

Skills training

A variety of behavioural techniques have been developed which are based on a skills deficit approach to behavioural problems. This approach analyses behavioural problems not in terms of behavioural excesses (e.g., he is too aggressive) but as behavioural deficits (e.g., he lacks the verbal skills to deal with authority figures so he hits them). Once a problem has been re-conceptualised as a deficit rather than an excess, then a constructional approach (Schwartz and Goldiamond, 1975) can be adopted whereby new behavioural repertoires are constructed. Social skills training is probably the best-known example of a skills training approach. In social skills training the behavioural components of social interactions are taught using techniques of instructions, modelling, role-playing and feedback. Skills training can also be applied to situations such as job interviews, handling potentially aggressive encounters, controlling anger, dealing with authority figures and asserting one's rights.

Other techniques

There are numerous other behavioural techniques available, with names such as paradoxical intention, response prevention, negative practice, thought stopping, behavioural contracting and cognitive behaviour therapy. Readers wishing to explore these further should consult a comprehensive text such as Ullman and Krasner (1975).

From Techniques to Behavioural Analysis

The sixties saw the development of most of the techniques mentioned in the preceding section, but it was in the seventies that behaviour therapy matured as it made the transition from the use of single techniques to more comprehensive behavioural analyses. A behavioural analysis looks at all aspects of the problem behaviour, including its development and when and where it occurs, and from this formulates a comprehensive, broad-based, behavioural treatment programme.

For example, alcoholics used to be treated simply with aversion therapy.

Now, however, it is recognised that for long-term success one must also look at why the person is drinking too much. If he drinks because he is anxious then systematic desensitisation might be appropriate. If he drinks because he is lonely then social skills training might be appropriate. If he drinks following rows with his wife marital counselling might be appropriate. Additionally he might need help with other aspects of his life such as work and accommodation.

Behavioural analysis is a more refined and sophisticated approach, but also more difficult. It means one cannot provide a 'cook book' which will describe what technique to use with what problem, but it does reflect more realistically the true complexity of human behaviour.

BEHAVIOUR THERAPY WITH SEX OFFENDERS

For a number of reasons the treatment of sex offenders provides a good illustration of the practical application of behaviour therapy. Firstly, few sex offenders are mentally ill yet their behaviour is clearly disturbed; secondly, considerable research has been done with sex offenders and most behaviour therapy techniques are potentially applicable; and finally, the development of behaviour therapy with sex offenders exemplifies the transition from simple techniques in the sixties to more comprehensive behavioural analyses in the seventies.

For many years aversion therapy was seen as the behavioural treatment of choice for sex offenders and the earliest report of its use appeared in 1835. The assumption was that sex offenders were motivated by inappropriate sexual arousal and aversion therapy could be used to eliminate this. Subsequent studies have reported the use of aversion therapy to modify the sexual orientation of homosexuals, transvestites, sexual sadists, paedophiles and exhibitionists. The shock is either associated with the deviant stimulus in a classical conditioning procedure, or used to punish the deviant act, fantasy or erectile response using an operant conditioning procedure.

Results vary considerably depending on the technique employed, the client population, the experimental rigour of the study and the criterion for success. Overall it can be concluded that aversion therapy can modify sexual preferences, but the magnitude of this effect is not always great and the long-term effectiveness in the absence of other treatments is uncertain. The original hope that if clients could abstain from their deviant behaviour for a sufficient period of time, then other types of non-deviant sexual behaviour would fill the vacuum, has generally proved over-optimistic. This failure of the effects of aversion therapy to persist in the long term has led to the search for more effective behaviour therapy techniques to use with sex offenders.

It has increasingly become recognised that an approach which considers sex offenders as presenting only problems of deviant arousal is too narrow, and there has consequently been a shift towards more comprehensive behavioural treatment programmes designed to deal with all of the sex offenders' problems, and in particular the substitution of satisfactory rewarding non-deviant sexual activity (Crawford, 1979, 1981a).

Increasing Non-Deviant Arousal

Various behaviour therapy techniques have been used to increase non-deviant arousal and the clinical and experimental evidence on their effectiveness has been well reviewed by Barlow (1973).

Orgasmic reconditioning

The importance of deviant fantasies in maintaining deviant arousal patterns was highlighted in a paper by McGuire et al (1965) and subsequently a number of methods of changing fantasies during the course of masturbation has been developed under the general name of orgasmic reconditioning (Marquis, 1970). They are based on the principle of switching to non-deviant fantasies just prior to orgasm so that they are strengthened by the powerful reinforcement of orgasm. Progressively the point of switching is moved forward in time so that gradually the deviant fantasies are eliminated and the previously less preferred non-deviant fantasies are substituted.

Classical conditioning

The ability of previously neutral stimuli to become sexually arousing by pairing them in a classical conditioning paradigm with stimuli which are already arousing has been demonstrated experimentally. Clinically, however, the results have been mixed. Some writers have reported success (Beech et al, 1971) but others have been less optimistic (Marshall, 1974) and it appears that the precise timing necessary for classical conditioning to take place is difficult to arrange when the response to be conditioned is sexual arousal.

Operant conditioning: shaping

There has been one report in the literature of shaping sexual arousal by reinforcing progressively greater increases in penile diameter using iced lime juice with a patient who was in a state of water deprivation (Quinn et al, 1970).

Operant conditioning: fading

An ingenious procedure was reported by Barlow and Agras (1973) whereby a male and female slide were superimposed, and as the subject responded sexually the brightness of the female slide increased and that of the male slide decreased. This was effective in increasing heterosexual arousal in homosexual subjects.

Biofeedback

With the development of sophisticated penile feedback systems it has become possible to use biofeedback to enhance sexual responsiveness in males. Biofeedback has been successfully used in a number of studies of patients with erectile difficulties, but its effectiveness with sex offenders has yet to be fully evaluated.

Systematic desensitisation

The ability of anxiety to inhibit sexual arousal is widely acknowledged and is the single most common cause of sexual dysfunction. If sex offenders experience anxiety in relation to non-deviant sexual activity this is likely to inhibit arousal and they can be helped by desensitisation to reduce their anxiety levels.

Decreasing Deviant Arousal

Covert sensitisation

The application of covert sensitisation to problems of deviant sexual arousal was first reported by Cautela and Wisocki (1971). It has subsequently been used by other workers and shown to be an effective procedure for reducing arousal. A typical treatment for a paedophile might involve him imagining making a sexual approach to a child, then starting to feel nauseous and finally vomiting all over the child.

Biofeedback

As well as its use to enhance non-deviant arousal, biofeedback can also be used in reverse to reward decreases in deviant arousal and thus teach offenders to exercise self-control over their deviant sexual responses.

Satiation

A technique developed by Marshall and Barbaree (1978) reduces deviant sexual arousal by satiation. The patient is instructed to continue masturbating for an hour after orgasm whilst verbalising his deviant fantasies. They demonstrated that this was effective in virtually eliminating deviant arousal.

Skills Training

Recognition that sexual behaviour is more than just a sexual response, and also involves complex social and interpersonal skills, has led to the incorporation of skills training in treatments for sex offenders.

Social skills

Although it is not true that all sex offenders lack social skills (Crawford, 1981b) it is clear that if an individual lacks the necessary skills to establish a social relationship that may subsequently develop into a satisfactory sexual relation-ship, he may resort to alternatives such as force, in which case we have the rapist, or children, in which case we have the paedophile. A social skills training programme is described in Crawford and Allen (1979).

Sex education

Incorrect or inadequate sexual knowledge is a problem for some sex offenders, and their ignorance serves to increase their anxiety towards non-deviant sexuality. A structured sex education programme with institutionalised offenders has been shown to increase sexual knowledge, and additionally to decrease anxiety and enhance self-esteem (Crawford and Howells, 1982).

Where to Seek Help

Although behaviour therapy is now well established and widely practised by clinical psychologists, and to a lesser extent other professions, serious sexual offenders are fortunately uncommon, with the consequence that the majority of therapists will have had little direct experience of treating them. Someone seeking treatment may therefore experience considerable difficulty in finding a suitable therapist. The first approach should be to the local National Health Service Department of Clinical Psychology which will usually, though not always, be based in a local mental hospital, to see if they will take the referral or if not can suggest someone in the locality with appropriate expertise. Secondly, there are psychologists employed in the prisons and special hospitals, some of whom will be able to offer advice, although it is unlikely that they would be able to provide treatment other than privately. Finally, there is a small number of clinical psychologists in private practice who could be approached, but as there is at present no statutory registration of psychologists care should be taken to deal only with properly qualified clinicians with some relevant experience and expertise.

CRITICISMS OF TREATMENT FOR OFFENDERS

Practical Problems

The increased use of behaviour therapy with offender populations has not been without its critics. Practical problems are considered here, while ethical issues will be dealt with in the next part of this chapter.

The most damning criticism of treatment programmes with offenders is simply that they do not work. The most influential proponent of this view has been Robert Martinson, who reviewed reports of 231 prison treatment programmes and concluded that 'Nothing works' (Martinson, 1974). However, his views have not gone unchallenged and careful study of his research reveals that his conclusions are an over-simplification. The identical studies have been re-examined by Palmer (1978) who concluded much more optimistically that 45 per cent of them yielded positive results. It is, therefore, premature to reject out of hand treatment programmes with offenders, but nevertheless there are real problems which merit consideration. Only brief coverage is possible here and readers wishing to pursue these issues in greater depth should read articles by Blackburn (1980) and Crawford (1980, 1982).

The wrong model of crime

One criticism of treatment for offenders is that crime is a product of a sick society, not a sick individual, and treatment is therefore inappropriate. However, research has shown that a proportion of offenders are variously mentally ill, alcoholic, inadequate, institutionalised, deficient in academic attainment and social skills, have low self-esteem and are prone to anxiety and other emotional problems. So treatment in the broadest sense of the word, to include rehabilitation, vocational training, skills training and education, would seem appropriate for significant numbers of offenders, and in particular mentally abnormal offenders. Indeed American courts have established the right of detained patients to receive treatment, otherwise their continued detention is illegal.

The wrong setting

A second criticism of treatment for offenders is that it is often conducted in the wrong setting. Offenders are removed from the environment which precipitated their crime to an alien, secure institution. The secure environment poses problems for both assessment and treatment because it places restrictions on access to every-day items like alcohol and money, disrupts work and leisure activities and restricts social contacts, especially with women and children. In spite of all these very real difficulties, evidence reviewed by Blackburn (1980) showed that institutional treatments are as successful as community treatments, thus providing no support for the more strident critics of institutions.

The wrong behavioural targets

A third criticism of treatment programmes is that they concentrate on the wrong behaviours. By their very nature most serious crimes are isolated events, which means they cannot be directly observed or modified within the treatment settings. It is necessary, therefore, to identify behaviours which have played a significant causal role in precipitating the offence and direct treatment towards these. It is hoped that by changing these behaviours the subsequent likelihood of offending will be reduced or eliminated. But there is a danger that the behavioural targets selected will not in fact be relevant, and many treatment programmes have concentrated on convenience behaviours, which seem primarily designed to aid the smooth running of the institution and to serve the custodial aims of the management.

The paper by Blackburn (1980) has some evidence which would support this criticism. He found that programmes which concentrated on skills training (such as academic, vocational or personal) were twice as likely to be successful in reducing recidivism as those that concentrated on convenience behaviours. Treatment should therefore be directed towards teaching new skills rather than simple compliance with institutional rules.

Ethical Problems

Behaviour therapy has given rise to considerable concern, and guidelines for its use have been published both in America, and more recently in Britain. To some extent behaviour therapy has been a victim of its own methodology, with its clear specification of goals and its admission that its aim is to change behaviour. Although many behaviour therapists would argue that their approach raises no unique ethical problems, this argument has not generally been accepted.

Causes of ethical concern

There certainly have been cases where the methodology of behaviour therapy has been misused. Examples such as long-term solitary confinement described as time-out, administration of apomorphine to induce violent vomiting and, most notoriously, the use of unmodified electroconvulsive therapy and with-holding food to force Vietnamese patients to work (Cotter, 1967), have all given behaviour therapy a bad name. Moreover, some treatment programmes, in particular those at Napsbury Hospital which resulted in the setting up of a DHSS Working Party to formulate ethical guidelines for behaviour modification, have been described as behaviour modification yet would not be accepted as such by the majority of professionals working in the field.

However, there are many other treatments which are open to abuse or misuse, and unethical practice is not confined to behaviour therapy. So why have ethical worries arisen to a disproportionate degree in relation to behaviour therapy? The answer appears to lie in the *means* employed and the *ends* they are designed to achieve.

The use of an aversive stimulus whose intended purpose is to inflict pain and discomfort raises ethical concerns greater than for an equally unpleasant treatment but where the pain is an unfortunate by-product. Withholding of food, the restriction of privileges, and limitations on basic rights of freedom, privacy and comfort, quite rightly cause concern, even when they are used in the best interests of the patient.

However, it is not only the means which have come in for ethical criticism. Behaviour therapy is explicit that its goal is to modify human behaviour. Any attempt to change behaviour involves a judgement of the propriety of one behaviour compared with another, a subjective value judgement that is potentially open to abuse. Whereas in the medical model the goal of treatment is a healthy individual, the behavioural model has no such absolute norm towards which to strive.

A further problem can arise because behaviour therapy techniques are not the sole prerogative of any one profession, and as knowledge is more widely disseminated so the likelihood of abuse increases. Programmes set up by competent professionals with appropriate expertise may end up being run by inexperienced staff.

Ethical Safeguards

Proscription

One approach to providing ethical safeguards has been to proscribe certain techniques such as aversive stimulation or withholding of food. For example, the Florida Guidelines for behaviour therapy state that *regardless of efficacy* aversive techniques should not be generally used if people believe them to be cruel or inhumane.

The problems with a blanket proscription of certain techniques are that it allows no room for flexibility for individual cases, it can be circumvented by giving a proscribed technique a new name and it offers no positive guidance on more general ethical standards. The implication is that a programme which does not include any proscribed techniques is, by definition, ethical.

Professional standards

This approach aims to maintain ethical standards by exhorting or enforcing adherence to general principles of good professional behaviour such as respecting a patient's rights, providing the best care possible in the most humane manner, and preserving the dignity and worth of the patient at all times.

The problem with such high-sounding and generalised principles is that they are hard to define and even more difficult to enforce. If aversion therapy appears to be the treatment of choice is it unethical to withhold it or unethical to use it? Gross injustices can be perpetrated in the best interests of the patient, and systems of intra-professional monitoring lack independence and do not have public confidence. A more satisfactory variation on the professional standards approach is the requirement of specified qualifications and experience to be held by the personnel supervising behaviour therapy programmes. It is still left, however, to the individual professional to make the final judgement as to whether a given treatment breaches acceptable ethical standards.

Public scrutiny

A third alternative is to ensure that all behaviour therapy programmes are open to public scrutiny by relatives, friends, staff, the press and interested pressure groups, and posssibly by independently constituted review bodies. The Minnesota Guidelines, for example, lay down the need for the establishment of local review committees to evaluate programmes, obtain annual progress reports and ensure that staff are properly qualified and consent procedures are followed.

The problems with this solution are that it can be cumbersome and expensive and can result in very cautious policies influenced by emotive or political factors rather than the patient's best interest. It also can breach patients' confidentiality, itself an ethical concern.

National Health Service Guidelines

In 1980 the British government published the 'Zangwill Report' (RCP, RCN and BPS, 1980) which formulated ethical guidelines for the conduct of programmes of behaviour modification in the National Health Service. The report identified six main areas of concern and made recommendations.

Information

Full information concerning the programme should always be available to the patient, his relatives and staff in the hospital. A patient's closest relatives should have unrestricted access unless specifically limited as part of the programme, but in no case should restrictions exceed two weeks.

Consent

Oral consent to participate should always be obtained from the patient, or nearest relative if the patient is incapable, and consent can be withdrawn at any time without prejudice.

No patient should ever be deprived of professional care but the rescheduling or restricting of food, money, visits or leave, or the use of isolation or physical restraint are permissible, although in such cases consent should be obtained in writing.

Control

All patients have a right to a high minimum standard of care including professional attention, and adequate diet, acceptable accommodation, clothing and the right to retain their own goods and money; these basic rights and privileges must be meticulously respected, and reinforcement should normally involve the provision of goods or privileges which improve on this basic standard.

Mild aversive procedures such as time-out are acceptable if used sparingly, but techniques causing discomfort such as electric shock should be employed only as a last resort.

Responsibility

Behaviour modification should be practised by a multi-disciplinary therapeutic team, within which each member of the team is legally responsible for his or her own behaviour.

Review bodies

The working party initially recommended the setting up of Regional Review Committees to scrutinise all programmes of behaviour modification, but this recommendation was reluctantly withdrawn in view of substantial objections which were voiced.

Training

The importance of training is stressed and an inter-disciplinary approach advocated. As a first stage, individuals with substantial knowledge and experience should be identified to offer guidance and advice, and as a second stage, workshops should be developed to offer in-service training.

CONCLUSIONS

Behaviour therapy has an especially important role in the treatment, training and rehabilitation of abnormal offenders because it is often their behavioural disturbance rather than their mental illness that has resulted in them being detained. The full range of behaviour therapy techniques developed for clinical use is potentially applicable to mentally abnormal offenders, and they have a right to receive the best treatment currently available.

However, the closed nature of the institutions in which most mentally abnormal offenders find themselves requires special ethical consideration, particularly in relation to consent. With adequate public scrutiny such problems should be insuperable, and mentally abnormal offenders can benefit from the rapid progress made in the field of behaviour therapy over the past two decades.

REFERENCES

Ayllon, T. & Azrin, N.H. (1968) *The Token Economy*. New York: Appleton-Century-Crofts.
Bandura, A. (1971) Psychotherapy based upon modelling principles. *Handbook of Psychotherapy and Behavior Change*. In Bergin, A.E. & Garfield, S.L. (eds.). New York: Wiley.
Barlow, D.H. (1973) Increasing heterosexual responsiveness in the treatment of sexual deviation: a review of the clinical and experimental evidence. *Behavior Therapy*, **4**, 655–71.
Barlow, D.H. & Agras, W.S. (1973) Fading to increase heterosexual responsiveness in homosexuals. *J. Appl. Behav. Anal.*, **6** 355–66.
Baum, M. (1970) Extinction of avoidance responding through response prevention (flooding). *Psychol. Bull*, **74**, 276–84.
Beech, H.R., Watts, F. & Poole, A.D. (1971) Classical conditioning of sexual deviation: a preliminary note. *Behavior Therapy*, **2**, 400–2.
Blackburn, R. (1980) *Still not Working? A look at Recent Outcomes in Offender Rehabilitation*. Paper presented at the Scottish Branch of the British Psychological Society Conference on Deviance, University of Stirling, February 1980.
Boren, J.J. & Colnman, H.D. (1970) Some experiments on reinforcement principles within a psychiatric ward for delinquent soldiers. *J. Appl. Behav. Anal.*, **3**, 29–37.
British Psychological Society (1973) Memorandum of evidence to the Butler Committee on the law relating to the mentally abnormal offender. *Bull. Brit. Psychol. Soc.*, **26**, 331–42.
Burchard, J.D. (1967) Systematic socialisation: A programmed environment for the habilitation of anti-social retardates. *Psychological Record*, **17**, 461–76.
Cautela, J.R. (1967) Covert sensitisation. *Psychological Reports*, **20**, 459–68.
Cautela, J.R. & Wisocki, P.A. (1971) Covert sensitisation for the treatment of sexual deviations. *Psychological Record*, **21**, 37–48.
Cohen, H.L. & Filipczak, J. (1971) *A New Learning Environment*. San Francisco: Jossey-Bass.
Cotter, L.H. (1967) Operant conditioning in a Vietnamese mental hospital. *Am. J. Psychiat.* **124**, 23–8.
Crawford, D.A. (1979) Modification of deviant sexual behaviour: The need for a comprehensive approach. *Brit. J. Med. Psychol.*, **52**, 151–6.
Crawford, D.A. (1980) *Deviant Behaviour: Problems and issues*. Paper presented at the British Association of Behavioural Psychotherapy Annual Conference, Sheffield, July 1980.

Crawford, D.A. (1981a) Treatment approaches with paedophiles. In *Adult Sexual Interest in Children*. Cook, M. & Howells, K. (eds.). London: Academic Press.

Crawford, D.A. (1981b) The assessment and training of social skills with mentally abnormal offenders. Unpublished PhD thesis, July, University of Reading.

Crawford, D.A. (1982) Problems for the assessment and treatment of sexual offenders in closed institutions: and some solutions. In *Issues in Criminological and Legal Psychology, No. 2*. Black, D.A. (ed.). Leicester: British Psychological Society Publications.

Crawford, D.A. & Allen, J.V. (1979) A social skills training programme with sex offenders. In *Love and Attraction: An International Conference*. Cook, M. & Wilson, G.W. (eds.). Oxford: Pergamon.

Crawford, D.A. & Howells, K. (1982) The effect of sex education with disturbed adolescents. *Behavioural Psychotherapy*, **10**, 339-45.

Hall, J. & Baker, R. (1973) Token economy systems: breakdown and control. *Behaviour Research and Therapy*, **11**, 253-63.

Hallam, I. & Rachman, S. (1976) Current status of aversion therapy. In *Progress in Behavior Modification*. Hersen M., Eisler, R.M. & Miller, P.M. (eds.). Vol. 2, New York: Academic Press.

Karacki, L. & Levinson, R.B. (1970) A token economy in a correctional institution for youthful offenders. *Howard Journal of Penology and Crime Prevention*, **13**, 20-30.

Laws, R.D. (1974) The failure of a token economy. *Federal Probation*, 33-8.

Lawson, R.B., Green, R.T., Richardson, J.S., McClure, G. & Padina, R.J. (1971) Token economy program in a maximum security correctional hospital. *Journal of Nervous and Mental Disease*, **152**, 199-205.

Mann, R.A. & Moss, G.R. (1973) The therapeutic use of a token economy to manage a young and assaultive impatient population. *Journal of Nervous and Mental Disease*, **157**, 1-9.

Marquis, J.N. (1970) Orgasmic reconditioning: changing sexual object choice through controlling masturbation fantasies. *Journal of Behavior Therapy and Experimental Psychiatry*, **1**, 263-71.

Marshall, W.L. (1974) The classical conditioning of sexual attractiveness: a report of four therapeutic failures. *Behavior Therapy*, **5**, 298-99.

Marshall, W.L. & Barbaree, H.E. (1978) The reduction of deviant arousal: satiation treatment for sexual aggressors. *Criminal Justice and Behavior*, **5**, 294-303.

Martinson, R. (1974) What works? Questions and answers about prison reform. *The Public Interest*, **35**, 22-54.

McGuire, R.J., Carlisle, J.M. and Young, B.G. (1965) Sexual deviations as conditioned behaviour: a hypothesis. *Behaviour Research and Therapy*, **2**, 185-90.

Miller, N.E. (1969) Learning of visceral and glandular responses. *Science*, **163**, 434-45.

Palmer, T. (1978) *Correctional intervention and research*. Lexington: D.C. Heath.

Quinn, J.T., Harbison, J.J.M. & McAllister, H. (1970) An attempt to shape human penile responses. *Behaviour Research and Therapy*, **8**, 213-16.

Rachman, S. & Teasedale, J. (1969) *Aversion therapy and behaviour disorders: An analysis*. London: Routledge & Kegan Paul.

Rim, D.C., de Groot, J.C., Boord, J., Heiman, J. & Dillon, P.V. (1971) Systematic desensitisation of an anger response. *Behaviour Research and Therapy*, **9**, 273-80.

Royal College of Psychiatrists, Royal College of Nursing and British Psychological Society (1980) *Behaviour Modification (the Zangwill Report)*. London: HMSO.

Ryle, G. (1949) *The Concept of Mind*. Harmondsworth: Penguin.

Schwartz, A. & Goldiamond, I. (1975) *Social casework: A behavioral approach*. New York: Columbia University Press.

Skinner, B.F. (1953) *Science and Human Behavior*. New York: Macmillan.

Skinner, B.F. (1974) *About Behaviourism*. London: Jonathan Cape.

Steffy, R.A., Hart, J., Crane, M., Tormey, D. & Marlett, N. (1969) Operant behaviour modification techniques applied to a ward of severely regressed and aggressive patients. *Can. Psychiat Ass. J.* **14**, 59-67.

Tyler, V.O. & Brown, G.D. (1968) Token reinforcement of academic performance with institutionalised delinquent boys. *Journal of Educational Psychology*, **59**, 164-8.

Ullman, L.P. & Krasner, L. (1975) *A Psychological Approach to Abnormal Behavior* (2nd edn.). New Jersey: Prentice-Hall.

Wolpe, J. (1958) *Psychotherapy by Reciprocal Inhibition*. Stanford: Stanford University Press.

Wootton, B. (1963) *Crime and the Criminal Law:* London: Stevens.

28

The Results of Treatment

Michael Craft

There are some who doubt the success of treatment with severe mentally abnormal offenders and feel life imprisonment is safer for the community. The trial of Peter Sutcliffe, the Yorkshire Ripper, with all medical evidence favouring schizophrenia, is a case in point. Others would concur with Mr Justice Marshall's remark on making a hospital order recently: 'The interests of the public are best served by curing this patient.' Yet what is cure for mentally abnormal offenders?

To study whether any or many are 'cured', one can best consider the effect of 'treatment' by maximum security hospitals in Britain and other countries. It is to these that the most severely mentally abnormal offenders are sent.

TREATMENT RESULTS FOR SPECIAL HOSPITALS

More than half the residents in Broadmoor, Rampton and Moss Side are 'psychopathic' or the often interchangeable synonym 'subnormal'. There has always been pessimism concerning success of treatment with these. Some have believed cure to be virtually impossible (Cleckley, 1964). Others doubt that it is treatable (Gould, 1959). Some believe that genetic misendowment (Heaton-Ward, 1963), others that damage to the developing fetus (Stott, 1962) and early adverse childhood experiences (Scott, 1963) militate against later treatment success. Unfortunately we are handicapped by the lack of long-term follow-up studies on the natural history of the condition.

Searching Western literature for follow-up studies as to how psychopaths 'develop' or 'mature', one is first baffled by the lack of agreed definition, and then by finding that the diagnosis usually marks the point at which the patient is removed from his 'natural development' in the community into some secure abode. This present follow-up concentrates on extreme examples of the disorder admitted to a more secure abode, the special hospital system of Britain. If it can be shown that subjects with psychopathy or subnormality and mental illness in Rampton, Moss Side and Broadmoor improved with the passage of time or treatment, or both, then it follows that lesser degrees of these disorders admitted elsewhere might have similar if not better prospects of alleviation.

1   Special Hospital studies must start with that of Tong and McKay in 1959. They followed 587 patients, predominantly male (average age, IQ and convictions not given) discharged from Rampton in 1945–1956. Direct information

436

was obtained for 423 of the 587 cases, central criminal files being searched for the rest. Of the 587, 171 had further offended, 86 had been convicted by the courts, the other 85 being returned to Rampton from local hospitals. Only two received a prison sentence over three years. Relapse offences were less serious than before, 19 being violent (67 before admission), 12 with heterosexual offences (23 before), nil for property damage (8 before) but 63 for breaking and entering (48 at original admission). Rampton treatment had lasted 7.4 to 12.8 years according to sub-group. Post discharge, follow-up duration, and employment position were not given. Of the 587, we find 416 had not further offended and 'most' (number not given) were reinstated in the community from the sub-normality hospital to which they were first transferred from Rampton.

2   Moss Side is reported upon by Craft (1965) who followed 100 consecutive admissions from 01.01.51 onwards. By ten years later 70 had been discharged to ordinary psychiatric hospitals and five transferred to Rampton or Broadmoor. Of the 70, nine had been readmitted to one of the three special hospitals within the ten years. No average IQ, age, convictions or length of treatment were given. The author gives reasons for supposing that the type of patient had not materially changed with the passage of the Mental Health Act, and most would have earned the label psychopathic disorder under this Act. In an extension of this study (Craft, 1966) discharges were followed up from among the 382 average patient population between 1951 and 1959, 10.2 per cent were discharged each year to local hospitals, jobs, home etc., of whom about 10 per cent (1 per cent overall) relapsed and were returned to Moss Side each year.

3   Gathercole, myself and others (1968) followed up 76 Moss Side discharges over a four-year period using a variety of criteria, the 'failure rate for the current sample being 19 out of 76 or 26 per cent'. Of the 76, 8 per cent were convicted (4 per cent imprisoned), and 22 per cent returned to a special hospital for further offences, mostly less in severity than on first admission. However, another 29 per cent were not discharged from the provincial hospital to which they had been transferred, and this despite a seven-year period of treatment. This was the first study following consecutive admissions through to community placement and meant that of patients so severely disordered as to need treatment in one of the three special security hospitals of England, just half (49 per cent) returned to the community were unconvicted and did not need further admission seven years after first admission.

4   Acres (1975) followed up 93 previously convicted patients discharged from the three special hospitals in 1971 direct to the community. Two years later half were in their own homes or lodgings, 17 per cent in special hospitals, 13 per cent in prison, two per cent in NHS hospitals. Most had settled, stable sexual relationships. 'Although 60 per cent were working within one month of discharge, 17 per cent had no work in the whole two-year follow-up period.' Forty per cent received regular supervision, and the presence of supervision and its frequency lessened the chance of re-conviction.

5   The Aarvold Committee (Home Office, 1973) met to consider safeguards necessary prior to release of special hospital patients. This was after public concern at the repeat poisoning by Graham Young, an ex-Broadmoor patient,

allowed access to poisons during after-care supervision. It examined a four-year follow-up of those on Section 65 Orders and found that the majority of those discharged unconditionally were re-convicted (70 per cent), as were 56 per cent of those released on expiry of the Section 65 Order. The best re-conviction rate of 16 per cent was for those discharged conditionally, and of these three-quarters were neither recalled nor re-convicted during the four-year study. They concluded that 'licence' under supervision was to be the preferred method of discharge from special hospitals.

6   Dell and Parker (1979) examined all 929 admissions to the special hospital case registers for 1971–4. Most were admitted after conviction, only 10 per cent of men and 57 per cent of women in 1974 being non-offenders admitted from local psychiatric hospitals. The analysis underlined the admission policy; Broadmoor tending to take male patients from the courts who were mentally ill, although a quarter had psychopathic disorder; Rampton and Moss Side taking one-third psychopathic, one-quarter subnormal, one-quarter mentally ill and one-fifth severely subnormal. Since this time there has been a decreasing number of admissions labelled subnormal, an increasing use of the term psychopath, and the proportion of male admissions from court has increased. Most admissions were for violence, including homicide; men were usually convicted prior to transfer, women often unconvicted and transferred on Section 26 from local hospitals. Dell (1980) followed up 105 special hospital discharges two years after transfer to local hospitals, finding seven recalled (two following management difficulties, four following violent behaviour, the last for arson). Three others committed serious offences, leaving 95 in local hospitals or in the community.

7   Black's special hospitals follow-up is described in Chapter 25. Of 128 men discharged direct to the community from Broadmoor, half remained there over the five-year study period, 20 per cent were re-admitted to Broadmoor, 20 per cent to local hospitals. In all 50 had mainly trivial court appearances, but 29 were imprisoned, 13 for personal violence. However, six were violent after the follow-up, two committing homicides. The best indicator for re-conviction was prior conviction; previous psychiatric treatment the best predictor of relapse.

8   Tennent (1983) followed up 617 discharges from English special hospitals for 12 to 17 years. Of these, 55 per cent committed offences during this period, 21 per cent being for violence. Of all violent offenders, 70 per cent were psychopathic or subnormal and 19 per cent previously mentally ill; of non-violent offenders 71 per cent were psychopathic or subnormal, 13 per cent had been mentally ill. Of non-offenders 42 per cent were psychopathic or subnormal, 46 per cent mentally ill. The remaining numbers consisted of multiple offences and multiple diagnoses. Nearly half of the violent offenders had been discharged abruptly by a mental health review tribunal.

Other Studies

9   Walker and McCabe (1973) followed up a country-wide cohort of 1963–64 patients admitted to psychiatric hospitals under Sections 60 and 65 of the Mental

Health Act, whilst Robertson (1981) later followed them for a total of 15 years. The majority of these court admissions were to ordinary psychiatric, a minority to special hospitals. Bowden (1981) quoting a personal communication says:

> For men diagnosed as mentally ill at the time of the order, subsequent offences of severe violence and of a sexual nature were very rare (4 per cent). For men with mental handicap, severe violence and sexual offences were very uncommon (7 per cent), despite the fact that 28 per cent of the orders had been made for sexual offences. [These findings should be related to the more general observation that sexual offenders tend to have fewer re-convictions than other criminals, Christiansen et al, 1965.] Men with a diagnosis of psychopathic disorder had the highest rate: most of them re-offended, although serious violence was unusual (9 per cent). It should be pointed out, however, that the three groups were so different on the crucial variables of age and number of previous convictions that the relevance of diagnosis remains uncertain. For example, the extent of criminal history contributes to the diagnosis of psychopathic disorder, but it is also the most reliable indicator of future offences.

10 Herstedvester was a 200-bed Danish hospital under the Danish Penal Department admitting criminal recidivists from the courts under a special law. It has been extensively described by Stürup (1968). The criteria of admission were:
(a) males aged over 15;
(b) convicted of three crimes within three years;
(c) needing psychiatric treatment;
(d) not having psychosis or IQ under 70.

Stromgren (1965) on being questioned, reported that the repeatedly convicted psychopath was by 1965 rarely found in penal units outside Herstedvester or its sister institution, Horsens, which opened in 1955. Between 1935 and 1953, Herstedvester had admitted 900 from the courts (Stürup, 1968). The 1963 follow-up showed 780 of these discharged into the community; 56 were still in their various penal units or returned by courts to local mental hospitals; 60 had died; four were abroad. The original group of 900 had been aged 15–73 on admission (mainly 25–29 age group), IQ 70 upwards, and on average had four previous convictions. Despite the considerable recidivision of the intake, total treatment was surprisingly short. As a result of the gain in treatment confidence from the 1930s and 1950s (together with an effective system of compulsory after-care and placement of all discharges in residential jobs) almost all property offenders could be discharged inside four years, and 97 per cent of sex offenders within the first year provided they accepted voluntary castration! Under the Danish Act follow-up was both compulsory and indefinite, although after a period of five years the order was usually annulled by the court which made the original order after receipt of medical report. As might be expected under these circumstances, at any one time 90 per cent of those being supervised within the community on compulsory indefinite after-care were holding employment, and the few who were not were either between jobs or temporarily unemployed. Whilst in 1963 780 (87 per cent) of the 900 admitted before 1953 were back in the community (and only 56, 6 per cent of the total, were still under detention in any institution), one does not know how many of the 87 per cent had been re-convicted in the intervals. One can only conclude that among the most serious psychopathic and criminal recidivists allowed under the Danish penal code the vast majority seemed to improve with time.

United States Studies

11   Steadman and Halfon (1971) followed up the 969 patients released from two institutions for the criminally insane in the USA as a result of the judicial decision in the case of Baxstrom, despite medical evidence supporting continued detention on the grounds of dangerousness (also discussed in Chapter 18). The main findings were the high proportion of patients returned to the community after transfer to other psychiatric hospitals and examination by other doctors, and the low percentage who later needed re-admission. Once more the arrest rate of patients on a short term follow-up was similar to that of the non-insane criminal population, and although further arrests were found over a slightly longer follow-up (McGarry 1971), Steadman and Halfon still doubted the need to retain the Baxstrom patients for an average of 13 years in an institution for the criminally insane prior to their unexpected discharge.

12   The state of Maryland built Patuxent as a 620-bed security hospital on the Herstedvester model. Boslow and Kohlmeyer (1963) report on 81 'parolees' from this hospital. Criteria for admission were similar to those of Herstedvester, under a similar law. Few details are given of average age, IQ, treatment length or follow-up, except that by 1963 the hospital population was 430, and of the 81 parolees 28 were re-convicted during the follow-up period of 1957–63, 13 being re-hospitalised. However, this is not a fair estimate of Patuxent treatment, as newspaper reports during building led to strong local antipathy and difficulty in employment and residence on discharge. It was a good example of answering one problem only to create another.

13   The much criticised US 'sexual psychopath' laws are still in being in Washington State. Saylor (1980) gives a recent review. The Western and Eastern state hospitals have a 180-bed semi-secure psychiatric facility practising group and therapeutic community treatment for court-referred sex offenders aged 15 upwards. After screening for 90 days and a court report, suitable patients are accepted on indeterminate order for a minimum stay of 18 months (average 20–24 months) with minimum of 18 months outpatient and residence, and job supervision thereafter. The 'sexual psychopath' laws allow treatment of first offenders and 'youth facility rejects' under 17. Saylor writes, 'sixty-five per cent have never been incarcerated previously. Fifteen per cent have been incarcerated where a sex offence was involved and 20 per cent on some other basis.' She goes on, '23 per cent have committed rape, 24 per cent statutory rape (this usually means under-age intercourse with consent), 33 per cent indecent liberties, 3 per cent indecent exposure, 6 per cent incest' and 11 per cent other varieties of lesser offences. 'In 81 per cent of the cases no force was used ...' She reports that '... from December 1967 to May 1979, we have a recidivist rate of 22 per cent or, of 402 graduates, there have been 89 re-offenders'. The conclusion drawn is optimistic: 'A number of storms have been weathered without compromising the effectiveness of treatment.'

CAN THE PSYCHOPATH BE 'CURED'?

As might be expected, the answer depends on how one defines 'psychopath', and how one defines 'cured'. If one talks in terms of those examples of psychopathy so extreme that they merit admission to special hospitals, then the answer is both 'yes' and 'no'. Accepting that in special hospitals 'subnormality' and 'psycho-pathy' are interchangeable titles for the dull normal personality-disordered, such patients comprise 55 per cent of inmates at Rampton and Moss Side, and some 25 per cent at Broadmoor. Only about a third of special hospital admissions are released in under four years (Tennent et al, 1980). Dell and Parker (1979) give the length of stay of the convicted mentally ill as 11.4 years on average (SD 7.3), unconvicted 7.7 (SD 2.3). However, the vast majority of admissions do leave eventually, and following discharge some of the variables underlying success or failure have been teased out in follow-up studies succeeding the Aarvold Report (Home Office, 1973). Many of these extreme examples of psychopath do re-offend, principally for trivial offences, but 9 per cent for serious personal violence including homicide.

Acres (1975) showed that after discharge about 60 per cent gain work within one month, although 17 per cent were unable to find work in a two-year follow-up period thereafter. By this time half had their own homes or lodgings, but one-third were back in institutions. The 40 per cent who received continuous statutory supervision and a similar number who had voluntary supervision did better than tribunal discharges without supervision. Thirty per cent in Broad-moor (mainly mentally ill), 49 per cent from Rampton (mostly psychopaths) and 79 per cent of Moss Side (mainly psychopaths) had been re-convicted during the two-year follow-up period, mostly for trivial offences; 64 per cent overall being property offences. Black showed that at five years after discharge half remained in the community, 20 per cent were back in their special hospitals and 20 per cent in other local hospitals. Other studies show that re-conviction among convicted special hospital patients ran at a similar level as convicted members of the population of similar age; and that psychiatric hospital admission also ran at a similar level to those of similar age previously hospitalised.

As judged by the severity of criminal offence, the dangerousness of these people substantially decreased with the passage of time or treatment or both, so that, although all patients on follow-up (see, e.g. Acres, 1975) were originally admitted for serious offences, after release only 13 per cent were re-convicted of similar offences. Again, re-conviction rate of similar persons in the general community decreases with the decades, also the severity of crime for which convicted. Time, treatment or chance factors clearly result in the 'maturation' or 'cure' of some if not most psychopaths. There is some evidence (see Chapter 24) that their death rate is higher than the general population, due to suicide, violent death, alcohol, misadventure, or to overall poor personal care. Walker and McCabe (1973) presented the first major analysis of the results of treatment with those certified as subnormal under the English and Welsh Mental Health Act; Robertson (1981) with Gibbens give follow-up studies over a 15-year period, of the results of treatment and follow-up concerning these subnormals.

There are also figures, quoted above, of the results of treatment and follow-up studies among subnormals in the special hospitals.

All these analyses must be viewed against the common clinical practice of special hospitals, using these two terms subnormal and psychopath almost synonymously. In practice, in the England and Wales of 1982, a substantial proportion of those receiving Section 60/65 order as subnormal under the Mental Health Act went to the special hospitals, provincial mental handicap hospitals usually taking such offenders on a probation order with a condition of residence for psychiatric treatment. Of those on a Section 60/65 order as subnormal, most went to Rampton or Moss Side together with psychopaths of average or full normal ability, where they comprise well over half the patient population. Brighter psychopaths go to Broadmoor. The surveys reviewed in Chapter 12 suggest that the term subnormal would apply to duller psychopaths from courts and include a greater number of unconvicted severely behaviourally disturbed patients from provincial mental handicap hospitals whose prognosis is therefore slightly better than the general run of psychopathic patients sent straight from Crown Courts to special hospitals.

Statistics bear this out. The duller psychopaths (that is labelled subnormal) on Robertson's 15-year follow-up were compared with mentally ill; and

With regard to the total extent of their offending behaviour these male groups were found to be very similar and to differ significantly from the third classification group within the Mental Health Act, namely, the psychopathically disordered ... although there are some differences between the [mentally] ill and the handicapped in terms of *types* of offence committed, these groups do not differ in terms of the total number of offences committed and the total number of court appearances made. Nor do they differ significantly as regards prison experience. However, this broad similarity makes fundamental differences between the two groups regarding the pattern of their criminal careers ...

The most important difference between the mentally handicapped offender and the mentally ill offender is that of age. The mentally handicapped men were some ten years younger than the mentally ill group on average and this primary difference is reflected in important criminological variables, such as age at first conviction.

He goes on:

In the handicapped [subnormal] group there is a pattern of juvenile larceny, usually committed in late adolescence, which develops into more sophisticated types of acquisitive offending, such as breaking and entering. Apart from a higher incidence of sexual offending, this pattern is very similar to that found in the general criminal population. It is certainly much closer to that norm than it is to the pattern followed by the mentally ill offender population ...

For those labelled subnormal the follow-up studies show they had fewer violent offences, more sexual offences, rather less prison experience overall than mentally ill offenders. In summary, they had a markedly better prognosis as far as re-offending was concerned than brighter psychopaths (actually labelled psychopaths) and the mentally ill. Since they also had more frequent hospital admissions, it could be argued that they were more 'protected' than the other two groups by re-admission to local hospitals at times of stress, risk or danger. This can of course, be argued both ways.

Other detailed research and statistics concerning re-offending by the mentally ill population is discussed in detail by Tony Black in Chapter 23.

Where the reader is attempting to evaluate the chances of a particular individual breaking down psychiatrically, socially or legally, statistics such as the above present a compound amounting to only one variable that can only be a guide to results which may not be appropriate for an individual with his assets and deficits. It has been shown earlier in this book that the term 'subnormal' can often be a duller variant of the term 'psychopath' and that the two labels have interchangeable diagnostic validity. For the mentally ill offender population there are diagnostic terms of greater reliability such as schizophrenia and depression, although even these diagnostic labels can be effectively destroyed by an efficient cross-examination as Paul Gerber shows in the Epilogue. Thus in the mentally ill, the prospects really depend on the inherent variability of the illness process compounded by such environmental variables (discussed in Chapter 8) as drugs, emotional relatives, day occupation, personal will-power; with finally the sheer elements of chance, a *femme fatale*, the chances of employment, recession, and war itself, all outside the calculations of professional, subject or court.

CONCLUSION

Each individual is unique. Many of those who need maximum security because of manifest violence improve with treatment and time. One knows that inhumane conditions of care can cause further personality warping. One can see in practice that many have the ability to respond positively to good care surprisingly late in life. Thus, there should be available constructive lines of advance for those who are able and willing to respond, also bearing in mind public safety. One of the oldest psychopaths in the Garth series (see Chapter 24), having been in prisons or hospitals almost continuously since 1915, asked for a community placement after 30 years in special hospitals. At 74 there were still a few happy years to be spent walking along a seaside promenade with his boarding-house landlady, a retired Liverpool prostitute.

With constructive treatment, careful planning and support, many erstwhile mentally abnormal offenders can and do fit back into society.

REFERENCES

Acres, D. I. (1975) The after-care of special hospital patients. Appendix 3. *Report of the Committee on Mentally Abnormal Offenders*. Cmnd. 6244. London: HMSO.

Boslow, H. M. (1965) Personal communication.

Boslow, H. M. & Kohlmeyer, W. A. (1963) The Maryland defective delinquency law. *Amer. J. Psychiat.*, **120**, 118–24.

Bowden, P. (1981) What happens to patients released from the special hospitals? *Brit. J. Psychiat.*, **138**, 340–345.

Christiansen, K., Elerts-Neilson, M., Le Maire, M. & Stürup, G. (1965) *Scandinavian Studies in Criminology*. London: Tavistock.

Cleckley, H. M. (1964) *The Mask of Sanity (4th Edn.)*. St Louis: C. V. Mosby.

Craft, M. J. (1965) *Ten Studies into Psychopathic Personality*. Bristol: John Wright.

Craft, M. J. (ed.) (1966) *Psychopathic Disorders*. Oxford: Pergamon Press.

Dell, S. (1980) Transfer of special hospital patients to the NHS. *Brit. J. Psychiat.*, **136**, 222–34.

Dell, S. & Parker, E. (1979) *Special Hospitals' Case Register, Triennial Statistics, 1972–4*. Special Hospitals Research Report No. 15, DHSS.

Gathercole, C., Craft, M., McDougall, J., Barnes, H. & Peck, D. (1968) A review of 100 discharges from a special hospital, *Brit. J. Crim.*, **8**, 419–424.

Gould, J. (1959) The psychiatry of major crime. In *Recent Progress in Psychiatry*. Fleming, G. W. T. H. & Walk, A. (eds.), Vol. 3.

Heaton-Ward, W. A. (1963) Psychopathic disorder. *Lancet*, **i**, 121–3.

Home Office (1973) *Report on the Review of Procedures for the Discharge and Supervision of Psychiatric Patients Subject to Special Restrictions (Aarvold Committee)*. Cmnd. 5191. London: HMSO.

McGarry, A. L. (1971) The fate of psychotic offenders returned for trial. *Amer. J. Psychiat.*, **127**, 1181-84.

Robertson, G. (1981) The extent and pattern of crime amongst mentally handicapped offenders. *Apex, J. Brit. Inst. Ment. Hand.*, **9**, 3, 100-3.

Saylor, M. (1980) A guided self-help approach to treatment of the habital sex offender. In *Sex Offenders in the Criminal Justice System*. West, D. J. (ed.). Papers presented to the 12th Cropwood Round-Table Conference Dec 1979. Cropwood Conference Series No. 12. Cambridge.

Scott, P. (1963) Psychopathy. *Postgrad. Med. J.*, **39**, 12-18.

Steadman, H. J. & Halfon, A. (1971) The Baxstrom patients: backgrounds and outcomes. In: Greenblatt, M. and Hartmann, E. (eds.) *Seminars in Psychiatry* **3**, 376-85.

Stott, D. H. (1962) Evidence for a congenital factor in maladjustment and delinquency. *Amer. J. Psychiat.*, **118**, 781-94.

Stromgren, E. (1965) Personal communication.

Stürup, G. K. (1968) *Treating the 'Untreatable'*. Baltimore: Johns Hopkins Press.

Tennent, G. (1983) The English Special Hospital: a comparison of violent, non-violent re-offenders and non-offenders (in press).

Tennent, G., Parker, E., McGrath, P. & Street, D. (1980) Male admissions to the special hospitals – 1961-5: a demographic study. *Brit. J. Psychiat.*, **136**, 181-90.

Tong, J. E. & McKay, G. W. (1959) A statistical follow-up of mental defectives of dangerous or violent propensities. *Brit. J. Delinq.*, **9**, 4, 276-84.

Walker, N. & McCabe, S. (1973) *Crime and Insanity in England*. Vol. 2. Edinburgh: University Press.

29

Conclusions

Michael & Ann Craft

This book started by emphasising the frequency of crime and of mental abnormality. Two such common things frequently occur together from chance as well as being causally linked. The frequency of each varies considerably between societies. Within the United Kingdom or the United States, urban and rural crime have different patterns; both will differ in incidence and severity from politically motivated black youth in Capetown, or internecine feuds in South America. The desperate activities of the latter groups are of a different order to the delinquency of the former.

The results of research into the causes of delinquency in recent Anglo-American literature have been considerably more pessimistic than in earlier decades. There is now a general consensus that no one cause can be responsible. Gone are the days of the beliefs that maternal deprivation or biological abnormalities such as genetic misendowment or brain damage can be sole or even principal causes of later delinquency or personality disorder. As Walker has put it, 'A quest for a general theory that will account for all instances of crime or deviance or misbehaviour makes no more sense than would a search for a general theory of disease' (Walker, 1977). Nevertheless, there is now much sound statistical information available on causative factors. The effects of gross childhood deprivation are universally recognised as commonly resulting in both repeated convictions and personality distortion (see Friday, 1980). The London DHSS research inaugurated by Sir Keith Joseph into late effects of deprivation has supported these findings and is described by Brown and Madge (1982). Similar results are found in Robins (1978) and Cline (1980). Alternatively, following up from age eight to 25, a cohort of 'normal' youngsters attending state schools in the poorer districts of London's Camberwell, West (1982) reaches the conclusion that most, if not all, severely deprived youngsters acquired convictions if not personality distortion. He says the next subjects for research are how best to teach intervention or coping strategies, and why the few who stayed unconvicted were not as damaged as their siblings. The lack of response of psychopaths to praise and punishment may suggest resistance to the socialising process. This may be due to biological factors and is recently reviewed by Loeb and Mednick (1977). The newer investigative techniques of brain function can show loss of tissue, the gross disparity in functional dominance of one cerebral hemisphere over another (Yendall and Wardell, 1978), temporal lobe or other birth damage (Waldrop et al, 1978, Bonnell, 1980) and are clearer biological causes of impulsive and deviant behaviour. Yet, as Fenton describes in his detailed review of the subject in Chapter 13, it is rare for a neurological abnormality to provide the sole or even major cause for recidivism or personality disorder; environmental factors are usually the main causal factors. After a lifetime of research (with Nigel Walker) at the Cambridge Institute of Criminology, Donald West (1982) puts it this way: 'Research indicates that delinquency is the end result of complex causal paths determined by the interaction of a multiplicity of social and personal factors ... The totality of youthful crime includes occasional offences by vast numbers of different individuals and repeated offences by a small number of versatile and persistent delinquents.'

INCIDENCE

It is characteristic of offences that their incidence will vary according to time and place. In small-scale simple societies, where everyone knows each other, criminality is likely to have a low incidence, and the mentally ill to be cared for at community level. In *Culture and Mental Disorders* Eaton and Weil (1955) describe such an ideal society, made up of some 8000 Hutterites following Bible precepts of concern and care for one's neighbours. The few community members who either offended, or who became mentally ill, were lovingly cherished and re-occurrence was rare. In fact the initial incidence of both phenomena was so low that it warranted research into the reasons, ably reported in Eaton and Weil's book.

In large-scale, complex societies, tending towards impersonal interactions and more diffuse social control, the incidence of both offence and mental abnormality is much greater. But whereas, in former times, the part played by mental illness in an offence was of little importance in the sentencing of those who broke the law, developments over the last 150 years have led increasingly to considerations of the motivation behind the crime and thus to the legal issue of mental abnormality. The position is now that '... judges are finding more and more offenders whom they do not wish to punish, that is, people who ... do not seem to deserve punishment, or to be likely to respond favourably to it, yet behave in such a way that some form of control over their activities is essential in the public interest' (Ormrod, 1975). So as a society becomes more sympathetic to the causes that lead a person to commit an offence, its legal system attempts to respond more selectively and appropriately towards offenders.

THE TIMING OF MENTAL ABNORMALITY

The timing of the onset of mental abnormality in its relation to the offence is of crucial importance. Research among recidivists shows that many have long-standing defects of personality which play a substantial part in steering them on collision courses with authority, in the commission of offences and their being caught. These constitute the phenomenon of the stage army, being highly visible and creating mayhem outside expensive institutions, seemingly well and well-behaved within.

Mental disturbance immediately prior to an offence can be the result of an acute mental illness such as depression, or a gross situational stress like the loss of wife or possessions.

Mental abnormality occurring after the offence, usually as the consequence of it, is also common. For both this and the preceding group, Lawson (Chapter 11) makes a strong appeal for the safety of prison, but others would prefer to use a psychiatric hospital. Crucial here is the degree of security for patient and community, often minimal or absent in modern acute general hospital units. The use of 'Butler' style medium secure units is the most recent variation on this theme.

DEGREE OF RESPONSIBILITY: LEGAL PRINCIPLES

The smaller the community the more likely are law enforcers to be satisfied for mentally abnormal offenders to be dealt with other than by court conviction, providing public safety is not jeopardised. Elsewhere the degree of responsibility for the offence is arguable at law, particularly where intent and motivation are in doubt. It is an area fraught with misunderstandings between lawyer and psychiatrist. In the most serious of offences, homicide, diminished responsibility is defined with phrases such as 'abnormality of mind' and 'substantial impairment of mental responsibility'. These, says Sir Roger Ormrod (1975), '. . . are lawyers' terms and it is for the court, whether judge or jury, to decide if [the psychiatrist's] evidence about the accused brings him within them. It is a common mistake for solicitors and counsel to ask psychiatrists whether "this man's mental responsibility is substantially impaired". Psychiatrists are quite entitled to say "I will tell you what I know about his mental condition. It is for you to say whether on that evidence he fulfils your criterion".' This holds true for all psychiatric statements made in court.

THE PREDICTION OF DANGEROUSNESS

Once facts have been presented in court, and a verdict given, sentence can direct towards punishment or treatment. In either case, a major issue is that the public should be safeguarded as far as is possible against a repetition of the offence. A long prison sentence ensures that an offender deemed to be a high risk is kept out of circulation for what is hoped will be a sufficient period of time. A hospital order or certification, renewable as thought necessary, has the same effect. The difference is that eventually a prison sentence is served and the offender goes free; with a hospital order judgements are regularly made as to an offender's current dangerousness. American law has recently concentrated on the issue of imminent dangerousness as a touchstone to measure likelihood of repetition of offence. The legal writers in this book reflect the current views of their professional colleagues in the degree of satisfaction they express in estimation of dangerousness. Psychiatric writers also reflect current views in their conclusions that dangerousness is the result of a number of personal and situational factors. It is rarely possible to predict accurately how many of the personal factors will recur (perhaps a second wife being unfaithful) or chance factors such as a pub brawl.

THE AGE FACTOR

Age has a close relationship with the proportion of offenders found mentally abnormal. Of all those convicted half are aged less than 21; if one excludes immaturity as a label, the incidence of mental abnormality is small. Contrariwise, the aged are least convicted, but mental abnormality is common and diminution of brain function readily demonstrable by modern methods of investigation.

In general the dangerousness of offenders decreases as age advances, and more of these offenders can be cared for within existing systems of community care than those in younger groups. One conclusion is the view expressed in this book that courts should make increasing use of probation officers and other social agents in ensuring that community systems can take proper care of aged offenders.

THE RESULTS OF TREATMENT

The treatment of the acutely ill mentally abnormal offender has this in common with other ill members of society needing care; that at the early stages there may be a need for intensive care and supervision, but such measures can usually be relaxed in the sub-acute stage. After this, there may be a need for a longer-term period of residence, with a variable period of after-care with greater or lesser need for change in habit of employment. This scenario can hold good for those who commit offences as a result of acute depression, elderly confusional episodes, alcoholic furores or adolescent states of acute excitement.

Although there have been a number of controlled studies of treatment of longer-term personality disordered, few have been statistically validated. The few which have are very well reviewed by West (1982) who concludes that although most systematical evaluations of treatment projects have failed to demonstrate any significant decrease in later arrests, or personality disorder, one should not conclude that 'nothing works'. He notes that Ross and Gendreau (1980) have published a collection of reports of treatment evaluations that yield positive results, at least in part by choosing studies that selected variables that could be influenced directly. He says, 'It is rather sad that the discipline of sociology, which has done so much to expose the pressures that provoke offending, has become associated with opposition to therapists who try to help individual offenders. As for judges and penal administrators who are always sceptical about claims for treatment, their disillusionment ... may last a long time.' Once more it seems best to rely on a many sided approach to treatment rather than rely too much on one avenue. Although the charismatic enthusiast clearly may accomplish much, the future would seem to depend on attention to all aspects of prevention and care, such as individual treatment, teaching coping strategies, counselling, home stimulation, daytime occupation and the quality of the supervisory officer to whom much can be left. Using meticulous supervision and long-term compulsory after-care, McGrath was able to prevent relapse for the decades of follow-up of a group of Broadmoor murderers; whilst Stürup using Herstedvester for severe psychopaths over a 30-year period could promise that they would have few if any re-convictions on entering his lifetime service. Such systems are expensive and not always politically acceptable. In the 1970s in Denmark there was a political swing away from the use of maximum security systems like Herstedvester for severe psychopaths, and the Council of Europe has recently come to much the same conclusion in ruling in favour of tribunal or court hearings for those mentally abnormal offenders withdrawn from licence. Britain was among the laggards in Europe in this judicial review of treatment; the 1983 Act now codifies practice for restricted patients.

THE MENTAL HEALTH ACT 1983

The 1959 English Mental Health Act was at the time innovative and widely copied in English speaking legislatures round the world. The new Act, twenty-four years later, introduces some major changes in the law. In attempting to forecast the effect of the changes, the most important shift has been in public opinion, now much against compulsory treatment. In the 1950s there was a substantial minority of patients in psychiatric hospitals under compulsory orders; now even offenders sentenced by the court are commonly admitted on a psychiatric probation order.

A number of the new measures introduced by the 1983 Act follow the recommendations of the Butler Report and allow the courts more flexibility in arriving at the most suitable disposal of those defendents thought to be suffering from one of the specified forms of mental disorder. Providing in each case arrangements have been made with the hospital for the reception of the accused, a Crown Court or magistrates' court can remand a person to hospital' before sentence for the purpose of reports on his mental condition. The initial remand period is not more than 28 days, but can be renewed for up to a total of 12 weeks in all. With similar time limits a Crown Court may remand to hospital for medical treatment an accused person, who on the evidence of two medical practitioners is suffering from mental illness or severe mental impairment. When a person has been convicted of an imprisonable offence and there is reason to believe it might be appropriate for hospital order to be made, a third new power enables a Crown Court or a magistrates' court to impose an interim hospital order. This authorises admission and detention for a specified period not exceeding 12 weeks. The interim order can be renewed for further periods of 28 days up to a total of six months in all. This allows the possibility of a trial of treatment for those offenders about whom there is some uncertainty as to the benefit of the imposition of a S37 Order. After considering the evidence of the responsible medical officer the court can either terminate the interim order in favour of a full hospital order, or deal with the offender in some other way. These new powers are likely to be of considerable benefit when used by hospitals dealing with forensic psychiatric patients, and to be useful additions to current compulsory and psychiatric probation orders for short-term treatment.

Considerable changes in the rights of restricted patients mean that Britain is now brought into line with recent verdicts of the European Court of Human Rights. The Mental Health Review Tribunal can now determine the need for detention of a restricted patient each year, and will also consider the case of each patient who is recalled from licence, within a month of the recall. Thus the indefinite powers of the Home Secretary are much curtailed, and a proper review of the need for continuation of treatment has to be formally made on a regular basis for each restricted patient. The powers of the tribunals themselves are both clarified and further amplified.

The most contentious part of the new Act is the clarification of consent to treatment for compulsorily detained patients. Such treatment is divided into three parts. Psycho-surgery and other treatment specified in the Act can only be carried out with the consent of the patient, a certificate from a doctor and two other persons, whose duties are laid down by a newly-formed Mental Health Commission. An unexpected addition to the amending Act, put in at a late stage, extends now to voluntary psycho-surgery operations and is highly contentious. The second part of the new consent to treatment provisions concerns administration of medicine for three months or longer, ECT and further treatment yet to be specified. These can only be carried out with either the consent of the patient or second opinion. If consent is withdrawn by the patient then possible continuation must be regarded as a new treatment. The third and final part of compulsory treatment is concerned with interventions necessary to save the life of a patient, and certain other urgent instances. This is specified in detail and also contains provision for a second opinion. Doctors and nurses will continue to be protected against civil proceedings against negligence or bad faith, but the specified necessity for prosecution to be brought by or with the consent of the Director of Public Prosecutions.

One of the most interesting parts of the new Act concerns the foundation of a Mental Health Commission in England and Wales. Scotland has had its own since the Scottish 1960 Act, and its successful working has clearly inspired England and Wales to follow the Scottish example. This commission is required to set up codes of practice and of standards, particularly for the treatment of compulsory patients. Its powers and duties may further be extended, and many hope that it will act, both to raise care standards by the professions and to raise material standards of hospitals by pressure on government and staff alike.

RESIDENTIAL ASPECTS OF CARE

Throughout the developed world there is increasing interest in the provision of community care for needful groups. This interest pursues both the idea of a more humane pattern of care, and the practicality of conserving resources in a world of declining assets. Translated into the field of mentally abnormal offenders this means an increase in the provision of hostels, small group homes and sheltered workplaces. Unfortunately, these ideals remain mostly unrealised. Indeed in many countries there are calls for bigger and better prisons, England in particular having proportionately one of the largest long-term prison populations in Western Europe. In the United States, although there is ostensibly much interest in the provision of secure care only for those who are particularly and 'imminently' dangerous, there remains a strong tendency to blame care staff for the release of those who subsequently re-offend. Similarly, in Australia and in Britain the community has a strong retributive feeling, but public education by way of the media can lead to a greater awareness of the part that mental abnormality can play in offences, and the possibility of treatment rather than punishment.

THE ISSUES OF COMPULSORY CARE

When compulsory treatment orders are made, release of a person with a mental disorder of uncertain outcome becomes a matter of difficult judgement. The arguments for indefinite care orders versus the tariff system of sentence for mentally abnormal offenders have been set out at several points in this book. Suffice it to say that all beg the question of after-care, adequacy of provision of job, home and supervision. The nub, of course, is that neither system responds in synchrony with the needs of the offender. On the one hand they may have to stay years longer in a maximum security setting than they actually need to in terms of risk; or alternatively they may be prematurely (in the judgement of their psychiatric consultants, therapists or prison staff) discharged from maximum security to community by tribunal, court decision or end of sentence, with very little preparation. There remains the question of who has the right to make, and more importantly to act upon, judgements about the potential dangerousness of those who have been labelled mentally abnormal offenders *prior* to the committal of any re-offence. Has preventative custody enough safeguards for the individual? The new Mental Health Act has gone some way to introduce more accountability.

The psychiatric probation order is one example of a flexible way of disposing of mentally abnormal offenders who do not pose major security problems. Providing that the treating psychiatrist, the probation officer and the offender are reasonably clear about the commitment and responsibility of each, the order offers a system of in- or out-patient treatment, social work support and adequate follow-up (for an extensive review see Lewis, 1980).

Mentally abnormal offenders are a vulnerable group of people. Rather like being on a roundabout, many come to the attention of the police, courts and hospitals again and again. They do not always, and perhaps seldom, fit easily between law and medicine, between punishment and treatment, between the concept of personal responsibility and the concept of impairment of judgement due to mental illness or deficit. Peter Sutcliffe (the so-called Yorkshire Ripper), Michael Fagan (who pestered the Queen) and John Hinckley, jun. (who shot at President Reagan) are recent *causes célèbres* who highlight the difficulties that can be presented to lawyers, psychiatrists and to ordinary members of the public. The considerations are not simply legal or penal, not simply medical, but involve politics and public security. Political decisions and cases involving the protection of society may well infringe individual rights, and we should not duck this issue. As Gunn (1979) says:

> It may be right for society to protect itself under certain circumstances against particular individuals who have clearly demonstrated that they can be destructive, but if we are to detain people much longer than we would otherwise punish them, then we must establish proper rules for doing this, and allow plenty of opportunity for an appeal against that decision ... Justice is justice whether the recipient is bad, mad or both.

That justice should also include the right to treatment, for as matters currently stand, it is by no means unknown for a mentally abnormal offender to be refused hospital admission on the grounds that he is likely to be destructive or violent. This brings us back to the need for a range of treatment, venues and options, and it points to the need for professional education in the area of forensic psychiatry.

It is a matter of politics how a community deploys its assets in raising the general standard of living, rewarding the worthy, or assisting the deprived. The severely deprived, as DHSS research shows, produce far more than their fair share of mental abnormality and offenders, in Britain as in any other community (Brown and Madge, 1982). There are a number of strong arguments for attempting to break the vicious circle of deprived adults producing deprived children, including the statistics of crime. There are additional economic arguments for aiding voluntary and religious agencies to increase community support measures for the deprived, so reducing the number and the expense of institutional placements.

We conclude by suggesting that where residential admission is considered, on whatever grounds, it behoves judges, psychiatrists and other professionals to mitigate the personal or family damage done by such procedures, in particular:

1 To clarify the circumstances under which the mentally abnormal or illegal act took place, so that defence counsel, court or treatment givers can decide how far the circumstances were unique. If, for example, a depressed patient attacked his wife because she was unfaithful, but as time goes on they are divorced, he recovers from his depression and gets a new girlfriend, the risk of repetition may be minimal. Expressed intent and a change of heart by the client can then be reported as positive features to hasten discharge.

2 If the probation services, social worker, voluntary agency or the client's family offers a community based measure which avoids custody but gives good guarantee of public protection, this measure should be considered carefully. When a

Queensland desert rancher in the practice of one of us became paranoid about a neighbour's wife and shot at her, the outback court accepted his family's offer of help from Adelaide, a thousand miles distant. The condition of residence in another state was effective banishment, but at least not personally destructive.

3   Where admission is necessary, the co-operation of the client in treatment or retraining would be more constructive than penal custody alone. The availability of hostels, community homes or supervised lodgings to serve as asylums for those who fear hurting others, feel 'irresponsible impulses', or who are inadequate is an essential element of the care system. This applies to a far larger group of long-term prisoners than most believe; West and Farrington (1977) say it is a simple majority. For some, prisons are a costly and unnecessary luxury. For the minority who, on the grounds of dangerousness, do indeed need hospital/ prison care the secure milieu should be as constructive, humane and caring as safety allows. At the very least, it should not cause a person to return to the community more brutalised than when he came in.

4   With such current scepticism on benefits from custody, there is even more need for an initial treatment plan, for effective after-care, and for supervision which encourages and promotes personal responsibility.

REFERENCES

Bonnell, M. L. (1980) *Child at Risk: A Report of the Standing Senate Committee on Health Welfare and Science*. Ottawa: Canadian Government Publishing Centre.
Brown, M. & Madge, N. (1982) *Despite the Welfare State*. London: Heinemann.
Cline, H. K. (1980) Criminal behavior over the life span. In *Constancy and Change in Human Development*. Brim, O. G. & Kagan, J. (eds). Cambridge, Mass: Harvard University Press.
Eaton, J. W. & Weil, R. J. (1955) *Culture and Mental Disorders*. Glencoe, Illinois: Free Press.
Friday, P. (1980) International review of youth crime and delinquency. In *Deviance and Crime: International Perspectives*. Newman, G. (ed.). New York: Sage.
Gunn, J. (1979) The law and the mentally abnormal offender in England and Wales. *Int. J. Law Psychiat.*, **2**, 199–214.
Lewis, P. (1980) *Psychiatric Probation Orders*. Cambridge: Institute of Criminology.
Loeb, L. & Mednick, M. A. (1977) A social behavior and electrodermal response patterns. In *Biosocial Bases of Criminal Behavior*. Christiansen, K. O. & Mednick, S. A. (eds.). New York: Gardner.
Ormrod, R. (1975) The debate between psychiatry and the law. *Brit. J. Psychiat*, **127**, 193–203.
Robins, L. (1978) Sturdy childhood predictors of adult antisocial behaviour: replications from longitudinal studies. *Psychol. Med.*, **8**, 611–22.
Ross, R. R. & Gendreau, P. (1980) *Effective Correctional Treatment*. Toronto: Butterworths.
Waldrop, M. F., Bell, R. Q., McLaughlin, B. & Halverson, C. F. (1978) Newborn minor physical anomalies predict short attention span, peer aggression and impulsivity at age 3. *Science*, **199**, 563–5.
Walker, N. (1977) *Behaviour and Misbehaviour: Explanations and Non-Explanations*. Oxford: Blackwell.
West, D. J. (1982) *Delinquency: Its Roots, Career and Prospects*. London: Heinemann.
West, D. J. & Farrington, D. P. (1977) *The Delinquent Way of Life*. London: Heinemann.
Yendall, L. T. & Wardell, D. (1978) Neurophysiological correlates of criminal psychopathy. In *Human Aggression and Dangerousness*. Beliveau, L., Canepa, G. & Szabo, D. (eds.). Montreal: Pinel Institute.

Appendix

The Professional Criminal

Michael Craft

This appendix presents an essay on professional criminals, as a counter-balance and contrast to the personalities and activities of mentally abnormal offenders. By definition the successful professional criminal is of stable personality, high in intelligence and able to plan carefully ahead with considerable judgement and forethought. He cultivates an image of 'normal' appearance and behaviour to protect his enterprise, is well aware of the penalties of failure, and takes care to avoid risk. In these respects he differs from most mentally abnormal offenders detailed in this book, although in some cases such as the professional 'heavy' who enjoys violence for his own personal satisfaction there may be overlap.

The professional criminal can be defined as a person using persistent illegal behaviour in the continuing pursuit of personal or material reward. The career pattern may be of careful training by a criminal mentor or father, or that of a technician such as a computer programmer who discovers he may make more money using his skills illegally, than legally.

Criminological writers divide professional criminals into three main groups:
1 The individual professional, working alone and using his individual skills for individual reward. These people avoid violence and publicity to escape identification. The pick-pocket, shoplifter, burglar, sneak-thief, confidence swindler and some sexual molesters are often successful, if lonely, people who develop their skills of professional activity to achieve a fair amount of personal success. Lacking, if not actually avoiding associates, their chances of arrest are much reduced until carelessness, over-confidence or bad luck results in discovery by police. The possession of a stable character, a cool wit and the intelligence to plan ahead, good judgement and foresight so essential to success place them in marked contrast to the unstable personality who repeatedly offends, does so on impulse and often gets caught. Dr Lawson, prison medical officer at Risley, says in Chapter 11 that all his repeated offenders must have defects of character to get caught!
2 The professional 'heavy' criminal uses his skills for financial or material gain. This involves the use of force, violence or threats. Such crime is a great deal more visible and more likely to be reported to police or legal sources, unless undertaken with associates who may afford a degree of protection. Crime here includes armed robbery, personal violence involving property acquisition, sometimes burglary, arson for insurance, kidnapping, hi-jack and trafficking in drugs and prostitution. Professional 'heavy' crime particularly suits the aggressive person-

ality whose motivation may arise from a broken or unstable home or neighbourhood schooling.

3 Those involved in what is called organised crime pursue enterprises with a material reward dependent on the skills of a number of operatives. This is particularly successful in areas that are already illegal or nearly so. Services such as prostitution, loan sharking, gambling, narcotics traffic, stolen goods, gun-running and assassination are well-known areas of operation. From the psychiatric point of view, persons involved in these enterprises are much more likely to be trained in or by families for the family business, and the more stable the personality, the more intelligent and careful the person, the more likely, as in other business, is success.

THE HISTORY OF PROFESSIONAL CRIME

All writers are agreed that the development of city life was a necessary background to the development of criminal careers. Farm and rural life means that local personalities and their activities are very well known to each member of the community, and professional crime depends on a degree of amorphism for its success. There are references in ancient Chinese writing and Egyptian papyri to laws for repeated offenders, Judges 9:4 in the Old Testament has a reference to Abimelech who hired professional assassins to dispose of his seventy legitimate brothers who were heirs to the throne ahead of him, whilst in Roman writing Plutarch described the lives of thieves.

Today, organised crime is best known for its American and Italian exponents. Professor Inciardi's (1975) well known history on careers in crime traces back organised crime in the United States to both Italian and Elizabethan English antecedents and shows the derivation of many of the words used among professional circles to be of Elizabethan origin. Professional thieves, swindlers and prostitutes are well depicted by Shakespeare, Daniel Defoe and Dickens, but there are also a number of Elizabethan tracts and pamphlets which describe the life and times of thieves and cozeners. They have recently been re-published and are described in Professor Inciardi's books, from which much of the following is taken. He says the earliest account of English professional criminal life appeared in the works of the poet John Skelton beginning with his book *The Tunning of Elinour Running* (1483). This offers one of the earliest accounts of contemporary 'low life' with the use of the terms 'bowsy' for bloated by drinking, and 'stall' to lure to decoy. Other words derived from this time are said to be the 'beak' of 1573 to describe a police judge, a 'fence' of 1700 as receiver of stolen goods, 'lifting' of 1592 as removing objects from another person and 'moll' of 1600 as a faithful sexual companion (*Moll Flanders* by Daniel Defoe).

The Italian mafiosa is said to have had its origins in the revolt of peasantry in 1282, known as the Sicilian Vespers, against the oppressive government of the French. Throughout the centuries of mis-government and conquest in Sicily that followed there was a prevailing sense of primitive chivalry and silent resistance to oppressors pervading society, resulting in two levels of government and 'taxation', namely that imposed by the foreign government of the time, and that taken as tribute by local organisations. It is said that the first use of *mafia* in the criminal context was the result of a play performed in Palermo and dedicated to the men of the local gaol in 1863. Although the term mafiosi has been commonly used since, actual mafiosi dislike it, preferring the term 'friends of friends' or more recently 'our friend'. The Mafia has recently been the subject of considerable investigation by the Italian government, but Professor Inciardi, writing from Miami, concludes that 'as such the Mafia is a de-centralised and unregimented congerie of semi-aligned groups having no bearing on, and little in common with the operations of organised crime in the United States'.

Elsewhere in Italy, Naples developed La Camorra, a similar organisation for similar reasons to Sicily. The Camorra were a loosely-knit group of gangs in Naples, founded in prostitution, violence and loan sharking, which became sufficiently visible and unpopular that riots occurred in 1911 and it was banned. Before this there had been upwards of three million Italian emigrants to the United States, and many who settled in New York and similar port towns dominated by the New England establishment, formed themselves into protective groups similar to those in their homeland. In New York and other ports the first and second generation Italians developed *La Mano Nera* (the black hand) and *Cosa Nostra*. Sub-groups spawned across the United States to other areas of depression and oppression, where first and second generation immigrants congregated, such as Chicago, Pittsburg and elsewhere. It is said that the Mafia as such never flourished as an organisation in the United States, but its two off-shoots Cosa Nostra and Camorra adapted to the new American society and were amalgamated as a result of the bosses gaining control of liquor operations during the prohibition era. The evidence indicates that Johnny Torrio masterminded a 'crime cartel' in the early 1930s and his associates included such well-known names as 'Dutch' Schultz, Al Capone and 'Lucky' Luciano.

Professor Inciardi suggests that organised crime by the Cosa Nostra is limited and decreasing at this present time due to the increasingly successful efforts of the Federal Bureau of Investigation and surveillance by communication media. He says that production of illegal alcohol is now clearly unproductive. Prostitution is risky because it is difficult to organise and discipline. The illegal import of narcotics has now shifted to the south of the United States. Cannabis was said by a federal indictment of 1964 to be proscribed by Cosa Nostra law because of its lack of appeal and to be overtaken by the proliferation of government methadone maintenance programmes for addicts, but evidence suggests cannabis consumption is widespread and commonly locally grown. However, gambling, particularly in Las Vegas, is extremely successful and is said to give a yield of between seven and fifty billion dollars annually with twenty-one million dollars being the profit from narcotics. During a recent trial of the New York Cosa Nostra (*The Times*, 22 June 1980) the FBI testified that the current annual profits of the 26 Cosa Nostra families were of the order of twenty-five billion dollars. By way of contrast, the annual turnover of Exxon, the largest US company, is two to three billion dollars.

It is said that dissatisfaction and local squabbles over the hierarchy have resulted in the break-up of the old family training network. Advancement in syndicates is now said to fall to those of higher qualification, such as lawyers, accountants and communication system personnel.

British Organised Criminal Networks

That there are networks organised for successful criminal activities in England is well known from the exposures at the Kray brothers' trial, and the 1981 Inland Revenue trial of Soho 'one armed bandit' syndicate operators, who paid the Revenue seven million pounds in order to leave the country without indictment. Organised crime in Britain depends heavily, as in America, on fringe activities such as gambling, commercial 'game' operations, and the use of prostitution in London's Soho and elsewhere. The recent Countryman investigation of the London Metropolitan Police shows that the ramifications of organised crime extend into the police force itself. Compared with the United States, two of the big differences in the UK are that there is a national police force with extensive power able to operate across county or country boundaries, such as into Scotland, and that the law of libel is much more extensive, so that the type of personal investigation and exposures enumerated by Inciardi are more risky.

RESEARCH INTO ORGANISED CRIME

By its very nature, the type of university research common in other areas is limited with regard to organised crime. The search for evidence concerning professional criminals can best be discussed in terms of the three groups given at the outset.

The careers of professional criminals who operate alone, such as shoplifters, pick-pockets, burglars and sexual molesters, can be followed from their individual autobiographies and biographies. They do not have the inclination nor the time to give an account of their career, until a prolonged period of banishment or incarceration allows them scope. Sociological investigations of such people have been made and reported in the literature.

Professional 'heavy' criminals, who repeatedly use violence to gain rewards, are sufficiently visible to be more often convicted than the foregoing group. Persistently aggressive male factors form a small but important group of convicts who are discussed from the psychiatric point of view by West in *The Habitual Offender* (1963) and suggested further reading is given at the end of this chapter. Jimmy Boyle (1977) gives an interesting autobiography which is a classic example of this group. Boyle was born in the Gorbals district of Glasgow, his father a professional 'heavy'. Although reared by a warm and caring mother in a close family, the deprivations of tenement life introduced him early to acquisitive crime, and his father and friends taught him that violence paid. When Boyle was 12 years old his father died as a result of one of his 'heavy' operations going wrong, and Boyle himself developed thereafter into a successful heavy, who later became associated with the Kray twins' organised syndicate in London. Judging from his autobiography, far more of his heavy operations went right than wrong, and whilst violence was occasionally used, the threat of it usually persuaded people to part with their goods. The rewards of this kind of life led Boyle to considerable affluence, yet he was finally gaoled for murder and has written his autobiography during the life sentence.

The difference between the professional heavy using violence and the non-violent skilled criminal appears from the many personal accounts available, to be partly one of aptitude, partly of upbringing and personal inclination. As Sutherland (1937) pointed out, both groups can start their occupational life in legitimate employment and can come from all classes of society. The steady worker with steady inclinations can by chance or temptation easily re-ply his trade whether he be waiter, hotel clerk or secretary. As Reckless (1967) points out, the pathways to recruitment are more accessible to some: 'The etcher becomes a counterfeiter; the skilled worker or foreman with the lock company becomes a safe cracker; the worker in the stockbroker's office gets into hot bonds'. And 'Human documents indicate that skilled thieves stem from all class levels; they may shift from legitimate occupations to a career in crime, others graduate from petty to criminal crime, some are recruited directly without the benefit of prior criminality or occupational experience. Characteristic of many of these individuals was a series of social and personal contingencies and opportunity structures that led to their career'.

Accounts of organised crime depend partly on the unravelling of organisations as recounted in court where four American Presidents' Commissions have been particularly instructive. The McClellan Committee (see Presidents' Commission, 1967c) identified 5000 men as mafiosi throughout the United States, but ten years later two-thirds were found to be in gaol, under indictment or dead, and 'those promoted to replace the fallen gangland members have been inept' (Inciardi, 1975). As a result, in 1972 syndicate bosses attempted to import a large number of Sicilian born mafiosi into the United States, but this resulted in collision with local Americans, and despite originally lacking dossiers, fingerprints, photographs and disenchanted wives or jealous neighbours to tip off federal services, most became well known to the FBI.

As might be expected, the most successful members trained by a family for organised crime are those who could have all the talents for a successful business career outside the syndicate; a stable background, quick brain, well developed intelligence, harmonious personal relationships with other members of the syndicate or family, steady dependable adult behaviour, low neighbourhood profile, in short no sign of mental illness or abnormality. Indeed there is much advantage in the recruit being as normal looking and normal behaving as to incur as little attention as possible. The successful operation of a major enterprise often depends on split-second timing, and reliability on the part of members to do their job in the face of considerable stress is an essential requirement. Clearly the emphasis on personal recruitment will be along standard business lines of maximising profits and minimising risks in the particular enterprise followed.

Interestingly enough, most writers note that the fall-out rate of members of organised crime systems is less from long-term penal incarceration than retirement in affluence and law-abiding security to distant shores. Like other normal members of society, it seems the successful professional criminal has a dream of affluent comfort in security, and tries to make his dream come true!

CONCLUSION

Aristotle once wrote, 'Men come together in cities in order to live; they remain together in order to live the good life'. Yet cities are the breeding grounds for crime, and from the Greek city-state onwards, cities have bred fear in their citizens of the violence they might suffer, or the goods they might lose at the hands of others. It is in the big cities such as Naples or New York that professional crime is at its most dangerous, but the bigger the city, the more likely there are to be numbers of lawless adolescents, the most active age-group in personal crime. It is at a personal level that efforts to minimise this last group are most successful, but for professional group only community attitudes, governmental strengths and economic well-being can set standards which reduce their acceptability or success.

REFERENCES

Boyle, J. (1977) *A Sense of Freedom*. Edinburgh: Cannongate Publishing. An autobiographical account of a British 'heavy' professional criminal.
Cameron, M.O. (1964) *The Booster and the Snitch*. New York: Free Press of Glencoe. An interesting account of contemporary shoplifting in the United States.
Inciardi, J.A. (1975) *Careers in Crime*. Chicago: Rand McNally. A source-book for this chapter. It describes the origin and development of professional criminals with respect to Britain and the United States, together with a considerable bibliographical reference list. An indispensable history for those pursuing the subject.
Inciardi, J.A. & Chambers, C.D. (1972) Criminal involvement of narcotic addicts. *Journal of Drug Issues*, 2 (Spring), 57–64. This concerns the predominance of shoplifting among 15 male addicts (1272 crimes over a four year period) and 15 female addicts (2556 instances over a three year period).
President's Commission on Law Enforcement and Administration of Justice (1967a) *Task Force Report: Crime and its Impact: An Assessment*. Washington DC: US Government Printing Office.
President's Commission on Law Enforcement and Administration of Justice (1967b) *The Challenge of Crime in a Free Society*. Washington DC: US Government Printing Office.
President's Commission on Law Enforcement and Administration of Justice (1967c) *Task Force Report: Organised Crime*. Washington DC: US Government Printing Office. The Federal Government's investigations into the Mafia and organised crime.

FURTHER READING

Alexander, A. & Moolman, V. (1969) *Stealing*. New York: Cornerstone. Employee pilferage in departmental stores.
Jackson, B. (1969) *The Thieves' Primer*. London: Macmillan. Jackson also discusses what happens to professional thieves on 'retirement'.
Jennet, J. (1964) *The Thieves' Journal*. New York: Grove Press. A famous French novelist and playwright and reformed thief. This is an autobiographical account.
Judges, A.V. (ed.) (1930) *The Elizabethan Underworld*. London: George Routledge. This author has reprinted many of the Elizabethan pamphlets concerned with pickpockets, prostitution, shoplifting etc. It includes Thomas Dekker's *The Bellman of London*.

Lombroso, C. (1911) *Crime: Its Causes and Remedies*. Translated by Henry, B. Horton. Boston: Little, Brown. The 'father' of modern criminology.

Radzinowics, L. (1966) *Ideology and Crime*. New York: Columbia University Press. The first British professor of criminality writing from the University of Cambridge. The book gives the history of organised crime and criminal investigation with special reference to Britain.

Reckless, W.C. (1967) *The Crime Problem*. New York: Appleton-Century-Crofts.

Sutherland, E.H. (1937) *The Professional Thief*. Chicago: University of Chicago Press. Professor Sutherland elaborates the hypothesis that crime is a learned behaviour, and the more stable the personality the better can the learning be achieved. He also discusses exits from the profession.

Tristan, F. (1842) *London Journal*. Translated by Jean Hawkes (1982). London: Virago Press.

Wallace, S.E. (1968) *Skid Row as a Way of Life*. New York: Harper and Row. This concerns the prevalence of aged thieves and confidence tricksters on Skid Row.

West, D.J. (1963) *The Habitual Offender*. London: Macmillan.

Epilogue

Psychiatry in the Dock – A Lawyer's Afterthoughts

Paul Gerber

Perhaps at the outset I had better declare myself as a former (now retired) barrister who practised in the 1960s and 1970s in both Queensland and Victoria, Australia. I was in much demand for cases – both criminal and civil – in which much depended on medical testimony. I appeared for a number of psychopaths, including John Andrew Stuart, the alleged 'mastermind' behind the nightclub extortion racket, which culminated in the firebombing of the Whiskey au Go Go night club, killing fifteen young people. During the trial, Stuart kept swallowing crosses made of wire, held in a vertical position by elastic wire. I also appeared in the celebrated Southport multiple rape case where five adolescents were charged with the rape of a 58-year-old cripple. After a hung jury at the first trial, a mistrial and a re-trial, there was an acquittal after a psychiatrist, who attended throughout the trial, deposed that, in his opinion, the prosecutrix was an hysteric, and that it was impossible to insert three erect penises simultaneously into the mouth of a woman wearing a cervical collar – one of the allegations relied on by the prosecution. However, my major contribution to psychiatry was that I once proved that it was more probable than not that schizophrenia was caught from bananas, despite – or perhaps because of – the expert testimony of five schizophrenologists to the contrary. I have now opted for the quieter life, although I am a regular contributor to legal and medical journals, and am Honorary Lecturer in Medical Jurisprudence in the Medical School of the University of Queensland.

Looking back over my years of legal practice, I have little doubt that the cross-examination of psychiatrists offered me the greatest forensic challenge. It was a kind of blood sport. English gentlemen like to hunt, shoot or fish; my hobby was catching psychiatrists. At a time when there was still the death penalty for capital offences, much could turn on the meaning of such phrases as 'disease of the mind', 'psychotic', the ability to distinguish between 'right and wrong'; schizophrenia was a very fashionable disease, though there seemed little diagnostic agreement as to what constituted this 'in' condition. Unfortunately, the death penalty was finally abolished, and much of the excitement went out of murder. After that, I began to build up an opinion practice. However, it is undoubtedly a fact that when your client's life is, literally, in your hands, when competent cross-examination can make the difference between an accused having a neck and losing it, most counsel are prepared to study the

461

mysteries of psychiatry, if only to increase the odds slightly in their client's favour.

Let me say at once that I have nothing against psychiatry – some of my best friends are psychiatrists – but speaking as a barrister, I must say that I have always found non-organic (or functional) psychiatry very easy to demolish. It is not always simple to talk yourself out of a broken leg, particularly if the plaintiff comes along with a clear-cut X-ray. Your best hope is to show that it is possible that there has been a mix-up in the radiological department. When, however, the issue involves the mental state of a witness, I rarely had any logistic problems in convincing a jury – or even a judge – that the accused was, or was not insane, schizophrenic or not schizophrenic, potentially violent or not, the result depending merely which side I was on. This is not meant to imply that I had any special talents, but rather that psychiatrists lacked them. In this epilogue, I will try and set out how these tricks are performed. Unlike magic, which is based on illusion, the barrister's art is to make the best of the props he is provided with. A good barrister tries to make the props do what he wants them to. If this is seen as a form of manipulation, I remain wholly unrepentant. In our legal system, the roles of the advocate and the expert witness are quite different. The expert witness is – or ought to be – objective and unbiased (it is remarkable how often psychiatric witnesses disagree on an issue like, say 'insanity'; biased invariably in favour of the side which has retained them). The barrister has to do his best for the client within the rules of evidence. He is – or ought to be – wholly indifferent to the client's guilt or innocence. That is a matter for the jury. In fact, I have rarely, if ever, appeared for a client whom I believed to be innocent. People are very rarely charged with offences they have not committed. True, the police have been known to give a little 'shove' to the evidence to ensure a conviction, but that only adds to the professional challenge to gain an acquittal. Indeed, I invariably viewed a conviction as an affront to my pride as an advocate. Like police manufacturing evidence, I was not, at times, above using psychiatry for my own ends – and these ends were not always the ends of justice. But, as I said before, that is not what barristering is all about. Let me hasten to add that I practised law at a time when psychiatry had less right to be called a scientific discipline than it has today.

The secret of success at the bar is to know – and use to best advantage – your opponent's weaknesses. In the case of psychiatry, it was its sloppy methodology. It is one thing to get up and prove a witness has a broken leg, it is quite another to demonstrate that he is psychotic. It is, after all, trite to say that a scientific statement depends for its validity on the demonstrable fact that it is correct; it is said to be reliable if it can be confirmed by others in the sense that there is a majority of reputable scientists who will agree with the statement. This is where I found psychiatry to be most vulnerable. Perhaps, given the vast spectrum of psychiatric 'schools', it is not surprising that there should be also vast areas of disagreement. However, what is disturbing is that – given this vast area of disagreement – the issue of liberty versus custodial care should be made to depend on psychiatric judgements. From a lawyer's point of view, it was therefore critical to come to grips with the methodology of psychiatry, if only to show that it was neither valid nor reliable. Thus, if it can be demonstrated that a statement that the accused is psychotic, or is likely to prove dangerous if released, is one with which a large body of psychiatrists are likely to disagree, then that testimony has little or no evidentiary value. And since psychiatrists are alleged to have special expertise in predicting violence, or be able to tell when a person can distinguish between right and wrong or suffer from diminished responsibility, it is a lawyer's duty to learn the methodology of psychiatry.

HOW RELIABLE ARE PSYCHIATRIC OPINIONS?

A number of early studies produce a gloomy picture. These have been usefully collected in a seminal article by Ennis and Litwack (1974) entitled 'Psychiatry and the presumption of expertise: flipping coins in the courtroom'. At the outset, they highlight the distinction between reliability and validity. Thus a diagnosis of 'dangerousness' is said to be reliable if representative pairs of psychiatrists looking at a representative sample of patients usually agree that each individual is dangerous. Thus, if each and every psychiatrist agrees that the person in the dock would commit a dangerous act if released, that judgement would be reliable. But if that person were released and did *not* commit a dangerous act, the opinion would be wholly invalid. After reviewing the extensive literature on the subject up to that time, Ennis and Litwack conclude that psychiatric opinion is not only not reliable, but not sufficiently valid to justify its admission as expert testimony. Unkindly, the authors add that the literature suggests that psychiatrists have no greater expertise in predicting, say, violence than have grocers, and since the latter are traditionally disqualified from giving opinion evidence on states of mind, so too should be psychiatrists. Their conclusion certainly receives some support from the literature which analyses specific psychiatric diagnoses under test conditions to determine the degree of correlation. Thus, the authors detail the following studies set up to measure diagnostic agreement: Ash (1949), Mehlman (1952), Schmidt and Fonda (1956), Norris (1959), Pasamanick et al (1959) and Beck et al (1962); and note the comment of Zubin (1967):

The degree of overall agreement between different observers with regard to specific diagnoses is too low for individual diagnosis. The overall agreement on general categories of diagnosis, although somewhat higher (64–84%), still leaves much to be desired. The evidence for low agreement across specific diagnostic categories is all the more surprising since, for the most part, the observers in any one study were usually quite similar in orientation, training and background.

Spitzer and Fleiss (1974) likewise surveyed the studies by Beck et al as well as those of Schmidt and Fonda (1956). In addition, they analysed similar studies by Kreitman (1961), Sandifer et al (1968), and the US–UK Diagnostic Project undertaken by Cooper et al (1972) who conducted a series of studies comparing diagnostic practice in the United States and the United Kingdom. Two studies were analysed involving several hundred consecutive admissions to New York and London mental hospitals, where patients were examined by the hospital physician according to his usual practice, and subsequently by members of the project using a structured interview schedule. The agreement measured was between the hospitals' psychiatrists and those of the project (most of the latter having received their training in London). Spitzer and Fleiss (1974) report on further research where 100 consecutive admissions to a New York psychiatric institution were studied, each patient being diagnosed by one of 15 admitting residents on admission, and also seen within three months after admission by one of two supervising psychiatrists after they had reviewed the case records prepared by the admitting resident psychiatrist. After incorporating a statistic named kappa, which contrasts the observed proportion of agreement with the proportion expected by chance alone, and using the formula kappa $= (p_o - p_c)/(1 - p_c)$, where p_o is the observed proportion of agreement and p_c is the proportion expected by chance (Spitzer et al, 1967) they produced a table (Table E.1)

Table E.1 Kappa coefficients of agreement on broad and specific diagnostic categories from six studies.

Category	I	II	III	IV	V New York	V London	VI	Mean
Mental deficiency				.72				.72
Organic brain syndrome	.82	.90					.59	.77
Acute brain syndrome				.44				.44
Chronic brain syndrome				.64				.64
Alcoholism					.74	.68		.71
Psychosis	.73	.62		.56	.42	.43	.54	.55
Schizophrenia	.77		.42	.68	.32	.60	.65	.57
Affective disorder					.19	.44	.59	.41
Neurotic depression			.47		.20	.10		.26
Psychotic depression				.19	.24	.30		.24
Manic-depressive				.33				.33
Involutional depression			.38	.21				.30
Personality disorder or Neurosis	.63			.51	.24	.36		.44
Personality disorder			.33	.56	.19	.22	.29	.32
Sociopathic			.53					.53
Neurosis		.52		.42	.26	.30	.48	.40
Anxiety reaction			.45					.45
Psychophysiological reaction				.38				.38

From Spitzer et al (1967).

which presents the values of kappa calculated from the data presented in the various aforementioned reported studies. The authors conclude:

In spite of the obvious unreliability of psychiatric diagnosis, there exists evidence of sensitivity and agreement on the major psychiatric problems experienced by a patient. Gurland et al (1972), in a detailed analysis of data on the patients in the US–UK diagnostic study, found that hospital psychiatrists were sensitive to patients' psychopathology. A number of patients in the New York sample were identified by the project psychiatrists as suffering from severe depression but not from any signs of schizophrenia. The hospital psychiatrists diagnosed most of these severe depressives as schizophrenic, but treated the majority of them with anti-depressant medication or with ECT. The hospital staffs obviously recognised the depression in their patients when it was present, but failed to incorporate that recognition into their diagnoses.

As one of its studies of diagnostic practice, the US–UK diagnostic project showed videotape recordings of a small number of psychiatric interviews to large numbers of American, British and Canadian psychiatrists (Copeland et al, 1971; Kendall et al, 1971; Sharpe et al, 1974). Some of the interviews gave rise to strikingly large diagnostic differences between the three countries; in one case, two per cent in the British Isles to 69 per cent in the United States, the proportion for Canadian psychiatrists being intermediate. In another study, Sandifer et al (1968) reported substantial diagnostic differences between American, English and Scottish psychiatrists.

Quite apart from the fact that these kinds of statistics must cause some disquiet among responsible psychiatrists, they are a gift of the gods in the hands of a skilled cross-examiner who has done his homework and faces an unwary psychiatrist in the witness box (who probably has not). The following is a semi-fictional piece of court drama, although not unlike many in which I and others have participated. For purposes of this epilogue, the proceedings are considerably pressure-cooked and extend only over a few lines of transcript. In the real world of court battles, I have had psychiatrists under cross-examination for up to three days – much to their annoyance when they (i) did not expect their judgement to be questioned, and (ii) cancelled only one patient in between a busy consulting practice.

'Doctor, you have used such terms as "psychosis" and "schizoid personality". I wonder would you mind explaining for the benefit of the court exactly what you mean by these terms?'

'Well, ah, I would say that the accused suffered from a condition which we describe as "paranoid-schizophrenia".'

'Well, doctor, you have really only substituted one technical term for another. I doubt whether that really helps us very much. Anyway, who are "we"?'

'By "we" I mean psychiatrists in general.'

'Do I take it then, doctor, that all your colleagues would agree with the diagnosis of "paranoid-schizophrenia", whatever that might mean?'

'Generally, yes!'

'Ah, doctor, I see that you have qualified your evidence. You use the word "generally". Does that mean that there may be doctors who might not accept that diagnosis?'

'No, I did not mean that. Although I am sure you'll produce some doctor who'll say the opposite to me. That's part of the game, isn't it?'

'Doctor, this is a serious matter; we are not playing "games" as you call it. Anyway, you are not here to question me. Just answer my questions. Do I make myself clear?'

'Yes.' (Witness begins to perspire).

'Well, doctor, what I put to you before you started to cross-examine me was: are you inferring that there may well be reputable psychiatrists who might not accept your diagnosis of paranoid-schizophrenia?'

'I doubt it. This was a fairly clear-cut case.'

'Well, doctor, you are hedging your bets again. You have "DOUBTS" about peer group agreement; this is a "FAIRLY" clear-cut case. I take it, then, there can be more straightforward cases than this?'

'No case involving a state of mind is ever "straightforward" as you put it!'

'Doctor, I didn't "put" anything. It was YOU who put the proposition that the accused was psychotic, suffers from paranoid-schizophrenia and God knows what else. And, really, apart from saying that you believe that psychiatrists "generally" would agree with what you have just told us, you haven't said anything much, have you?'
(After an uncomfortable pause, counsel will then bang his fist on the bar table and say – or shout – 'Well, HAVE you?')

I will stop this hypothetical cross-examination at this point for two reasons. First, readers will identify with the witness and feel acutely uncomfortable. Second, they will abreact their discomfort and begin to harbour feelings of deep resentment against the legal profession in general, and this contributor in particular. I will therefore mute my sado-masochistic instincts and limit myself merely to *describing* what happens next.

The witness will be asked how he arrived at his diagnosis of paranoid-schizophrenia. If the reply is that the man claimed that he'd heard voices, counsel will feign astonishment and wail, 'Is THAT all?' He will pick up a stack of heavy medical texts and journals and flick through them, painfully, one by one. The witness will be asked, for example, if he has ever heard of Professor Rosenhahn. It is no disrespect to the learned professor that the answer is unlikely to be 'yes'. The witness is then carefully taken through the Rosenhahn experiment in which eight psychologists, each presenting with only one feigned symptom of schizophrenia, were admitted to various US mental hospitals with that diagnosis. Once admitted, they ceased to display any abnormal symptoms and behaved perfectly normally. Too late. Once a patient is labelled, according to Rosenhahn (1973) 'all of his other behaviours and characteristics are coloured by that label'. Thus, when several of these pseudo-patients began to take notes about their experiences, this was promptly noted as 'an aspect of the pathological behaviour'. No doctor likes pseudo-patients, and our psychiatric friend in the witness box is no exception. He will bristle and airily dismiss such an experiment as having 'no scientific value'. Anyway, EVERYBODY knows that American diagnostic practices are notoriously unreliable. Well, that's one up to the witness. After all, it is a fact that nosology has not been one of the most outstanding characteristics of American psychiatry. But, of course, you don't tell the witness that. Instead, you will ask him whether he has heard of Dr Clare, the eminent British psychiatrist. The question will be put in a way which suggests that everyone has heard of him. You will then pick up Clare's *Psychiatry in Dissent* (1979), thumb through it, and assert that it fully supports the witness' view on American psychiatry. The cross-examination will go something like this:

'Doctor Clare suggests that if Rosenhahn were to present to a British mental hospital complaining of auditory hallucination, he might well be advised to go home like a good man, get a decent night's rest, and come back in the morning.'

'I wholeheartedly agree with Dr Clare.'

'Doctor, we seem to be at cross-purposes, or perhaps you've missed the point. You see, Dr Clare does not seem to attach much significance to a complaint of a single auditory hallucination. Yet you seem to have based your entire diagnosis of paranoid-schizophrenia on this one complaint.'

You now have the expert on the run and are ready for the kill. All you need to do now is to take him slowly through the medical literature in which both the reliability and validity of psychiatric judgements have been seriously questioned and he will be ready to admit that, yes, there may well be other psychiatrists, and reputable ones, who would come to a different conclusion from his own. That, in a criminal trial, is enough to raise that degree of doubt that entitles the accused to the benefit of it. As I said at the outset, I have never been involved in a criminal trial in which there was even basic agreement between 'opposing' psychiatrists.

It may be that when psychiatry reaches greater consensus on the more controversial diagnostic categories and definitions of mental disorder, it may be able to demonstrate improved diagnostic reliability. The latest toy – Diagnostic and Statistical Manual (DSM) III – may well provide the kind of multiaxial evaluation system that can provide for greater unanimity. Frankly, reading about the heated controversy, and the number of drafts drawn up before reaching some kind of consensus, does not make me very hopeful that DSM-III will provide the Rosetta Stone which will harmonise all the earlier barnacle-encrusted terminology, ranging from Jung through to the neuropsychopharmacologists who see mental states in terms of polypeptides, and will shortly prove that 'God' is a mental state to be found among the 31 amino acids in the endorphins. I understand that homosexuality was deleted by majority vote from the classification of mental disorder in 1973; necrophilia is no longer a disorder unless the individual complains of the symptoms (cf. Spitzer et al, 1980). So be it. Come the millennium, there may well be a DSM-IV which, by narrow majority, has voted schizophrenia out of the psychiatric vocabulary. Hallelujah. Meanwhile, one can only hope that the new systematic formulation of psychiatric conditions, with agreement on the separate clinical variables, will result in improved diagnostic reliability and validity.

ASSESSING DANGEROUSNESS

This is one area where the courts frequently rely on psychiatric judgements. Since it is an aspect that has been dealt with elsewhere in this book, I will merely content myself with the aftermath of the decision in *Baxstrom* v. *Herold* and allow the reader to draw his own conclusion. In that case, the United States Supreme Court (the highest US court of appeal) held, on constitutional grounds, that prisoners whose terms of imprisonment had expired, could not be detained within the prison system merely on medical grounds, or because psychiatrists believed that they were too dangerous to be released. They either had to be released or committed to a civil mental institution. Some 967 patients, who fell into either of the two classes, were thereupon transferred to civil hospitals.

Over a four-year period (1966-70) 49 per cent were released. Of these, 20 per cent were re-arrested, but only 7 per cent were convicted (the vast majority for minor offences such as vagrancy or intoxication). In a sample of 98 released patients Steadman and Cocozza (1975) found only two had committed a 'dangerous' offence; a robbery and an assault. As Ennis (1970) put it,

> In statistical terms, Operation *Baxstrom* tells us that psychiatric predictions are incredibly inaccurate. In human terms, it tells us that but for a Supreme Court decision, nearly 1000 human beings would have lived much of their lives behind bars ... all because a few psychiatrists, in their considered opinion, thought they were dangerous *and no one asked for proof*. [My italics.]

It would seem that psychiatrists, in evaluating 'dangerousness', base their decision not so much on the information at their disposal, but on their perception of that information, that is, the conceptual model of the particular disorder, which may be medical, social, behavioural or psychological (Williams, 1979). According to Siegler and Osmond (1966), there may even be 'moral' and 'conspiratorial' models.

One cannot help wondering whether there is not here an element of 'defensive psychiatry', one well justified by the legal development of the common law, which postulated a duty of care in circumstances where the harm in suit was reasonably foreseeable. It was put succinctly in a decision of the Supreme Court of California.

> As a general principle, a defendant owes a duty of care to all persons who are foreseeably endangered by his conduct with respect to all risks which make the conduct unreasonably dangerous. (*Tarasoff* v. *The Regents of the University of California* 1976 at 342.)

It is significant that the above is taken from a (majority) decision of that court and involved the liability of a psychiatrist. The facts of that case were as follows. Psychiatrists at the University of California hospital saw one Poddar who exhibited signs of dementia and informed the therapists that he intended to kill his girlfriend (unnamed, but readily identifiable if investigations had been carried out). At the request of the head therapist, the campus police detained Poddar, contacted the head therapist and informed him that in their (i.e. the campus police) informed view the man 'appeared rational'. He was thereupon released, and the head therapist ordered that no further action be taken. Shortly afterwards, Poddar killed the girl. Her parents brought a successful action against the University of California (as employers of the psychiatrist and thus vicariously liable for any negligence committed in the course of the psychiatrist's employment). The issue ultimately turned on whether the damage was too 'remote'; alternatively, whether in the circumstances the doctor owed a duty of care to the plaintiffs. (Lawyers frequently use 'remoteness' and 'duty of care' interchangeably.[1])

In the above case, the majority concluded that:

> a denial of a duty of care begs the essential question – whether the Plaintiffs' interests are entitled to legal protection against the defendant's conduct of the sum total of those considerations of policy which lead the law to say that the particular plaintiff is entitled to protection. (At 342.)

---

[1] cf. Lord Denning, M.R.: *Spartan Steel & Alloys Ltd.* v. *Martin & Co. Ltd.* (1973) QB 27.

It is worth quoting the dissenting opinion of Clark J.

Until to-day's majority opinion, both legal and medical authorities have agreed that confidentiality is essential to effectively treat the mentally ill, and that imposing a duty on doctors to disclose patient threats to potential victims would greatly impair treatment ... The issue whether effective treatment for the mentally ill should be sacrificed to a system of warnings is, in my opinion, properly one for the legislature. (At 354–5).

I have developed elsewhere (1981) the parameters of medical liability and the extent to which confidentiality can be pleaded by way of defence. Suffice it for present purposes that I adhere to the view that confidentiality must yield where public danger begins. Put into the present context, could a doctor who recommends the release of a potentially violent patient, who subsequently causes physical harm to person or property, be liable at the suit of the victim? I wonder. Thus in *Home Office* v. *Dorset Yacht Co. Ltd.* the House of Lords held the Home Office liable for damage done to a yacht by escaping Borstal (delinquent) boys. It is a firmly entrenched principle of our common law that those who have custodial care of patients who may pose a threat to others (or even to themselves) must take adequate measures to ensure that others are not harmed. In the circumstances, it is perhaps not surprising that psychiatrists tend to err on the side of caution and over-predict potential violence. I tend to agree with Mr. Justice Clark that this is a matter 'properly one for the Legislature'.

SCHIZOPHRENIA AND BANANAS: THE QUEENSLAND CONNECTION

Finally, and more as a *jeu d'esprit*, having boasted of having proved a link between schizophrenia and bananas, I should perhaps set out in brief outline how this forensic 'breakthrough' was achieved. P.F., a 46-year-old banana farmer, was the eldest of five children. Two brothers, an uncle and the paternal grandfather were known schizophrenics. In 1962, there was a banana glut in Queensland and the patient's farming venture ran into severe financial difficulties, with the bank (as mortgagee) threatening to take over. Shortly afterwards, the patient was found in a 'queer' state under a banana tree, taken to the local doctor and treated for a 'back condition'. However, as his 'back' got progressively more delusional, he was taken to Lowson House (the psychiatric unit of the Royal Brisbane Hospital) where he was found to be suffering from an acute florid episode of schizophrenia and given electroconvulsive therapy and anti-psychotic medication. He was discharged after some six weeks and returned to his farm. He soon became convinced that dieldrin (an insecticide used in the banana industry) was poisoning mankind and began to undertake some 'research' on the subject, which he reduced to a monograph and sent a copy to (i) HM the Queen; (ii) the head of the British Broadcasting Corporation and (iii) the Secretary of the Royal Society in London. Shortly afterwards, he left the farm, and built himself a small bark hut somewhere in the Australian bush where he has been living happily ever since, drawing (thanks to this contributor) weekly payments of workers' compensation.

One of the few rational things the patient had done was to take out what was then known as a Voluntary Insurance Policy pursuant to which he was to be provided with the same benefits as are provided in the case of a worker within the meaning of the Workers' Compensation Acts (Q) in the event of 'injury by accident' (which, by definition, includes any disease to which the employment is a contributing or causal factor). The plaintiff made a claim under his policy, alleging that the florid episode was 'caused, aggravated or accelerated' by the depressed state of the banana industry, and that his chronic schizophrenia was in turn precipitated by the florid episode on the farm. It was, perhaps, drawing a long bow. Certainly, I could not get a single psychiatrist to support such a proposition. The presumptive inference which this sequence of events would naturally inspire in the mind of any commonsense person uninstructed in psychiatry was impressive.[1] Here you had a man happily growing bananas. Suddenly he is threatened with bankruptcy – and promptly goes 'bananas'.

I tried my theory out on my own general practitioner who agreed with me (he was also a qualified lawyer). Anyway, we gave it a run. My GP was my only expert witness. He modestly disclaimed all knowledge of psychiatry but claimed to have seen many elderly patients – bank managers and the like – who managed to plod along quite nicely until some major crisis entered their lives, like retirement, bereavement or the like. Many become acutely depressed; some quite psychotic. He claimed the plaintiff classically fitted that picture.

Having disclaimed all knowledge of psychiatry, the witness was barely cross-examined. The defence was eagerly awaiting the arrival of the plaintiff's medical experts. In fact, the only specialist called was an agricultural economist attached to the Department of Primary Industries in Canberra. The defence saw it as a test case and had retained four of Brisbane's leading psychiatrists. Each point was bitterly contested, and they now faced the task of demolishing what little evidence there was in the tenuous chain between chronic schizophrenia and the banana glut. However, there was just enough for a submission of 'no case to answer' to fail. Four psychiatrists marched in, for once in total agreement – the plaintiff suffered from chronic schizophrenia, the condition was hereditary, and given the plaintiff's family history, one did not have far to look for the cause of the plaintiff's breakdown. Schizophrenia, they hooted, had nothing to do with bananas. However, what appeared to be an impregnable position was soon to crumble. Again, for the sake of brevity, only a short extract from the cross-examination is included.

'Doctor, you have given evidence that schizophrenia is a condition of heredity; you are convinced about that?'
'Yes, certainly.'
'How is it transmitted?'
'I'm sorry, I don't understand the question.'
'Doctor, the question is simple enough: what theory of transmission do you favour?'
(Long pause, the witness appears to be deep in thought when counsel interrupts.)
'Doctor, let me help you. Is it a Mendelian dominant or is it recessive?'
'I'm sorry, I can't answer that!'

---

[1] Cf. per Rich, A.C.J. *Adelaide Stevedoring Co. Ltd.* v. *Forst* (1940) 64 CLR 538.

'My goodness me, doctor. You come along here as an expert witness, you mouth phrases like "hereditary" and you don't even know how the condition is transmitted? Surely the court can expect more assistance than that?'
(With a 'heaven lend me patience' look counsel announces that there seems little point in cross-examining this witness further and sits down. Exit witness.)

The next expert, also no geneticist, was floored by the statement, garnered from some exotic American psychiatric journal, that the incidence of schizophrenia amongst African natives in their tribal surroundings was negligible; yet over 50 per cent of American negroes living in the ghettos of New York have at least one episode of a schizophrenic nature in their lives. The obvious question is: if schizophrenia is indeed hereditary, how come there is this vast difference in incidence between different groups of the same genetic stock? Now there may be a perfectly respectable answer to this conundrum; it may be that the nosology of African witchdoctors differs from that of their New York brethren. Whatever the answer, the proposition seems self-evident – environmental stresses can play a part in precipitating schizophrenic episodes in predisposed subjects. And that is all I had to prove. The plaintiff won, and two appeals to higher courts were dismissed. In a rage, the State Insurance Office persuaded Parliament to abolish that kind of policy. The moral of the story is that medical witnesses should never go to court unless fully prepared. There were no 'lawyer's tricks' or unfair questions in the whole of the case. There was, however, some light relief when a famous forensic psychiatrist, the late Dr Howard Tait, neatly turned the table on counsel. I asked the witness to suppose that he had a camel with a pre-morbid personality; it had nine straws on its back and was just able to creak along. Dramatic pause. Then

'Now doctor, you place the tenth straw on this camel's back, and down it goes. Doctor, if you were asked "which straw broke the camel's back", what would you say?'

I just KNEW what the answer would be – you never ask a question unless you know the answer, a cardinal rule. The answer I expected was 'You can't pick any one straw, they ALL played their part'. That is the answer I wanted – it was, after all, a workers' compensation case. Instead, the answer I got was:

'I am sorry, Dr Gerber, I can't answer that. I don't treat psychotic camels.'
(Me: 'Touché'.)

In parenthesis, unbeknownst to either party, and contemporaneous with the 'banana case' was a High Court decision – *Commonwealth of Australia* v. *Rutledge* – which involved a claim for total incapacity made under the Commonwealth Workers' Compensation Acts. The facts and decision become sufficiently clear from a short extract from the judgment of Menzies, J.

The (worker's) ordinary employment with the appellant in which she had been engaged for about four and a half years was to sort out and file trunk line dockets of telephone calls at the Spencer Street Post Office. But for about a fortnight from 12 September, 1961, her special confidential employment had been to detect suspected malpractices by other employees with regard to bookmakers' telephone calls. On 27 September 1961, she suffered a break-down. It seems that she was a paranoiac person and became an active psychotic person. Dr Springthorpe, speaking of her spying work, said: 'One could hardly have chosen a job more likely to stir up a paranoiac person than the one she had, and it only took some fourteen days, I think, from when she started this special job, before she had this pretty drastic break-down'.

Upon this and like evidence, I am not disposed to disturb the finding made by the learned County Court judge, that the (worker's) conversion from a latent paranoiac, as she was, into an active psychotic person, as she became, was due to the nature of the employment in which she was engaged, (225).

CONCLUSION

I have done little more than to set out – perhaps somewhat provocatively – that psychiatry is presently too inexact to be let loose in the courts. Indeed, having observed scores of psychiatrists giving evidence, I wonder whether there may not be more than a grain of truth in Edward Glover's (1932) assertion that 'normality may be a form of madness which goes unrecognised because it happens to be a good adaptation to reality'.

CASES

Baxstrom v. Herold 383 US 107 (1966).
Commonwealth of Australia v. Rutledge (1964) 38 ALJR 222.
Home Office v. Dorset Yacht Co. Ltd. (1970) AC 1004.
Tarasoff v. The Regents of the University of California (1976) 551 P 2d 334.

REFERENCES

Ash, P. (1949) The reliability of psychiatric diagnosis. *J. Abn and Soc. Psych.* **44,** 272-6.
Beck, A.T., Ward, C.H., Mendelson, M., Mock, J.E. & Erbaugh, J.K. (1962) Reliability of psychiatric diagnosis: 2. A study of consistency of clinical judgments and ratings. *Amer. J. Psychiat.,* **119,** 351-7.
Clare, A.W. (1979) *Psychiatry in Dissent: Controversial Issues in Thought and Practice.* Philadelphia: Institute for Study of Human Issues.
Cooper, J.E., Kendall, R.E., Gurland, B.J., Sharpe L., Copeland, J.R.M. & Simon, R. (1972) *Psychiatric Diagnosis in New York and London.* (US-UK Diagnostic Project). London: Oxford University Press.
Copeland, J.R.M., Cooper, J.E., Kendall, R.E. & Gourlay, A.J. (1971) Differences in usage of diagnostic labels amongst psychiatrists in the British Isles. *Brit. J. Psychiat.,* **118,** 629-40.
Ennis, B.J. (1970) The rights of mental patients. In *The Rights of Americans.* Dorsen, N. (ed.). New York: Random Press.
Ennis, B.J. & Litwack, R. (1974) Psychiatry and the presumption of expertise: flipping coins in the courtroom. *Cal. L. Rev.,* (Pt. 2), 693.
Gerber, P. (1981) Medical confidentiality – a battered baby. *Med. J. Aust.,* **2,** 542-4.
Glover, E. (1932) Medico-psychological aspects of normality. *Brit. J. Psychol.,* **23,** 152-66.
Gurland, B.J., Fleiss, J.L., Sharpe, L., Simon, R. & Barrett, J.E. (1972) The mislabeling of depressed patients in New York State Hospitals. In *Disorders of Mood.* Zubin, J. & Freyhan, F.A. (eds.). Baltimore: Johns Hopkins Press.
Kendall, R.E., Cooper, J.E., Gourlay, A.J., Copeland, J.R.M., Sharpe, L. & Gurland, B.J. (1971) The diagnostic criteria of American and British psychiatrists. *Arch. Gen. Psychiat.,* **25,** 123-30.
Kreitman, N. (1961) The reliability of psychiatric diagnosis. *J. Ment. Sci.,* **107,** 876-86.
Mehlman, B. (1952) The reliability of psychiatric diagnosis *J. Abn. and Soc. Psych.,* **47,** 577-8.
Norris, V. (1959) *Mental Illness in London.* Maudsley Monograph No. 61.
Pasamanick, B., Dinitz, F. & Lefton, M. (1959) Psychiatric orientation and its relation to diagnosis and treatment in a mental hospital. *Amer. J. Psychiat.,* **116,** 127-32.
Rosenhahn, D.L. (1973) On being insane in insane places. *Science,* **179,** 250-8.
Sandifer, M.G., Hordern, A., Timbury, G.C. & Green, L.M. (1968) Psychiatric diagnosis: a comparative study in North Carolina, London and Glasgow. *Brit. J. Psychiat.,* **114,** 1-9.

Schmidt, H.O. & Fonda, C.P. (1956) The reliability of psychiatric diagnosis: a new look. *J. Abn. and Soc. Psychol.*, **52**, 262–7.

Sharpe, L., Gurland, B.J., Fleiss, J.L., Kendall, R.E., Cooper, J.E. & Copeland, J.R.M. (1974) Some comparisons of American, Canadian and British psychiatrists in their diagnostic concepts. *Can. Psychiat. Assoc. J.*, **19**, 3, 235–45.

Siegler, M. & Osmond, H. (1966) Models of madness. *Brit. J. Psychiat.*, **112**, 193–203.

Spitzer, R.L. & Fleiss, J.L. (1974) A re-analysis of the reliability of psychiatric diagnosis. *Brit. J. Psychiat.*, **125**, 341–7.

Spitzer, R.L., Cohen, J. & Fleiss, J.L. (1967) Quantification of agreement in psychiatric diagnosis: a new approach. *Arch. gen. Psychiat.*, **17**, 83–7.

Spitzer, R.L., Janet, B.W., Williams, M.S.W. & Skodol, A.E. (1980) DSM III: The major achievements and an overview. *Amer. J. Psychiat.*, **137**, 151–64.

Steadman, H.J. & Cocozza, J.J. (1975) We can't predict who is dangerous. *Psychology Today*, **8**, 32–5 and 84.

Williams, P. (1979) Deciding how to treat – the relevance of psychiatric diagnosis. *Psychol. Med.*, **9**, 179–86.

Zubin, J. (1967) Classification of the behaviour disorders. *Ann. Rev. Psychol.*, **18**, 373–406.

This book is the property of
LIVERPOOL AREA HEALTH AUTHORITY (1)

Abbreviations

AHA	Area Health Authority
ALI	American Law Institute
CAT	Computer axial tomography
CNV	Contingent negative variation
DHSS	Department of Health and Social Security
ECT	Electroconvulsive therapy
EEG	Electroencephalogram
ESN	Educationally subnormal
FBI	Federal Bureau of Investigation
GMC	General Medical Council
HMT	Hospital management team
IRU	Industrial Rehabilitation Unit
ITU	Industrial Therapy Unit
MAOI	Monoamine oxidase inhibitor
MIND	National Association for Mental Health
NGRI	Not guilty by reason of insanity
NHS	National Health Service
OHE	Office of Health Economics
RMN	Registered Mental Nurse
RMO	Responsible Medical Officer
RNMS	Registered Nurse for the Mentally Subnormal
TBR	Terbeschikkingstelling van der Regering (detention at the government's pleasure – Holland)
TLE	Temporal lobe epilepsy

Principal Author Index

Subject Index

Cases Index

Note: *n* denotes footnotes.